IMPERIAL
COMMONWEALTH

IMPERIAL COMMONWEALTH

by

LORD ELTON

Fellow of Queen's College, Oxford

Collins

14 ST. JAMES'S PLACE LONDON

1945

COPYRIGHT
PRINTED IN GREAT BRITAIN
COLLINS CLEAR-TYPE PRESS : LONDON AND GLASGOW
1945

FOREWORD

I HAVE tried to write a history, sufficiently founded upon the authorities, yet capable of being read with enjoyment by the ordinary reader, of that greatest and most fruitful of recorded political achievements, the British Empire. This is a story of which at present, thanks largely to the indifference of schools and Universities, the British themselves know next to nothing. And knowing so little of the nature of the achievements by which their ancestors changed the destiny of mankind, they necessarily know all too little of the vast opportunities and obligations of the Empire-Commonwealth of to-day, while for three generations past they have cherished illusions as to its character and record which would have been unthinkable among an even moderately instructed people.

Yet it is not chance that, save Holland, every one of the great rivals and assailants of the Empire-Commonwealth has been a despotic state. Once England, and three times the Empire Commonwealth, has saved itself, and Europe, from a tyrant— from Philip of Spain, from Louis of France, from Napoleon and from Germany of the Hohenzollerns. These words are written before the long struggle against the fifth despotism, the Germany of Hitler, has ended. But if there is to be any future for freedom in the age to come, it seems certain that, as pattern, or even, it may be, as nucleus, of the world organisation of the future, there will be a vital rôle to be played by the one world community in existence—which discovered and spread abroad the art of self-government, and has already established permanent peace among a quarter of mankind. It will not be easy, however, to render mankind that last great service, so long as the bulk of our citizens remain in almost total ignorance of the character and achievements of our own world society.

For an elaborate bibliography the reader is referred to the Cambridge *History of the British Empire*. I have confined myself here to listing, at the end of each "book," for the benefit of those who may wish to investigate further, a number of the most useful and accessible secondary authorities. Finally, I must express my gratitude to the distinguished historian, Mr. Milton Waldman, for the great assistance I have derived from his kindly and penetrating criticisms.

CONTENTS

Book IX
IMPERIALISM AND CHAMBERLAIN

Book X
THE CLAIM TO SURVIVAL

Book XI
THE GRAND ORDEAL

Epilogue

LIST OF MAPS

Prelude

CHAPTER ONE

THE LIFTING OF THE VEIL

(1485-1558)

ONE who peered, towards the end of the fifteenth century, among the scrolls and Tritons of some fantastic map of the world, as men then believed the world to be, found little enough that resembled the shape of the earth we know. Yet England, in squat, just recognisable, outline, was there; then as now, despite the prodigious lacunæ of primitive cartography, a mere pinpoint against the sprawling world-mass. Nothing could have forewarned the most speculative muser over that early chart that three hundred years later other maps would show that insignificant island off the north-west angle of Europe as metropolis of a world-wide society; and after another century as nucleus of a world Empire, vastly altered in ground-plan and composition. Nor, however much he knew or guessed of the material forces of his own and the succeeding age, could one who mused over a world-map of Behaim have deduced the unfolding of the vast design. For on any reckoning of such factors the probabilities must have told overwhelmingly against so unprecedented a physical expansion, so tremendous an impact upon the future of mankind.

§2

Certainly no human foresight could have discerned, as the New Year of 1485 broke over England, that the distracted and insignificant island was one day to become metropolis of the most extensive Empire known to history. For the last thirty years the English, with the Welsh about three million all told, had lived in anarchy. For thirty years no king's writ had run secure all England over. The Earl of Northumberland made war upon the Earl of Westmorland, Cheshire upon Shropshire, the students of Oxford upon its citizens. Fortunate the dweller in the quiet English shires who had never chanced upon the corpse by the wayside, or watched the grey spire of smoke from a neighbour's burning rafters above the crest of the greenwood, or heard the arrow humming down the glade. And these evils did not spring from the mere license of dynastic ambition: the Wars of the Roses were the death throes of a system.

Nor was it by any means only the decay of their own social structure which, to all seeming, doomed the English to permanent insignificance. Nature herself appeared to have set their island overfar from the main tide of human affairs for them to play any significant part in world history. Since time out of mind the currents of trade and civilisation had lapped the shores of the land-locked Mediterranean. The misty and tempest-girt isles of Britain lay upon the very fringes of the continent, facing the vast inhospitable spaces of an ocean which was the world's end. The scanty wares which the islanders exported to the mainland—for long mainly wool, but now increasingly woollen cloth—must wait upon the tempests. Whatever impulse of expansion they had mustered must needs spend itself upon the Continent; yet those parts of the Continent which were accessible had never been likely to take the impress of the island civilisation, which, although already strangely virile and individual, was as yet more primitive than their own. The tedium and tragedies of the Hundred Years' War had cured ordinary Englishmen for ever of any ambition to fight their way back on to the mainland from which their own rulers had once sprung. And now that formidable new portent, the rise of powerful national monarchies in France and Spain, had conclusively barred and bolted a door which had already ceased to be inviting. What then was to be looked for now save a long anæmia, and aspiring youth condemned to dream in damp, sequestered manor houses of the barren, receding glories of Henry the Fifth?

And yet even then, discernible only to an eye which could pierce the outer semblances, there slumbered in England forces of immense potency. Chief among these was the stubborn individualism of the English themselves. All, save one, of the five rival states which the English were to encounter overseas, would be authoritarian in structure, and their expansion the deliberate bid of a government for world power. But the expansion of England would be the work of individuals and voluntary associations, instinctive and spontaneous growth rather than design, and therefore at once more natural and more likely to endure. The idea which transforms human society comes slowly to maturity, but already it was growing in England, against the day when it would be her destiny to plant it abroad in the five continents. Their consciousness of the absolute value of personal liberty and individual initiative had already given Englishmen Magna Carta. It was yet to shape the pattern of their domestic history, and to give the world a new destiny. Even in 1485 a score of signs pointed to what was unique in the English way of life. Thus in France feudal society, a rigid structure of noble, priest and peasant, with no place in it for a middle class, endured into the eighteenth century, substantially unchanged, and then perished abruptly at the hands of the excluded middle class in the sudden explosion which we call the French Revolution. In England on the other hand feudalism had already begun to yield to the infiltration of the new middle class as early as the fourteenth century. The instinct which bade the Englishman follow his own judgment, or seek his own fortune in his own way, was too strong for it. By the fourteenth century the immemorial custom of the manor was beginning to give place to the free play of economic forces, with men bargaining for wages according to opportunity and their own lights. Lollardry, and then the Reformation itself, stood for the claim to reject authority, to exercise one's own judgment, even in religion. In all these ways the individual was breaking through the ancient crust of custom sooner than anywhere else in the world. And the new middle class, in whose gradual ascent all these tendencies were reflected, brought with it the very blend of soberness and enterprise best fitted for the great adventure which lay ahead. This middle class had survived the anarchy virtually unscathed; it was the feudal nobility which had bled itself white for the rival Roses. If ever wider opportunity were to beckon to this people, it would be seized, one might already conjecture, not by the Crown and its ministers, working to a deliberate system, but by countless enterprising individuals, following, largely at haphazard, their own adventurous instincts.

§3

At this juncture two unforeseeable processes abruptly swept away the obstacles which had hitherto condemned England to insignificance. Henry VII, the first of the Tudors, seized the throne in 1485, and established a new form of monarchy, ending not only the anarchy of the Roses, but the more deep-seated malaise of which it had been a symptom. And the Portuguese and Spanish explorations, suddenly calling a new continent into existence beyond the Atlantic, transformed the western ocean from a barrier to a highway. England thus not only became a vigorous national state but moved suddenly from the circumference to the very centre of the world. This alone, needless to say, does not of itself account for what was to come. For it was not to England only that opportunity now beckoned. Other, and much more powerful, nation-states of the new pattern faced westward across the same mysterious and alluring ocean. Nevertheless, these great political and geographical changes would make it possible for the English to exert their qualities in the world arena. It was on the nature of those qualities that the outcome would depend.

Henry VII gave England peace abroad, he gave her order at home, he replenished the royal exchequer. Above all, he gave the new middle class its opportunity. These small landowners and merchants who were to make the Empire were no clear-cut caste, or rather outcasts, as in France. The small landowners, squires as they would be called a little later, formed a social bridge between the great land-owners of the countryside and the merchants of the towns, with both of whom they had close connections. This was no self-contained or rigidly defined class; it had come into existence, indeed, by forcing its way into a hierarchic feudal structure—of noble, priest, peasant—which held no place for it. But, for all that, it was clearly recognisable as a class, and it was from this class that the makers of the new and greater England would chiefly come. In an age ruled by custom they came of the only social stratum, the only social stratum perhaps in any country, already bred to change. These were the men who were to pit their individual courage and enterprise against the governments of foreign states.

§4

Just as the administrative reorganisation of England by the new monarchy was providing the English with new channels for energies hitherto restricted by the rigid feudal structure, or wasted in domestic anarchy, there commenced an astonishing twofold ex-tension, mental and physical, of the whole horizon of mankind. From Italy, the home of the Renaissance, the new studies began to reach Oxford in the last two decades of the century. The lovely long-lost world of Hellas was taking shape again, with all its passionate cult of beauty and learning, and that restless zest for inquiry which acknowledges no confines of the human mind. The anti-clericalism of Latin civilisation has its roots in the secularism of art and science at the Renaissance, and its segregation from the Church; but in England clergy and laity combined to welcome the influences of the new age, and in the coming expansion overseas the religious instinct of the people would always play a central rôle. In spite of which the new appetite for beauty and luxury, which sprang from the Renaissance, undoubtedly contributed its impulse to the dawning age of adventure, urging men on to seek in unknown lands overseas the gold and jewels, the fine stuffs and spices and all the various wealth with which to build and adorn the new many-windowed Italianate palaces which would soon be replacing the grim defensive keeps and castles of the era of feudal anarchy now coming to an end.

The Reformation is not only a unique event, at a crucial moment, but is closely intertwined with the story of the Empire itself. Were not the greatest rivals with whom England was to struggle for her stake in the new world and for her own existence most Catholic Spain and most Catholic France? It cannot be denied that the Reformation was accompanied by flagrant abuses, above all by that exaggerated individualism for which, within the limits of the law, the individual is absolute master of his own, an irresponsible owner, without obligation to God or society. Yet the vices of the new individualism would play a far smaller part in the record of English expansion than in our own domestic history, for the men who sailed from home to trade or settle overseas were mostly of too humble or too godly an origin to be liable to its worst excesses. And the claim, even in the greatest matters, to judge for oneself was the supreme manifestation of that uprush of moral energy with which all England was now pulsing.

§5

It is hard now to imagine the stir and astonishment in men's minds at the sudden expansion of the terrestrial globe which accompanied the sudden expansion of human knowledge. Bliss was it, no doubt, for eager spirits, in that dawn to be alive, when every few years some fabulous new territory took shape beyond the ocean, and to meet a shipmate of Cabot's rolling down the streets of Bristol must have been like encountering a voyager returned from Mars. The world was very young again; anything might happen, anything be achieved.

Almost every great discovery, every liberating idea, can be seen to have arrived gradually, by trial and error extended over many generations, in broken gleams revealed to many far-separated minds. And a long, uncertain prelude to the great new departure stretches back into the furthest mists of antiquity. Norse colonists from Greenland almost certainly discovered America in the late tenth century. It is possible that the Canary Islands were found by the

Genoese in 1270; they were certainly discovered by the Portuguese in 1341. An Englishman may have happened upon Madeira in 1370. But these were haphazard ventures; men were blown far out of their course, sailed after strangely shaped clouds which they took for land, sighted or struck upon some unknown island, often, no doubt, only for their strange experience to pass unrecorded out of history. Meanwhile the scientific instruments of exploration slowly accumulated; science and empirical, unlettered seamanship were slowly converging.

Meanwhile America waited; and from time to time mariners would puzzle over monstrous canes or curiously wrought timbers floating on the lonely waters, or huge pine trunks, which no European soil could have bred; or a corpse of outlandish aspect would be washed up upon our western beaches. The unknown was sending forth its silent summons to investigation.

The first example of systematic exploration was set by Prince Henry of Portugal. When he died in 1460, though there had been no great discovery, some great discovery was only a question of time. The Spaniards were next to step on to the world stage, close on the heels of the Portuguese. A Genoese sailor, Christopher Columbus, had long been convinced that, since the world was round, it must be possible to reach the Indies by sailing west from Spain. The reasoning, like most great innovations, was simple. Columbus, moreover, was prepared to prove its validity himself by sailing into the unknown. It was not till 1492 that he found any one rash enough to provide him with ships for a venture much more perilous than the first Atlantic aeroplane flights, based on a theory which seemed as dubious as that of the philosopher's stone. Like the Portuguese adventurers, Columbus had secured a royal backer, no less a person than His Majesty of Spain. It was on a later voyage that he came upon a mainland, and realised to his astonishment that this was not India but a vast new continent of whose existence men had not dreamed. Before the end of the sixteenth century both Spain and Portugal had built Empires on these foundations—Portugal, which had not the resources for distant conquest and administration, a chain of trading centres; Spain, a strictly administered military Empire, including Mexico, Peru and the West Indies.

The English came next. Although they were at present less wealthy and powerful than the Spanish they possessed advantages which in the long run would enable them to outstrip their rivals. For one thing, being islanders, they could turn their backs upon the continent and concentrate, if they wished, upon expansion over-seas. Hedged in by the main, as Shakespeare would soon observe, they were secure and confident from foreign purposes. The island was rich in inlets and seaports, and the shallow waters round its coasts nurtured a numerous and hardy fisher folk, so that a high proportion of its population was bred to the sea, and to the faith, courage and hardihood natural to sailors. They were adventurers, too, by nature, and not accustomed to look to a government to plan their adventures for them.

On May 2, 1497, the *Mathew*, a small, frail vessel, but fully rigged and decked, put out from Bristol, and, heading boldly westward, presently disappeared over the silver rim which for so long had marked the limits of the world. No state expenditure supported this enterprise, as it had that of Columbus. The *Mathew* contained the Genoese John Cabot, possibly Sebastian Cabot, his son, another citizen of Genoa, a Burgundian, a Jew, some Bristol merchants and about a dozen English sailors. Seven hundred leagues, as he reckoned, from home Cabot struck land, which he confidently believed to be the north-eastern fringe of Asia. It was probably, but not quite certainly, Newfoundland, the first English colony. Of this desolate and mysterious shore Cabot took formal possession, planting there the standards of England and St. Mark. He then sailed hurriedly south along the coast—for three hundred leagues says one of the very few contemporary authorities—far enough at any rate to satisfy himself that this was indeed Asia, and that somewhere south and west of him lay the fabled riches of Cathay or Cipango. Here and there he landed, but found no inhabitants— doubtless to his satisfaction since this small, privately financed adventure, typical of so much of the British colonisation to come, had sailed not to fight or to conquer, but, in the interests of commerce, to spy out the promised land. With his crew of eighteen, now the sole repositories of a secret which would astound the world, Cabot was not tempted to take risks. Now and again (say the records) his men came upon signs of human habitation—curiously notched trunks, snares set for game, a bone tool like a fisherman's netting-needle. The little landing-party must have peered anxiously into the dense woodlands, but nothing stirred. Maybe they were watched by unseen eyes, but the natives, if they observed them, remained prudently in hiding. This time the two races did not meet. By August 6 the *Mathew* was safe in Bristol harbour. Four days later Cabot was in London and had had audience of the king, who gave him ten pounds from the privy purse, with promise of a permanent pension to come. Cabot apparently remained nearly a fortnight in London. "He is called the Great Admiral, and vast honor is paid him . . . ," noted a contemporary, "and these English run after him like mad, and indeed he can enlist as many of them as he pleases. . . ." It is curiously suggestive of the lionising of one of the early Atlantic fliers, more than four hundred years later. The Government clerk, his mind doubtless running on those ancient legends as to what lay beyond the ocean which the explorers would now so soon outmode, entered the royal benefaction to Cabot as "to him that found the new isle." Had Cabot himself made the official entry he would doubtless have recorded himself as having reached Asia and the "country of the Grand Khan." What he had in fact discovered, however, was the British Empire.

Cabot sailed again in 1498, this time probably with five ships, one of them a comparatively large vessel equipped at the king's cost. His object was to follow the new-found coast south to the spice regions of Cipango, or Japan, to which he still believed it would lead them. The expedition set forth in early summer, and from that day to this, save for one ship which put back from the outward voyage, damaged, into an Irish port, neither Cabot nor any of his crews can be conclusively proved to have reappeared out of the unknown. The indirect and presumptive evidence, however, that they reached America again, and that some of them returned, is very strong. Like most of the pioneer work of the British Empire, this had been a commercial venture, but it had failed.

§6

From the death of Henry VII to the accession of Elizabeth English voyages of discovery went on, but spasmodically, for Wolsey chose to plunge his country back into the barren whirlpool of continental politics. In 1501 an expedition was planned to plant a permanent colony, but there is no evidence that a colony was founded. An expedition of 1536, which, for some mysterious reason, included numerous London lawyers, was reported to have run out of food in Newfoundland, to have been driven to cannibalism and eventually to have attacked a French ship and seized its provisions. This particular ship's crew might perhaps have been expected to encounter some unusual fate, but it is difficult to believe that hunger can have reduced even a shipload of lawyers to cannibalism and piracy in the midst of the most productive fisheries in the world. In the 'fifties there were several voyages, some of them very profitable, to Africa, and in 1553, in the course of an attempt on a north-east passage to Asia, Sir Hugh Willoughby discovered Nova Zembla, and froze to death in Lapland, while Richard Chancellor landed at Archangel, went overland to Moscow and founded English trade with Russia.

The English might not, like Spain and Portugal, between whom the Pope divided the new world in 1493, have reaped riches overseas; yet, while Spanish and Portuguese sailed over tranquil waters to lands of pearl and gold, the hardy English in their stormy north were acquiring the tradition of seamanship and sea adventure which would soon stand them in good stead. And, between them, the two Henrys had created the Royal Navy. The birth of a new age was at hand.

CHAPTER TWO

THE ELIZABETHANS

(1558-1603)

§1

IT WAS Henry VIII who made the English Navy, which was to make the British Empire. At the end of his reign he had amassed a Royal Navy of forty-five vessels—roundships, galleys, galleons (fifteen of them) and pinnaces. From 1530 onwards his fleet was powerful enough to guarantee him against invasion from the Continent. In 1539 and again in 1544, invasion was threatened, but each time it came to naught. For the first time England was indeed an island; the turning-point in English history had been reached. At last England can dare to be herself. She pursues her own English destiny. The consequences would be prodigious, lasting and world-wide; but they were also immediate. Forthwith Henry's diplomacy is transformed. His earlier caution is flung to the winds; he breaks with the Pope, flouts the Emperor, challenges France and Scotland. All is changed; is he not now armed? The Reformation itself was made possible by the English Navy.

The Henrys had thus given England the beginnings of a fighting Navy, while as yet her rivals, like the Romans and Carthaginians, had got no further than putting soldiers on to ships; when the Spaniards beat the Turks at Lepanto in 1571, their methods were still those with which the Greeks had won the battle of Actium in 31 B.C. While the fires of Smithfield burned under Mary, the navy fell into decay. It mattered little, since all legitimate seafaring trades were now swallowed up in privateering. Many a young English blood with small interest in the new religion could see nevertheless that the persecution, and Mary's Spanish husband, threatened the independence of England, and sailed out to avenge the martyrs in the Channel. It was a superb school of seamanship. When Elizabeth came to the throne Henry's great ships might be dismantled and his coast-fortresses abandoned, but the English were a nation of seasoned fighting seamen. From now on their naval superiority steadily increased. To contemporary observers this superiority, no doubt, was not apparent. For success in warfare depends ultimately upon the social pattern of a country, and upon its morale; and contemporaries could hardly have been expected to perceive that a new type of social structure, and a new élan of national self-confidence, were emerging in the small northern island of heretics. Spain was the chief of the new national states, and, particularly after the annexation of Portugal, was well placed for maritime adventure. Moreover she already possessed unbounded wealth, a vast Pacific empire and the most formidable army in Europe. For contemporaries the conclusion was irresistible—the Spanish Navy, too, must be invincible. Only after the catastrophe of the Grand Armada did men begin dimly to perceive that the foundations of naval strength are other than the foundations of military strength, and that a sea power had arisen which was stronger than Spain.

Spain was a military, feudal and hierarchic state, and this social complexion was reflected not only in its Empire but in its fleet. Nurtured on their tradition of slave-rowed galleys, the Spaniards thought of a warship as a means of transporting soldiers to fight other soldiers on their own, or the enemy's, decks. The sailors who worked and manœuvred the great floating barracks inherited the servile tradition of the galleys, and were treated with harshness and contempt. The Spaniards had no tradition of individual enterprise, no private merchants and sea-adventurers to man their ships, no energetic middle class to bridge the feudal gulf between landowner and peasant. With the English it was otherwise. On their ships even in the reign of Elizabeth the sailing and fighting services were virtually indistinguishable. And the adventurous of all classes were taking to the sea in a spirit of cheerful camaraderie which to the Spanish would have appeared altogether barbaric. Above all, although the world was not yet aware of their revolutionary invention, they had already discovered, and were regularly practising, the new naval tactics—of the speedy ships which sailed close to the wind and manœuvred not to board, but to discharge their broadsides. " Were regularly practising"—here was another clue to the victory which would soon astonish the world. For the ocean-going vessels of Spain were not warships, and the Spaniards only began building a fighting navy on the eve of the outbreak of war with England. But every English ship was a warship, since in the reign of Elizabeth commerce and war were hardly to be distinguished. In these years of public peace and private hostilities, every merchant who put to sea knew that he would be lucky if he made his home port again without having had to fight a pirate or a foreign rival. Indeed commerce could only be carried on at the cannon's mouth. For the Spaniards attacked all merchants who attempted to trade with America, while the Portuguese fell upon those who approached the African or Indian coasts. Again, the Spaniards had no commerce, they only imported treasure from the new world. But English commerce was growing fast, and for England commerce meant warfare now, as afterwards it was to mean the Empire. The trading voyages to the Guinea coast of West Africa, which had to go on more or less surreptitiously under Mary—her husband, Philip of Spain, insisted that they must be banned—went on openly year after year under Elizabeth, who often hired out her royal warships to the merchant adventurers. The Guinea trade itself led to a desultory and irregular oceanic war with Portugal, which Elizabeth's great minister, Cecil, whatever he may have thought of the provocation of Spain, did nothing to discourage. But more than this, Spain, now busy extinguishing Dutch Protestantism in a sea of blood, was the sword of the Papacy, whose spiritual suzerainty the English had themselves so lately cast off, the dark cloud menacing all freedom everywhere. And for them, they had no manner of doubt, a triumphant Spain spelled slavery, and the fires and dungeons of the Inquisition in every English town. Elizabeth and her ministers might doubt and ponder, perplexed by high policy and reasons of state, but the people saw more clearly because they saw by instinct. Tyranny was the brutal negation of the Idea slowly maturing within their own island, and, as so often in centuries to come, their instincts drove them to resist it to the death. And so for years the Channel was the scene of desperate encounters past numbering. And far in the uncharted oceans of the new world Drake and Hawkins were seizing and plundering the treasure ships of King Philip, harrying his subjects and sacking his ports.

§2

But it was Francis Drake, greatest of privateers and greatest of admirals, who most fully embodied the spirit of lawless and lighthearted daring in which the English navy was now cradled. Son of a Protestant naval chaplain, he was brought up on a hulk anchored in the Medway, brought up to swim, to row and to handle a sailing ship in all weathers.

In November, 1577, after careful preparations, which Walsingham and the war party warmly encouraged, but of which Cecil must on no account hear, he sailed out of Plymouth Sound in the *Pelican*, a ship no larger than a modern racing yawl, accompanied by the *Elizabeth*, which was smaller by a third, a couple of sloops about half the size of the *Elizabeth*, and a twelve-ton pinnace, in which a yachtsman of to-day would hardly risk a summer cruise round Cornwall. With three ships he reached Magellan's Straits on August 20, which is midwinter in those climes. For three weeks they groped their way through the tortuous channel, overhung by wild and icy mountains. No sooner had they reached the Pacific than a fierce gale drove them far to the south-east, beyond Cape Horn. They thus discovered, what no one had suspected hitherto, that Tierra del Fuego did not stretch to the South Pole, and that the Straits of Magellan were not the only passage between the two oceans. South of America, Atlantic and Pacific met in open water: Terra Australis Incognita was a myth. Drake was careful not to divulge this great discovery to the Spanish prisoners captured later in his voyage, and it was many years before the Spaniards knew the truth.

But Drake had solved his problem. He had reached the Pacific. Upon the age-old peace of those remote waters he descended, terrible and unannounced, like a falcon from the blue. The whole western seaboard of the Americas was at the mercy of one small ship and a handful of Englishmen. The Spaniards had plenty of garrisons on land, but they had not dreamt of an attack from Europe, and at sea they had taken no precautions whatever, And the *Golden Hind* could outsail and outgun every Spanish vessel in the Pacific. They were taken completely unawares, and throughout the whole of an adventure during which he captured many prizes and a fabulous booty Drake seems not to have slain a single Spaniard. In September, 1580, the *Golden Hind* (for so the *Pelican* had been renamed) entered Plymouth harbour, having been gone three years, and traced the first circle round the globe, and changed the balance of power for generations to come. For in the oceanic era now opening English primacy was assured.

Drake was a pirate, but at a moment when piracy was the only means of assailing those who were preparing the destruction of England. And so, although a pirate, he was the first of the great English seamen who have saved our liberties and made the Empire.

And Drake was also the symbol of war. If he had failed, the peace party at Court might have had the upper hand, and Spain would have been left to dominate the new age. More than this, he was the symbol of achievement. The miracle of Drake ranked with the miracle of Columbus. All England thrilled with a sense of great things done, and the instinct that greater things were to be.

§3

In 1582 Philip of Spain began to build the Armada. Spain was undoubtedly the first nation of Europe. Within the space of fifty years the Spaniards had enlarged the boundaries of the world; they had conquered Mexico and Peru, colonised South America and seized Cuba, the West Indies, and the Philippines. They had built stately cities beyond the sea, and filled Spain with the fabulous riches of the west. And all this they had accomplished while they were holding the Turks and the Moors off Europe. Indeed they were the first nation in Europe and in the world, first in power, first in wealth, and first in achievement. And yet to be first was not sufficient. Could they remain first in an age of change? For the issue of great wars is decided by the whole pattern of civilisation in the contending states, upon which the strength and character of their war-making depends. And the civilisation of the Spaniards was neither pliable nor elastic enough to adapt itself to the needs of the new age. They were traditionalists in an era of change. Their rigid feudal hierarchy was capable of no new plans for the sea-battles to come, and although now, with the dark menace of Drake hanging over them, they began to build sailing men-of-war for the Armada-to-be, they followed a Portuguese model, high-castled, light-gunned troop-carriers, long obsolete in England, and destined to find themselves all but helpless against the swift heavy-gunned battleships which John Hawkins was now steadily turning out at Deptford. The Spaniards counted upon the favour of Providence to give them victory over the heretics, and upon the notorious dissensions among the heretics themselves, much exaggerated by the optimism customary, then as now, among refugees. English civilisation, emancipated from the rigid feudal mould, was much more fertile of innovations in war. Moreover if the English survived the coming struggle they were likely one day to found, as Spain could not, a new kind of Empire, not an Empire of priests and soldiers and racial arrogance, but a Commonwealth of merchant adventurers, with freedom as its foundation. This much was sufficient to save England from the mortal stroke which Philip intended. And this was all which the defeat of the Armada would ensure. England survived. She did not destroy the Spanish Empire, nor found an Empire of her own. More would be demanded of her, her strength and spirit must be tested in other and yet more searching trials, ere that could be.

The nation had been stung to anger, it is true, by the constant conflicts on the high seas, by the wrongs inflicted there and the wrongs endured, and above all by the highhanded cruelties of the Inquisition. Scarce a village of English seafolk but knew of some likely lad starved or tortured to death in prison, or toiling in the galleys or burnt alive because he owned an English bible or said an English prayer. Yet, half-consciously, perhaps, profounder impulses were at work. Riches and power, men believed, were to be won beyond the ocean, but they could not be shared with the Spaniards who claimed a monopoly of the new world. The new world must be fought for, or left to others. With such a choice before them, though their government might be in two minds, Englishmen did not hesitate.

It was the native qualities of the islanders which saved them, not their government. Elizabeth's indecision, and her natural parsimony—augmented and excused by the niggardliness of her Parliaments—did almost everything to ensure the Armada's success. Her navy had suffered both from partial neglect, and from corrupt administration. And even now she would not put her best ships into commission. What ships she had she starved of ammunition and food. The Armada sailed on the twenty-third of July; by the last week of the month the desperate English sailors were left with half-rations for a week, and powder for two days. Had they been properly supplied with powder and shot, the whole Armada might have been sunk off Plymouth in the first day's fighting. It was much the same with the militia. The men were ready, but they had been given no arms or stores with which to fight the first army in Europe, if it should land. Between them, Crown and Parliament had come near to betraying England. But her private citizens did not fail her. The gentlemen of the coastal regions came out in their own vessels and at their own charges to meet the enemy. In no other country in the world at that time, save the Low Countries, could the nation in this way have spontaneously saved itself.

The English ships could not only outsail but outgun the enemy. The Spanish soldiers who crowded the great galleons were waiting impatiently to board. Instead, they were mowed down by the broadsides of ships of twice their speed and agility, ships with which they were powerless to close, and which their own cannon could seldom reach. Every schoolboy knows how the miserable survivors of the catastrophe in the Channel were wrecked and massacred far along the inhospitable coasts of western Ireland. Of the thirty thousand who had set forth, a sick and starving remnant of nine thousand was all that at long last crept painfully back to Spain. The valour and devotion of these Spaniards had been worthy of victory, but the civilisation of Spain was static, and could not adapt itself adequately to the opportunities of the new age. She had founded an oceanic empire, but she had failed to become a naval power.

Despite their government the English seamen had saved England, and though they hardly knew it had made possible an English Empire. Victory they owed to their superior seamanship, and their superior seamanship to their own native qualities. They had faith, but so had the Spaniards. They were courageous but the Spaniards were courageous too. But their courage and their faith were of a new kind, and cradled in the Reformation. They did not, like the Spaniards, believe that if they prayed hard enough, and performed their religious duties with due devotion, and were valiant in battle, God must give them the victory. The English believed rather, as their adage has it, that God helps those who help themselves. They trusted in God to help them, but they knew that they must trust in themselves too. They must trust in God but they must also keep their powder dry. In this distinction lay the germ of the new age, of its virtues and, assuredly, of its vices too. Nevertheless it was well for the world that English seamen saved not only England but the world from the universal dominion of Spain and the Inquisition. For the virtues of Spain were not the imperial virtues, and her vices must have made her Empire a prison-house, dark with cruelty and oppression.

§4

Despite this sudden acquisition of naval supremacy, in the course of the desultory warfare which followed the defeat of the Armada England seized no part of the Spanish possessions. She had saved herself, but she was not yet ready for Empire. The pattern of her civilisation could already give her sea-power, from which all else would one day spring, but it was not adequate to support an offensive war upon the grand scale, and she had as yet neither the wealth nor the population for overseas expansion, or an empire of her own. Nor had she yet been tried sufficiently in the fires. And it was fortunate for England that she was not ready. For if in these years Drake or Grenville or Hawkins had wrested their overseas possessions from Portugal and Spain, English colonisation might have been diverted to tropical climes. The first foundations, it is true, might have been easier to lay there, and might have been laid sooner. But in that far, soft south the moral energy of the first settlers would soon have died away. As it was, no English colony took root in American soil during the reign of Elizabeth.

Tudor England prepared the sea routes to the new world, it was left to Stuart England to use them. Before Elizabeth died, Gilbert had declared English sovereignty over Newfoundland, Drake had annexed the coast of California for his Queen, and from Raleigh's efforts at least the name Virginia would survive; but no permanent settlement overseas, and no foundations of empire therefore, had been established. During these years, however, the English were both accumulating the necessary knowledge and making their first attempts, premature and ill-starred, at the settlement of America. The systematic, and indeed scientific, study of exploration, geography and colonisation owed most to Richard Hakluyt, the younger, who systematically collected, studied, preserved and published documentary records of maritime adventure and colonisation, and was recognised, abroad as well as at home, as a leading consultant geographer and advocate of colonial enterprise. But he was more than this. It is as an authentic picture of his own gallant contemporaries and of a young world full of mystery, beauty and adventure that Hakluyt's *English Voyages* lives. Reading these unassuming records of happenings heroic and fantastic, we are conscious of a light that never was, in our time at least, on land or sea, and feel, with Froude, that, although the blood of the Elizabethans is flowing in our veins, something since their day—not bravery, maybe, nor strength, nor wisdom, but *something*, not youth only but an indefinable grace, a zest, a confidence—has departed from us for ever.

Meanwhile the first crude attempts at colonisation were reproducing the pattern of the first voyages of discovery. Once again the government had no plan, and supplied no initiative. This was not the dawn of any sort of state expansion. Once again it is a story of individual enterprise, backed by a royal grant or charter, and by what was hardly so much the assistance, as the connivance, of particular persons in high place. Of the numerous individuals who, between the defeat of the Armada and the death of Elizabeth, helped to launch the first small, fumbling colonial ventures, and made the first inevitable mistakes, Sir Walter Raleigh was at once the most distinguished and, despite, or rather because of, his many-sidedness, in many ways the most characteristic. Politician and court favourite (two callings which under Elizabeth it was not always easy to distinguish), sailor and soldier, historian and philosopher, he was also a promoter of buccaneering expeditions, a sea-captain who had himself sailed the Spanish Caribbean to search for the gold of Guiana, and almost the first systematic coloniser of the new Continent.

Deep in the distracting business of the court, enmeshed in the

Queen's favour, Raleigh would fling, as it were, a handful of Englishmen at the vast and distant coast. They would disappear into the silence, and when, after many months, word of them found its way to England, it seldom made cheerful hearing. The first expedition sailed home, well pleased after landing on Roanoke Island and learning a little of the region and its natives. Elizabeth named the new country Virginia. The second venture, in 1585, deposited there Master Ralph Lane with one hundred and seven gentlemen, commoners and mariners. Here they remained for a year, and then took ship home with Drake, who had chanced that way. Fifteen men, left behind to keep the colonists' claim alive, were killed by Indians, or drowned while attempting to leave the island.

However daring or well organised, almost all the early attempts at colonisation, of which Raleigh's were characteristic, were doomed to eventual failure by the mere fact that they were the ventures of individuals. Only a constant flow of fresh colonists and fresh supplies could have ensured survival in such arduous and primitive conditions, and this was just what the promoters, whose capital had usually been exhausted on the original venture, could not contrive. Investors were not attracted by the prospect, as it appeared to them, of flinging good money after bad, and so colonies, which might have survived if vigorously reinforced and replenished from home, withered like untended seedlings in a drought. In colonisation private enterprise was far more adventurous than any government, but only when the Chartered Company had made co-operative adventure possible could it succeed.

Raleigh's third expedition, of 1587, for the first time included women and children. Here, for the first time, were the germs of a permanent and organic settlement. Seventeen women, two of them pregnant, and nine children, made that perilous voyage. What induced them to face the almost unimaginable discomforts and dangers of an Atlantic crossing in 1587, the terrible uncertainties of an attempted settlement? We do not know. We only know that they deserve a place of honour in the story of Empire. We only know that the whole colony vanished without trace.

BOOKS FOR FURTHER READING

J. A. Williamson, *The voyages of the Cabots* . . .; Callender, *The Naval side of British History;* J. A. Froude, *English Seamen in the Sixteenth Century;* J. A. Froude, *Short studies on great subjects*, vol. I; C. M. Andrews, *Our earliest Colonial Settlements;* J. D. Upcott, *Sir Francis Drake;* J. A. Williamson, *The age of Drake;* Dr. Frank Aydelotte, *Elizabethan seamen in Mexico and Ports of the Spanish Main;* Hakluyt, *Voyages.*

Book I

BIRTH OF A NEW WORLD

CHAPTER ONE

THE NEW AGE

FOR THE PROCESS now beginning to take shape there were no precedents. The Empire of Spain was already doomed, for it was an oceanic empire founded by a nation which had already lost the mastery of the sea, and which had never possessed, or in Spanish South America would speedily lose, the energy needful for a vast creative rôle. Nor were there precedents in the great Empire of the past whose boundaries had once been those of civilisation itself. For Rome had for the most part conquered inhabited provinces and held them with soldier settlers and military stations; her citizens had not streamed out, like the English, to make new homes in empty lands. Rome had spread her civilisation far and wide, but she did not give birth to new nations. The Roman Empire was the creation of the state, centralised, despotic and uniform; the expansion of England would be the work of individuals, and the growth of her Empire would be spontaneous and diverse. For the greatest community grows inevitably to the model of its inmost cell, and the Roman Empire did but mirror the Roman family, in which the *patria potestas*, the authority of the father, was despotic; whereas the tradition of the English family was to train its sons for an independent life of their own. For the same reason religion, which would send so many of the English to seek new homes overseas, played no part in the expansion of Rome. The slavery upon which the Roman Empire, like the Roman family, was founded, rendered it yet more uniform by setting up a ubiquitous class distinction which served to obliterate the barriers of race. Rome knew nothing of the representative system, which the English were already beginning to perfect, and perhaps for that reason nothing of the federal idea. Rome's was a close-knit military Empire of the land, with the long straight roads radiating from the forum at Rome to every corner of the known world, with only the friendly, landlocked Mediterranean and the English Channel to cross; the English would found a straggling civilian-minded Empire of the seas, and long before the day of the sailing-ship had passed they would be crossing seas yet undreamed of to settle in the remote Antipodes. Why did the Roman Empire fall? It would be wiser perhaps to inquire why it endured so long—Roman provincial administration, reckons Arnold, lasted seven hundred years; and if, with Bury, we see the Eastern and Western Empires as essentially one, the rule of Rome may be said to have survived for sixteen centuries. Partly no doubt it was its moderation which preserved the Roman Empire; for, unlike Athens, Rome knew when to be content with what she had, and moderation, we shall see, counterpart of their hereditary instinct for compromise, would be the saving principle of the English also. But the final answer must be that in a static age Rome gave the world what the world most needed. The Empire of the English, we may conclude, would endure so long as, in an age of change, it too enshrined a principle of which the world had need.

We are in the presence of one of the epochal moments of history. And like all such moments it is mysterious. It can be explained, but it can only be partially explained. Why did this small island, sparsely populated, by no means wealthy and now increasingly distracted by civil strife, launch itself upon so vast an undertaking as the colonisation of the New World? What urgent motives sufficed to impel eighty thousand Englishmen to cross the Atlantic and brave the wilderness, before the outbreak of the civil war in 1641? The final answer to questions such as these must be sought at levels of reality more profound than those with which history usually concerns itself.

It will assuredly not be found among the glib economic theories and reasons of state which the political economists of the day, as we should call them, were so ready to bandy about. Their views had already been clearly set forth before 1590, in terms which were constantly echoed during the next sixty years, and indeed would need little substantial modification for the next two hundred. Colonies, the economists said, must be profitable because they would supply commodities otherwise necessarily imported from foreign lands, and so promote that favourable balance of trade to which the so-called mercantilist theory of the time attached such excessive importance. To produce the goods required, Englishmen must settle overseas, and, once established there—an additional advantage —the colonists would themselves import manufactured goods from England. Again, strangely enough at first sight, it was generally believed by contemporaries that even Elizabethan England was over-populated. There were no statistics, of course, but men's imaginations were haunted by the growing army of disorderly and

vagrant poor, most of them uprooted from the soil by the agricultural revolution of the sixteenth century. The still familiar
Hark, hark the dogs do bark, The beggars are coming to town . . . commemorates a grim everyday possibility, which must have sent a
frisson of disquiet through many a nursery in the age of the great
enclosures when the rhyme was first sung. Colonies, it was held,
might draw off this dubious surplus of unemployed paupers, "living
altogether unprofitable and oftentimes to the disquiet of the better
sort." But though an expedition overseas did sometimes occasion
something like a gaol-delivery of local n'er-do-weels and unfortun-
ates, the importance of this element in migration was deliberately
exaggerated by contemporary publicists and politicians in order to
placate the Spaniards, who would be earnestly assured that an
expedition had sailed, not against His Majesty of Spain but "to drive
from here thieves and traitors to be drowned in the sea." By some
advocates of colonisation its strategic advantages were also stressed,
for the later stages of the Spanish war had suggested the need of
military bases in the West from which to strike at the Spanish
colonies. And closely coupled, as always, with this commercial and
self-interested individualism was a genuine missionary impulse.
"Far be it from the hearts of the English that they should give any
cause to the world to say that they sought the wealth of that country
above or before the glory of God and the propagation of His
Kingdom"; so wrote Robert Gray in 1609.

Such were the grounds on which statesmen or publicists saw fit
to advocate colonial enterprise. But the effective impulse to migration came not from statesmen, but from individuals. And they, we
may be certain, thought little of trade balances or population, and
much of more personal incentives, the prospect of adventure, of gold
or of land, the desire for fuller political liberty, or for freedom to
worship God in their own way. But beyond, or beneath, all such
superficial motives, public or private, forces more deep-seated and
compelling were at work. For there are moments in history when
a whole nation suddenly responds to opportunity or inspiration,
seeming to accept a mysterious summons from destiny, as birds will
obey the obscure impulses of migration. There are moments when,
in the words of Lord Grey of Fallodon, "there is more in the minds
of events than in the minds of the chief actors." At such moments
neither reason of state, as seen by the man of affairs, nor yet the
various incentives of which the individual is conscious, nor even
all these together, will fully account for the outburst of energy
which ensues. The nation itself may be said to be responding,
altogether instinctively, to impulses of which it is never consciously

aware, and to laws of which as yet we know little. We may say, if we will, that destiny beckons to it. As in dreams the subconscious mind of the individual can sometimes foresee the future, so, it is possible, the subconscious mind of the nation is sometimes aware of what awaits it. Few, no doubt, of the multitude of individual adventurers who crossed the Atlantic were moved by any such prescience; only, beneath the immediate personal motives, economic, political or religious, to which they knowingly responded, there will often have been a dim impersonal instinct that they were serving larger and remoter ends.

§2

The defeat of the Armada had ensured the survival of Protestantism and freedom in England. It had made Empire possible. The question now was, what use would be made of the new opportunities? It was for a new generation to find the answer, for by 1600, Leicester and Walsingham, Grenville and Frobisher, Hawkins, Drake and Burghley were all dead. The Elizabethan age had ended, and with it a primal grace and energy, not to be seen again. From the seventeenth century, the era of the Stuarts and of Parliamentary conflict, the bloom of youth and confidence seems to have vanished. Seen in a merely national and European setting it appears but a prelude to the revolutionary settlement of 1689, and save for a few years under Cromwell's Protectorate, England seems to have sunk once more to the degree of a third-rate power. View it, however, against the larger imperial background, and the age of the Stuarts takes on a new dignity and significance. For now the first colonies were planted in the West, and the foundations of English power laid in the East. And during these years the Spaniards and the Dutch fell behind in the race for expansion, and the arena was cleared for the imperial contest with France in the eighteenth century. Nor did the Stuarts and their ministers, whatever their other faults, lack wisdom or energy in their handling of the first colonial problems. And if England was partially paralysed by its own internal conflicts, Europe was altogether distracted, from 1618 to 1648, by the Thirty Years' War.

Even so it is strange enough (and far stranger than our time-honoured tradition, of over-estimating the importance of our domestic political history, usually allows us to recognise) that the age of the Stuarts, a century, it would seem, all distemper and civil strife, should have laid the foundation of Empire so firm and wide—

long before, as we are taught to believe, the nation found its true self in the Glorious Revolution of 1689. For there would have been no Empire, of that we may be sure, if those who laid its foundations had not possessed some quality of absolute value, some virtue of which the world stood in need. Nor is this paradox, of the unstable and divided society at home and the enduring foundations overseas, to be explained merely by reminding ourselves that the Englishmen who sailed across the ocean, and indeed the English people as a whole, were superior to their governments. Their governments indeed, even the Stuart governments, possessed very solid merits; only—and here the seeming paradox is accounted for—at home the virtues of government and people were incompatible. For the Stuart government, at its best, stood for benevolent authoritarianism; Strafford and his *Thorough*, for example, did much to protect the poor against the self-seeking individualism of the middle-class merchants and capitalists who backed Parliament against the king. Yet at home this virtue in the Stuarts did but assist their vices, their arbitrary oppression, unreliability and bad judgment, to ensure their fall. For, until control of the state had been wrested from the crown, state interference, which was to become the favourite watchword of a later age, ran clean counter to the hereditary English instinct for personal liberty. And so, lest its saving virtues be extinguished, the excesses of individual enterprise must persist for two centuries yet unpruned. And at home the island people, ready and eager now, before any other people in the world, to govern itself, must fight to the death against the authoritarian monarchy which stood between it and its destiny of spreading freedom across the world. The Petition of Right against the autocracy of Charles the First, and the Declaration of Rights prepared for William the Third, are thus two further stages in the great process which began with Magna Carta, the process by which England was not only enlarging her own liberties but preparing herself for her imperial task. At home all this meant conflict between a nation whose deepest instincts warned it of its destiny and a monarchy whose qualities were even more dangerous than its defects. But overseas the virtues of government and people were not incompatible; indeed they were complementary. There free enterprise and authoritarianism need not yet come to grips. The people were the pioneers; it was the free initiative, the courage or the piety of countless individual Englishmen which drove them across the ocean to tame the wilderness and endure the horrid sufferings of the first plantations. Nevertheless the government could come much nearer to seeing the pattern as a whole. The English colonies in America might recognise no mutual bond, but for the king's government each was but a part of the king's dominions, and in this era it was the government, and the government only, which could conceive of some sort of unity among them. And when the impulse which carried the first settlers overseas had begun to flag, the government did much to foster a new sort of plantation.

§3

The reign of the first Stuart did not open promisingly. Raleigh was in the Tower, and the Navy began to fall on evil days. For James disliked fighting men and desired the friendship of Spain, and it seemed unlikely that he would look favourably on adventure overseas. The final tragedy of Raleigh indeed, though deferred till 1618, was typical of James, or at any rate of James at his worst. From the Tower Raleigh staked all that was left of his own and his wife's fortune, his honour and the trust of his friends, on an expedition to find a gold mine in Guiana. The king wanted gold, and though he did not want piracy, was not averse to showing Spain by his intrusion that his friendship was worth courting. As for Raleigh, doubtless he desired his liberty; probably he hoped to render war with Spain inevitable, and thereafter to do her terrible injury; he may have hoped to capture the Plate fleet; and almost certainly he believed in his gold mine, which he had found more than twenty years earlier on the Orinoco, then unvisited by Spaniards. But he consented to bind himself to assail no Spaniard on his voyage, and, even if he did not know at first that since he last saw Guiana Spaniards had settled between his gold mine and the sea, he can hardly have expected to fulfil such a pledge. From the first fortune deserted him. While he waited on guard at the river-mouth, his men took the Spanish town but did not reach the mine. His son was killed and his crew mutinied. But though he knew that the king had communicated all his plans to Gondomar, the Spanish ambassador, and that he was returning to renewed imprisonment, and probably to death, he came back. He was soon in the Tower again, and before long was condemned to be beheaded. Raleigh was a wayward genius, and a fanatic of Empire, who combined passionate sincerity with a fatal habit of prevarication in detail, thanks to which, in the final crisis of his fortunes, he was quite unnecessarily disbelieved in his main assertions. He had toiled, and suffered, greatly to inspire his fellow countrymen with his own vision of an imperial destiny. When the English navy deserted Charles I at the outbreak of the Civil War, the ghost of Raleigh may be said to have pursued the Stuarts to their downfall.

But all this was still unguessed when James came to the throne, and set himself to come to an accommodation with Spain. The Treaty of London, which, in 1604, gave its quietus to the slowly expiring Spanish war, failed altogether to settle the wider imperial issue. Spaniards still held that no foreigner was entitled to occupy territory in the New World, theirs by right of prior discovery and the authority of Papal bulls. The English still claimed the right to settle in any lands "not actually possessed," as the charter of Virginia put it, "by any Christian prince or people." And at that the Treaty left it. The upshot was dictated by force of circumstances, and more or less justified the English contention. Spain was naturally unable to keep Englishmen out of America, but naturally, too, foreign settlers steered clear of the territories already effectively occupied by Spaniards or Portuguese, that is to say the western mainland of America from the Florida Channel to Buenos Ayres, with the exception of Guiana. But these were no narrow limits. Virtually the whole of what is now the United States of America lay open, awaiting the European intruder.

CHAPTER TWO

VIRGINIA

(1606-1641)

§1

ON THE North American mainland the two main theatres of the strange and memorable scenes now to be enacted were Virginia and New England. Between them they illustrate to admiration not only the main types of the crude, experimental machinery of early colonisation, but the courage, enterprise and idealism which gave the clumsy mechanism life. The contrast between the two stories moreover sharply illustrates the variety of motive which sent Englishmen to face the hazards of the New World.

Unlike the later colonies in New England, whose first settlers were religious enthusiasts determined to set up a City of God upon earth, Virginia was a commercial venture of hard-bitten soldiers of fortune, adventurers, younger sons and rapscallions. The Charter of 1606 placed the whole of the vast and unknown territories between latitude north 34° and 45° under the authority of a Royal Council of Virginia, in England, which seems to have been intended to become an embryo Colonial Office, or at least a sort of privy council for colonial affairs. The foundation of this, as of all early colonial enterprise, was a charter. For while the government had not the enterprise to undertake colonisation, the individual adventurer lacked the resources to withstand the long financial drain of an attempted settlement. The Chartered Company was the device which met the new needs, one of the earliest of that long series of voluntary associations which have been so distinctive a trait of the English genius, a characteristic attempt to combine effective corporate action with the highest possible degree of individual self-expression. It was a direct descendant of the mediæval trade corporation, whose novel features were the limited financial liability of the individual shareholder and the free transference of his shares. This new mechanism, which steadily adapted itself to experience, canalised and concentrated the restless energy and heterogeneous motives of the early English adventurers. Thus chartered, and optimistically authorised for twenty-one years to make what profit they could of a duty on all non-members who might one day trade

with their still non-existent colony, the Virginia Company's first
small expeditionary force set sail in December, 1606. Two-thirds of
its members were to perish before the year was out.

The most remarkable character in that ill-starred company was
a certain Captain John Smith. Into the eleven years since he was
apprenticed, at fifteen, he had already crowded the adventures of a
lifetime. He had served in the Dutch, French and Transylvanian
armies, had been robbed and beaten by outlaws and thrown into the
sea for a heretic. He had been slave to a Turkish pasha, and fought
three Turkish champions in single combat, decapitating each in
turn. On the strength of the reputation thus acquired he had been
selected as one of the resident council which was to direct affairs
in Virginia; a prescient choice, as it was to prove. Meanwhile his
remarkable talent for hairbreadth escapes did not desert him: on
the outward voyage he was charged with conspiracy, and kept under
arrest until three weeks after the settlers had landed at Jamestown,
when he was admitted to the council. He bore more than his full
share of the labours and perils of the first year, during the early
months of which a good deal of the surrounding wildwood was
explored, and, despite a certain amount of fighting, a precarious
understanding was come to with most of the neighbouring Indians.
(On one of their voyages up river during this period the settlers
sighted "a Savage Boy about the age of ten yeeres, which had a head
of haire of a perfect yellow and a reasonable white skinne," not
improbably a descendant of one of the lost colony of Roanoke.) On
June the 22nd, 1607, Captain Newport, who had been in command
of the ships, sailed for England, promising to be back within twenty
weeks with fresh supplies, and leaving behind him a company of
one hundred and four "verie bare and scantie of victualls, further-
more in warres and danger of the Savages." The outlook was now
almost as black as it could be. Having been five months on their
voyage, instead of two, as they had expected, the settlers had arrived
too late in the season to plant crops. And now the full heat of the
Virginian summer blazed down upon them. Where they had
scratched some sort of tillage in the forest glades, weeds, briars and
bushes began to spring up with uncanny speed and luxuriance.
Unenviable indeed was the plight of the starving and undisciplined
amateurs, struggling with their unaccustomed tools alone in the
parched fields amid the malarial and Indian-haunted forest. And
from August onwards the small company began to die off very
quickly of typhoid, malaria and the various diseases which starvation
breeds. The narratives of the survivors become a mere chronicle
of deaths:

Our men were destroyed with cruell diseases, as Swellings, Flixes, Burning Fevers, and by warres, and some departed suddenly, but for the most part they died of meer famine. There were never Englishmen left in a forreigne Countrey in such miserie as wee were in this new discovered Virginia. Wee watched every three nights, lying on the bare cold ground, what weather soever came, [and] warded all the next day, which brought our men to bee most feeble wretches. Our food was but a small Can of Barlie sod in water, to five men a day, our drinke cold water taken out of the River, which was at a floud verye salt, at a low tide full of slime and filth, which was the destruction of many of our men. Thus we lived for the space of five months in this miserable distresse. not having five able men to man our Bulwarkes upon any occasion.

All day the great forests, harbourage of the ever treacherous Indians, shimmered in the heat, and by night the fort was loud with the groans of the sick and dying; and often enough, when dawn broke, there would be three or four corpses "like Dogges to be buried." Such were the origins of the English Empire in America.

All this while Smith was foremost in encouraging those who could still work to mow, thatch and build, himself working longer hours than any. The survivors were saved by supplies opportunely brought in by the Indians, or procured in adventurous trading expeditions by Smith—whose courage and genius for Indian diplomacy could always obtain much better value in supplies than the feckless majority of the settlers.

In the course of an unusually long expedition into the interior Smith was taken prisoner. He was three weeks in the hands of the Indians, who seem to have regarded him with a mixture of superstitious reverence and alarm. During his captivity he instructed them in the elements of astronomy and geography, enlarged upon the wonders of Europe, and insisted upon the omnipotence of the God who had created all these marvels, of whom the Indians learned to speak with bated breath as "the God of Captain Smith." Despite his unbounded influence over the Indians he would have been executed—so marvellous a being was obviously dangerous—but for the last-moment intervention of the King's young daughter, Pocohontas.[1] He returned to the fort, now held by less than forty sickly survivors of the original hundred and five, only to be arrested

---

[1] After many adventures and giving much help to the settlers, Pocohontas married an Englishman, John Rolfe, and became "the first Christian ever of that nation, the first Virginian ever spake English, or had a childe in mariage by an Englishman."

and condemned to death by the Council, which was already seething with faction. He escaped hanging by the timely return of Captain Newport, and seems then to have resumed his place as the natural leader of the little community, the chief source of its energy and confidence and a name to conjure with among the surrounding Indians. With them, as with his fellow settlers, he was ready to be ruthless. Orders from England were to do them no harm, and in the story of Empire John Smith was the first of many men on the spot (to use a phrase which became familiar long afterwards) who found it advisable to disregard his orders. He doubtless consoled himself by reflecting that the men who issued the instructions had had no experience of being ambushed by a scalping party. In his last two years in Virginia, he boasted afterwards, not a single settler was slain; "whereas before we had sometimes peace and war twice in one day, and not a week passed without some treacherous villainy or other, they were now in such fear and obedience that Smith's very name would sufficiently affright them."

In September, 1608, he was formally elected President of the Council, and as President proceeded to replan the fort, train the guard and drill the whole company on an improvised parade-ground, named Smithfield after himself. As President he carried the settlement safely through many and varied emergencies, sometimes outwitting the ever unreliable Indians, sometimes attacking and chastising them, and sometimes overaweing them by sheer force of personality. His tenacity and resolution alone held the colony together. His rule was doubtless virtually martial law, but the resolute leader cannot be over-squeamish when his followers are starving in a wilderness. Nor, meanwhile, did his most characteristic gift desert him; he continued to escape by the skin of his teeth from a succession of appalling perils. It was fortunate indeed for Virginia that neither attempted assassinations, Indian ambushes, nor a hand to hand fight with the Paspaheigh Chief could dispose of, or even perturb, its President.

There was little enough now to tempt fortune-seekers, one would have thought, in the precarious settlement, so constantly on the verge of starvation, and reduced during Smith's Presidency by the depredations of rats among the stores to billeting most of the settlers among the Indians. Yet each new Supply from England brought not only a few much needed commodities but fresh settlers, of whom only the toughest survived the diseases which regularly assailed the unseasoned. It was with the coming of the Third Supply, in 1609, that Smith's Presidency came to an end. For "to redresse those Jarres and ill proceedings," by which the colony had so far been distinguished, a revised Charter had been framed, and the office of President, the colonists now learned, no longer existed. The resident Council, arena of so many quarrels and intrigues, had been suppressed. A Governor, subject only to the Council in England, was to reign supreme. Few who have read the early accounts of the constant factions and intrigues which persisted even during Smith's virtual autocracy will be inclined to blame the constitution-makers at home for this reversion from oligarchy to dictatorship. Sir Thomas Gates, the new Governor, with his brand new Commission and a hundred and fifty of the five hundred settlers with whom he set sail, was wrecked en route on the Bermudas and did not reach Virginia until May of the following year. The new-comers, meanwhile, proved to include three of the original expedition who had returned home, and now reappeared, only too ready to renew the fierce quarrels of which they had already been the storm-centre. In the midst of the ensuing disputes Smith's customary genius for hairbreadth escapes temporarily deserted him, and he was so severely wounded by the accidental explosion of a bag of gunpowder that (although, recovering his natural aptitude, he survived a plot to murder him shortly afterwards) he was incapable of defending himself effectively against the various charges which his enemies, and many who had resented his discipline or suffered his punishments, now hastened to bring against him. He decided to sail for England with the returning vessels of the Third Supply, and departed early in October, 1609.

Captain John Smith possessed not only tenacity, courage and intelligence, but another gift, at least as uncommon and at least as necessary, the capacity to deal wisely and firmly with savage races. Without him there could have been no Indian trade worth having; without him, indeed, the colony would have starved or been massacred almost at once. The survivors, it is true, were not particularly virtuous or valiant, or of any social consequence. But they were the germ of something greater than themselves and, if only because of their sufferings, they deserve respect. Smith had saved Virginia in its infancy, a feat at least as arduous as many better remembered and more widely recorded. He was the prototype of many others who have figured in the British story, well known, little known or not known at all, men of infinite determination and resource who were usually forthcoming when need arose, in however remote a corner of one or other of the five continents. It has been the almost miraculous abundance of such individuals, rather than the statesmen, the merchants or the economists which has made the Empire.

§2

Like Smith himself, Virginia had survived thus far by the narrowest of margins. After the coming of the Third Supply, with its riff-raff of new unsuitables, the outlook grew darker still. On Smith's departure there followed the grim six months long remembered as the Starving Time, during which the settlers were reduced to living on roots, acorns and berries, and even to cannibalism. Ten more days, the survivors reckoned, and when Sir Thomas Gates and Sir George Somers, having built a new ship in the Bermudas, at length sailed up the James River, on May 23, 1610, they would have found the silence of death brooding over the skeleton of Jamestown. As it was, sixty emaciated wretches crawled out to meet the newcomers.

The hundred and fifty new settlers were no doubt horrified by the appearance of their predecessors. They must have been just as unpleasantly surprised by their background—the palisades torn down, the fifty wooden houses neglected or half-burned, the tools and arms traded to the savages, the domestic animals eaten, the clearings abristle with weeds and undergrowth. After a fortnight in which to deliberate, and listen to the stories of the survivers, Somers and Gates agreed to abandon Virginia. More than eight hundred persons had landed since the spring of 1607; sixty survivors, with nothing but the rags they stood up in, embarked for home on June 7, 1610, bidding farewell, for ever as they supposed, to the wreck of Jamestown and its grim memories. But "God would not have it so abandoned." At the mouth of the river they were astonished to perceive a ship's boat being rowed towards them, and on being boarded by its English crew, to learn that Lord de la Warr, with three well-stocked vessels, was off the Capes. The combined flotillas returned to Jamestown. Three days after leaving it, as they supposed, for ever the colonists disembarked once more, and, reviving fading memories of their drilling by Captain Smith, actually drew up in military array to receive their new Governor. For de la Warr had been appointed Governor and Captain General of Virginia for life. His firm hand, and the fresh supplies which he had brought, soon restored discipline and confidence, but after less than a year a succession of illnesses compelled him to leave, and even now the settlement had hardly taken root.

The early colonists had laboured under two crippling disadvantages, communal ownership and its inevitable consequence, martial law. The business of all proved to be the business of none;

men would not work for the common store as they would have
worked for their own families or for themselves, and Smith and his
immediate successors had to drive on their reluctant followers with
savage threats and punishments. In such a setting the English
genius could not flourish. The effects of a very partial introduction
of private property under Sir Thomas Dale were startling and
immediate. Each man was given three acres of his own, but still
had to work eleven months out of twelve for the general store.
Even so, the lazy turned industrious almost overnight:

> When our people were fed out of the common store, and
> laboured jointly together, glad was he could slip from his
> labour, or slumber over his taske he cared not how, nay, the
> most honest among them would hardly take so much true
> paines in a weeke, as now for themselves they will doe in a day;
> neither cared they for the increase, presuming that howsoever
> the harvest prospered, the generall store must maintaine them,
> so that wee reaped not so much Corne from the labours of
> thirtie, as now three or foure doe provide for themselves.

Gradually, but only gradually, the authorities in England came
to realise that communal ownership and compulsion must go hand
in hand, and that even if the colony had not at first consisted so
largely of ne'er-do-weels, the primitive communism which it
practised would have compelled early Presidents and Governors to
resort to the martial law which was for long the subject of acute
controversy at home. As long as all labour was for the community
only, savage sanctions were needed to ensure that it was properly
performed. In 1618 the Company gave Virginia the first written
Constitution in America, a "great charter of priviledges, orders and
Lawes" which provided not only a governor and Council but a
General Assembly. Parliamentary institutions began as communism
ended. On July 30, 1619, a memorable date, the first legislative
assembly to be convened on the American Continent met in the
church of Jamestown, in the persons of the Governor, six members
of Council and twenty burgesses, two from each of ten settlements.
England had begun her long task of spreading self-government
about the world.

Neither opposition nor the arts of obstruction troubled this first
Assembly, and it proceeded to pass a prodigious number of measures
in five days. But the *Proceedings of the Virginia Assembly* are not
remarkable only for their quantity. No one who comes upon them
fresh from the record of worldliness, violence and disaster, which

appears to fill the early years of the colony, can fail to be astonished at the high proportion of measures which seem to be inspired by a strict Puritanism. The sumptuary laws against idleness, gaming, drunkenness and "excesse in apparell" were perhaps to be expected, but the Virginian burgesses went much further than this. In the elaborate code which they proceeded to lay down for their own moral and religious discipline we almost seem to be breathing the austere air of a New England theocracy. All Ministers are to read divine service, and catechise the young every Sunday. The Ministers and Churchwardens are to present the incontinent and, if need be, excommunicate them. After being thrice admonished for swearing, the culprit is to pay the church five shillings for every offence. Every one is to attend divine service and sermons every Sunday, both morning and afternoon, upon pain of a three shilling fine. And all these admirable measures were enacted within a stone's throw of ground on which a few years earlier Virginians had been reduced to cannibalism. Yet they are characteristic; for whenever the English were most truly themselves there lay beneath their expansion overseas a certain sense of moral obligation, a conscious-ness of something owed to the world, rather than the expectation of what might be acquired from it.

But the days of the Virginia Company were now numbered. Everything seemed to conspire against it. For one thing, King James and the Company quarrelled long and bitterly over the tobacco duties. Above all, the Company had been formed to make a profit for the shareholders, it was not making anything of the kind, and without gold, and without a trading monopoly, there seemed little prospect of its ever doing so. In 1624 its patent was revoked. Virginia thus became the first royal colony—for Bermuda remained for another fifty years in the hands of a company. Under the new constitution it was to be managed by an English Council, itself entitled to appoint a Governor and twelve assistants in the colony. The General Assembly of Virginia, which had met for five years, from 1619 to the fall of the Company, resumed formal sessions from 1630 to 1638, although there is no evidence that the Crown had empowered the Governor to summon it. The English Ministers, in all probability, had not made up their minds. The action of the Virginians forced them to decide, one way or the other. And as so often in English history, theory was compelled to follow on the heels of practise, and authority flung its belated mantle of respecta-bility over experiment. In instructions of 1639 and 1641 the English Government authorised the Governor to summon the legislative assembly of Virginia every year. The Virginians had forced the

King's hand. A precedent had been established for all America. Government was not to be by Governor and Council, but by Governor, Council and Assembly; that is to say, as at home, by King and people. In the long perspective of history this is the true justification of the sufferings of the first settlers of Virginia.

CHAPTER THREE

THE PURITANS IN NEW ENGLAND

(1620-1660)

§1

VIRGINIA had survived its infancy for destinies still unimaginable in 1624. Yet it is possible that if Virginia had remained the only English colony Englishmen would before long have tired of the arduous business of colonisation. Fortunately a colonial story of a very different kind was now opening, of so different a kind, indeed, that the Pilgrim Fathers of New England are generally accorded the credit of having been founders of the United States, although the *Mayflower* did not sail from England until Virginia had been founded fourteen years, and had held its first General Assembly.

While elsewhere in the New World—in Newfoundland and the West Indies, in Bermuda, about the Orinoco and the Amazon and in parts of New England itself—colonisation on the Virginian model was being attempted or achieved, in New England a new motive, and a new colonial model, were to appear. Everywhere—even, as we have seen, among the scandals and disasters of the early days of Virginia—religion furnished one of the motives, and contributed largely to the rules of conduct, of the first colonists. Only in New England was religion all, the sole inspiration of the founders and the sole basis of the society they set up. In its heyday Puritanism, that offspring of the Reformation which had turned its back upon the Renaissance, was the most otherworldly of religions, consistently treating this life as what all forms of Christianity have professed to believe it, a mere antechamber of eternity. The heyday of Puritanism in England, however, was brief, scarcely more than fifty years, with Cromwell as its statesman, Milton as its poet and *Paradise Lost* as its swan-song. It was during these years of its dynamic activity, while Puritanim was the storm-centre of both religion and politics in England, that Puritans settled Massachusetts Bay. From the first, with such origins, the history of Massachusetts was bound to follow a very different course to that of Virginia and the other settlements. Here a colony, or rather perhaps a religious community, came into existence full grown. There would be no slow and precarious development, no painful fumbling for rough and ready means of self-discipline and defence, no haphazard despatch of rogues and adventurers, scarcely any serious friction among the leaders, no disasters so frightful as to threaten the existence of the settlement, and for more than fifty years no effective interference from without. Certainly Puritanism justified itself in the eminently practical business of settlement overseas; the other-worldly were not un-worldly. It is not to be wondered at that America has been so ready to instal the Pilgrim Fathers of New England as its founders *par excellence*.

Until the great Puritan migration, which carried twenty thousand English people across the Atlantic within twelve years, all previous attempts at plantation in New England, or all but one, had come to an untimely end. Before 1629, New England contained only a few hundred scattered fishermen, fur-traders and nomads, without cohesion or government of any kind—these, together with a small group of Pilgrim Fathers at Plymouth, where a small religious community, rather than a colony, had taken root. These Puritans of Plymouth were the forerunners of the full Puritan migration which was to mould New England into a new colonial model. A number of the "persecuted flock of Christ" from the village of Scrooby in Nottinghamshire and Gainsborough in Lincoln-shire had migrated to Leyden, in Holland, in 1607. There, after ten years, though they had lived under the Dutch government, practis-ing their Congregational worship "with much peace and liberty," they began to reflect on the manifold inconveniences of life in a foreign land, and "how like we were to lose our language and our name of English." After the Lord had been "solemnly sought in the congregation by fasting and prayer to direct us" they dispatched two envoys to England, to persuade King James to allow them "to enjoy their liberty of conscience under his gracious protection in America." Their entreaties were supported by powerful friends at Court, including the principal Secretary of State, and James was in any case never averse to seeing Puritans leave Europe. He had an eye, however, for the commercial aspects of the proposal:

> This his Majesty said was a good and honest motion, and asking what profits might arise in the parts we intended (for our eye was upon the most northern parts of Virginia) 'twas answered, Fishing. To which he replied with his ordinary asseveration, "So God have My soul, 'tis an honest trade, 'twas the Apostles' own calling."

The applicants were given to understand that His Majesty was willing enough, as Governor Bradford put it, to suffer them without molestation, though he would not confirm it by any public act; in other words, he would connive at their going, very much as Elizabethan ministers had connived at the exploits of Drake. In 1619 they obtained a patent from the Virginia Company, and on September 6, 1620, about one hundred and twenty of them set sail from Southampton in the *Mayflower*. They were not the first colonists of North America, nor yet were they the Puritans who spread the Puritan model of government over New England, and beyond it. But this was the first Puritan migration, these were the Pilgrim Fathers, and posterity has accepted them as the parents of the great democracy to be. They sought, not their own fortunes, but a city of God on earth, and their leave-taking was naturally different from that of the first Virginians, fourteen years earlier. One of them has left a picture of the parting from the rest of their community in Leyden:

> And when the ship was ready to carry us away, the brethren that stayed having again solemnly sought the Lord with us and for us, and we further engaging ourselves mutually as before, they, I say, that stayed at Leyden feasted us that were to go, at our pastor's house, being large; where we refreshed ourselves, after tears, with singing of psalms, making joyful melody in our hearts, as well as with the voice, there being many of the congregation very expert in music; and indeed it was the sweetest melody that ever mine ears heard . . . and after prayer performed by our pastor, where a flood of tears was poured out, they accompanied us to the ship, but were not able to speak one to another for the abundance of sorrow to part. But we only going aboard . . . we gave them a volley of small shot and three pieces of ordnance, and so lifting up our hands to each other, and our hearts for each other to the Lord our God, we departed, and found his presence with us in the midst of our manifold straits he carried us through.

They landed at Cape Cod in November, and in December founded the colony of Plymouth, in New England. The hardihood of the Pilgrims, and their families, so characteristic of the English adventurers, may be judged from the fact that a child was born on the *Mayflower* at sea, and christened Oceanus, and another, Peregrine White, in Cape Cod harbour. It is pleasant to note that, as recorded in his obituary notice in the fifteenth number of the *Boston News Letter*, the first newspaper printed in New England, Peregrine died in Marshfield, New England, in 1704, at the age of eighty-three, "vigorous and of a comely aspect to the last." At first, however, there was the usual mortality, so that by the following March, as a survivor recorded, "of a hundred persons scarce fifty remain;[1] the living scarce able to bury the dead; the well not sufficient to tend the sick, there being, in their time of greatest distress, but six or seven, who spare no pains to help them." All traces of the burials were carefully obliterated, lest the Indians should discover how the numbers of the colony were diminishing.

A visitor to Plymouth, that summer of 1621, would have seen, as he landed, between a high bluff and a swift little stream, a rough log house, about twenty foot square, which contained the common property of the settlers. Beyond it he would have passed, up a gentle slope, between two rows of cabins, nineteen in all (the number of the families in the settlement) some of them empty since the death of all their tenants in the first epidemic; and so to a hill, its summit levelled for cannon. At work in the enclosures about the huts, or fishing in the harbour, or going to the woods for game, he might have counted twenty men, while six or seven women, busy with household tasks, and some twenty children, gave the rude scene a domestic background.

§2

But the story of these first Pilgrims of the *Mayflower* is the story of a small enterprise, illumined indeed by faith, hope and charity, but limited by scanty numbers and slender resources, and far removed from the central currents of English life. History has glorified the *Mayflower* fathers, but it was with the founding of the Colony in Massachusetts Bay that the veritable Puritan migration began, organised by men of public authority and wealth, and deliberately aimed at founding in the New World not a colony, but a powerful Puritan state. How did this great enterprise, portal to such vast consequences, come about?

It was due partly to events in New England, but mainly to the rapid slide, during the sixteen-twenties and thirties, toward religious and political crisis at home. These new Puritan emigrants were not only a "persecuted flock of Christ" seeking to found a city of God on earth, they were also refugees, fleeing from the disasters threatening their native land. The great conception of an independent Puritan Commonwealth has been credited by various writers and at

---

[1] Actually Prince, who had Governor Bradford's notebook with a register of births and deaths, reckoned forty-four deaths out of a hundred.

various times to more than one individual: it is more likely that it grew fragmentarily and by degrees, from mind to mind, and under pressure of circumstance here and overseas. Indeed it is not difficult to trace its steady development through a succession of more or less related events. Thus in 1623 the Reverend John White, Rector of Dorchester, and a group of West Country merchants, had planned a permanent fishing settlement in New England. And that summer a shipload of fishermen and planters sailed from Weymouth and landed at Cape Ann, but the settlement was a dismal failure. By 1626 it had broken up, save for a remnant of twenty or thirty, under Roger Conant, who took the Indian trail to Naumkeag, destined in due time to be familiar as the prosperous port of Salem. Even now, however, the seminal idea, of a Puritan Commonwealth, had, in all probability, not been born. And while Conant and the Old Planters were clinging to the Salem that was to be, in a few thatched shacks through the rigours of a New England winter, in old England the indefatigable Rector of Dorchester was persuading a handful of West Countrymen to found a "New England Company for a Plantation in Massachusetts Bay," which obtained a generous patent from the Council for New England in March, 1628. Their motives had expanded, and they purposed now not a fishing settlement but a colony. In June of that year they sent out John Endecott, some fifty settlers and, more surprisingly, a considerable consignment of beer, wine and spirits, to reinforce Conant and the Old Planters. Their patent, however, was dubious, overlapping other grants made, somewhat lightheartedly, by the Council for New England to other would-be colonists, and soon White and the rest were busy negotiating for a royal charter. By March of 1629, after how much intrigue and, it may be, bribery, it is impossible to say, but at any rate "with great cost, favor of personages of note, and much labor," they had obtained it, and were duly incorporated as the Governor and Company of Massachusetts Bay in New England. That same spring three hundred new colonists went out to Salem, among them two clergymen, chosen to organise the first church there. And at this point the Puritan motive begins to obtrude itself.

For one of the two clerics, Higginson, was one of the best known nonconformist clergymen in England. His farewell sermon was preached from the text, "And when you see Jerusalem compassed with armies . . . then let them which are in Judaea flee to the mountains," a suggestive reminder of that refugee mentality which was to be a permanent and powerful element in the Puritan migration. As the ship passed Land's End, Higginson called his children, and some other passengers, to the stern of the ship, and exclaimed

"We will not say, as the Separatists were wont to say at their leaving of England, Farewel *Babylon*! Farewel Rome! But we will say Farewel Dear *England*! Farewel the Church of God in England, and all the Christian friends there! We do not go to New England as Separatists from the Church of England. . . ." Yet this was precisely what they were doing. Within a month of their arrival the church of Salem was organised upon a Separatist, or Congregational, model. At first sight the *volte-face* is surprising. Such Separatists as had not left England for Holland twenty years back, and thence for Plymouth, New England, had discreetly gone to ground; Separatism was little known in 1629, and in the whole of England there probably were not more than half a dozen Separatist Congregational churches. In New England, however, there was already the Congregational model set up by the Pilgrim Fathers at Plymouth, and Samuel Fuller, the Plymouth physician, who was summoned to Salem to cope with an outbreak of scurvy, seems to have brought persuasion with him as well as pills. And many an Anglican of energy and character, but humble birth, in Stuart England, and, for that matter, for long afterwards, must have fretted at the impossibility of playing any rôle of consequence in a parish church controlled, in effect, by the parson and the squire. Non-Conformity, and particularly Congregational Non-Conformity, meant the fullest opportunity for the fervent and capable layman to play a leading rôle in his Church, and this not unnaturally (as Robert Baillie put it) "made it very suitable and lovely to a multitude who had lately stepped out of the Episcopall thraldom in England, to the free aire of a new World." That heady new World air it was, and the sudden opening of un-dreamed-of scope for self-expression, together with the example of the established Congregational polity at Plymouth, at least as much as the spread of Puritanism in England, which led settlement after settlement in the coming years to set up its Separatist church and its oligarchy of Ministers and elders. Two members of Governor Endecott's original Council in Salem, who insisted on reading services from the Book of Common Prayer—and were promptly shipped home on the ground that "New England was no place for such as they"—were but the first to suffer under a nonconformist orthodoxy which soon became more oppressive than the rule of Laud in England.

But if the all too human instinct of self-assertion is conspicuous enough in both the first origins and the later organisation of American Puritanism, its deep religious sincerity was even more unmistakable. For what, after all, were the Puritans? Those, first and foremost, who believed that the Bible was the whole word of

God. Politically, in old England at any rate, the early Puritans were democrats and Radicals, but this, perhaps, was largely due to the chance that in Old England at this time a High Church Archbishop who suppressed Puritanism was hand in glove with a monarch who would have liked to suppress Parliament. In New England, at any rate, the Puritan oligarchy showed itself both conservative and autocratic. It seems likely that what the democracy of America owed to the English Puritans, it owed to their Englishry rather than their Puritanism.

§3

In 1629, it was clear to many earnest Englishmen, England was going to the dogs, as it so often has since. And as so often since, the apparent decadence proved to be the starting point of a new outburst of moral energy. Manners, it seemed to the Puritans, were changing fast, and for the worse. Riches and poverty were both increasing. If the powerful Laud, soon to become Archbishop, was of the High Church, was not the Queen a Catholic? Were there not suspiciously many Catholics to be seen at Court? The Government, true to a long, if intermittent, tradition of "appeasement" in English foreign policy, had refused to lift a finger to save the French Huguenots or the Protestant Elector Palatine. A plague was devastating the Continent and must soon reach England. Parliament had been dissolved, and its Puritan leaders lodged in the Tower. What could all this portend but a Catholic reaction, a return to the persecutions of Bloody Mary, and, in due time, the vengeance of the Lord? "My dear Wife," wrote John Winthrop, on May 15, 1629, "I am verily persuaded, God will bring some heavye Affliction upon this lande, and that speedylye. . . ." And so thought many others. In many a prosperous and influential English household serious men and women were beginning reluctantly and anxiously to consider fleeing from the wrath to come by transporting themselves and their children to the New World. Among them were several members of the new Company. To some of these a novel and revolutionary idea presented itself. Why not transfer the whole Company to New England, government, charter and all? Such a thing had never been done before, but in these days of crisis why stand upon precedent? If they were to make a home overseas worth the sacrifice of leaving the home of their fathers, if they were to found a model community in which they could obey the voice of God, free from worldly interference and unhampered by authorities to whom the voice of

God seemed to mean singularly little, then surely they must found, not a colony controlled from England, and still exposed to the changes, chances and distempers of the English body politic, but an independent Puritan Commonwealth. And this they could only hope to do if they severed the strong legal link which bound them to England, and carried not only their government, but their Charter, with them. On August 26, a number of Puritan gentlemen met at Cambridge. John Winthrop, who was to be Governor if the Company went overseas, was there, fresh from a conference with sundry Puritan friends at Tattershall, the Earl of Lincoln's mansion in Lincolnshire. Here on August 26 "for the better encouragement of ourselves and others that shall join with us in this action" twelve of them signed and dated a compact, binding themselves to be ready to embark for New England on the first of March next, "provided always that . . . the whole government, together with the patent . . . be first by an order of court legally transferred and established to remain with us and others which shall inhabite upon the said plantation." Transferred the patent was, by decision of the General Court of the Company two days later; but whether legally, is another matter; a matter which the Company discreetly refrained from investigating. And so these twelve prosperous, sober and influential Puritan gentlemen stood committed by their signed compact to remove themselves and their families to unknown hardships across the seas. Their lead and example were followed widely and speedily. Within nine months a thousand emigrants had assembled at their various ports, and sailed for New England—and this in an age with no means of rapid communication and transit. It was a remarkable achievement, and not only on physical grounds. For the gently nurtured pioneers must have known what was in store for them. If not a speedy death, then danger, discomfort, privations and an utter parting, unrelieved by any reliable means of communication, from those they left behind. "And now (my sweet soale)," wrote John Winthrop from Cowes harbour, to his wife, who remained behind till Groton Manor could be sold, "I must once againe take my last farewell of thee in old England. It goeth verye neare to my heart to leave thee. . . ." And so on the eve of departure from Bristol or Plymouth or Southampton wrote, or thought, many Englishmen during the next eleven years. Because Englishmen, unlike the men of many other nations, were prepared to face these agonising separations there would be an English Empire. The great migration had begun. The manifestation of energy was to be vast, and in one respect, it will be noticed, not altogether healthy. For not only the natural instinct for expansion was at work; the migration sprang also from a deep schism in the State, and these colonists carried with them a sense of grievance which never wholly abated, and was to play its melancholy part in the later history of America.

§4

By mid-June they had anchored in the North River, near Salem. Half a dozen townships were founded before winter set in. The trading Company was no more; the Commonwealth had been born. But the founders of the Commonwealth had still to get rid of the authority of the State, if they could, for how else could they build a model city of God? They insisted accordingly, a manifest sophistry, that the Crown in granting them a Charter had abandoned all claim to control them. They maintained, on equally inadequate grounds, that the statute law of England was no concern of theirs. And they did in fact succeed in entrenching themselves for fifty-four years in virtual independence. They drove out all, whether Anglican, Antinomian or Quaker, who would not conform ·to their own nonconformist regime. Indeed they could do worse than this. When two women of the new sect of Quakers came to Boston in 1656, the Puritans burnt their books, imprisoned them for five weeks in solitary confinement behind boarded windows, and shipped them off for Barbados. As more Quakers came, it was enacted that the heretics should be imprisoned and flogged before expulsion, and, if any ventured to return, his ears should be cut off and his tongue pierced with a red-hot iron. But still the stream of Quakers grew, and at last the Puritan Council decreed the death penalty. And when Quakers still came, deliberately courting martyrdom, there were actually some executions, though not without a strong public sense of guilt, so that the procession to the gallows would go furtively through the back streets. Naturally this persecuting conformity among the nonconformists bred yet further nonconformity. Roger Williams, who objected to a State church, and then Anne Hutchinson, who objected to almost everything, were both expelled, and took the chief part in founding the Rhode Island communities, which became to New England as a whole what New England was to the mother country. And when other small Puritan theocracies had been founded in New England—Connecticut in 1635 and New Haven in 1638, wholly without authority from the Crown—the rulers of Massachusetts became acknowledged leaders of a New England Confederation of Bible Commonwealths, of 1643 (from which only the schismatic Rhode

Island was excluded). It was the first significant appearance of the federal principle in American history. They prospered and grew fast, for in 1633 Laud had become Archbishop, and enforced a uniformity so stringent that almost the only loophole left to the English Puritan was emigration.

New England was strong enough now to survive the inevitable struggle with the Indians, a desultory and intermittent, but terrible, affair of ambush, scalping and sudden massacre, of punitive expeditions and wigwams flaming in the forest, and women and children butchered by both sides. And inevitably, since the Englishman everywhere is a political animal, by process of trial and error, and not without heated controversy, the Commonwealth developed a constitution. The officers of the Company became the Governor and executive council, as well as the Upper House and supreme court of justice of the colony. With a lower House of Deputies they were elected on a franchise soon widened to include every church member, that is to say every communicant—admitted only after the brethren had satisfied themselves that he was one of the "visible saints." This church oligarchy ruled with sombre and conscientious severity, awarding stocks and pillory, fines and flogging for immorality as well as crime. The potent seeds of a democracy had undoubtedly been sowed by the Pilgrim Fathers, yet for free speech and toleration, for a wide franchise and the idea of equality, and indeed for the whole theory and practice of democracy as we know it, the men who ruled Puritan New England in the seventeenth century would have had nothing but condemnation and contempt. And naturally, for democracy, at bottom, is a passionate conviction of the fallibility of rulers. And, with their bibles in their hands, or fresh from seeking the Lord in solemn fast and prayer, the brethren knew that they were inevitably right—or as nearly right as sinful man can hope to be.

It is well to remember that this high-aiming and God-fearing theocracy was the foundation of the British Empire, and that never, even when the Empire was at its most worldly, did the influence of the Puritans wholly die away. It is easy enough for the twentieth century to smile at the Pilgrims, their narrow horizons and their rigid standards. With our far greater store of knowledge, our vastly extended liberties, our infinite, and perhaps excessive, toleration in belief and conduct, our expanding material comfort and our pathetic faith in continual progress, we have been only too ready to look down with complacent superiority upon all past history, and have felt in a special sense superior to the men and women who inhabited this particular nook of space and time. Yet to reflect upon their story is to realise that the complacency of the twentieth century has been the vulgar complacency of the *nouveau riche*. These men and women had faith, and, having faith, they had courage, loyalty and discipline too. In their would-be theocracy there was too little liberty for our taste, but—barring, if you will, the Salem witch-trials—there was no license. There was little tolerance, but no cynical indifference to moral standards. There was nothing that we should have called comfort, and all the less temptation to suppose that increased comfort is the goal of human endeavour. There was less knowledge, but was there so much less wisdom?

§5

The third main archetype in this first age of experiment was a reversion to the Elizabethan tradition of the proprietary patent, the grant, that is, of a whole area to an individual English subject, the method which had failed in the premature exploits of Raleigh and Gilbert. George Calvert, Secretary of State under James I, who became a convert to the Catholic faith and retired from public office in 1625, obtained a patent in 1632 to the lands immediately north of Virginia, which, at Charles' suggestion, were named Maryland, after his Catholic queen. Thus was founded the first permanent proprietary colony. The proprietor, who had been raised to the peerage as Lord Baltimore, became its monarch in miniature. Inevitably, however, since these were Englishmen, Parliamentary government took root. Maryland, like Virginia, was ruled by Governor, Council and Assembly, the colonial version of King, Lords and Commons. Moreover, Maryland was the first community in the world to embody the principle of toleration in law. For the Baltimores, fully intending toleration for their fellow Catholics, were well content to permit toleration for every other faith. "No person," ran the Maryland Toleration Act of 1649, "professing to believe in Jesus Christ shall from henceforth be any waies troubled or discountenanced for, or in respect of, his or her religion nor the free exercise thereof within this province." It was some years after this that the Puritans of Massachusetts were executing Quakers for being Quakers.

And so, despite some frontier troubles with the Virginians, Maryland speedily settled down, with far less than the usual sufferings and tragedies of the infant colony, into a simple but prosperous tobacco- and corn-growing community. The government of the Colony remained in the Baltimore family until the Declaration of Independence.

§6

There were no more American colonies until after the Restoration. In 1660 English settlement still showed as two narrow and separate strips along the coast, to the north the six New England states; Plymouth, Massachusetts, New Hampshire and Maine, over both of which Massachusetts exercised jurisdiction, Rhode Island and Connecticut; then a gap occupied by the Dutch colony of New Netherlands and some scattered settlements of Swedes along the river Delaware; and two hundred miles to the south of New England, Maryland and Virginia. Besides these, there were only the Island outposts; to the north, Newfoundland, which since Gilbert's unlucky venture of 1583 had known a series of precarious settlements along its south-eastern shores; to the south, the Bermudas—inadvertently occupied, as we have seen, by Sir George Somers when he ran his *Sea Adventure* ashore there in a hurricane, on his way to Virginia in 1609, and first known as the Somers Islands.

West of the frontiers of occupation, and it took a century to push them a hundred miles from the coast, still stretched vast expanses of virgin forest, somewhere within which the warriors of the Five Nations, and other Indian tribes with whom the settlers had yet to try conclusions, went stealthily about their business. Westward again, a chain of formidable natural barriers, the Alleghany Mountains and the Great Lakes, seemed placed by Providence to bar the colonies for ever into their narrow ocean littoral; to which use indeed the French, with growing settlements, north-east and north-west of the New Englanders, in Acadia and New France, already showed signs of intending to put them. And further still beyond the primitive settlements which housed the few thousand English emigrants, far and far to the west, stretched the vast unexplored continent, of whose true size and shape no man had as yet more than the most speculative and uncertain knowledge. Physically what had so far been accomplished was insignificant. In the domain of the spirit it was prodigious.

Books for Further Reading.

Professor Vincent Harlow, *Ralegh's Last Voyage;* A. G. Bradley, *Captain John Smith;* Alexander Young (ed.) *Chronicles of the Pilgrims;** L. G. Tyler (ed.) *Narratives of early Virginia, 1606-1625;** J. G. Palfrey, *History of New England;** S. E. Morison, *Builders of the Bay Colony.*

* Published in America.

Book II

FOUNDATIONS OF EMPIRE

CHAPTER ONE

OLIVER

(1649-1660)

§1

IN 1642 Charles I had raised his standard at Nottingham, and the Great Rebellion had begun; in 1649 the King was beheaded in Whitehall, and England became an oligarchy ruled by the victorious Puritan middle-classes; in 1653 Cromwell expelled the unrepresentative Rump of the Long Parliament, and set up his strange military-religious despotism; in 1660 Charles II was restored amidst universal rejoicings, and in 1688-9, amidst rejoicings almost equally universal, his brother, James II, was driven overseas. Such is the familiar framework. At first sight it is sufficiently remarkable that while England was distracted by this revolutionary epoch the English colonies should have grown notably in number and strength, and that England should have survived the challenge of the second of her great rivals, the Dutch, and laid the foundations of her eventual victory over the third and greatest, the French. It is scarcely less remarkable that rival English statesmen, who spent so much time failing to solve their own domestic quarrels, should have evolved, in something like unanimity, new and far-reaching principles of colonial policy. The truth is that whereas the domestic settlements of 1660 and 1689 were still the work of a part of the nation only, a half-conscious instinct drove the whole people towards expansion overseas. And it is characteristic of our long blindness to the greatest of our achievements that the traditional estimate of both Cromwell and Charles II should have so completely ignored the imperial policies of each.

The growth, and even the survival, of the English settlements under Charles II is all the more remarkable in view of the alarming naval decadence of England under James I. Corruption in the dockyards and neglect of the seamen had bred such inefficiency at sea early in the century that contemporary pessimists concluded that England itself was decadent, and that the Dutch had "taken up our wonted valour." Nevertheless, feeble though it had become, English sea power sufficed to shelter and sustain the infant settlements in America. Fortunately for England, the period of acute civil discord at home almost exactly coincided with the Thirty Years' War, which desolated, and distracted, Europe from 1618 to 1648. And, fortunately too, just as Europe was beginning to awake from that long nightmare, the Navy was handed over to the care of the victorious Ironsides. In three years they had added forty-one men-of-war to the Navy and turned its crews into Ironsides of the sea. Better still, they had made Robert Blake, a successful, though hardly a leading, Parliamentary general, into an Admiral. At the age of fifty, and, so far as is known, with no more previous acquaintance with the sea than was to be acquired from his experiences as a Bridgwater merchant in time of peace, he received command of the fleet. Within ten years he had won a number of resounding victories, and left a name revered by the Navy with those of Drake and Nelson.

§2

With the Navy once again a formidable fighting force, the Commonwealth was free to frame and pursue an imperial policy. Frame, perhaps, is not exactly the word. The Ironsides did not, like the French Minister Colbert and so many European statesmen then and since, think out a precise and coherent system, and then proceed to put it into force. Rather, as is the English way, they fumbled, often enough hard put to it, from expedient to expedient. And yet, as we look back at their expedients, we see—and perhaps, though not so clearly, they could see themselves—that a policy was there. And why not? To no small extent their policy was born less of their own volition than of the instincts of the people. Moreover from the fifteenth century onward, a steady stream of pamphleteers and publicists had been canvassing colonial affairs, and by now conscious and coherent trends of opinion were discernible, to which the Ironsides, being at once opportunists and revolutionaries, were more sensitive than any government of mere theorists could have been. Moreover their profoundest instincts and prejudices, like those of all the English, even the English revolutionaries, were deeply conservative. Like many other iconoclasts, they conceived of themselves not as uprooting and overthrowing, but as rescuing and preserving, ancient liberties. They had undertaken their work of destruction with deep reluctance—"I have sought the Lord that He would rather slay me," said Cromwell, as he suppressed Parliament, "than put me upon the doing of this work"—and they turned now with relief to revive the dream of the Elizabethans, and reconstruct an oceanic Empire.

Three main imperial tasks awaited the regicides; to reduce the revolted colonies to obedience, to frame a domestic policy for the young Empire, and to adjust its relations with foreign powers, if need be by war. Each problem was involved with, and complicated by, the others, and all had to be solved speedily and simultaneously. Indeed if the English government did not strike swiftly and successfully, there would soon be no imperial problem to solve, for by 1650 almost all the colonies were in open revolt. And although the rebels mostly made a somewhat unconvincing profession of royalism the various risings were in fact directed not so much against the victorious regicides as against English suzerainty itself. For with the outbreak of the civil war in England the two principal ambitions of the colonists had been realised with sudden and intoxicating completeness. The home government could neither interfere with their politics nor confine their commerce to English ports. For eight years now they had been enjoying both legislative autonomy and free trade with all the world. But now that the Roundheads, and the merchants who had backed them, were firmly in power it was certain that political interference, and, worse, trade restrictions, would be revived. And accordingly the colonists revolted, not against the Commonwealth but against their subjection to the English mercantile interest. They flew the royal standard, but nine out of ten of them felt much more strongly about the sugar, or tobacco, trade than about the wrongs of His Majesty. Indeed if the King had won the civil war he would probably have had to suppress a colonial revolt himself, and for the same reasons. But a naval expedition reduced the rebellious colonies to obedience with surprising ease in 1651 and 1652. The most urgent problem was solved. The speedy suppression of the Colonial revolt was the first clear warning that the power of the Navy would be indispensable to Empire.

§3

While thus disposing of its first imperial problem, the colonial revolt, the Commonwealth was attacking the second, the need of a new colonial policy, with methods which formidably complicated the third, the adjustment of the foreign relations of the Empire. In 1650 and 1651 it passed its two notable Navigation Acts. These measures have been almost uniformly misunderstood by modern economists. In our age of easy-going materialism, for which progress came to mean little more than a higher standard of living, economists, and even historians, have unreflectingly assumed that the true object of economic policy must everywhere and always be material Plenty. And since it is easy to show that the Navigation Acts cannot have contributed to Plenty, they have been patronisingly condemned by almost all recent writers.[1] But the Navigation Acts were most certainly not intended to increase Plenty. For that earlier and sterner age, concerned to build rather than to enjoy, the first purpose of policy was not Plenty but Power. And the object of the Navigation Acts was to restore the Power, without which Plenty could not be. The reasoning of the men who framed them is not difficult to follow. Our wealth, so ran the argument, depends upon overseas trade, and overseas trade can never be secure without a powerful Navy. But in an era when it was not easy for the state to maintain a powerful Navy in peace time, trade itself must be made to foster the elements of sea power. The more large merchant vessels therefore the better. And, above all, the more sailors the better; for the State could not afford to maintain a great naval establishment in peace-time, and the men who could sail a merchant-man could sail a warship. And so commerce must be promoted, and particularly long-distance colonial commerce, in which large ships and large crews were employed, primarily in order that England might possess as many large merchant vessels as possible, and that on these as many Englishmen as possible should be trained to the sea. It followed that if commerce with the colonies was indeed to become a nursery of naval power, the foreigner must not be permitted to encroach upon it. The Navigation Acts, in short, were precisely what their authors called them, Acts of Navigation. They were intended, not to increase trade, but to promote the use of English ships by English seamen. The first of them, passed in October, 1650, would be memorable, if for nothing else, as the first Act which treated the English colonies as a whole, and as an integral part of the mother country. It was, however, frankly a war measure, designed against the revolted colonies, which, as the preamble of the Act puts it, "are and ought to be subordinate to and dependent upon England." It asserted that the Parliament of England possesses legislative supremacy over the colonies, and forbade foreigners to

[1] But for an exception see J. A. Williamson, *Cambridge History of the British Empire*, vol. i, chap. 7.

trade with any of them. This was explosive matter, and it provoked from Barbados a tart rejoinder which anticipated all the arguments of the colonists, more than a hundred years later, in the American War of Independence. A year later, before the colonies had been subdued, Parliament passed a second Act, "for the increase of the shipping and encouragement of the navigation of this nation," in which this policy of restriction in the interests of power was considerably elaborated. Manifestly this was not, and was not intended to be, good for trade. It was not, as it has often been represented to be, an unsuccessful attempt to plan (as the modern economist would say) material prosperity by men unfortunate enough not to have had the opportunity of learning from Adam Smith the blessings of free trade. Rather, it was a determined effort to promote national power by statesmen sufficiently clear-sighted to see that without power the infant Empire could not survive, and stout-hearted enough to endure sacrifices, if need be, to achieve it.

§4

For there were formidable rivals in the field. And the Navigation Acts had been designed not only as a stimulus to English shipping but as a blow to that of the Dutch. The Dutch moreover, great traders though never great colonists, had rooted themselves so firmly, thanks to their trading-posts and their powerful merchant Navy, within the English Empire that our imperial legislation touched them almost as closely as if they were Englishmen. And so the second imperial problem of the Ironsides, the framing, with the Navigation Acts, of a new colonial policy, involved them, whether they liked it or not, in the third, the framing of a new foreign policy. What is more, they soon found themselves committed, so powerful were the awakening imperial instincts of the nation, to a diplomacy which ran clean counter to most of the Puritan prejudices, and all the Puritan traditions. For the Ironsides of the army, who had no interests in the colonies or in colonial commerce, and whose most ardent sympathies had always centred on Puritanism, could hardly be expected to welcome war with the most Protestant nation in Europe. For them, and for many other Englishmen, religion, not empire, was the key to policy, and alliance, not war, with the Dutch seemed to lie in the logic of history. In October, 1650, the month of the first Navigation Act, the bellicose Dutch Stadholder died and there appeared to be every hope of negotiating a treaty of friendship. Unlike every other imperial rival of the English,

Holland was not even a despotic state. But to the surprise and consternation of many worthy citizens in both countries the English
mission to the Hague was a complete failure. Barely three years had
passed since the close of the Thirty Years' War, which had laid
Europe waste in the name of religion, but now Europeans were
breaking into a new, unpeopled continent beyond the Atlantic, and
into the unguarded treasure-house of the East; and inevitably a
new era of imperial conflicts had dawned, and, despite the religious
sympathies which the two nations shared, newer and more potent
forces were driving them into rivalry. And for England there were
now only two ways of dealing with the Dutch. To go on permitting
them to absorb a steadily increasing share of the trade of our own
colonies would spell the decay of English naval power, and this
possibility accordingly the Navigation Acts were now decisively
ruling out. Either, therefore, it must be alliance, and a division of
the vast imperial arena between the two powers, or else a war to
the death for supremacy in the whole of it. The religious motive
had failed to secure an alliance, the field was clear for the imperial
motive, and it was bound to lead to war. The immediate occasion
of the Dutch war, into which Blake and van Tromp stumbled almost
unintentionally in May, 1652, was trifling, a dispute over the law
of contraband and the English claim to a salute from foreign ships
in the narrow seas. But the underlying causes were of vast consequence. Spain, whose mortal challenge England had survived in
1588, had been the first claimant to empire in the new worlds
opened by naval and geographical discovery; and Spain was now
entering upon her long decline. France stood on the threshold of
her rapid ascent under Louis XIV, hardly yet recognisable as an
imperial rival. Only the Dutch appeared to bar the way. To some
European power it must fall to be foremost in setting its impress
on the backward and unpeopled continents. Was that power, in the
years to come, to be Holland or England? That so great an issue
awaited decision was the true cause of the Dutch war.

§5

The Dutch had underrated the English Navy, unaware of its
recovery from the early Stuart decadence. Moreover the Dutch lived
by trade, and their trade routes, to western Europe, the Mediterranean and the ocean, all passed close to the southern and eastern
shores of their enemy. The English were still predominantly
agricultural, and able, if need be, to dispense with trade and manu-

facture. They could therefore concentrate upon attacking Dutch trade, without exposing their own, so that the war developed into a series of escort actions in which the Dutch admirals would seek to pass great convoys, sometimes of as many as four hundred and fifty merchant vessels, down the Channel or round the north of Scotland, where the English soldier admirals, Blake and Monck and Deane, barred the way. The Dutch had more seamen, the English stouter ships—we built for seventy years, said an English captain, the enemy for seven. As for the Ironside admirals, they had little skill in naval tactics, but a profound moral conviction and a dour readiness to fight every action to the bitter end. The fortunes of war varied, but the Dutch were necessarily on the defensive, their vulnerable trade was exposed as ours was not, and inevitably they suffered the most. By the spring of 1654 they were ready for peace. In April they had agreed to give the salute and pay belated compensation for the Amboyna massacre,[1] to recognise the Navigation Act and accept a defensive alliance, while England acknowledged the freedom of the North Sea fisheries. This hardly suggests a decisive victory, but the true result of the war is to be read elsewhere than in the terms of the peace treaty. The Ironsides and their sea generals had dealt their chief imperial rival a wound, not deadly indeed—there were to be two more Dutch wars—but shrewd enough to ensure that they should not overwhelm our overseas trade in the infancy of the new colonial policy.

§6

It was during the Dutch war that Cromwell had suppressed Parliament, and become, as we should now say, dictator, "in substance a re-establishment," as Vane and Ludlow complained, "of all we engaged against." Now Oliver was a soldier, and commercial interests mattered less to him than to most of the Parliament men whom he had bundled so unceremoniously out of Westminster in April, 1653. For him Spain, not Holland, was still the national enemy, and like many other Puritan soldiers he had never felt comfortable about the Dutch war. When, after the signing of the treaty of peace with Holland, he entertained the Dutch envoys in Whitehall, he made them sing the hundred and thirty-third Psalm, "Behold how good and pleasant it is for brethren to dwell together in unity." And unity, he firmly believed, was possible. For him religion was still the key to European politics, and he dreamed of a

[1] See p. 79.

new and more triumphant Protestant League to crush the Catholic
Powers and root out the Inquisition. But he was an imperialist too,
and—for here too his mind was firmly rooted in the past—an
imperialist in the Elizabethan tradition. And it was doubtless the
Elizabethan tradition which impelled him to reconcile as best he
could, and indeed to combine, his two dominant motives, religion
and imperialism. For what was the Elizabethan tradition if not the
struggle to found an Empire, in conflict with the greatest Catholic
power in the world? Thus no religious bias can have prompted the
treaty which Oliver concluded in 1654 with the Portuguese, for the
Portuguese were Catholic; the treaty, however, gave English merchants and English shipping much the same privileged status within
the Portuguese Empire as the Dutch had managed to acquire in the
English colonial trade during the Civil War, and in effect, another
blow to Dutch ambitions made possible by the Dutch war, had
constituted England heir presumptive to the moribund Portuguese
Empire.

For long Oliver sought to weave into one coherent texture the
two designs he had inherited from the past, the European-religious
project of a new and greater Protestant League, and the oceanic-
imperial vision of a powerful English Empire overseas. For the
years of his Protectorate fell in a watershed of history, when one
political force, religious strife, was spent, and its successor, national
expansion, whether in Europe or overseas, had not yet fully gathered
momentum. It was natural therefore that Oliver's policy should
seek to embody both old and new—although even the new for him
was always coloured by the past. His long attempt to combine the
incompatibles is nowhere more clearly illustrated than in a project,
launched with his approval during the negotiations for the Dutch
peace, for a Protestant League, of England and Holland, which
should monopolise the oceanic trade and the colonial Empire of the
whole world. Thus would the old European continental conception
of a Protestant Grand Alliance be transplanted and reborn upon the
world-wide oceanic plane. It was a design of Napoleonic dimensions,
but it was at once too old-fashioned and too novel for its day. Men
had ceased to fight, and to ally themselves, for religion; they had
hardly begun to think in terms of world Empire. Nevertheless the
conception was characteristic of the man—of one who, as history
may one day hold, played a more fruitful rôle in the development
of the English Empire, and of the maritime supremacy on which it
was founded, than in the domestic strife to which, so far, he chiefly
owes his fame. For, dictator though he was, Oliver first among
Englishmen may be said to have foreseen the nature of the enduring

Commonwealth which was one day to be, that Empire which was not a mine of material advantage but the embodiment of a missionary idea.

The Protestant world-empire was not to be, but the Protector could at least persist in expanding the Empire of Protestant England. And soon his Council of State found itself compelled to purchase a new atlas, and to have a world-globe ever handy in the Council Chamber. For English politics had entered upon a new dimension. The Empire must be expanded, Oliver had decided, at the expense of that of Catholic Spain. It was not so easy a choice as it may sound. With the power which Providence had committed to him it was for England to deal a blow for the Protestant interest, of that the Protector was certain. He would not strike at Holland therefore, even though to strike elsewhere would surely forfeit him the sympathy of the powerful new commercial middle classes. But was it to be a blow against Catholic Spain or Catholic France? For these two powers were still engaged in the struggle which the rest of Europe had thankfully abandoned in 1648, and in Flanders England might intervene against either with decisive force. And at first it had been Spain which made friendly advances to the hated but formidable republic of regicides, recognising the Commonwealth in 1650 and allowing Blake to base his ships on Spanish ports for his blockade of Prince Rupert's royalist fleet in Lisbon. Moreover France continued to prey on English shipping, and English Puritans were as much incensed by the persecution of the French Huguenots as their fathers had been by the doings of the Spanish Inquisition. Why then did the Protector loose his bolt against Spain? Partly, no doubt, because for him Spain was still both the traditional enemy and the Catholic power *par excellence*, but chiefly because war with France could not offer imperial prizes so rich and various as would an attack on Spain. And so the Protector chose Spain for victim, and framed his Western Design for a great marauding adventure in the Caribbean. He was the first great English ruler to follow that same deep-seated instinct which drove the eighteenth century statesmen, fortified by his example, to shun European quarrels and the cramped old battlefields of Europe, and spend British energy overseas.

Unfortunately the strategy and organisation of the Western Design was greatly inferior to the political instinct which lay behind it. The expedition was to seize some important Spanish Colony—Cromwell deliberately withheld precise instructions—and if all went well might even develop into the conquest of all Spanish America. But all did not go well. Cromwell sent out (at the close of 1654) not so much an army as an armed mob, which after failing pitifully at Hispaniola and San Domingo, seized the almost undefended Jamaica —a valuable prize, as it proved, but an inglorious trophy. Nor were the European repercussions of the Design what its author had expected of it. Spain accepted the assault on her Empire as a declaration of war, and Cromwell was driven into the arms of Mazarin, who thus reaped the reward of long patience under provocation. In 1656 England and France became allies, and in 1658 captured Dunkirk and triumphantly invaded the Spanish Netherlands. Blake meanwhile had blockaded the Spanish ports, and eventually, himself already a dying man, destroyed the entire Spanish fleet in the harbour of Vera Cruz. The consequence of all this was the Treaty of the Pyrenees, of 1659, by which England obtained Dunkirk, and France part of the Netherlands, but whose true significance was that Spain passed for ever from the centre of the imperial stage, and France moved forward to take her place. The age of Louis XIV had begun. The third and deadliest rival of the English Empire was all but ready for the struggle. And again it was a despotic power.

§7

The Empire scarcely grew under Oliver. His military despotism stifled the free, adventurous England out of which the impulse to expansion had come. Had the system of Oliver endured indeed, England would have been denied her historic mission to spread the idea of liberty across the world, and at best her Empire would have been but one more grasp at world dominion, doomed to the transcience of all merely selfish power. Nevertheless Oliver was a man of vision, and imperial vision was not denied him. He saw that the English destiny was overseas. He saw that there could be no Empire without a powerful navy. He saw that Gibraltar might become one day the cornerstone of an oceanic Empire. Above all, in an age to which colonies were too often but commercial enterprises, he first clearly saw the English Empire in its true guise as the acknowledgment of an obligation, and the spread of an Idea. It was his habit, it is true, to think of that Idea as Protestantism, but, though Protestantism to him was religion and philosophy and politics and way of life, the Idea for which he sometimes groped was more English even than Protestantism, something primeval and instinctive, something of which he was dimly conscious but did not wholly understand, alien to his own despotism and deep-buried in the folk-mind of the nation.

CHAPTER TWO

THE RESTORED STUARTS

(1660-1689)

§1

THE DICTATORSHIP which might have strangled the Empire died with Oliver. But the Protectorate handed on at least one evil tradition to the returning Stuarts, the custom of sending bad citizens overseas. For the theorists and pamphleteers—economists, as we should call them nowadays—had changed their minds, as economists will, about emigration. They no longer believed that England was over-populated, and they now regarded every sound citizen who settled overseas as so much loss to the mother country. Hence the practice of peopling the Plantations as far as possible with British undesir-ables, with foreigners and above all with negroes. The undesirables and the foreigners probably did the colonies little harm. For the undesirables were undesirable largely owing to their environment, and in the new world often became new men. Unintentionally too, by driving overseas English Quakers, Irish Catholics and Presby-terians, and, later still, Scottish Jacobites, the rulers of the empire continued to people it with some of the choicest British stock. But if the growing habit of planting colonies with misfits and ne'er-do-weels did less harm than might have been expected overseas, it did a good deal at home. For it accustomed the English politicians who had to legislate for the colonists to thinking of them as inferiors.

§2

Whatever may be thought of the domestic record of Charles II —and recent historians have been revising some of the harsh judg-ments which were so long fashionable—the imperial administration of the restored monarchy possessed solid merits. Perhaps indeed this is an understatement. The outburst of energy at the Restoration has been compared to that of the Elizabethans. After the unnatural repressions of the Cromwellian era the instincts of the English reverted to their natural channels. And two at least of Charles'

Ministers, Clarendon and Shaftesbury, were, in imperial affairs, men of vision, energy and judgment. And so the two great trading companies, moribund under the Puritans, revived; and new enterprises on the grand scale, the Royal African Company and the Hudson's Bay Company, were founded. The colonial Governors of the period, too—always a pretty reliable indication of the quality of a home government—are unexpectedly impressive; they were neither undistinguished placemen, like so many of their eighteenth century successors, nor did they lose all contact with the home administration, like so many of their seventeenth century predecessors. The gallant Lord Willoughby in Barbados, the indefatigable Sir William Stapleton in the Leeward Islands were good men well chosen; and—another sign of grace—Charles' government did not confine its choice to royalists; it could select Sir Thomas Modyford, who had been responsible for the capitulation of Barbados to the Commonwealth, to govern Jamaica. Again, it was the Restoration which gradually put together the first administrative machinery of the Empire. By 1675, after experiments with various Committees of Trade and Plantations, a Committee of the Privy Council, known as the Lords of Trade, with a permanent Secretary, had become the recognisable forerunner of the Colonial Office of to-day.

Our domestic history has been more continuous, diversified by fewer contrasts, fresh starts and revulsions, than that of any other ancient civilisation. In our imperial history, where jealousies of creed and class have counted for even less, there have been even fewer abrupt frontiers, and the transition from Protectorate to Restoration was almost imperceptible. In Charles' first year the Commonwealth's Act of Navigation of 1651 was re-enacted with the additional provision that the colonies might export certain "enumerated" raw materials only to England, Ireland, Wales and Berwick-on-Tweed. Its sequel and appendage, the "Act for the Encouragement of Trade" of 1663, provided, in effect, that all European goods destined for the colonies must first be brought to England, unloaded there and thence reshipped overseas. Nor, though colonies were still held to exist for the advantage of the mother country, were the benefits, it must be remembered, by any means all reaped by her. The English taxpayer had already commenced the long task of sustaining almost single-handed the burden of imperial defence, without which the colonists would have been helpless victims of foreign aggression. And colonial shipping shared the privileges of English shipping, and colonial merchandise, though debarred from Europe, was heavily protected against foreign competition in the English market.

Expansion, too, came early. In 1663 eight powerful public men received a patent of proprietorship of the still unoccupied coastline southward from Virginia to the Spanish territory of Florida, the great stretch of empty coastline on which Raleigh's successive colonies had settled and perished. Clarendon and Shaftesbury were both among the eight new proprietors, and it is symbolic of the continuity of colonial policy that one had been a royalist exile and the other an associate of Cromwell. Their motive was doubtless profit, but probably not so much profit as patriotism; they intended their new colony to supply England with certain commodities— wine, silks, oil and fruits—not obtained from the other colonies. The northern part of the new settlement was first occupied by Virginians and became North Carolina. In the south a party collected from England, Barbados and Bermuda settled at the harbour now known as Charleston, the nucleus of South Carolina. Many of the settlers of Carolina, it will be noticed, came not from Britain but from other colonies. And in general colonial growth under the Stuarts was less a further expansion of England than a first expansion of colonial America itself. For in a number of the established colonies there were citizens ready for various reasons to re-emigrate. New England in particular had begun to send forth a stream of hardy adventurers, toughened by the rigours of its climate and its discipline, but not unwilling to escape them. Such immigrants were hardly likely to prove docile, and for many years Carolina harboured a rude society, in which, as a Virginian severely observed, "they have no established laws, and very little of the Gospel."

Overseas too the transition was of the smoothest. Virginia reverted readily to a Governor who had been appointed by Charles I, and ousted by the Commonwealth. Maryland pursued a placid and prosperous course, less chequered, after the Restoration, by religious faction, under the Lords Baltimore. In New England, Massachusetts, it is true, was pretty constantly at loggerheads with the Restoration ministers, but Massachusetts, which carried on a flourishing illicit trade in contravention of the Navigation Acts, would have had its differences with any English government. Not till 1684 did the home government take drastic action and revoke the charter of the colony. Meanwhile, unaffected by political upheavals, the grim Puritan tradition flourished unabated. All through the Sabbath, which began at six on Saturday morning, all work, every sport and every amusement, rare enough on week days, was rigidly prohibited. The streets were empty, If a citizen, even of the highest repute, moved from home while a last ray of the setting sun still shone on

Sunday evening he was liable to punishment for Sabbath travel. A maidservant who smiled in church was threatened with banishment; those who absented themselves for more than one Sunday without sufficient excuse were set in the stocks, or whipped. And in the barn-like churches the two hour sermon and the hour's prayer would be followed by crudely worded hymns, given out by leaders, a line at a time, and chanted, in terrible discord, by a congregation which knew five tunes at most. Such was the austere and melancholy atmosphere which helped to breed the Salem witchcrafts, that transient madness during which twenty persons were executed on the gallows, and hundreds committed to prison, as reputed witches.

§3

The second Dutch war, of 1665 to 1667, makes yet another link between the imperial policy of Restoration and Commonwealth. The Dutch had recovered from their punishment in the last struggle; Charles' government was acting vigorously overseas; commercial rivalries accumulated, as they had accumulated under Cromwell, and a renewed conflict became inevitable. It was remarkable as the first war in English history fought solely on colonial issues. France came, reluctantly at first, to the assistance of her Dutch allies in 1666. Her power was soon to overshadow Europe, and she was about to become our great imperial rival, albeit never so formidable as she might have been, if all her power had ever been directed overseas. Like the previous struggle with the Dutch, the new war was hard-fought and equal, an alternation of costly reverses with almost equally costly victories, one of which was won by the Duke of York, the future James II. But the plague of 1665, and the great fire of London in 1666, greatly impoverished the country; and partly for this reason, and partly because it could not control, and did not wholly trust, the government, Parliament refused to vote it adequate supplies. Before the war was over accordingly Charles was compelled to lay up his best ships and disband their unpaid crews, so that, while the treaty of peace was still being negotiated, the Dutch were able to sail up the Medway and burn some of our finest warships off Chatham. The disaster made no apparent difference to the terms of peace, but the memory of it bit deep into popular imagination, and somewhat unfairly has told heavily against Charles' credit ever since. By the treaty of Breda (1667) we surrendered Surinam in Guiana to the Dutch, but, what was vastly more important, the Dutch retired finally from the North American mainland. For the

Dutch settlements which were to become New York and New Jersey
had been captured in the course of the war, and were not returned.
The Dutch Empire was destined henceforth to be an Empire of
trading stations in the tropics. The peopling of vast temperate
regions from the mother country, the spread of their own way of
life across the new continents, all this and how much more, had
they only known it, they were abandoning to the English. Here too
a historic achievement must be ascribed to the government of
Charles II. How far the men who framed the treaty of Breda foresaw
the consequences of what they did it is impossible to say, but at
least some instinct must have warned them where the English
destiny lay.

New Jersey received the first organised emigration of the hardly
used Quakers from England, and, after some vicissitudes, passed
eventually, by the complaisance of the Duke of York, into the hands
of a Quaker syndicate, headed by William Penn. For the Catholic
James had struck up an unexpected friendship, which does credit to
both parties, with the gifted Quaker son of that Admiral Sir William
Penn, who had fought with him in the Dutch wars, and shared with
him the victory off Lowestoft of 1665. The Duke took to the younger
Penn "as a singular and entire friend, and imparted to him many
of his secrets and counsels." Largely, it seems likely, out of Penn's
friendship with James came the charter which he obtained from
Charles in 1681 as proprietor of a new colony of Pennsylvania—it
was Charles who insisted on adding "Penn" to the proposed
"Sylvania." The territory granted him lay just inland from New
Jersey, between Maryland and New York; it was the first American
colony without a coastline. Charles intended it to enlarge the
British Empire, "and . . . be a benefit to the King and his dominions,"
Penn as a Holy Experiment and a refuge for the persecuted Quakers
of Europe. Its subsequent history partly, but only partly, realised
both ambitions. Once again, however, a powerful religious tradition
had been planted by England in the new world.

§4

Five new American colonies—North and South Carolina, New
York, New Jersey and Pennsylvania, and, as we shall see, a great
expansion in India—was no inconsiderable achievement. The reign
of Charles II, customarily thought of as the reign which saw the
Dutch in the Medway, was also, and more significantly, that which
saw them quit North America. But it was also the reign in whose

closing years were played the opening scenes of the imperial struggle with France. And the one remaining Stuart enterprise of imperial expansion in America, the founding of the Hudson's Bay Company in the far north of Canada in 1670, was cradled in conflict with the French. Long before this, like every other new land on which the English entered, Hudson's Bay had taken heavy toll of such adventurers as had reached it. It was as though Nature wished to test the mettle of the pioneers before she allowed them to breed a new race. Henry Hudson himself, who found it, was set adrift there in a shallop with his young son and eight sick men by a mutinous crew in June, 1611, and never, save in Indian folk-lore, was heard of again. Most of Sir Thomas Button's crew next year died of scurvy. Others tried their luck in 1614 and 1615, and were caught in the ice, or groped blindly among vast islands of rock and frost. All these men had been seeking the fabled northern passage to the South Seas. For many years after 1620 the great inland sea lay undisturbed in the loneliness of death; and from its shores the wild peninsula of Labrador, the impenetrable forests to the south, the great territories of the Northwest, spread their mysterious immensities unexplored. And then in 1667 two French explorers were at the court of Charles II. They had roamed vast inland tracts of northern America, had reached Hudson's bay by land, and found there an old log cabin, scored by bullets, perhaps a relic of Hudson's last hours. In 1668 Prince Rupert and other gentlemen packed them off in a couple of English ships to search the Bay for the passage to the south, but also, and in particular, to trade in furs. They spent the winter where the snow fell day afer day, week after week, and the aisled forests were bowed with white, and the iron earth whooped and roared in the frost at night. They did not find the passage, but they brought back furs, enough furs apparently to encourage their backers to apply for a Charter. They received it in May, 1670, and the Company embarked upon its long career of trade and government. Already the English were displaying their strange instinct for administration. A governor and thirty-two men kept the whole "South Shore," a slice of the Hudson Bay territory about the size of the Hohenzollern Germany of 1914, in impeccable order.

At first the Company made no attempt to settle its vast and undefined territories, but confined itself to developing the fur trade. For twelve years, thanks to France's European war of 1672 to 1678, all went well. For already France had begun to sacrifice what might have been her imperial destiny to the more spectacular, but less permanent, prizes of European battlefields. And the true significance of the war, which to contemporaries appeared to have established Louis

XIV at the zenith of his glory, can be seen now to have been that it permitted the foundations of the Restoration Empire to be securely completed, and provided England with the sources of the wealth which helped her eventually to overthrow France in both America and India. But in 1682 the French began to raid Hudson's Bay. With a thousand miles of swamp, forest and cataract to the south, the iron cold to the north, and uncharted wilderness to the west, and with France and England at peace, the small English garrison of Hudson Bay had felt itself secure enough. Suddenly French ships appeared in the Bay, and then, incredibly, a party of French bush-rovers, and Indian auxiliaries, who had made their way a thousand miles overland through the inhospitable wildwoods from Montreal. And for several years now on that remote and barren shore was waged a war of fierce ambushes and bloody assaults, a war almost without quarter, a war whose perils were multiplied and embittered by the constant struggle of both parties against Nature herself. Prisoners were tortured, Indian fashion, for their secrets, turned out to perish in the wilderness or used as slaves by the conquerors. The combatants knew, what their homelands scarcely yet suspected, that they were fighting not for a fur trade but for a Continent. In 1682 the French bush-rovers took one of the Company's forts, and in 1686 six out of the seven, but on each occasion European diplomacy induced the rulers of France to order the conquests to be restored. Charles' secret and dishonourable understanding with Louis XIV was not without its imperial advantages.

§5

In Europe both war and diplomacy wore another aspect, and it is of their European motives and consequences that contemporaries were conscious, and by these that history has judged them. Not that English policy in these years is easy to read clearly. This was a frontier of time, when the Dutch were yielding place to the French as our chief imperial rivals, and men's minds moved uncertainly back and forth, between old and new antagonisms. And other potent and distracting forces were at work. There was the steady disclosure of Louis' vast European ambitions, which even Englishmen, for all their insularity, could perceive and fear, and which, with Spain fallen on decay, Austria distracted by the Turk, and Germany and Italy still subdivided into impotence, there was no continental power, save Holland, to resist. And there was Charles' secret design, with French gold and French countenance, to mould

England to the impressive French model, as a Catholic autocracy. Urged this way and that by so many conflicting considerations, English diplomacy faltered and retraced its steps. In 1668 Sir William Temple negotiated the Triple Alliance, of England, Holland and Sweden, which at once halted the French advance in the Low Countries. But the alliance with the Dutch could not last. Against it worked not only Charles' subterranean preference for France but English jealousy of Dutch world commerce; Sir Josiah Child reckoned that of fifteen vanished English trades almost all had been lost to Holland. To Spanish imperial rivalry a term was set in 1670, when Spain abandoned at last her claim to monopoly in the New World, but the Dutch seemed as formidable as ever, and in the oceanic struggle still far more formidable than the French. This much colour had Charles for his French intrigue, and this much excuse his subjects for accepting, at first, a reversal of the Dutch alliance. In 1670, only two years after the Triple Alliance, the Treaty of Dover was signed with the French. Its published terms provided for an attack on Holland and the partitioning of its possessions; and there is no doubt that Charles hoped to seize Dutch ships, colonies and commerce. But he had more questionable ends in view, and in the secret terms, undisclosed for a century, Louis undertook to assist Charles, with French gold, and, if need be, with French troops, to declare himself a Catholic and raise Catholics to dominance in England. "Surely," noted Evelyn in his diary, when war came in 1672, "this was a quarrel slenderly grounded and not becoming Christian neighbours." But Evelyn could not know the king's secret, and even the declared grounds of war were not so slender, nor its consequences slight.

For two years Holland managed to survive, and there was time for Englishmen to reflect that, if Dutch independence were extinguished, France would be in possession of the delta of the Rhine. Two great unchanging motives have driven England into all her major continental wars—fear of the dictatorship in Europe of a single nation, and fear lest the Low Countries be held by a strong and hostile power—"a pistol," as Napoleon would put it, "pointed at England's head." And by 1674 these same twin spectres, of French supremacy over a prostrate Europe and of a French threat, from Antwerp, to our sea communications, were beginning to haunt men's minds. Reinforced by popular resentment at Charles' Declaration of Indulgence to his Catholic subjects, these misgivings were sufficient to compel the government to abandon the war in 1674. For all its ambiguous aspects there can be no doubt that it had earned its imperial dividends.

Henceforth the Dutch were no longer formidable competitors. The second of the great imperial rivals of the English had shot their bolt. Their resources had been overstrained; and the great man who now led them, William of Orange, was interested in the old world, not the new. Moreover during the war, which France prolonged to 1678, Louis' effort to establish his dominion over Canada was abruptly interrupted. Not for the last time the French had sacrificed imperial to European interests. Even so in America France was already a formidable rival. In the closing years of Charles a Frenchman descended the Mississippi to the Gulf of Mexico; and with both the Mississippi and the St. Lawrence under French control the English colonies in America seemed likely to be hemmed in by French territory on all sides save the sea. Yet during the four years of English neutrality, which followed our withdrawal from the war until France and Holland came to terms in 1678, England acquired a great carrying-trade, and the nucleus of the wealth and power which would enable her, so soon now, to overcome French rivalry overseas. Contemporaries could see only that the France of Louis XIV was far more splendid and far more powerful than the England of Charles II. Yet even now the foundations of English predominance were being laid, for while France sought glory and the hegemony of Europe, England pursued her oceanic destiny.

CHAPTER THREE

MERCHANT ADVENTURERS

(1600-1702)

§1

To INDIA the English had come not less early than to America, but after another fashion. As soon as the defeat of the Spanish Armada released them from ever-present anxiety for their own defences, they turned instinctively to more adventurous trade overseas. They had neither the strength nor the desire to wrest any part of her empire from Spain. But the world lay open to them, and for distant adventures of trade, and the fighting which was then its inevitable accompaniment, they were more than ready. There had been chance contacts with India ere this. One Ralph Fitch left England with three companions by the overland route for the Far East in 1583, and was long given up for lost. In 1591, however, he reached home again, with a strange tale of his journey by way of the Euphrates and the Persian Gulf, and eventually, in manacles, to Goa, of his release through the influence of an English Jesuit resident there, of his visit to the Mogul court of Agra, and of the riches, iniquity and incompetence of the Portuguese. Reports such as these, eagerly circulated, encouraged the already impatient merchants of London, and in 1591 they dispatched three trading vessels to the Far East, an act of presumption which greatly astonished and enraged the rulers of Spain. One ship only survived to reach the Malay Peninsula, and load a cargo of pepper and spices. On the homeward voyage she was swept across the Atlantic to Hispaniola and Labrador. Half dismantled, with a handful of mutinous survivors on board, she eventually struggled back to Plymouth. Her captain, James Lancaster, was landed at Rye by a French vessel, much later, in 1594. But he had at least proved that the voyage was possible. On December 31, 1600, the East India Company received its charter, and entered on its long career of trade and Empire.

It hardly seemed destined for a long life. Indeed its members were so little disposed to look ahead that at first it was their practise to wind up their accounts, and return all capital to the investors, at the end of each voyage; a practise which began to cause increasing confusion as soon as the company found itself maintaining resident agents in the East. With the modification, however, that capital was raised for a period of years, instead of for a single voyage, the cautious original methods persisted until 1657, when the Company raised permanent capital, and became a joint-stock concern in the modern sense. There were many other early perils to be survived. The Crown, for one thing, was apt to expect, in return for the monopoly conferred by the charter, something more than one trading venture every two or three years. For the merchants of the Company, on the other hand, each voyage was a dangerous gamble, and they were naturally reluctant to gamble too high and too hard. With each expedition the frail cockleshells of their miniature fleet carried their capital into the unknown. Disease and tempest, the hostile attentions of Spaniards, Portuguese and Dutch, and countless other unknown hazards must be survived before, more than two years later, a messenger spurred up to London with word that the *Ascension* or the *Red Dragon* was back in Plymouth. And although, like James Lancaster's first voyage if 1601, the fleet might have carried home more than a million pounds of spices, the home market could not hurriedly be flooded with so much, and years might pass before the accounts were wound up and the final dividends pouched. Thus the profit on the first two voyages totalled something like ninety-five per cent, but with their money locked up for eight years the members' actual net gain was reduced to rather less than twenty per cent, by no means an extravagant return for the risks they had run. Many an anxious London merchant in the audience at the Globe, must have listened with heartfelt sympathy to Salanio, in *The Merchant of Venice*, speculating on his own feelings if he had staked his fortune on such a venture:

> *I should be still*
> *Plucking the grass, to know where sits the wind;*
> *Peering in maps for ports, and piers, and roads;*
> *And every object that might make me fear*
> *Misfortune to my ventures, out of doubt,*
> *Would make me mad.*

The merchants wished to trade; they knew that if they were to trade successfully, their servants would sometimes have to fight, but they wanted as little fighting as possible. They were not so squeamish as to object to the boarding of an occasional Spaniard or Portuguese provided that the risk seemed small and the prospective plunder considerable, but they had no desire to send out fiery gallants who would be likely to prefer fighting, for its own sake, to trade.

They had resolved, they discreetly informed the Lord Treasurer, "not to employ any gentleman in any place of charge"; they wished "to be allowed to sorte their business with men of their own qualitye, lest the suspicion of the employm^t of gentlemen being taken hold of by the generalitie, do dryve a great number of the Adventurers to withdraw their contributions." As for the Company's servants in the East, their life was perpetual hazard, of tempest, disease and the violence of foreign foes. Lancaster is said to have used lemon-juice as a specific against scurvy, but later its virtues were forgotten, and for two hundred years the death-rate among seamen, from this sickness alone, was prodigious. Under the constant shadow of death the light-hearted cynicism of some of the pioneers of the East suggests the traditions of the pirate ship rather than the civil service: "Walker dyed, laughing, Woodes and I staked two pieces-of-eight on his body, and after a long play, I wonne."

§2

The founders of the Company had no designs on India. They had formed it to trade in spices with the East Indies, the archipelago of islands, that is, off the south-east coasts of Asia. The Company eventually turned its attention to the sub-continent which we now call India reluctantly, as an altogether inferior alternative, and because it had been expelled from its chosen hunting grounds by the Dutch. For the Dutch had commenced trading with the islands six years earlier, and, like all the rivals of the English, they depended far more upon state enterprise, so that their United East India Company was virtually a department of state, with a vast capital, subscribed in perpetuity. At the outset their greater resources gave them a formidable advantage. A treaty with the Dutch, which James compelled the Company to accept in 1619, dangerously weakened its position. The English were to be allowed a third of the trade of the islands, and to pay a third of the expenses of the civil and military administration. In general the result was that the more numerous Dutch controlled all the fortifications, and forced the English to pay excessively towards the cost of them, charging "large and unreasonable reckonings thereof to the common account." The tragic and long remembered climax came in 1623, at Amboyna, in the Moluccas.

Here was a particularly strong Dutch fortress garrisoned by two hundred soldiers and a company of Dutch burghers, and defended by eight ships. Nearby, virtually unarmed, dwelt the agents of the

English Company, eighteen all told, under Gabriel Towerson. Despite constant difficulties over "the common account" and other matters, Towerson seems to have been well content with the "courtesies" and "love" of Van Speult, the Dutch Governor. Van Speult, however, was only biding his time. In February of 1623, he seized one of the thirty Japanese soldiers of the garrison, who had put some casual questions to a Dutch sentinel as to its strength. Under torture the Japanese was induced to confess that he had been concerned in a plot, with other Japanese, and the handful of unarmed English, to capture the fortress—defended by two hundred Dutch soldiers, eight ships and twenty guns. Other Japanese were tortured for confirmation of this quite incredible story. The eighteen English were then seized by a subterfuge. All of them denied any knowledge of the alleged conspiracy, but under eight days of savage torture some sort of confession was extorted from all of them, except perhaps from Towerson himself. On February 27, ten English merchants and nine Japanese soldiers were executed in the presence of the native population. Some of the prisoners, after their torture, contrived to write protestations of their innocence in prayer-books or diaries which eventually found their way back to England.

The news did not reach England till next year. It roused widespread horror and indignation, and for the first time disclosed the Dutch as the new imperial rivals. James wept as the tale was told him, but did little more than weep. Brutality, however, usually defeats its own ends. For a century the English people did not forget the massacre, or that no Dutch statesman had expressed regret for it, and every Dutch war was fought with greater zest because of Amboyna. It was left to Cromwell to exact some belated compensation for the surviving relatives of the victims in the peace treaty of 1654.

The massacre went far towards founding the British Empire in India. For it brought English trade with the Spice Islands to an end. And two years later the Company had abandoned the farthest East altogether and was concentrating its energies on trade with India, where fortunately it had for some while been establishing a hold. Here the chief obstacle was not the Dutch but the Portuguese, already established at Goa and on the Malabar coast, and in possession of Ceylon, and now aiming at a monopoly of Indian trade both with Europe and with the Far East. Here too therefore, however much the Company disliked it, and with or without orders, its servants would have to fight. As yet, indeed, trade could be had on no other terms. And here too it would be fighting not with the native populations but with jealous European rivals, and here too it would not be formal warfare, declared and organised by governments, but the inevitable clashes with would-be monopolists, ranging from the murderous onset in some dark nook of the bazaar to pitched battles, and miniature campaigns, on sea and land. Once again all would depend upon the courage and resource of individual leaders and small, isolated parties, far out of reach of the authorities they served, and almost unsupported by their own government.

There would be no English trade with India if the Portuguese could prevent it, as they certainly would unless they were overcome by force. The fighting soon began. At the end of it, the Portuguese, who had been considerably reinforced, turned tail, after losing several ships and three hundred men. The two English ships were still intact, and only three Englishmen had been killed. The Mogul Governor of Surat, who had remained an interested but passive spectator of these prolonged hostilities within his jurisdiction, readily acknowledged the victory by authorising at Surat, in 1612, the first permanent English trading post in the dominions of the Grand Mogul. In 1614 the Portuguese Viceroy of Goa made a supreme effort to expel the intruders, mustering nine ships, and sixty native barges, with two hundred and thirty-four guns, two thousand six hundred Europeans and six thousand natives against Captain Nicholas Downton's eighty guns and four hundred men. After fighting which lasted more than three weeks the Portuguese drew off to Goa, with the loss of five hundred men. The English factory at Surat was secure, and, though the Company did not dream of so astonishing an outcome, and certainly did not desire it, the earliest foundations of an Indian Empire had been laid. After this, the collapse of the Portuguese Empire proceeded steadily. The Spanish government, it is curious to note, maintained an apparently unbroken indifference to the disappearance of its vassal Empire; so that for three years not a solitary official communication from Europe was received by the Portuguese authorities in Goa.

From 1615 to 1618 Sir Thomas Roe was able to reside as ambassador at the court of the Mogul in Agra, and, though handicapped by lack of a competent interpreter, and by Jehangir's reluctance to make, or keep, promises, he was able to do not a little for English interests, and incidentally to acquire a nice taste in the selection of presents acceptable to his hosts; four or five cases of burgundy, he eventually concluded, would be esteemed "more highly than all the jewels in Cheapside." An English factory was established at Masulipatam, half-way up the eastern coast, in 1611, and from Masulipatam, much to the annoyance of the unambitious Directors, Francis Day acquired for the Company sovereignty of a strip of land in Madras, on which he erected Fort St. George, the first fortified factory in India. At so remote a distance the Company could exercise little control over its factors in India, and the eventual development of English rule there, little designed or desired by the men on the spot, was even less to the taste, or according to the plans, of the Directors in Cheapside.

But sufficient proof that Indian trade would be a rich field to till was the mere fact that the Company's agents continued to develop it in spite not only of the dangers and obstacles in India itself but of an almost complete cessation, for nearly a quarter of a century before the Protectorate, of effective support from home. And then Cromwell turned his attention to the Company's affairs. Conflicting interests clamoured for his favour. Some wanted no regulations at all, a fair field and no favour. Some demanded a regulated company, whose members, however, would be free to trade as they pleased and on their own accounts. And some wanted the *status quo*. In 1657 Cromwell made his decision. The Company's monopoly was to be maintained, and, with a permanent capital, it was at last to become a joint-stock concern in the modern sense.

§3

Even more than the history of America, the history of India during the thirty years which followed is evidence that the reign of Charles II cannot be understood by historians for whom English history is only the history of England. In India as in America the men of this generation seem to rival the energy and confidence of the Elizabethans. And even more perhaps in India than in America were outstanding individuals needed, and forthcoming. The era of Charles II moreover was seminal in the history of India. It saw a startling change, not of their own choosing, in English methods, and the first pregnant stages in the transformation of a Company of merchants into an imperial administration. At the beginning of this period the President of Surat is the local manager of a trading concern; at the end of it he is President of Bombay, head of an executive government, with law courts, a standing army and a system of taxation of its own.

The first step towards still unimagined ends came, scarcely noticed, at the very outset of the reign. A new charter, in 1661, added to the old privileges a wider jurisdiction over all Englishmen in the East, and new powers to raise troops and maintain fortifications. Charles doubtless intended no more than that the Company should be able to defend itself effectively against its European rivals. None the less he had begun to entrust merchants with the instruments of government. And in 1668 he made over Bombay to the Company, for a rent of ten pounds a year. It had been part of his Portuguese wife's dowry, but as a Crown Colony it had brought no profits, and entailed heavy expense. From the first, and against every probability, the Company believed stoutly in the future of its new acquisition. Four hundred of the first five hundred English inhabitants of Bombay perished there, very many of a terrible new disease, cholera. The average life of an English factor in the east was reckoned at three years. As one of them wrote: ". . , in five hundred, one hundred survives not; of that one hundred, one-quarter get not estates; of those that do it has not been recorded above one in ten years has seen his country." But they buried their dead, and toiled on. They fortified the pestiferous city of Bombay, and gave it some sort of sanitation. In ten years its population rose from ten to sixty thousand.

And now a change of incalculable import slowly overshadowed the Indian scene. It became apparent that the Mogul Empire was breaking up. Hitherto the English had counted on trading within the peace kept by the Indian lords of India. They had not dreamed of conquest or administration. They might have to defend themselves, but it would be against their European rivals. But now the great empire whose writ had run throughout northern India, and beyond, was overtaken by the traditional doom of eastern despotisms. The viceroys of its outer provinces began to revolt. Inevitably anarchy spread, and soon the Mahrattas were plundering central India far and wide. Sir George Oxenden beat off a Mahratta raid from the unfortified walls of the English factory at Surat in 1664. It was the beginning of the end of unarmed trade, the system which the English had light-heartedly assumed would last for ever. The shadow of Aurungzeb was no longer sufficient to protect them. They must defend themselves. A new era had begun.

§4

The Company could hardly have survived the long and unforeseen ordeal now opening but for the quality and fibre of its servants in the east, and the sturdy vein of Puritanism in its own making.. It is easy to forget that the English came to India in the age of the *Mayflower*, and that the Company long wore the impress of that serious and stalwart era. Thus at the departure and homecoming of their ships it was the custom of the shareholders to attend a solemn service, and hear a special sermon. The Company provided its chief settlements with chaplains, whom it selected with much care, after solemnly attending in a body to hear candidates preach upon a selected text. It sent out religious literature, and schoolmasters to give secular instruction to the children of English, Portuguese, or any other nation, without charge. For the Company's servants the factory was a large trade-household in which they lived under the authority of the President, very much like undergraduates in a strictly disciplined college. There were fines for swearing, for absence from prayers (twice as heavy on a Sunday as on weekdays), for staying out at night or coming in after the gate was shut, and for drunkenness and "thereby prostituting the worthiness of our nation and religion to the calumnious censure of the heathen." For striking or abusing the natives "they are to be sett at the gate in irons all the day time, and all the night be tyed to a Post in the house." Those guilty of persistent profanity and debauchery were liable to be shipped home "as unworthy to reside in a Christian Plantation." Writing from Bombay in 1672, a youthful servant of the Company reports public prayers morning and night, and strict observance of the feasts and fasts of the Church. Indeed his picture of life in the factory is almost too good to be true. In their spare time, he assures his parents, the Company's servants

. . . have much more Discourse of Religion, Philosophie, the government of the Passions and affections, and sometimes of history, than of trade and getting money for ourselves, though that allsoe be in noe manner neglected on the Company's behalfe, yet for our owne Particular I believe there is noe Marchants have less regard to it.

The young man's account may have been coloured by a pardonable anxiety to reassure a censorious parent—three years earlier indeed the chief factor in Bengal was protesting "that we have divine service once on the Sunday is as much as can be expected in these hot countries; for neither a man's spirit nor his voice can hold touch here with long duties." Both pictures, however, were probably substantially true to life, for under the constant shadow of death men are apt to grow either unusually reckless or unusually serious. The Company rewarded its servants but meagrely for their services, and for facing the appalling risks of life in India. The humble "writer" drew £5 a year, about as much as it cost him to board and lodge for a month. Even Governor Pitt of Madras, grandfather of the great Earl of Chatham, was paid but £300 a year in all. Yet he was able to purchase the famous Pitt diamond from the mines of Golconda for a prince's ransom in 1702. The fact was that already the Company's servants, almost without exception, borrowed money and traded on their own account, and frequently amassed considerable private fortunes. The practise was pardonable, and under the circumstances inevitable, but before long it would endanger the whole moral fabric of the English system in India.

It was fortunate for the Company, as it moved doubtfully into the new era, that so many of its servants were men of constancy and courage, prepared to dare, and suffer, to the end. For once again it would be for the men on the spot to make or mar all. It was Gerald Aungier, President of Surat from 1669 to 1677, who inspired the heroic persistence with which, despite a fearful death-rate, and the Company's reluctance to send out engineers, the English built and fortified Bombay out of swamp and rock and sand. Indeed he was ever pressing for some fresh enterprise, so that the cautious directors at home groaned at the very sound of his name. Madras, where they had allowed Francis Day's fort to fall into decay, they would have abandoned in 1674, but changed their minds at the eleventh hour, and refortified it, so that three years later it held off the Mahrattas, and induced Aurungzeb, too, to keep his distance. In Bengal, after years of oppression, injustice and violence at the hands of the Mogul's viceroy, it was clear by 1686 that the English must choose between resistance and withdrawal. Job Charnock, the Bengal agent, a hard, unlovable person, who had occasioned scandal by marrying a Hindu wife and taking to Hindu habits, was a man, nevertheless, of clear vision and indomitable purpose. And he had an eye for strategy. He was a hundred miles from his fleet at the river's mouth; this was no site for the merchants of the sea. He shipped men and merchandise downstream to a bleak mudbank near the river-mouth. Protected on one side by pestilent swamp and jungle, its deep anchorage commanded by the high river bank, this repellent spot, he perceived, was defensible, and it could be supplied from the sea. Many clearly would perish of disease there, but what matter? The Company's servants were accustomed to disease and death. In tents and boats under a savage sun the English held on. Forced by the Mogul's army to evacuate their port in 1687, they were back again before the close of the year. Once again Charnock was ordered to leave, but in 1690 he returned, this time to stay. Still "death overshadowed all," and the merchants under his command yearned for the earlier upriver settlement, where, though they might be dependent upon the unreliable favours of the Indian potentate, they could at least hope to survive. But Charnock held them grimly to the new site, and, though he died in 1693, they stayed on. In 1697 Fort William was built there, and slowly thereafter rose the city of Calcutta. Here, for the first time, the Company possessed rights of justice and police over native inhabitants. In general, however, the aggressive policy had been a failure. It had led to the abandonment of Bengal and the loss of Masulipatam, and had gravely imperilled Madras. The President of Bombay had had to make humble submission, and the Nawab of Bengal was mollified by an indemnity in cash.

Despite all, however, the Company continued to prosper, and therefore to incur increasing jealousy at home. And as the era of the Stuarts drew to a close it became involved in the growing political tension at home. A dissident minority of shareholders, imbued with the liberal ideas fashionable among the Opposition, desired to abandon the monopoly. It was defeated, but after the Revolution it perceived that a monopoly based upon a royal grant could now be readily abolished by legislation, and returned to the attack. An Act of 1690 duly recognised a New Company, but Sir John Child and the old Company fought stoutly on, the inexperienced New Company had little success in the East, and in 1702, after ruinous competition, the rivals agreed to amalgamate. Such was the state of English fortunes in India when the long struggle with France began. Thus far it had been the story of a handful of merchant adventurers. But great issues were in the making. Soon soldiers would be needed, and statesmen; and then the acceptance, by the whole nation, of wholly new moral and political standards.

BOOKS FOR FURTHER READING.

E. Lipson, *Economic History of England*, vol. 3; John Buchan, *Oliver Cromwell;* W. Hull, *A topical biography of William Penn;** H. C. Lodge, *A short history of the English Colonies in America;** Anon, *An historical account of . . . South Carolina & Georgia* (1779);** C. H. Haring, *The Buccaneers in the West Indies;* Agnes C. Laut, *The Conquest of the great North West;* Beckles Wilson, *Ledger and Sword;* Edward Thomspon and G. T. Garratt, *The rise and fulfilment of British rule in India.*
                        * Published in America.

Book III

THE HUNDRED YEARS' WAR BEGINS

CHAPTER ONE

BRITAIN AND FRANCE ON THE EVE

§1

To describe the imperial struggle with France, ushered in by
the Revolution of 1689, as a hundred years' war is no exaggeration. Between the Revolution of 1688 and the battle of Waterloo in
1815 we waged seven great wars; five of them were throughout,
and the other two soon became, wars against France. European
quarrels complicated the issues in some of them, but all were, in
essence, wars of Empire. And although we were officially at war
for not more than sixty-four years of the hundred and twenty-six,
little enough attention was paid by those who conducted the
imperial contests overseas, either in India or America, to the peace
treaties which from time to time put an end to hostilities in Europe.
It was while France and England were officially at peace that Clive
defended Arcot and Braddock was routed at Fort Duquesne.

It has been said that the Glorious Revolution of 1689 was neither
glorious nor a revolution, and there is a measure of truth in both
assertions. Nevertheless it was certainly glorious in that it was
bloodless, and it was a revolution in that it substituted a Parliamentary oligarchy of landowners and merchants for a monarchy which
had aimed at despotism. Whig historians have long schooled us to
see the settlement of 1689 as the main source of our national greatness. And if, as Whig historians have mostly taken for granted,
British history means British domestic politics, there is a good deal
to be said for this view. But those who see the chief significance of
British history in the growth of a British world society will hardly
accept the roseate traditional view of the Whig Revolution. For
although the Revolution released the energies which made Britain
mistress of the seas, and although it gave her more freedom and
more justice, and so in due time rendered possible the second Empire
and the enduring Commonwealth, the Revolution was almost

equally responsible for that gross coarsening of moral fibre which had first to be expiated by the loss of the American colonies. Perhaps the balance sheet of the Whig Revolution is most simply struck by saying that it gave Britain the virtues with which she defeated France and the vices with which she lost America. And for those who would understand the British Empire it is well to remember that the American colonies were founded by austere Puritans in the seventeenth century and lost by dissolute rationalists in the eighteenth.

The era of Parliamentary oligarchy which now set in brought with it, it is true, an altogether novel vigour, without which the vast spiritual and physical effort of the coming centuries would have been impossible. For the supreme virtue of the Revolutionary Settlement was that it was a settlement. Under the Stuarts constant conflict with Parliament had deprived the Crown of finances, denied it armaments and paralysed its diplomacy. Divided within itself, the state was never able to put forth its full power. And so when the long struggle was finally settled, in favour of Parliament, in 1688, the country achieved not only more freedom but more efficiency. No longer distracted by constitutional conflict at home it could exert its full strength abroad.

There is no mistaking the energy of the new age. It did not possess the wisdom and moral discipline without which the nation would never achieve its true destiny, but the rough, male tang of eighteenth century England, with its hard drinking, gambling and duelling, its hunting and cock-fighting, its self-seeking politicians and its vitriolic pamphleteers, was appropriate enough for an age of constant warfare and almost instinctive expansion. To a foreigner the life of the island might seem tumultuous and in some respects anarchic, but, if so, it was the tumult of energy and the anarchy of life. Throughout its hundred years' war Britain was governed by an oligarchy of the landed aristocracy, and one way of understanding why Britain defeated France is to contrast the exquisite trifling of Watteau's modish nymphs and gallants with some country conversation-piece by Gainsborough of a florid young landlord with his gun under his arm, his dogs at his heels and his lady, in stiff blue silks, at his side. Unlike the French *noblesse*, who possessed much privilege but no power, the Whig and Tory lords actively administered both the country and the countryside. Theirs was a full-blooded, exuberant life, from the day when the little lords fought each other through twenty rounds with bare fists at Eton to the robust rough-and-tumble of the debates at Westminster. The tastes of the British aristocracy were coarser than those of the French, because its vitality was so much earthier and more energetic. It governed with the same self-confident zest as that with which it gambled, drank, read Horace or rode to hounds. These men believed in their country, their institutions and themselves; and if they sometimes seemed to think of the Almighty as a superior Whig nobleman somewhat handicapped by owning no pocket boroughs, the fact remains that, before 'its close, the eighteenth century produced both Wesley and Wilberforce.

§2

And not only at the outset of the long duel with France did England become a Parliamentary state; she also became Britain. The accession of James the First had meant union of the crowns of England and Scotland, but the Parliaments and laws of the two countries had remained separate. Scotland at this time was a poverty-stricken land of mediæval agriculture, scanty industry and about a million inhabitants, half its area under the tribal rule of wild Highland chieftains. Hitherto the Scots had had no legitimate share in the English Empire, and the Navigation Acts had excluded them from colonial trade as rigorously as any other foreign country. But they must have been conscious of the gifts which qualified them above almost every other nation for a great imperial rôle, and between 1695 and 1698, by a supreme effort, they raised the capital for a Company of their own which was to found a trading colony on the Isthmus of Darien, or Panama. Five ships left Leith, amidst great public enthusiasm, towards the end of 1698, but after much sickness and sufferings the colony was abandoned by the survivors next June. A relief expedition, which arrived five months later, ignorant of the failure of the pioneers, was likewise decimated by disease, and capitulated to a Spanish force next year. Throughout the ill-starred adventure the English had stood somewhat contemptuously aloof, and no assistance had been sent to the Darien settlement from their West Indian colonies. Scotland seethed with anger and mortification, and it seemed likely that on the death of Queen Anne there would be a Jacobite restoration in Edinburgh. The establishment of the House of Hanover in England was likely to be delicate and dangerous enough, without such complications across the border, and the obvious alternative to a separation of the Crowns was a union of the Governments. When this was at length effected in 1707 both partners were conscious of gaining immense advantages; England political unity at home, Scotland admission, on equal terms, to the Empire. But both were gaining more than they knew. For though few can have suspected it in 1707, the needy Scots farmers who mused or argued over their Bibles in cabins of turf or unmortared stone would prove a race supremely qualified to administer and enrich an Empire. Particularly valuable was this rich tributary stream at the outset of a hundred years of war with France, during which Englishmen were still apt to sneer at the Scots adventurer on the make, and Dr. Johnson thought that the fairest scene of nature a Scotsman could behold was the highway which led to England.

§3

Nevertheless the cynicism and the materialism in the new England is as unmistakable as the new energy which they partly clogged and the new virtues which they did much to mar. And here we have the dark underside of the Whig Revolution. For from the first the Revolution, and the new power of the commercial interests, coarsened and degraded public life. The appetites of materialism were now unleashed.

For the Stuarts, even at their most perverse, had had their ideals. They had been empire-founders, not empire-losers, albeit they could not keep their own crown. Whatever their faults and errors, Strafford, Laud and Clarendon were high-minded and high-aiming men, and the objectives of all of them were moral rather than material. And there is a grossness about the cynicism of eighteenth century politicians, which Whig historians, ever ready to censure the more graceful cynicism of the court of Charles II, have been apt to overlook. For worse as well as for better, the imperial history of the eighteenth century bears the impress of the greatly increased political power, and the greatly increased wealth, of the commercial classes. In the eighteenth century the economic begins to overshadow the political motive, and the moral sentiment disappears, until, largely for that reason, the first Empire dissolves. The prosperity of their own expanding industries at home is now the too exclusive concern of British statesmen, and there is at least as much suspicion of favouritism and self-interest in the imperial legislation of Parliament after 1688 as in the Court administration which preceded it.

The mechanism of colonial administration, too, deteriorated for the time being. The old Lords of Trade, and the salaried Board of Trade with which William III replaced them in 1696, had acted with vigour and intelligence. But with the coming of the Hanoverians the considerable salaries of the Board proved too tempting to the growing army of place-hunters, and by 1740 its proceedings had become a farce. Unfortunately perhaps the political settlement of the Whigs did not extend to the Empire. Except in New England, the flight of James II neither interrupted nor diverted the currents of colonial history. For William, at this turning point of time, there was surely an opportunity to overhaul both the theory and the practise of Empire, to attack, and perhaps to solve, the increasingly formidable problem of colonies which were economically subject, yet otherwise very free, colonies whose population was doubling itself every twenty years and which were three months' voyage from the mother country. If so, it was an opportunity which he did not take.

And so eighteenth century England would know disasters as spectacular as its triumphs, and as richly earned. The Whigs and their Revolution made a Britain which was gross and self-seeking and lost the American colonies, but they retained their courage and their energy, and so defeated France, and because, despite all its defects, they built their political system upon the hereditary English sense of the absolute value of individual personality, they ensured for their country the primacy of the age to come.

§4

Once again Britain was to be pitted against a despotic state, and once again to all contemporary Europe it seemed inevitable that the despot must triumph. For the island which was now to sustain a century of conflict, and, despite the secession of all its American colonies, to emerge at last as mistress of the most widespread Empire the world had ever seen, itself now contained a population of not more than five and a half millions. Across the narrow Channel its new rival, still to all appearances richer, much more powerful and universally admired, contained more than twice that number. But France was still a feudal society, strictly hierarchic and rigidly over-centralised. The new wealthy middle classes had not, as in England, acquired their proper influence in the state, or lent it the full impulse of their energies. Louis XIV spoke true when he boasted that the French state was himself. Only, in his early years he had been sustained by the counsel of the great Colbert, and now the master hand of Colbert was withdrawn. Louis himself never even fully perceived that sea-power was indispensable to an Empire overseas.

Like authoritarian Spain at the dawn of the oceanic age, authoritarian France on the eve of a world-wide struggle, to be fought by new methods and for new prizes, was too rigid, too unadaptable, too firmly set in the mediæval moulds. English society was far more fluid, and therefore far more adaptable. In England the infiltration of the middle classes, for whom the feudal system had provided no place, had proceeded steadily for three hundred years, and the feudal structure had long since disintegrated. There were classes, but no castes.

It was to be a struggle not only of peoples but of systems, of what we should now call ideologies. In France the king's words were actually law. Of the Rule of Law, of judicial independence, ministerial responsibility or the control of taxation, all now established in England, the French as yet knew nothing. All these meant a new potency in action, but they meant more than this. For in the last resort they stood for respect for human personality. And respect for human personality was the great new public virtue which on the moral plane gave England her title to victory. There was cynicism and materialism in plenty in eighteenth-century England, and she would yet pay dear for them, but even the cynics and the materialists would be dimly conscious, as the long struggle wore on, that they were defending something more precious than their own wealth or their own power.

The triumph of England over the Grand Monarch in the first round of the long contest, the wars of Marlborough, would greatly astonish a world which had supposed that despotism, on the French model, was the secret of efficiency. And the prestige acquired by Parliamentary institutions in this ordeal by battle was eventually responsible in Europe for the intellectual movement towards liberty in Church and state which marks the second half of the eighteenth century. This is the great achievement on which historians have usually concentrated their attention. But it was an even greater achievement that England did not merely set Europe an example of liberty which Europe would repeatedly forget, but, through her victories overseas, would in due season spread free communities across the entire world. For the grand historic significance of the eighteenth century is not the rise and fall of Parties in the new Parliamentary arena. It is that twofold drama—first the long conflict with France on land and sea, and then, interwoven with it, the searching moral ordeal in America and India, which would end one age, and lay the foundations of another.

§5

In America itself the contrasts of our island of free institutions with the feudal despotism of its more populous neighbour were in some ways curiously reversed. In America, for one thing, it was the British who were the more numerous, two hundred thousand of them against a mere fifteen thousand Frenchmen—and this because the British represented a genuine migration, the initiative of generations of individual citizens, while the French were rather pawns of royal policy planted in Acadia at the will, and by the authority, of the Crown. Frenchmen have seldom made ready or natural colonists, for they seldom cease to regret France, and in a plantation overseas were apt, as Dr. Johnson put it, to lead "a laborious and necessitous life, in perpetual regret of the deliciousness and plenty of their native country." And to the French of the eighteenth century, and later, *la gloire* reaped on a European battle-field was apt to appeal a good deal more strongly than expansion overseas. The French were not naturally colonists. When Napoleon sneered at the British as a nation of shopkeepers he was thinking of a race for whom colonial expansion had meant, first and foremost, trade, and who had never been distracted from colonial enterprise by the will-o'-the-wisp of European glory. Again, whereas in the world-wide conflict between the mother countries free institutions proved themselves more formidable than despotism, for the struggle in America certain clear advantages, at any rate at first, were enjoyed by the French model. For the English colonists refused to combine, and indeed at first, save for Massachusetts, would hardly act in their own defence. The colonies remained jealous separate communities, recognising no bond save British sovereignty and without a notion of their common interests or of combining to achieve them. In 1754, when the final struggle for mastery of the continent began, Virginia refused all military aid, and the Quakers of Pennsylvania openly declared that they would accept French rule, rather than surrender a point in the trifling dispute which each assembly was carrying on with its governor. Without the individualism of the English there would have been no British America, but now British America was a raw new world of individualists, which had never known the discipline of monarchy or feudalism. The French Canadians, on the other hand, like most French colonists down the centuries, had to the best of their ability carried old France with them overseas. French Canada itself was feudal, and *seigneur* and *curé* played their time-honoured rôles, in the new world as in the old.

To have transplanted to America a social system which, by English standards, was already three centuries out of date in Europe was hardly of good augury for the political future of the French in the new world. But in the opening of the conflict at any rate their feudalism stood them in good stead. For they were accustomed to obedience and to concerted action. And it was this tradition of discipline, and the royal regiments stationed in Canada, which together enabled them to make headway against the massive superiority in numbers of their neighbours.

It was in fact a prologue to the spectacle, so often enacted since, of the free nation unready for war, and at first slow in action, and divided in purpose, in conflict with a despotism far better prepared, far swifter in action and far more single of purpose. Indeed the analogy can be carried a good deal further. This was in embryo the struggle, so often to be repeated, of industrial democracy with military centralisation, and down the centuries both democracy and its great rival have continued to make precisely the same mistakes. "If those not immediately concerned," writes Colonel Heathcote, a member of the New York Council, in 1715, "only stand gazing on while the wolf is murthering other parts of the flock, it will come to every one's turn at last." For the French understood, as the British at first did not, the greatness of the prize, they eagerly studied their rivals' weaknesses and carefully matured ambitious plans for defeating them. For a while all the military advantages were on one side, until the numbers, wealth and natural vigour of the British colonies—the fact, in other words, that they were true colonies—and the sea power which sustained them, slowly turned the scales.

Politically, the American colonies were not ready for the conflict. The Stuarts had designed the consolidation of British America; when in 1686 Sir Edmund Andros arrived in Boston, it was as governor, not of Massachusetts, but of all New England. In 1688 his authority was extended over New York and New Jersey. Under one administration from the Delaware to the borders of Nova Scotia, British America seemed to be moving fast towards unity. But in 1689 James fled from England, and with him fell Andros and the Dominion of New England. With the revolution the northern colonies reverted to separatism, and the Stuart design of consolidation was abandoned for ever. Paradoxically enough, in relation to the Empire the revolutionary differed from the Restoration settlement only in a slight additional emphasis on the power of the Crown. The colonists continued to exercise representative, but not responsible, government. Their assemblies could voice their grievances, but could not enforce their wishes; they could initiate legislation, but could not replace the executive. Later experience has repeatedly shown that representation without responsibility is the most dangerous of halfway houses to democracy. And not later experience only. This, after all, was precisely the condition of the Commons of England under James I and Charles I, and, to a lesser degree, in the later years of Charles II. In England it had produced civil war in 1641, and revolution in 1689. What induced the revolutionaries of 1689 to perpetuate in America the system which they had risen to destroy for ever in England? The answer, it is to be feared, is that the American colonists were not Whig and Tory noblemen. For here a later generation was expiating that dangerous sense of the colonist as an inferior, which had been nourished by the Stuart tradition that derelict wastrels, broken men and felons were the fittest persons to send overseas. Nor did the eighteenth century abjure the error which it had to expiate. Publicists continued to hold that it was better for the mother country to lose mischievous or useless citizens than to see the virtuous and industrious migrating overseas, and that in any case transportation to the new world was the likeliest means of reforming criminals. And after 1719, under two statutes of George I, several hundred convicts were shipped annually to Virginia. The Annual Register of 1766 contains a lively picture of "the convicts . . . passing to the waterside in order to be shipped for America with pipes playing before them ' Thro' the wood, laddie.'" And Georgia, the last of the thirteen colonies, was founded in 1733 by the philanthropic General James Oglethorpe expressly for the moral reformation of the inmates of English debtors' prisons, "who," as he put it in his *Brief Account of the Establishment of Georgia*, "would otherwise starve and burden England." The paradox did not escape contemporary satirists. *And on sure grounds the gospel pile to rear*, Britain, wrote Churchill in 1764, *Sends missionary felons once a year*. Such gentry, the Whig lords were only too apt to feel, could scarcely expect to be entrusted with powers as complete as these of the British Parliament.

CHAPTER TWO

THE WARS OF WILLIAM AND MARLBOROUGH

(1689-1713)

§1

THE FIRST WAR was William the Third's, the war, as the text-books call it, of the League of Augsburg, and it would last from 1689 till 1697. Five years of uneasy peace, and it is followed by Marlborough's war, fought against the same enemy, and ended in 1713 by the triumphant peace of Utrecht. Both wars, as the men who fought them knew well enough, were waged for our classic aims in Europe —against the domination of the continent by one power, and against the occupation of the Low Countries by a formidable enemy. But both, though few who fought in them suspected it, were fought for vaster ends than these. During both a fierce struggle was waged with the French along the American frontiers, but, save perhaps for a brief period under the Tory administration of Harley and St. John which took office in 1710, this was a natural counterpart and concomitant of the war in Europe rather than an integral element in the strategy of those who directed it. Inevitably, however, and even when English ministers were least aware of it, it was the imperial issue which was being fought out in Europe. The wars of William and Marlborough ensured that French despotism should not overshadow all Europe, and that the ruler of France should not acquire the crown of Spain, or its Empire overseas. Both these decisions were of great moment for the imperial struggle, but, what was far more significant, these wars gave to Britain the mastery of the seas. Before the Treaty of Utrecht Britain was a great naval power, after it she was the naval power—paramount on every sea.

§2

Yet at the outbreak of William's war the French were actually for a short while more powerful at sea than England and Holland combined, and possessed in Tourville the ablest commander afloat. In June, 1690, they defeated the combined Dutch and English fleets off Beachy Head, and burnt Teignmouth. But Versailles was incurably land-minded, and the pregnant moment passed unexploited. And in 1692 the French, who had designed an invasion of southern England, were defeated in the Channel by a superior allied fleet, and lost fifteen of their finest ships in the battle of La Hogue. The action was in no way discreditable to Tourville or to French seamanship, but the effect upon French public opinion was calamitous. This, together with the strain of the continental war, and the inveterate failure of French statesmen to perceive the full significance of sea-power, was responsible for the steady decay of the French fleet, which fought no other general action during the rest of the war. In years to come the French navy would breed fine sailors, fight great battles and know moments of victory, but its doom was sealed. From now on, the relative power of the English Navy steadily increased; within ten years it was everywhere supreme, and indeed unchallenged. "No decisive encounter between equal forces, possessing military interest," observes Mahan, "occurs between 1700 and 1778." All this while, nevertheless, English sea-power was the determining factor in the history of Europe and the world, everywhere exercising its relentless, invisible pressure, and making possible a score of victories in which it seemed to play no part. It is curious perhaps that the supremacy of England on the seas should date neither from a spectacular victory nor from the career of a great sea captain. It may be curious, but it is certainly significant. For the English overbore the French at sea partly because they were undistracted by continental commitments and ambitions, and because their statesmen had by now learnt to think instinctively in terms of the sea; but above all because more fully and naturally than the French they were a sea-going people, and their sea power was broad-based upon the free maritime enterprise of the whole nation. As for the Dutch, their bolt was shot and they were no longer rivals. Year by year they contributed a diminishing quota to the allied armaments, year by year their finance and commerce dwindled. The military and artistic glories of seventeenth century Holland were no more. It was a small state, distracted, like France, by its land frontier, and during the period of its greatness its resources had been overstrained. After the Treaty of Utrecht Holland ceased to be a great power, and withdrew from the wars and diplomacy of Europe. The lists were cleared for the struggle of England and France.

§3

Inevitably we remember the war of 1702 to 1713 as that in which England astonished Europe by producing one of the great generals of history. But even Marlborough's extraordinary victories were made possible by English sea-power. Sea-power protected the commerce upon which depended the subsidies by which the continental forces were sustained, it linked Marlborough's armies securely with the home ports, and by ruining French commerce it exhausted France. But it did more than this. It maintained meanwhile the campaigns on the Spanish peninsula, and made possible a vast expansion, even in war-time, of English overseas trade, so that in 1713 5807 ships cleared from British ports, as against 3550 in 1710. Moreover in 1704, on his own initiative, Admiral Sir George Rooke bombarded Gibraltar, and captured it forthwith by an assault in small boats. The significance of Gibraltar had been foreseen, fifty years earlier, by Cromwell; with Minorca, captured by General Stanhope in 1708, it gave English sea-power the bases which established it firmly in the western Mediterranean. From now on our predominance at sea powerfully influenced the character of society in these islands. It dispensed us from the necessity of maintaining one of those large standing armies which everywhere on the continent proved an obstacle to the development of free institutions. Moreover since there was no military conscription here, British citizens never experienced that regimentation which might in time have cramped their characteristic individualism. The drawback to this fortunate immunity was that they were also spared from familiarity with discipline, and in times of prolonged peace were specially tempted to forget that no nation can remain great without sacrifice.

§4

Naturally, since France and England were rivals for the new world, no sooner were they at grips in Europe than the American frontiers burst into flame. It was the sporadic, small-scale fighting of scanty numbers in a vast arena, but, thanks to the ruthless use by the French of their Red Indian allies, it was often savage and pitiless. On the English side at least during the wars of William and Marlborough no grand strategy co-ordinated the campaigns in both continents. Always our imperial wars were wars of the people rather than the government. With the brief and ill-fated exception of Bolingbroke, English ministers were as ready to leave the colonies to a savage, unprofessional scramble in their own backwoods as were the colonists to ignore the European conflict on which their own fate ultimately depended. In 1705 Vaudreuil, the French governor, even proposed a treaty of peace, or neutrality, to the New Englanders, while the mother countries were still at war. Even within their own arena the English colonists were quite unable, and quite unfitted, to plan a campaign. As yet indeed they had not even fully perceived the vastness of the issues at stake. Shut in by the Alleghanies, each colony lived a life of its own, little dreaming of a future collective greatness which the possession of the West must confer upon the eventual victor.

As soon as William's war began, Frontenac, the Governor of Canada, loosed his Red Indians on the frontiers of New England and New York. At first it was sporadic harryings and murders, but in the second year of war Frontenac planned three separate forays in force of French and Indians, in the course of two of which Schenectady and Salmonfalls, small wooden townships of civilians, were surprised at night and burned to the ground, and their inhabitants butchered or carried off into captivity among the Indians. A third, and more formidable, raiding band, mainly French, drove into Maine and captured Falmouth and its garrison of seventy. There was a formal surrender, with quarter for all, and an escort to the nearest English settlement, promised by the French; but as soon as the English had laid down their arms the Indians were let loose on them, and the French Commander, Portneuf, looked on while the prisoners, and their women and children, were massacred. Many a similar atrocity was to follow in the years to come. A soft people might have been tamed by them, but the New Englanders were not soft. Against such tragedies their most effective defence was some form of attack. For a substantial military effort their resources and organisation were of the most primitive, but sometimes, against all the apparent probabilities, they were successful. Early in the second year of war the Court of Massachusetts publicly advertised for a navy, offering two armed sloops, and all the booty they might capture, to any who would use them against the French in Acadia. It was the tradition of the Elizabethans, the adventurous private citizen tempted to repair the deficiencies of his government by patriotism and the prospect of licensed plunder. By April an expedition of seven hundred men was ready to embark in eight ships. Their commander, Sir William Phipps, whose energy was largely responsible for this unexpected muster, had been born, thirty years before, the son of a poor settler near Pemaquid, had been left an orphan, and turned ship's carpenter, and later ship's captain. As such, with the patronage of the Duke of Albemarle, he found and salved the cargo of a sunken Spanish treasure-ship. With sixteen thousand pounds, his share of the prize, he became a man of wealth, and, with the knighthood conferred on him, a man of mark. 1690, and the Court's invitation to privateers, found him ready for further adventures at sea, and not unaware that a successful attack upon the French settlement might well win him further favour in high quarters in England. Long and publicly though the English expedition had been prepared, with every appointment in it canvassed for weeks or months by the general gossip of Boston, it nevertheless found the French Acadians totally unprepared. Port Royal surrendered as soon as Phipps had landed his men. In the summer of that year there was a council of war at New York at which the New England states were represented. The middle and southern states, needless to say, paid no heed to the troubles of the northerners. Yet even this much co-operation was unaccustomed, and owed something, no doubt, to the recently fallen Andros and the defunct Dominion of New England. A most ambitious project was hatched. Nearly nine hundred men were to march upon Montreal, along the valley of the Hudson, while the indomitable Phipps with the Massachusetts fleet, thirty-two ships strong, and no less than two thousand two hundred men, set sail to attack Quebec. It was an enterprise of scope and moment too great for the colonies' resources. The land expedition quarrelled, sickened of smallpox, ran short of food and turned back. Phipps with his flotilla reached Quebec and hopefully summoned it to surrender. But Frontenac was in Quebec, and this time the fate of Jericho was not re-enacted. After an unsuccessful cannonade, and some skirmishing of a landing-party, the English fleet withdrew. It was not a glorious episode, yet it was something to have shown French Canada that the New Englanders had learned that to defend themselves they must attack, and that they knew the place at which to strike; it was something for the ship's-carpenter from Pemaquid to have led his fellow-citizens into the conflict which would one day decide the fate of the New World; it was something, as Parkman says, to have been, even partially and with such scant success, the forerunners of Wolfe.

§5

The struggle in the far north was even fiercer. Here Nature herself took a grim hand in the game, and the garrison which lost a fort might be driven out to survive, if it could, the terrible winter in the woods. The French were led by d'Iberville, a blend of Garibaldi, Robin Hood and blackflag pirate, who found time, in the intervals of capturing English forts in the Arctic circle, to raid the English settlements in Newfoundland and harry the English frontier in New England. By 1686 the French were in complete possession of the south of Hudson's Bay. In that year England and France concluded a treaty of colonial neutrality, but no one who knew the story of Hudson's Bay can have seriously supposed that an official signature in Europe would put an end to the ebb and flow of surprise, stratagem and sudden assault among the adventurers in the furthest north. Indeed Louis issued secret instructions to the French woodrovers that they should "leave of the English forts on the Northern Bay not a vestige standing." And it was while peace remained still, officially, unbroken that d'Iberville performed some of his most characteristic feats in Hudson's Bay, canoeing across the ice-floes to Albany, for whose recapture a couple of English ships had just sailed down from Nelson; hiding his men in a tamarisk swamp while the English disembarked, and then sailing off in one of their ships, laden with their furs. At the straits he encountered an incoming English fleet, and was locked within gunshot of them by the ice, but, quite undisconcerted, ran up an English flag on his stolen ship, and was signalling the English commanders to pay him a friendly visit when the ice cleared, and he was off. Three years after the outbreak of war, three years during which d'Iberville was busy with frontier raids on New England, the English surprised and recaptured Albany, leaving its garrison, as their own men had been left when the French ejected them, to winter in the woods. But by 1697 the Company had only Albany left, and was all but bankrupt. And at this depressing juncture the Treaty of Ryswick ended William's war and left Hudson's Bay to the *status quo*. In the same treaty, Acadia, which had been conquered by the New Englanders, was restored by the home government to the French.

§6

Within five years of the end of William's war in 1697, Marlborough's war had begun. The failure of tortuous and protracted diplomacy to prevent a union of the French and Spanish crowns, and therefore of the French and Spanish empires, raised an imperial issue of the first consequence, so that as Marlborough pursued his triumphal course from Blenheim to Malplaquet he was in fact saving the future of the British Empire on the battlefields of Europe. Few, however, of the Whig and Tory statesmen who intrigued and quarrelled over the *Conduct of the Allies,* and few of the lesser tribe of pamphleteers and penmen who spat punctual venom at their Party's orders, saw far beneath the majestic European façade of his campaigns. And for the greater part of the ten years' war the English in America were left once again to work out, if they could, their own salvation. Once again the burden fell upon the New Englanders, or, more strictly, upon Massachusetts, New Hampshire and Maine. Between Canada and New York there was a virtual peace, for neither was anxious to disturb the illicit middleman's trade carried on between the two by the Caughnawaga Indians. In August of 1703 the Indian raids commenced in earnest along two hundred miles of frontier. Many an English settlement in these first months of what Cotton Mather called the *decennium luctuosum,* or woeful decade, suffered much the same fate—the raiding party, French and Indian, lying hid in the woods till close on dawn, the stealthy approach to the palisade, the sudden warwhoops, the burning houses, the butchered inmates, and the huddle of terrified captives. Sometimes the English would have time to rally to some fortified house, with loopholes and projecting upper story, and would manage to drive off the assailants. More often the assault was too sudden for effective defence to be possible. For it was not easy to be always on guard, and the shadow of danger never lifted. At any moment the scalping party might come leaping from the neighbouring woods, where it had lain hidden, perhaps for days together, watching for its chance. And when its work was done the encircling woods would swallow it up again and silence descend once more upon the ravaged settlement. For the English this was a testing time indeed. To face such insidious and everpresent dangers, year in and year out, demanded a more obstinate courage than the most arduous campaign. And yet even in the darkest days of the "woeful decade" the outlying settlements were never abandoned. The English have sometimes forgotten their true selves in prosperity, but seldom in affliction. Moreover the heart of the settler was buried in his soil, while the dwellings which the Indians destroyed were of the rudest simplicity—the log cabin of the richest man in Wells contained two bedrooms and a kitchen, the kitchen equipped with a table, a pewter pot, a frying-pan and a skillet, but no chairs, cups, knives, forks or spoons, and the bedrooms each with a bed, a blanket and a chest.

A characteristic ordeal was that of Deerfield, a township of forty-one dwellings, on the north-west frontier of Massachusetts. Here, in the winter of 1704, about fifty English were slaughtered, and a hundred and eleven carried off into captivity. Their captors were converted Indians of the French missions. Of the subsequent sufferings, and the strange and varied fates, of the prisoners there survive vivid accounts by the pastor of Deerfield, John Williams, and his son Stephen, who was eleven years old when captured. For a while on their journey through the woods, Williams tell us, he was allowed to walk beside his wife, who had lately borne a child, and was clearly too weak to struggle far. But soon he was driven to the head of the column, and heard no more of his wife until, resting for a moment at the summit of a snowy hill, he questioned his fellow prisoners, one by one, as they struggled painfully by, and learnt at last that, being quite unable to climb the hill, she had been slain with one blow of the hatchet. Many of the women and children ended thus. At the mouth of the White River the party broke up, and Williams' surviving children were carried off in various directions by their respective captors. After great sufferings he himself reached Chambly, not far from Montreal. Hereafter his chief anxieties centred on the persistent efforts of the Jesuits to convert the prisoners—by bribes, by threats and even by fraud or violence. "I mourned," he writes, "when I thought with myself that I had one child with the Maquas Indians, a second turned papist, and a little child of six years of age in danger to be instructed in popery." Eventually Williams himself, and two of his children, were exchanged, and returned to Deerfield. The youngest the Indians would not release; she was converted to Catholicism and married to an Indian. More than thirty years later she paid a brief visit to her relatives at Deerfield, accompanied by her husband, and in all respects an Indian squaw. Not a few of the English children carried off to Canada suffered similar fates. Two became Caughnawaga chiefs. Others married fellow captives, or Indians or half-breeds. "If," writes a French Abbé, "one should trace out all the English families brought into Canada by the Abenakis, one would be astonished at the number of persons who to-day are indebted to these savages for the blessing of being Catholics and the advantage of being Canadians."

§7

The cordon of militia which the harassed colonists were compelled to maintain along their northern frontier was immensely expensive; it was estimated that it cost Massachusetts about a thousand pounds to kill an Indian. As before, the most effective method of defence was attack, and the most obvious objective French Acadia, from which a vicarious penalty might be enacted for the sins of French Canada. Highly unprofessional and somewhat half-hearted expeditions sailed from Massachusetts in 1704 and 1707. The colonists fought their own battles in their own unpredictable and amateurish way. Their expeditions were a mob of peasants, fishermen and artisans, hastily collected for the occasion, and officered by farmers, tradesmen, blacksmiths and deacons of the church. The wonder is not that there should have been quarrels, indecision and confusion but that they should occasionally have dealt a telling blow. After the ignominious failure of two scrambling attacks on Acadia a more ambitious scheme was hatched. The prime mover, Samuel Vetch, a Scot who had held a commission in the English army, proposed to conquer not only Acadia but Canada, and possibly New Foundland as well, and in 1709, taking fire from his enthusiasm, the General Court of Massachusetts, which usually fought shy of English troops and their somewhat supercilious officers, dispatched an address to Queen Anne, begging for men and ships from England. It was the reverse of the process customary with France, where it was the government which ordered the colonists into action. But even the New Englanders could not fight all their wars unaided and henceforth they would look increasingly to the mother country for aid. Most unexpectedly the English government proved to be complaisance itself. A squadron of five regiments were readily promised, and Vetch, who had borne the colonists' petition, hastened back to New England early in 1709 with orders that the colonists should muster with all speed. Spurred by the prospect of these unprecedented reinforcements the New Englanders sprang to arms. Even New York abandoned its neutrality, and its trade with French Canada; even Pennsylvania and New Jersey, despite their Quaker traditions, raised three hundred and fifty men between them. Fifteen hundred, it had been decided, were to march on Montreal by way of Wood Creek and Lake Champlain. Twelve hundred would join the regular troops, when they arrived, in an attack on Quebec by the St. Lawrence. The twelve hundred duly reached Wood Creek, and there awaited word that the English fleet, promised by the English Government in mid May, had reached Boston. But English expansion was seldom the work of English governments. Weeks and months went by. As mid-summer drew on disease began to decimate the troops. Meanwhile at Boston the New England contingent had likewise been waiting since the twentieth of May, ready to embark for Quebec at ten hours' notice. The troops drilled, Vetch cursed, the Assembly fasted and prayed, and the Governor wrote urgent letters to Sunderland in England. But there was no sign, and no word, of the English ships. At last on the eleventh of October a letter from Sunderland announced that the English forces had been diverted to Portugal. It had been written on the 27th July, more than two months after the troops were due in Boston, and it had been eleven weeks on its way. Such was the English government's first attempt at combining with the colonists in a colonial campaign.

The New Englanders were profoundly disappointed, but they did not despair. They begged for four frigates and five hundred men by the end of March. Indeed with an eye to the future, New York decided that it would be well to impress the Five Nations—whose enmity would block the overland route to Quebec—with the splendour of Her Majesty and her realm, and five Mohawk chiefs were dispatched to England on the next boat. The grave Indians were fêted all over London as the nation's guests, arrayed in fancy dress, attended by liveried servants and saluted by ships' guns. Steele and Addison wrote essays on them, Verelst painted them, the archbishop presented each of them with a Bible. What they made of it all will never be known, but at least their visit advertised the war in America, and it may have helped to incline the Ministry towards the New Englanders' proposals. These at least were accepted, and though the English ships arrived late—they had been asked for in March and reached Boston in July—this time they did arrive. On the eighteenth of September, 1710, after a banquet to the chief officers at the Green Dragon, the expedition sailed. By October 2, after comparatively little fighting and a good many elaborate courtesies between the rival commanders, Port Royal surrendered, and with it, since there was no other fortified town in the country, Acadia passed to England. Twice before it had been captured by New Englanders and handed back in a subsequent treaty by the home government. This time, renamed Nova Scotia, it was to be retained.

§8

Next year, in 1711, for the first time a powerful Minister in London turned his attention seriously to the war in America. His motives were certainly not exclusively, and perhaps not even primarily, imperial, and the consequences of his departure from the ruts of the conventional European strategy proved to be ignominious in the extreme. None the less the departure was made, and this in itself was highly significant. In October, 1710, the Tories had been returned at what was perhaps the first General Election fought in the modern sense, and fought bitterly, on Party lines. Harley and St. John led the triumphant and reunited Tory party. Their mutual rivalry, perhaps the best known personal quarrel in our political annals, first took shape over the project of a British expedition against Quebec, which the fiery and enterprising St. John had vehemently taken up in January, 1711, and which the prudent and slow-moving Harley as vehemently opposed. The Ministers were hotly divided over St. John's plan, and it might have gone no further, but for the accident that in March Harley was stabbed by a French spy, and disappeared for several weeks from the political scene. While from his sick bed Lord Treasurer Harley, supposing himself *in extremis*, sent his "dying request" to the President of the Council that the Canadian project should be abandoned, Mr. Secretary St. John pushed on the preparations with inflexible determination. In part no doubt his motive was to efface the prestige of Marlborough and the Whigs. "If it succeeds," he himself wrote to Harley of his project, before he despaired of Harley's co-operation and before their open quarrel had begun, "you will have done more service to Britain in half a year than the Ministers who went before you did in all their administration." Yet there was both patriotism and vision beneath the Party-man's calculation. For the enemies of Marlborough had long contended, as Swift venomously proclaimed in the *Conduct of the Allies*, that his grandest triumphs spelt more advantage for Holland or Germany than for Britain. In a sense it was the first appearance in British history of the long contention, so familiar in our own time, between the advocates of the far-flung expeditionary force and those who believed in concentration on the main European front, or in conquering America on the battlefields of Europe. Moreover we see here the first, faint foreshadowing of an imperial policy; it had long been the Tory doctrine that the sea and the colonies were the proper sphere for an English war effort, and that its diversion to the European mainland had been a heresy

of Dutch King William and the Whigs. And to make Canada a
British colony, and indeed North America a British sub-continent—
for St. John's vaulting ambition did not stop short of the larger
goal—might well, to any who had once grasped that Britain's future
lay overseas, seem worth more than all the resounding European
triumphs from Blenheim to Malplaquet. Few who have read his
Patriot King will doubt that St. John, Lord Bolingbroke, was capable
at times of penetrating insight into the deepest springs of human
action, insight such as Harley and Walpole, his duller but more prudent rivals, could hardly compass; and it may be that he saw further
into the future of the British Empire than any Minister before him;
it is at least not without significance that Disraeli always looked
back to Bolingbroke as the wisest and most prescient of eighteenth
century statesmen. Unfortunately although in the width of his
general view he may have been far in advance of his times, as soon
as he descended to the particular his administration became typical
of his own day at its most unedifying. As he revolved his American
strategy the patriot may have predominated over the partisan; when
he began to issue his orders the partisan undoubtedly gained the
upper hand. For general of the expedition he chose a genial man
about town who lacked every recommendation for command save
one; the Queen's new favourite, Mrs. Masham, was his sister. And
if the mystery of St. John's general is that he possessed only one
qualification, and that of the most ambiguous character, the mystery
of his admiral is that he possessed no qualifications at all. And so,
since Admiral Walker was incapable of reaching Quebec it mattered
the less that, weakly though it was defended, General Hill would
almost certainly have been incapable of taking it.

Seven seasoned regiments, five of them from Flanders, were
dispatched. On June 24th the fleet reached Boston and disembarked
its troops. The New Englanders looked on with mixed feelings.
The imperious mien and professional discipline of the military was
impressive, but the unaccustomed and exacting demands which
followed in their train were uncomfortable reminders of other
aspects of the home country. The Assembly, however, was determined to rise to the occasion. Prices were fixed, troops raised and
compulsorily quartered on the citizens, technicians were impressed by
warrant, liquor seized and deserters rigorously rounded up. In five
weeks all was ready, and the citizens of Boston watched the fleet set
sail with hearty wishes for its success and hearty relief at its departure. Admiral Hovenden Walker, as his *Journal* reveals, was
already in an agony of apprehension. It was not the eventual
prospect of fighting which alarmed him; indeed he seems hardly

yet to have begun to concern himself with that, so formidable, it seemed to him, were the natural obstacles which had first to be surmounted. Supposing they should contrive to reach Quebec, as to which he was far from confident, how was he to protect his ships from the river ice, which would freeze, he was convinced, "to the bottom"? Moreover if they had reached Quebec, he afterwards persuaded himself, the entire expedition must have perished of cold and hunger, after being reduced to cannibalism, and "drawing lots," as he puts it, "who should die first to feed the rest." With the Admiral in this strangely unheroic frame of mind it was hardly of good omen that the fleet should have carried with it no pilot who was familiar with the St. Lawrence. The Admiral lost his bearings in a fog, supposed himself off the south shore of the river mouth, made north, discovered to his astonishment that he had all the while in fact been off the north shore, and lost eight transports, with about seven hundred soldiers, on the rocks. He was now all for retreat, and Jack Hill was not the man to raise objections. Walker must have known that Phipps, with his New England fleet, and even less practised pilots, had sailed safely to Quebec in 1690, but nothing now would reassure him, and soon the New England transports were steering for Boston and the British fleet for the Thames. On receiving the unexpected news, the land expedition, which had been waiting once more at Wood Creek, burned its forts, marched home and disbanded. The first serious British attempt to combine in a major military operation with the American colonists, the first serious attempt to drive the French from North America, had ended in ignominious failure, and left ruffled tempers on both sides of the Atlantic. The colonists, it seemed, would be wise henceforth, as in the past, to rely upon themselves. And at home the advocates of concentration on the European front seemed doubly justified when at the Peace of Utrecht in 1713 Marlborough's victories secured far greater concessions from the French in America than the fighting there had justified.

For in Hudson's Bay too Marlborough's war passed without any signal British triumph, and indeed almost without military incident. Left by the Peace of Ryswick with only one fort, the Company was too exhausted for any serious offensive. It contrived, however, to maintain a lucrative trade in furs. Half involuntarily moreover it found itself beginning to explore the vast, wild hinterlands. For with the French in occupation of the greater part of the bay the best hope of trade was to intercept the Indian canoes far up in the forests before they came down to the coast. Characteristically enough much of this early exploration was due neither, it goes without saying, to government, nor even to Company but to a London street-arab, Henry Kelsey, who disregarded the strict rules of the fur-posts, broke bounds and ran off with a party of Assinbouie Indians. Meanwhile, cut off by English privateers from their home supplies, the French garrisons on the bay came near to starving. As soon as it was clear that France was beaten on the Continent the Company began to press its claims on British ministers—for a huge indemnity and the return of all their posts. They did not get their indemnity, but they got the Bay.

§9

A succession of Whig historians has soundly rated the Tories who made the Treaty of Utrecht, which ended Marlborough's war in 1713, and its principal authors certainly showed little consideration for their allies, or indeed for their colleagues. It is doubtful, however, whether for the Empire at least the Whigs would have done so well. There is something in the boast of St. John (soon to become Lord Bolingbroke) that "this agreement contains more advantages for your Majesty's Kingdom than were ever, perhaps, stipulated for any nation at one time." In India there had been no fighting with the French, but in America there were now substantial changes. Britain retained Acadia, or Nova Scotia, with an inland boundary which was never defined, and without Cape Breton Island, off its east coast, on which the French proceeded to erect Louisbourg, "the Dunkirk of North America." Newfoundland, too, was handed over by the French, with the reservation of certain fishing rights, and that although during the war they had three times captured the lightly held port of Saint John's. These acquisitions meant that the British were now solidly established both at the gates of French Canada, at the mouth of the Saint Lawrence, and in its Arctic rear, on Hudson's Bay. Bolingbroke was no doubt well aware that in the failure to draw the Acadian frontier clearly, to secure Cape Breton or to define the Newfoundland fishing compromise precisely, lay the seeds of future conflict; indeed the Council of Trade and Plantations had advised him clearly on all these matters. But he was in a hurry, no more than the French could he afford to risk rekindling the war, and he had had to fight long and hard for what he had gained. And he had gained much.

Some of the European terms of the treaty also profoundly affected the Empire. Gibraltar, the key of the Mediterranean, was retained. Moreover the European possessions of Spain passed to the

Austrian crown, and among them the Netherlands, so that, since Austria was an inland power, the secular English apprehensions as to a naval threat from the Rhine Delta were allayed. The foundations of the Empire, our sea communications and our sea power, were safe. Also the treaty of Utrecht brought a vast and dubious accession to British world commerce. The Asiento (or Contract) with Spain permitted Britain, alone of foreign powers, to send one ship to trade with Spanish America, and to transport thither close on five thousand negroes, every year. The Spanish doctrine of the *mare clausum* in the West, against which Drake and Hawkins had fought long ago, was now at last finally abandoned. And on this slender official foundation a considerable edifice of illicit trade was soon erected. The Asiento itself had been granted to foreigners for many years past, and, after the Portuguese, Germans, Dutch and Genoese had all had their share of it. But the slave trade was a much older story. The Portuguese had been the first regular slave-dealers, and the Spaniards the first great slave-owners. Hawkins was the first Englishman to take a hand in the traffic, and for nearly a hundred years after him there was no other. In the seventeenth century the Dutch were invading this branch of commerce, as they invaded many others, and it was they who introduced the first negro labour into Virginia, in 1620. About 1650, English traders, who were competing with the Dutch in every other trade, began to compete with them in the slave trade also. The demand for slaves was now very great. Brazil and Hispaniola had long imported negroes, the West Indian planters were looking for labour which could support their climate, the traffic with the American plantations had begun. From 1662 an African Company, chartered in London, supplied the English plantations. In 1700 it was shipping somewhere about twenty-five thousand slaves; the number had multiplied five times over during the previous twenty years. Towards the end of the century, when Wilberforce and the evangelicals were launching their successful campaign for the abolition of the trade, the yearly export from Africa to America had reached a hundred thousand. Its economic advantages were obvious. "The impossibility of doing without slaves in the West Indies," wrote a publicist in 1764, "will always prevent this traffic being dropped." Without it, since the white man is physically incapable of the daily work of the plantations in the latitudes between Virginia and the River Plate, tropical America could not have been developed, and cotton, sugar and coffee must have remained the luxuries of the rich. And if Britain alone withdrew from so vast and lucrative a carrying-trade her maritime strength, in comparison with that of less scrupulous rivals, would be dangerously impaired. Yet in the long run, and even judged by purely economic standards, the trade did more harm than good. By superseding white labour, negroes slowed down, and even put an end to, normal immigration. Moreover the primitive character of their labour tended to discourage experiment and confine production to a few traditional staple crops, while, by associating all manual work with racial inferiority, it was indirectly responsible for the backwardness of slave-holding settlements in manufacture and industrial invention.

On moral grounds there can be only one verdict. Slave-holding, at any rate in the British American colonies, was often based on kindly human relationships, but slave-trading was everywhere and always iniquity. During the two centuries of its heyday it was responsible for an unimaginable aggregate of human suffering. If the world had owed the slave trade to the British, it is impossible to believe that a British Empire could have endured. But nowhere in the world as yet had men learned to see that slavery was evil, and many good men believed that a negro was lucky to become a slave. It was inevitable therefore that there should be a slave trade, and, since a major share of all world trade was now in British hands, a major share of the slave trade was bound to be there also. From time to time a Baxter or a Warburton would denounce it; the Quakers and then the Wesleyans condemned it; but it went on. What can be chiefly said in our defence is that Englishmen were not the first to begin the trade, and were the first to end it. It reached its zenith while eighteenth century Britain was in its most cynical and materialistic mood. Within four years of the loss of the American colonies Wilberforce and the Evangelicals would launch their successful campaign for abolition. The suppression of the trade would be the first incontestable evidence that the nation had begun to learn the lessons of adversity.

CHAPTER THREE

THE WALPOLE TRADITION

(1713-1742)

§1

STRENGTHENED immeasurably, and far more than she could yet know, by her emergence, after the Peace of 1713, as the unchallenged mistress of the seas, Britain now passed into a quarter of a century of peace, during which she was exposed to dangers different, but not less deadly, than those of war. For almost the whole of these twenty-five years she was ruled by the mellow and pacificatory genius of Walpole. Genius is doubtless a questionable term in relation to the arts of political management as exercised by this genial, earthbound Norfolk squire; yet when we remember how critical were the years of his power, what perils he avoided and how much he achieved in firmly establishing not only the House of Hanover and the Cabinet system, but that tradition of moderation, of tolerance, of empirical sagacity and of mutual give-and-take without which political democracy cannot survive, it hardly, at first sight, seems excessive. For twenty-one years, from 1718 to 1739, Walpole at least gave Britain peace abroad, and growing prosperity at home. And those for whom material prosperity is the measure of civilisation naturally hold him to have been a great statesman. It needs a longer and a wider view to see him for what he was, a ruler capable of conferring on his country every benefit save that which in the hour of victory it needed most, moral discipline. With that fatal reservation, Walpole was wise. It was his wisdom to hold aloof from the war of the Polish succession, which raged in Europe from 1733 to 1735, and in which neither of the great traditional British interests, neither resistance to a projected dictatorship of Europe, nor the defence of the mouth of the Scheldt, was involved. It was the timely self-restraint of his "Let sleeping dogs lie," the *Pax Walpoliana*, which enabled both the country to recuperate its strength and the unprepossessing Hanoverian dynasty to take root.

Yet the defects of his great qualities were deadly. It was the system of Walpole, so shrewd, so cynical and so materialistic which rendered inevitable the dangers and disasters, in West and East, to which in the second half of the century the Empire succumbed, or which it so narrowly survived. In the hour of victory, when dangers dislimn, effort is relaxed, and wealth and comfort beckon, what a great nation most needs is a leader who will protect it from moral decadence. The Old Testament, and indeed the history of mankind itself, is but a record of brief interludes of prosperity punctuated by the catastrophes to which the prosperity itself gave rise, because in prosperity men forgot their true selves. The rule of Walpole was almost perfectly adapted, not to quell but to enhance the insidious effects upon the moral sense of the nation of its new power and its new wealth. Indeed, even within the clear but narrow scope of his own political objectives, thanks largely to the robust egoism of his temperament, he was only partially successful. Thus, paradoxically enough, although his main purpose was to establish George I securely on his throne, it is probable that Walpole's own methods gave the Jacobite menace what reality it possessed. For by so persistently and jealously excluding the Tories from office, when he might conceivably have built a national party, he kept alive in the Opposition that sense of grievance on which the exiled Stuarts chiefly founded their hopes of restoration. And by repeatedly denouncing all Tories as dangerous Jacobites, when in fact, as no one knew better than Walpole himself, not one in ten of them was ready to go further than an occasional fuddled toast to the king over the water, he went some way to making a reality of the bogey which served his party ends. But the essential tragedy of Walpole was that he encouraged the conscience and the spirit of the nation to slumber in those years of dawning world power when what Britain most needed was a blend of the spirit of the Elizabethans with the conscience of the Puritans. The Empire as a business concern or an estate he could have managed as shrewdly as any merchant or agent in Britain; of the Empire which Cromwell had already foreseen, the Empire which was an Idea and an obligation, he was not even aware. Under his long hegemony the life of the nation coarsened and its moral sinews relaxed. As Bolingbroke complained in *The Patriot King*, the spirit of the people was asleep, and a measure of its slumbers was the strange general apathy which permitted five thousand wild Highlanders to march from Edinburgh to Derby in 1745, without either encountering resistance or receiving aid. Yet that this was slumber, not decay, was proved by the moral energy to which the elder Pitt so speedily roused the nation in the Seven Years' War.

Walpole, needless to say, was not passionately interested in the colonies—perhaps he was not passionately interested in anything except his gamekeeper's reports—but even the colonies owed material benefits at least to his cynical but far-ranging sagacity. He removed many duties on the export of British manufactures and the import of raw materials. He allowed the rice of Carolina and Georgia to be shipped to ports south of Finisterre without passing through the customary entrepot in these islands—so that it soon supplanted the rice of Egypt and Italy in the markets of Europe. Later he performed much the same good offices for the West Indian sugar trade. Colonial commerce expanded notably during his administration. For Walpole at least had perceived that it was all to Britain's interest that the colonies should prosper and that their enterprise should have free play. Unchecked by interference from the mother country, American manufactures, too, began to grow. Overseas as well as at home Walpole's instinct for letting sleeping dogs lie had its material advantages. And with the Duke of Newcastle as Secretary of State no policy could be more natural and easy to pursue. Indeed that nobleman's all-embracing incompetence, and roomful of unopened colonial dispatches, ensured not only that there would be no undue interference, but that there would be no interference at all. It was Newcastle's methods which Burke described as treating the colonies with salutary neglect, and the contrast with them which suggested the aphorism that Grenville lost America because he read his dispatches. Walpole's system had obvious material advantages, its vice was that it had so few others. And in the final estimate everything which he did well is overshadowed by what he did ill, or did not do at all, by his fatal insensitiveness to moral values. He was fully aware of what might be gained from Empire, but blind to what was owed to it. And so he sowed the disasters of the seventeen-seventies. He was not the man to resolve political tensions, or modernise administration, overseas. He did nothing to improve colonial defence, and neglected the fighting services at home. In 1727 there were eighty-four ships-of-the-line and forty fifty-gun ships in the British Navy; by 1734 the totals had fallen to seventy and nineteen. But these were the superficial aspects of Walpole's failure. Underlying all was the deep-seated materialism of his un-aspiring regime. As in every era in which its leaders have encour-aged it to think first of prosperity and comfort, the moral fibre of the nation had coarsened, and its energies grown sluggish. Com-menting on the indecisive naval battle, fought off Toulon, after five years of the coming war, in 1744, Mahan, the historian of sea-power, draws attention to what he calls the "unpreparedness of mind" of the British captains, and adds:

There is not in modern naval history a more striking warning to

I.C. H

the officers of every era, than this battle of Toulon. Coming as
it did after a generation of comparative naval inactivity, it tried
men's reputations as by fire. The lesson . . . is the danger of
disgraceful failure to men who have neglected to keep themselves
prepared, not only in knowledge of their profession, but in the
sentiment of what war requires.

"The sentiment of what war requires"; this, certainly, since war
requires, above all else, self-sacrifice, discipline and faith, the system
of Walpole had not been calculated to inspire. Nor was this the last
or only moment in our history when self-indulgence and materialism
had in due course to be expiated in suffering and failure.

§2

Indeed his consciousness that the nation was neither morally nor
physically prepared for the effort must have done a good deal to
stiffen Walpole's natural reluctance to yield to the popular clamour
for war with Spain which beset him in 1739. The sudden war-fever
was partly the work of the bitter, and now heterogeneous, Opposition
which Walpole's masterful policy of exclusion had inevitably raised
up against him, and which, with the irresponsibility too often
characteristic of Oppositions, did not hesitate to move a reduction
of the army while continuing to clamour for war. But even without
the Opposition the popular demand would have been insistent, and
difficult to withstand. In part, no doubt, but only in part, it represented no more than a vulgar craving, appropriate to the age of
Walpole, for military adventure and commercial gain at the expense
of an ancient, and now enfeebled, enemy. In part too it was a
reaction, natural enough in a proud and vigorous people, from the
humdrum materialism of Walpole's rule. For all that, this was the
same current of democratic patriotism which the elder Pitt was soon
to touch to finer ends. The resolution of the Commons that "it was
the undoubted right of British subjects to sail their ships in any
part of the seas of America" held wider implications than any mere
commercial claim. And once again the instinct of the people was
wiser than the calculations of its rulers; in looking to the new
world for its objectives it showed an understanding not only of the
future but of the past. For the settlement at Utrecht had revived,
and exacerbated, the very quarrel with Spain which had resounded
through the Elizabethan era, and which the peacemakers supposed
themselves to have ended. By recognising and legalising a strictly

limited trade with their possessions in the west the Spaniards had finally relinquished the principle of the closed Empire. But the illicit traffic with Spanish America, which had gone on more or less unbrokenly since the days of Elizabeth, persisted, and now with two vital distinctions—that, with the rest of our commerce, it was expanding, and that, once the sacred principle of total exclusion had been abandoned by Spain, the survival of the ancient embargo on the greater part of our commerce seemed a doubly irritating anachronism. The grotesque Captain Jenkins' legendary lost ear became the symbol of the nation's resolve to break down the commercial barriers which had so long provoked and thwarted it. Moreover the Spaniards, whose energies had somewhat revived since the brief rule of Alberoni, were taking more vigorous measures to enforce their laws of contraband. And soon Spain was as hot against the crimes of British buccaneers as was Britain against the cruelty of Spanish coastguards, and the terrors of Spanish dungeons. War was inevitable. It was a war for commercial prizes even more than a war to right the wrongs of British seamen. But beneath the greed, the clamour and the catchwords the deeper instincts of the people, as so often, had fastened on an essential truth. Behind Bourbon Spain, they suspected, despite the Treaty of Utrecht, stood Bourbon France, secretly planning to destroy British world power. They scented a danger of which Walpole was scarcely conscious. Perhaps indeed no British citizen embarked on war more reluctantly than the Prime Minister. He must have known that the *Pax Walpoliana* was hardly likely to have bred or maintained the simple, fundamental virtues by which wars are won. He must have suspected that the desire for trade advantage, which was the most conscious motive of the war party, though a natural consequence of his regime, made a poor moral basis for a nation at war. He certainly knew that after twenty years of his administration our military resources were in confusion and decay. He must have foreseen that war of any kind would be the end of his political system.

§3

The struggle of 1739 to 1748 has passed into history as the war of Jenkins' ear. No great commander or statesman arose to lend his name to it, and for those who dislike that derisive title there is no more alluring alternative than "War of the Austrian Succession," made familiar by generations of historians for whom all history was the history of Europe. It is certainly not the drab dynastic complexities of the Austrian succession which give these years their significance in British history. And yet, though it was one round in a tremendous conflict for tremendous ends, the war of Jenkins' ear deserves perhaps its undistinguished label, and that not merely because its pretext was questionable and its outcome indecisive. For its failures, its lost opportunities and its half-successes, may be regarded as part of the price which Britain was called upon to pay for the fleshpots of the regime of Walpole, the expiation which prepared her for the triumphs of the Seven Years' War.

Inevitably, since its essence was a struggle for the great quadrilateral of trade and empire bounded by Britain, Newfoundland, the West Indies and the African slave coast, it soon became a war against France, as well as Spain. Inevitably therefore it was fought in India too, where the rival Companies, left by their home governments even more completely to their own resources than the colonists in America, rose and fell, at first with the emergence, on one side or the other, of leaders of genius, but in the last resort by the possession of sea-power. The West Indian islands were never a major element in the strategy of the series of wars now opening, presumably because Britain, the combatant most capable of an offensive overseas, was mainly preoccupied with the North American continent. And so, although the West Indies were the scene of numerous naval actions, the islands tended to be treated as valuable ships or convoys, tempting prizes to be picked up as occasion presented itself. They changed hands repeatedly, but the upshot was to leave the greater part of them in British hands. Essentially the coming wars would be a struggle for the possession of North America and India fought out between France and Britain, each of whom was in varying degree, and for different reasons, distracted by its European commitments.

In 1740, within a year of the outbreak of the war of Jenkins' ear between Britain and Spain, the death of the Austrian Emperor Charles VI plunged all Europe into the intricate welter of perfidy and violence which is known as the war of the Austrian Succession. With the whole continent aflame, another war between Britain and France could not be long delayed, and under the circumstances it is surprising that Walpole should have retained office until 1742. He toppled to his fall in a series of passionate debates and narrowly contested divisions—defeat by four votes, victory by seven, by twenty-four, by twenty-one, defeat again by four, by one, by three. The taunts, the cheers, the tense waiting on the outcome of the divisions made exciting Parliamentary history, but the destiny of the nation was being decided elsewhere than at Westminster, and by other means. And the Parliamentary machine might have responded less slowly and uncertainly to the manifest needs of the moment, if the Opposition which was hunting down the great peace minister had itself shown any signs of containing a leader upon whom the country could rely in war. Pitt indeed was of the Opposition, but Pitt was still a young man, whose powers were not yet generally suspected, and to replace Walpole first by Wilmington and then by Pelham and Newcastle, though it meant much to the politicians who contrived it, was of little service to the nation, or the men who fought its battles overseas. England, in the words of Frederick the Great, was still in travail; fourteen years were to pass before she produced a man.

CHAPTER FOUR

JENKINS' EAR (1) AMERICA

(1739-1748)

§1

UNDER the new ministry, Britain became an ally of Austria, against whom France was already engaged, but, by an odd convention of the times, since it was as an auxiliary, and not a principal, that she had entered the continental war, and although at sea France was already fighting as an auxiliary to Spain, neither country regarded itself as officially at war with the other. It was not until later in that year that the two countries were formally at war; which mattered all the less in that, while fighting in Europe had begun before the declaration of war, fighting in both America and India would continue after the declaration of peace.

This time both countries suffered from European entanglements. The rulers of France were intent, as usual, upon traditional objectives, the humiliation of Austria, the advance on the Rhine, the conquest of the Netherlands. They ignored, as usual, the opportunities of expansion overseas, and neglected its instrument, the Navy. Outside the charmed circle of Versailles, however, there were by now a considerable number of Frenchmen, drawn mostly from impoverished noble families of military and naval tradition, who were sick of the spider's-web diplomacy and barren battlefields of Europe, and looked to imperial aggression for the aggrandisement of their country and the enrichment of themselves. This was the France which produced de Bussy and Dupleix, Lally and Montcalm. Fortunately for Britain it was not the France which directed French policy or controlled the French Navy.

In Britain, although the nation was far more awake to the opportunities of the new age, several factors, besides feeble ministries, and the moral and material unreadiness which was the legacy of Walpole, now combined to obstruct the needful concentration on imperial issues. For one thing, Britain was linked, through her monarchy, to the unpredictable fortunes of Hanover, now helplessly exposed to the predatory armies of the Continent. Hanover consequently must either be defended by British troops and British gold, or else ransomed, when peace came, by the surrender of imperial conquests overseas. Again in this war France directed her main offensive upon the Austrian Netherlands, reviving the traditional British apprehensions as to the ownership of that coast, and compelling British strategy to preoccupy itself with the fighting on the Continent. Nor should it be forgotten that, until after 1745, the cause of the Stuarts was still alive and the menace of a Jacobite invasion an ever-present anxiety. In short, the European war of the Austrian succession, supervening so soon upon the Anglo-Spanish war of Jenkins' ear, deflected hostilities from their natural course, and postponed for another fifteen years that decision on vastly greater issues, which concerned Britain, France and Spain far more significantly than the fortunes of the Austrian empress. At the close of it, France was triumphant on land but impotent on the seas; she had conquered the Austrian Netherlands and parts of Holland itself, but her navy was annihilated, her commerce largely destroyed and her communications with her colonies cut off. Britain, on the other hand, remained dominant, though not yet fully effective, on the seas, but found herself enmeshed in an unsuccessful continental war which she had not desired and was ill qualified to conduct. Under such circumstances it was only natural that the peace settlement of 1748 should have assumed the character of an indecisive exchange of conquests. Nor had British trade benefited. The Asiento was not renewed: all that remained of British trade to the Spanish Indies was the illicit commerce from the West Indies, now no longer camouflaged by the Asiento, and an indirect trade of reshipment. The Spanish right of search, which nine years earlier had roused the war party to such eloquent frenzy, was not so much as mentioned.

§2

The real interest, as well as the real significance, of the nine years' fighting, from 1739 to 1748, is to be found overseas. Here the rival imperial systems measured their strength in a struggle in which sooner or later sea-power must prove decisive, but which for the time being, thanks to the indifference, or the distractions, of the home governments, turned largely upon the character and abilities of the leaders on the spot. And in America, in the intermittent co-operation with the colonists of British squadrons or British troops, were being forged traditions which before long would powerfully affect the political history of both countries. After a generation of Walpole's rule, and whether the Whig political manipulator who professed to wield it was Walpole himself or Wilmington or New-castle, the American colonists could scarcely expect any very courageous or well planned use of British sea-power. And at the very outset of the war a naval episode, part grotesque and part heroic, illustrated to admiration both the pitiable military in-adequacy to which Britian had been reduced, and those stalwart qualities in her captains which Pitt, but not her present rulers, would know how to use.

In 1740 Anson was instructed to round Cape Horn, attack the Spanish colonies on the west coast of South America, and prey on the rich commerce of the Pacific. He was given five warships, with three auxiliary vessels, and as their complement of troops, for any land fighting that might be becessary, five hundred out-pensioners of Chelsea Hospital. The historian of Anson's voyage, who was chaplain of his flagship, and seems to have written his account more or less from Anson's dictation,[1] assures us that even of this " decrepit detachment" no more than two hundred and fifty-nine actually reported for duty on board. All those who were still hale enough to walk out of Portsmouth had already deserted, leaving only the invalids, most of them old gentlemen turned sixty, and some upwards of seventy, years of age. Such, in one domain at least, were the fruits of twenty years of Walpole and letting sleeping dogs lie. And yet, astonishingly, despite many misadventures and infinite suffering, Anson's voyage was a success. His squadron was scattered by violent tempests off the Cape, but he rallied three ships, pillaged the South American coast and then crossed the Pacific, and there, with the one ship now left to him, captured a Spanish galleon with a cargo worth half a million, and so, by way of the Indian Ocean and the Cape of Good Hope, completed his circle of the globe, and reached home, with one-fifth of his men surviving, in 1744. His voyage had occupied nearly four years and was of little military importance; but there is an Elizabethan flavour about it; and its many misfortunes, and the calm persistence with which its com-mander turned them all to good account, have earned it a justifiable renown. Meanwhile Vernon had captured Porto Bello, which Drake knew as Nombre de Dios, in Panama, and, in 1740, owing to an outbreak of fever and his own quarrels with the general in command of the landing force (which Smollett compares to those of Caesar and Pompey), failed miserably before Cartagena, and in a descent on the coast of Cuba. The miseries of his plague-stricken crews have been immortalised in *Roderick Random*. This was virtually the sum total, hardly worth the oratory which had introduced it, of the

---

[1] Richard Walter, *Anson's Voyage*.

Anglo-Spanish war of Jenkins' ear. But elsewhere the fires which it had helped to light burned steadily and long.

§3

For America had for some while been ripe for another war. The crucial Anglo-French boundaries, left undefined by the treaty of Utrecht, had still to be determined, and the growing French design of a chain of forts to link Louisiana and the mouth of the Mississippi to Canada was beginning to threaten the very existence of the British colonies. The final struggle for the mastery of all North America could not be long delayed. Even so, war with France beyond the Atlantic did not begin until after news that Britain and France were officially at war in Europe reached the colonists, in the spring of 1744. Four years before this, news of the outbreak of the war of Jenkins' ear had been received with cheers in Boston, where a Protestant and merchants' war against Papist and monopolistic Spain not unnaturally stirred responsive chords. Massachusetts even raised a contingent of five hundred men, of whom only a tenth ever saw New England again, for Vernon's ill-fated attack on the Spanish West Indies in 1740. Its outcome, like most military co-operation with the mother-country hitherto, had done little to inspire the colonists with confidence or respect. One agreeable, if little known, Anglo-American consequence of the expedition, however, survives to this day. Lawrence, the elder brother of George Washington, had been one of the volunteers from Virginia, and Mount Vernon, well known to countless pilgrims as the home of the first President of the United States, commemorates the name of the English admiral.

In 1744 the French struck first. News that the parent countries were officially at war reached Louisburg before it came to Boston, and the French seized and burnt a fishing hamlet on the straits between the mainland and Cape Breton Isle, and then failed to capture the crumbling, ill-guarded ramparts of Annapolis, capital of Acadia. Neither expedition was authorised by the French government and a contemporary French commentator saw reasons for regretting the precipitancy of his fellow countrymen. "Perhaps," he reflected sadly, "the English would have let us alone if we had not first insulted them. It was the interest of the people of New England to live at peace with us, and they would no doubt have done so, if we had not taken it into our heads to waken them from their security." But short-sighted though the British colonists undoubtedly were, they could hardly, even without the French provocation, have remained passive much longer while the rulers of Canada pieced together their plans for excluding them from the entire hinterland of North America. And exasperation now prompted them to an undertaking of unexampled audacity. They would attack Louisburg itself. The French government had spent thirty million *livres* over the last twenty-five years on fortifying this nest of privateers, their only naval base in America, according to the system of the celebrated Vauban. Its garrison included regular troops and commanded the main approaches to Canada. The prospects of capturing it with a few thousand raw New England militiamen did not seem bright. Such indeed was undoubtedly the opinion of the General Court of Massachusetts when in January, 1745, Shirley, their enthusiastic Governor, invited them to prepare forthwith to reduce the famous and formidable fortress. With the notion of some day lending aid to an attempt on Louisburg by a British expeditionary force they had already toyed, but to be asked to assail it themselves, without the consent of the home government, without trained officers or troops, and at their own financial risk— this was altogether too breath-taking a proposal, and after a brief investigation they discreetly declined it. The Governor, however, was not easily discouraged. Before long he had set the merchants of New England petitioning for a reconsideration, and the Court duly deliberated, and voted, again. This time the advocates of the adventure carried the day, by one vote. Troops were raised forthwith, from New Hampshire and Connecticut, but mainly, as usual, from Massachusetts. William Pepperell, a popular and respected merchant, son of an emigrant from Wales, was appointed commander; the clergy blessed the expedition, or even joined it in person, arming themselves, in some instances, with axes wherewith to hew down the Popish altars of Antichrist. Within seven weeks of the Governor's first proclamation the expedition was afloat. Against every apparent probability it was triumphantly successful.

It owed much to the presence—due less to the home government's orders than to a generous interpretation of them—of a British naval squadron, which blockaded the harbour, protected the land forces, lent them the trained gunners they lacked, and greatly discouraged the garrison by capturing a French warship which was bringing it munitions and provisions. But much, perhaps most, of the credit must go to the amateur New England soldiers. They broke all the rules of an army in the field, which may perhaps have contributed to their success. Behind the front line they were noisy, disorderly and sometimes drunken, they played quoits, wrestled and ran races, or wasted their scanty ammunition on shooting competitions. For a siege which consisted so largely of bombardments they seem to have learned their gunnery to a surprising degree by process of trial and error in the field, and their cannon burst repeatedly owing to unskilful loading. When, prematurely, it is true, their commanders ordered a general assault, the army signified in no uncertain fashion its "great dissatisfaction" at the prospect, and the plan was at once abandoned. They scorned the traditional military science of trench and earthwork, preferring to trust to darkness, fog or mere good fortune. In spite of all they succeeded where rigidly disciplined troops might have failed. They improvised the art of war as need arose. Barefooted and in tatters they dragged their artillery, two hundred men to a gun, over two miles of marsh and rock swept by fire from the batteries of Louisburg. And under every hardship they remained cheerful and undaunted. The surrender of Louisburg was greeted with no less astonishment and delight in London than in Boston. Illuminations and rejoicings came all the more readily perhaps because there had been so little else to justify them. Pepperell was made a colonel in the British army, and received a baronetcy, "the only native of New England," as the title page of his New England biographer records, "who was created a baronet during our connection with the mother country."

Inevitably, since the Duke of Newcastle was Secretary of State, the success at Louisburg was not followed up. Action of any scope and consequence in North America was impossible now without joint action on land and sea, and effective co-operation in a remote arena between Navy and Army, always a searching test for the most efficient of governments, was all but unthinkable under Pelham and Newcastle. In the course of her long history Britain has more than once had cause to complain that the politicians who ruled her were only politicians, but never surely better cause than when for a few perilous years the destinies of America and India were entrusted to amiable borough-mongers who understood how to manipulate votes but understood little else. But nations acquire the governments which they deserve, and the rule of Walpole had doomed Britain to some such fate; it was left to the tough fibre of her people to keep her from irremediable disaster until worthy leadership was again forthcoming. And now there was a twofold reason for energetic action. The fall of Louisburg had greatly encouraged the New Englanders, who were now ready for the most ambitious undertakings against Canada; and it had stung the French government into a fixed resolve to recapture it at all costs.

And now the energetic Shirley, Governor of Massachusetts, the prime begetter of the assault on Louisburg, had commenced a long and thankless bombardment of Newcastle with grandiose projects of further aggressive action in America. French and British, he argued, could not live indefinitely upon the same continent; at this triumphant moment twenty thousand colonists could be raised for the grand assault; all that was required was support from the British Navy, and orders from His Majesty. Most unexpectedly, though it was not in the nature of that indolent nobleman to take fire from these, or any other, proposals which did not involve the fate of a borough or the manufacture of a majority, Newcastle at least responded favourably to them. He even went so far as to dispatch a circular to the Governor of every American colony, as far south as North Carolina, bidding them raise as many men as possible from their respective assemblies. Newcastle promised eight British battalions. But with this, his fit of apparent energy came to an end. The British troops did not arrive, and all thought of an attack on Canada in 1746 had to be abandoned. Months later Newcastle explained that the British regiments had been delayed by contrary winds, and that in any case they were needed in Europe. Meanwhile France had launched her counterstroke. A powerful fleet under d'Anville sailed in June, 1746, convoying thirty-four transports with more than three thousand veteran troops on board. It was to retake Louisburg and Acadia and lay waste the seaboard of New England. The alarm and excitement in Massachusetts has been compared to that which stirred England in 1588. The unbroken succession of natural disasters which befell this Armada, however, relieved the British fleet and the colonial militia of the necessity of engaging it. By the end of 1746 its remnants had struggled back to France without having dealt a solitary blow at the enemy. In May of next year another French fleet sailed from La Rochelle, part of it designed to recapture Louisburg, part to support Dupleix in India. Within four days it was intercepted, and totally defeated, off Cape Finisterre, by Anson. But the colonists, who had too often seen at close quarters the consequences of British apathy, scarcely noticed that once again, in this distant action, they had been shielded by the British Navy.

Meanwhile the French did not cease to attempt the recovery of Nova Scotia, their lost colony of Acadia. Its inhabitants had taken an oath of allegiance to King George, but they were wholly French and were constantly incited to disaffection by their priests. Shirley clearly perceived both the crucial importance of Acadia in the coming struggle for Canada and the urgent need of defending it energetically forthwith, and throughout 1745, 1746 and 1747 he tirelessly bombarded Newcastle with warnings, exhortations and advice. "I am afraid," he writes, in one of his infrequent phrases of apology, "your grace will think from my incessant Representations of the State of Nova Scotia, that I imagine that Province should be the sole Object of your Attention." If, which is unlikely, Shirley in fact imagined anything so remote from probability as this, he sadly mistook his man, and if Newcastle was aware of the geographical whereabouts of Acadia, and, less certainly, of Annapolis, this, together with an uneasy impression that its inhabitants were a source of constant annoyance to himself, and that a growing number of dispatches concerning their troubles awaited his attention, may well have represented the sum total of his information on the subject. Since Newcastle, whose duty it was to protect Nova Scotia, did nothing, Shirley did what he could. The defence of this Canadian province lay quite outside the functions of the Governor of Massachusetts, but its safety closely concerned all New England, and, as so often in British history before and since, the subordinate on the spot must needs do more than his duty because the ruler at home did less than his. And so towards the end of 1746 we find Shirley raising and dispatching a thousand New Englanders to meet a threat from Canada, and when they had been surprised and defeated at Grand Pré, a further draft of Massachusetts militia to reinforce them. If Nova Scotia was still in British hands when the Peace of Aix-la-Chapelle was signed in 1748, the credit was due not to Newcastle and his Whig manipulators but, after the British Navy, to the Governor of Massachusetts and the New England colonists, whose own borders throughout these years had suffered, as before, the tragic and futile depredations of Franco-Indian raiding parties. Their reward, when the terms of peace were known, proved to be the return of Louisburg and Cape Breton Isle which they had captured, to the French. To the exasperated colonists the rôle of the home country appeared to be to fail ignominiously in its military duties in war-time, and to hand back the conquests of New England at the subsequent peace. What they could not see was that to obtain the return of Louisburg the French had evacuated both Flanders and Madras, and that these would be far more essential in the decisive world-struggle soon to come than the fortress which loomed so large in their own calculations. For Flanders was the dagger which could always be pointed at the heart of British sea power. And with the command of the sea the British could always retake Louisburg, while without it the French could never hold Madras.

CHAPTER FIVE

JENKINS' EAR (2) INDIA

(1742-1748)

§1

IN INDIA, too, there was bound sooner or later to be a struggle with France, but as was natural, the struggle had developed more slowly. For so long as British and French alike were but the owners of a handful of insecure and insignificant trading stations within a majestic, ordered and alien empire, there was little cause for conflict between them. It was only after the growing anarchy of the whole sub-continent had compelled them to arm, only after they had involved themselves competitively in the murderous rivalries of native rulers, and the invincibility of European military discipline had become apparent, that France and Britain found themselves facing each other in an unavoidable struggle for survival. Neither William's nor Marlborough's war had spread to India. Tenderness for the fortunes of the East India Company moved Walpole, it is true, to a rare and transient mood of belligerency, when the Austrian Emperor Charles VI, to whom the Netherlands had passed at the peace of Utrecht, encouraged the founding of three Belgian trading stations in India, and in 1722 chartered the Imperial and Royal Company of the Austrian Low Countries. When, three years later, a treaty with Spain had opened the south American ports also to the Austrian Company's ships, and greatly alarmed commercial interests in Britain, Walpole mobilised the fleet, and Spain, accepting the challenge, besieged Gibraltar. But before the conflict could become general the Emperor had given way, and the new Company was suspended, and then abolished. It was an incongruous interlude of aggression in the pacific career of Walpole, but the brief conflict had not touched India, and when the war of Jenkins' Ear began, the French Company proposed that in India the traders of the two countries should observe a strict neutrality. It was a sign of the changing times both that regional neutrality should no longer have been taken for granted, and that, after some hesitation, the British Company should have rejected its rival's overtures.

The Company had grown greatly in solidity during this comparatively tranquil first half of the eighteenth century, thanks partly to the tranquillity, but partly because the new United Company combined the staff, the traditions and the prestige of the old Com-

pany with the Parliamentary charter of the new. It would need all
its staying-power to weather the storms ahead of it. For the disintegration of the Mogul Empire, which was well under way in the
second half of the seventeenth century, was proceeding with cumulative and alarming rapidity in the first half of the eighteenth. As
the Emperors became more feeble and more debauched, the *subahdars*
of their six provinces had grown into virtually independent sove-
reigns. But now the lesser *nawabs* and rajahs of the subordinate
states were similarly repudiating the authority of their overlords.
The political structure of the whole subcontinent was in dissolution.
And, as so often before when deprived of strong central rule, it was
becoming the helpless prey of the marauder. Persian and Afghan
raiders swept over the north-western frontiers, and returned laden
with booty or remained to found dynasties by the sword. The
Mahrattas plundered the centre and the south, overwhelming the
lesser Mohammedan governments which had emerged from the
wreck of the Mogul Empire. Sikhs and Rajputs rose victoriously.
Nadir Shah of Persia advanced on Delhi itself; only disorderly mobs
barred his path. The Mogul ministers offered him vast bribes to
spare the capital. He accepted the bribes but sacked the city. India
was now one vast anarchy, its markets deserted, its fields untilled,
its people an unprotected and leaderless multitude, eager to cling to
any ruler or any system which seemed capable of discharging the
most elementary functions of government. Once again, as so often
before in her long history, India awaited a conqueror. Conquest
might have come to her in many forms; in another Mohammedan
invasion from the north, in a Mahratta Empire, in a partition
between powerful Indian princes. In 1740 any of these destinies
might have been regarded as probable. What no man could have
foreseen was that a London trading Company, separated from India
by a six months' voyage, and possessing but a few acres of Indian
soil, would within a hundred years have subjected the greater part
of India to a rule more potent than the greatest of the Moguls had
ever established.

Yet now, at the moment when the whole logic of history proclaimed that the tremendous prize, and the tremendous burden, of
dominion over India must pass to some ruler strong enough to
conquer anarchy and civilised enough to organise order, it chanced
that there were present in India some twelve thousand representatives
of two European powers, each of which, though they scarcely knew
it yet, was infinitely more adept in the arts both of war and of peace
than any native potentate. Inevitably suzerainty over all India
would sooner or later devolve upon either France or Britain, for,

as disorder spread, the Dutch withdrew from India to concentrate upon the archipelago in which they had no rivals. But the French and the British remained, and they could not indefinitely stand aloof from the formidable tide of events. Either they must end the welter of lawless violence, either they must modernise the mediæval patch-work of petty, warring princedoms, or perish. It was not for this that they had come to India, and they accepted their destiny slowly, and with reluctance. Only gradually, and as it were by fits and starts, did a few clear-sighted men in both nations come to perceive that if they could dispose of their European rivals it would be possible, in course of time, to impose order upon all India. And fewer still, of the few who could read this much of the future, welcomed what they saw. Conquest by themselves was the last consummation they desired. For they were not soldiers or administrators but traders, and to their century trade seemed more important, and government less important, than to our own.

§2

If during the opening years of the conflict the French were in the ascendant, it was because the slow pressure of sea-power had not yet been brought to bear—Britain was at war with both France and Spain, and was not yet decisively superior to both Navies combined—and because a leader of genius had appeared among the French in the east, but not, as yet, among the British. In 1744, Dupleix had been three years Governor-General at Pondicherry, Robert Clive was still a junior clerk of nineteen in Madras.

Dupleix had gone to Pondicherry, from eleven years Governor-ship of Chandernagore, in 1741, and almost from the moment of his arrival he had been preparing for the coming struggle with the British. He found French prestige high among the Indians, thanks to the bold front with which his predecessor had scared off a Mahratta incursion; he found too that la Bourdonnais, the gifted French seaman who was Governor of Mauritius, was preparing for more energetic action in India than the aged and cautious Fleury was likely to approve. Soon after war had broken out in Europe in 1744 British warships seemed likely to capture Pondicherry, and Dupleix induced the Nawab of the Carnatic to forbid hostilities within his jurisdiction—a veto which did not prevent Dupleix himself from sending la Bourdonnais to attack Madras next year. That admirable commander, deprived by the vacillations of the French government of the warships on which he had counted, had detained every French merchantman which reached Mauritius, overruled their commanders, and, with the belated accession of a single man-of-war, led the whole flotilla to the Coromandel coast. Here he fought an indecisive action with the British squadron, but reached Pondicherry, and, after some hesitation, yielded to the insistence of Dupleix, and sailed to attack Madras. The British Governor appealed to the Nawab to enforce neutrality on the French, as it had already been enforced upon the British, but he appealed without the appropriate bribe, while Dupleix judiciously undertook to hand over his prospective conquest to the Nawab, who readily concluded that there was no reason for interference. The defences of Madras, as of most European stations in India at this time, were quite inadequate, its Governor was a man of little resolution and after five days' bombardment it capitulated, 10th September, 1746. The terms of surrender provided that on payment of a ransom, which La Bourdonnais promised should be moderate, the town should be restored intact, and that the British inhabitants should be prisoners on parole. But this clement procedure was quite incompatible with the vast designs which Dupleix had now begun to revolve, and a furious quarrel broke out between Governor and Admiral. While it still raged, the breaking of the monsoon shattered the greater part of the French squadron off Madras; on his way home the unfortunate La Bourdonnais was captured by a British cruiser and, when he eventually reached France, suffered the too frequent fate of French commanders who had deserved well of their country overseas, and was flung into the Bastille. Dupleix meanwhile announced that, despite the terms of capitulation, he intended to retain Madras. He gave orders that the town should be systematically plundered, carried off the Governor and a number of the leading servants of the British Company and paraded them in a triumphal procession through the streets of Pondicherry. A few of the prisoners escaped, disguised as Indians, to Fort St. David, a minor British station not far south of Madras, which they prepared to defend. Among them was Robert Clive.

Before attacking Fort St. David Dupleix had first to beat off the Nawab from Madras, which, despite his promise, he had no intention of handing over to that incensed potentate. When, in the new year of 1747, the French were free to proceed against the town all their attacks failed, and at the approach of a British squadron they raised the siege. The youthful Clive had received a commission, and took an energetic part in the defence. By December it was known that the war in Europe had ended eight months ago. Not long afterwards came word that the peace treaty required Madras to be restored to its owners.

For the British it had been an inglorious opening to the great contest. The spiritual legacy of Walpole lay heavy on them. It is doubtful indeed whether they had as yet realised upon how great a contest they had embarked. Largely for this reason, perhaps, they had been unsuccessful and, what was worse, unenterprising. The return of Madras did something, it is true, to restore their fallen reputation, as the Indians saw Dupleix in the flush of triumph compelled by a mysterious and invisible power to disgorge his gains. Nevertheless in general Indians who knew something of the rival European Companies thought poorly of the British prospects. And so most certainly did Dupleix himself. For Dupleix perceived that India was ripe to be conquered once again, and this time, as he judged, by Europeans. He confidently intended that its conquerors should be the French. Not only had he been in all probability the first European to frame this vast ambition; he also perceived the means by which it might be achieved. He had realised that a handful of European troops, or even of Indians trained and led by Europeans, would suffice to rout the largest native armies, and also that in the present welter of disorder a judicious combination or two might make it easy to rule vast realms through puppet princes, to set up and put down native monarchs, and so at last maybe to pass, in the ancient tradition, from kingmaker to king. Towards all this the indispensable first step was clearly to dispose of the rival Europeans. These were vaulting ambitions indeed, and though they sorted ill with the placid commercial ends for which both the rival Companies had been founded—and to which, to do them justice, they would greatly have preferred to continue to confine themselves—for the French in India it was just now of signal advantage that Dupleix should have conceived them. For all their policy, save in so far as the weakness or ignorance of the distant home government could interfere with it, would now be framed by men who clearly understood that a struggle to the death had begun, and for prodigious ends.

Books for Further Reading.

A. J. Mahan, *The Influence of seapower on history;* G. B. Herz, *The old Colonial system;* Lord Morley, *Walpole;* F. S. Oliver, *The endless adventure;* J. A. Doyle, *The colonies under the House of Hanover;* Francis Parkman, *Half a century of Conflict;* Usher Parsons, *The Life of Sir William Pepperell;** A. G. Bradley, *The fight with France for North America;* Beccles Wilson, *Ledger & Sword;* Edward Thompson and G. T. Garratt, *The rise and fulfilment of British rule in India;* Lord Macaulay, *Essay on Clive;* Sir Charles Wilson, *Clive.*

* Published in America.

Book IV

PITT AND TOTAL VICTORY

CHAPTER ONE

WILLIAM PITT

(1748-1763)

§1

THE FIFTEEN YEARS which follow changed the destiny of the world. They culminate in the world-wide victories organised by the genius of Pitt, and, in particular, in the wonderful year during which "it rained victories," and, what is more, victories of that rare kind which open new epochs in the history of man. In 1763 Britain would have reached the first climax of her power. She had ruined the imperial ambitions of her third great rival, France. Overseas her strength now seemed unchallengeable. The American colonies were still closely bound to her, and there was no apparent reason why she should lose them. She was the wonder and envy of the world. The virtues of eighteenth century Britain, her vigour, her courage and her free institutions, had been responsible for these great results. In 1763 the retribution so soon to be visited upon her vices, upon the greedy materialism and political corruption of the age, was still beyond conjecture. It was a golden moment. If the years from 1748 to 1763 be considered in themselves, and without relation to their sequel, the loss of the American colonies, they present an exhilarating picture of national resurgence after the long enervation of the rule of Walpole, of a people recovering its virility under the stimulus of adversity and the magic wand of Pitt. But if these years are viewed against the background of the two decades which followed them we are faced once again with the melancholy spectacle of a nation rising superior to its vices in war-time and succumbing to them in peace. Yet if the horizon be yet further expanded the scene is not so dark. For although Britain was so soon to lose the American colonies, in saving them from France in the Seven Years' War she would save North America for free institutions. And because, after the colonies were lost, she was able most notably to learn the lessons of adversity, much of what she gained in that war would go to the making of the Commonwealth yet to be.

But although the Seven Years' War is prologue to the failure in America, and even, at longer range, to the enduring Commonwealth to be, it is also, let us not forget, in its own right a splendid and memorable episode. The traditional text-books, preoccupied with European affairs and our own Parliamentary history, have paid too little attention to these great events. There have even been writers who have done their best to avert their gaze from them altogether, in the strange belief that "war decides nothing." Of this weak modern illusion the war between France and England from 1756 to 1763 should of itself alone be a sufficient exposure. For it would be truer to say that it decided everything. It is not difficult to see to-day that this war, or, to be more particular, the inmost quality and structure of the two peoples as now tested in war, decided the distribution of world power for an unknown period to come, decided the moral, social, political and economic texture of all North America, and of great nations still unborn, and profoundly affected, it is not too much to say, the future of every people in the world. Above all perhaps, it launched the British Empire upon its greatest task, the spreading of free institutions, in place of despotism, into every continent of the world.

This vast world struggle dwarfs into insignificance the Parliamentary history which has preoccupied so many British historians. It overshadows the official war in Europe, that Seven Years' War, from 1756 to 1763, whose very title proclaims the blindness of our historical conventions to the paramount issues, since the world war was no seven years' affair, but continued, ignoring the European peace treaty of 1748, almost without pause. Indeed the chief importance both of the war in Europe and of the fall of Newcastle, was that each profoundly affected the world-conflict. The Seven Years' War may have been fought because Frederic of Prussia had robbed a neighbour of a province not half the size of Bengal, but it brought the governments of France and Britain officially to grips again, so that the *tempo* of the struggle already going on in America and India was heightened, and deadlier and more purposeful blows were struck. And the fall of Newcastle was not merely the end of the most adroit of all borough-mongers and place-pedlars, of the Walpole tradition, of an era of materialism, contentment and inertia; it was the arrival of the greatest war-minister Britain had yet known, or would know again for close on two centuries, of the first statesman since Cromwell who could speak, over the heads of the politicians, to the nation, and rouse the moral energies which slumbered but had never died.

§2

William Pitt, who came of a long line of minor Dorsetshire squires, had been the favourite grandson of rough old Governor Pitt of Madras, the poacher turned gamekeeper, who made a fortune, bought, and eventually sold, his famous diamond, and founded a great family. After Eton and Christ Church, for neither of which he cared particularly, Pitt became a cornet in Cobham's horse, and, unlike most cornets, devoured every military book he could lay hands on—early studies which may have contributed twenty-five years later to his penetrating insight into world strategy. But his chief ambitions were political, and he attached himself, as one of "Cobham's cubs," to the Opposition which, under Bolingbroke's leadership, was attacking, as is the way of Oppositions, almost everything which the government did, but in particular its gross indifference to all the finer spiritual and intellectual instincts of the country. In 1735 he entered Parliament as Member for Old Sarum. In a later controversy his constituency would become the most notorious of the rotten boroughs, but at least Pitt could claim that its grass circles and haunted mounds had lain within a stone's throw of his own nursery windows. His maiden speech, in 1736, with its satirical allusions to the notorious dissensions in the royal family, delighted the Opposition and enraged Walpole, who characteristically determined to "muzzle this terrible cornet of horse," and promptly dismissed him from the army.

He could hardly have hit upon a more effective means of furthering the young man's political ambitions. Such heavy-handed vengeance on a mere subaltern for his political opinions enraged the army, gave the Opposition a welcome theme and at once made Pitt a public figure. That summer, as if to draw attention to the poverty to which he had been reduced, he travelled about the country in a one-horse chaise without a servant, and is said to have been received everywhere with acclamation. The incident is curiously characteristic. Like most great orators Pitt was always an actor; and what is more, he would be the first statesman of his century to make a practice of appealing to popular sentiment, and looking, beyond the precincts of Westminster, to the people as the true source of policy. But for this sensitive contact with the instincts of the people, indeed, he could never have become a great imperial statesman. By next year his friends were already comparing him to Cicero and Demos-

thenes, and in 1739, after his philippic against Walpole's Convention
of the Prado, a speech which a Minister described as "the prettiest
words and the worst language he had ever heard," he received the
formidable tribute of a public embrace from the Prince of Wales.
The essential quality of even accurately reported oratory escapes in
print, and no accurate report of a speech by Pitt survives, but all
accounts agree that on his hearers the effect of his orations was
tremendous. There was a terrifying quality in him—"when he was
angry or speaking very much in earnest," said his grand-daughter,
"nobody could look him in the face"—and in his maturity he could
hush a turbulent House as though it were a pack of frightened
schoolboys. Once as he was limping goutily out of the Chamber
he caught the opening words of a new speaker who had announced
that he proposed to reply to Mr. Pitt. Pitt turned, and fixed the rash
member with his awe-inspiring glance, then hobbled slowly across
the floor of the Chamber, lowered himself painfully into his place,
and ejaculated fiercely "Now let me hear what the honourable
gentleman has to say to me." But the unhappy man had already
collapsed in his seat, incapable of saying more. Asked if no member
had laughed, the narrator of this episode replied, "No, sir, we were
all too awed to laugh."

From the record of Walpole's administration after the outbreak
of war in 1739—and there is evidence that he carefully studied the
details of Vernon's abortive attack on Cartagena—Pitt must have
learned some useful lessons as to how a war should not be managed.
He continued the most tireless and formidable of critics, despite his
uncertain health—there is a tradition that he already suffered from
gout at Eton, by 1744 he was ill for the greater part of the year,
and attacks ever more severe and at shorter intervals recurred for
the rest of his life. In 1746, at the age of thirty-eight, he became
Paymaster of the Forces, and the next nine years were the most
peaceful and inconspicuous in his stormy career. As a minor minister
in the drab administration of the Pelhams he was no longer tempted
to oppose the government's policy, and, being outside the Cabinet,
had no hand in framing it. The public attacks on him, and the
public eulogies, died down. Those who did not know the real Pitt
may have supposed that age was mellowing him, or even that, like
the lesser fry of politics, he could be silenced by a place. The Pay
Office indeed was traditionally most lucrative. For the Paymaster
was accustomed to invest his large unexpended balances for his own
private profit, and even to accept commissions from the rulers of
allied nations to which war-time subsidies were being paid. It is
said that the Duke of Chandos built Canons from his profits as Pay-

master in Marlborough's wars, and Henry Fox notoriously lined his pockets handsomely from the office. By the standards of the age all this was in no sense corruption; it was legitimate profit fully sanctioned by precedent. Yet from the first, Pitt refused to use the public funds for his personal advantage; his balances were lodged in the Bank of England, and he never touched a penny of interest on them. It has been said, on somewhat dubious authority, that Pelham himself, who was Paymaster from 1730 to 1743, had similarly refused to profit by his invested balances, but that his self-restraint never became known to the public. Be that as it may, it must be admitted that typical of Pitt though this strict integrity undoubtedly was, the speed with which it became known to the public was no less characteristic. For, unlike his contemporaries, for whom the only political reputations which mattered were those which were made or lost at Westminster, he was always most sensitive to popular opinion, and was a master of what we should now call the arts of publicity.

These were pleasant, fallow years, during which he found leisure for his reading, his varied friendships (which included Fielding and Garrick) and his landscape-gardening. In 1754, after a brief and sudden courtship, he married Lady Hester Grenville, his friend Grenville's sister, whom he had known for twenty years. He stood now on the threshold of his years of storm and greatness, and it was well for him that his melancholy and impatient spirit should have known the haven of a marriage whose happiness remained unclouded to the end. As the nation stumbled through the ill-starred colonial prologue to the Seven Years' War under Newcastle's palsied rule, Pitt, recognising the drift to disaster, began to lash the government, of which he was still a junior member, with merciless philippics, in that fierce and daunting vein to which the House had not listened for close on ten years. Newcastle's half-hearted and reluctant attempts to conciliate Pitt were rejected one by one, for Newcastle wished to obtain his support, without giving him power. In November, 1755, after a particularly formidable onslaught on the government, Pitt was dismissed from the Pay Office. He devoted himself now to speeches which would not only expose the ineptitude of the ministry but rouse the spirit of the people. In particular he pressed for a Militia Bill, to raise British forces instead of German mercenaries, for the defence of Britain, and to end the humiliation of having to "send . . . money abroad to buy courage and defence." And while Pitt thundered his denunciations, and Newcastle was pelted by the mob at Greenwich, the official war had begun in Europe and the bad news poured in by every post.

§3

In Europe the French planned to invade England and to capture Minorca. British sea power was sufficient to prevent the army of invasion from embarking, but Port Mahon, the capital of Minorca, surrendered in June, after Admiral Byng had fought an indecisive action in its defence with an inadequate fleet, and had then withdrawn to protect Gibraltar. The alarm and indignation in Britain were such that, to save his government, Newcastle had Byng court-martialled; courts-martial of senior officers were only too familiar to the Navy in the state to which the rule of Walpole and Newcastle had reduced it. The unfortunate admiral, whose personal courage was completely vindicated, was condemned and shot on his own quarter deck, neither the first nor the last sacrifice of a fighting man by the politicians who were themselves chiefly responsible for his misadventure by their failure to provide him with adequate arms. No success elsewhere relieved the gloom of the first year of war. The fortunes of the country, and, what was worse, its spirit, were at their lowest ebb. To such a pass had thirty years of materialism, borough-mongering and letting sleeping dogs lie, reduced a proud nation that, as the bad news poured in by every mail, it even seemed to cease to believe in its own destiny. "It is time," wrote Horace Walpole, "for England to slip her cables, and float away into some unknown ocean." Men saw everything that was done, done badly, they knew that they had no leaders, and that Newcastle believed neither in his country nor in himself. The utmost strength of the British army on every front was thirty-five thousand, while the French had fifty thousand in the Channel ports alone. A foreign landing was expected hourly; there were moments of panic in London, and gloom and disaffection everywhere. George II despaired of Britain and concentrated his remaining hopes on his beloved Hanover. To many sober minds it seemed that only a miracle could save the country. Yet what the country needed was not a miracle, but a leader. The ancient virtues and the vast resources were still there, but not the man to rouse and use them. Here was a crucial test of the Parliamentary system. During the last thirty years Parliament had done none too well for the country. If it had failed now to bring forth a man worthy of the hour, it could not have long survived. But at the eleventh hour it did not fail. On November 15, 1756, Pitt was appointed Secretary of State; on December 4 he received the seals of office. No wonder, for he dominated Parliament, and in its dark hour the whole country looked to him as the only statesman it could trust. No wonder, for it was Pitt himself who said, "I know that I can save this country, and that no one else can."

§4

His first ministry did not last six months. He was in power only on sufferance, with a façade of Whig respectability provided by the Duke of Devonshire. He had been forced upon the king, and in a sense upon Parliament, by the country. To Newcastle his displacement by a man who had no boroughs in his pocket and cared nothing for the arts of political corruption, seemed a transient interference with the laws of nature, and, when he judged that Pitt's popularity in the country was flagging, he whistled up his henchmen in the House. The outburst of popular indignation, when it was known that the borough-mongers had got rid of Pitt, has scarcely a parallel in the history of Parliament. The Press, almost without exception, was for him. Led by London, the chief towns of the kingdom voted him their freedom; for weeks, as Lady Hervey said, "it rained gold boxes." The king, who suspected, with good reason, that Pitt would not fight the war on sound Hanoverian lines, struggled desperately against the inevitable, and for nearly three months the country was at war without a government. But by the end of June, 1757, he had had to give way, and this time there was a clear understanding. Pitt was to direct the war and rule the country, Newcastle would look after the places and the pensions. Both the parties to this arrangement were well content, for each found himself in his natural element.

The wave of popular confidence which had restored Pitt to power, despite the king and the wirepullers, was deeply significant. For in his brief first ministry Pitt had had no time to win victories. But in those few months he had done more than win victories; he had provided the indispensable foundation for them; he had recalled the nation to its true self. For though Pitt was a great war minister, he was more than a great war minister; he played the part of the prophets of old, summoning an erring nation to repentance and revival. He had found "a gloomy scene for this distressed, disgraced country," a nation contemptuous of its government, distrustful of its military commanders, dispirited, divided and relying on foreign mercenaries for its own defence. In a few months he had compelled Parliament to raise a militia, and entrust the defence of Britain to it; he had raised two regiments from among the very clansmen who

had marched on England in '45, and thereby ensured the reconcilia-
tion of the Highlands; he had infused a new spirit into the Admiralty, and started the building of many more ships. But above all he
had made clear to the nation what it was fighting for, and given it
the assurance that victory was possible. But victory, he knew, would
only come when Britain had deserved it, by ridding herself of the
vices of the long, gross years of peace. His task was to see that the
nation learned the lessons of adversity. "I fear we do not stand in
the smile of Heaven," he wrote. "May a degenerate people profit in
the school of misfortune." "We are no longer a nation," Lord
Chesterfield had written in July. Pitt's mission was to teach Britain
that she was a nation, the first nation in the world.

He was a superb war minister. His own energy was daemonic,
and he infused energy into everyone and everything. When an
admiral protested that his task was impossible, "Sir, I walk on
impossibilities" replied Pitt, pointing to his crutches. When Anson,
the head of the Navy, told him that he could not find the ships he
needed, Pitt replied simply "I shall impeach you, if you do not."
His rule over his cabinet of mediocrities was absolute. The war plans
were his plans. Their breadth and impetus were born partly of his
natural genius, partly of his unremitting mastery of detail. For he
would turn from planning the sweep of one expedition across half
a continent, to reminding the War Office of the ammunition-flints
needed for another. He worked with a staff of two under-secretaries,
and nine clerks. He never entered his office save in full dress, and
never allowed his under-secretaries to sit in his presence. He
revolutionised the business methods of his department, and, to ensure
complete lucidity, would labour for hours over the wording of a
dispatch. He spent more than five hours one night weighing every
word in an important note to Prussia. "I would not spend such
another evening," said Holderness, his fellow Secretary of State, "for
the king's revenue, or for what is perhaps still more valuable, Mr.
Pitt's abilities . . . for I neither can nor will be detained for hours
upon the introduction of a monosyllable." But Pitt spent himself
upon monosyllables as readily as upon campaigns. And, like all
great administrators, he was learning all the time. "The first time
I come in to Mr. Pitt upon any matter I find him extremely ignorant,"
said one informant, "the second time I come to him I find him
completely informed upon it." That rarest gift, the power of
choosing men, he possessed in abundance. And the captains whom
he chose took fire from his genius. "No man," said Barré, years
later, in his funeral oration, "entered the Earl's closet, who did not
feel himself, if possible, braver at his return than when he went in."

CHAPTER TWO

CLIVE IN INDIA

(1748-1760)

§1

THE SCENE which unfolded itself before Pitt, when he took office at the end of 1756, was sombre indeed. The imperial war with France, which in India and America had proceeded almost unbrokenly since 1748, had gone ill, and the official declaration of war between the two governments in 1756 had let loose that flood of disasters which so often since has been ensured by the failure of British governments to shoulder their obligations in time of peace.

In India the salvation of the British, as so often, would be the emergence at the fateful moment, and in the fateful place, of a man of genius. Robert Clive was twenty-three when the Peace of Aix-la-Chapelle was signed, the son of a small Shropshire squire. From early childhood, to the growing disquiet of his relations, he had shown every sign of possessing a strong will, a hot temper and dauntless courage. An uncle remarked with distaste that as a boy he was "out of measure addicted" to fighting, and the worthy citizens of Market Drayton long remembered with what horror they had seen him seated astride a stone dragon's-head spout at the summit of their lofty steeple, and how, anticipating by some two hundred years the business methods of the American gangster, he had got together a troop of young ruffians, and levied from the local shopkeepers a regular tribute of apples and coppers, in return for an undertaking that their windows should remain unbroken. Few, if any, of our greatest leaders have shone at school, whatever variety of school they have attended, and Clive, who was at four schools, was no exception. One pedagogue, it is true, more perceptive or more complaisant than the rest, is said to have prophesied that if the boy "lived to be a man, and if opportunity enabled him to exert his talents, few names would be greater than his," but in general Clive seems to have been regarded as a scapegrace, of whom little good could be expected. It was probably with relief that his family shipped him off, at eighteen, to sink or swim as a junior Writer in the service of the East India Company. The Empire owes much to the abundance with which Britain has produced adventurous and gifted young men, and the readiness of their impoverished relations to see them seek their fortunes overseas. In Madras Clive must have suffered much at first. There was always a streak of morbid sensitiveness in his complex nature, and he was lonely, homesick and in poor health. Twice he is said to have attempted suicide, and twice the pistol, after he had pulled the trigger, failed to fire. Then came the war with France. He witnessed the tame surrender of Madras and escaped from Pondicherry. At Fort St. David he obtained his commission as an ensign. As if by magic he began to shed his old faults, and to display new and unsuspected qualities. Courage and audacity he had always possessed, but now he displayed a ready discipline, and a cool, mature judgment of which few had hitherto suspected him. For he was no longer, as he had been among the ledgers, a misfit. The founder of the British Empire in India was entering upon his true career.

§2

In India the rival forces, separated by a voyage of many months from Europe, depended even less than in America on direction by ministers at home, and even more upon the quality of their leaders on the spot. And, at first sight, it is something of a paradox that even in the twilight of her fortunes in the East France should have been served by a succession of men each of whom, in his own way, showed an authentic touch of genius. Besides Dupleix himself and de la Bourdonnais there was the Marquis de Bussy, who came near rivalling Clive as a general, and the Comte de Lally, fearless and headstrong, who had saved the day for France at Fontenoy. Yet none of these was great as Clive was to show himself great, both in council and in the field. The French leaders moreover seldom agreed among themselves, and were usually but half trusted by the rulers of France. Charges of treachery or corruption, with which Frenchmen have often been only too ready in times of public misfortune, seemed specially plausible when levelled against men whose business had been kingmaking among the fabulous treasure-houses of the East. It is no coincidence that of these four gallant men, each of whom served France devotedly according to his lights, de Lally should have been guillotined, and de la Bourdonnais sent for three years to the Bastille, while the great Dupleix ended his days in poverty and public contempt. There was another sense, however, in which in the far East French and British were more dependent upon their home governments than in America. The European forces, of whose small numbers disease or warfare took constant toll, must for ever be reinforced and re-equipped from the mother country. Without adequate replenishment from France Dupleix' sublest combination of native alliances must sooner or later collapse. And here the invisible barrier of British sea-power played its deadly part. By 1757, the fleets which should have attacked the British stations, or carried succour to the French forces, in America or India, were being relentlessly blockaded in the ports of France. Montcalm as well as Dupleix was hard hit by the foe he never saw, but it was Dupleix who suffered most.

Dupleix, however, thought that he saw his great opportunity dawning in the year of the peace, 1748. Native pretenders had appeared to the thrones of the great southern vice-royalty, the Deccan, and of the Carnatic, its rich dependent province. Together they invaded the Carnatic. Here, Dupleix perceived, was his long-awaited opening. If he could set up a puppet Nizam of the Deccan, a puppet Nawab of the Carnatic, what vistas of power and glory awaited him! He at once espoused the cause of the pretenders. Four hundred French soldiers and two thousand French-trained sepoys turned the scales in the decisive battle against the reigning monarch. The conspirators at once became masters of almost the whole of the Carnatic. A few more months, and the Deccan was theirs also. To French eyes it was an impressive picture. The candidate for the Deccan whom the British favoured had been murdered by his own subjects. The son of the defeated Nawab of the Carnatic, whom the British had even attempted, feebly, to assist, was closely besieged in Trichinopoly. To emphasise even more starkly the swollen power of Dupleix, the new Nizam was killed in a scuffle on the way to his capital, and de Bussy, who was escorting him, coolly selected and enthroned a substitute. The new beneficiary could not well be mistaken for anything but a French puppet. *Te Deums* were sung in Pondicherry. The new Nizam journeyed there, to pay his respects to his allies, and was welcomed by Dupleix in the guise of a brother monarch. This was Dupleix's great hour. He became the chief channel of profit and honour at the Nizam's court. He was the most powerful potentate in India. He erected a column, on whose four sides four inscriptions recorded his triumphs, in four different tongues. Around it arose Dupleix Fatihabad, the City of the Victory of Dupleix.

All this while the British hung back, dismayed and bewildered by the rapid transformation of a rival trading Company into a great oriental power. They continued, it is true, to recognise Mahomed Ali, the son of the dispossessed and slaughtered Nawab of the

Carnatic, but recognition was of little value to that unfortunate prince so long as he continued to be closely besieged in Trichinopoly by the French and their allies. And the British were backward in action. To be backward in action of the kind of which Dupleix was setting the example was indeed natural to the servants of a trading Company, and if the Governors in London could have shaped the pattern of events, backward they would have remained. Not for war or Empire had they come to India. It had been only slowly and with reluctance that after nearly three-quarters of a century of peaceful trade the British had found themselves compelled, if they were not to abandon India and their trading altogether, to arm themselves for defence. And now it was only slowly and with reluctance that they came to realise that, if they were not soon to be forced to abandon India and their trade there altogether, they must needs follow the example which, equally without the countenance of his superiors at home, Dupleix was now setting, and launch boldly into war and kingmaking. The British would eventually conquer India, but nothing could be falser than the too familiar charge that it was for conquest that they went there. They only began to fight when fighting was forced upon them, and, as so often since, they did not put forth their full powers, or find their destined leader, until their situation seemed all but hopeless.

§3

Clive had become a civilian again after the peace of 1748, but he had been employed as commissary to the troops, and so had seen with his own eyes the desperate situation of the British protégé, Mahomed Ali, in Trichinopoly. He now applied for a commission, and was granted the rank of captain. He was twenty-five. It is evidence both of his own great qualities, and of the military unpreparedness of the Company, that he should already have been universally regarded as the chief British officer in the Carnatic. After a dangerous personal reconnaissance he returned to propose a desperate stroke to Saunders, the new and energetic Governor of Madras. If Trichinopoly fell, he believed, the French would become virtual masters of all India. And with their limited resources the only hope for the British of saving Trichinopoly was to strike an unexpected blow elsewhere. Let them seize Arcot, the capital of the Carnatic, which the new Nawab, not dreaming of interference from the now despised British, had emptied of troops for the siege of Trichinopoly. Saunders could give Clive only two hundred

Europeans and six hundred Indian sepoys, and even this would leave less than a hundred and fifty soldiers to garrison both Fort St. David and Madras. But he believed in Clive, and he agreed. With this little force, and eight officers, four of whom were clerks who had imitated their commander in abandoning their desks, Clive hurried to Arcot and captured it without a blow. When the garrison, recovering from its panic and considerably reinforced, returned, three thousand strong, to the attack, he surprised it in a night assault, cut it up and put it to flight, without the loss of a single man. But the trial of strength was yet to come. Before long about ten thousand Indians, many of them detached, as Clive had foreseen, from the siege of Trichinopoly, with the valuable aid of a hundred and fifty Frenchmen from Pondicherry, were investing Arcot. During the brief respite allowed him Clive had done what he could to repair the ruinous walls and to improvise defences on the inadequate ramparts. For fifty days the handful of defenders held the widening breach against the constant pressure of an army twenty times their number. Clive's spirit dominated and animated them all. When provisions ran low the sepoys assured him that the water in which the rice had been cooked would suffice for them, and urged that the Europeans, who were accustomed to more solid fare, should be given all the available grain. Meanwhile the fame of the siege had spread abroad, and a Mahratta chief, who had been engaged to assist Mahomed Ali but had hitherto held back, believing that his cause was doomed, declared that he was very ready to come to Clive's assistance now that he had seen, for the first time, that the British could fight. The besiegers determined to storm Arcot before assistance could reach it. They were beaten off with heavy loss after a desperate struggle in the night, in which Clive served a gun himself. When day dawned, the enemy had vanished, leaving a number of guns and much ammunition behind them. Arcot was safe. This was the turning-point of British fortunes in India.

Before the year was over Clive had defeated Dupleix' Nawab, and his French allies, at Arni, and the British began to overrun the Carnatic. In the course of these operations Dupleix' monument of victory and its city of Fatihabad were rased to the ground. These things, after all, were symbols, and Clive understood the workings of the Indian mind. Early next year Major Lawrence, who had commanded the Company's forces in 1748 and 1749, returned to India. His arrival might well have been a disaster. He was a major, an exalted rank for the Indian service in those days, he was a regular soldier, and, worse still, he knew his textbooks. Luckily he also knew military genius when he saw it. He had treated Clive kindly in the past, and Clive readily placed himself under his orders. The combination, while it lasted, proved fortunate; Lawrence made full use of Clive's brilliant gifts, Clive learned all he needed of Lawrence's professional lore. All hung now on the fate of Mohamed Ali, the British protégé, in Trichinopoly, which but for Clive's performance at Arcot would have fallen long since. Lawrence and Clive defeated the French commander of the besieging force, and then the reinforcements sent by Dupleix to extricate it. In due course the reigning pretender to the Carnatic was captured, and the French army surrendered. Mohamed Ali assumed his throne, and Clive and Lawrence spent the remainder of the year 1752 in mopping up, as we should now say, the French garrisons in the Carnatic—with troops, both British and Indian, sometimes so raw that on occasion Clive had to expose himself constantly to the enemy's fire to shame them into spirited behaviour. Next year Clive, whose health had suffered from the climate and his great exertions, sailed for England. Only three years earlier Dupleix had been erecting his column of victory; now his plans, like the column, seemed fallen into ruin. And the prime author of that rapid reversal of fortune was the young captain now on his way home with a newly married bride and the secret ambition of becoming a Member of Parliament.

§4

Fortunately for his country, this was an ambition which he failed to achieve. Elected for a Cornish rotten borough, he was unseated by one of the petitions which were part of the routine of eighteenth century politics. In 1755 he sailed again for India as a lieutenant-colonel in the British army and Governor designate of Fort St. David's. Dupleix meanwhile had not despaired. While de Bussy conquered the coast province to the north of the Carnatic, he embarked, with varying fortunes, on a lengthy struggle with Lawrence in the south. But in the long run he could not succeed without regular reinforcements from home, and regular reinforcements he did not receive. The directors of the French Company understood little of his imperial designs, and what they understood they cordially disliked. In the summer of 1754 the bolt fell. His successor arrived in Pondicherry, with orders for his immediate return. The man who had taught the British how an Indian Empire might be built, the man at whose rise all India had marvelled, and who had so lately seemed to stand upon the threshold of final triumph, sailed in black despair for home, leaving his life's work thwarted and broken behind him. In France he lingered for another nine years, impoverished and disgraced. In France, though not in India, he was soon forgotten. He had deserved better of his countrymen than this, yet it was well for India that he did not triumph there. For during the five thousand years of her subjection to successive foreign conquerors all the rulers of India hitherto, save only the transient Empire of Alexander, had aimed exclusively at power and wealth, and there is no evidence that Dupleix had other ends than these. Clive was to do more than found an Empire; before he had finished, he would set it on the road to becoming an Empire of a new kind.

Despite the fall of Dupleix, in 1755, when Clive returned to India, the scales had hardly yet tilted. In the Carnatic indeed all was well for the British. Dupleix' successor had undertaken to recognise the rightful Nawab, whom Clive and Lawrence had enthroned, and French and British even optimistically agreed that henceforth there should be no interference in native quarrels. But further north de Bussy was still busy and powerful in the Deccan. And further north still, in Bengal, there was now to begin a series of terrible events which in due course would lead inexorably to British sovereignty in India. Here, about the delta of the Ganges, stretched the wealthiest province of India, where Hindu masses, timid, sedentary, intelligent and voluble, were ruled by a Mahommedan conqueror from the north-west. Here the bleak mudbank on which Job Charnock had pitched seventy years earlier was now the pleasant city of Calcutta. The French were a short way further up the river at Chandernagore, the Dutch at Chinsura. Thus far, however, there had been no fighting in Bengal; all three powers still traded peacefully side by side. For in Bengal there had hitherto been a native power capable of exercising authority, and the European merchants accordingly could remain merchants, as they had always been. In 1756, however, the ruling Nawab of Bengal was succeeded by his nephew, a cruel, dissolute and feeble-witted youth whose name is usually anglicised as Surajah Dowlah. Surajah Dowlah would in any event have been very ready to attack Calcutta, for he hated the British, and believed that it would be highly profitable to plunder them. He had been brought up, among flatterers and buffoons, to suppose that his every whim was law, and there was now the pretext that the British, who knew that war with the French was about to break out, had begun, without his permission, to improve the fortifications of Calcutta. They had also given offence by sheltering a wealthy refugee from his summary methods of justice, and by allowing native merchants to trade duty-free under British passes. Surajah Dowlah had heard moreover how in the south native princes were becoming clients under French or

British protection, and to escape a similar fate he resolved to strike at once.

The British in Bengal were still merchants. No Dupleix had compelled them to turn their hands to soldiering, and when Surajah Dowlah marched on Calcutta, with a large army, although (despite Macaulay's picturesque but inaccurate account) they showed great gallantry, they could not resist for long. A few soldiers and a medley of untrained civilians defended themselves for three days against immense odds, but their new batteries were on the river front, where a French attack might be expected, and the landward defences were nugatory. With the city, large numbers of British residents fell into the hands of Surajah Dowlah, and there followed the famous tragedy of the Black Hole of Calcutta, perhaps the only episode in Anglo-Indian history of which Macaulay's familiar phrase is approximately true, and every British schoolboy knows something. The Black Hole was the garrison prison-cell, twenty foot square. At the summer solstice, and in the climate of Bengal, it would have been cruelty to compel even a solitary European to spend a night in it. Into this grim chamber one hundred and forty-six British prisoners were herded by the Nawab's guards. Surajah Dowlah may not have given the order, but only Surajah Dowlah could have countermanded it, and he was sleeping off a debauch, and must not be disturbed. The Indian guards held lights to the bars of the cell, to see and mock the torments of the prisoners within. Twenty-three ghastly survivors were dragged forth at dawn; the rest of the hundred and forty-six had perished. After systematically plundering the Company's premises the Nawab marched off with flying colours, and a number of British prisoners, half-starved and manacled, in his train. He was a despot, and he had always assumed that a despot could do as he pleased without fear of consequences. He did not expect that the British would trouble him again.

But little though he guessed it, the dealings of Surajah Dowlah with the British had ensured that they would become the next rulers of India. For the tragedy of the Black Hole had dispelled their last wishful illusion that it might still be possible for them to remain in India as traders and no more. There was an outrage to avenge, and at last they were more than ready to fight. News of the fate of Calcutta, in May, 1756, did not reach England till June, 1757. But it came to Madras in August. And by now Clive had returned there. Sailing from England in 1755 he had landed in Bombay and spent some little while, with a squadron under Admiral Watson, in extirpating the pirates who had terrorised the coast to the south for a century. War with France was known now to be imminent;

in fact it had broken out in May, but the news, even now labouring towards India on the high seas, would not arrive until December. A powerful French expeditionary force, destined for the Carnatic, was said to be fitting out in Brest. It seemed certain that there would soon be work for Clive in Madras, and the shocking news from Calcutta set the Council an ugly and unwelcome problem. At once, however, they decided to take the risk of leaving their own province virtually defenceless. Nine hundred British infantry and fifteen hundred sepoys were despatched, under Clive, to recover Calcutta, and exact reparation. It was a small enough force in relation to the resources of the great principality which it was to attack, but the siege of Arcot had shown that numbers were not indispensable for success. The whole of the naval squadron under Admiral Watson was to accompany it. Friction and misunder-standings as to the respective authority of king's and Company's officers delayed the expedition, and it did not reach the mouth of the Hugli till December, 1756. Such was the state of affairs when, on December 4, Pitt received the seals of Secretary of State, and a new era opened.

§5

In India particularly, from six to twelve months distant, Pitt could not control the struggle as he could control it in America. Moreover in India it was primarily the Company's war. It was for the Company to provide the troops, both British and Indian, and count itself fortunate if it could look for a few regular regiments and a warship or two from a sympathetic government at home. India was won because Clive was there. But even Clive needed support from home, and this Pitt, as no British statesman before him, was qualified to give. Bred by his grandfather to the East Indian tradition, he knew by heredity and instinct what India meant. "Mr. Pitt," remarked Clive himself in 1760, "seems thoroughly con-vinced of the infinite consequence of the East India Company to the nation." No one moreover had a quicker eye for genius than Pitt, and for him, in his desperate search for youth and talent among the elderly red-tape generals of the regular army, to find a Clive ready-established in command must have seemed a special dispensa-tion of Providence. "Clive," as he put it, "that man not born for a desk, that heaven-born general. He . . . never learned the arts of war or that skill in doing nothing, which only forty years of service can bring!" And he reinforced Watson's squadron, and allowed the men of the only regular regiment in India to be enlisted into the Company's army.

At the moment when Pitt took office, Clive was at the mouth of the Hugli on his way to recapture Calcutta. In January, 1757, he took it with the utmost ease. An army forty thousand strong, sent by Surajah Dowlah to eject the British, was roughly handled by Clive's small forces, and the Nawab decided to treat. He offered Clive everything which he had come north to exact. Clive now found himself in something of a quandary. He would have liked to pursue and chastise the ruler who had been responsible for the tragedy of the Black Hole. But by now news of the outbreak of the Seven Years' War had at long last reached India; and this both at once transformed the French nearby at Chandernagore into potential allies of Surajah Dowlah, and exposed Madras, which had stripped itself of troops for the liberation of Calcutta, to obvious dangers in the south, where the French threat was still imminent. Clive decided to treat. From this moment, though his greatest victory was yet to be won, what Clive did as statesman becomes even more important than what he did as soldier. For vast problems of diplomacy and administration now shaped themselves swiftly in the fluid anarchy which was India. Neither Leadenhall Street nor Downing Street could solve them, for eighteen months, at the very least, must pass between the dispatch of an inquiry from India and the arrival of a reply from either Company or government. These apparent obstacles were, however, wholly harmonious with the British genius, whose greatest and most lasting achievements have been less the outcome of long-considered and clearcut design than of the successive solution of immediate problems by the hard-pressed men who were confronted with them. And when the Select Committee, as it was called, of Calcutta suggested to Clive that he should now surrender his special powers and place himself under its orders, he replied, as might have been expected, "You will excuse me, gentlemen, if I refuse to give them up." Inevitably, then, it was to Clive that it fell to grapple with the portentous problems which now crowded thick and fast upon the British in Bengal, and by the manner of his solving them to determine the destiny of all India.

Clive desired to return to protect Madras, but could not safely leave Bengal until French Chandernagore had been reduced. Surajah Dowlah's consent for an attack was still needful, and complicated negotiations followed with that fickle and distracted tyrant, who veered by fits and starts from preparing to attack the British to pledging them undying friendship, and from hailing Clive as his friend and protector to intriguing with the French in Chandernagore and with de Bussy in the Deccan. Clive saw that he must act, and with Watson and his fleet, took Chandernagore, after a brief but desperate resistance, in March, 1757. But Surajah Dowlah, though still afraid to strike, had manifestly not ceased to be anxious to wound. And now a revolution was brewing in his own palace. Powerful courtiers, weary of a cruelty and treachery excessive even for an oriental despot, planned to set their own nominee, Mir Jafar, upon the throne of Bengal, and communicated their plans to Clive. It seemed a golden opportunity for the British to depose a despot who had inflicted on them unforgettable cruelties and would certainly destroy them if he could, and to replace him with a reliable protégé of their own. Clive decided to back the conspiracy. He sent Surajah Dowlah what he described as "a soothing letter," and, by the hands of the same courier, a message bidding the British agent at the Nawab's court "Tell Mir Jafar to fear nothing. I will join him with five thousand men who never turned their backs."

For now Clive had embarked upon intrigue against a master of intrigue, and in a land where intrigue was the very air men breathed. He could not succeed, he believed, if he declined to use the weapons of his opponents. For the ambiguous methods which he now employed he has been censured by historians, as he was censured by his contemporaries at home. Macaulay remarks that the belief that the word of the British was their bond has made the fortune of British rule in India, and that, on the lowest grounds, such an asset should not have been thrown away for a temporary advanatge over a treacherous enemy. No one who believes in absolute standards of morality, valid at all times and under any circumstances, will dispute that what Clive now did was wrong. Nevertheless it is easy to exaggerate its wrongness, by forgetting its background. For Clive was not acting for an established authority, he was grappling desperately in the dark with adversaries who would stick at nothing. Europe and its traditions seemed very far away, and for the moment he abandoned them, as a prize-fighter, set upon by an assassin in a dark alley, will discard the rules of the ring. He used treachery to deceive the treacherous, very much as to this day, without complaint from the most censorious, the state uses it against the blackmailer. The blackmailer indeed makes an appropriate analogy, for one Omichund, a wealthy Hindu agent of the negotiations with Mir Jafar, threatened suddenly to betray the whole design, if he were not promised a million sterling from the Bengal treasury when Surajah Dowlah had been dethroned. Clive's response was to draw up two versions of his agremeent with Mir Jafar. One, on white paper, contained no mention of the vast bribe to Omichund; the other, on red, conceded his demands, but was to be disavowed. Omichund saw the red treaty only, signed by all the British leaders in Bengal, and was content. He did not know that even in this ambiguous document one signature had been forged. Watson had refused to set his name to it, and the others had added it for him.

§6

In mid-June Clive marched from Calcutta with three thousand men, eight hundred of whom were British, to one of the decisive battles of history. As he neared Plassey he was seized by unaccustomed misgivings. Surajah Dowlah, with an army of fifty thousand, and fifty heavy guns, was hard at hand. Mir Jafar, it had now become obvious, would not desert, as he had promised, with the troops under his command. The rains had set in, and the Hugli, if once the British crossed it, would bar their retreat. Clive called a council of war, and it pronounced against attacking. It was the only council of war he ever summoned, and if he had listened to its advice the British might not have conquered India, for Empires are not won by committees. After the council Clive spent an hour alone in a grove of trees in silent meditation. He came back with his mind made up, and gave the order to cross the river. Early on the next morning but one, June 23, 1757, near the orchard of mangoes known as Plassey Grove, he dispersed Surajah Dowlah's army in irretrievable ruin. At the cost of thirty-six men he had defeated an army seventeen times as large as his own, and decided the fate of India.

Mir Jafar, who had hung on the outskirts of the battle without committing himself to either side, rode in next day to congratulate the victors. Clive greeted him without a hint of reproach, saluted him as Nawab of Bengal, Behar and Orissa, and within a few days installed him, with high ceremony, in the capital. Surajah Dowlah fled, was betrayed and captured, and murdered by the son of Mir Jafar. As for Omichund, he came greedily to receive his expected reward. The treaty on white paper was produced, and Clive, who spoke no Urdu, turning to one of his staff, said calmly, "It is now time to undeceive Omichund." The shock of disappointment was too much for the unfortunate traitor; he lingered for a few months in semi-idiocy, and died. As for Clive, his real difficulties were only now beginning. The British had set Mir Jafar upon his throne, and now only the British could keep him there. They had taken up arms to protect their trade, but more than ever it was apparent that there was no turning back. To resume the status of mere traders would mean a relapse into universal anarchy. For the moment the only course open to them was that of which Dupleix had already set them such clear examples; they must rule, as best they could, through Mir Jafar. Clive indeed had already perceived that the logical consequence of what he had done was full British sovereignty. And in a letter to Pitt, in January, 1759, he set forth the vast prospects and vaster obligations which were opening before the Company, and went on:

> But so large a sovereignty may possibly be an object too extensive for a Mercantile Company; and it is to be feared they are not of themselves able, without the nation's assistance, to maintain so wide a dominion. I have therefore presumed, Sir, to represent this matter to you and submit it to your consideration, whether the execution of a design that may hereafter be still carried to greater lengths, be worthy of the government's taking it into hand.

More than a century before India passed completely under the British Crown the founder of British rule there had foreseen the inevitable event. The difficulty, as Pitt saw, was that, although "the Company were not proper to have it," the Crown was not proper either, "for such a revenue would endanger our liberties"—by making the Crown independent of Parliament.

Clive spent the year 1758 in reducing the outlying princelings to obedience to the new Nawab, and early in 1759 defeated a formidable invading army of forty thousand men, sent by a coalition under the Nawab of Oudh. For these services Mir Jafar, who knew that only Clive could maintain his throne, and now regarded him with superstitious awe, presented him with an estate worth thirty thousand pounds a year, of which the Company itself was the tenant. But Mir Jafar was no more reliable than his predecessor. Before the end of the year he was in secret communication with the Dutch at Chinsura. A Dutch squadron had appeared in the mouth of the Hugli, carrying troops which, since Clive had had to send reinforcements to the Carnatic, were superior in numbers to his own. Holland was nominally a friendly power, and Clive knew that if he attacked the Dutch on the Hugli he might be disavowed and punished by the British government. He knew too that at the moment much of his personal fortune was in the hands of the Dutch East India Company, for remittance to Britain. But he knew also that if he allowed the Dutch vessels to pass up the river to Chinsura, Mir Jafar would promptly join them, Bengal would again be plunged into anarchy, and all would be to do again. When Colonel Forde, whom he had dispatched with a small force to bar the way to Chinsura, sent in great perplexity to ask whether he should attack, Clive was engaged on a rubber of whist. He turned only for a moment from the game to scribble in pencil on a scrap of paper torn from Forde's note: "Dear Forde, Fight 'em immediately, and I'll send an order of Council to-morrow." Nothing loth, Forde proceeded to rout the Dutch troops, and capture the Dutch ships. Chinsura surrendered, and the Dutch promised to erect no fortifications, and keep no more than a hundred and twenty-five European soldiers in Bengal. In February, 1760, Clive sailed home from India for the second time. He left behind him vast problems of administration, which he himself, when he returned for the third and last time to India, would take a principal share in solving.

§7

Meanwhile, while Clive in Bengal was laying the foundations of British rule in India, French power in the south was crumbling no less fast. The death stroke came when the indomitable Lally, quarrelling persistently with his officers, and followed by a mutinous army, set out late in 1759 to besiege the fortress of Wandewash, in the Arcot country. Here Eyre Coote, who had been one of Clive's officers at Plassey, fell upon him. de Lally's cavalry refused to obey his orders, de Bussy was captured, de Lally was wounded and his army fled. This was the end. One by one the French strongholds, and then Pondicherry itself fell, and with it the last vestige of a French Empire in India.

Order must one day be restored to India by some European power, and now there was only one European power in the peninsula. The British had survived the onslaughts of the French; and the medley of anarchic princedoms which was India was unlikely to constitute a lasting obstacle if Britain was drawn into the task of establishing order. British endurance and valour had cleared the path to Empire, though as yet this was a path which scarcely any desired to tread. It remained to be seen whether they could also resist the manifold new temptations of oriental power. Not unless they survived this peril also could the foundations of a new order in the East be firmly laid.

CHAPTER THREE

WASHINGTON AND WOLFE

(1748-1759)

IN AMERICA the scene which confronted Pitt at the end of 1756 was even darker, for in America there had been no Clive. As soon as the Treaty of 1748 brought peace to the northern frontiers both French and British were freed for fresh encroachments elsewhere, and it is at this juncture therefore that the Ohio and the Mississippi enter history. Sooner or later they were bound to play their part in the conflict for the mastery of America, as any one who glances at a map will readily perceive. No pressure of population, needless to say, drove the British westward, or the French south. But for the French, the British might have remained contentedly for generations hemmed in by the western barrier of the Alleghanies. But for the British, the French might never have conceived the notion of linking Canada to the delta of the Mississippi by a chain of forts. But given the mounting rivalry between the two nations, given those mountain barriers and that river highway, the twin impulses were inevitable. Why should not the French bar the British for ever from the vast unexplored hinterland? Must not the British forestall such a stranglehold by themselves pouring westwards across the mountains? A generation ago the French had made their first moves. After 1748 the *tempo* quickened. Next year small parties of French troops were moving down the Allegheny River and the Ohio. Meanwhile, in their own less deliberate fashion, the British too had begun to move. There had been British traders on the Ohio as early as 1740, and after 1748 several companies were formed in Virginia to trade and settle beyond the mountains. It was becoming clear that more formal conflict could not long be delayed. The strength and the weaknesses of the rivals were illustrated to admiration in the characteristic and contrasting methods of their advance. It was the French who had taken the initiative, and their movements were part of a clear-cut aggressive design, carefully planned by their government, and almost entirely military. The British were a far more civilian, and a far less disciplined, community. With them there was at first no military design and indeed no coherent government policy; only once again the instinctive reaction of an uneasy commercial and civilian society, suddenly awaking to a threat to its existence. Given

153

time, a people is stronger than any government, but only if it is given time. In the course of time the British would outstrip or overthrow their rivals because their rivals were dependent upon governments while their own expansion was an impulse of the people, constantly able to take its own course despite the timidity or indifference of their rulers. But such a process is like a flooding dam, irresistible when the water has begun to spread but easily contained at the outset. And the danger to the American colonies now was that the French government would contrive to complete their dam before the British population had begun to flow westwards in force. It was a danger which the colonial governments did little to forestall.

The Governor of Virginia, Robert Dinwiddie, though obstinate and cantankerous, was, it is true, a man of great energy and some vision, but his energy was hampered by the too familiar disputes with the Assembly of his own colony, and by the discreditable apathy of all the others. Nowhere was there any conception of a united English-speaking Commonwealth, nowhere even any serious notion of joint action to meet a common danger. In the three central colonies the considerable influx of German settlers was a natural obstacle to any sense of a common British cause, and in Pennsylvania the pacifist principles of the original colonists served as excuse for the inaction of timid or factious politicians. Though Pennsylvanians were soon to suffer terribly from Indian marauders, they would not lift a finger to secure an Indian alliance when an alliance was still possible. Yet there were advantages on the British side. The long French tentacle reaching down from Canada was slender, artificial and dangerously extended. There might be no concerted rejoinder from the British colonies as a whole, yet the civilians who began to stream across the mountains westward from Virginia represented an energetic community far more numerous and much nearer to the disputed territory.

In 1753 Dinwiddie dispatched a formal message to the French commander, warning him that the French were now occupying a fort upon land "notoriously known to be the property of Great Britain," and that "it is my duty to require your peaceable departure." The messenger would have to travel about five hundred and sixty miles, over lofty mountains and through a trackless wilderness; and it was desirable that, besides conducting himself, when he reached his destination, with dignity and tact, he should also seize the opportunity of inconspicuously informing himself as to the strength, arms and disposition of his hosts. It was a delicate, as well as an arduous, mission and it is one of the minor curiosities of history that Dinwiddie, who must have had an eye for men as well as measures, should have selected for it a young land-surveyor and major of militia of twenty-one, whose name, destined to become one of the most famous in all history, was George Washington. Next year, Washington, now a lieutenant-colonel, was sent, with a force amounting to three small companies, to recapture a British post at the confluence of the Allegheny and the Monongahela which the French had taken, and rebuilt as Fort Duquesne. He defeated a French garrison and killed its commander, under circumstances which were subsequently much disputed, but a stronger French force compelled him to retreat, and eventually to capitulate, with the honours of war, at Great Meadows. With the action in Great Meadows French and British were unmistakably at war again—and Washington was launched upon his strange military career.

§2

The danger to the British colonies was now obvious. The French were disciplined, united and victorious. Impressed by their successes, the Indian tribes were increasingly ready to support them. The British meanwhile did little save quarrel. Only the undaunted Dinwiddie showered letters among neighbouring Governors, urged on his own Assembly, and by his mere energy became, without any commission from the Crown, something like commander-in-chief of the reluctant colonial defence. Meanwhile the British government had resolved to act; only, since it was the government of Newcastle and Pelham, it could be relied upon to act on insufficient information and with insufficient force. By the odd convention of these times—in which official persons usually cared little for the imperial contest—war confined to the colonies was not war, even when waged by troops from the home countries, and in November, 1754, the King's Speech at the opening of Parliament congratulated Lords and Commons on the prevalence of peace, although at that moment a thousand men were preparing to embark for Virginia. For their commander the government had selected General Edward Braddock, a courageous, honest and not particularly intelligent officer who, according to Horace Walpole, had been "adored" when he commanded at Gibraltar, and might conceivably have distinguished himself in a European campaign, but in the backwoods of America would thoroughly deserve the verdict of his secretary, a son of Governor Shirley, that he was "most judiciously chosen for being disqualified for the service he is employed in, in almost every respect." And since his best chance of success would have been to rouse the unstinted support of the reluctant and contentious colonists, the final condemnation of Newcastle's choice is conveyed in Benjamin Franklin's characteristic verdict that Braddock "had too mean an opinion of Americans and Indians." Perhaps even a Washington could not yet have roused the colonists to united and decisive action. Four hundred and fifty Virginians was the limit of the support which Braddock at any rate could elicit from the colonies which he had come to defend. The most that the Assembly of Pennsylvania could be persuaded to do was to vote twenty thousand pounds, subject to a special, and quite irrelevant, proviso that a minor domestic controversy at issue between itself and its governor should be determined in its favour. Braddock set out with a thousand British regulars and the four hundred and fifty Virginian militia-men, whom he characteristically proceeded to make "as much like soldiers as possible," and incidentally to disqualify for frontier warfare, by the traditional methods of the British barrack-square. He had refused the assistance of a party of colonial frontiersmen, long skilled in forest warfare, who painted themselves like the Indians against whom they had sworn a vendetta, and though he had had the perspicacity to appoint Washington one of his aide-de-camps he rarely accepted his advice.

Washington was often heard to say in later life that he had never seen a more magnificent spectacle than the British troops on the morning of the ninth of July, 1755. Every man was faultlessly attired in full uniform, the columns were perfectly aligned, the sun gleamed upon their highly polished arms. It was magnificent, no doubt, but unfortunately it was not war, not, at any rate, the right kind of war. The enemy did not, strictly speaking, ambush Braddock because the discipline of their Indian allies was not good enough for an ambush, but they attacked the head of his column suddenly, and well concealed behind trees and bushes. Such tactics had figured in none of Braddock's textbooks. Battles, he had been brought up to believe, were won by courage; to fire from behind a tree seemed to him cowardly in the extreme; and when his regulars showed signs of imitating the invisible enemy, and, for that matter, their own Virginian companions, and making some use of cover, Braddock drove them out into the open with the flat of his sword, and did his best to form them into parade ground platoons. It is hardly surprising that first confusion and then a complete rout ensued. Braddock, blindly courageous and hopelessly bewildered to the last, received a mortal wound. Washington was among the few officers who survived; but his experiences under Braddock may well have coloured all his subsequent career. He had lived at close quarters with a British general who manifestly despised colonials as inferiors, yet himself displayed the crassest and most obstinate ignorance of the very elements of colonial warfare. The final slaughter in the woods must have bitten deep into Washington's imagination, with Braddock as the symbol of an old world too arrogant and too dull to learn the needs or customs of the new. Washington had his full share of colonial sensitiveness—at the outset of Braddock's enterprise he had resigned because colonial officers were to rank junior to all those who held the king's commission, and he never forgot that a later British commander charged him, quite mistakenly, with unsoldierly conduct. These months may have helped to make any British government hereafter for him as arrogant and narrow as Braddock, and as little to be feared. But the immediate and visible consequence of Barddock's disaster was to open the frontiers of Virginia and Pennsylvania to the enemy. Redskins under French leaders poured over the mountains to burn and slay among the outlying settlements. Amidst the dangers from without and the lethargy and selfishness within, two men remained unweariedly active and steadily undismayed. Dinwiddie quickly roused his own Assembly to action, and sent another shower of notes, exhortations and remonstrances throughout the length and breadth of the neighbouring colonies. And Washington laboured on, amidst disaster and calumny, strenuous, patient and serene. He was now twenty-four, and a contemporary preacher spoke of him, with more prevision than he could know, as "that heroic youth whom I cannot but hope Providence has hitherto preserved in so signal a manner for some important service to his country."

§3

No ray of success lit the American scene in 1756. The Marquis de Montcalm, the new French commander, captured Fort Oswego; the new British commander, the Earl of Loudon, did nothing. Such in India, in America and at home, was the melancholy spectacle which confronted Pitt when he assumed office. It was the darkest hour of his country's fortunes. Yet within two years an unbroken tide of British victories was flowing in every continent. At the touch of the magician's wand the country was transformed into its earlier, its true, self. And yet Pitt used no magic. He could rouse the spirit and the moral energies of his fellow countrymen, instead of their appetites; he could plan victories and pick men of valour and vision to win them, that was all. That was all, but it was enough.

But victory did not come at once; how could it? The short-comings and the blindness of the past must be expiated first. Nations do not survive unless they are fit to survive, and unless there are still tasks which they are needed to perform. "May a degenerate people profit in the school of misfortune," Pitt himself had said. The British Empire has survived chiefly because not once nor twice only it has proved able to learn the lessons of adversity and fit itself through suffering for the tasks of a new age. Victory could not now be earned until the nation had recovered its true fibre, and deployed its full energies. Moreover the fields of battle were distant and communications precarious and slow, and time was needed before Pitt's plans and Pitt's spirit could reanimate the whole scene.

Pitt had taken office too late to make 1757 a year of victory, and it too ended, as it had opened, in gloom. The hopeful march of events in India was still unknown. February the eleventh was appointed by Royal Proclamation a General Fast, and on that day many sermons similar to that which Mr. Thomas Fothergill of Queen's College preached before the Mayor and Corporation of Oxford, bewailed our disasters, and acknowledged that every symp-tom seemed to point to imminent and final destruction. After referring to our defeats, our lack of allies and our vast national debt, Mr. Fothergill complained of faction in Parliament—"what betrays the strongest Symptoms of a State being devoted to Ruin; not even these Dangers are sufficient to unite our divided Councils"—and went on to catalogue the shortage of bread among the "numberless poor," and the virulent diseases which were destroying sheep and cattle alike:

> In Fine, there are few Calamities incident to a Nation, which our own at present does not in some Measure feel: so that many among us are ready to cry out with the Servants of *Pharaoh*, "Knowest Thou not yet that Egypt is destroyed?"

The only hope of deliverance for Britain, he insisted, as for Israel of old, was national repentance. Mr. Fothergill could have come to no sounder conclusion, though it is unlikely that he knew that Pitt too wholeheartedly shared his views, and was determined that the nation should learn those lessons of adversity without which it could not deserve victory. But no gleam of the coming triumphs lit the gloom of 1757. From India no word of Plassey had yet been received. And in America, while Pitt toiled at his plans for victory in 1758, all still went ill. The Earl of Loudon sailed to take Louisburg again, spent six weeks at Halifax, where he set his troops planting cabbages, found the French fleet at Louisburg stronger than he expected, and sailed back to New York. Meanwhile Montcalm ascended Lake Champlain and Lake George and captured Fort William Henry. The garrison marched out, to be escorted by the French to a place of safety; but Montcalm's Indians fell upon them, massacred about a hundred, and carried off six hundred captive. Montcalm and other French officers did all that was possible, short of using force, to hold back the savages. But force they did not dare to use, for to have used force would have spelled the end of their alliance with the Indians, and with the loss of the Indian alliance French Canada must have perished. Montcalm knew that he could not do without his Indians. Had he not been compelled to spend days sharing in their savage ceremonies, the monotonous war songs, the ritual boastings, so that it needed all his fortitude to conceal the terrible tedium in his heart? But Montcalm, though he was bitterly denounced by the British, was not the culprit; Montcalm at least risked his life to save the victims. It was the French in Canada who were to blame. For a century, to compensate for their own inferiority in numbers, they had deliberately encouraged and profited by Indian savagery. The massacre at Fort William Henry was but the culmination of decades of Indian atrocities. But it bit deeply into men's imaginations because this massacre, perpetrated despite the French commander's pledge, and in his presence, seemed at once the culmination and the symbol of four generations of the terror on the frontiers. Like so many of the atrocities perpetrated upon the British, before and since, it helped to defeat its own ends. For the British fight best when they are roused to anger. And after this, *Remember Fort William Henry* became the menacing war-cry of many a subsequent engagement, so that the first impulse of a captured Canadian was to explain, if he was able, that he at least had not been present at that unforgotten scene. And when the final victory had been won, the British, still embittered against all Canada, for once in a way were not disposed to compromise, and inflexibly demanded the expulsion of the French from the entire continent.

§4

For 1758 Pitt planned to pin the French down in Europe, by attacks, of the type we have lately learned to call commando raids, upon their coast, by a strict naval blockade, and by giving all the help possible to Frederic of Prussia, and to Hanover. With France thus fettered by our dispositions, and her own Austrian alliance, the real war, the American war, must be waged and won. It is unfortunate that a phrase of Pitt's about "conquering America on the plains of Germany," spoken on a later occasion and in a different context, should have been so long, and so well, remembered. For to conquer America upon the plains of Germany was precisely what Pitt did not propose to do. Through 1755 and 1756 he had steadily denounced the subsidies to princely German soldiers of fortune which were almost the sum total of George II's notion of waging war. Hanover, Pitt had urged, should be left for the time being to its fate; victory overseas, victory on the grand scale which he designed, would restore Hanover, and much else, when it came to making peace. But in 1758 he let British subsidies go to Germany, and British troops fight in Hanover under Ferdinand of Brunswick, because all this now helped to distract and deflect France from the main theatre of war, which was America. And there was light in Germany now. In November, after a number of disasters, Frederic had given the French under Soubise at Rossbach the soundest beating they had received since the days of Marlborough. At one stroke that forbidding Prussian sceptic had become the "Protestant Hero" of countless British toasts, inn-signs and perorations, and had confirmed Pitt's confidence in his new policy—subsidies and military aid for Prussia, and every ounce of Britain's available strength for the battlefields which would make or mar her overseas.

In 1758 the impact of Pitt's genius upon the war began to produce its effects. A new spirit, the old spirit, was abroad, and in the remotest skirmish men remembered the leader who was confident of victory, and who believed in taking risks. The design of holding France down in Europe, until the mortal strokes could be dealt in America, fell visibly and successfully into the great pattern. Pitt's commando raids on the French coast kept the enemy in constant uncertainty and alarm; they were costly, and not always successful—Horace Walpole spoke of breaking windows with guineas—but Pitt claimed that they kept many times their own number of the enemy off the hard-pressed Prussians in Germany. Above all, the British navy, which had quickly recovered its ancient spirit, blockaded the French ships which might have carried rein-forcements to America, or destroyed them if they contrived to sally forth. In the last resort the fate of Montcalm in Canada, of de Bussy and de Lally in India, would be sealed by the ships they never saw. Meanwhile the main British offensive was being launched against Canada, no longer, as under the Newcastle regime, a scrambling and haphazard affair mainly dependent upon colonial levies, but a triple attack, carefully timed and co-ordinated, prepared with all Pitt's tireless eye for detail, and entrusted to regular troops.

Ticonderoga was to be attacked by Abercromby, and Fort Duquesne by Forbes; and in February a powerful naval and military expedition under Boscawen and Amherst had sailed for Louisburg, carrying with it a gawky, serious young brigadier of thirty-one with red hair, a pale complexion and a somewhat receding chin. His health had never been good, and he invariably suffered agonies from sea-sickness, so that he did not look forward to the voyage; but he was on active service again, and he was well content. For James Wolfe not only came of an army family, but was passionately devoted to his profession. His father was a general, who had served in the wars of Marlborough, and again in the '45; his younger brother died on his first campaign. And when James was scarcely out of his nursery in the small Tudor house on the outskirts of Westerham in Kent, at the tender age of thirteen, and despite his mother's tears, he had actually contrived to get himself attached as a volunteer to the regiment of marines which his father was to command in the ill-starred expedition to Cartagena. Fortunately a childish malady prevented his embarking, and he was sent home, and thence packed off to school. But he was not baulked for long. At fifteen he received his commission in the 12th Foot, and at sixteen he served as adjutant on the field at Dettingen. In the '45 he was a brigade-major. After the peace of 1749 followed eight years without active service, during which Wolfe fell in love, sedulously studied his pro-fession and, while stationed in Glasgow, engaged two tutors to teach him Mathematics and revive his "almost lost Latin." Mathe-matics he did not care for, judging, perhaps rightly, that "they have a great tendency to make men dull"; but he thought that they were necessary to his profession and stuck to them grimly. He was too conscientious as well as too adventurous to care much for peace-time soldiering. This was a serious young man, though not too serious to learn dancing in Paris. And he had no illusions as to the short-comings of the army under the Newcastle regime, seeing there the exact counterpart of the defects with which the tradition of Walpole had infected the civil population. "We are lazy in times of peace," he wrote, after hearing of Braddock's disaster, "and of course want vigilance and activity in war. Our military education is by far the worst in Europe, and all our concerns are treated with contempt or totally neglected. It will cost us very dear some time hence."

In 1758 Wolfe was thirty-one. His health was poor—he refers to his "meagre, consumptive, decaying figure"—but he was an ardent soldier, one of the comparatively few who studied his profession assiduously and constantly, and though he was somewhat too serious, too temperate and too outspoken to be popular with his contemporaries, he got on well with his superiors and was loved and trusted by his men in the Twentieth, which he had turned into one of the finest regiments in the army. In short he had every qualification for high command, except those which in his day had hitherto counted most, senility and friends at court. But Wolfe was almost the only man who came with credit out of an unsuccessful "commando" raid on Rochefort in 1757. Wolfe himself was in despair over our performance there. "Little practise in war," he wrote, in words which since his day have more than once again been true of Britain, "ease and convenience at home, great incomes and no wants, with no ambition to stir to action, are not the instruments to work a successful war withal; I see no prospect of better deeds." But tough old Admiral Hawke had noticed Wolfe's conduct at Rochefort and praised him to Anson at the Admiralty. And Pitt, always eager for youth and talent, and always starved of it, leaped at the news that there was another able young officer at his disposal. And so it came about that Wolfe's Christmas holiday, at Bath and Exeter, was cut short by the news that he was to be one of the three brigadiers in the attack on Louisburg.

§5

A million sterling had been spent on the fortifications of Louisburg since it was last restored to the French, and it was now strongly garrisoned both by land and sea. But the spirit of Pitt was abroad among the assailants from the moment when, at the beginning of June, Amherst with two of his brigadiers—one of them Wolfe, still suffering excruciatingly from sea-sickness—surveyed the coast through his glass from a rowing boat in a heavy sea, and saw that only three landing places were possible, even in calm weather, and that these were all heavily defended. It showed itself in the élan with which Wolfe's men, their frail boats climbing and dipping on the great Atlantic rollers, landed under heavy fire in Kensington

Cove and drove the enemy from their trenches with the bayonet. It showed itself, no less characteristically, in the detachment of picked marksmen whom Wolfe trained to skirmish, to make full use of cover and to wear a costume more suitable than parade-ground regimentals for the purpose. All of which would doubless have been accounted a disgrace to the army by the unfortunate Braddock, or by Newcastle's elderly generals. But Braddock was dead, and Newcastle's elderly generals were fortunately at home, and to the young brigadier it seemed the most homespun common sense to adapt his tactics to the nature of the ground. It is said that on seeing this unconventional light infantry a fellow-officer, who knew his classics, remarked to Wolfe that it reminded him of the Kardouchi spoken of by Herodotus. "That is exactly where I got the idea," replied Wolfe; "only these people never read anything. . . ."

Before the end of July the much battered Louisburg had unconditionally surrendered. The British government, and not colonists or Company, had at last struck a telling blow in the colonial conflict. The French fleet was destroyed, and with it the French navy disappeared from the North Atlantic. And, since Halifax, with an even better harbour, lay so near, the British Government decided that Louisburg should be no more. In 1760 a motley crowd of workmen and soldiers toiled for six months to wipe the fortress city from the map. And soon the only traces of the Dunkirk of America, which for a century and a half had been among the most famous cities in the world, were the green moulds which hid the ruins of its bastions, and the faint lines marking what once were busy streets, where now the sea birds cried and swooped over the lonely, surf-beaten shore.

Meanwhile Forbes had found Fort Duquesne burnt and empty; its garrison had retreated on Canada; already the French had abandoned the Ohio, the much disputed region in which the world conflict had begun. Abercromby, however, had been less successful. At Ticonderoga he was terribly repulsed, after a succession of hopeless, heroic frontal assaults on Montcalm's *chevaux de frise* of fallen trees. A battery would have blown away the French defences in an hour, but Abercromby had left his guns behind him. He could have starved the enemy into surrender without firing a shot. But Abercromby belonged to the old school, like Braddock. He preferred to send his men in with the bayonet, and the invisible, unreachable enemy shot them down in swathes. The Black Watch, one of Pitt's first Highland regiments, performed prodigies of useless valour, and lost five hundred and one out of its thousand men. No Tennyson commemorated "the attack of the Retrenchment of Ticonderoga," as the memorial tablets have it on cathedral walls, and it has been almost forgotten. But it was a bloodier, a braver, and a stupider business even than the charge of the Light Brigade. And the fall of Canada was postponed for another year.

§6

1759 was to be the *annus mirabilis* of triumph, the year of crowning mercies when, as Horace Walpole said, "our bells are worn threadbare with ringing for victories." Already, before it opened, Pitt had begun to sow the seeds of victory elsewhere than in India and America, in Germany and the home waters. Now that the fall of Louisburg had reasonably assured the eventual conquest of Canada, he had allowed himself to look further afield, on the whole great Atlantic quadrilateral of trade and Empire. In 1758 he had sent a small expedition against the French slaving settlements in West Africa. In November, by which time it had taken Fort Louis on the Senegal, Pitt was able to spare it Admiral Keppel with five ships of the line, and the year of victories was inaugurated by the news, which reached England early in the new year, that Keppel had taken Goree, the other slaving centre, on December 29, and that with it the whole French slave trade, so integral to the sugar plantations of the West Indies, had collapsed. Six weeks later came word that Hopson had landed on Guadeloupe. Pitt was not one of those who believed that the West Indian sugar islands were the supreme colonial prize, but he was anxious for a conquest which could conveniently be exchanged for Minorca at the peace settlement. On June 13 London knew that Guadeloupe was captured, and on August 5 that Marie Galante, an island to the south of it, had fallen. Next day all thought of the conquest, however lucrative, of Caribbean islands was swept from men's minds by the intoxicating news of Minden, where six British battalions had borne the brunt of the fighting in Ferdinand of Brunswick's brilliant victory over the French. Every house in London, it was said, was illuminated, and there were two bonfires in every street. Even Frederic's disastrous defeat at Kunersdorff on August 12 did not seriously damp the public ardour. For men knew now that, thanks to Pitt, the long tide of disaster had turned, and that, thanks to Pitt, they were capable of anything. Even the menace of a French invasion—with a fleet of the flat-bottomed boats which so often since have vainly threatened England—did not seriously perturb them now. Newcastle, it is true, was scared and did what he could to scare his friends, but Pitt trusted his Navy and his Militia and declined to divert a single man from his offensives overseas. And in this same August Boscawen chased and caught a French squadron which had slipped out of Toulon, past Gibraltar, and destroyed it in Lagos Bay.

On September 8 news of the American victories began to come in, the capture of Niagara, the fall of Ticonderoga and Crown Point, as Amherst struck from Lake Champlain towards the St. Lawrence and Montreal. This was one of the two main thrusts against Canada which Pitt had devised for 1759. But Amherst was not on the St. Lawrence yet, and of the other stroke the packet brought no news at all. And on the fortunes of that other venture Pitt hung even more anxiously. He had sent a combined expedition, under Admiral Saunders and young James Wolfe, for a direct assault upon Quebec. Wolfe had gone with local rank as major-general for the campaign only. A temporary major-general of thirty-two was portent enough; for Pitt to have given him permanent rank would have seemed to Newcastle an assault on the British constitution itself. The last news from the expedition had reported it off Cape Breton Island on June 6. Pitt had to wait till October 14 for more, and then Wolfe's dispatches, written on September 2 and 5, brought cold comfort. Superlative seamanship had brought them safely to Quebec, through tortuous channels where the experienced French pilots rarely ventured; "the enemy," reported the Frenchman de Vaudreuil, "have passed sixty ships of war where we dare not risk a vessel of a hundred tons by night or day." But Montcalm, who knew that there would be no reinforcements from France, believed that he had made Quebec impregnable. When the British disembarked on the Isle of Orleans on June 27, they beheld four miles to the west across the sunny water a city strangely and symbolically different from the great trading centres of brick and wood with which they had filled their own colonies, a city whose tiers of spire and belfry, battery and barrack proclaimed it at once for what it was, the capital of a country of soldiers and priests. With fourteen thousand men in his inaccessible Beauport lines along the high six-mile ridge to the east of the city Montcalm barred all direct access to it. Wolfe could bombard the city when he had taken Point Lévis to its south, and he could rake Montcalm's left when he had seized the far side of the Montmorency gorge to the east. But he could not reach the Beauport lines, and there was no way round them. Montcalm would not stir, and time was running short, for Wolfe's army would have to embark for home before the Canadian winter fell.

Canadian and New England woodrangers skirmished and scalped each other with hereditary ferocity; the guns from Point Lévis made

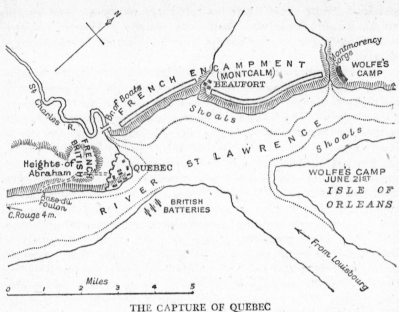

THE CAPTURE OF QUEBEC

a heap of ruins of lower Quebec; and a frontal attack on the steep hill which formed Montcalm's left, delivered suddenly and contrary to all orders by the rank and file of the Grenadiers and Royal Americans, was a costly failure. But still time passed, and still Montcalm did not move. And at home in the coffee-houses sage heads were shaken and it was common talk that Mr. Pitt's young general was a failure. Wolfe's feeble constitution began to flag under anxiety and toil. "Don't talk to me of constitution," he had said, "spirit will carry a man through anything," but on August 20 he lay helpless with fever, and full of black despair. By the 25th, "to the inconceivable joy of the whole army," he was pronounced out of danger. On September 1 he was up, his head full of his last desperate plan. For the next few days a series of sudden bombardments, and feints by troop-laden boats and warships, kept the French constantly on the alert, but completely mystified. On the 5th Wolfe was prostrate again with fever, aggravated by his chronic rheumatism and gravel, but he besought the doctor to "patch him up sufficiently for the work in hand; after that nothing mattered," and on the 6th he had struggled up again. With the fleet and some 3600 men he moved up eight miles west of the city, to Cap Rouge, where for the first time the high cliff barrier dipped, and Bougainville stood on guard. Meanwhile, the screen of general activity down stream convinced Montcalm that a general assault was imminent where the River Charles flows into the St. Lawrence under the city walls. But Wolfe and his brigadiers were carefully surveying that sheer line of cliffs to the west of Quebec, which Montcalm had confidently declared that a hundred men could hold against the whole British army. Beneath one of the small posts on the summit, a mile and a half west of the city, Wolfe perceived traces of a zigzag path up the bush-studded cliff face. Here, at the Anse du Foulon, he secretly determined to make his assault. Here, while the French either massed much further to the west, or lay in the Beauport line to the east, the high ground just above the city was practically undefended. On the night of September 12, while Bougainville anxiously guarded the cliffs well to the west, and Montcalm hourly expected the apparently imminent assault upon his Beauport lines to the east, sixteen hundred of Wolfe's men at Cap Rouge dropped quietly into their boats and with muffled oars rowed and drifted down towards the Anse du Foulon under the shelter of the high north bank. It was, as Wolfe said himself, a desperate plan, requiring both fine seamanship and good fortune if there was to be even a chance of success. There were two French posts to be passed, and from one of them they were challenged, and a Highland officer replied in French that this was a convoy of provisions. A good many recent authorities have discredited the famous story that as they moved stealthily downstream Wolfe murmured passages from Gray's *Elegy in a Country Churchyard*, and remarked, "I would rather have been the author of that piece than beat the French to-morrow." That he recited the Elegy at some time on September 12 is, however, generally agreed, and on the whole the evidence,[1] I think, is in favour of the traditional version. In any event Wolfe's copy of the *Elegy*, liberally underscored, and with his autograph comments in the margin, still exists to prove his devotion to the poet. Young Captain Howe, brother of the much loved Lord Howe who fell at Ticonderoga, was to lead the ascent up the path with a handful of picked men. The troops followed so eagerly that they left the path and hauled themselves up somehow by the overhanging bushes all along the cliff face. As the first streaks of dawn showed in the east they reached the summit and overpowered the astonished French picket. Beneath them in the half-light Wolfe's men were swarming up the cliffs. It was not till six in the morning that Montcalm, east of Quebec, received the shocking news that the British army

[1] The evidence for the story, which ultimately depends on the authority of John Robison, subsequently Professor of Natural Philosophy at Edinburgh, is clearly summarised in an appendix to W. T. Waugh's *Wolfe* [New York, 1928]. See also English Historical Review XV. [1900].

was on the plateau to the west. By that time Wolfe, whose tactical arrangements had been flawless, was moving on the city. He encountered Montcalm on the Heights of Abraham. The French colonials, who made about half of Montcalm's army, were admirable behind cover or in the forest skirmish, but in the open they were no match for the discipline of British regulars, who awaited their straggling advance in complete silence and barrack square alignment. At forty paces the British fired, so perfectly that the volleys from the six battalions sounded like six reports from one gigantic gun. They advanced twenty paces and fired again. One more volley, and a charge, and the French army was a flying mob, among which groups of white-coated regulars stood their ground to offer a brief but hopeless resistance. Wolfe, who had put on a conspicuous new uniform for the occasion, had been hit on the wrist, and then in the groin, but scarcely seemed to feel his wounds. "His countenance," said one who was there, was "radiant and joyful beyond description." It seems to have been just after the British had fired their first volley that he was wounded in the right breast. He was carried about three hundred yards to the rear, and laid on the ground. He had fallen into a coma when a soldier nearby cried out, "They run!" As if waking from sleep, Wolfe stirred and asked, "Who runs?" On being assured that it was the enemy, he summoned all his energies and said, "Go, one of you, to Colonel Burton; tell him to march Webb's regiment to the Charles River, to cut off the retreat to the bridge." Then, turning on his side with a sigh, as if to sleep again, he murmured, "Now I die content," and so passed away—"in the moment," as Pitt said afterwards, "when his fame began."

§7

News of the victory reached England on October 16, hot on the heels of Wolfe's last gloomy dispatch. Not even Pitt could then estimate the vast influence on the future of mankind of the brief episode on the Heights of Abraham, but all men knew that this was victory, and victory in its most stirring guise. Once more there were bells and bonfires everywhere, save in Westerham, where Wolfe was born, and Blackheath, where his widowed mother mourned in a darkened house. Wolfe was voted the thanks of Parliament and a monument in the Abbey, but the government characteristically declined to spend the trifling sum needed to enable his executors to fulfil the terms of his will, and the last years of his mother were embittered by a dispute over the pay said to be still owing at his death.

Canada was not yet conquered, for Amherst had failed to reach the St. Lawrence—he was a thorough, but not a dashing, soldier, and the southern colonies, freed from the menace of French and Indians, displayed neither gratitude nor energy, reverting thankfully to the accustomed routine of tobacco-planting and wrangles with their Governors. Canada was not yet conquered, but it was manifestly doomed.

Before October ended came news of the astonishing victories of Clive and Forde in India. And in November the Comte de Conflans brought out his fleet from Brest and was chased by Hawke into Quiberon Bay. Here he counted on shaking off the pursuit, for a gale was blowing, the bay with its rocks and shoals was notoriously dangerous, and to enter it in a storm seemed foolhardy enough, and to fight a naval action in it unthinkable. But Hawke was weary of the long blockade of an enemy he never saw, and was determined to destroy the French fleet at any risk. And so he followed Conflans into the bay, and soon the thunder of the guns was added to the thunder of the storm and of the surf upon the rocks. And while, if he had known it, at home Hawke was being burnt in effigy for his supposed inaction, he took and destroyed six of the French fleet while four others were so damaged that they never put to sea again. The battle, a signal feat of skill and daring, was the Trafalgar of the Seven Years' War, the *coup de grace* to Choiseul's invasion plans, and the end of French naval power for a generation. It brought the year of victories to a fitting close. The war was but half over, but what followed was in a sense an epilogue. Thanks to the genius of Pitt, and the spirit which he had roused in the nation, total victory was now in sight. Britain had learned the lessons of misfortune.

CHAPTER FOUR

THE INSTINCT OF MODERATION

(1760-1763)

§1

ALTHOUGH the second half of the Seven Years' War was in a sense
an epilogue to the *annus mirabilis*, it was not lacking in great events.
In Canada indeed one moment of peril remained to be surmounted.
By April of 1760 the troops left to garrison Quebec, under General
Murray, had been reduced by scurvy and starvation from seven
thousand to three thousand men. The French marched upon them
from Montreal with an army of eight thousand; and when the
British, who could dig no trenches in the frozen ground, came out,
somewhat foolhardily, from the shelter of the city to meet them,
they lost a third of their little force, and had to retire within the
broken walls to stand a siege . All now hung upon the Navies of the
two countries. If the first ships up the river, when the ice melted,
proved to be British, the French would be doomed; if they should
be French, Wolfe's work would have to be done again. On May 9
a warship hove in sight, and there was a horrid moment of suspense.
Then her colours ran up, and they were British. Once again sea-
power had triumphed. The garrison mounted the parapets, in full
view of the enemy, and cheered itself hoarse for an hour. Soon the
disconsolate French were hastening back to Montreal, and there,
with the converging of Murray from Quebec, Amherst from Oswego
and Haviland from Lake Champlain, the long-drawn drama ended.
On September 8, 1760, the last French Governor of Canada surrendered
unconditionally—Amherst remembered the Indian atrocities and
refused to allow him the honours of war—and all Canada passed to
the British Crown. The future of North America was to be freedom,
not despotism.

§2

With the fall of Canada, Pitt was able in 1761 to reinforce
Ferdinand in Germany and, with the most successful of his "commando" raids, to capture Belleisle near the mouth of the Loire.

Dominica, too, in the West Indies was taken, to be followed next year by Martinique, and, after that, by St. Lucia, Grenada and St. Vincent. But George II had died in October, 1760, and with the accession of George III, who came before long to regard the great minister as "a trumpet of sedition," began a series of events which was to thrust Pitt from power. For beneath all the diplomatic haggling with Choiseul, the great French minister, and all the domestic political intrigues, the core of the complicated transactions which followed was the conflict between Pitt and the majority of his colleagues as to the nature of the coming peace. The new king and his Scots tutor Lord Bute, and not a few members of Pitt's own Cabinet, were more than ready to see him fall, but none would have ventured to oppose him openly but for the irreconcilable differences which opened between them as the tentative peace negotiations proceeded in 1761. And, curiously enough, it was the lesser men who were right. For now, as so often before and since, the very virtues of a great war minister, or perhaps the triumphant exercise of them, seemed to render him incapable of judging rightly the necessities of the post-war age. At this moment Pitt stood upon the pinnacle of his fame. His situation, says Macaulay, "was the most enviable ever occupied by any public man in English history. . . . He was the first Englishman of his time; and he had made England the first country in the world." Both for the statesman and for the nation such a moment is always perilous. Many men, and not a few peoples, have been ruined because the world was at their feet, and they chose wrongly. Pitt possessed great abilities and had used them greatly, and measured by his heroic scale his colleagues are apt to show as timid or time-serving mediocrities. Nevertheless, despite Carlyle, it is not always the hero who is right. Pitt's colleagues were average Englishmen, and if the average man did not sometimes see more clearly than either hero or philosopher there could have been no democracy. It is well that at this pregnant moment this handful of Whig noblemen should have defied the imperious minister who had so long overawed them, for the problem which they now faced reached to the very foundations of morals and politics, and their answer to it saved their country from the course by which sooner or later every Empire in the past had been destroyed.

For Britain in 1761 was all-powerful. Thanks to her paramount naval power, every overseas settlement and the commerce of every ocean lay within her grasp. No other nation could rely upon reaching what colonies it still retained. No other nation could retain a colony save by the favour of Britain. Had George II died a little later, had Pitt kept his health and his influence with Crown and Parliament

a few years longer, he might well have stripped France, Spain and
Holland of every inch of territory outside Europe. And when
Choiseul opened negotiations in 1761 it became evident that Pitt
was bent upon a peace which would leave France permanently
powerless at sea, and Britain in control of every ocean. This, it
seemed to him, was the logic of his conquests—the final crippling
of the hereditary rival. His resignation, on October 5, 1761, came
ostensibly because, now that Bourbon Spain had signed its third
Family Compact with Bourbon France in August, and was manifestly preparing to attack Britain, he was for an instant declaration
of war—and, as Pitt said, "the Council trembled." Here Pitt was
probably right; but comparatively this business of declaring war
on Spain was a trivial matter; indeed war with Spain duly opened
on Spain's initiative early in 1762. The gulf which finally sundered
Pitt from his colleagues was the nature of the terms to France.

There were men in the cabinet, and outside it, who stood aghast
at the unchallengeable ascendancy which their country had now
achieved, and trembled to think that Pitt might perpetuate it. The
most explicit spokesman of this instinctive recoil from the sudden
vision of world supremacy was the Duke of Bedford. Bedford had
lately come into conflict with Pitt as an unsuccessful Lord Lieutenant
of Ireland, and there were personal grounds for his opposition in the
cabinet. But he had deeper and sounder motives than these. It has
been one of the virtues of the British aristocracy that at crucial
moments there has always been some member of it to voice the
sentiment latent among the unvocal masses, and the Radical strain
hereditary in the house of Russell was strong in the fourth Duke.
He was a passionate, eccentric man, quite unfitted for administration
or diplomacy, but he possessed energy and eloquence, and a certain
native shrewdness and integrity, reinforced by all the natural
independence of a great nobleman. In part the demand for moderation of which Bedford became the spokesman represented no more
than the instinct of Polycrates in the myth, who desired to sacrifice
some treasured possession lest excessive prosperity be visited by
Nemesis in the years to come. But, more than this, Bedford and his
friends did not believe that France could be kept permanently in
subjection, taking the view, more familiar to our own day, that, if
excessively humiliated, a vigorous people will always reassert itself
and seek revenge. And, looking deeper still, he could appeal to history
and to morals against the prospect of such universal predominance
of one power. And here, there can be no doubt, he voiced not only
his own instinct, but the national tradition. "The endeavouring to
drive France out of any naval power," he wrote to Bute on July 9,

is fighting against nature, and can tend to do no good to this country; but, on the contrary, must excite all the naval powers of Europe against us, as adopting a system, viz.: that of a monopoly of all naval power which would be at least as dangerous to the liberties of Europe as that of Louis XIV was, which drew all Europe upon his back.

When he argued that British naval predominance would be as dangerous to the liberties of Europe, such as they were, as the military despotism of the Grand Monarch, Bedford overstated his case; yet fundamentally the historical argument here was unanswerable. It was not for the power which had saved Europe from the dictatorship of Louis XIV—and would save it from the dictatorship of Napoleon and of Germany—to set up even the semblance of a dictatorship itself.

As an opponent of annexation Bedford went further than his colleagues; he would have handed back Canada to the French. The project was chimerical; neither the American colonies nor the British public would have tolerated it; yet there is a genuine prophetic insight in his argument:

> . . . the neighbourhood of the French to our North American colonies was . . . the greatest security for their dependence on the mother country, which I feel will be slighted by them when their apprehension of the French is removed.

Bedford was even prepared to argue on grounds of abstract morality: "to do as we would be done by is the most golden rule as well in what relates to the public as private life." His colleagues in the cabinet, who carried their point against the all-powerful Pitt, would hardly have claimed to be acting upon such high principles as these. Yet, just as Bedford can be recognised as a forerunner of the Radical tradition in British foreign policy, so these Whig noblemen, recoiling partly from undue harshness to a defeated rival, but even more perhaps from the prospect of unchallengeable imperial supremacy, stood for that principle of tolerance and moderation which, as much as anything else, would preserve the Empire in the years to come. It was the tradition of compromise, of pushing no principle to extremes, already long familiar in domestic affairs, extended, at this critical moment, to foreign policy. This after all is that moderation which for the Greeks was the cardinal virtue, so that their tragedy is for the most part a study of the penalties which await the overweening. Power corrupts, and absolute power corrupts absolutely. And in our own day we have known a war which may even have been lost because the ruthless pronouncement that the vanquished must disappear from history so vastly intensified the world-wide resistance to Germany. It is not merely that to tower too high for rivalry breeds hatreds which cannot be allayed. An Empire which has ceased to fear rivals is doomed; for it soon forgets the virtues by which it rose. The men who now insisted that Britain should not leave herself without rivals did more for her than they knew, for they were laying the cornerstone of a system which, whatever its faults, would not be intolerant or exclusive, and would survive because it never grasped too much.

§3

The core of the difference between Pitt and his colleagues was the Newfoundland fisheries. Determined that France should never again challenge British naval power, he was resolved not to restore to her any share in that famous training-ground of mariners. Reluctantly they yielded to his imperious insistence. But when he demanded a declaration of war on Spain they would not yield. This, though it was the occasion of Pitt's going, was a trivial matter in comparison with the nature of the coming peace. For Spain herself declared war early in 1762, and while Bute's ministry resumed negotiations with France it found itself, somewhat to its own surprise, continuing to win victories in the manner of Pitt, with the instruments which Pitt had bequeathed to it. Spanish possessions began to fall like overripe fruit. Havana, the capital of Cuba, famous and formidable since the days of Drake, surrendered, with a fifth of the Spanish navy, in August, and Manila, the capital of the Philippines, in October. And meanwhile Bute hurried on his peace, and Bedford was sent to Paris to settle the final details. It was to be pre-eminently a peace of restitutions, and there were even serious discussions as to "whether Guadeloupe was more important than Canada." Some of the proposed terms had leaked out; British conquests, it was known, were being surrendered, and Frederic of Prussia was to be betrayed. Half Britain was seething with indignation ; and at the Guildford Assize dinner the Sheriff and guests declined to drink Bute's health when it was proposed by the Treasury Solicitor. Not even Bute and Bedford, however, could deprive Britain of great acquisitions. The definitive Treaty of Paris was signed on February 10, 1763. France withdrew finally from America. This was the grand achievement of the Seven Years' War. Britain received all Canada, Nova Scotia and Cape Breton Island; Louisiana France ceded to Spain in compensation for Spanish losses elsewhere:

only their fishing rights in Newfoundland and the Gulf of St. Lawrence, and two small island fishing-stations were restored to the French. In the West Indies Britain retained Grenada, St. Vincent, Dominica and Tobago, and in Africa, Senegal. The other conquests in the West Indies, and Goree in Africa, were restored. In Europe Belleisle was handed back to France, and Minorca to Britain; and all French conquests in Hanover, Hesse and Brunswick were evacuated and restored. From Spain Britain received Florida, which lies between South Carolina and Louisiana. In India the captured French trading-stations were returned, but they were returned unfortified, and without the hinterlands on which their trade depended. And so, though Bute may have supposed that he was making substantial restitution, Clive's victories remained decisive. The European empire, which had become inevitable in India, would be British, for it could not now be French.

Manifestly these were very great results. The peace may be said to have been a gamble on the loyalty of America, but it was manifestly a triumphant peace. After despotic Spain, despotic France. This time it was the French who had challenged Britain in the new West and in the ancient East, both of which the oceanic age had laid open to Europe, and in both of which in the long run sea-power must prove decisive. And France, who would have brought despotism to each, had been expelled from both America and India. In the West Indies too Britain had notably extended her hold. On all the oceans her fleets were supreme. Bute's hurried scramble for peace, it is true, had not been of the most dignified, and in his haste he had abandoned Frederic of Prussia to his fate, an act of treachery which Europe, and in particular Germany, remembered for more than a century. Nevertheless Britain was admired and envied all over the world. Her prestige was as pre-eminent as her power. Few in this golden hour can have guessed—what both Pitt and Bedford, for different reasons, had foreseen and feared—that within twenty years the Empire as they knew it would have received its death-blow.

Pitt had believed that for a nation which had climbed so far to world ascendancy to hesitate at the final step was fatal; Britain must put it for ever out of the power of a people whom she had deprived of so much to fight a war of revenge on the high seas. Bedford on the other hand had desired to shield Britain from a war of revenge not by leaving France powerless but by treating her generously. The Treaty of Paris did not altogether satisfy either; it neither weakened France sufficiently to please Pitt, nor conciliated her enough for Bedford. Yet perhaps, in the nature of things, neither Pitt's peace nor Bedford's could have achieved the objects which each had in view. For the future good of the Empire and the world Bedford's doubtless was the sounder policy. But the great events which were about to unfold in the immediate future cannot be held to have wholly proved either Pitt or Bedford wrong. For the Empire as they knew it would be destroyed not in the last resort because France had been rendered too weak, nor yet because she had been left too strong, but because British colonists and British statesmen were selfish and obtuse. No empire can survive that is not for ever learning, and for the most part from its own mistakes. The British Empire was about to be presented with an opportunity of learning upon the vastest of scales, so vast that at length the choice would be no less than between extinction and world leadership in a wholly new form.

Neither Pitt's policy perhaps nor Bedford's could have spared Britain this dilemma. For in the last resort all hung upon the qualities of the nation. It had possessed the energy and the valour to survive the ordeal of war; did it possess the wisdom and the self-restraint to survive the even more searching ordeal which now awaited it? One who cast an appraising eye over British society in that moment of time, might well have doubted its fitness for any high and enduring destiny. He would see Johnson in his garret and the nabobs in their mansions, the time-serving bishops and the heartless great ladies, the coffee houses, the gaming-tables, the cockpits and the press-gangs, a thousand aspects of a highly coloured, full-blooded and little-disciplined society full of zest and energy and appetite, but seldom able to see beneath the surface glitter or beyond the immediate advantage; a society, in short, still better fitted to conquer than to lead. For Britain had yet to learn the final lessons of the school of adversity, and be touched to finer issues by Wesley and Wilberforce before she was ready to fulfil her destiny.

BOOKS FOR FURTHER READING.

Basil Williams, *The Life of William Pitt, Earl of Chatham;* Brian Tunstall, *William Pitt, Earl of Chatham;* Frederick Harrison, *Chatham* (*American Historical Review,* vol. xlviii); Lord Macaulay, *Essays* (on *Clive* and *Chatham*); Beckles Wilson, *Ledger and Sword;* Sir Alfred Lyall, *British Dominion in India;* Edward Thompson and G. T. Garratt, *The rise and fulfilment of British rule in India;* Sir A. J. Arbuthnot, *Clive;* John C. Fitzpatrick, *George Washington himself;** Jared Sparks, *The life of George Washington . . . his diaries and speeches;* A. G. Bradley, *The fight with France for North America;* J. A. Doyle, *The colonies under the House of Hanover;* W. T. Waugh, *James Wolfe, man and soldier.**
* Published in America.

Book V

TIME OF TESTING

CHAPTER ONE

THE QUARREL WITH AMERICA
(1763-1775)

§1

DESPITE her victories, Britain had not yet earned a great imperial rôle. She was now to be subjected to a twofold ordeal, both in the West and in the East, a test of her fitness to survive more searching even than that of the Seven Years' War, since this time she would be required to conquer not so much her enemies as herself. Both in America and in India Britain stood at one of those moral turning points of history which are more decisive than any battle. In both the essential issue was the same. Could Britain learn to exercise power in the interests of those over whom she ruled? In the East, after a convulsive struggle and a public debate on profound ethical issues which divided and enthralled her for a decade, she would emerge triumphant. The moral foundations of dominion over dependent races would be laid. Not only would Britain earn survival for herself, but before long, through her, man would take a long step forward in his slow political ascent. In the West she would fail. The wisdom, the moral restraint needful was not in her. And yet here too in due time she would wrest triumph from defeat. For, unlike the Empires of the past, she would learn the lessons of failure and in the years to come build up a new and enduring world society upon the principles which, had she only known it, would have saved her now. And so because Britain failed in part, but did not wholly fail, the outcome of her ordeal would be that although the old Empire would perish, a new Empire would be born, and within it the living germs of the Commonwealth to be.

Although this twofold ordeal ended in the clash of arms, the new world war was but an epilogue to the true struggle, registering the previous success of the British, and their failure, on the moral plane. The French, whose vengeance Pitt and Bedford had so dreaded, proved to be but minor actors in the closing scenes of the great drama, lending their aid in that secondary and material conflict whose issue was already predetermined. Their role was vengeance, not creation. No French Empire grew from their intervention in the Anglo-Saxon dispute, for despite all their military and intellectual gifts, they were not an imperial people.

§2

In the West the ordeal would be more intricate and more searching. The same lesson was to be learnt, but it would be harder to learn it. And the melancholy and menacing panorama which would present itself to British citizens in 1778 would be far more directly of course the outcome of the schism with the New World. The nature of that schism, whose complexities at the best of times are difficult enough to unravel clearly, has been partly obscured by the fashion, so long current among British historians, of treating British history as primarily the history of our own Parliament and our own politicians. To them the dispute with the American colonies which flared up so suddenly in the early years of George III naturally appeared as a series of political blunders by the King and Lord North and their Tory claque. And so they could hardly help overrating the relative importance of the final controversy, and the protagonists in it, and usually overlooked the extent to which the whole dilemma was an inevitable outcome of the very nature of the Empire of that day, and our failure to solve it a judgment upon certain long-standing defects in the British on both sides of the Atlantic. A century of Whig historians have enshrined in a hundred text-books the luminous but misleading phrases in which the great Whig orator Burke idealised the relations of Britain with her colonies before the accession of George III, and under the rule of the Whigs. But in fact the colonial policy of the Whigs was no more enlightened than that of the Tories, and from the first there had been in the fabric of the old Empire elements making for an eventual rupture, which only a supreme exercise of self-restraint and foresight could now have averted. As long as to Britain the Empire could mean primarily her rights against the colonists, it was doomed, and its dissolution but a question of time. Only if the British learned to see their Empire primarily as an obligation to the world could it endure. Such a moment of vision had come, and passed, with Cromwell; there could be no hope of it under Walpole, or the tradition of Walpole. And so, from the first there had been men who saw the Empire clearly for what it was, and could not see it as it might be, who had prophesied disruption. In Cromwell's day Harrington in his *Oceana* had foreseen separation as soon as the colonies outgrew their infancy, and this forecast, or foreboding, had been repeated by discerning, but not sufficiently discerning, observers at regular intervals ever since. Indeed the French statesman Vergennes had confidently anticipated it as a consequence, of the British conquest of Canada. These tendencies might perhaps have been reversed; indeed the Dominion of New England projected by James II was a step towards one possible solution. But the most promising opportunity for revision was altogether neglected by William III and the authors of the Glorious Revolution, who thought too much of their advantage and too little of their obligations. And even during the crisis of the dispute under George III, it occurred to nobody, not even to Chatham or to Burke, that the whole current conception of colonies, that ideal of a self-sufficient Empire regulated by the mother country, which we know as the Old Colonial System, might need to be abandoned. To have perceived this would have required a moral strength which Britain did not yet possess. This is not to say that separation was inevitable when once the treaty of 1763 had permanently disposed of the French menace to the colonies; indeed then, and for some years longer, there were still good grounds for the reassuring words of that clear-sighted observer Benjamin Franklin, at this time agent of Pennsylvania in London. If the colonies could not agree, he wrote,

> to unite against the French and Indians, who were perpetually harassing their settlements, burning their villages, and murdering their people, can it reasonably be supposed that there is any danger of their uniting against their own nation . . . with which they have so many connexions, and ties of blood, intercourse and affections, and which it is well known they all love much more than they love one another.

" The seeds of liberty," Franklin observed: are universally found there, and nothing can eradicate them. And yet, there remains among the people so much respect, veneration, and affection for Britain that, if cultivated prudently, they might be easily governed still for ages without force or even considerable expense.

The seeds of liberty had indeed been sown in American soil and by the earliest settlers, and they were bound to ripen. Yet liberty was not incompatible with union, if Britain could perceive her duties as well as her rights. But the conquest of Canada had removed the most powerful of practical restraints upon the growth of separatism; and if the colonies were now indeed to be governed "for ages without force" not prudence only would be needed, but generosity, self-restraint and some prophetic glimpse, beyond the Empire, of that Commonwealth which waited in the womb of time. Vision, assuredly, was required, the kind of vision which is born of high moral qualities—and these the rule of Walpole had not been calculated to evoke. Chatham at least had vision, and perhaps if Chatham had retained his political authority, and his mental powers, he might have made of the spirit which he had evoked for the conquest of France the even finer spirit needed for the preservation of America. Certainly he was regarded in America with a veneration and affection felt for no other British statesman, and his papers prove that he had repeatedly meditated the imperial problem. But Chatham did not even retain his mental powers, and it is one of the tragic ironies of an era full of tragic ironies that Charles Townshend's clever, shortsighted American taxes, a long stride, as it proved, down the primrose path to open rupture, were imposed by a ministry of which Chatham was the nominal head, but at a time when Chatham himself remained inaccessible at North End, unwilling or unable to reply to the despairing appeals of his bewildered colleagues, and sitting silent hour after hour with his head in his hands in a profound stupor of melancholia.

§3

The main moral and political problem set to the British was certainly formidable, and their rulers had hardly prepared them for solving it. And the complicating factors were formidable too. For it has to be remembered that with the passage of time what had once been one nation divided by a seven weeks' tossing on the Atlantic was fast becoming two. America was far more equalitarian than Britain. It had its rich and poor, but there were far fewer extremes of opulence and penury. In America, wrote a French observer, "no useful profession is the subject of ridicule or contempt. Idleness alone is disgrace." Britain on the other hand was ruled by a small and cultured, but just now cynical and ostentatious, coterie, society was strictly hierarchic, and the lingering tradition of the age of Walpole, with the sudden relaxation, and the sudden wealth, which had followed the world victory of 1763, was coarsening all its upper strata. There was no leader to do for Britain in peace what Pitt had done for her in war, and evoke the spirit which might have surmounted the temptations of ease as it had surmounted those of war. The middle class, in which the English Puritan tradition was much stronger, and which would have been much better qualified to understand and sympathise with the simpler and more strenuous American scene, as yet exercised little influence in politics. But it is doubtful whether even a middle class administration would have been capable of the vision and altruism which Britain now needed. Certainly the polished and cynical aristocrats who ruled her could not rise to the formidable moral effort required of them. And in the eyes of the colonists Britain was represented by the gross, hard-headed, brilliant society which ruled her, wholly alien to the still Cromwellian standards and sympathies of the greater part of America, so that to all appearances at this moment of time the two branches of the British race were more unlike each other than they had ever been before, or perhaps would ever be again. The racial composition, too, of the Americans was changing fast. By now Dutch predominated in New York; there, as well as in Virginia and South Carolina, there were many Huguenots; and from 1709 for many years there had been something like a torrent of German immigrants. Although the German colonists showed themselves at this time on the whole not hostile to British claims, it is clear that the America of the close of the Seven Years' War was less likely even than the sensitive and cantankerous New England Puritans of the seventeenth century to allow national sentiment to offset what it conceived to be its political rights or its material interests.

Nevertheless sentiment there was in plenty in America to evoke in Britain, if Britain were wise, an answering generosity, perhaps even a glimpse of the closer, yet freer, unity which might one day be. Britain was still constantly spoken of in America as "home." "They may be looked on as foreigners," wrote Franklin of his fellow countrymen, "but they do not consider themselves as such." John Adams might declare that no relation for whom he cared a farthing had been in England for a hundred and fifty years, and that he himself was purely American, but the Americans who knew the mother country thought of it with admiration not untinged with envy. "Why should that pretty island," wrote Franklin,

which is but like a stepping-stone in a brook, scarce enough of it above water to keep one's shoes dry, enjoy in every neighbour-hood more sensible, virtuous and elegant minds than we can collect in ranging a hundred leagues of our vast forests?

But sentiments such as these, on which a wise government might even have built a bridge from Empire to Commonwealth, could hardly be expected to survive political humiliation or material loss. And long before 1763 the colonists had been only too conscious that in many respects the British colonial system had sacrificed their interests to those of the mother country. In the course of the controversy indeed most of them came to believe that they were systematically exploited by Britain, just as before long many of the British believed that all the colonists were ungrateful traitors. In fact, however, although most of the economic advantages of the old colonial system may have been enjoyed by the mother country by no means all of them were, and the fundamental failure of the British was that they lacked the magnanimity which would have sacrificed even unquestionable rights in the interests of closer union,

§4

The constantly avowed object of the old colonial system was clear-cut, intelligible and, within its narrow limits, reasonable—a self-sufficing Empire, whose supplies should not be dependent upon any foreign power. And by a self-sufficing Empire men understood a system in which the colonies produced the raw material and the mother country the manufactured goods. There was no inherent reason why such an ideal should have bred friction. It might indeed as naturally have led to some form of federal union, and the Commonwealth-to-be. All depended upon the spirit in which the economic adjustments which the system made inevitable were effected. Fundamentally, as always, it was a moral, rather than an economic, problem. For clearly self-sufficiency could not be achieved without some interference with the natural development of manufactures and the natural flow of trade, just that kind of interference in fact of which the nineteenth century apostles of *laissez faire* disapproved almost as strongly as they disapproved of the self-sufficiency which was its object. Much of the regulation of trade required for self-sufficiency told unmistakably against the interests of the colonist. Thus colonies were expected to produce raw materials, not finished goods, and a number of manufactures likely to compete with British industries had been suppressed altogether— wool and bar iron in 1719, felt hats in 1732, molasses in 1733 and steel furnaces in 1750. Such restrictions were certainly not what Adam Smith would characteristically call them, "a violation of the most sacred rights of mankind," for the most sacred rights of mankind are not economic; and, like all other legislation of this kind at this time, the prohibitive acts were far from effectively enforced. All the same, unless considered in relation to the advantages which offset them, they seemed unfair, and, what was worse, humiliating. Again, since 1651 the Navigation Acts had in effect restricted colonial trade to British ships, for colonial shipping was in its infancy, and could only carry about an eighth of the tobacco exported. In default of foreign competition the British shipowner could always charge exorbitant freights, and to the colonial exporter who paid them it was doubtless small consolation to reflect either that the Navigation Acts too were never completely enforced, or that their ultimate object had always been to foster the British Navy, on which the safety not only of the British Isles but of the colonies themselves ultimately depended. Again, the regulation that many "enumerated articles" might be exported to Europe only by way of Britain was often a serious handicap to colonial producers in competition with foreign rivals. It was for this reason, for example, that the British West Indians lost the Spanish markets to the French. Colonial importers too had reason to resent this restrictive policy. They are said to have paid twenty-five per cent more for the wine, oil and fruit which they bought, but might not ship direct, from Portugal and Spain.

All the same there was another aspect of all this. There were disadvantages for the colonies in the old colonial system, but there were corresponding, if not compensating, advantages. For it was implicit in the ideal of a self-sufficient Empire that Britain and her colonies were to be complementary to each other; and so if colonial manufactures were obstructed, colonial raw materials were deliberately and actively fostered. Thus large bounties were accorded, not only by the British Government but occasionally by a private "Society for the Encouragement of Arts and Commerce," to colonial commodities likely to make Britain independent of foreign countries. Tobacco, flax, raw silk, logwood, turpentine, pitch and tar, hemp and indigo and more than a dozen other colonial products were artificially assisted in this way. Special bounties, from the pocket of the British taxpayer, promoted the prosperity of the American timber trade, so essential to the British Navy, and travellers would remark on the flourishing saw mills round New York, or the fifty mills to be seen on one river in North Carolina alone. Moreover, if colonial industries were apt to be suppressed, so were British raw materials. Tobacco growing in the west of England, for example, was ruthlessly extinguished. Nor, as Benjamin Franklin himself admitted, was the Navigation Act itself without its solid compensations for America. If it protected British shipping against foreign competition, it protected colonial shipping too. If it fostered the Royal Navy, it fostered the shipyards of Boston and Philadelphia and the New England fisheries no less. British shipbuilders clamoured for protection against their American competitors, but clamoured in vain. If the colonists paid artificially high for wine, oil or fruit from Spain, the British paid monopoly prices for Empire-grown sugar. In general both parties to the implicit bargain were intended to reap advantages, and both were expected to shoulder burdens. And if a strictly economic balance-sheet is struck, although the colonists doubtless had the worse of the bargain, it is difficult to see that they had intolerably the worse. That they should have somewhat the worse was made inevitable if by nothing else by the materialist appetites of a Britain *nouveau riche* after the world-triumph of 1763.

But seldom indeed in human affairs is the sole, or even the dominant, motive economic, and dissatisfaction in America had long been due primarily to psychological causes. It was not only that by a familiar human failing the colonists, so conscious of their own sacrifices, were scarcely so much as aware that any sacrifices had been accepted by the mother country, nor yet that few indeed of them had ever recognised how fully they owed their survival to the British Navy. The most deep-seated source of suspicion was the mere fact that the imperial system had never been a bargain between equals. It was the creature of the British Parliament, and inevitably the colonists assumed that British politicians, with British merchants and manufacturers ever at their elbows, had seen to it that very much the best of the bargain was theirs. And when in Boston or Philadelphia men recalled that the ultimate author of some regulation which pressed hard upon their economic interests was the remote and irresponsible Parliament at Westminster, what had been a grievance would transform itself into a humiliation.

§5

Up to 1763 the system had been tolerated. The seeds of a quarrel had been latent within it, but it had been tolerated. And it had been tolerated because it had never been enforced. Thanks partly to the cheerful inefficiency of British ministers, but partly too to the British instinct for compromise, the restraints on trade had always been in large a part dead letter, and smuggling was a flourishing industry. About nine-tenths of the wine, fruit, tea, sugar and molasses consumed in the Colonies was contraband. And during the late war American merchants had even supplied the French armies with stores and provisions. All this, the treason as well as the illegality, had been winked at. And then abruptly the final conquest of French Canada transformed the whole situation. Without native European rivals or enemies in the whole of North America the colonists no longer now felt themselves dependent upon the protection of the mother country. The mother country on the other hand had incurred heavy financial burdens in fighting what was generally regarded as a war on behalf of the colonists, and looked forward without enthusiasm to the obligation of garrisoning its conquests. A standing army of ten thousand, it was expected, would be necessary in America. Indeed its necessity was demonstrated in the very year of the peace. For in that year an Indian rising under Pontiac captured many forts, slew, tortured or drove off thousands of settlers, and devastated their lands. It was put down with great difficulty, and much gallantry, by British regular troops. The colonists had scarcely provided a man; the Assembly of Pennsylvania indeed would not hear of lifting a finger in self-defence—until a number of their own frontier-dwellers, who knew what the Indian raiding-party meant, first invoked the protection of the British against their own fellow-countrymen and then marched upon Philadelphia in protest. It was calculated in London that three millions a year was being spent upon colonial defence, to which the colonies contributed not a penny. To British statesmen it seemed proper that the colonies should shoulder some part of the obligations. It even, at first, seemed proper to some leading Americans. "It is very possible," wrote Benjamin Franklin in 1764,

> that the Crown may think it necessary to keep troops in America thenceforward, to maintain its conquests and defend its Colonies, and that the Parliament may establish some revenue arising out of the American trade to be applied towards supporting those troops. *It is possible, too, that we may, after a few years' experience, be generally very well satisfied with that measure.*

But it was not to be. For the era of compromise was ending, the era of Secretaries who did not read their dispatches, and were too sensible, or too lazy, to push a principle to its logical conclusion.

Shortly after the ratification of the Treaty of Paris public indignation at the terms of peace scared the unpopular Bute from office, and he was succeeded by Pitt's brother-in-law, George Grenville, a courageous, industrious and narrow-minded man whose qualities and failings were equally calculated to render him dangerous to the Empire. "He took public business," said Burke, "not as a duty he was to fulfil, but as a pleasure he was to enjoy." His task, as he conceived it, was clear. He was to restore the national finances, and prepare the defence of the Empire against the expected Bourbon revival. No anticipation of vaster issues clouded his resolution. Grenville had been bred to the law and, as lawyers sometimes will, he understood affairs better than he understood men, and was stronger in logic than in tact. His portrait by Reynolds suggests that a certain self-satisfaction mingled with determination and obstinacy in his makeup, and when it is added that he feared neither king nor people, we have a statesman not without solid virtues but at this particular juncture almost perfectly adapted for doing harm. He began by an attack on the laxities of the colonial administration. Many of the customs officials, he found, lived comfortably in England, contentedly pocketing the difference between their own salaries and the exiguous sums they paid to the deputies who did, or professed to do, their work. The whole customs revenue amounted to about two thousand pounds a year, and this it cost seven thousand pounds to collect. Grenville immediately packed the astonished officials off to their posts. He gave orders that the laws of trade should be actively enforced. And next year, 1764, he added several new commodities to the list of enumerated articles. The Molasses Act of 1733, whose prohibitive tariff had been one of many sleeping dogs once conveniently allowed to lie, had been enforced during the Seven Years' War, as a means of cutting off trade with the French West Indies. The colonists had assumed that, with the advent of peace, the Act would relapse quietly into a dead letter; they were horrified to see it revived, as the Sugar Act, with lowered duties, intended now not to keep out French sugar but to add to the public revenue. In all this, Grenville had been introducing no new principle; he had only been applying principles which his predecessors had accepted, but neglected to enforce. And this in itself amounted to a revolution. Taxes, after all, are tolerable enough as long as they are not collected, and, as a colonist indignantly observed, a little later, "it is this new invention of collecting taxes which makes them burdensome." And yet with all his disturbance of vested interests and enforcing of neglected regulations Grenville had merely succeeded in making the colonial customs approximately pay for the cost of collecting them. He was determined to do more than this. The colonists would not raise the men or the money for their own defence; British troops must be stationed in America; he would therefore impose an imperial tax to contribute towards their support. In 1765 he passed his famous Stamp Act, and so initiated the American Revolution.

To Grenville's essentially legal mind the case for the Act was overwhelming. Parliament indeed appeared to share this view, and took little interest in the measure. "There has been nothing of note in Parliament," wrote Horace Walpole, "but one slight day on the American taxes." Grenville had decided that £100,000 would be a reasonable contribution from the colonies to the costs of imperial defence. How else was he to raise £100,000 so simply? How else could he raise it at all? By the old constitutional method, replied Benjamin Franklin, of application through the Governors to the several Colonial assemblies. But this could hardly be regarded as a serious alternative. There was little prospect, as their agents admitted, that the Colonial assemblies would even agree as to their respective quotas in a voluntary levy. Colonies whom indolence or mutual jealousies had more than once prevented from raising a single soldier for self-defence when their own frontiers were ablaze were hardly likely to vote substantial sums of money for that purpose in a time of profound peace. On the contrary, the Americans were now exhibiting a tendency which democracies have so often and so disastrously since repeated; after a victorious war they were only too anxious to fling away their arms and forget their obligations. Grenville's method, a single duty imposed directly on all the colonies, obviated the interminable delay of separate appeals to a dozen reluctant legislatures, and seemed to be simplicity itself. Stamp duties, after all, on a more oppressive scale, had long been levied in Britain, and there were precedents,[1] though not many precedents, for a revenue tax on the colonies. It was simple, indeed it was too simple. It lit a flame in America which soon astonished the Americans themselves. At first indeed some of those who before long were to be prominent as leaders of the colonial revolution themselves gladly accepted posts as stamp-distributors under the Act. But the year's delay conceded by Grenville between his Resolution and his Act gave the colonists time to appreciate the inconveniences of the new measures against smuggling. And with his Stamp Act, they soon realised, Grenville had enabled them to transfer their objections to the suppression of smuggling to more respectable and constitutional grounds. They bitterly resented the stricter enforcement of the Acts of Trade, but nobody could pretend that their enforcement was unconstitutional. It was easy, however, to argue that the Stamp Duty was unconstitutional, and soon the cry of No Taxation without Representation was being raised, not

[1] 25 Car. II, cap. 7; 2 & 7 Wm. & Mary; 1 & 9 Anne; 3 Geo I, cap. 7.

only by the few whose first doubts had been of the propriety of the Stamp Act but by the many whose real grievance had always been the Customs duties.

The novelty of the Stamp Act was not so much that it was imposed by a Parliament in which the taxed were unrepresented. For this, as we have seen, there were precedents; and as recently as 1758 no less a body than the Assembly of Massachusetts had expressly acknowledged the constitutional omnipotence of the British Parliament. "The authority of all Acts of Parliament which concern the Colonies . . . ," it declared, "are ever acknowledged in all Courts of law . . . and we know no inhabitant within the bounds of this Government that ever questioned this . . . authority." This was, needless to say, the general view in Britain, where nine persons out of ten who had thought about the matter at all also assumed that Parliamentary supremacy implied, as in Britain, the right to tax. No charter, said John Wesley, had ever given an American colony "the illegal privilege of being exempt from Parliamentary taxation." Pitt, who subsequently poured out his eloquence for the repeal of the Act, accepted British Parliamentary supremacy as axiomatic, but drew a distinction between taxation and every other legislative act:

> . . . this kingdom has no right to lay a tax on the Colonies. At the same time I assert the authority of this kingdom over the Colonies to be sovereign and supreme, in every circumstance of government and legislation whatsoever. . . . Taxation is no part of the governing or legislative power.

By now it had come to subtleties, and this is a dangerously subtle argument. At home, it goes without saying, the power of taxation had always been accepted as an integral feature of the supremacy of Parliament, and, save by the legalistic fiction of "virtual representation," the unenfranchised majority of the British nation in 1765 could hardly be said to be more effectively represented than the American colonists. The real novelties of the Stamp Act were not so much taxation without representation, as internal taxation, in contrast to external taxation in the seaports, and taxation for revenue as distinct from taxation for trade. On the whole the colonial critics at first used the latter argument, while at Westminster Chatham and Camden preferred the former. Logically neither is an easy position to defend. Thus the original Molasses Act of 1733 had been prohibitive, that is to say by excluding French sugar it regulated trade, and was therefore, on the colonists' theory, constitutional.

Grenville's Sugar Act halved the duty, in order to admit sugar and raise revenue from the customs, and was therefore, on the same thesis, illegal. It thus became constitutional to impose a tax of sixpence and unconstitutional to lower it to threepence. Absurdities of this kind were inevitable as the quarrel plunged further away from its moral origins into a jungle of legal niceties. And the logical strength, or weakness, of the ground first occupied by the insurgents mattered all the less since it was so frequently shifted. Many Americans objected to seeing old claims newly enforced with the avowed object of extracting money from them; even more objected to being compelled to realise that they were indeed subject, and not in some remote and amiable theory only, to a Parliament at West-minster which seemed to have singularly few moral claims to their obedience. With Chatham only intermittently and unpredictably a political force, and Burke, whom posterity has learnt to revere, in his own day scarcely a political force at all, there was no British statesman who could command a following overseas, and very few who could even command respect. "The whole venal nation is now at market," wrote Benjamin Franklin of a British General Election in 1768, "and will be sold for about two millions, and might be bought . . . by the very devil himself." In the last resort Britain lost the American colonies because her moral qualities did not command their respect. For a proud people, cradled in idealism and now beginning to glimpse the vast possibilities of its future, there was a peculiar humiliation in conscious subjection to the unreformed Parliament of the eighteenth century. Why, Otis asked, should America be governed by the electors of Old Sarum?

For the British the economic problem—should they tax the colonies—was in essence a moral problem: could they perceive their duties, looming beyond their rights, a Commonwealth beyond the Empire? Could they bring themselves to renounce an authority for which there was a sound basis in law and equity, and which they believed to be highly advantageous to their own material interests? But the fundamental moral problem, which was so often argued in terms of economics, can equally well be seen as a searching test of the political instinct of the nation. In England Parliament had gradually subordinated the executive to the control of the legislature. Already a century of expansion had made it clear that it would be the mission of Britain to spread free institutions overseas. Could not the colonial legislatures be accorded the powers recently acquired by the British Parliament which was their model? If in course of time respect for human personality had bred Parliamentary control of taxation and the Rule of Law in Britain must not the same premise lead to the same conclusions in America? If the destiny of Britain was not to spread free institutions round the world, what was her claim upon the future?

The same history, stretching back to Magna Charta, was shared by mother country and colonies alike. Townships in America managed their affairs after the fashion of English boroughs; each colony possessed a constitution in the Parliamentary tradition, with Governor, Council and Assembly representing King, Lords and Commons. Yet from their common past each drew contrary conclusions. For the British the Colonial Assemblies were but municipal governments at a distance, passing by-laws under the supervision of the imperial Parliament at Westminster. For the colonists on the other hand each Assembly was a Westminster in miniature, entitled to powers as plenary as those of the Mother of Parliaments herself. The deadlock was formidable, yet it might have been resolved. To resolve it, however, would require a high degree of wisdom and altruism in the mother country. The British Parliament had acquired its own powers after civil war; another civil war could only be averted if it was prepared itself to make the resignation which it had once exacted from the Crown, and recognise the supremacy of an American Congress in American affairs. But of this much wisdom and altruism Britain was not capable. The Parliamentary oligarchy of the eighteenth century could only think of the colonists as inferiors, inferiors whom it was too often tempted to exploit.

As free and equal partners of the mother country the colonies would doubtless have been ready and thankful to preserve the unity of the English-speaking race, but to make them free and equal partners what moral and political revolutions were needed! Of such a conception we know that democracy is capable; and it is just possible that the Stuart monarchy might have risen to it, for the Stuarts never forgot that the Americans, equally with the English, were their subjects. That ideal did even then have its advocate, under the eighteenth century Parliamentary oligarchy. In his remarkable *Administration of the Colonies* Thomas Pownall, a former Governor of Massachusetts, advocated, in place of a paramount mother country and subject colonies, "a grand marine dominion—united into one Empire," in which the "different members should stand to each other as do Yorkshire and Middlesex." And in the later stages of the struggle the colonial leaders who, while snapping link after link with Britain, continued to protest their allegiance to King George, had clearly come to think of the only possible union as independence within the Empire, and subject to the Crown. Thus even now was prefigured the enduring Commonwealth, and the solution to which men came, after many struggles and much suffering, more than a hundred and fifty years later, when the Empire opened a new era of history with what had come to be known as Dominion Status. Perhaps that great lesson could only be learned after the tragedy of separation. Perhaps it required a vision and an altruism only to be learned in the school of failure and adversity. And if that be so, since the learning of that lesson was a condition of survival, even separation, it would seem, was a price worth paying. Certainly the conception of Dominion status lay far, immeasurably far, beyond the political horizon of the eighteenth century. Although at the eleventh hour their argument may have pointed to independence within the Empire, no more than the mother country did the colonists dream of what, for the Empire and the world, freedom with unity might have meant. Even the admission of colonial representatives to the British Parliament, which Pownall and others had advocated, and to which George Grenville did not object, was not seriously considered in Britain, and was actually dreaded in America. It has always to be remembered that hitherto the American colonies had not been thought of, and had not thought of themselves, as one nation, but as a number of separate, and often mutually hostile, entities. It was the quarrel with Britain which by giving them a common cause and a common rallying-cry began to fuse them into one.

§6

Once the issue had been fairly joined the dispute proceeded, with that steadily increasing momentum which seems characteristic of all revolutions, to its inevitable climax. Most of the claims which the American leaders were advancing towards the close of the dispute, and the political and philosophical grounds on which they justified them, were such as a few years earlier they had either not dreamed of, or had expressly repudiated. Tempers, needless to say, were lost, and foolish things were said, on both sides of the Atlantic. Even so wise a man as Dr. Johnson could declare that the malcontent colonists were "a race of convicts, and ought to be thankful for anything we allow them short of hanging." Any one with a taste for studying the shortsightedness of politicians may turn to the scene at Westminster in 1767 when, without the approval of his glum, bewildered colleagues, Charles Townshend, that lighthearted master of all the Parliamentary graces, outlined his strictly "external," or sea-port, taxes on glass, paper, painters' colours and tea, which so cleverly exploited the colonists' first thesis that only "internal" taxes were illegal, and so inevitably drove them to adopt a new one. Those who find the self-contradictions of revolutionary philosophers more engrossing will prefer to study the paradox of the American apostles of the Rights of Man denying even elementary justice to their loyalist fellow-citizens, or the theorists of universal liberty who continued to own slaves, and denounced the Quebec Act of 1774 for permitting the Roman Catholics of Canada to practise their own faith.

The Stamp Act was a fiasco from the first. No one would use stamped documents, there were riots and a boycott of British manufactures. In the following year, 1766, the Marquis of Rockingham, who had succeeded Grenville, repealed the Act. Pitt devoted some of his best remembered eloquence to demanding the repeal, Grenville and Bedford angrily opposed it. In America there was a sudden revulsion of gratitude and loyalty. New York even put up a leaden statue of George III, destined before long to be melted into bullets for shooting down his soldiers. Six months after the repeal, John Adams of Massachusetts, a Radical leader who had no desire to see America contented, noted regretfully that "the people are as quiet and submissive to Government as any people under the sun; as little inclined to tumults, riots, seditions, as they were ever known to be since the first foundation of the Government." But Rockingham did not confine himself to repeal. He passed two other measures, each destined to revive the quarrel. One was the Declaratory Act "for securing the dependency of the colonies." In this way, while withdrawing the tax, the Government proclaimed its unabated insistence on the right of taxation, "and thereby," in Shelburne's words, "naturally suggested to the Provinces that the timidity of the British Parliament kept pace with its ill dispositions towards them."

This was the kind of quarrel in which the national instinct for compromise has more than once served a British Government noticeably ill. Ministers should either have been more generous or more severe. As Shelburne remarked, they ought either to have enforced the Act by every means in their power, or else to have withdrawn both the Act and the claims on which it was founded. Rockingham's other provocative measure was a modification of the Sugar Act, which reduced the duty from threepence a gallon on foreign molasses to a penny on British and foreign alike. The impost thus ceased to be a prohibitive and protective tariff and became a tax for revenue purposes, and the logical forerunner of Charles Townshend's ill-starred budget in the following year.

Before then Rockingham had fallen, and William Pitt, transformed into that tragic and enigmatic figure the Earl of Chatham, had become the chief figure in the Ministry with which the king hoped to break down Party, and whose heterogeneous membership Burke, in a famous passage, compared to a tessellated pavement. The composition of the Ministry appeared to ensure that, like Chatham himself, in colonial affairs it would favour concession. But the tragi-comedy of error and mischance had not run its course. Very soon Chatham was on the borderline of insanity, hopelessly incapable of public business, and Charles Townshend, so gifted, so ambitious and so erratic, was light-heartedly committing his indignant colleagues to the famous budget of "external" taxes which was wholly at variance with their wishes. But in 1767 there was no strict tradition of collective cabinet responsibility, and Chatham, the only Minister who could have brought the Chancellor of the Exchequer to heel, was brooding in inaccessible melancholy at North End. It was thus by a Ministry to which the great architect of Empire still lent his splendid name, and in which not only he but almost all his colleagues strongly disapproved of further taxation, that the quarrel was revived and final rupture ensured. Townshend's budget had allowed tea, coffee and cocoa exported to America a rebate of the duties paid on their importation into England, which meant that tea in Boston was sold at half the price of tea in London. But even this was regarded as an abuse, largely because the proceeds of the taxes were to go to provide government officials in America with a permanent civil list, and would thus make them no longer dependent for their salaries upon the Assemblies. More provocatively still, the Customs service was reorganised and improved, with a Board of Commissioners at Boston. It became evident that the government intended to do its best to stamp out smuggling altogether. Once again the practical irritants necessary for a new agitation had been provided. But once again, the colonial leaders recognised, they would have to shift their theoretic ground.

Townshend's new taxes, after all, were undeniably "external," and therefore, according to the thesis which had served against the Stamp Act, undeniably constitutional. This indeed was precisely why that too ingenious Minister had imposed them. Moreover to argue that the suppression of smuggling was unconstitutional was clearly an even less hopeful enterprise. The distinction between internal and external taxation, it was obvious, would have to be abandoned. Henceforth all taxation by Parliament of any kind whatsoever, whether internal or external, must be denounced. At this advanced stage in the argument it was inevitable that the Rights of Man and the Laws of Nature should begin to figure prominently; for the Rights of Man and the Laws of Nature are phrases which, while genuinely representing the consciousness latent in most human beings of their title to a certain elementary justice, are nevertheless extremely difficult to define and have in fact been conveniently found, by most of those who at various times have attempted to define them, to include all the privileges which they desired for themselves and singularly few of those which were claimed by their opponents. The Assembly of Massachusetts which, in January, 1768, petitioned the King against the new taxes, and pleaded feelingly "the fundamental rights of nature," had no intention whatever of allowing freedom of worship to Catholics or liberty of opinion to Loyalists.

Townshend's measures sufficed to keep discontent in America simmering for another three years. Sons of Liberty instigated merchants to pledge themselves once more to import no British goods. By 1769 close on four thousand British troops were quartered in Boston, among a population of seventeen thousand. Before the day of police forces troops were the only means of protecting unpopular officials, but to keep even highly disciplined troops cheek by jowl with a resentful populace was bound sooner or later to provoke an ugly incident. For the uniform, in which so lately the British had scaled the heights of Abraham and saved the colonies from the conspiracy of Pontiac, was everywhere the object of mockery and insult. The officers were boycotted in society, and there were even instances of British soldiers, convicted in the local courts of felony, being sold into slavery. As Professor Egerton remarks, that such proceedings should have been meekly borne hardly savours of tyranny. Nevertheless the manners of the troops were doubtless not pleasing to a society which still contained a powerful strain of Puritanism, and their mere presence was inevitably regarded as a symbol of tyranny. A civil police force enforces its authority because it has behind it the law courts, and indeed society; the British regiments in Boston had neither. In 1770 a solitary sentinel at the Customs House was threatened and insulted by a large crowd, which refused to disperse when the guard of six men and a corporal was called out. A soldier was knocked down, the guard opened fire and four of the crowd were killed. The soldiers were subsequently tried for their lives, and, to the honour of the American courts, acquitted. But the incident passed immediately into the martyrology of the revolution, and for years, and indeed for decades, afterwards "the horrid massacre at Boston" was celebrated, with a public anniversary of its own, and with every variety of exaggeration and distortion, as evidence of the ferocious tyranny of British rule.

§7

Even so there was to be one more lull in the long dispute. Chatham had resigned in 1768, his successor, the Duke of Grafton, had been in a minority in his own Cabinet, and in 1770 the King sent, not as was generally expected, for Chatham again, but for a chief Minister of a very different type, Lord North. Thus George the Third renewed the experiment, which he had attempted prematurely at his accession, in the administration of Bute. The Ministry was to be the king's mouthpiece. The Whig Revolution had ensured that Parliament, not Crown, should be supreme, and now accordingly, George was determined, the Crown should rule through Parliament. And this time there was every prospect of success. The Whig Opposition was divided and discredited. The court Party of King's Friends was disciplined and powerful. George himself was a first-rate Party manager, and North, shrewd and cool-headed, a skilful Parliamentary tactician and an adroit debater, asked no more than to do the King's pleasure. Thus was forged the strange alliance of virtuous and obstinate King with shrewd and complaisant Minister, which despite disaster after disaster abroad, and the splendid eloquence of Chatham and Burke at home, survived for twelve years, and lost the American colonies. To the shortcomings of North's administration must, in fairness, be added those of the Colonial officials who reported to him, and through whose too often jaundiced eyes accordingly he usually viewed the American scene. In a sense, as Sir George Trevelyan truly says, "his own Governors and Lieutenant-Governors wrote King George out of America." Benjamin Franklin has analysed the process by which the Governor would begin with arrogance and so earn unpopularity, and then, knowing himself unpopular, would become malicious. And then:

> their malice urges them to continual abuse of the inhabitants in their letters to administration, representing them as disaffected and rebellious, and (to encourage the use of severity) as weak, divided, timid and cowardly.

A decade of such advice from the men on the spot had not prepared any British government to see the American problem steadily or whole. And beneath all this lay the inadequacy of Britain in the mid-eighteenth century for the formidable moral ordeal with which she was confronted. By the time that North took office it is probable that nothing short of a miracle, not even Chatham with a free hand and at the height of his powers, could have preserved America. It is very certain that North could not have.

Nevertheless North started well. He at once abolished all Townshend's taxes, save that on tea; indeed it was only by a majority of one that the cabinet decided to retain even the tea tax. It might have been wiser to let the tea tax too go, for its survival too obviously served the same purpose as the Declaratory Act—it reserved the right to tax. And so the agitators were presented both with a victory, in the withdrawal of three duties, and a grievance, in the survival of one. Even so agitation died down, and for three years was little more than a sullen smoulder. Once again the British public, ever only too ready to forget unpleasant circumstances, settled down thankfully to put America out of its thoughts, as it fondly supposed, for ever. "The great defect here," noted Franklin from London in 1773, and many observers since have made the same observation of Britain, "is in all sorts of people a want of attention to what passes in such remote countries as America." Across the Atlantic extremists did what they could to fan the embers with Committees of Correspondence, which served to exchange propaganda, suppress Loyalism and provide the framework of a revolutionary organisation. But for three years the American scene presented an illusory effect of quiescence. The relief and optimism induced in Britain by this unaccustomed tranquillity was rudely dispelled in 1773, and on the initiative of the British Government. This was the year, as we shall see, of Lord North's Regulating Act in India, and to compensate it for the Government's encroachment on its political monopoly the East India Company, whose finances were in a poor way, expected some commercial concessions. In order to provide them North in an ill-omened hour turned once more to that source of so many previous troubles, the American tea-trade. Thanks largely to the American boycott, vast mounds of unsold tea cumbered the Company's warehouses. Hitherto it had sold its tea by public auction in London, and on tea re-exported to the Colonies there had been a rebate of three-fifths of the duty paid on its import into Britain. North's Act provided that the Company might now export its own tea to America in its own ships and sell it there through its own agents, and allowed it a refund of the whole of the British import duty. In this way, he calculated, since the Company's tea would be much cheaper than any they could procure, he would neatly put the smugglers out of business, and incidentally halve the cost to the American consumer. Of the inevitable political consequences of the measure, despite all the lessons of the last decade, he seems to have had no notion whatever. And yet he need hardly have altered his Act if his prime object had been to outrage every American interest. Both the merchants who had hitherto handled the export trade and the smugglers who would now be undersold, were threatened with ruin—and there were prominent colonial leaders in each of these categories. Every American who had taken any interest in the political dispute felt himself concerned to prevent the landing of the tea, whose cheapness must mean a ready sale and the collection by the Government of the threepenny duty. And even hesitating patriots were antagonised by the extension to America of a monopoly which was suspect even in Britain. The consequences of this neat, logical and supremely foolish measure were not slow in unfolding. At New York and Philadelphia not a chest of tea could be landed. At Charleston it was landed, but not sold. At Boston, on the day before the Company's three ships were to discharge their cargo, a party of men disguised as Indians boarded them and threw the tea into the water.

§8

This was in December, 1773. By March of next year North was proposing punitive measures to Parliament, and the stage was all but set for the final explosion. Here once again he was foolish. It would have been wiser, as Chatham protested, to postpone a Bill of pains and penalties until voluntary reparation had been invited and refused. But it mattered less now if North continued to be foolish, since even wisdom could hardly have averted a conflict. By now nothing would have contented the colonists short of complete self-government under the Crown. But such a short cut to the coming Commonwealth could not be; only after further adversity would Britain be ready for the new era. Dominion status, the goal at which the Empire was to arrive so much later and by such different paths, might have arrested the slide to catastrophe, but who was there in Britain with the vision to understand or champion Dominion status now? For Chatham and Burke, who have left us so many famous passages of eloquence in denunciation of the American taxes, both believed in the legislative supremacy of Parliament, and Chatham believed in the self-sufficient Empire as well. Doubtless the colonies looked more hopefully to George III than even to

Chatham; a warm loyalty to His Majesty and a growing suspicion of both Houses of Parliament had long been characteristic of many prominent Americans besides Benjamin Franklin. "America," declared Franklin and Alexander Hamilton, "is no part of the dominion of Great Britain, but of the King's Dominions." But George had no notion of an Empire over which he would reign but would not rule. His duty, he believed, was to rule, but to rule through Parliament, whose authority, now that it was subject to his will, he had no wish to see displaced. And so, in default of any of their rulers, there remained only the mass of the British people. And that many of them, even if they were blind to the full grandeur of the issues at stake, were at least disposed to sympathise with the American cause there can be no doubt. "With regard to the sentiments of people in general here concerning America," wrote Benjamin Franklin in 1773,

> I must say that we have among them many friends and well-wishers. The Dissenters are all for us, and many of the merchants and manufacturers. There seems to be, even among the country gentlemen . . . a disapprobation of the harsh measures with which we have been treated, and a wish that some means might be found of perfect reconciliation.

Franklin may have been a trifle optimistic. The Dissenters were not in fact all for the Americans: John Wesley himself argued the orthodox British view in a series of eloquent tracts. And two years later Burke was lamenting the universal indifference of the public. "As to the good people of England," he wrote to Lord Rockingham, "they seem to partake every day, more and more, of the character of that administration which they have been induced to tolerate."

But neither the minority which actively sympathised with America, nor the majority which was indifferent or hostile, had begun to dream of an independent American Dominion, linked to Britain by the Crown. They had not even yet risen—and this was perhaps the most fatal defect in British statesmanship—to the conception of common membership, under whatever Parliamentary machinery, of one great community, on both sides of the Atlantic. Here and there farsighted observers urged this wide, imaginative view. Thus Joseph Galloway, a former Speaker of the Assembly of Pennsylvania, who subsequently sacrificed everything as a Loyalist, wished to see Britain and America fused into "one grand and illustrious empire," and advocated a federal union with a Parliament on each side of the Atlantic. But voices such as these were few and far between, and to the average American such views, at once moderate and highly theoretic, were far less easy to understand than the simple zeal of the Radical politicians or the republicanism of the Congregational ministers who for "the kingom of heaven" would now read "the Parliament of heaven" each Sunday. It was easier to sympathise even with the simple calculation of the American merchants who owed large sums to British creditors and were all for a rupture and repudiation. And so Galloway and his like were ignored or persecuted in America—and subsequently neglected in Britain. And, as North and Parliament prepared their pains and penalties the ultimate catastrophe was inevitable, for agreement had ceased to be possible. Boston port was to be closed and its custom-house removed to Salem. Troops, it was enacted, were to be quartered on the town; officials indicted for murder in the course of their duties, that is for bloodshed in the suppression of riots, might be brought to England for trial; and the charter of Massachusetts was virtually annulled.

§9

That summer a measure of a very different character equally enraged the Americans. This was the Quebec Act, which gave the French Canadian Catholics complete freedom of worship—a presage at last of the liberal Empire to be, and a most surprising example of enlightenment and tolerance from men who had displayed such short-sighted intransigence in dealing with their own kin. The American colonies were horrified, not merely because the Act also extended the Canadian boundary south and west into their own hinterland, and gave Canada a military Governor and a nominated council, but because, while most of them were still violently opposed to religious tolerance, the French Canadians, as an American pamphleteer complained, were to "have the Catholic religion established among them, and are even allowed a Popish bishop in the British dominions with the French language and customs." Chatham, Burke and the Whigs denounced this rare act of wisdom and generosity with the same eloquent fury which they had lavished upon the most foolish measures of repression. But Parliament passed it, as it passed everything with which the King and North chose to present it, but on this occasion with better reason than its customary complaisance. Religious freedom had been promised to Canada in the peace treaty of 1763. And since then the first two Governors, Murray and Carleton, finding themselves in charge of a province in which Catholics outnumbered Protestants by a hundred to one, had granted them not only religious freedom but measure after measure of civil equality. For a kindred reason—that the Roman Catholic majority preferred to do without it—they had opposed the setting up of a representative assembly. The Bill of 1774 was based upon the experience of these years. Not only the American colonists but Chatham and Burke assailed it because it gave the French in Canada the religious liberty which they did want, without forcing upon them the representative institutions which they did not. Happily, as so often in British history, experience was preferred to theory, and the Act of 1774 established the great new principle of equality between British and non-British settlers, and its corollary that British conceptions of law and administration must be modified to meet the needs of the newcomers. It is not surprising that when the Congress of Philadelphia appealed to the Canadians to join the revolutionary cause they should have declined. But vaster consequences than these were to grow from that first half-instinctive, half-empirical act of wisdom, whereby Britain, in the midst of her failures, gave proof that she would not always fail. Here, at the moment when she was turning her back upon her own destiny, she had firmly grasped one of the principles by which that destiny would one day be fulfilled.

§10

But south of the Canadian border, the sands were running out, and as the punitive measures took effect, the prospect steadily darkened. In that December of 1774 General Charles Lee wrote to Burke:

> I have now run through almost the whole colonies, from the north to the south. I have conversed with every order of men, from the first estated gentleman to the poorest planter, and cannot express my astonishment at the unanimous, ardent spirit reigning through the whole.

Representatives from every colony save Georgia had travelled that summer, feted and feasted on the way, to a Continental Congress at Philadelphia. Little enough share in the election of these delegates had been permitted to Loyalists, to whom the Rights of Man were tacitly assumed not to extend; and who were less likely to vote for a delegate than to be tarred and feathered or driven off their farms and even out of their country. Even so it was only after a struggle that the extreme party gained the upper hand. And despite the Declaration of Rights which the Congress hastened to adopt, and which was in effect an ultimatum to the British Government, its proceedings contained considerable evidence of a desire to placate moderate opinion. Thus though the Declaration demanded the repeal of thirteen Acts of Parliament passed since 1763, the Quebec Act among them, it expressly acknowledged the right of Britain to regulate external trade. And though formally approving the "Suffolk Resolves," in which Massachusetts had already virtually declared its independence, Congress was lavish with protests of a desire for reconcilation, and in an appeal, over the heads of their rulers, to all British citizens of good will it denounced the calumny that the colonies were aiming at separation. A Declaration of Rights was in itself a tacit appeal to the history of British liberty, and if at this eleventh hour Britain could have responded to it she might have fulfilled her own full destiny so much earlier as to have transformed the history of the world. Despite their pacific phrases, however, the assembled delegates committed themselves to an Association for excluding all British merchandise forthwith, shrewdly permitting themselves, however, another year in which to export to Britain themselves, if Britain would accept their goods. This was to assume the functions of a national legislature, and though few delegates perhaps realised fully the significance of what they were doing they had brought both war with Britain and their own unity very close. On the twentieth of October the Assembly of Pennsylvania entertained Congress to a banquet in the City Tavern, and the whole ceremony rose to acclaim the toast, "May the sword of the parent never be stained with the blood of her children." Soon the delegates were jogging gravely homeward. Next spring the fighting began. The long ordeal was over. Britain had been tried, and found wanting. How should those who unsheathed the sword in 1775 foresee that, beyond these troubles, a new, and perhaps a greater, destiny awaited her?

CHAPTER TWO

INDEPENDENCE

(1775-1783)

§1

THE ISSUE of the war was certain as soon as the first shot was fired. If the American colonies wished to be independent they could not be retained by force. Even if they could have been conquered, Britain would have had to give them almost everything they had been fighting for as soon as peace was signed. But how could they be conquered? Such a war Britain could only have won if her people had both believed wholeheartedly in their cause and clearly perceived the true value of what they were defending. But thanks to Grenville, Townshend and North they did not believe wholeheartedly in their cause. Many even of those who were readiest to fight, when it came to fighting, and who knew least of the niceties of the quarrel, were dimly aware that for long there had been something unworthy in the American policy of British ministers. And they had little notion of the immense prize which was now slipping from their grasp, still seeing in the colonies what Walpole, and not what Cromwell, had seen, a source of material advantage to the mother country, rather than a vast moral obligation, the embodiment of a missionary Idea.

Viewed in such a light this was not a cause in which a united nation was likely to put forth its full powers, or endure to the end. And certainly the nation was not united. There was always an influential and vocal opposition to the war. In the famous orations which turned few votes but are among the noblest classics of the English tongue Burke warned his fellow-countrymen that coercion could only end in disaster; "it is not what a lawyer tells me that I may do; but what humanity, reason and justice tell me I ought to do." And although their policy as a Party was neither unanimous nor particularly intelligible, there was always a small but distinguished body of Whigs to applaud Burke's angry eloquence. The surrender of a British army at Saratoga was greeted by a section of the Opposition with whoops of delight. Chatham, though he had always opposed coercion, would not hear of granting independence once war had begun. Yet he would not allow his own son to fight against the colonists, although later, when France and Spain had entered the war, he sent him, with his blessing, to take part in the defence of Gibraltar. These delicate distinctions were typical of the varying degrees of misgiving and mental confusion which beset many worthy citizens, few of whom could long forget that this was a civil war. Many must have suspected that to fight at all was a form of self-betrayal, and that, in Chatham's words, "be the victory to whichever host it pleases the Almighty to give it poor England will have fallen upon its own sword." In general no doubt the people supported the government—the election of 1774, for what such evidence is worth, gave North a thumping majority, and Burke repeatedly complained of the defection of the commercial classes which "ought to have supported with efficacy and power the opposition to the fatal cause of all this mischief." Yet there were influential voices to keep the nation's conscience uneasy. Hume, the philosopher, objected to "mauling the poor unfortunate Americans." And though Wesley airily brushed aside the American case, Dr. Price, the nonconformist clergyman who later crossed swords with Burke over the French Revolution, defended the colonists in a widely circulated tract which powerfully influenced his co-religionists. And the *Common Sense* of Thomas Paine, the English Radical who fought for the Americans with sword as well as pen, circulated in tens of thousands throughout the length and breadth of the colonies. The chief influence of Paine's pamphlets may have been in America— an American historian estimates his services to the revolution as "beyond calculation"—but they represented a genuine, if restricted, element in British opinion.

The Americans themselves, it is true, were even more divided. Like all revolutions this was the work of a minority. It has been estimated that the average vote cast in Boston during the height of the controversy between 1765 and 1775 amounted to not more than one in six of the qualified electors. And even among the convinced rebels there was an inevitable nostalgia for the past. "We might have been a free and great people together" regretfully exclaimed Thomas Jefferson, the publicist of the Revolution, in his draft of the Declaration of Independence. The Continental Congress deleted these words before the great manifesto was approved on July 4, 1776, but they represented the sentiments of many unquestioned patriots. Loyalists, too, were numerous; numerous enough to provide fourteen regiments to fight for King George against their fellow-colonists, so that this was in a double sense a civil war. A steady stream of loyalist articles, poems and pamphlets denounced and derided the revolution. In May, 1778, the editor of the *New York*

Gazette was still describing the rebel leaders as "an infernal dark-designing group of men . . . the refuse and dregs of mankind." In 1779 Joseph Galloway, the Pennsylvanian Liberal who had advocated federal union with two co-equal Parliaments, in Britain and America, testified before a Committee at Westminster that "many more than four-fifths of the people would prefer a union with Great Britain upon constitutional principles to . . . independence." This was no doubt an exaggeration but the harsh treatment of the loyalists is in itself evidence that the insurgents considered loyalism formidable. In the early stages of the controversy with the mother country loyalists had been tarred and feathered and their homes had been wrecked. After war had broken out official repression gradually took the place of unofficial persecution, and soon concentration camps, confiscation of property and surveillance were the order of the day. Thousands of loyalists fled to Britain, Canada or other parts of the Empire. The insurgent States found the greatest difficulty in raising armies and keeping them in the field. After the first flush of enthusiasm had waned, the colonists deserted to the royal armies in hundreds and to their own homes in thousands. Generous grants of money and land were offered to volunteers, and freed negro slaves were enlisted in substantial numbers—in 1778 there were on an average fifty-four negroes in each of Washington's battalions. Even so, desperate efforts were needed to maintain between thirty and forty thousand fighting men, out of a population of three million. Indeed the supreme achievement of George Washington, the heroic figure in command of the revolutionary armies, was not brilliant strategy, for his strategy was seldom brilliant, nor dazzling victories, for his victories were few, but the indomitable resolution with which, somehow or other, in adversity or prosperity, he contrived to keep some sort of army in being. Despite jealousies, internecine strife and immense confusion he kept his sorely tried battalions on their feet; and in the end he triumphed, for he was the soul of America. In him was incarnate that calm, deep, unconquerable faith which always must triumph in the end, and which there was no British leader to embody because among the British at this time faith of this supreme quality did not exist. It was no accident that this Washington was the same young officer whom Governor Dinwiddie had once sent into the still empty West to grapple with the French. For Washington could see beyond this immediate quarrel. No British statesman had yet perceived the tremendous future which would await a tolerant British Commonwealth. But Washington had already surveyed the empty spaces and sensed the vast destinies of an independent America.

Washington, not the British generals, knew that he was fighting for the future.

§2

Inevitably the war was a scrambling, unsatisfactory, protracted affair, in which neither side seemed capable of inflicting a mortal wound. Not until the French had entered the struggle, and, some while later, made their first serious effort to assist the colonial armies in America, was a decisive blow struck. As for the British army, as usual at this time it consisted in the main of the sweepings of the streets and the gaols, officered by aristocrats. For the British were an adventurous, but a profoundly unmilitary, society; the middle classes had never entered the army, and as yet it had occurred to no one that they should. After France's entry into the war a considerable body of British troops was pinned down in England by the customary threat of invasion, now apparently more formidable than ever before. And so for the American campaign the government had to augment its own slender resources with several thousand German mercenaries, whose conduct endeared neither them nor their employers to the colonists. If the eyes of the British had been open to the stakes for which they were fighting there would have been no need of mercenaries. It was of course a formidable handicap that they had to fight on the further side of three thousand miles of water, but it was a handicap more formidable still that the Colonial Office should have been under Lord George Germaine, and the Admiralty under the Earl of Sandwich. If the British had not lost the American colonies because their ministers did not know how to administer them, they would have lost them because their ministers did not know how to fight a war. One aspect of the fundamental moral failure of eighteenth-century Britain was the bad old system of place-jobbing and sinecures which obstructed the promotion of able men, and prevented the nation putting forth its full strength. An occasional almost fortuitous meteor such as Pitt only illumined the darkness of the surrounding scene. And in general the industrious placemen, promoted because they, or their relations, had obliged the reigning administration, were neither worthy of the nation nor fit for their responsibilities. That every man has his price had been, characteristically enough, the tradition of Walpole, but it was under George III, exploiting it to the limits in the interest of his personal hegemony, that a bad tradition reached its nadir. Had it endured, there could have been no national recovery; so it was significant of what might yet be that Dunning's celebrated motion that "the power of the Crown has increased, is increasing and ought to be diminished" was carried in 1780, the year before the culminating disaster of Yorktown.

§3

The strategic problems which faced British generals in America were of the kind least likely to be solved by text-book maxims or the traditions of the parade-ground. There were vast distances and wild country to be covered, and the colonists were often a most elusive foe, soldiers melting into civilians, and civilians turning soldiers, according to the fortunes and necessities of the campaign. Conceivably there was no Wolfe, no Clive available now for high command; and even if there had been, Lord George Germaine was certainly not the man to discover or appoint them. Sir William Howe, commander-in-chief during the first crucial years, had always been an opponent of coercion and had even declared that, if called upon, he would refuse to fight the Americans. His political views therefore were unlikely to spur him to swift and energetic action or ruthless punitive measures, and his political views were reinforced by natural indolence. He believed that by holding New York and Philadelphia, and by blockading the coast, he could wear his opponents down. Conceivably, if the French Navy had not intervened, he might have succeeded, and been hailed as a Fabius Cunctator who had conquered at the cost of the least possible legacy of bitterness. But Howe was not energetic enough even for his own cautious strategy; in a sudden burst of activity he would fight a successful action or two, and then retire for a prolonged spell of inaction in city quarters. And for Howe, whose tastes were luxurious, every city proved a Capua. Sir Henry Clinton, who succeeded Howe, was less indolent but not more skilful. As for Lord Cornwallis, he lacked any military qualification whatever. A country whose heart and soul was in the contest would hardly have tolerated a Lord George Germaine as Secretary of State, and even if compelled to accept such a fate would somehow have burst the shackles of the system of Parliamentary jobbery, and contrived to throw up a soldier capable of embodying its will to victory. But Britain was not heart and soul in the contest; how could she be, when she believed that she was fighting for her rights against the colonists, rather than for her duty to the world?

Though Howe entered New York in 1776, he made little impression upon his opponents. September of next year saw him settle down, after defeating Washington at the Brandywine river, to another long spell of inaction in Philadelphia. Meanwhile the unfortunate General Burgoyne, little suspecting that his superior had marched south, was coming down from Canada, in the confident expectation of joining forces with Howe's army marching north from New York. Howe had either been foolish enough to suppose that Burgoyne would need no assistance or, as some say, had not received the crucial instructions, for the sufficient reason that Lord George Germaine had forgotten to dispatch them. And so about the time when Howe was installing himself comfortably in Philadelphia, Burgoyne, still relying on his aid, and the remnants of Burgoyne's 7000 men, were being encircled by 20,000 Americans in difficult country on the Hudson. By October 17 Burgoyne had surrendered the remnants of his army to General Gates at Saratoga. Despite the small scale of all these operations the loss of seven thousand men, half of them Germans, was not a decisive blow. But it brought France into the war.

§4

Vergennes had been patiently waiting for his moment. Before the ink on the Treaty of 1763 was dry, de Choiseul had commenced to reconstruct the French navy. For the first time since the days of Colbert France was governed by a Minister who fully understood the sovereign importance of sea-power. Within seven years de Choiseul had trebled the fighting quality of the French navy. Nor was naval rearmament the only means by which this great minister set himself to ensure a reversal of fortune in that renewal of the long imperial conflict which he impatiently awaited. From the day when Canada passed to the British Crown he had believed a revolt of the American colonies to be inevitable. Indeed de Vergennes, who was to succeed de Choiseul as chief Minister, but was at the time Ambassador at Constantinople, is reported to have made to an English traveller a remarkably accurate forecast of the results of the British conquest. "The consequences," he said,

> of the entire cession of Canada are obvious. I am persuaded England will ere long repent of having removed the only check that could keep her Colonies in awe. They stand no longer in need of her protection; she will call on them to contribute towards supporting the burdens they have helped to bring on her; and they will answer by striking off all dependence.

And to ensure that the coming opportunity should be exploited to the full de Choiseul prepared a close alliance with Spain; to recover Canada formed no part of his design—indeed he seems to have regarded its loss with relief—but he fully intended that in the coming war France should be strong in the Mediterranean and the West Indies. But for all his high abilities de Choiseul was an impatient man and he moved too soon. For seven years he eagerly watched the growing tension between Britain and the American colonies, and in 1770 he judged that his time had come. But his attempt to thrust Spain into a war with Britain, which France would at once have joined, was premature. Spain drew back, the aged and cynical Louis XV was both irritated and alarmed, and de Choiseul was dismissed. French plans, however, were not deflected. The new Minister was de Vergennes, de Vergennes who had so confidently prophesied one of the consequences of the Treaty of Paris. And de Vergennes, whose patience was greater than his predecessor's, continued to watch and wait—and to prepare.

His agents had fomented discontent in America and discreetly aided the party of insurrection. But he had made no overt move. Since the November of 1776 Benjamin Franklin had been in Paris, one of a mission of three angling for French aid. Franklin quickly became the rage of the salons, a household word, indeed, all over France, the virtuous sage of classical antiquity returned to earth; but still Vergennes had not moved. Now at last the surrender at Saratoga decided him that he need wait no longer. The news arrived on December 2; within a fortnight France had recognised the United States as an independent power. On February 6, 1778, treaties of commercial and military alliance were signed, and shortly afterwards France declared war. The quarrel with the colonies was now merged in another world war, and the American threads interwoven with an older theme, the struggle of European nations for imperial power. The odds against Britain were heavier, to all appearances, than ever before. Not only did France, last of her defeated rivals, challenge her once more. Soon hostile shades were rising from a remoter past. Spain, the first great imperial enemy, joined the conflict in 1779. And to complete the muster of spectral Empires, Holland, the second rival, now so long outstripped, allowed her West Indian island, St. Eustatius, to become a vast depot for the supply of munitions to America, so that North declared war on her in December, 1780. Add to this the Armed Neutrality of the minor European sea-powers, gradually banded together to resist the British doctrine of blockade, and the isolation of Britain was complete.

§5

No other nation would have survived such an onslaught. The world took it for granted that the whole British Empire was doomed. Yet paradoxically Britain, bewildered and blundering, with her incompetent ministers and her disorganised resources, seemed to draw strength from the vast extension of the conflict and the onset of so many foes. The American colonies she could not save, for the American colonies were already lost. But despite the failure in America the British had not condemned themselves to losing their entire Empire. And defending it against their ancient rivals they were conscious of a cause far more fully theirs, a cause far less hedged with moral reservations, than the struggle with their own colonies. For all that in America they, or their leaders, had blindly rejected their own high destiny, the folk-mind of the nation was not unconscious, perhaps indeed was all the more conscious for the failure in America, of a destiny awaiting it elsewhere. The British moreover seldom fight their best save against long odds. Thus it was that, against all apparent likelihood, the nation was able gradually to stem the tide which had threatened to engulf it.

Nevertheless George III and his advisers continued to misdirect the war, and to misdirect it because they misunderstood it. It took nearly four years more for the war in America to drag to its fore-doomed conclusion. The British generals managed to capture towns and win battles, as well as lose them; in 1780 indeed Clinton captured nearly 7000 insurgent soldiers in Charleston, South Carolina. But their armies could never effectively occupy even the areas which they overran, and they never had a coherent plan of campaign. Until 1781 the French gave the colonists little effective aid even at sea, and by then Washington's troops were mutinous, diminishing in numbers and short of supplies. "We are at the end of our tether," he wrote, "now or never our deliverance must come." But in that year a fine force of French regulars was in the field, the French admiral de Grasse with a powerful fleet obtained temporary command of the sea off the American coast, and Washington's exhausted armies rose to their opportunity. The result was the siege of York-town, and the surrender of the British General Cornwallis with his entire army. After this George III continued to believe that "if measures are well concerted, a good end may yet be made to the war," but nobody else did. The nation by now was heartily sick of "the King's war," and increasingly conscious that there was a moral blight on it. The independence of the colonies was not formally recognised until 1782, but the surrender at Yorktown was virtually the end of the American fighting.

§6

In the world struggle with her ancient enemies Britain, needless to say, was not to revive the glories of Pitt and the Seven Years' War yet gradually she put forth something of her true self. Despite all the corrupt politics, corrupt as Britain had never known them before or since, for all the selfishness and the grossness, eighteenth century Britain was a proud, virile and courageous society. But for this indeed she could not have survived. The landlords and merchants who lost America would ere long defeat Napoleon. The great families which ruled Britain and the Empire may have been jobbers and sinecurists, they may have taken the lion's share, but, as Sir George Trevelyan says, they also played the lion's part. They fought, and died, in every quarter of the globe; a commission in the army or navy at least was no sinecure. And an aristocracy with courage and vitality cannot be wholly bad. The very dignity and beauty, the innate good taste, of almost everything, from cottage to palace, which they built was perhaps a presage of the novel forces already stirring beneath the incompetence and corruption of the age of North. For if North and his placemen were still in the centre of the stage, Wilberforce and Wesley, the younger Pitt and Grey were in the wings, and from the ashes of the American catastrophe would spring the phœnix of spiritual revival and political reform. And though for the present Parliament gave the nation no leaders at home, at least there was Warren Hastings in India, Carleton in Canada, Eliott at Gibraltar and Rodney with the fleet. And so, shorn of its American colonies, the Empire survived. But it was by a narrow margin. There were the combined fleets of France and Spain, and later of Holland, to contend against, and the now familiar threat of an invasion across the Channel revived in its most formidable form. In 1781 and 1782 the fleet of France and Spain sailed the Channel menacingly, but there was no landing, and a Dutch squadron was defeated by Sir Hyde Parker in the North Sea. Eliott held Gibraltar firmly through a siege which lasted for three years and seven months; that there should have been a siege at all was some evidence of the odds against which the British navy was contending. In and out of the West Indies the rival fleets manœuvred according to the hurricane season, occasionally capturing an enemy island. In 1781, in the dark days after Yorktown, most of the British islands fell, and the French and Spanish were preparing an assault upon Jamaica when Rodney returned from England and on April 12, 1782, routed the French fleet, capturing the French admiral de Grasse and seven French battleships. Rodney had also defeated the Spaniards off Cape St. Vincent, but this was the one resounding victory of the war over the French, and it came in the nick of time. Thanks to this eleventh hour revival of her supremacy at sea, when the war died away amid the general exhaustion of all the combatants early in 1783 Britain had held all her possessions against the Franco-Spanish onslaught, save Minorca and Florida, which had both fallen to Spain.

In India meanwhile Hastings had saved Bombay from the Mahrattas in 1780. And in 1781 and 1782 the victories of Sir Eyre Coote saved Madras from Hyder Ali. The French trading stations fell easily; the enemy failed to seize the command of the sea in Indian waters, and in 1782 and 1783 Sir Edward Hughes, with fewer ships, fought five fierce actions against the French Admiral Suffren, without decisive victory for either side. When the war ended British India survived virtually unscathed. Hastings had saved it by his own energy and his own resources.

§7

Fortunately for Britain the preliminary articles of peace with the United States were signed (on 30th November, 1782) before terms were negotiated with France and Spain, and without their cognisance. In this way the treaties recognised the true nature of the war, and the old Empire expiated its failure without robbing the new of its future. Shelburne, now chief Minister in an administration "on a broad bottom," failed to protect the American loyalists from their fellow countrymen. The most that he could secure was a stipulation that there should be no further persecution, and that Congress should recommend the individual States to restore their confiscated property. But these provisions were ignored by the States, and the loyalists fled, or were driven, from their homes, most of them to settle in Canada or Nova Scotia, where the British Government compensated them for some proportion at least of their losses. The lands between the Ohio and the Mississippi, annexed in 1774 to Canada, were handed over to the States. And the sovereign independence of the United States was formally recognised. The great schism was complete. No man can yet measure its full significance for good or ill. "We might have been a free and great people together," Jefferson had exclaimed, as he drafted the Declaration of

Independence. This was not to be, yet at least, independently of the other, each nation would itself become free and great, with a freedom and a greatness, which, while preserving a strong family resemblance, would follow a pattern of its own. It may be that it was well for the world, and for the community now dissolving, that separation should be. It may be that it was well that those who parted then should, by parting, all unconsciously have ensured that in time to come there would survive, as supreme world influences, not only the British way of life, but the British way of life as enriched and deflected by the vast cosmopolitan emigration from Europe to America in the nineteenth century. It may well be so, but to ensure it two consequences of the secession of 1783 were necessary, neither of which could the men of 1783 foresee. The British must learn, and learn nobly, the lessons of their failure, building a wiser and a wider Commonwealth on the wreckage of the old Empire. And sooner or later British and Americans, both free and both great, must come close to each other again if that ideal of freedom, which was the foundation of both their histories, was long to survive.

France, Spain and Holland, the ancient enemies, did not succeed in dismembering what was left of the Empire. They did not even maim it. In the course of negotiation their first ambitious demands were considerably abated, and in the end the peace treaty was mainly a mutual restoration of conquests. Minorca and Florida went to Spain, and Tobago in the West Indies to France. And in Africa France gained Senegal. But these were scratches, not wounds. Despite the loss of Minorca, Gibraltar (which some of the British ministers would have liked to exchange) still gave access to the Mediterranean. And now that her own colonies north of it were gone, Florida meant little to Britain. The wealthy West Indian islands were virtually intact. In Canada, larger than the whole territory of the United States from ocean to ocean, the United Empire Loyalists had planted the British way of life, and the nucleus of an English-speaking population, so that here Britain would yet be able to shew whether she had learnt the lesson of the lost colonies. In India the British were stronger than ever before. The French and Dutch trading stations were handed back, but all knew now that if there were war again Britain could take them as and when she pleased. And one of the Dutch posts, Negapatam, was not even handed back. Henceforth there would be no European rivals for the British in India.

Here was the nucleus of a great empire still. Accustomed by now to the speedy decline of defeated imperial peoples the world looked to see Britain sink to the rank of a second-rate power. But the

vitality of her people was unexhausted, and their mission still un-
discharged. They were still the most homogeneous and the most
enterprising people on earth. The Idea of freedom, which they had
lately betrayed, but still embodied, was now as before an expanding
and explosive force, and they were capable still not only of adventure
in every quarter of the globe but, at home, of inventions, political
and economic, which would transform the world. No man could
then foresee the rapid growth of the second Empire. But it was not
growth which mattered most. The discovery of unknown lands, and
the long struggle for existence against yet another tyrant, would add
vast, unlooked for territories to the Empire. But only self-discipline
and spiritual revival, only the wisdom which learns from failure,
could keep its soul alive.

CHAPTER THREE

CLIVE AND THE NABOBS

(1760-1774)

§1

MEANWHILE the same problem in another guise had been posed to the British in India. In was indeed but a heightened version of the moral problem of all rule everywhere. For here too they were required to learn that (in Burke's words) "all political power which is set over men ... ought to be some way or other exercised ultimately for their benefit." It was the same lesson which they had failed to learn in America, and, failing, had been compelled to part from their own flesh and blood. In India amid all the temptations of the Arabian Nights they did not fail. But despite Clive and Warren Hastings they did not succeed quickly, so that the laying of the moral foundations of British rule in the East became part of the revival which followed the loss of the American Colonies.

Clive had left India, for the second time, in 1760. By then his victories had already ensured that the British trading Company would not succumb to the flood of universal anarchy which threatened every Indian landmark, and that the new European administration which must succeed the dissolution of the Moghul Empire would be not French but British. The French had attempted to direct the disruptive forces released by the break-up of the Moghul Empire to the overthrow of their British rivals, and, thanks to Clive, they had failed. This much was already settled. But the nature of the new British administration, and the manner in which it would surmount, or conceivably fail to surmount, the manifold perplexities and temptations with which it was now beset, all this was still one vast interrogation mark.

Clive had returned to England very wealthy and very popular. With the doubtful exception of Wolfe, he was the greatest British soldier since Marlborough, and when his victories began he had been only twenty-five, an age at which, without the assistance of a veteran staff, no great commander, save Napoleon, has ever given equal proof of military genius. His public rewards, however, were not so great as he was entitled to expect. He was raised to the peerage, but after two years, and to an Irish barony. And the Court of Directors at East India House cooled noticeably towards him, as the first enthusiasm of the public wore off. It remembered no doubt the acid and outspoken strictures in a communication which he had dispatched to it shortly before he left India. Moreover Clive's suggestion to Pitt, that sovereignty in India might be transferred to the Crown, had become known, and had not endeared him to the rulers of the Company. Clive was, however, very wealthy—"no Englishman," says Macaulay, "who started with nothing has ever, in any line of life, created such a fortune at the early age of thirty-four." And his wealth made it easy for him to obtain a seat, and a small following, in Parliament (his Irish peerage did not debar him from the Commons) and, what is more, to spend a hundred thousand pounds on acquiring support in the Court of Proprietors of the Company, where every owner of five hundred pounds' worth of East India stock was qualified for a vote. He spent much money too in less ambiguous ways, giving large sums to his sisters, and to various poor friends and relations, and settling five hundred a year on his former commander, Lawrence, who was now in straitened circumstances, and eight hundred a year on his parents. It was not long before the votes at East India House proved useful. In the Court of Directors Laurence Sulivan enjoyed at this time a complete ascendancy—"he follows the same plan," Clive had written in a private letter to Bengal, "of keeping every one out of the direction who is endowed with more knowledge or would be likely to have more weight and influence than himself." And Sulivan now regarded Clive as a dangerous rival. He disliked his proposals for reform, and was jealous of his popularity. In politics too they were at variance, for on Pitt's retirement Clive had attached himself to Grenville, while Sulivan was an adherent of Bute. "The consequence has been," wrote Clive, "that we have all along behaved to one another like shy cocks." In the annual election of Directors in 1763 Clive, for all his votes, failed to overthrow Sulivan's ascendancy, and in revenge for the attempt Sulivan had orders sent to Calcutta prohibiting any further payments to Clive from the estate which he had received from Mir Jafir. This was a most high-handed proceeding, for the best English legal opinion held the grant valid, and the Company, which held much property in Bengal on precisely the same authority, had long acquiesced in it. Clive promptly replied by filing a bill in Chancery against the Directors. Such were the unedifying relations between Clive and the Company when the whole complexion of affairs was transformed by the increasingly grave news from Bengal, and the events were set in train which led to Clive's triumph in the Court of Directors, and to his return to India for that brief last period during which his services as statesman were even more splendid than those he had already rendered as soldier.

§2

The five years of Clive's absence in England make the darkest page in the history of British India. Bengal presented a gloomy scene of avarice and extortion among the rulers, and misery among the ruled, unrelieved by any spark of merit save the continuing prowess of the British soldier. British rule seemed to be earning speedy and ignominious collapse. It is strange that an administration destined to become famous for an integrity such as the East had never dreamed of should have been cradled in a corruption at which a Verres might have blushed. And yet it is not difficult to understand. For this was an interregnum between the old system and the new. Power had come too swiftly, and the Company was not ready to face its new obligations. Indeed it hardly yet recognised their existence. For although it had set up a puppet government in Bengal, although it controlled the revenue and provided the defence, it still persisted in thinking of itself as a mere trading organisation, and of the welfare of the Indian people as the concern of Indian princes and officials. The Company in short was doing its best to combine the new power of the military overlord with the old irresponsibility of the merchant adventurer, and the attempt, like all attempts to enjoy privilege without its corresponding obligations, could only end in disaster. Power without responsibility will always breed temptations which few human beings are qualified to resist. And at this particular moment and to these particular human beings the temptations were specially formidable. For these were men bred to commerce and thinking naturally in terms of wealth rather than welfare. And in Britain, too, and indeed in Europe, this was the age of the placeman and the sinecure, the age in which even men long trained to politics were apt to think of them largely as opportunities for self-enrichment. The task now set to the British in India therefore was to rise superior to a vastly exaggerated variety of the very temptations which they had not yet learned to overcome in Britain. It was a formidable task, which the spirit of Pitt might master but not the spirit of Walpole. It was a formidable task, yet if they failed in it, as so many earlier Empires had failed, the British Empire too was doomed. It was a formidable task, and the failure of those who were first so unexpectedly faced with it is not difficult to understand.

For Vansittart, the weak Governor of Bengal, and his subordinates, down to the most junior writer, found themselves suddenly all-powerful among fabulous riches, riches which could apparently be theirs for the asking. The only authority to which they owed allegiance was the Court of the Company, factious, ill-informed and so remote that it took eighteen months to receive an answer to a dispatch. Which is as much to say that in effect they were subject to no authority at all.

The Company moreover, itself not a government but a trading organisation primarily concerned to make money, had always not so much permitted as compelled its servants to enrich themselves through private speculation, by persisting in paying them salaries on which, so far from being able to save, they could not hope to subsist. And from legitimate private trading it seemed a short step to accepting from an Indian potentate gifts which would represent in England anything from a comfortable competence to a princely estate. It seemed a shorter step still for the junior officials, who could hardly hope thus to tap the Bengal treasury itself, to sell their traditional claim to trade free of tolls and dues to a medley of unprincipled native adventurers who mercilessly fleeced the soft Bengali population under cover of the British flag. While they traded tax free, the Bengal merchants in general paid a duty of forty per cent on every article of merchandise. In this way the Company's servants exploited, not for the Company but for themselves, almost the whole internal trade of Bengal. Meanwhile the Calcutta Council had deposed the ageing Mir Jafar, whom Clive had installed as Nawab after Plassey, and replaced him, to the accompaniment of a rich largesse to themselves, by Mir Cassim. When Mir Cassim proved recalcitrant and began to train his army by European methods, they defeated him and restored Mir Jafar. When Mir Cassim returned to the attack, with powerful allies, in 1764, his army of 50,000 was defeated with great slaughter by Sir Hector Munro with twelve hundred British soldiers, and eight thousand half-mutinous sepoys, at Buxar, a battle only less decisive than Plassey, which made it clear that, for all its early vices, British rule in Bengal could not be overthrown by force. Next year there was again a vacant throne to fill, for Mir Jafar himself had died, and the Councillors of Calcutta, selecting the illegitimate son instead of the legitimate grandson, again contrived to pocket prodigious sums. To these melancholy abuses was added all the inevitable confusion of two overlapping administrations, interdependent yet mutually hostile, the Indians retaining at least the appearance of civil jurisdiction, and the British all the effective authority of military power.

Pigot in the Carnatic, like the distracted Vansittart in Bengal, could
dictate high policy, when he pleased, through a puppet Nawab; but
meanwhile the day to day administration remained in the hands of
venal and ineffective native officials who had lost the respect even
of their own fellow-countrymen. Clearly these improvised arrangements were almost perfectly adapted to make the worst of both
worlds. Out of the medley of corruption and confusion it was for
Clive and the Directors to fashion a more honest and a more stable
system. If they proved unable to do so, Britain would have proclaimed herself unworthy of imperial power in the East.

The Directors were already seriously alarmed. Each vessel from
Calcutta seemed to bring some new tale of misgovernment or
extortion. And while the Company's trade steadily contracted its
servants were transmitting huge private fortunes to this country.
It was this aspect of the disastrous Indian scene on which, naturally
enough, the Directors fastened first. To lose their good name was
serious enough, to lose their dividends also was intolerable. And in
an indignant official survey they denounced the " unheard of ruinous
principle" among their servants, "of an interest distinct from the
Company," which "showed itself in laying hands upon everything
they did not deem the Company's property," so that "whilst the
Company were sinking under the burden of the war, our servants
were enriching themselves from those very funds that ought to
have supported the war." In their predicament Directors and
Proprietors alike turned instinctively to Clive. Let the man who
had laid the military foundation of British supremacy in India
return to add the moral and political foundations without which
military conquest would prove worthless, and all must soon founder.
The proposal was hotly resisted by Sulivan and his associates, but
the general body of shareholders was now much too alarmed to
listen patiently to the once all-powerful Chairman of the Directors.
By an enormous majority the Court of Proprietors invited Clive to
return to India as the first Governor General of all the Company's
Indian territories. As to the dispute over his Indian estate it was
hurriedly proposed that all proceedings should be dropped. Only
the sternest sense of duty compelled Clive to accept the formidable
proposal that he should return to India. How much pleasanter to
enjoy wealth and ease in England, rather than sacrifice his popularity,
and perhaps his reputation, by wielding the axe of the reformer
among the abuses, and the vested interests, of the East! But an
inner compulsion drove him, at any cost to himself, to save, if he
could and since no one else could, the future of British dominion
in the East. And so to the flustered Proprietors he replied with

dignity that as to the income of his estate he would make a proposal which he hoped would be satisfactory to the Directors, but that he could never undertake the government of India while Sulivan, his avowed enemy, remained Chairman of the Company. Amidst the ensuing uproar Sulivan was shouted down, and Clive was nominated Governor and Commander-in-Chief. He provisionally accepted the formidable commission, but stubbornly refused to take his departure until Sulivan had been dethroned. He knew enough already of the trials of the man on the spot not to be willing to have them added to by a hostile authority at home.

The next election of Directors was to be in April, 1764. The Company's ship waited on, in harbour, but Clive would not sail. And then, on the evening of April the twenty-fifth, it was known that in the new Court half the directors were supporters of Clive and half of Sulivan, but that, with the support of the new Chairman and deputy Chairman, Clive would have the preponderance. It was a narrow margin, but it was sufficient. Sulivan at least had fallen. And although the Council could not quite bring itself to accept Clive's suggestion that he should be free to overrule its decisions, in its anxiety to propitiate him it hit upon the cumbrous alternative of conceding this power to a Select Committee which he was to nominate, and of which he would be a member. Clive sailed in June, 1764.

§3

He was met, on his arrival at Calcutta, in May, 1765, by news of the Council's latest and most lucrative auction of the throne of Bengal, that which had followed the death of Mir Jafar. It wrung from Clive a cry of despair. "Alas!" he wrote to an intimate friend,

> how is the English name sunk! I could not avoid paying the tribute of a few tears to the departed and lost fame of the British nation—irrecoverably so, I fear. However, I do declare by that great Being who is the searcher of all hearts, and to whom we must be accountable if there be a hereafter, that I am come out with a mind superior to all corruption, and that I am determined to destroy these great and growing evils, or perish in the attempt.

These are the words of a man determined to do his duty at all costs. He knew that if he chose, and without exercising the slightest pressure on princes only anxious to load him with gifts, he could within a few months make himself the wealthiest subject in Europe. But it was to suppress such traffic that he had come to India, and he consistently declined to take the least advantage of his prodigious opportunities, and courteously but unequivocally refused every proffered gift. A legacy bequeathed to him by Mir Jafar he made over to the Company as a fund for soldiers invalided in its service. After a year and a half of such opportunities of self-enrichment as no European perhaps has ever enjoyed he left India poorer than he reached it. Perhaps this timely example was his greatest service to the East.

He knew too that to suppress the rampant abuses effectively must raise up enmities which would pursue him rancorously to the end of his days, yet he did not hesitate. His first action was to suspend the powerful and flagitious Council of Calcutta, and substitute for it the Select Committee of his own choice. He prohibited the taking of presents from Indians. He prohibited the private trade of the Company's servants. And since he knew that this unofficial commerce, which had been the origin of all the frightful corruption in Bengal, was nevertheless a long-recognised tradition, and that a Company which did not even pay its officials a living wage could hardly expect them to abstain from every source of private profit, he made arrangements to appropriate a part of the revenue of the salt monopoly to increasing the salaries paid by the Company. These measures were not immediately and completely successful. Private trade and private presents persisted after Clive's departure. About two years later the Company substituted for the salt monopoly a percentage of its own net revenue as the source from which to supplement salaries. Nevertheless Clive's reforms were decisive. The cleansing of the Augean stable had begun. What might have been corruption in the oriental tradition and of oriental dimensions would become something very different. Britain had by no means yet earned the moral right to rule India, but Clive had made it possible for her to earn it. By the whole tenor of what he did, and above all perhaps by his own personal example, he set a new standard which in due time would become ubiquitous and un-questioned. This was a more splendid achievement than Plassey itself.

The prevailing laxity had spread to the Company's troops, and during Clive's mission two hundred British officers, enraged at a reduction by the Directors in their pay, conspired to resign their commissions simultaneously, confident that this early example of collective bargaining would speedily bring the authorities to their knees. But they had reckoned without Clive. He arrested, tried and cashiered the ringleaders, sent for loyal officers from Madras, and issued new commissions to civilians. The sepoys, for whom the name of Clive stood for almost supernatural powers, remained as steady as a rock. The mutiny collapsed ignominiously and at once.

It remained for Clive to strike at the diarchy which was paralysing the administration of Bengal, a task which involved far-reaching decisions not only constitutional but diplomatic. A formidable coalition of native princes which had been threatening Bengal laid down its arms at the mere rumour of his landing. The Mogul wished Clive to extend a British protectorate over Delhi and all northern India, where of late Mahrattas and Afghans had been alternating in conquest. But Clive, like most British statesmen of the time, believed in the maxim of Pericles, *do not add to Empire*, and had no wish to extend his country's power or responsibilities. "Never consent to act offensively against any power" he wrote. The British had not come to India for warfare, and once again they were slow to recognise that the logic of history would force Empire upon them. Moreover a sure instinct warned Clive that his fellow-countrymen were not yet morally prepared for wider power in the East. And so he made Oudh into a buffer state between the native powers and Bengal, whose government he proceeded to establish upon an altogether new footing. In return for a regular subsidy the Mogul ceded to the Company the *diwani*, or right of administering the revenues. In Bengal the Company thus became the supreme civil, as well as military, authority, not only *de facto* but *de jure* ruler of the province. Henceforth its Nawabs, though they retained for the present the administration of justice, would be but royal pensioners and subjects of the British Company, dignified but powerless symbols of the past. "The power," Clive reported, "is now lodged where it can only be lodged with safety," and he seems to have thought of this significant transaction only as permanently securing the Company's position in Bengal. Nevertheless he had here set in train a process which would continue until in one form or another all India had acknowledged the Company's authority. At the end of January, 1767, he sailed home for the last time. The fortunes of the Carnatic, to which he had been able to devote scarcely any attention, were just now not bright; it had been invaded by Nizam Ali, and then by Hyder Ali of Mysore, and there had been war with these two free-booters, each of whom had seized his own throne by violence, and with the Mahrattas. But just now what was of most moment was the settlement in Bengal, and the foreshadowing there of new standards of public morality, the germ of all that was to come. And by the courage and wise moderation which he had shown in Bengal

Clive had won a place among the select band, headed by Cæsar and Napoleon, of great soldiers who have also been great statesmen, and had almost earned Macaulay's verdict that "our island, so fertile in heroes and statesmen, has scarcely ever produced a man more truly great either in arms or in council."

§4

He did not, on his return to England, find his contemporaries disposed to take this view. His old enemies among the Directors were implacable, and a host of new enmities, bred by his reforms in India, pursued him home. In England he was to fall a victim to popular resentment at the abuses which in India he had done so much to suppress. For the British public was by now profoundly disturbed by what it knew of the course of events in India. And here, dimly and gropingly, it was beginning to display its fitness to play a great new imperial role. British citizens did not know much of India, but they believed that their fellow-countrymen there were guilty of corruption and injustice, and they were angry and indignant. They had yet to hear Burke proclaim that Britain was morally responsible for the welfare of dependent races; but the man in the street could not help but be aware that something was gravely wrong with British administration in the East, and an innate sense of justice and moderation came to his aid. And naturally enough his indignation focused upon the homecoming "East Indians," whose wealth and ostentation would in any case have rendered them unpopular, and who provided a constant reminder of the abuses, with which rumour was now so busy, in the East.

For the shower of gold which had descended on the Company's servants in Bengal, was already producing its curious social consequences at home. The tide of returning "Nabobs" had set in. Wealthy, too often very wealthy, and accustomed to abject subservience in the east, they could find no niche for themselves in the society, at once aristocratic and democratic, of their own country. Too wealthy and pretentious to associate readily with the classes from which they mostly sprang, they were too vulgar, too grotesquely *nouveaux riches*, to be accepted by the aristocracy to which they aspired. They were apt accordingly to fall victims to a complex of inferiority which drove them to even more extravagant ostentation, and, as such complexes so often do, towards the politics of the Left, so that Burke reckoned "the East Indians" Jacobins almost to a man. Add to all this the general belief that the wealth which they so brazenly flaunted was the fruit of cruelty and corruption, and it is not surprising that they became the targets of universal hatred and contempt, denounced in the pulpit, satirised in literature, lampooned in art and derided on the stage. The instantaneous revulsion in Britain at the first hint of excesses such as those which undermined the virtues of republican Rome was evidence of that vein of robust austerity in the national character which would fit it for an imperial rôle.

That Clive himself, who had done so much to repress the very vices with which he was charged, should have been the first conspicuous victim of his countrymen's indignation was a tragedy indeed, but a tragedy which so underlined the pregnant lessons to be learned that it may perhaps be said that in his dark closing years he was rendering no less lasting service to India than in the days of his splendour and power. The tragedy of Warren Hastings, the moral fervour of Burke's accusing eloquence would be needed before Britain moved unmistakably down the right path, but already she had turned her face towards it. In 1768 it was not difficult to see Clive, the latest and greatest of the returned East Indians, as but the wealthiest, and there were enemies to whisper, the wickedest of the Nabobs. Soon there were plenty of honest citizens for whom the great Captain had become the personification of all the mysterious abuses of the East, including the abuses which he had himself sacrificed health, ease and popularity to suppress. In 1772 the storm broke in Parliament. A Committee was appointed to inquire into Indian affairs. It cross-examined Clive unsparingly, and sifted laboriously and hungrily through much ancient history—the fraud practised on Omichund and the gifts received from Mir Jafar. Clive, who bitterly resented the whole proceedings, told the Committee bluntly that as to the deception, if he found himself in the same circumstances he would unhesitatingly do the same again, and as to the presents he need only have said the word and he could have had ten times as much:

A great prince was dependent on my pleasure; an opulent city lay at my mercy: its richest bankers bid against each other for my smiles; I walked through vaults which were thrown open to me alone, piled on either hand with gold and jewels! Mr. Chairman, at this moment I stand astonished at my own moderation.

At length, after stormy debates, the Commons resolved "that all acquisitions made under the influence of a military force . . . do of right belong to the state," and that for private persons to appropriate them is illegal. They resolved, too, that Clive had obtained large sums from Mir Jafar. But they declined to censure him explicitly. And they concluded by accepting, without a division, a further resolution that "Robert, Lord Clive did at the same time render great and meritorious services to his country." These characteristically illogical conclusions did credit to the assembly which passed them. Clive had not been explicitly censured, yet at the very outset of British rule in India Parliament had issued a stern public warning against corruption. In Clive the Commons censured all the nameless Collectors and Councillors who had shown so much more greed and rendered so much less service. More than this would have been unjust to one who had wrought lasting good and displayed great self-restraint; less would have proved Parliament unfit to rule an Empire. Clive himself did not long survive this partial acquittal. The brief remainder of his life was passed under a cloud. He had always been liable to melancholia, and as he sat lonely and inactive amid the splendours of his mansion at Claremont, it preyed upon him increasingly. In November, 1774, at the age of forty-nine, he died by his own hand.

CHAPTER FOUR

WARREN HASTINGS

(1772-1795)

§1

MEANWHILE the vast, confused problems of India accumulated menacingly. In Bengal the revenues, though administered by the British, continued to be collected by native officials, to the traditional accompaniment of corruption and oppression. A third of its population perished in the famine of 1769 and 1770. The Company's servants continued, though less flagrantly, to enrich themselves. It was evident that in many directions Clive's reforms must be extended. As to the Madras Presidency, it was constantly in dispute, and often at war, with turbulent native neighbours. And in Bombay, whose tranquillity had long made it a welcome contrast to the Company's other possessions, the Council would soon back a pretender to the Mahratta throne, and become involved in war with that formidable race. In addition to all this, the ubiquitous Mahratta marauders, now again masters of Delhi, were penetrating into Rohilkand on the frontiers of Clive's buffer state of Oudh. And in all the vast areas of India which lay remote from direct contact with the Company's territories anarchy and rapine throve and grew. It was a dark and disquieting scene, and it was fortunate indeed for British India that at this juncture there should have occurred the only event which could have given it the resilience to survive the stresses of the coming world war—the emergence as Governor of Bengal of Clive's greatest successor, who, like Clive, would save British India, and, like Clive, be arraigned by his fellow-countrymen.

§2

Warren Hastings came of an ancient and illustrious family, whose main stock, though there had been earldoms among its junior branches, had been so impoverished by the civil wars that his great-grandfather had been compelled to part with the family seat at Daylesford in Worcestershire. Hastings's father, grandson of the last Hastings of Daylesford, was not, as Macaulay says,[1] "an idle worthless boy," who "married before he was sixteen"; he was already in Holy Orders when the future Governor General was christened in 1732. But he was very poor, and when the boy's mother died a few days after his birth, he left the child to be brought up by its grandfather. From his earliest years Daylesford, the lost home of his family, haunted young Warren's imagination; in later life he told a friend that "when I was scarcely seven years old, I well remember that I first formed the determination to purchase back Daylesford." It was a dream which never left him, and whose eventual realisation, against every apparent probability, many years later, cheered the darkest years of his life. At the age of ten he was sent to Westminster School, where he became the senior scholar of his year and showed such promise of distinction in the classics that when the uncle who had become responsible for him decided to ship him off at sixteen, as a junior writer, to India, his headmaster begged hard that he should be allowed to stay on. If the pedagogue had had his way, Hastings would have gone to Oxford or Cambridge, would in all probability have obtained a Fellowship, and might conceivably have rivalled the learning of Porson or Bentley. He was destined for a wider stage than the University, and for a career more splendid and more stormy than that of a classical don.

By 1761 he was a member of the Council in Calcutta, and during the years of corruption which followed it was all too easy for a member of the Council to enrich himself. But Hastings remained poor. Despite his secret ambition to repurchase Daylesford, avarice was never one of his failings. His passion was not wealth but power, and power he desired for his country even more than for himself. He was a man of vivid personality and an insatiably active and inquiring intellect. Everything interested him, and he loved the teeming heterogeneity of India, and respected, and understood, its inhabitants, to a degree hardly equalled by any subsequent Governor General or Viceroy. When he became Governor of Bengal in 1772, his most formidable task, he soon found, would be to raise the money for which the Directors at home were always pressing, and of which the government in India never had enough. And almost all the faults subsequently charged against him were the faults of a ruler eager to increase the power of his government, usually by enriching its depleted treasury. It was to increase the power of his government that, with the authority of the Directors, he transferred the collection

[1] In the famous *Essay on Warren Hastings*, where he takes his facts from Gleig's *Memoirs of the Life of Warren Hastings*. Macaulay also has the Christian name of Warren's father wrong. The facts as to Hastings's parentage will be found in Sir Charles Lawson's *The private life of Warren Hastings*, 17-20.

of the revenue to British officials and dealt the death blow to the
dual system of administration. It was to enrich it that, for a payment of four hundred thousand pounds, he lent one of the Bengal
army's three brigades to the Nawab of Oudh, to enable that monarch
to annex Rohilkand. It is true that, as Macaulay says, the Rohillas
were a courageous and accomplished race whom only British troops
could have conquered, and that the cowardly and usurping Nawab
of Oudh soon reduced their prosperous territory to the uniform
squalor of his own dominions. But it is also true that Rohilkand,
whose integrity was important to Oudh and therefore to Bengal,
was being raided by the all-conquering Mahrattas, and that the
Rohillas were themselves alien usurpers of very recent date.

§3

In the year after Hastings became Governor, Lord North, who
was so soon now to lose America, decided that he could no longer
postpone trying his hand at the reform of India. Pitt, who had by
now "fallen upstairs" and was Earl of Chatham, had regarded Indian
reform as "the transcendent object" of his last ill-starred administration. The Indian provinces, he held, must be claimed, and governed,
as dominions of the Crown. But when the inquiry, which he
instigated, began, Chatham, though still chief Minister, was inaccessible in his sick-room, on the verge of insanity, and his colleagues
made nothing of the business. And now North, the king's mouthpiece, a very different physician, was compelled to try his hand at
a remedy. Chatham, temporarily recovered, approved from a
distance. "India," he wrote, "teems with iniquities so rank as to
smell to heaven and earth." And "the hearts and good affections
of Bengal are of more worth than all the profits of ruinous and
odious monopolies." He saw that if there was to be a British Empire
in the East there must be a drastic cleansing. He saw, but he could
not act. North did not think in these terms, but even he could not
help seeing that something must be done.

The relations between the Company and the home government,
and between the Company as merchant and the Company as ruler,
could not be left in their present indescribable confusion. Let no one
suppose that the rare political talent so often displayed by the
British Empire came to it naturally and without effort, by a sort
of divine afflatus. The art of government can only be acquired by
experience, and the distinctive quality of British rule has always been
its instinct for the empirical, its ability to learn by trial and error—

and it may well be that at this time, in the infancy of European experience in the East, no British statesman could have framed a satisfactory constitution. What is certain at any rate is that North and his colleagues were peculiarly incapable of doing so. There was one salutary feature in their Regulating Act of 1773, and only one. They unified Indian administration. Henceforth Madras and Bengal were all alike subject to the jurisdiction of a Governor General at Calcutta. And Warren Hastings was to be the first Governor General. This prudent process of centralisation, and more particularly the choice of Hastings as the ruler of all the Company's territories, would save, but only just save, British India in the coming world war. But for this, Lord North would in all probability have gone down to history not only as the man who lost America, but as the man who lost India also. For here the wisdom of the Regulating Act came to an abrupt stop, and the rest was *a priori* pedantry in its crudest form. Democracy has always had a dangerous weakness for committees, and eighteenth century theorists of the constitution had a peculiar taste of their own for checks and balances. And so the Governor General was saddled with a Council of Four, appointed, like himself, by Parliament. Each of the five was to have one vote, unless their opinions were equally divided, in which case a casting vote went to the Governor. If three of the Council opposed the Governor he was powerless. And as if thus to have organised systematic deadlock was not sufficient, the legislators proceeded to divide power between the Company and the British Government with such meticulous nicety that it became virtually impossible to decide which was the responsible authority. For Parliament appointed the Governor General, but he took his orders from the Directors. The Directors in turn were required to submit to the ministry all the instructions they sent out to India, and the ministers could disallow them. But ministers were not responsible, to Parliament or to any one else, for the consequences of their interference. Finally the Act set up a Supreme Court—and a bitter dispute was soon raging between the first Governor General and the first Chief Justice (who were old schoolfellows and personal friends) as to their respective jurisdictions. In part perhaps Lord North and his colleagues were misled by the national instinct for compromise. They may have supposed that if power were distributed as evenly as possible between rival authorities, policy would naturally follow a golden mean. In any case they had produced a constitution which came as near to being completely unworkable as was humanly possible, and must indeed have been fatal but for the fortunate accident that Warren Hastings was a ruler of genius, and that a succession of chances, and the vast distance between India and England, enabled him to shake himself free from most of its paralysing restrictions.

§4

In their infatuated belief in checks and balances the authors of the Regulating Act had selected as three of the first four Councillors men known to be convinced opponents of the Governor General, thus yet further ensuring that their constitution should be all check and no balance. One of them, Philip Francis, a person of peculiar malevolence, was almost certainly the author of the *Letters of Junius*, the most famous and the bitterest literary invective in our language. All three were new to India; and reached Calcutta in October, 1774, profoundly ignorant of Indian problems and Indian habits, but unalterably convinced that everything the Governor General had done, or was likely to do, must be wrong. In a sense they represented a public opinion at home which was suspicious, and rightly suspicious, of most things Indian. But they carried first suspicion, and then personal rancour, to unnatural lengths. Hastings and Barwell, the only member of the Council besides himself who knew anything of India, received them with ill-concealed misgivings, and with a salute of guns which fell provokingly short of the customary complement. Barwell was a fussy and loquacious person, but by now he was won over to boundless admiration of Hastings' great abilities, and he proved a tower of strength in the years of conflict now beginning. Francis and his allies, Sir John Clavering and Colonel Monson, had their own grounds for complaint. Hastings was a man of vast ability, striking good looks and immense personal charm, but, fortunately as it proved, he was also by nature a benevolent despot. During the years when he had been Governor of Bengal only, his Council had been entirely complaisant, he himself had been the government, and he had developed to the full the dictatorial and solitary habits of thought and action which became his permanent characteristic as Governor General. He was admirably informed on Indian affairs by an extensive network of agents, but he disclosed as little as possible of what he knew or what he intended to his colleagues. They for their part at once made it clear that they regarded the Governor General as a man already on his trial. They demanded to see all the official correspondence which had passed since he assumed office, and set themselves as a matter of routine to vote down all his plans and reverse all his decisions. The affairs of every Presidency were soon plunged in steadily increasing confusion. And within six months of their arrival Francis and his allies were presented with what appeared to be a heaven-sent opportunity of destroying the Governor General.

Raja Nuncomar,[1] a wealthy and powerful Brahmin, handed them a document purporting to show that Hastings, who was a bitter personal enemy of his own, had been guilty of corruption on a vast scale. The triumvirate received it with unbounded satisfaction. They had not perhaps fully realised that, in the words of Macaulay, "large promises, smooth excuses, elaborate tissues of circumstantial falsehood, chicanery, perjury, forgery, are the weapons, offensive and defensive, of the people of the lower Ganges"; or that it was only necessary for it to be suspected by the native population that the dominant power would have no objections to seeing a particular individual ruined for it to be furnished unasked within twenty-four hours with an abundance of the most damning charges supported by the most circumstantial evidence. Even the known fact that Nuncomar himself, though the highest of religious dignitaries, had in the past been repeatedly detected in criminal intrigues, including forgery, did not deter them. Their triumph seemed to be complete. All native Bengal believed that the Governor General was now doomed and that henceforth the triumvirate was the power to reckon with. Nuncomar held a daily levee in almost royal state, crowded by obsequious compatriots. But he had reckoned without one novel feature of Lord North's act. Of a sudden Calcutta was electrified by the news that Nuncomar had been arrested, charged with another forgery, six years old and in no way concerned with high politics, and committed to the common gaol. For under the Regulating Act the High Court was wholly independent of the Council, and it was the Chief Justice, Sir Elijah Impey, who had been at Westminster with Hastings, who had ordered Nuncomar's arrest. Before Impey and a British jury the unfortunate Brahmin was tried, condemned and sentenced to death. Abruptly Bengali opinion was transformed; the Governor General, after all, and not his enemies on the council, was the power with which the prudent must reckon. No one doubted now who was master in Bengal. In due course Nuncomar was hanged, the triumvirate having coolly ignored his petition for a respite. At Hastings's trial twelve years later these strange events formed one of the principal charges against him, and they have been hotly disputed ever since. No man will ever now

---

[1] This is the Anglicised form of the name made famous in the course of the long controversy. Some modern historians, more accurate or more pedantic, write it Nandakumar. But there is no finality in the spelling of Indian names.

know the whole truth concerning them, but some facts are indisputable, and they seem to warrant certain conclusions. The trial and execution of Nuncomar at that particular moment undoubtedly saved Hastings from much embarrassment and danger, and proved the turning point in his struggle with the triumvirate. Impey, who set in motion the formidable machinery of justice, was an old friend who certainly knew how convenient for Hastings it would be that Nuncomar should be disposed of. The trial was impartial and the verdict in all probability just, and in English law (though not in Scotland or North America) forgery was a capital offence. Yet to award the death penalty for forgery was as hopelessly foreign to Indian sentiment as to British citizens to-day would be the hanging of a man for travelling in a first-class railway compartment with a third-class ticket. As far as is known, no Indian, before or since, has ever been hanged for forgery.[1] It is hardly surprising that all Hastings's enemies, and most of his friends, assumed that he was the real instigator of the proceedings. And if he was so, the undoubted fact that Nuncomar was guilty of many other crimes for which he was not tried is no mitigation. In defence of Hastings, whom most recent historians have been disposed to acquit, it remains the chief argument that, although his entire public record was sifted and resifted by hostile critics during his own lifetime as that of no statesman ever has been before or since, no scrap of evidence has ever been produced to connect him with the affair. It is too much perhaps to suppose that the prosecution of that particular individual at that particular moment was nothing but coincidence, with Impey as a miraculous *deus ex machina*. But it does seem probable that, although Impey may have instituted the prosecution because he knew that it would be of service to the Governor, the Governor watched events with relief and satisfaction no doubt, but without active participation.

In this ambiguous fashion Hastings had thus survived the first great threat to his Governorship. He survived a second when, not long after, the Government, learning of his differences with its three nominees, decided that he ought to be recalled. But here Lord North found himself hoist by his own petard. Under a characteristic provision of the Regulating Act the Governor General could be removed by the Crown, but only on an address from the Company. And by a narrow margin of votes the Court of Proprietors declined to oblige. Hastings's final release from domestic perils and obstructions came when Monson, and then Clavering, died, in 1776 and

[1] Despite an ambiguous sentence in the *Oxford History of India*, 515. See Thompson and Garratt *Rise and Fulfilment of British Rule in India*, 137.

1777, leaving of the implacable triumvirate only Francis. Their successors, one of whom was Sir Eyre Coote, victor of Wandewash, were more amenable. Hastings could now go his own way. It was high time. In Madras the party of corruption had actually imprisoned its governor. Bombay was deeply involved in its struggle with the Mahrattas of Poonah. And it was in 1778 that Vergennes judged that his time had come, France joined the revolted American colonies and another world war had begun. It was time that Hastings's hands were freed. Under the checks and balances of the Regulating Act as exploited by dissidents in the Council, British India must infallibly have perished under the weight of its own shortcomings and the onslaught of its enemies. Left at last to his own devices, the great Governor General just, but only just, contrived to preserve it in the troublous years to come.

§5

When the storm burst in 1778, British rule in India was threatened with an alliance between its European enemies and one or other of the powerful Indian military adventurers who flourished upon the ruins of the Mogul empire. But hostile armies were by no means the only danger which Hastings had to face. While Britain grappled with the American colonists, the fleets of France, Spain and Holland and the political hostility of almost all Europe, he could not expect supplies from home. And some of the measures by which he filled his own war-chest earned him in later years the famous impeachment whose consequences would do so much to establish the moral basis of British rule in India. Moreover in war as in peace he must continue to create an administration virtually out of the void. He had dissolved the corrupt dyarchy and transferred power to British hands but he was still building up the vast and complex machine of government—when he left India he could boast that every public office in Bengal was his own creation. Despite what by British standards was a complete lack of experienced administrators and official traditions he created a government and reduced anarchy to order. Civil problems as formidable as the war itself beset him continuously. It was after war had begun that he had to crush the pretensions of the independent judiciary under Impey, which had established something like a reign of terror among the natives and seemed about to usurp supreme authority for itself. And all this he achieved while constantly bombarded with censures from home, and bitterly opposed by the members of his own council. But Hastings possessed what was perhaps even rarer than his cool judgment and his inflexible will, an imperturbable patience. And so he triumphed over all difficulties, political and military. Before the struggle with France began he was already involved in a preventive war with the Mahrattas of the west, from whom he had expected the chief danger, when the Carnatic was suddenly invaded and overrun by the formidable Hyder Ali of Mysore, greatest of all the native adventurers who during the last few decades had carved themselves kingdoms out of the anarchy of India. In three weeks the British Empire in the south was on the verge of collapse; a French expeditionary force would shortly descend upon the Coromandel coast; all was at stake. Hastings acted with his usual calm resolution and energy. The quarrel with the Mahrattas was hastily patched up, troops and money were poured into Madras, the Governor of Fort St. George was suspended, and Sir Eyre Coote, the victor of Wandewash, a veteran but still the first captain in India, was bundled off to stem Hyder Ali's advance. In a few months the signal victory of Porto Novo had saved the Carnatic. And so while in Europe, Africa and America Britain was compelled to give ground, in India, and India only, she actually extended her power during the world war of Independence. Hastings's administration closed in serene tranquillity. For the first time for many decades peace and prosperity reigned in Bengal. The Governor General left India in 1785 admired and beloved by the entire British community, civilians and soldiers alike, and with the reverence and gratitude of the peoples over whom he had ruled. He returned not, as he expected, to new honours and new power, but to a lingering personal tragedy. The explanation of that paradox is an explanation of the new Empire.

§6

Hastings had had to find the money not only to fight an expensive war, but to continue the necessary remittances to his expectant masters at home. He found it largely from the treasuries of neighbouring states. In the general anarchy of India all the long-descended and legitimate governments were either mere phantoms, or in the last stages of decrepitude, while all the vigorous and effective monarchs had won their thrones lately and by the sword. In such an environment it was not difficult for a ruler of Hastings's resolution and resourcefulness to find pretext for exactions as to whose legality the subtlest lawyer would have been puzzled to pronounce. Was the Rajah of Benares a great feudatory of the

British Empire, properly subject to what the feudal system would have called tallage for the necessities of his overlord, or was he an independent sovereign, liable for a fixed tribute indeed, but liable for nothing more? No man could say for certain, but Hastings squeezed him for steadily increasing sums. Again, the Nawab of Oude was degenerate and incompetent and his miserable subjects could only be protected from marauders by the loan of a British brigade. Was Hastings entitled, when the Nawab boggled at the payments for these troops, to wring twelve hundred thousand pounds out of the Begums, or royal ladies, of Oude? No; yet without the money he could not have saved British India. The charge against Hastings therefore was not corruption, for his personal record was scrupulously honourable, nor was it misrule, for he had given Bengal the best government it had known for centuries. The charge was that on certain notable occasions he had oppressed or despoiled his defenceless neighbours. Already, before his term was over, Parliament had severely censured some of his measures, and had tried, and failed, to have him recalled.

At first when he returned to England, all went well; he found "everywhere and universally . . . evidences . . . that I possess the good opinion of my country." A peerage, a seat on the Board of Control, seemed within his grasp. But he had reckoned without Francis and without Burke. His services to India were not yet complete. He had still to stand his trial. Not till the thunder of Burke's accusing eloquence had died away would Britain have made good her moral title to dominion in the East.

Francis, who had ended his Indian career by fighting a duel with the Governor General, still nursed his malevolence, and was now a member of Parliament. As for Burke, that wise and eloquent Irishman knew everything which was to be known about India, except all that which could only be learnt from living there. He could see that there had been oppression, but for all his splendid powers of imagination he could not fully grasp the nature of the stresses under which Hastings had been compelled to act. Nevertheless he knew that there had been oppression, and for him that was enough. The new conception which he had firmly grasped, and would now nobly proclaim, of Britain's responsibility before God and man for the defenceless natives of India, would become the moral basis of British rule in Asia and Africa, and marked a long advance in civilisation itself. That Burke's righteous indignation should soon have come near to monomania, that he should have lashed himself into a sustained passion which could see the great Governor General only as devil incarnate, all this may have been the tragedy of Warren

Hastings, and indeed of Burke himself, but it does not impair the vast significance of what Burke did. The attention of the thousands who devoured the opening speeches of the trial in Westminster Hall in 1788 may have been fastened upon the pageantry and the eloquence, but, even so, unconsciously an enduring lesson was burned into their minds. And it was a lesson which made the second Empire possible, and would lie at the foundations of the Commonwealth to be. The doctrine of imperial trusteeship was born of Burke's speeches in Westminster Hall.

That there was a trial at all was largely the doing of Hastings and his advisers, in particular of the egregious Major Scott. Over-confident and ill-advised, Hastings had first provoked the Opposition with a challenge and then, when summoned to the Bar, bored the House by reading it a long, prosy memorandum. The issue in the decisive division was turned by a speech from Pitt, a speech whose logic was so obscure that many, even some among his friends, were convinced that his motive had been petty jealousy. But years after-wards Wilberforce, who had been Pitt's confidant, declared that he had given the case "as much impartial attention . . . as if he were a juryman." And though the reasons Pitt gave for voting for an impeachment may have been over-subtle, and though impeachment was a hopelessly antiquated and cumbrous process, it was well that there was a public trial. For if Britain, the ancient enemy of auto-cracy in the West, was herself henceforth to play the autocrat in the East—and autocracy was the only government which the East understood—Parliament must accept full responsibility for what the Governor General did there. And if the British were to learn to recognise themselves as trustees for backward peoples, Parliament must see that its servants were faithful to their trust.

The trial itself began by being over-dramatised—the grey Hall of Westminster bright with the scarlet and ermine of peers and judges, and crammed with great dames and famous beauties, ambassadors and wits, with Fox, Sheridan and Burke eager to display their matchless eloquence and Mrs. Siddons and Georgina, Duchess of Devonshire, their celebrated charms. The ladies who sobbed or fainted, the fifty guineas paid for a single ticket, Sheridan ending his peroration by falling exhausted into the arms of Burke, all were true to the theatrical atmosphere which lay heavy over the great spectacle from the start. But if its opening was theatrical its close was unredeemed anticlimax. For the Lords had other business besides the impeachment; there were Bills to attend to in their House and partridges to shoot on their estates. In its second year only seventeen days were given to the trial. It lingered on, half forgotten, for nearly eight years. Long before the end the result was a foregone conclusion, and when the acquittal was at last pronounced in the spring of 1795, it seemed, as Hastings himself said, as if the case had been opened before one generation, and the verdict pronounced by another. The accused had been almost beggared by the expenses of the trial, and all the ambitions with which he returned from India had been thwarted. All, rather, save one; thanks to the generosity of the Company he was able to repurchase and restore Daylesford. In his old age another generation was at pains to do him honour. He became a member of the Privy Council, and on several occasions was treated with signal deference by the Prince Regent. When, in 1813, he appeared once again at the Bar of the Commons, this time as an expert witness on Indian affairs, members received him with acclamation and rose and uncovered as he withdrew. At Oxford the University gave him an honorary degree, amidst the frantic applause of the undergraduate audience. To the end of his life, in adversity and prosperity, he preserved the noble equanimity with which he had faced every crisis of his Governor Generalship.

§7

If the career of Warren Hastings was a tragedy, it was a tragedy which history cannot regret. Like Clive, he had served Britain and India no less as defendant than as Governor General. He had preserved British India in the hour of danger; he had built up an entire administrative system; he had given the subjects of the Company security and prosperity such as they had not known for generations; more than any other man he had initiated the tradition of just and efficient government in India. He had held power in a time of deadly peril, constantly compelled to improvise his own resources, and here and there, in the stress of crisis, he had used his power tyrannically. A century and a half later we have ourselves seen great European nations daily and officially practising abuses of power beside which Hastings's most flagrant lapse seems a mild and amiable virtue. We can see to-day that Hastings's ultimate objects were the same as Burke's, and that the charges against him were wildly exaggerated, yet we cannot regret that they were made. For although it was only under stress of a great emergency that Hastings acted oppressively to certain neighbouring princes, and although long after his day the rule of many whom their countries have called great has been incomparably more oppressive in times of profound peace, it cannot be denied that Hastings often acted as though he believed that the necessities of the state must override morality, *salus populi suprema lex*. No doctrine can more speedily sap the moral sense of a nation, and it was well for Britain that Burke should have proclaimed a contrary creed. For nation and Empire now stood at the crossroads. If the British had not become conscious that their power in the East must rest henceforth upon a new moral principle, if they had not begun, haltingly at first, to put that principle into practise, their Empire would now have gone the way of all other Empires. When Burke declared that "all political power which is set over men . . . ought to be some way or other exercised ultimately for their benefit" he was proclaiming the moral charter of the new Empire, and making possible the future Commonwealth. It was of crucial importance that Britain should have mastered the worst temptations of power in the East when she had just failed so disastrously to rise to her opportunities in the West. Because George III and his ministers had lost America the Empire perished. Because Clive, Hastings and Burke had saved India, the Empire would be reborn.

Books for Further Reading.

G. B. Herz, *The Old Colonial System;* J. A. Doyle, *The Colonies under the House of Hanover;* Basil Williams, *The Life of William Pitt, Earl of Chatham; The Correspondence of George III with Lord North;* Sir G. O. Trevelyan, *The American Revolution;* Sir A. J. Arbuthnot, *Lord Clive;* Sir Charles Lawson, *The Private Life of Warren Hastings;* Lord Macaulay, *Essays* (on Clive and Warren Hastings); Edward Thompson and G. T. Garratt, *The rise and fulfilment of British rule in India;* Sir Alfred Lyall, *British Dominion in India.*

Book VI

RE-BIRTH

CHAPTER ONE

THE END AND THE BEGINNING

§1

AND SO Britain seemed to have rejected her destiny. The haphazard enterprise of a nation of seafarers in an age when the world lay empty had enabled her to people a new Continent, but she had lacked the wisdom and self-restraint needful for the mastering of the novel problems bred of her success. And so to all seeming one more Empire had passed. For according to all precedent the loss of the American colonies should have been the end of the British Empire. Like imperial Spain and imperial Holland Britain should now have shrunk to secondary stature. Like so many ancient Empires, her Empire should have bled to death. Something of this sort indeed was confidently anticipated by foreign observers. They had noted the failure in America; they had failed to note the foundations of success in the East. And neither the success nor the failure did they understand. Yet the British still held the key to the future in their hands. For if they could accept the doctrine that power is trusteeship in one Continent might they not learn one day to practise it in every Continent? That this was indeed the key to the future the British themselves had not yet realised. Yet it is difficult to resist the impression that the folk-mind of the people, still aware of its own vigour, was instinctively conscious that somehow, at some other time and in some other place, a high destiny still awaited it. Indeed even in the immediate outlook they saw no cause for misgivings. At home the loss of the thirteen colonies was followed by no wave of pessimism or self-distrust. In general politicians and people still looked upon the diminished Empire of 1783 as a solid and hopeful concern. Indeed there was almost a sense of relief when the long struggle was over and the American colonies had finally parted company. For in the eyes of most British citizens who had reflected on imperial matters at all, brought up, as they had been, in the mercantilist tradition, these thirteen continental colonies of settlers had long seemed a divergence from the normal pattern of a maritime Empire, an anomaly not easy to fit into the imperial scheme. No wonder, they thought, that there had been trouble with America. And now that the Empire was reduced to narrower limits but, as it seemed to them, to a more intelligible pattern they set themselves contentedly enough to develop it. So far were they from having lost heart or forgotten their ancient energy that within five years of recognising the independence of the United States they were founding New South Wales in the newly discovered continent of Australia, destined before long to present them with that same problem, of a distant population of British settlers, which in America they had so misunderstood, and of which they now thankfully supposed themselves to have seen the last.

Reasons such as these, for which it seemed natural to contemporaries to view the loss of the American colonies with little regret, were, needless to say, entirely misconceived. In the narrow old tradition they were still, consciously or unconsciously, thinking of an Empire and its constituent elements primarily as a source of material advantage to the mother country—a conception to which the West Indian islands answered much more readily than New England. Which is to say that their notions even of a colony were primitive, while of a Dominion, self-governing but subject, like themselves, to the British crown, despite the speculations of Thomas Pownall and Joseph Galloway, they had as yet no notion at all. Had their philosophy of Empire remained lastingly at this low level the British would indeed soon have been reduced to a minor rôle, and the vast access of power which awaited them would have been unthinkable. But the reflections with which they consoled themselves after the secession of the United States hardly did them justice. They were fully conscious of their own energy and enterprise, and a profounder instinct warned them that some high destiny still awaited them. And this instinct they rationalised in terms of the old colonial theories, the only doctrine of Empire with which they were as yet familiar. And so still believing in their own future they wholly misconceived the nature of what that future held in store for them. For what were the facts? The promise ever latent in the old Empire had been that, through their own kindred overseas, unlike previous Empires, they should deliberately spread the idea of liberty through the world, and that, unlike previous Empires, they should learn to protect and educate backward races, and not merely to exploit them. This latent promise had been partly, but only partly fulfilled. North America indeed they had saved for free institutions, and in the long perspective of history this was an achievement upon the heroic scale; yet they had failed to grant Americans sufficient freedom. In India Clive, Hastings and Burke had already taught their countrymen something of the moral obligations of power over weaker peoples, but this lesson they were as yet but beginning to digest. And the trade in African slaves still flourished. Even so the old Empire had moved further towards the twin goals of liberty and justice than any of its predecessors; not far enough to merit survival in its present guise, but far enough surely to have earned a second chance.

And already there were signs that the British would not fail to take their chance. As indispensable foundation of the higher qualities which would be needful, their rich individuality and hardy, enterprising vigour endured unabated. In was in 1769 that Captain James Cook charted the coastline of unknown New Zealand, and, first of all explorers, sighted the eastern shores of Australia, and so called a new continent into existence. For two hundred and fifty years the Spaniards had dwelt in South America, growing ever richer and ever lazier; in 1606 they had discovered the coast of the mysterious southern continent, *Terra Australis*, but for eight long generations from 1513 they had neglected to explore the Pacific. Had such an opportunity come to the British, it is safe to say, every island in the ocean would have been discovered long since. Cook, a poor boy who had run away, like countless other poor English boys, to sea, had not only contrived to make himself the most scientific navigator the world had yet known, but was a man of iron courage and untiring energy. Because Britain continued to breed such men in abundance an imperial future was still open to her. Yet this alone was not sufficient. Courage, enterprise and vigour had been plentiful in the past; the future demanded, in addition, a new spirit.

And of that new spirit. if any had been concerned to search for it, even before the old Empire fell there were already signs. For since the seventeen-forties John Wesley and his fellow-evangelists had been slowly rousing the masses to a new spiritual life. Religion was waking from its long slumber; the age of rationalist churchmen and Let Sleeping Dogs Lie was drawing to its close. As early as 1773 Parliament had censured the great Clive for enriching himself from the nation he had conquered. It was in 1772 that Granville Sharp pleaded the cause of a negro slave in England, and Lord Mansfield ruled that a slave became free when he set foot on British soil; it was in 1780 that Dunning carried his motion against the influence of the Crown. From these inconspicuous sources would derive the great crusade of Wilberforce and the evangelicals, which was to abolish first the slave trade and then slavery itself, and the new imperial doctrine of moral responsibility impressed upon the national conscience by Burke's denunciations of Warren Hastings. From them too would flow the current which brought the Reform Act of 1832 and was to transform the character of the government of the Empire. Wilberforce, Burke and Grey of the Reform Bill all in their various ways represented a moral idealism utterly alien to the age of Walpole, Newcastle and North. Wilberforce and Burke between them taught the nation a sensitiveness to the rights of backward races which had been unknown to any previous imperial power, and would in course of time develop into a deliberate doctrine of Colonial Trusteeship. Grey and the reformers founded a Parliamentary tradition capable, as the Parliament of George III and North had never been, of according responsible government to British settlers overseas, and at length of rising to the conception of a Commonwealth of self-governing Dominions. All this was a moral resurrection indeed, and without it there would have been no resurrection of the British Empire. Its fountain head was doubtless the religious revival of Wesley, but no religious revival could so speedily have transformed public life, had not the nation as a whole been disposed to learn, and learn nobly, the chastening lessons of adversity. For although in 1783 the British looked forward with confidence and optimism, they were well aware that much was rotten in the Britain which had lost the American colonies, and as they turned their faces to the future they were very ready to turn their backs upon the past. And so because they were able to learn from their own failures the Empire would be reborn.

§2

The first and most spectacular appearance of that new spirit which would revitalise and transform the Empire was in the strange series of events, already traced, which culminated in the impeachment of Warren Hastings. Already, before that lengthiest and most celebrated of trials commenced, the government of India had been radically reformed. Fox, during the brief and ill-fated Coalition of 1783, had wished to transfer the political power of the Company bodily to the Crown. But both Fox and his Coalition with North were generally and deeply suspect, his proposal to transfer all Indian patronage to seven Commissioners was inevitably denounced as a design to provide him with the means to corrupt Parliament, and on this measure the Coalition fell. Next year the nettle was grasped by the youthful Pitt. By more discreet and devious means he did what Fox had set out to do. The commercial functions of the Company were left intact, but its political authority was subjected to a Board of Control, representing the British Cabinet, and in effect the Board of Control became omnipotent. Patronage, save for the greatest offices, remained nominally with the Company, but it was soon notorious that in practise it was exercised by Pitt's henchman, Henry Dundas, as head of the Board. In India Pitt was wise enough to free the Governor General from all control by his Council, so that, though subject to the Cabinet at home, he was an absolute ruler in the East, where at present only absolute rule was understood. This long step towards the acceptance by the nation of responsibility for India was taken two years before Warren Hastings left India. But what was responsibility to mean? That would be determined by the trial of the great Governor General.

CHAPTER TWO

§1

EVEN while Burke and the trial in Westminster Hall between them were ensuring that the British would recognise their moral obligations to India, Wilberforce and the Abolitionists had begun their long crusade for a moral revolution in their treatment of Africa. The campaign for the abolition of the slave trade, no less than Burke's enunciation of the doctrine of imperial trusteeship, enshrines the new spirit which made the new Empire possible. Both the Abolitionist crusade and Burke's vision of the responsibilities of Empire stand out in such sharp contrast to all the works and ways of North or Newcastle that they manifestly mark a moral frontier and initiate a new age. Yet both movements had their roots in the past. Even while eighteenth-century Britain and its rulers were at their most cynical there had been stirrings in the conscience of the nation. The general reprobation of "the Nabobs," Parliament's censure of Clive, the strictures which it passed on Hastings before he left India—all these were a prelude of which the natural development was the scene in Westminster Hall. As for the slave-trade this was a more ancient abuse, and the protests against it begin much earlier. It is not surprising that an organised movement for abolition should have been slow to mature when we remember that the trade was thought to be indispensable to the prosperity of the West Indies, and (by Rodney at least) to our strategic hold on them, that any interference with it was bound to provoke bitter resentment in the colonies, that traders and plantation owners together now wielded great political influence, and that in no other country, save little Denmark, was there any serious opposition to the trade at all. Nevertheless even in the seventeenth century there had been denunciations by Anglican and Nonconformist divines; in 1724 the Quakers condemned the trade, and in 1761 disowned all Friends who continued to have a hand in it; Aphra Behn had chosen a negro hero for her novel *Oroonoko* before the end of the seventeenth century; Defoe, Pope, and Thomson of *The Seasons* denounced slave traders.

And it was not humanity that the British lacked, only imagination. As long as slavery remained a remote tragedy in a distant clime they accepted it as one of the inevitable evils of creation. But planters and merchants from the colonies had a habit of bringing their own slaves with them on their visits home; and sometimes the slaves would escape, and there would be advertisements and pursuits, and startled citizens would see reluctant negroes haled back to captivity through the streets of London. Such spectacles profoundly shocked them. All their ancestral passion for personal liberty stirred irrepressibly. Surely in England at least there could be no slaves? The only justification they could think of for what they had seen was that the victims were benighted heathens. Often enough, however, a runaway slave would dispose of this poor shred of excuse by getting himself baptised—he could always find sympathetic citizens ready to act as godparents. And not infrequently when the slave's owners attempted to carry him home with them overseas, one of his new godparents would threaten a lawsuit. Interference of this kind became so common that as early as 1729 the West Indians appealed to the Law officers of the Crown for an opinion on it. The Attorney General and the Solicitor General obliged with the pronouncement that neither residence in Britain nor Christian baptism affected the master's property in his slave. They were reversing an earlier opinion of Chief Justice Holt that every slave entering England automatically became free. Reassured, the West Indians threw discretion to the winds. Not only did they advertise rewards for runaways; they even announced slave-auctions in the British Press. Once again they had forgotten that the British public will never long tolerate cruelty which it can see with its own eyes. The Abolitionist movement at once began to take shape. Granville Sharp, its father, had already saved several slaves from their owners —one by a writ of *Habeas Corpus* from a ship about to sail for the West Indies—and published *The Injustice . . . of tolerating Slavery in England*, when in 1772 Lord Chief Justice Mansfield arranged with him that the dispute over one James Somerset, a captured runaway, should be treated as a test case. Mansfield's judgment in the Somerset case—"the power claimed never was in use here or acknowledged by the law"—put the matter beyond further dispute. Henceforth any slave setting foot in Britain became instantly free.

§2

But slavery on British soil overseas, and the slave-trade itself, remained. And if these were ever to be ended, the formidable task of persuading Parliament to end them must be undertaken. By 1783 there was a small committee of Quakers in existence " for the relief and liberation of the negro slaves in the West Indies and for the discouragement of the Slave Trade on the coast of Africa." And philanthropists outside the circle of the Friends were collaborating with them—in particular Granville Sharp himself, James Ramsay, an Anglican clergyman who had returned from nineteen years in St. Christopher to write a series of pamphlets against slavery, and Thomas Clarkson, a Cambridge scholar who in 1787 determined to abandon his clerical career and devote the rest of his life to the campaign against the slave trade. In that same year the Committee for the Abolition of the Slave Trade was formed, with the original Quaker group as its kernel and Granville Sharp as its first Chairman. By now signs were multiplying of a stirring of opinion against the trade. Adam Smith and Paley condemned it, Bishop Porteous preached against it and a series of ineffective resolutions was even moved in the House. The American colonies had been lost, the country was in a chastened, although not a despondent, mood, and its best minds were very conscious that the hour called for reform in every department of national life. But on any reckoning the task which faced the new Committee was prodigious. Only Parliament could put an end to the trade, and Parliament was apathetic or hostile. Their only hope, the Abolitionists decided, was to rouse public opinion in the country, and then somehow focus it on West-minster, as a means of breaking down Parliamentary reluctance. For both processes they would have to invent their own technique, for there were no precedents for either in 1787. And the dead weight of resistance which already confronted them was to be enormously increased by the French Revolution, the Jacobin Terror and finally by the outbreak of war with revolutionary France in 1793. A nation at war has seldom much interest to spare for controversial reforms, and a nation at war with revolutionaries is ready to see the mildest reform as a revolution. The Abolitionists could not hope to achieve their goal unless the nation proved specially sensitive to a moral appeal, unless they themselves rapidly improvised the then virtually undiscovered art of reaching and rousing public opinion, and unless their case in Parliament were in superbly competent hands.

Already in 1787 they had discovered their destined champion. William Wilberforce possessed in abundance all the rare qualifica-tions needed. Brought up a gay and popular member of the most modish society, at twenty-five he had been profoundly influenced by the evangelical Milner, and for the rest of his life, despite Parliament, high society and his own great practical abilities, he was a pro-

foundly religious and otherworldly man. For all his new seriousness
he remained immensely popular. "Dined Lord Chatham's," his
private diary would record at first, "Duchess of Gordon, Lady
Charlotte, Duke of Rutland, Graham, Pitt, Dundas, etc. How ill-
suited is all this to me! How unnatural for one who professes himself
a stranger and a pilgrim!" And yet he was no prig. Few could
mistake the gay, accomplished, bright-eyed little man for anything
but a saint; certainly none who knew anything of his private life,
of his prayers and vigils, his anguished self-questionings, his regular
giving of a fourth of his income to the poor, his surrender of all
personal ambition. For the Abolitionist cause he was an ideal
spokesman and figurehead, a man whom the nation could recognise
as single-minded and opponents could not deride as a crank, a man
of position and influence, an Anglican and a Tory, a friend of Pitt's,
clear-headed and eloquent, capable of mastering the intricate detail
of his brief, and of returning repeatedly to the charge at Westminster
without boring the House. It is significant of the growing consciousness of the need for higher standards, the sense that the nation must
earn survival by self-reform, that Wilberforce's first concern should
have been an attempt to improve public morals; "God Almighty,"
he wrote, "has set before me two great objects, the suppression of
the Slave Trade and the reformation of manners." But before long
the suppression of the Slave Trade engrossed all his attention. And
little wonder, for progress was heartbreakingly slow. Wilberforce
opened the attack in the House in May, 1789, in a speech of which
Burke said that it "equalled anything I have ever heard in modern
times, and is not perhaps to be surpassed in the remains of Grecian
eloquence." He was supported by Pitt, Fox and Burke himself, an
unequalled trio, but all that the Commons would agree to was to
hear evidence in Committee. The hearing of evidence dragged on
through two years, and in 1791 Wilberforce's motion for a Bill "to
prevent the further importation of slaves into the British islands
in the West Indies," though again supported by Pitt, Fox and Burke,
was rejected by 163 to 88.

For a long while Wilberforce would not come so near success
again. For now the shadow of the Jacobin terror in Paris fell across
British politics, and soon Jacobin France had invaded the Low
Countries and proclaimed her intention of assisting all countries
rightly struggling to be free. Inevitably the traditional British
anxieties revived, for the old twofold threat was taking shape, of a
hostile power at the mouth of the Scheldt, and a dictatorship of
Europe. In 1793 Pitt declared war on France, and Parliament could
no longer be interested in controversial domestic reforms. The only

hope was to mobilise opinion outside Parliament. The Abolitionists set themselves to promote a nation-wide campaign, the like of which Britain had not known before. Before long a wholly new phenomenon had made its appearance, possible only in a country with a genius for politics. In the nineteenth century many foreign nations supposed themselves to be setting up their counterpart of the British political system by the comparatively simple process of establishing Parliamentary government. But they overlooked that integral element of the British system which had first taken shape during the Abolitionist crusade. Without roots in the nation a Parliament must wither away; it can only survive and flourish if in constant and intimate contact with the electorate. And such contact is not to be taken for granted, or maintained without much talent and much organisation. Intimate contact between the British Parliament and the British people dates from the Abolitionist campaign. With their Corresponding Committees all over the country, their pamphlets and touring propagandists, their mass meetings and the petitions carefully timed to coincide with Wilberforce's motions in the House, the Abolitionists worked out what was then a wholly novel technique, archetype of the countless social and political movements which have diversified our public life ever since. It is characteristic of the close-knit texture of British life, and the power of religion in it, that the political propaganda of the Abolitionists should so obviously have been closely modelled upon religious evangelism. The Abolitionists after all were evangelicals, heirs of the Puritan tradition, and in the Puritan tradition politics and religion were closely interwoven. And so the Corresponding Committees of Wilberforce and his friends represented the local communities of the faithful, their pamphlets and touring speakers the tract and the itinerant preacher; and their speeches, in phrasing and substance, were often closely akin to sermons. Thus both the new democracy and the new Empire would have their roots in religion.

The crusade proceeded slowly and painfully, by fits and starts, with defeats and long interludes, and victories followed by further defeats. Every weapon of controversy was employed against Wilberforce, and particularly the charge that he was an unpatriotic revolutionary. "If anything happens to our island," said Lady Malmesbury, "I should certainly, if I were a planter, insist on Mr. Wilberforce being punished capitally." Peace came with revolutionary France in 1801 and two years later war with the France of Napoleon; then from 1803 the life and death struggle against yet another authoritarian foe shelved all domestic reform; Trafalgar and Austerlitz were fought; Pitt died, and then Fox. At last, in

1806, nearly twenty years after Wilberforce had first pledged himself to the cause, the final scenes were enacted, and as the Bill at last approached its goal, the House of Commons rose to its feet and cheered him, round on round, while he sat with his head in his hands, and the tears streaming down his cheeks. The foundations of a new age had been laid.

§3

The British slave trade was no more, but the British Government had to bribe or browbeat other nations by slow degrees into following its example, and for years one of the British Navy's chief tasks would be to chase slave-ships and suppress slavery. And slavery itself still flourished on British soil overseas. Before long the final crusade was on foot. Like the campaign against the trade itself it was obstructed by the political circumstances of the time—by the closing stages of the struggle against Napoleon, and the social and economic difficulties of the first years of peace. But Wilberforce remained unshakably confident in the British people. "Because the people of England are religious and moral, loving justice and hating iniquity . . . I rely upon the religion of the people of this country." In 1821 Thomas Fowell Buxton accepted Wilberforce's invitation to become Joshua to his Moses, and assumed the Parliamentary leadership of the crusade. But as late as 1833, within a few months of his death, Wilberforce was addressing a public meeting on behalf of final Abolition. He died in the September of that year, but not before Parliament had put an end to slavery, voting twenty million pounds in compensation to the planters. The abolition of slavery in the British Empire, imitated in course of time by every civilised country in the world, is one of the milestones of history, marking a new stage in the slow upward journey of mankind. It ensured that when, later in the century, Africa was virtually partitioned by the great powers, Europe should not be corrupted, as Rome had been, by the proximity of a great slave-market to her southern shores. And in Britain the tradition of the Abolitionists would live on. Thus the great Trek of the Boers in South Africa in 1835 was chiefly prompted by their resentment at the clemency shown by the British Government to the native races. And the Minister responsible, Lord Glenelg, was the son of one of Wilberforce's intimate associates, Charles Grant. Henceforth there would always be a vocal and influential section of opinion in this country ready to protest at anything which looked like cruelty or exploitation overseas. More-

over the London Missionary Society had been founded in 1795 and
the Church Missionary Society in 1799, while the Society for the
Propagation of the Gospel in Foreign Parts dated from Stuart times.
Henceforth missionaries and the missionary societies would play an
influential part in the shaping of colonial policy. To them is chiefly
due the survival of the native population in the Pacific Islands and
elsewhere. Their desire was to prevent white settlers and traders
from intruding upon native races lest they obstruct the missionaries'
task of teaching them Christian civilisation. In Africa and India
and the West Indian colonies they were already busily at work.
Sierra Leone in West Africa had been founded by Wilberforce and
the Evangelicals as a colony for redeemed slaves in 1787.

The victory over Napoleon greatly increased the material power
of Britain. Once again British sea-power was unchallenged. But,
more than this, the long resistance to tyranny had added enormously
to the country's moral prestige. The British had displayed courage
and endurance, but so had many imperial peoples before them. They
had saved themselves by their exertions and Europe by their example.
But it was of even deeper historical significance that a wholly new
conception of the moral obligations of Empire was now visibly
taking shape among them. In a world given over to various types
of tyranny they had long stood for freedom, and their most signal
stroke for liberty was the victory over Napoleon. But now the moral
forces of the Empire had been strengthened and enriched. It is not
too much to say that the instincts roused and personified by Wilberforce and Burke had ensured that the second British Empire would
endure, because they had ensured that it would be an Empire of an
altogether new kind. The nation which had led Europe against
Napoleon, and the world against slavery and exploitation, had
earned other forms of leadership in the years to come.

CHAPTER THREE

CAPTAIN COOK AND TERRA AUSTRALIS

(1768-1823)

§1

IT HAD needed Burke and Wilberforce to direct the energy of the
nation to moral ends; but the energy itself had never flagged. The
disruption of the old Empire had not been due, as had been the
decline of the imperial power of Spain or Holland, to failing vigour
or overstrained resources. In the last two decades of the eighteenth
century the British were no less hardy and enterprising than their
forebears. And now with the perfecting of the art of navigation a
new era of maritime discovery in the remoter seas was opening.
Britain was the dominant sea-power of the world; inevitably and
all but involuntarily, she found herself founding a new Empire,
and an Empire of white colonists, of the kind to which, as she
supposed, she had said farewell for ever in 1783. Equally inevitably,
the victory in the long struggle with authoritarian France presented
her with the opportunity, which she used with remarkable moderation, of making a number of strategic additions to that commercial-
maritime Empire which had survived the war of Independence, and
in which she still believed. In India too, since British rule was now
firmly established, a focal point of order and security in the anarchy
of the sub-Continent, the Empire was bound to extend. And so
within a few decades of the secession of the American colonies,
which to many foreign observers had seemed to mark the end of
Britain as a great power, the British found themselves in control of
a more extensive Empire than ever before, while already on the
horizon, in the struggling new settlements of white colonists,
loomed those formidable problems and vast opportunities of which
they supposed that destiny had finally relieved them in 1783. The
new expansion, made possible by adventurous exploration in the
Pacific, a protracted war in Europe and vigorous administration in
India, was unforeseen and uninvited. It would not have come if the
nation had not retained its virile qualities; it could not have
endured if the nation had not accepted new moral standards.

§2

It was before the American colonies had yet been lost that Captain James Cook called a new world into existence, which would in due course redress the balance of the old. Inevitably the great navigators of earlier times had clung to the shortest practicable route across the Pacific, between Central America and the Philippines. With their small, unseaworthy ships, their unscientific navigation and their inadequate provisions they had done the utmost that human courage and endurance could compass, but they could not venture further afield. Of what lay north and south of the track between Panama and Manila they knew next to nothing. And particularly in the south they had given free rein to their imagination, picturing a vast, circular Antarctic continent. Tasman had sailed round Australia in the seventeenth century but with too wide a margin to sight its eastern shores; William Dampier, an Englishman, had landed on its western coast in 1688 and 1699; but in 1763 opinion was still divided as to whether or not Terra Australis Incognita stretched unbroken to the South Pole. The final conquest of the ocean awaited more serviceable ships, exacter navigation and wider knowledge, above all perhaps some sort of antidote to the scurvy.

By the second half of the eighteenth century the necessary equipment was available. Between 1764 and 1768 Commodore John Byron and Captains Wallis and Cataret discovered a number of Pacific islands. But the great navigator of the new age of discovery was James Cook, the son of an agricultural labourer of the Cleveland district of Yorkshire who had run away to sea. Many an English boy ran away to sea like James Cook; many, like him, possessed an iron constitution and a complete indifference to danger, discomfort and privation; had they not indeed they would hardly have sailed before the mast in the eighteenth century. But few, if any, can have been endowed with the scientific gifts and the immense industry which Cook must have possessed. For somehow or other the boy who had gone to sea on a collier at thirteen rose by the age of thirty to be navigator of a king's ship. He was with the fleet during the siege of Quebec and was entrusted with the difficult and dangerous task of taking the soundings in the channel of the St. Lawrence, directly in front of the French camp. This he contrived with such signal success that the admiral commissioned him to chart the river below Quebec. "Of the accuracy and utility of this chart," says his eighteenth-century biographer, "it is sufficient to say that it hath never since been found necessary to publish any other." How had the labourer's son acquired this highly specialised knowledge? Presumably during his four years in the Royal Navy, rather than the thirteen he had spent on small merchant vessels. But who provided him with books, whether he had any teaching, how he found time and opportunity for study it is impossible to say. Certainly he must have possessed immense aptitude—his early biographer roundly asserts that he had "scarcely ever used a pencil" before he charted the St. Lawrence—and, as certainly, immense industry. His industry, indeed, is everywhere apparent in the record of his voyages, for he seemed to his companions to be tireless—a tall, thin, grave man, austere in habits and explosive of temper, feared and trusted by his crews.

Cook sailed on his first voyage of discovery in 1768. Its prime object was to enable Sir Joseph Banks and other scientists to observe the transit of Venus from a Pacific island. But after this, Cook's instructions were to "prosecute the design of making discoveries in the South Pacific Ocean." He succeeded beyond all expectation. After the transit had been duly observed, he sailed to New Zealand, then a mere name, circumnavigated both islands and made the first accurate chart of their coastline. Thence he held on westward and on April 30 reached the east coast of Australia, on which no European had hitherto set eyes. On August 23 he noted in his log that he "took possession of the whole eastern coast by the name of New Wales"—or, as he wrote in a letter and in his journal, "New South Wales." Banks, much impressed by its fertility, called the bay in which they had first anchored Botany Bay; already he had made up his mind that one day the British must colonise this land. From April to August of 1770 Cook pushed northward for two thousand miles, assiduously charting the eastern coast of Australia. Thence he passed through the Torres Strait, which separates Australia from New Guinea, establishing the fact that these are separate islands. No one voyage before or since has added so much new territory to the known world. As usual the deaths from scurvy had been prodigious. The astronomer and two others of Banks's party had died; the surgeon, the first lieutenant and the master, two midshipmen, the boatswain, the carpenter, his mate and two of his crew, the sailmaker and his mate, the corporal of marines, the cook and a dozen seamen. In a ship's company of eighty it was a terrible, but a typical, death roll. On his next voyage, Cook determined, his crew's diet should be radically improved. No longer should they have to live day after day on weevily biscuit and a fibrous mass of highly salted meat. Next time accordingly he carried with him a number of new commodities, some of which proved to have valuable antiscorbutic properties. The second voyage lasted from 1772 to 1775. In three successive summers Cook penetrated into the southernmost ocean up to the great southern ice-wall. He had given the final quietus to the myth of a Southern Continent, Terra Australis Incognita, that earthly paradise full of varied riches and inhabited by a highly civilised people, in which up to now so many learned persons had insisted on believing. If there were land further south than this it must clearly be a land of perpetual ice. In 1776 Cook sailed for the North Pacific. He charted new islands and discovered the Sandwich group, all the while methodically recording in his journal the manners and customs of the strange races he encountered. He explored the Alaskan coast and sailed through the Bering Strait, but decided that there was little hope of a passage through it into the Atlantic. Next summer, after wintering in the Sandwich Islands, he intended to try the Straits again. But before next summer he was dead, killed in a ridiculous quarrel with the natives of the Sandwich Islands, who had at first taken him for a god.

§3

In a twofold sense Cook was the father of Australia. He was the first explorer to reach and chart its eastern coast. But, more than this, he had instantly realised the fertility and promise of the country. The Dutch had found and mapped the western portions of it long before Cook, but they reported it as barren and repellent. But Cook realised at once that in those eastern shores he had discovered a new habitation for civilised mankind. "In this extensive country," he wrote,

> it can never be doubted but what most sorts of grain, fruit, roots, etc. of every kind, would flourish were they once brought hither . . . and here is provendor for more cattle, at all seasons of the year, than ever can be brought into the country.

Here in effect was an invitation to colonise Australia. And Cook's views were rapidly and widely known. For his *Voyages* became the most popular work on travel ever published. They were translated into many foreign languages, and read by both Louis XVI and Napoleon. A hundred years later, in 1890, Sir Walter Besant could still write of Britain, "Every boy has read Cook's *Voyages*; not only every library but almost every house with a row of bookshelves contains some account of them. . . ." Certainly Australia owed more to Cook than its discovery.

Yet it was not until 1788, eighteen years after Cook first anchored in Botany Bay, that New South Wales, the first Australian settlement, was founded. The loss of the American colonies had a good deal to do with the venture. For one thing, of the American Loyalists who clung to the British connection a certain number had come to England with the returning British troops. And most of these were now destitute. Moreover there was the problem of the convicts, who could now no longer be annually transported to America, although the judges did not cease to pass sentences of transportation. In 1779 Sir Joseph Banks recommended to a Committee of the House of Commons that convicts should be sent to Botany Bay, whose wealth of plants he still remembered with pleasure. A few years later an even brighter idea occurred to Admiral Sir George Young. Why not send not only the convicts but the Loyalists to New South Wales? Pitt took to the suggestion, at any rate as far as the convicts were concerned. If he had had any inkling that he was about to found a new nation, with vast consequences to human history, he would probably have sent the Loyalists, who were at least experienced colonists, as well. But Pitt was not so much founding a colony as disposing of a difficulty. He even defended the project with the uninspiring argument that "no cheaper mode of disposing of the convicts could be found." Nevertheless Pitt had vision, and although his first object may have been to ship off the convicts he cannot have been altogether unaware that greater consequences might ensue. Indeed when Captain Phillip sailed in 1787 with an expedition of 1100 persons, including 750 convicts, his instructions were to annex the entire eastern half of Australia and the adjacent islands. And certainly Phillip and his officers had no doubt but that they were sailing on an imperial mission.

§4

This migration of convicts and soldiers is the one great exception to the British tradition of expansion through individual enterprise, and inevitably it was not long before private adventurers began to pour in, and transformed the character of the undertaking. But first the colony had to survive. If it had not happened so often before in the history of the Empire that a leader of courage, common sense, practical ability and vision was forthcoming when most needed, it might be said that New South Wales was fortunate beyond expectation or deserts in its first Governor. "The gentleman, the scholar, and the seaman," wrote a close friend, were combined in Phillip, and perhaps it was from the scholar in him that he derived the sensitiveness and imagination which made him so excellent a Governor. "Upon my soul, Butler," observed Captain Fortescue to a clerical acquaintance, "I do believe God Almighty made Phillip on purpose for the place." And certainly Captain Phillip did for New South Wales very much what a century and a half earlier Captain John Smith had done for Virginia. He carried it, almost on his own shoulders, through the first precarious years of infancy. His difficulties, it is true, were not the same as Smith's. The stone-age aborigines of Australia were far less formidable than the Red Indians of America; the mortality from disease was not so terrible; the first settlers, thanks largely to the forethought with which Phillip himself had provisioned the First Fleet, were much better equipped. But there were two special dangers with which Phillip had to contend. One was the wretched human material he had brought out with him. Many of the convicts, he reported, "have been brought up from their infancy in such indolence that they would starve if left to themselves." "The anarchy and confusion which prevails throughout the Camp," wrote Surgeon Bowes in February, 1788, "is arrived to such a pitch as is not to be equalled, I believe, by any set of villains in any other spot upon the globe." Even more disheartening at first was the universal absence of any vision of the future. At home a government which appeared to regard the colony as little more than a convenient refuse-dump; around him convict settlers even less likely to share his conception of their settlement as the germ of a great new civilisation. Beside this drab absence of ideals the threat of starvation in the early years seemed a transient and trifling trial. When nothing would have been easier than to view his task and his surroundings with cynicism or distaste—as the age of Walpole would undoubtedly have viewed them—it was Phillip's supreme merit never to have wavered in his belief in the essential nobility of his mission. "I am serving my country and serving the cause of humanity," he wrote. And however depressing the setbacks which his dispatches might be compelled to record he never forgot their insignificance when seen against the vast horizons of the future in which he so confidently believed. "Nor do I doubt," he would conclude some long chronicle of disasters, "that this country will prove the most valuable acquisition Great Britain ever made."

Botany Bay had not appeared a tempting site to Phillip's practised eye, and eight days after reaching it, on January 26, 1788, he unfurled the British flag in what he described as "the finest harbour in the world in which a thousand sail of the line may ride in the most perfect security." He gave it the name of Lord Sydney, the Secretary of State who had been responsible for the expedition. Here he did his best to reform his strange community by offering liberal concessions to the well-behaved. His powers were absolute but he exercised them with the utmost tact and moderation. At Parramatta he faced a mob of mutinous convicts with a calm dignity which immediately restored order. Though his discipline was strict, and his punishments could be "prompt and terrible," he was by nature a humanitarian, to whom his convict charges frequently referred as "our good Governor." Before 1792 he had established a farming settlement of the more industrious convicts at Parramatta, and had segregated two hundred of the worst of them on Norfolk Island, a thousand miles out in the Pacific, an unexpected second instalment of transportation which served incidentally to relieve the strain on the food supplies of half-starved Sydney. When ill-health compelled Phillip to resign at the end of 1792 the little community had many perils still to survive, but the first and worst of them had been surmounted. He had deserved well of the state, primarily because, like Regulus, he had not despaired of it. Characteristically enough, little notice was taken of him on his return home. He died inconspicuously at Bath in 1814. It was more than eighty years before his place of burial was rediscovered.

§5

Phillip's successor, Captain Hunter, did not arrive till 1795, and during the interregnum the colony was administered by officers of the special New South Wales Corps which had been raised in 1790. During this military interlude, as if to add one more fantastic touch to the handicaps of the colony, Phillip's prudent restrictions on alcohol were removed, large quantities were imported and became for a while something like the staple currency of the colony. The officers of the Corps grew rich on the monopoly of its purchase and distribution. In such a community the consequences were naturally disastrous. In 1798 the whole colony, soon to be one of the chief wool-producing areas of the world, was without adequate clothes by day or blankets by night. In 1800 the British Government thought seriously of abandoning it, but was dissuaded, it is said, by the ever-optimistic Sir Joseph Banks. And gradually free settlers increased and commerce developed. Coal was discovered north of Sydney, and John Macarthur imported and bred a strain of sheep which bore excellent wool. And the convicts themselves, though all convicted of crime, were by no means all of criminal character. For in the early years of the nineteenth century a man could be sentenced to death for stealing a pocket-handkerchief, or to transportation for slaughtering butcher's meat without a licence. And there were the political prisoners—the Reformers, arrested as British Jacobins in 1793, and the Irish rebels of 1798. Macquarie, Governor from 1809 to 1820, came to the conclusion that the colony existed primarily for the benefit of its heterogeneous convict population and that emancipists, convicts who had served their time and become free men, should accordingly be treated in every respect as normal members of society. He began therefore to invite a number of them to entertainments at Government House, and insisted that they should be eligible for all civil offices. To this the officers of the 46th regiment—the New South Wales Corps had been disbanded—strongly objected. "The mess-table of the 46th regiment," they declared, "was regarded as the standard of society in the colony," and to the mess-table of the 46th they stoutly declined to invite any emancipist. When the colonel of the 48th, which succeeded them, inclined to be more accommodating and brought to the mess an ex-naval surgeon sentenced for dealings with the mutineers of the Nore, the junior officers left the table in a body. There was something to be said for both points of view; but there could be no satisfactory solution of the convict problem until transportation, to the mainland at least, was abandoned altogether in 1840. During its brief heyday it on the whole deserved the encomium of Darwin; "... as a means of ... converting vagabonds, most useless in one country, into active citizens of another, and thus giving birth to a new and splendid country ... it has succeeded to a degree perhaps unparalleled in history."

Meanwhile New South Wales continued to obtain some relief by retransporting the more villainous of the transported convicts. And after 1803 Norfolk Island was not the only destination to which they could be despatched. In that year Governor King, unnecessarily but not unnaturally alarmed by the explorations of a French vessel in the neighbourhood, decided to dispatch a settlement to Van Diemen's Land, the island to the south east which now bears the name of its discoverer Tasman. The intentions of the French were in fact no more formidable than the name of their vessel, the *Géographe*, implied, but French and British were now at war again, and the publication by the French explorers of a map bearing such titles as *Terre Napoléon* suggested that colonisation was their aim. It had doubtless not occurred to Governor King that authoritarian states seldom produce colonists, and he preferred to be on the safe side. To the small party of fifty landed on the island in 1803 were from time to time added consignments of the more ruffianly convicts, and an intermittent trickle of free adventurers drawn by the very primitiveness of life on the island. There were frequent escapes of felons, and in 1817 the familiar label "bushranger" was coined for them. It was a savage and graceless community, but at least it possessed toughness and tenacity and prepared the way for the civilisation which was to come.

§6

1803 was almost the last year in which there was any need for Governor King, or any one else, to cherish apprehensions as to French designs on Australia. For 1805 was the year of Trafalgar, and henceforth British command of the sea was so complete that no French aggression anywhere overseas was possible. Throughout the nineteenth century British colonisation of Australia could proceed undisturbed behind the shield of British sea power. For long the colonists were a mere pinpoint on a vast, unknown continent, as to whose very shape they were at first completely ignorant:

> Was it a vast desert? Was it occupied by an immense lake—a second Caspian Sea—or by a Mediterranean to which existed a navigable entrance in some part of the coast hitherto unexplored? Or was not this new continent divided into two or more islands by straits communicating from the unknown parts of the earth to the imperfectly examined north-west coast or to the Gulf of Carpentaria, or to both?

So wrote Flinders, one of the first explorers of the vast unknown. Thanks to its convict basis only a small proportion of the small community was free to risk its life on the mountain barrier to the west or the unknown coasts to the south, but as was to be expected in a British settlement, however scanty the available nucleus of explorers, exploration began at once. And as was to be expected it began with adventurous private individuals. Matthew Flinders and George Bass, midshipman and surgeon on the *Reliance* which had brought Governor Hunter to Sydney, were both Lincolnshire men, and combined a keen appetite for adventure with courage, fine seamanship and a gift for scientific inquiry. Bass had brought out on the *Reliance* a small tub, with an eight-foot keel and a five-foot beam.

In this he and Flinders explored the George River and discovered the site of Bankstown. A little later, in a borrowed whaleboat, Bass rounded the south-east corner of the continent and entered Bass Strait, showing that the old belief that Van Diemen's Land was an extension of New Holland was probably false. In 1798 the two friends together sailed clear through the Strait, reached the "monstrous swell" of the open ocean, and circumnavigated Van Diemen's Land, finally establishing its island shape. The Admiralty was at this time much too preoccupied with the French war to concern itself with exploration, and in 1803 Bass was lost on a trading voyage to South America. But exploration went on. In 1801 Flinders sailed along the south coast in the leaky *Investigator*, charting it so accurately that his maps remained in use for a century. He explored every considerable opening in the coast-line, to test the current belief that the continent was divided by a strait. But instead of a strait he found Spencer Gulf, to whose islands and capes and bays he gave Lincolnshire names, and Gulf St. Vincent where he landed, near the present site of the city of Adelaide, and gazed at a vast stretch of desolate forest, from which curled a solitary spire of smoke from the fire of some native bushman. In 1803 he circumnavigated Australia and mapped the continent as one vast island. He urged that since New Holland and New South Wales were now conclusively proved to be but western and eastern portions of the same huge country it would be convenient to give one name to the whole. The name, he suggested, might be "Australia," a title which had first made its appearance in the seventeenth century. Curiously enough Sir Joseph Banks and others objected, and Flinders had to publish his account of his explorations as *A Voyage to Terra Australis*; but although for some years New Holland survived in official usage, Flinders's suggestion gradually found its way into general use.

By 1823 the population of New South Wales was over thirty thousand. The time had come to give the colony a constitution and Parliament prepared to pass a New South Wales Judicature Act. The problem which the eighteenth century had so disastrously failed to solve, the problem of how to govern British settlers overseas, was beginning once more to take shape. With so much of the world still empty, with British sea power paramount and British vigour unabated, it could not be otherwise. The Empire could not long remain, as the men of 1782 had fondly supposed when they said farewell to the Thirteen Colonies, restricted to the tropical dependencies beloved of the mercantilist. The British were colonists as well as merchants. In New Zealand in 1823 there were as yet but a few adventurers living without law or government, but there also before long, as well as in Canada and South Africa, the same problem would be posed. It would be the old problem, but it was a new Britain and a new Empire which faced it. And its solution, for this time it would be solved, would in turn react upon British methods in India and in the tropical dependencies, until the Empire grew into one organic structure of ascending political gradations.

CHAPTER FOUR

NOT LIKE A GIANT

(1793-1815)

§1

WHILE British hardihood was thus laying the foundations of a new civilisation in the Pacific, the inmost qualities of Britain herself were being tried to the uttermost in the long struggle with Revolutionary and Napoleonic France. When at last in 1815 she had saved both herself and Europe, she had proved that for all its defects there was a vitality, an endurance and a moral strength in British society superior not only to the effete autocracies which had gone down like ninepins before the French hurricane, but to the new France itself. Defects, needless to say, there were in plenty. The era of the Napoleonic wars saw also the birth-pangs of the industrial revolution which was to distemper Britain for a century. It was the age of the enclosures for large scale agriculture, which turned the independent yeoman into the urban pauper. It was the age of the "Speenhamland" Poor Law, the first inhuman factories and the grim beginnings of the slums. It was an age of oligarchy, political and social. Even in these abuses, it is true, there were merits. Without the enclosures Britain might have been starved into surrender by the Continental System of Napoleon. And the industrial revolution into which Britain led the world, was itself evidence of enterprise, inventiveness and energy on the grand scale. And it was steadily increasing her wealth. As for the oligarchy, its leadership was cool-headed and stout-hearted, and its members fought and fell in the forefront of every battle. When we think of the unreformed Parliament as a nest of placemen and nepotism it is well to remember that ministers of the unreformed Parliament promoted Nelson at sea and Wellington on land—and made one of the most self-denying peaces in history. And there was a natural cohesiveness in British society, independent of all its injustices and inequalities. Sir Ralph Abercromby's last order, given as he was carried dying off the field at Alexandria, was the fine flower of a spirit whose counterpart could be traced all through society. "What is it you are placing under my head? Only a soldier's blanket! A soldier's blanket is of great consequence; you must send me the name of the soldier, that it may be returned to him."

And even as she fought, Britain was gathering the strength to reform her worst defects. There was no self-conscious public planning of the future, no suggestion that the common people were fighting for anything more than that well-loved familiar way of life which the dictator threatened to destroy. Yet in the first generation of peace the political monopoly of the landowners was swept away without a revolution, and the reformed Parliament began actively to lay the foundations of a modern state. And this was very far from all. For throughout the long wars the British were learning the lessons of adversity, as they had often contrived to learn them before. In the darkest hour of the country's fortunes Wilberforce's *A Practical View* (its full title, in the sonorous eighteenth-century fashion, runs to twenty-four words) was selling in spectacular quantities. This study of Christianity, full of scorn for moral complacency, was one more evidence of a new spirit awaking in the country, the spirit which would underlie the humanitarian reforms of Romilly and Shaftesbury, and the religious revivals of Newman and Keble.

The one failing for which Britain could find no remedy was, as usual, Ireland. Elizabeth and Cromwell had transferred the bulk of Irish soil to British proprietors, and for many years now the distressful island had lain quiet under the Protestant ascendancy and the Penal Laws against Catholics, but in the last quarter of the eighteenth century the old trouble began to stir in a new guise. To Pitt it appeared that the only hope now was a Union of the two Parliaments. An orgy of corruption in Dublin, and the promise of Catholic Emancipation, carried it, but Pitt found that he could not implement his promise. George, for one thing, had rationalised his objections to Emancipation by persuading himself that it was contrary to his Coronation oath. But the king's scruples were not the only obstacle. In Britain Parliament and people also were against Emancipation. Anti-Jacobinism and Evangelicalism were the dominant moods; and the anti-Jacobins did not care about giving political rights to traitorous Celts, while the Evangelicals mistrusted all Papists. And so Ireland was left to face the new century divided once more into two peoples, and nursing the memory of one more wrong, a broken promise.

Britain was the only power which fought continuously against revolutionary France, from 1793 to 1802, and after the brief peace of Amiens she was the only power which from 1803 to 1814 fought continuously against Napoleon. The outworn autocracies of the continent, Russia, Austria and Prussia, came and went, alternately stimulated by British subsidies to patch up a new coalition or swept ignominiously from the field by the armies of Carnot and Bonaparte. For the first two years of Napoleon's war, while there was no enemy but Britain, Napoleon's "Army of England" lay in camp at Boulogne, waiting to be shipped across the Channel in the familiar invasion barges. Not for the last time Britain and the British Navy stood alone between the world and its conquest by a military despotism.

As always, Britain was unprepared for war, and as always she paid a heavy price for her unpreparedness. Had she been ready, France of the Terror might have been crushed in 1793. Had she been ready, Nelson would have had the frigates for which he and St. Vincent had pleaded again and again, when on June 23, 1798, the British battle fleet passed unknowing through the course of the great French convoy carrying Bonaparte and an army of 40,000 Frenchmen to Egypt. With frigates Nelson would have sighted and closed with the ill-manned French battleships and the helpless transports, and sunk the heart and nucleus of the Grand Army, with its terrible chieftain, then and there, and so saved Europe the seventeen years of agony to come. But though once again Britain lacked the qualities which might have sent her ready-armed into the struggle, she displayed in greater abundance than ever before the enduring virtues on which pre-eminence in war and peace alike depends. They were virtues which found their supreme embodiment not so much in Pitt as in Nelson, at once the greatest and the best loved of all our fighting men. For "the Nelson touch" was more than penetrating intellect, brilliant imagination and inspired courage. It was all these upon a foundation of immense professional knowledge, lifelong industry and discipline, a burning patriotism and the simple piety of the Norfolk vicarage in which he had been brought up. Because the strength of Nelson and of his country derived from more enduring principles than the strength of Napoleon and of France, they prevailed. To defeat a Napoleon not material power only was needed but a spiritual force greater than his own. And in Napoleonic France, as in so many infidel and despotic systems, there was an ineradicable flaw. It worshipped itself, and therefore it lacked that moderation which is the foundation of all wisdom, and at last, like its master, it came to believe that it was above the moral law. And so Napoleon threatened the British not with defeat only and the dissolution of their Empire, but with the destruction, the whole world over, of the only kind of life they cared to live. In such a struggle there could be no compromise; they were bound to resist him to the end. And in the end their innate respect for the human decencies made them stronger than their enemies. The Britain of Pitt and Wilberforce, Wordsworth and Nelson rested on firmer, because juster and more humane, foundations than the France of either Robespierre or Napoleon. And so the victories of Nelson did not save Britain and Europe only. They gave the world, through the British Navy, a century of more unbroken peace than it had known since the age of the Antonine emperors of Rome. And to Britain they gave a century in which her reborn and re-inspired Empire would grow into a Commonwealth for which history has no precedent.

§2

At the Congress of Vienna, which wrote the peace treaties of 1815, Britain once again, as in 1763, might have held the world to ransom. As the only power which had fought all through the twenty years of war, as the soul and paymaster of every coalition, as the victor of Trafalgar and Waterloo, her claims on the allies were paramount. As the prototype of free institutions she repre-sented the chief motive force of the coming century. As the century-old enemy of ever-resurgent France she might have pleaded the right to a revenge such as should crush her rival for ever. As the one power which asked nothing in Europe save a strong, independent Holland and a balance of power on the Continent, she could play the honest broker between the rival ambitions of Austria, Prussia and the Tsar. Outside Europe the world was her oyster. Her navy was unchallengeable, her hands were full of the islands, colonies and ports of call which had fallen to her as prizes of war. She could have kept what she pleased, with none to say her nay. Had she been as greedy or as vainglorious as the Empires of the past she would have added vast new territories to her possessions—and in due time would have gone the way of the Empires of the past. Had she even been in Chatham's mood of 1763 she would have stripped and crushed France beyond possibility of revival. But even after the Hundred Days of Napoleon's return from Elba, even when Prussia was clamouring for revenge *à outrance* and the dismemberment of France, and while Prussian troops committed their characteristic brutalities upon the French population, Castlereagh and Wellington stood firm for "security not revenge."

And in the upshot, thanks chiefly to Castlereagh, that wise and liberal-minded aristocrat, France was spared. An independent Holland resumed the guardianship of the Scheldt. The balance of power in Europe was restored. Castlereagh could not foresee that of the central states, which he had laboured to strengthen against the Russian menace, Austria would rapidly decay and Prussia swell into imperial Germany, the highwayman and assassin of Europe. Much of the rapacity of the Continental powers in central Europe he could not check. But at least his wise moderation gave Europe a hundred years of peace. Had the peacemakers of 1815, like those of 1919, been in constant contact with the quick, hot moods of democratic politics at home, and all the unpredictable mass reactions to sudden release from so long a strain, they could hardly have made so clement and so wise a peace. They might well, like the men of 1919, have had to promise to hang the fallen tyrant and to squeeze the last farthing out of the defeated foe. Public opinion might even have hallooed them on to fill their pockets with imperial plunder while the world's treasure house lay open. Naval stations and ports of call, rather than white men's settlements, were still considered to be an Empire's most valuable prize by that generation, and of these there were few throughout the world which were not Britain's for the asking. For Britain's victorious allies were continental powers, and took no interest in overseas possessions; while her old imperial rivals, Spain and Holland, had fallen under the domination of France, and their possessions had therefore been laid open to the attacks of the British Navy. It almost seemed that all the kingdoms of the world, and all the power and glory of them, were being offered in one apocalyptic moment to the British peacemakers at Vienna. To their eternal honour, and to the lasting advantage of their country, they turned away from the temptation. Working in remote seclusion from public opinion at home, the small British coterie of aristocrats and oligarchs displayed a wise and generous moderation for which there were few precedents in history.

Castlereagh's just fame was delayed for a century by the accident that afterwards in the Commons he became the chief spokesman of Liverpool's Tory Cabinet, and so earned the bitter hostility of the political reformers. *I saw Murder pass this way, He wore a mask like Castlereagh*—Shelley would not have written thus if he had known or cared much about what happened outside these islands. But few British citizens cared much just now for Europe, and perhaps fewer still for the Empire. On only one issue in world politics was British opinion throughout alert and eager, and that was the suppression of the slave trade. Castlereagh did what he could to persuade the statesmen at Vienna to co-operate against it, and before long British ministers were urging France, and bribing Spain and Portugal, to do their part. But years of effort by British government and British Navy would be needed before the trade could be put down. On the continent, in which Russia, Austria and Prussia were predominant, the populations of Poland, Italy and Germany were bargained for and bandied about without the slightest reference to their own inclinations; and Poland, Saxony, the prince-bishoprics of the Rhine and the ancient Republic of Venice were carved up or extinguished as chanced to suit the interests of the three despots. But overseas the British plenipotentiaries could do virtually as they pleased. And at the outset they let it be known that "for the welfare of the Continent" Britain was prepared to sacrifice most of her colonial conquests, since "her object is to see a maritime as well as a military balance of power." Provided that the Low Countries were independent again all our colonial conquests, with a few named exceptions, would be regarded as objects of negotiation.

They chose to restore to France Martinique, Guadeloupe and Cayenne; and, save two, all of her West Indian islands; Pondicherry and all her Indian factories; and the cruiser base of Reunion. France was not even excluded from the disputed Newfoundland fisheries. To have excluded her, Castlereagh explained subsequently to the Commons, would have been "invidious, and would only have excited a feeling of jealousy." Rarely indeed has an all-powerful victor shown reluctance to render a defeated enemy jealous. To Holland our plenipotentiaries handed back her small West Indian islands; Surinam; and the rich Dutch colonies in the East Indies, Java, Amboyna, Banda and Ternate, the Moluccas and Malacca. This surrender was the more remarkable since even during the three years of British occupation the condition of Java had been vastly improved by Stamford Raffles, one of the greatest of British administrators and the first of any nation to turn science and humanitarianism to bettering the lot of a native population. Of the many prizes which had fallen to Britain during the war her representatives retained only Ceylon, as a strategic appendage to India; Malta, the fortress of the Mediterranean; St. Lucia, Tobago and one or two small Dutch islands in the West Indies; the cruiser base of Mauritius, from which French commerce-raiders had done immense damage during the war; and the Danish island of Heligoland which had served for smuggling goods into Germany. The Cape of Good Hope we kept as a naval base on the route to India, little suspecting that it would prove to be yet another white colony, with formidable problems peculiar to itself—and we paid the Dutch an indemnity of five million sterling. On this generosity a Dutch statesman, Falck, commented that the possessions which we retained were worthless to Holland and should have been abandoned; "what good fortune to find people complaisant enough to pay us for abandoning them!"

For the nation which had borne the main burden of twenty years

of war these acquisitions were by traditional standards trifling
indeed, and to Castlereagh, his colleagues and most of his contemporaries it seemed that Britain's true gains from the war were
not a few islands and ports of call, but the continued supremacy of
our navy and mercantile marine, henceforth threatened neither by a
hostile power on the Scheldt nor by a hostile dictatorship of Europe.
Nevertheless the maritime-commercial Empire had been greatly
strengthened, and free government had been preserved, to spread
in due course throughout the British settlements in Africa, Australia
and America. And to all this must be added the lasting prestige of
having been the only nation which Napoleon could not defeat, and
of having acquired a giant's power without using it like a giant.
These memories, sinking deep into the world's consciousness, would
do more than armaments to safeguard the Empire in the years to
come.

§3

Already therefore at the close of the French wars the second
British Empire was spread wide across the five Continents. And
already the main problems of its future had taken shape. British
colonists were bound to move towards self-government, for self-
government was essential to the British way of life. Could they
govern themselves without parting, as the Americans had parted,
from the mother country? Such was the vast interrogation mark of
Canada and Australia. Could British rule rise to the moral level
of the theory of trusteeship inherent in the doctrine of Wilberforce
and Burke, and bring justice and contentment to backward races?
This was a world-wide problem, posed in many and various guises
in Africa, in the East Indies, or the Pacific islands. And compounded,
as it were, of these two was a third even more complex, where, as in
South Africa or New Zealand, the future of white colonists was
inextricably involved with that of the primitive peoples among whom
they dwelt. Akin to all these, yet unmistakably distinct, loomed the
prodigious task of governing the vast, heterogeneous population of
the sub-continent of India. And these after all were but the separate
problems of the elements of Empire. How would British citizens
come to think of the Empire as a whole? Mercantilism was dead or
dying; the old ideal, of a closed, self-sufficient Empire ministering
to the needs of the mother country, would not suffice for the new
century. What would take its place? Would the Empire bring the
world good or evil? And how would the Empire as a whole, whatever the triumphs or failures in its constituent territories, commend
itself to the slow judgment of mankind?

CHAPTER FIVE

THE RIVAL DOCTRINES

(1815-1850)

§1

THE EMPIRE was reborn, but so far that was all. No new character had been stamped upon it, no new goal was clearly in view as the age of the machine drew on, and the tides of change grew swifter. Instinctively, without formulating a new imperial doctrine, and almost without acknowledging any imperial purpose, the nation had taken advantage of two great opportunities, the new age of discovery in the southern seas, and the long war against the French despotism. But as yet this new Empire was a framework without a soul. The various qualities personified by Cook, Nelson, Wellington and Castlereagh were alive in it, and they were undoubtedly the qualities of an imperial people, but as yet they were not directed to an imperial goal. Burke and Wilberforce, it is true, had voiced the new ideal of trusteeship for backward peoples but, despite Abolition and Emancipation, the ideal was far as yet from becoming a policy. And as to the future of the new British settlements overseas no one had even suggested an ideal. To forecast in 1835 that the Empire would move towards Trusteeship would have been a singularly hazardous guess, to forecast that it would move towards Dominion status would have been virtually impossible. In a sense, it is true, in British history such forecasts are always out of place, for the British have always felt their way from problem to problem with the minimum of conscious and formulated purpose. And even in the coming century much of what was done would be instinctive or empirical. But in this of all centuries, with the material environment of man changing further in a generation, thanks to the coming of the machine, than in the whole vast interval between George III and imperial Rome, with every social and political problem transformed and exacerbated, and the new democracy steadily taking shape amidst a prodigious clamour of discussion and controversy, in this of all centuries there was bound to be a nearer approach than ever before to a delibrate imperial policy. Yet even now, since the British did not yet think of themselves as an imperial people, in so far as their policy overseas was shaped by deliberate forethought at all, it was apt to be only in an indirect manner, a secondary consequence, as it were, of the various conclusions at which they had arrived with regard to domestic problems.

§2

For nearly half a century from 1832 the underlying assumption of all political thought was an all-pervasive Individualism. Men thought of society as an aggregate of individuals, and not of the state as a corporate personality with its own ubiquitous and over-riding claims. They believed in individual liberty and individual self-help, but for many years among many of the most vocal and influential of them this belief was coloured by other doctrines, kindred but distinct. Thus many of them were Utilitarians, profess-ing the greatest happiness of the greatest number as their goal and disposed to ask of every institution *cui bono*, what is the use of it—a question pertinent and fruitful enough in a swiftly changing age full of anchronism and anomaly, and yet, as posed by the highly rational Utilitarians, apt to ignore those more subtle and abiding values which cannot be weighed, measured or reduced to terms of formal logic. Many of them, too, were humanitarians, and in the field of Humanitarianism they achieved their most indisputable successes, sweeping away the savagery of the old penal code, and doing much to mitigate the cruelty with which society had so long been riddled. Other centuries had been more courageous, more chaste, more faithful or more just, but in none had men been so ready to be kind. All these moral and intellectual currents were embodied and personified in Jeremy Bentham, the acknowledged Master of reformers for half a century, so that Benthamism will serve as a label for them all. A crayon portrait of Bentham in old age, attributed to the youthful Watts, shows him a benevolent, apple-cheeked old gentleman, seated, hands folded over his walking-stick, at his garden-gate. And so he may have thought of himself, as scientific reformer, rationalist and utilitarian, for ever pursuing the greatest happiness of the greatest number, and for ever *kind*. But other portraits of Bentham give him a less benevolent air, and indeed there is a darker aspect of Benthamism. For Individualism always meant *laissez faire*, that determination to leave the individual free to pursue his own "enlightened self-interest," which Carlyle derided as the principle of "whatever goes on, ought it not to go on?"

And so the Benthamites who were so eager to sweep away aristocratic privileges and antiquated survivals were most of them equally eager to preserve the liberty of children of six to work eleven hours in the mines, and children of twelve eighteen hours in the factories. Nevertheless it was well for the Empire that this great age of expanding wealth and population should have begun as an age of Individualism, in which men believed, with Burke, that the Almighty Himself "obliges men, whether they will or not, in pursuing their own selfish ends to connect the general good with their own individual success." For so individual enterprise, by which the Empire had been created, would be left free to develop and transform it. And the moral insensitiveness in *laissez faire*, which tolerated the abuses of early industrialism overlong in Britain, meant much less to the Empire, in which there was as yet no industrialism, than the Humanitarianism which was so ready to concern itself with backward races. Such was the background of all political thought during the half century which followed the Reform Act of 1832, while Britain led the way into the industrial era and the British Navy kept the peace of the world. But certain strands in the complex texture were of special significance to the Empire, and certain sects among the disciples of Bentham disputed between them the right to shape its future.

§3

It was only natural that a powerful influence should be exercised by the small Radical group which represented what may be called the elixir of Benthamism. For Radicals bore the same relation to Individualism in the nineteenth century as did Socialists to Collectivism in the early decades of the twentieth. They were impatient, that is, to apply generally accepted principles, all-pervasive in the intellectual atmosphere of their time, with more thoroughness, more speed and above all more logic than was acceptable either to the majority of their own colleagues, to their political opponents or to the country as a whole. And, like the Socialists, they exercised a persuasive influence out of all proportion to their actual political strength. All Benthamites, and indeed the whole politically conscious public, were now inclined to be Utilitarian and to favour *laissez faire*, but the Radicals were the bleakest of Utilitarians and the most uncompromising advocates of *laissez faire*. As Utilitarians they ignored, or actively resented, all those imponderables not embraced by their own narrow and materialist formula. It was their weakness to rate sentiment, instinct and tradition excessively low, and commercial prosperity excessively high. Both prejudices inclined them to be hostile to the Empire. "Our dependencies," wrote Cobden, ". . . serve but as gorgeous and ponderous appendages to swell our ostensible grandeur, without improving our balance of trade." "The colonies, army, navy and church are, with the corn laws, merely accessories to our aristocratic government." The Empire, in other words, increased our prestige, and did not increase our bank balance. On both counts, Cobden had no doubt, the charge was damning. The sooner we disposed of so unprofitable a specula-tion, the better. And that the Empire, assessed in pounds, shillings and pence, was indeed an unprofitable speculation seemed to the Radicals to become clearer every day; they had themselves in fact done much to render it so. In the eighteenth century the ideal of the merchantilists had been a monopoly of trade with the tropical dependencies, and particularly with the West Indies. Thus in 1783 it had been intended that the West Indies should henceforth be supplied by Britain and Canada with the imports previously obtained from the seceding colonies. But Britain soon ceased to export food-stuffs, and the plan broke down. In 1822 Huskisson, a Tory Minister but a Benthamite, threw the West Indian trade open to all the world. In 1825 he opened the trade of all British colonies, provided that foreign powers extended similar advantages to British traders, and that merchandise was carried either in British ships or in those of the country of its origin. The leading maritime countries soon availed themselves of the offer and the mercantilist Empire was at an end. There ensued a tentative system of imperial preference. In British ports Canadian timber and corn and West Indian sugar paid but a fraction of the duties levied on foreign competitors. Upon these discriminations the Radicals fell in righteous fury, and between 1841 and 1852 the imperial preference which had succeeded imperial monopoly was swept away by the Tory Government of Peel and the Whig Government of Russell. All its fiscal advantages having now been eliminated the reiterated complaint of the Radicals that Empire was not a paying proposition became even more persuasive.

Cobden disapproved of the Army and Navy almost as whole-heartedly as he disliked the Empire. As early as 1836 he had derided the notion that some foreign power might be tempted to seize one or other of the British colonies, if they were left undefended. "Where is the *enemy*(?)" he asks sardonically, "that would be so good as to steal such *property*? *We* should consider it to be quite as necessary to arm in defence of our national debt." Obviously the sooner the Empire was liquidated, the better. The Master himself, indeed, had sounded the note of surrender at the very outset of his career. It is true that Bentham's *Emancipate your Colonies*, published in 1793, was addressed not to the British Parliament but to the French Jacobins, who had conspicuously neglected to comply with its advice; but its sub-title was *Showing the uselessness and mischievousness of distant dependencies to an European state*, and in 1830 it was published in England. Inevitably, since it came from Bentham, it exercised a wide influence during the next three decades. The Radicals were thus only too ready to see the last of the Colonies both because such "gorgeous and ponderous appendages" must be condemned by any self-respecting Utilitarian, and also because, with the spread of *laissez faire* principles in trade, Empire seemed no longer to pay. But political, as well as economic, *laissez faire* impelled them in the same direction. To what indeed could the principle of Let Be be more naturally applied than to colonial administrations, distant, tiresome and commercially unprofitable? Let the colonies shape their own course towards independence, while the mother country was careful only to ensure that the inevitable parting should be a friendly one. "Whether Canada is to remain for ever dependent on England or to become an independent state . . . it is still the duty and interest of this country to imbue it with English feeling and benefit it with English laws and English institutions." So spoke Huskisson in 1828, and such, in effect, is the theme of Sir George Cornewall Lewis's *The Government of Dependencies*, published in 1841, an influential work, typical of the Benthamite views of the day. And it is not too much to say that such was the opinion of most of those British citizens who reflected upon such matters at all. "The Colonies, instead of being an addition to the strength of the country," said Joseph Hume in 1823, "increased its weakness." And in 1852 even Disraeli could write, "these wretched colonies will all be independent in a few years, and are a millstone round our necks." For the Radicals indeed the young American republic was on the whole the ideal British Colony. For it still absorbed the surplus products and the surplus population of the mother country; it cost us nothing, and if it was unfriendly this was because it had been compelled to fight for its independence. Let Britain take Bentham's advice, emancipate her colonies and introduce universal free trade, and all would be harmony and prosperity.

§4

And yet even among Radicals there were some who held very different views, some who had already realised that in the British colonies a new world was coming to birth, and, while remaining

Benthamites and Utilitarians, and even professing faith in *laissez faire*, were determined that in the Empire at any rate they could not afford to Let Be. These men came to constitute the second of the sects which disputed the right to shape imperial policy in the age of Bentham. The source of inspiration of these Radical imperialists was that mysterious figure, Edward Gibbon Wakefield. Wakefield, who began his career by eloping with one heiress, went on, after her early death, to abduct another. He seems to have been a selfish and ill-balanced young gentleman—perhaps indeed there was always a kink in his character—and his trial, in 1827, revealed the abduction as a fantastic medley of fraud and foolishness. Yet it was during the three years' sentence which he then served in Newgate that Wakefield wrote the pamphlet and letters which appeared in book form, later in 1829, as *A Letter from Sydney*, and inaugurated a new era in colonisation. Presumably the ill-balanced and ambitious youth had been steadied by the shock of disgrace and misfortune, and for the first time in his life began to devote his great abilities to a serious and reputable task. He chose Australia for his subject partly because he had the vision to perceive the vast possibilities of the new Continent, while the planlessness of all our colonial administration seemed to cry aloud for the attention of an ambitious reformer, but partly too because New South Wales was a convict colony, to which he might so easily have been transported himself, and about which he had learned something from returned convicts. And, in view of all that had happened, his own best chance of a successful career seemed now to lie in some British settlement overseas. The *Letter*, published under a pseudonym, is admirably clear and lively, and describes so vividly the scenes on which its author had never set eyes, that it was generally accepted as emanating from New South Wales—" you could almost smell the dust." Once again, though in a much more reputable guise, Wakefield had perpetrated a fraud.

He left prison a fully qualified colonial reformer barred for ever from public eminence in Victorian England. Henceforth he must spend his life behind the scenes—writing anonymous articles, prompting politicians and inspiring societies which shrank from printing his name upon their publications. But he soon became the mentor on imperial affairs of a little group of active Radicals. By 1833 the National Colonisation Society, which he had founded in 1830, included among its forty-two members no less a person than John Stuart Mill, as well as Sir Francis Burdett, Charles Buller, Sir John Cam Hobhouse and Colonel Torrens, all Radically inclined Members of Parliament. Sir William Molesworth, too, a Radical

Member who was to become Colonial Secretary in Palmerston's Cabinet of the 'fifties, and the celebrated "Radical Jack," Lord Durham, of the Durham Report, worked closely with him. In the early days most of these apostles of *laissez faire* may have justified their enthusiasm for colonies which must inevitably grow up under the protection and control of the state by reflecting that in due time they would equally inevitably become independent democracies. Not a few of them, however, lived to hold very different views as to the future. "The experiment of keeping colonies, and of governing them well," Lord Durham would write in his great Report of 1839, "ought at least to have a trial ere we abandon for ever the vast dominion which might supply the wants of our surplus population." As for the prescient Wakefield, even from Newgate, in the *Letter from Sydney*, he had foreseen the colony of the future either represented in an imperial British Parliament, or, "if a mean jealousy on the part of the Englishmen should prevent such an arrangement, they might frame their own laws in a Colonial Assembly, under the eye of a viceroy, incapable of wrong, and possessing a veto like the king of England, but whose secretaries, like the ministers of England, should be responsible to the people! . . . This would render them happy in a most intimate connexion with their mother country. . . ." For 1829 this is indeed a remarkable prevision of the political machinery of the Dominion of to-day. At a time when so few troubled their heads about the Empire at all it meant much that, even though discreetly screened from the public gaze, this obstinate, far-sighted persuasive and disappointed man should have been so near the heart of affairs. He was often vindictive and often mistaken, but he rendered one invaluable service. He never ceased to believe in the future of the colonies.

Like the Radicals as a whole, Wakefield and the little group of Radical imperialists were influential out of all proportion to their numbers. What Canada, Australia and New Zealand owe to them we shall shortly see, but it is significant that, quite apart from their services to individual colonies, they should have conducted a steady offensive against the Colonial Office itself. This Department, which had been linked with the War Office in 1801, provided from many angles an easy target. And here the critics spoke not only as imperialists impatient for energy and vision in the administration, but as Radicals who instinctively preferred colonial self-government to bureaucratic interference. When all allowances have been made for tempers shortened in recent disputes, and for the exaggeration natural to controversy—by no means all Ministers and high officials, as no one had better reason to know than the Radical imperialists themselves, were apathetic nonentities—Charles Buller's famous caricatures of Mr. Mothercountry and The Sighing Rooms contained both truth and significance.

In some back room . . . you will find all the Mothercountry which really exercises supremacy, and really maintains connexion with the vast and widely scattered Colonies of Britain. We know not the name, the history or the functions of the individual, into the narrow limits of whose person we find the Mothercountry shrunk . . . he has a modest home in the outskirts of London, with an equally modest establishment, and the colonist, who is on his road to his office, little imagines that it is the real ruler of the Colonies that he sees walking over one of the bridges, or driving his one horse shay or riding cheek by jowl with him on the top of the short coach, as he comes into town of a morning . . .

There are rooms in the Colonial Office with old and meagre furniture, book-cases crammed with colonial gazettes and news-papers, tables covered with baize, and some old and faded chairs scattered about, in which those who have personal applications to make are doomed to wait until the interview can be obtained. Here, if perchance you shall some day be forced to tarry you will find strange, anxious-looking beings, who pace to and fro in feverish impatience, or sit dejected at the table, unable in the agitation of their thoughts to find any occupation to while away their hours, and starting every time that the door opens, in hopes that the messenger is come to announce that their turn is arrived. Those are men with Colonial grievances. The very messengers know them, their business and its hopelessness, and eye them with pity as they bid them wait their long and habitual period of attendance. No experienced eye can mistake their faces, once expressive of health and energy, now worn by hopes deferred and the listlessness of prolonged dependence. . . . Those chambers of woe are called *The Sighing Rooms*, and those who recoil from the sight of human suffering should shun the ill-omened precincts.

In the 'thirties jobbery was still one of Mr. Mothercountry's vices; "jobs," declares Charles Buller, "which even Parliamentary rapacity would blush to ask from the Treasury, are perpetrated with impunity in the silent realm of Mr. Mothercountry." But Sir James Stephen at least, who became permanent head of the Colonial Office in 1836, and had long been the chief influence there, was an energetic, and certainly an honest, man, and a good deal of the animus against him cherished by the Wakefield Radicals may have been due to their jealousy of the missionaries and Evangelicals to whom, like Lord Glenelg, Colonial Secretary from 1835 to 1839, he was always only too ready to listen.

§5

Here, in the Evangelical and missionary interest, we come upon the third of the political and religious forces which in the age of Bentham disputed the right to influence the future of the Empire. For twenty years at least before his death in 1833 Wilberforce had held a unique place in public regard; no other in that generation had been famous quite as Wilberforce was famous—save only Wellington, to whom Waterloo had given a pre-eminence different in kind but hardly greater in degree than that which Wilberforce had earned by the abolition of the slave trade. "When Mr. Wilberforce passes through the crowd," observed an Italian diplomat, "every one contemplates this little old man, worn with age and his head sunk upon his shoulders, as a sacred relic—as the Washington of humanity." For years Wilberforce had been "the keeper of the nation's conscience," and his unique position was primarily no doubt the tribute which the British will always pay to patent selflessness in a public man. But his vast prestige was certainly shared, and to some extent perhaps contributed to, by the Evangelical movement of which he had been the protagonist. And all through the 'thirties the Evangelicals, who had been chiefly responsible for abolishing the slave trade in 1806 and slavery in 1833, were alert and influential, particularly, thanks to their interest in missions, in imperial affairs. Wilberforce had been the chief originator of the British and Foreign Bible Society, as well as one of the founders of the Church Missionary Society in 1800. With the London Missionary Society, too, which dated from 1794, he was closely in touch. Founded under such influence, and with their roots in the Abolitionist crusade, these bodies were bound to keep a watchful eye on imperial policy. Indeed one of their chief duties, as they believed, was to see that humane and Christian standards were observed in the relations of their fellow-countrymen with native races. To some, "Exeter Hall," their London centre and symbol, stood for an unctuous humanitarianism, larded with texts, to others for a pack of pious and ignorant busybodies, for whom, whenever there was trouble in the colonies, the black man was necessarily right and the white man necessarily wrong. And in the 'thirties and 'forties, it must be admitted, Exeter Hall, without ceasing to play the strenuous part which it had mapped out for itself, would also figure from time to time in the rôles ascribed to it by its opponents.

South Africa and New Zealand were to be the chief battlegrounds for the Evangelicals and their opponents, but before this the varying fortunes of Wilberforce's long campaign to open India to the missionaries were typical of much that was to come. For, though Wilberforce had eagerly accepted Burke's doctrine of trusteeship, for him trusteeship was meaningless if it did not imply proselytism. Burke thought that we ought to govern India honestly and humanely, and do everything possible for its welfare, but with its ancient religions he saw no reason to interfere. "We ought to suffer all classes, without distinction," he had said, "to enjoy equally the right of worshipping God according to the light He has been pleased to give them." To Wilberforce on the other hand any talk of our promoting the welfare of India appeared merely farcical so long as we lifted no finger to save Indians from paganism and, as he believed, from eternal damnation. And so when the renewal of the Company's Charter was debated in 1793 he moved a series of resolutions declaring the conversion of India "by all just and prudent means" to be our bounden duty, and demanding schoolmasters and chaplains throughout the British dominions. But the Company had always scrupulously respected the customs and creeds of India, and had the strongest possible objection to missionaries. And this time the Company proved too strong. Twenty years later the Charter came up for renewal once more, and Wilberforce returned to the attack. By now he had come to believe that our indifference to Indian paganism was "the greatest by far, now that the Slave Trade has ceased, of all the national crimes by which we are provoking the vengeance and suffering the chastisement of Heaven." Already in 1812 Exeter Hall was mobilising its forces for the campaign. And this time the prospects were more hopeful. Although some Anglo-Indians remained adamant—even the circulation of the Bible, they considered, should be prohibited—India House had not stood still since 1793. From the original assumption that it was only in India to trade, the Company had been driven to accept the obligation of maintaining peace and order. And now that too was proving insufficient. For during the two decades since 1793 the new conception of trusteeship had taken root, and the Charter Act of 1813 allotted ten thousand pounds a year not only for "the revival and improvement of literature and the encouragement of the learned natives of India," but also "for the introduction and promotion of a knowledge of the sciences among the inhabitants of the British territories in India." Western learning was a tentative first step towards vaster ends than any could yet guess. But if Western science was to be admitted why not Western religion? Was Christianity to be the only benefit of civilisation which we refused to share with our Indian fellow-subjects? As he pressed home the dilemma Wilberforce was thrusting against a half-open door. And in the upshot the substance of the resolutions he had moved in 1793 was accepted. Henceforth a missionary refused a licence by the Directors was to be allowed to apply to the Board of Control, that is to the British government. Wilberforce had obtained all that he had hoped for. India was open to the missionaries. Henceforth they would not only spread the Gospel but serve as observant critics-on-the-spot of the standards of British administration. Within a year an Anglican bishopric had been created in Calcutta. The ending of the slave trade, the opening of India to the missionaries, and, twenty years later, the abolition of slavery—it was with three political achievements of the first magnitude already to their credit (the abolition of slavery indeed was one of the greatest events in the history of the world) that the Evangelicals and Exeter Hall would wage their contest for the soul of the new Empire with the Radicals, the Radical Imperialists, the uninstructed mass of Benthamite opinion and the dead weight of public indifference.

BOOKS FOR FURTHER READING.

Lord Rosebery, *Pitt;* Professor R. Coupland, *Wilberforce;* Sir Walter Besant, *Captain Cook;* Edward Heawood, *Geographical Discovery in the seventeenth and eighteenth centuries;* Ernest Scott, *A short history of Australia;* Professor Webster, *Castlereagh;* Professor Webster, *The Congress of Vienna;* Professor A. V. Dicey, *Law and Opinion in England* (on Bentham); Lord Morley, *Life of Cobden;* A. J. Harrup, *The amazing career of Edward Gibbon Wakefield;* Leslie Stephen, *The English Utilitarians;* Edward Gibbon Wakefield, *The art of Colonisation;* Edward Gibbon Wakefield, *A Letter from Sydney.*

Book VII

EMPIRE AS SELF-GOVERNMENT

CHAPTER ONE

DURHAM AND ELGIN

(1783-1854)

§1

SUCH were the three main groups which, against the sober background of a Benthamism principally concerned with domestic affairs, at various times and for various motives, friendly or hostile, interested themselves in the vast problems beginning to take shape overseas and contended for influence over them. One or other of them, or their mutual disputes, profoundly influenced the history of each of the young colonies. It was in Canada that the Radicals might have done most harm, with their rigid prejudice in favour of a general dissolution of the Empire and against what Hume would call "the baneful dominion of the mother country." It was in Canada that the Radical Imperialists, with their growing faith in the future, did most good.

§2

The survival of a British North America had first been assured by the migration from the thirteen seceding colonies, in 1783 and the following years, of somewhere about sixty thousand "United Empire Loyalists." Many of them had been men of the highest standing in their own states—judges, colonels, great landowners, eminent divines. Indeed some of the most distinguished British regiments during the War of Independence had been those raised from among the colonial loyalists. But despite their promises in the peace treaty, the victorious insurgents made the life of every Loyalist intolerable. Many would in any case have refused to live under a Republic, for the influence of the monarchy was very powerful—a high proportion of the earliest Loyalist townships in Canada were named after one or other of George III's children, which in that philoprogenitive family ensured a sufficiently wide choice. Rochefoucault, a French nobleman who visited Canada more than a decade later, records that while travelling with the British Governor he encountered an immigrant American family on its way from New York. "You are tired of the Federal Government," said the hearty old Governor. "You like not any longer to have so many kings. You wish again for your old father. You are perfectly right. Come along, we love such good royalists as you are. . . ." And the Loyalists streamed out of the States by land and sea, stripped of all their possessions, penniless, often half starved and bound for a country where, as they believed, "there were nine months of winter and three months of cold weather every year." They came by a dozen different routes, down the Hudson or the Oswego, the Black River or the Richelieu, across the Adirondacks or along Lake Champlain, but many died of exposure and disease, and "strong, proud men wept like children and lay down in their snow-bound tents to die." They were the Jacobites of the new world, sacrificing far more than the Jacobites of the old for what seemed a far more impossible loyalty and a far remoter kinship.

They poured first into Nova Scotia, whose western parts in 1784 became a separate province, named, like so much else, after the royal family, New Brunswick. As Nova Scotia filled, the Loyalists turned their eyes to the shores of the St. Lawrence, west of Montreal and Quebec. One of them has recorded the turning of the tide westward:

> In the meantime the Governor, in his perplexity, having heard that my father had been a prisoner among the French at Frontenac, sent for him and said, "Mr. Grass, I understand you have been at Frontenac in Canada. Pray tell me what kind of a country it is. Can people live there? What think you?" My father replied, "Yes, your Excellency, I was there a prisoner of war, and from what I saw I think it a fine country, and the people might live there very well."

Two shiploads led the way, the Pilgrim Fathers of British Canada. Thus, and by the influx along the inland routes from across the borders, the northern shores of the Great Lakes were peopled, in what is now the province of Ontario. With tools, and often clothes, provided by the government they built their log shanties and settled down to tame the wilderness. With the British Loyalists came many Indians of the Six Nations, who had fought for King George in the late war. The Mohawk tribe indeed crossed the frontier in a body, led by their chief Thayendanagea, or Joseph Brant, and settled along the Grand River, which flows into Lake Erie. Here they built the first church in Upper Canada, and here their descendants may be found to this day.

The coming of the Loyalists transformed the destiny of British North America. Hitherto, while a French population of perhaps a hundred thousand dwelt on the banks of the St. Lawrence between Quebec and Montreal, there had been a mere fourteen thousand British in Nova Scotia and New Brunswick, with some two thousand in the province of Quebec. The migration of somewhere about sixty thousand Loyalists to the maritime provinces and the valley of the St. Lawrence made it possible for Canada to become British in something more than name. It also vastly complicated the political problem to be solved by future generations.

§3

The problem began to take shape at once. In 1784, the very year of the Loyalist migration, petitions to the British Parliament for the "representation of the people" in the government of Canada began to cross the Atlantic. As they studied them, British statesmen began to realise, with a certain sinking of the heart, what a pretty tangle of issues confronted them. The maritime provinces at least were not at present involved; for Nova Scotia had been given a representative assembly in 1758, and New Brunswick when its separate existence began in 1784. And even Prince Edward Island (for so the Island of St. John was renamed in 1798, in honour of Queen Victoria's father, the Duke of Kent) had possessed an assembly, which met intermittently, since 1773. It was the province of Quebec which posed so many and such delicate problems. For here after all was a majority of French Catholics, whose training had been feudal, whose political experience was nugatory, and who were mostly either indifferent or hostile to the prospect of self-government. Side by side with them dwelt a minority of British Protestants, long accustomed to political life, most of them fresh from the terrible controversy over self-government which had laid their lives in ruins, and all of them after 1789 stimulated by the spectacle of the French Revolution and the promise, which it so signally failed to honour, of universal liberty. To grant the franchise to the British and withhold it from the French was not to be seriously thought of. Yet one constitution for the whole community must subject the Loyalists, who had so recently sacrificed everything to live under the British flag, to the permanent domination of an alien majority. And in addition to the constitutional problem it was necessary to grapple with the complex interrelationship of British Protestantism and British law with French Catholicism, French land tenure and the French legal code.

To Pitt and his advisers the simple solution seemed to be to divide Canada into two provinces. The new Upper Canada, just peopled by the Loyalists, should be British; Lower Canada, the original Bourbon colony, would remain French. And each should have its own assembly. It seemed simple, indeed to some British critics it seemed too simple. For one thing, there was the British minority in French Lower Canada, mainly merchants in the cities of Quebec and Montreal and recent settlers in the eastern townships—a minority which objected strongly to the prospect of being left high and dry, a politically impotent residuum in a French province. Again, Pitt hoped that "the division would remove the differences of opinion which had arisen between the old and new inhabitants, since each province would have the right of enacting laws desired in its own house of assembly," while Burke endorsed the project, declaring that "the attempt to amalgamate two populations composed of races of men diverse in language, laws and customs, was a complete absurdity." But even if Pitt was partly right, wondered the critics, might not Burke be wholly wrong? Might it be that to divide Canada into two provinces would but emphasise and perpetuate precisely that racial cleavage which it should be the first object of wise statesmanship to obliterate? So Fox at least thought. "It was most desirable," he said, "to see the French and English inhabitants coalesce into one body, and the different distinctions of people extinguished for ever." Was it of evil omen that the debate on Pitt's new Bill was the occasion, though not the cause, of the famous public severance of a life's friendship between Fox and Burke?

But Pitt saw no other way, and perhaps in 1791 he was right. And the Canadian Constitutional Act duly divided Canada into Upper and Lower, along the boundary which still separates Ontario from Quebec. Each province was to have its legislative council, nominated by the Crown, and its assembly, elected by the inhabitants. In each there would be a Lieutenant-Governor with a nominated executive council, and a Governor over the whole country. The elected assemblies were to have some control of taxation but none over the executive. Once again this was representation without responsibility. Land tenure was to be English in Upper Canada, French or English in Lower; the British criminal code would be enforced in both. The Catholics naturally retained the full religious freedom which they had been promised, and would continue to pay tithe to their own priests. And one-seventh of all Crown lands was to be set aside "for the support and maintenance of a Protestant clergy." At least the Act was clear-cut and logical. The new assemblies were certainly primitive; in their early days the representatives of Upper Canada occasionally met in a large tent. But they were the germ of greater consequences than their creators could foresee. And as for the tent, it had been round the world with Captain Cook.

§4

But before long danger from without was to teach the Canadians that they could be one people. From 1812 to 1814 a three years' war with the United States united all Canada in a patriotic effort of defence. The Orders in Council, the British Government's reply to the blockade imposed by Napoleon's Continental system, were ostensibly the root of the trouble, but there were other grievances south of the border, and the old enmities of the War of Independence still smouldered in the south and west. The Americans however were by no means unanimous. The maritime states of New England protested against the war, and there was some difficulty in enlisting new troops and inducing the militia to move. But in Canada, threatened with invasion and conquest, political differences were forgotten and all classes and both races prepared for a war of defence. The belief, widespread in the United States, that the Canadians were being oppressed by the British and would flock to the standard of a liberator, was falsified at once. When Hull, the invading American general, announced that the Canadians were to be "emancipated from tyranny and oppression" the Loyalists could only remember the oppression from which they had fled in the States, and the freedom which they had found in Canada. And there was nothing they desired less than to live under a Republic.

Three times, in 1812, 1813 and 1814, the tide of American invasion poured in, and three times, despite the scanty numbers of the Canadians, it was driven back. British and French shared the honours of the defence, in which the French have specially remembered de Salaberry's victory on the Chateauguay and the British the struggle in the dark which ended the final and decisive battle of Lundy's Lane. In 1814 the British fleet appeared in strength on the American coast and, in retaliation for wanton arson and destruction in many Canadian villages and towns, Washington, the Federal capital, was taken and burnt—an act of vandalism which still lies heavy on the conscience of British citizens, most of whom have forgotten, or never knew, that it was an episode in a war in which they were certainly not the aggressors. By the end of 1814 the long struggle with France was over and the rights of neutrals at sea ceased therewith to be an urgent issue; Britain had had her fill of fighting since 1793 and the Americans had learned that Canada was not, as they had supposed, a ripe fruit only waiting to be plucked. The New England states too, who were heavy losers by the war at sea, had become increasingly restive. There had been little point in beginning the war, and it was obvious to both sides that there was none whatever in continuing it. Peace was signed on Christmas Eve, 1814, and provided for "a mutual restitution of conquered territories and possessions." Britain and Americans had fought each other for the last time.

This little war proved to be a highly formative element in Canadian history. French and English, Scotsmen, Irish and even Americans had fought and died for the British connection. They began to be conscious of their nationhood and of a new self-confidence and self-respect. But the causes of Canadian resistance are even more significant than their consequences. Why had Canada so stoutly resisted assimilation to its great neighbour? Partly no doubt because it would have been assimilation through conquest. But chiefly, it would seem, because Canadians preferred a monarchy to a republic, and their own pattern of liberty to the American.

§5

All this seemed to mean that there was a great future for a British Canada; yet there could be no future at all unless the British themselves acquired a further instalment of political wisdom. If the record of the three years' war with the Americans foreshadowed a Canada one day united, stable and strong, the Constitution of 1791 still stood for all the myopia and inexperience which had lost the American colonies. A democratic assembly without real power and an executive which was the creature of the British government ominously suggested a re-enactment of the American tragedy, and made a particularly fatal combination in Lower Canada, where the French Canadians had no experience of any kind of self-government —"you will scarcely find a trace of education among the peasantry," one of Lord Durham's Assistant Commissioners would write. Both provinces were soon demanding further powers, Lower Canada pressing for the election of the executive council, Upper Canada for responsible government. But in Upper Canada at this time the words "responsible government" were used with many different meanings, and hardly ever in their proper sense of the collective responsibility of the executive to the majority of an elected Parliament. Responsible government in this sense would prove the corner stone of Canadian liberties, but it was brought to Canada from overseas by Lord Durham and Lord Elgin, without ever being put forward as a panacea by the Canadian reformers.[1]

In addition to all this, each province was divided by its own internal schism. In Lower Canada the French majority attacked the British as " *étrangers et intrus*," in Upper the so-called Family Compact of United Empire Loyalists had established itself as a narrow oligarchy, which imposed disabilities on newcomers and provoked increasingly violent opposition. But the rebellions which broke out in the two Provinces in 1837 were trifling affairs. For the dominant influence in Lower Canada was the Roman Catholic Church, and in Upper the United Empire Loyalists. And both were conservative and sincerely attached to the imperial connection. For the Catholic hierarchy had been won over by the unexpected tolerance of the British administration. Experience powerfully suggested that no such religious liberty could yet be looked for under American rule, while the atheism of the Revolution and the growing anti-clericalism under the Bourbon Restoration and the July Monarchy had discouraged nostalgia for France.

§6

The rebellions were never formidable and collapsed almost at once. It was only after their collapse that Britain came to one of those decisive moments of history, so often unrecognised by contemporaries, which can be seen in retrospect to have been a parting of the ways. For what was to be done now? The British had been granted a new opportunity; had they learnt a new wisdom? Once again, as in 1775, the problem was How could a healthy nationalism and a growing desire for self-government be prevented from bursting the bonds of Empire? If the Ministers of George III had put down the Americans as easily as the Canadian rebels were suppressed in

[1] This view is contrary to that of most of the best Canadian historians, who describe the Upper Canadians as having demanded "responsible government" without analysing what they meant by those words. But Professor Chester New, *Lord Durham* (1924), 336-342, makes it plain that they scarcely ever meant what we mean to-day, and what they eventually got.

1837 they would doubtless have riveted the old colonial system more firmly than ever on the defeated colonists. Because the Ministers of the young Victoria did otherwise they opened a new chapter in history, and made possible the growth not only of a new Canada but of a new Empire, and, it is not too much to say, of a new world. Little did the amiable Lord Melbourne and his Whig Cabinet know what they were doing, little perhaps did they care. What was done was due partly to the general acquiescence of Benthamite opinion, and particularly of the Radical minority, in the growth of freedom, and even in the prospect of an eventual disintegration of the Empire; to the paradox in fact that in the new age the British made a new Empire possible by ceasing to desire one. More conspicuously it was due to the sudden brief appearance and wise decisive rôle played by one man, the Earl of Durham. And not to Durham only, but to the handful of Radical Imperialists whom he chose to advise him, with Gibbon Wakefield characteristically active and indispensable, and characteristically in the background. And certainly not less to the insight, the courage and the superb self-restraint of Lord Elgin, the man who did what Durham himself could never have done, and turned theory into hard reality by painfully teaching what he had learnt from Durham to Canadian, and indeed to British, politicians. No country could have counted upon such political insight followed by such practical sagacity. And despite the long political experience of the British these qualities might never have been forthcoming at the crucial moment, but for the renewed apprenticeship to Empire which the whole nation had served since the loss of the American colonies.

Lord Melbourne's Government showed more than its usual perspicacity in its selection of a Governor General at this moment of perplexity. For John George Lambton, first Earl of Durham, was by no means an obvious choice. This Whig aristocrat, one of Lord Grey's chief lieutenants in the Reform of 1832, whom the *Morning Chronicle* had backed for the Premiership, instead of Lord Melbourne, in 1834, besides being hand in glove with the Radicals was unpredictable, quarrelsome and something of a genius—a most unlikely combination for a Whig Governor General. In 1834 he had commanded a great popular following as an aristocratic Radical—a crowd of a hundred and twenty thousand gathered to hear him speak on Glasgow Green that year. In many ways indeed his career foreshadowed that of Lord Randolph Churchill half a century later; there was the same popular appeal, the same independent programme of reform, the same brilliance and sudden end. Durham was a strikingly handsome man, "of medium height, dark and bright-eyed, like a fine Murillo." From manhood onwards he had been constantly tormented by terrible pains in the head, to which was doubtless due the violent temper, whose frequent outbursts in the cabinet or at some country house-party Creevey and Greville take a malicious delight in describing. His political opponents constantly derided him as irritable and arrogant; "the Monarch" and "the Angry Boy" are two of Creevey's nicknames for him. But his arrogance was of a simple and almost impersonal kind. "Instead of pluming himself on his talents," said his enemy, Brougham, "he really was chiefly fond of exalting his wealth and family." And he would travel with a great retinue of footmen and outriders because it was his duty, he believed, to maintain his position. But fundamentally he was a generous, friendly and even a modest, man. He had a very mean opinion of his own abilities, and though his quarrels were frequent he usually made them up within a week. On one occasion, it is said, he spoke rudely to his wife before their servants. After they had left the room she gently remonstrated with him. Instantly he rang the bell, summoned the whole household into the room and told the astonished servants that he had temporarily forgotten himself, and that if ever they heard him contradict the Countess again they should remember that he had thereby put himself in the wrong and that she was always right. Whereupon he apologised to her in their presence, and dismissed them. He did not always recover himself quite so quickly as this, but only with Brougham was he on bad terms for so long as twelve months, and it was to Brougham's rancour that he owed his premature return from Canada. Durham's sensitive irritability and apparent arrogance made it highly unlikely that he would prove a successful Governor General in normal times. But these were not normal times, and for the special task before him he was admirably qualified by his undoubted courage and generosity, his wide political knowledge—"he thinks completely upon politics" wrote Henry Fox, "it . . . entirely engrosses him"—his independent mind and his rare ability to pierce swiftly to the heart of a complex problem. With his qualities and his defects it is not perhaps surprising either that his Governor Generalship should have lasted only six months, or that his subsequent Report should have opened a new era in history.

How could Canada achieve self-government, and yet remain within the Empire? That was the problem posed to this impetuous Radical-aristocrat with his blinding headaches, his unpredictable fits of temper, his courageous independence, his strange political insight and his life-long confidence in democracy. And he would succeed in solving it, largely because he saw what scarcely anybody else had seen—that responsible government was the key to self-government. He owed little enough to the wisdom or support of colleagues at home. Melbourne, it is true, had written, "as far as I am concerned, and I think I can answer for all my colleagues, you will receive the firmest and most unflinching support," a promise which he signally failed to honour. But in the debates on the Bill which suspended the constitution of Lower Canada until 1840 most of the Radicals expressed the hope that there would be a speedy separation between Canada and the mother country, and almost all the other speakers agreed that, though the time for separation was not yet, separation some day was inevitable. "In a national way," said Brougham in the Lords, "I really hold those colonies to be worth nothing." But Durham was not only a Radical, he was a Radical Imperialist. He was President, for one thing, of the New Zealand Association, of which, behind the scenes as usual, Wakefield was the moving spirit. He already knew much about the colonies, and he believed in their future. And now that the time had come to select his staff he sat down and politely but firmly rejected the applications which poured in from influential persons whose friends had an eye on a Canadian appointment and a liberal salary. For the first time Canada was to be served by the best brains in Britain. Durham took with him a little group of Radical Imperialists, men who, like himself, knew and believed in the Empire. For Chief Secretary he chose Charles Buller, brilliant, witty and thirty-one, the most popular of the Radical Members. "The essence of his mind," wrote Carlyle, Buller's former tutor, after his death, "was clearness." Durham picked Wakefield too, planning to appoint him Commissioner of Crown Lands. But the emergence of Wakefield, and such an emergence, from behind his customary curtain would have been too much for public opinion at home. Lord Melbourne wrote, in great agitation, "if you touch G.W. with a pair of tongs it is utter destruction, depend upon it," and Durham had to assure the Prime Minister that Wakefield had withdrawn into his former obscurity and held no official position. "Oh, no," he wrote sardonically, "we never mention him; his name is never heard. Really, if it was not so very inconvenient, all this would be ludicrous." Fortunately, as usual, Wakefield's effacement did nothing to diminish his activity.

Durham was not only Governor but High Commissioner "for the adjustment of certain important questions depending in the provinces of Lower and Upper Canada, respecting the form of future government of the said provinces." In effect for the time being he was dictator. If he had had a year, considers the best Canadian judge,[1]

[1] Professor Chester New, *Lord Durham*, 387.

besides revolutionising the government of Canada and the character of the British Empire, he would have "removed all real grievances, satisfied every reasonable demand and established adequate systems of municipal govermnent and education in both Upper and Lower Canada." If he had had a year. But this British politicians, and his own past, would not allow him.

His first task was to settle the delicate problem of the rebels of Lower Canada. Three hundred and twenty-six had already been released, but a hundred and sixty-one remained to be tried and punished—nobody knew how. Some clearly must be punished, yet only a packed jury could be relied on to convict them, and Durham was the last man to pack a jury. He decided to select the eight most culpable, obtain from them a confession of guilt, and banish them, by ordinance, to Bermuda, a distant, but not a penal, colony. All the rest he would pardon. It was a masterly solution. An example had been made of the ringleaders, but without bloodshed. Canada was enthusiastic; the exiles themselves bore no grudge, and are said to have drunk Durham's health on board the ship which carried them to Bermuda. And many citizens of the United States, seeing this mild treatment of the leaders of an armed rebellion against the Crown, began to revise their opinions as to British tyranny. But Durham had made two slips. Technically a sentence of detention in Bermuda was beyond his powers. And he had neglected to supply ministers at home with full information as to his motives and procedure. And so when his enemies, led by the vindictive and disappointed Brougham, fell upon the illegality of the Ordinance as a means of wounding Durham and embarrassing the government, Melbourne and his colleagues, most of whom already lacked the will to defend him effectively, lacked also the means.

While this storm was brewing in the lobbies of Westminster, Durham was delving into the problems of Canada and beginning to touch the imagination of the Canadians. "Faith when it is sincere is always catching" he wrote himself, and faith, just now the rarest and most indispensable virtue for an imperial statesman, he possessed in abundance. "Your Lordship has been the first statesman," wrote Robert Baldwin, a leading Reformer in Upper Canada, "to avow a belief in the possibility of a permanent connection between the colonies and the Mother Country," and strangely though so sweeping an assertion reads to-day, it seems to be literally true. But at home the bolt had fallen. Parliament had disallowed the Ordinance. For Durham it was indeed a bolt from the blue. Lady Durham's journal records how the news reached them as they were coming back from a drive along the banks of the St. Lawrence:

I.C.   T

We were a merry party—the children, Charles and Caroline (I think) and Mr. Buller, enjoying the little adventures and difficulties of crossing the ferry, laughing at Mr. Cavendish and his drag following us—and delighted with the beauty of the scenery. As we returned we saw from the heights the steamer from Montreal, arriving with the post and bringing with it, tho' little did we guess it, the intelligence of those events whose fatal consequence we were, alas! so far from anticipating.

The steamer had brought letters from the Prime Minister and the Colonial Secretary warmly approving Durham's conduct—"my colleagues and I entirely approve," said Glenelg; "I have nothing to express but the most entire approval and concurrence," wrote Melbourne—and describing the Parliamentary attack, then just beginning, as impotent and foredoomed. In the bag from England this was all. But the steamer brought also a New York journal with the later news that the Ordinances had been disallowed. For Melbourne and Glenelg had been silent for fourteen days after sending Durham their thanks and congratulations, and had permitted him to read of the disallowance of his wise and healing measure in an American newspaper. The Government had found itself, it is true, in an awkward quandary. For its Law Officers had advised that so much of the Ordinance as related to Bermuda was *ultra vires*, and Melbourne had had to decide whether or not to introduce a Bill to supplement it. But such a measure would have been defeated by a combination of Tories and Radicals, and a defeat in the Commons would have been the end of the administration. And in the midst of the strange Indian summer of his romantic tutelage of the young Queen, Melbourne refused to sacrifice his government for a distant colony and a man he had always disliked. And so the Ordinance had been disallowed, and the Government survived. It was not so much Melbourne and his cabinet who were to blame as all those Party politicians who could be relied on to vote against the government if it stood by Durham, not because they cared one way or the other about Durham, Canada or Bermuda, but because it was part of the game to use the weapon chance had offered them against their political opponents.

In Canada Brougham was burnt in effigy and Durham was greeted with tremendous ovations. And from all over the country flooded in petitions begging him to remain. Once again Canada was united—because British politicians, pursuing Party advantage without thought of Canadian interests, had overturned the policy of a Canadian government. Some thought that Durham should have stayed on, to attempt out of this temporary unanimity to build permanent unity in Canada. But even if he had been the man to put up readily with a public affront, he believed, and perhaps rightly, that with Brougham and his allies on the warpath any major stroke of policy in Canada was likely to be reversed at Westminster. He decided to resign. Perhaps it was as well. He was not likely to make a successful Governor General for any length of time—his final proclamation was full of indiscretions—and the circumstances of his resignation doubtless strengthened his determination that, if anything he could now do could prevent it, the British Parliament should never again have power to sacrifice Canadian interests to its own parochial quarrels. Durham returned home with only a few months to live. He devoted them doggedly to the Report which was to be his imperishable service to Canada and the Empire. At last, on the threshold of the grave, his wayward temper, his pride and even his ambitions were forgotten. All were subdued to his great final task.

Either Durham's personality or the political situation alone would have ensured a blaze of publicity for the Report, but assurance was made doubly sure by the appearance on February 8, 1839, several days before the government presented it to Parliament, of a long first instalment in the *Times*. Unconfirmed tradition has it that this leakage was the work of Gibbon Wakefield, moving, half-perceived for once, behind the customary veil. Soon other British papers were printing the Report in serial form; and within a few months it was known throughout the British world. Despite its length, most of the Canadian Press published it in full. And not Canadian papers only. " It has now gone the round," wrote Wakefield that December, "from Canada, through the West Indies and South Africa, to the Australias, and has everywhere been received with acclamations." Naturally enough, for the Report is an admirable piece of writing, clear, courageous, inspiring and like all truth, dateless. And to even the least instructed reader it brought a sense of revelation. Durham's enemies put it about at once that the Report was not his work. "Wakefield thought it, Buller wrote it, Durham signed it," as a contemporary *mot* had it. As to which it is only necessary to say that Wakefield admittedly wrote most of the sub-report on public lands and emigration, but that all historians who have investigated the evidence agree that Durham was the author of his own Report.[1]

The core of the recommendations was twofold. The reunion of the Canadas was to be the indispensable first step. Durham was mistaken in hoping to merge the French Canadians in British

---

[1] See Appendix to Chester New, *Lord Durham*.

Canada; he was sometimes very much a child of his age, and he failed to perceive that those very qualities in the French which in the dawn of an industrial era seemed to spell backwardness might in course of time prove no less indispensable to Canadian civilisation than the alert commercialism of the British business men of Montreal and Quebec. Nevertheless without reunion neither responsible government in the 'forties nor Confederation a generation later would have been possible. And the crucial element in the Report is the recommendation of responsible government, so familiar now, so revolutionary then. Only, external trade, foreign affairs, unoccupied lands and the power of amending the constitution were to be reserved for the imperial Parliament. The words "responsible government" were used very loosely at that time, in many different senses, often meaning little more than "government by trustworthy persons"; but Durham made it clear that he had in mind the contemporary British model, "which has vested the direction of the national policy . . . in the leaders of the Parliamentary majority." Such a constitution you may call responsible government, because it implies the responsibility of the Canadian executive to the Canadian legislative, or self-government, because it thereby deprives the British Parliament of its overriding authority and vests ultimate power in the elected representatives of the Canadian people:

> I admit that the system which I propose would, in fact, place the internal government of the colony in the hands of the colonists themselves; and that we should thus leave to them the execution of the laws, of which we have long entrusted the making solely to them. Perfectly aware of the value of our colonial possessions and strongly impressed with the necessity of maintaining our connection with them, I know not in what respect it can be desirable that we should interfere with their internal legislation in matters which do not affect their relations with the Mother Country. . . . The colonists may not always know what laws are best for them, or which of their countrymen are the fittest for conducting their affairs; but at least, they have a greater interest in coming to a right judgment on these points, and will take greater pains to do so than those whose welfare is very remotely and slightly affected by the good or bad legislation of these portions of the Empire. . . . The British people of the North American colonies are a people on whom we may safely rely, and to whom we must not grudge power.

"Strongly impressed with the necessity of maintaining our connection with them"—the sovereign virtue and originality of Durham was that he combined the wisdom to perceive the virtue of self-government, and the courage to advocate it, with a firm faith in the value and possibility of permanent union. A Manchester Radical might have advocated colonial self-government, but he would have advocated it because it was a step, as he believed, towards separation. And while many high Tories viewed the prospect of self-government with deep mistrust, their mistrust was not due to any faith in the future of the Empire. But Durham not only proffered a novel solution of present problems, he pointed confidently forward to a hitherto undreamed of future. And it was this doubly prophetic quality in the Report which startled and stirred men like a wind blowing from another world. Here for the first time appears the conception of independent nationality within the Empire, the basis of the imperial structure of the future. Of Durham's recommendations a distinguished Canadian historian wrote ninety years later that with the passing years their wisdom had only become more apparent; "they undergird the life of Canada to-day at almost every point, and are reflected wherever British nations pursue their destinies under the inspiration of self-government and imperial partnership."

§7

Lord John Russell's Canada Act of 1840 united the Canadas and gave them a nominated legislative council, and an assembly of which half was to be elected from each of the two provinces. The executive was to be chosen by the Governor. Characteristically enough, this in itself was not responsible government so much as a framework into which responsible government could be built. Under the inspiration of the Report the building did not take long. Obviously from the first there was nothing to prevent a Governor from choosing his ministers from a Parliamentary majority. And Lord John's instructions of October 16, 1839, advised that in future the executive should not longer hold office virtually for life, but should be removed "as often as any sufficient motives of public policy may suggest the expediency of that measure." Thus at a stroke was made possible the rise and fall of ministries in accordance with the will of the assembly. Once again it was characteristic of the empiricism which has been responsible for most of our constitutional progress that the first Governor under the Act, Lord Sydenham, should both have cherished a profound mistrust of

ministerial responsibility and also have laid its foundations firmly
on Canadian soil. Sydenham formed a coalition Party commanding
in the assembly a majority from which he chose his executive
council. The executive council, as Durham had recommended, he
reorganised into a cabinet of Ministers, each responsible for his
separate department. He established the indispensable convention
that members of the cabinet must be members of the assembly.
And in general he familiarised Canadian politicians with the
Parliamentary technique through which a ministry rules by means
of the majority upon which it depends. In a less politically minded
nation all this would doubtless have been set down in black and
white in the original Act, with every probability that responsible
government would immediately have broken down. And if there is
something paradoxical in the spectacle of a Governor who steadily
refused to endorse the theory of ministerial responsibility industriously educating Canada in the practise of it, it is certain that no
other method could have given responsible government a likelier
chance of taking root. Thanks to Sydenham, Sydenham's successor
found himself reporting to the Colonial Secretary that responsible
government "virtually . . . exists." He spoke prematurely, for Peel's
Tory Government took alarm for a while and sent out Lord Metcalfe
to put the clock back, if he could. But in 1847, on the morrow of
the triumph of Free Trade, and with the Whigs in power again,
Durham's spiritual heir, Lord Elgin, went out to complete Durham's
work.

§8

Elgin was not only Durham's spiritual heir, and incidentally
his son-in-law, but his most timely counterpart and complement.
For Durham was a prophet, not an administrator, and understood
principles better than he understood men. But Elgin, who had
wholeheartedly accepted Durham's teachings, was primarily a great
ruler, the very man needed to consolidate and perpetuate the reforms
which were now making Canada the experimental laboratory of the
new Empire. If there was much of the poet in Durham, Elgin's
patient inductive statesmanship recalled the method of the scientist.
In the British Empire adjustments have usually been due not so
much to ministers and orators as to the administrator who marshals
and masters the facts on the spot. But here in Canada in these
critical years, when change was the only alternative to disruption
and decay, both the speculative and the practical genius was forth-

coming. James Bruce, eighth Earl of Elgin, son of the Lord Elgin who brought the famous Marbles from Athens, was a great administrator, yet to say that he was a great administrator is almost to damn him with faint praise; for his qualities evade such short descriptive labels as this. More completely than any statesman of that century, save perhaps Peel, he could analyse and understand the complex situations which he was called upon to control. But intellectual power alone would never have accounted for his achievement. Many of the moral qualities indispensable for the great ruler were native to his caste and his generation—the strict sense of honour, the reverence for justice, the courage, and, less familiar but not less important, the fine manners. For most of the crises of Empire have centred upon some form of racial cleavage or nationalist hostility, in which mere unperceptive rudeness can do irreparable harm; and the men who have done most for the Empire at such times have all been great gentlemen, winning their victories as much by their courtesy as their strength. And although there was a certain loneliness about Elgin—as one of his brothers put it he "lived a life apart from his fellows"—the impression he produced upon strangers was always of geniality and charm. But his rarest quality was the astonishing, the sometimes almost superhuman, patience with which he so often conciliated or disarmed, would rather carry his point than crush his opponents, and would even prefer a rebuff to a victory, when victory was likely to leave bitter memories behind it. But perhaps it was not patience so much as self-control. "May I command my temper and passions"; so the future Governor General had concluded a nursery prayer at the age of ten. And certainly some of the portraits of Elgin, with the tight lips, the broad nostrils and the somewhat stocky figure, suggest not so much patience as daemonic energy and strong passions constantly held in check.

"I have adopted frankly and unequivocally Lord Durham's view of government," wrote Elgin in 1847. And the basis of all that he did for Canada was the determination that if there was to be responsible government the Governor, like the Sovereign in Britain, must reign but not rule. He must withdraw from the arena of political controversy. He must support and advise his ministers, but henceforth it must be the Parliamentary majority which determined who those ministers should be and what policy they should pursue. On March 3, 1848, the Opposition carried an amendment to the speech from the throne, and Elgin at once invited the leaders of the Opposition to form a government. And so the first genuinely responsible ministry in Canadian history took office. It was a bold venture, for the new government was a coalition of ex-rebels, and

Elgin could not as yet be completely certain of the goodwill of either the French of Lower Canada or the Reformers of Upper Canada. And just now, to add to the apparent risk, preparations for an armed attack on Canada were going on among Irish Americans across the border. But Elgin had realised almost at once, what no Minister in Britain had yet managed to perceive, that, treated with justice and consideration, the French would become the most conservative element in Canada. And more than this, he had perceived that the interest taken by Canadians in general in political controversy was temporary and unnatural. Their natural interest was the land still to be cleared and tilled, the roads and railways yet to be built, and all the vast task of opening up a new country. Let one or two rankling grievances be removed and they would have little energy to spare for political controversy. Elgin was soon proved right; the main grievances he saw removed himself—the clergy reserves were secularised and the seignorial feudal tenures abolished—and very soon Canadian politics mellowed into a steady alternation of Conservative-Liberal and Liberal-Conservative administrations. Under Elgin, too, politics in Canada began to cease to wear the appearance of a racial feud. "I believe," he had written in 1847, "that the problem of how to govern United Canada would be solved if the French would split into a Liberal and Conservative Party, and join the Upper Canada Parties which bear corresponding names." And this, thanks to him, was precisely what they did.

But not at once. There were other lessons for Elgin to teach Canada first. The Canadian Tories, whose opponents Elgin had just admitted to office, and who still supposed themselves to be the sole champions of the imperial connection, were outraged by the spectacle of the former rebels in power. And when the government introduced, and passed, its Rebellion Losses Bill, proposing compensation in Quebec similar to that already granted in Ontario, their indignation became uncontrollable. Were French sedition-mongers to recoup themselves for sedition? The Governor General had gone far enough in admitting these men to office on the unconvincing grounds that they possessed a majority; surely even he would not give his assent to such a measure? But for Elgin the situation, though delicate, admitted of no doubts. He would take any risk rather than betray "Lord Durham's view of government," and disallow a measure passed by a constitutional majority. And so he gave his consent. There was rioting in Montreal, and he himself was twice pelted with stones. For some while after this he resolutely declined to appear in public. He knew that he could have provoked the rioters to put themselves still further in the wrong, and thereupon could have crushed them by force. He knew that all French Lower Canada would have risen as one man in support of the government. But he knew too that he, or his successors, would have one day to rule through the Tory politicians who were hallooing on the rioters. And he had no desire to earn the easy reputation of a strong man at the cost of bloodshed. Nothing he did must embitter the racial conflict. And so he held his hand, and let who would deride him as a coward. Never did his rare self-control serve Canada better. "" I own I would have reduced Montreal to ashes before I would have endured what you did," said a friend. "I have been told by Americans," wrote Elgin afterwards, "' . . . we could not understand why you did not *shoot them down*.'" As for Carlyle, the apostle of Great Men was contemptuously indignant. "Majesty's Chief Governor in fact," he wrote, "seldom appearing on the scene at all, except to receive the impact of a few rotten eggs, and then duck in again to his private contemplations." Very differently would one of his own Heroes have conducted himself. Elgin's indeed was a greatness which Carlyle was constitutionally incapable of understanding. But the spectacle of a British Governor insulted by Tory Loyalists, because he insisted on the right of a French Canadian majority to legislate as it pleased, had done more than years of argument to conciliate French Canada and establish responsible government. Thanks to the wise patience of his son-in-law, "Lord Durham's view of government" had triumphed.

CHAPTER TWO

THE MAKING OF AUSTRALIA

(1823-1850)

§1

IN THE vast new continent to the south the Radical Imperialists had a more conspicuous and a more controversial rôle to play. In 1823 what we now call Australia was a huge empty bulk, its south-eastern shores dotted with the few sparse settlements whose inhabitants knew nothing of their own hinterland, save that here and there a handful of explorers had penetrated a few days' journey into the unknown which stretched illimitably westward. Not till 1813 had they crossed the forbidding wall of the Blue Mountains, some fifty miles inland from Sydney. Thanks to Flinders and his successor, King, the coasts had been surveyed, but for the rest the continent remained for all practical purposes what it had been always, *terra Australis incognita*. But if during the next quarter of a century some celestial spectator could have kept the whole continent under observation he might have watched group after group of explorers working its way westward through the mountains from Sydney, and in their wake the agricultural frontiers creeping forward, as the squatters made for the new-found grazing-lands. He would have seen Stuart searching for the inland sea, into which the rivers running westward from the coastal watershed were believed to flow, until he came to the masked outfall of the Murray in Encounter Bay, where the city of Adelaide would one day stand. He would have seen Mitchell and McMillan pushing southward into the rich lands of what would be Victoria; and Leichardt making his way north-westward by the northern coasts, and then, a few years later, setting out to cross the centre of the Continent from east to west with seven companions, not one of whom was ever seen again. From each new city as it grew up, he would have seen the tracks of the explorers heading for the unknown. The fortunes of some journeys he might have been tempted to watch with special attention; perhaps that on which Eyre, afterwards as Governor of Jamaica the centre of a famous controversy, set out from Adelaide to explore the possibility of an overland route to Western Australia—set out with five Europeans and two native boys, and after journeying along

the barren shores of the Australian Bight came to Albany in Western
Australia, accompanied at last by a single native.

Gradually new names would appear upon the map, and even new
colonies would take shape. At home the officials of the Colonial
Office might wring their hands—"all schemes of this kind have been
of late years discountenanced as leading continually to the establishment of fresh settlements and fresh expense," wrote the Under-
Secretary in 1835—but inevitably where rich land was found
squatters poured in to claim it. Thomas Henty sells his Sussex
property for ten thousand pounds, when he is seventy, and sails for
Australia, determined to settle his seven sons on land of their own.
One of them discovers rich grass land on the south coast in Portland
Bay, where not a soul then dwelt, and by 1835 four of the brothers
are whaling, sheep-farming and cattle-raising in what will one day
be Victoria—before the government of Sydney has any notion that
a yard of land south of the Murray had been occupied. Here Major
Thomas Mitchell, the Surveyor-General of New South Wales,
discovered them to his astonishment, already established for two
years, and in possession of the only glass windows he had seen since
leaving New South Wales. Here in the south there were no officials,
no land laws, only rich empty lands; and other claimants were not
long in crossing the Bass Straits from Van Diemen's Land. Occasionally, like John Batman, they would assign themselves a vast acreage
in some preposterous pseudo-feudal document which the aboriginals
of the neighbourhood would be only too ready to sign in return for
a largesse of knives, mirrors and blankets. More often they simply
took what they wanted. And once again the Government found
itself compelled to regularise the *fait accompli*. To trail, scolding
ineffectually, in the wake of the pioneer is at best of times not a
dignified proceeding, but the Colonial Office, which treated the
pioneers with singular lack of generosity, contrived to make it
shabby into the bargain. None the less in 1850 a new colony,
Victoria, came into being. Like Victoria in the south, the northern
parts of New South Wales were bound to hive off in due course into
a new colony. Here the nucleus was a penal settlement at Brisbane,
and squatters moving in to the pastures of Darling Downs. The new
colony was proclaimed, as Queensland, in 1859.

§2

The British statesmen of the seventeen eighties had wished,
somewhat half-heartedly, for a remote convict settlement. Unknow-

ingly they had acquired a continent three-fourths of the size of all Europe, including Russia. For some decades they would probably have been thankful to give away large portions of it to any respectable government which had asked for them, and it was long before any notion of controlling so vast an area presented itself to them. All colonies, they believed, were a source of trouble, and they had enough troubles of their own at home. And soon there were Benthamites and Radicals in plenty to assure them that to do nothing was of itself a major virtue. Yet the wealth of the new continent grew with startling rapidity. Much of its soil was as rich as any in the world, and it was an unopened treasure-house of precious metals. Mr. Mothercountry might be in the mood to do as little as possible, but he could not help doing something. For after the explorers came the squatters and their sheep, and the value of the wool exported increased about thirty-fold in the thirty years after 1826. Wool made Sydney, and then Melbourne and Adelaide, into great seaports. Between the seaports and the squatters an expanding belt of farmland grew the food-stuffs for the mounting population. But who owned the land, and by what title? It was a fundamental question, but for long there was no answer. Or rather there were too many answers. John Batman of Victoria had claimed to hold his acres by virtue of twin parchments inscribed with a lawyer's rigmarole of livery and seisin, and "signed" by the "mark" of aboriginal black-fellows. For less imaginative squatters it was sufficient to maintain that all Australia belonged to the existing colonists, and that he who chose to appropriate unclaimed land was its rightful owner in perpetuity. Governors had assumed the right to give away great tracts for nothing. As for the British government, when forced to reflect upon the problem, it preferred the ancient feudal doctrine that all land belongs to the Crown. "The waste lands of the vast Colonial possessions of the British Empire," wrote Lord Grey in 1852, "are held by the Crown, as Trustee for the inhabitants of the Empire at large, and not for the inhabitants of the particular province . . . in which any such waste land happens to be situate." This in itself, however, solved no problems; the land might be Crown land, and held in Trusteeship, but the Crown was not likely to till or mine it; how then was it to be disposed of?

§3

Edward Gibbon Wakefield had no doubt that he knew the answer. It was to Australia after all that his thoughts had turned in Newgate, and the problems of Australia, still fresh, still awaiting their first answer, had engrossed him ever since. When Wakefield was in Newgate in 1830 the ineptitude of an Australian land settlement was topical news. A party of settlers on the Swan River in Western Australia had just afforded, it seemed to him, a permanent object lesson in all the most disastrous mistakes which government and colonists could commit. The government had been alarmed at rumours of French, or American, intrusion and had for once countenanced a project of colonisation. But it had been willing neither to spend public money nor to issue a proprietary charter to private capitalists in the traditional manner. It had presented huge blocks of land, virtually free of charge, to private persons willing to invest money in taking out labourers. The settlement had languished, on the verge of extinction, until 1832, when it began very slowly to take root. Wakefield had no doubts as to the reason. The grants of land were much too large and much too cheap. If land could be had for nothing why should one man work for another, and where accordingly was labour to come from? And if land was to be held in such vast blocks the settlers must inevitably be dispersed in isolated handfuls, incapable of any sort of mutual assistance. "The greatest pains," wrote Wakefield, "were taken to disperse the colonists, to cut up their capital and labour into the smallest fractional parts, whence a miserable failure with all the elements of success."

The first grantee took his principality at the landing-place; and the second, of course, could only choose his outside of this vast property. Then the property of the second grantee compelled the third to go farther off for land, and the fourth again was driven still further into the wilderness. At length, through a very brief process, an immense territory was appropriated by a few settlers, who were so effectually dispersed that, as there were not roads or maps, scarcely one of them knew where he was.

Between 1825 and 1830 the average emigration to Australia was about one thousand a year, and in 1831 the *Spectator* declared that "colonisation, worthy to be so described, has never been pursued by any modern Government." This was precisely what Wakefield was determined to alter. Shorn of its complexities, the gist of his doctrine was simple. Colonial land must be sold, not given away, and sold at a "sufficient" price; for as much, that is, as would ensure that immigrant labourers would have to work for a reasonable time before saving enough to become landowners themselves. The proceeds of the land sales should form a fund to assist further emigration. British politicians at this time were much exercised over their swollen poor rates, and Wakefield pictured his emigrants as "young pauper labourers of both sexes in equal numbers." News of the apparent failure of the Swan River Company, and of Captain Stuart's discoveries in South Australia, reached England about the same time. Wakefield and his friends decided that the time for action had come. They would found a model colony in South Australia.

The prospectus of the South Australian Association was issued from number seven Adelphi Chambers in December, 1833, with a Committee including Charles Buller and three other Members of Parliament. Wakefield's name, as usual, did not appear. Indeed after three years as producer-prompter in the wings an appearance before the footlights would have hampered his technique, and if he felt any resentment at his perpetual relegation to the half-lights, it was probably vented in the uncertain temper of which his colleagues so often had to complain. "Saw Edward Wakefield," notes Robert Gouger's Journal in April, 1834. "We disagreed materially . . . and this led to much unpleasant talk between us. It is unnecessary to sketch the conversation and its results. The sooner forgotten the better." But there was much to try Wakefield's temper besides his own equivocal status. The negotiations with Mr. Mothercountry were protracted and exasperating. For a while a favouring breeze filled the Association's sails when Spring-Rice, who had been at Westminster with Wakefield, became Colonial Secretary, and in August of 1834 a Bill "to erect South Australia into a British province" was actually passed. But this was only the beginning of the affair, and delay followed delay with depressing regularity. "At the Colonial Office," wrote Wakefield to Leigh Hunt, "Right and Wrong have nothing to do with it. The only rule for getting on *there* is Importunity, which includes a good deal of impudence. Mr. Rice must be pressed. Not this or that man, but the abstract Colonial Minister of England necessarily attends from time to time only to that affair which presses most." Lord Aberdeen followed Spring-Rice, and the favouring breeze died away. And early in 1835 Wakefield was prostrated by the death of his seventeen-year-old daughter, the one human being he really loved, and from now on his temper was even more uncertain. In April there was yet another change at the Colonial Office, and the new Secretary, Lord Glenelg, advanced so far as to approve the list of Land and Emigration Commissioners. Next month, however, the Commissioners fixed the price of South Australian land at twelve shillings an acre. Wakefield was horrified, for twelve shillings was not a "sufficient" price. Without his sufficient price, what matter if the Government had adopted his principle of forming an emigration fund from the proceeds of the land sales? "If they start with 12s.," he wrote, "the Colony will be a second Swan River." Come what may, the price must be high enough to prevent the labourer from buying his own land at once, and low enough to enable him to buy it after two or three years. Prophets are seldom accommodating, and, however many of his friends might accept the Commissioners' ruling, the sufficient price was still Wakefield's principle.

Before long he was estranged, not only from the Commissioners but from most of his former colleagues, and had washed his hands of the South Australian venture. And at the outset the colony seemed likely to justify his worst forebodings. In 1840, after four years, South Australia was virtually bankrupt. But in May, 1841, a young army captain of twenty-eight with a confident and imperious bearing and piercing blue eyes disembarked at Adelaide and informed the Governor that he had been sent to supersede him. Once more the crisis had produced the man; another of the great public servants of the new Empire was commencing his career. George Grey forced the overgrown population of Adelaide on to the empty land awaiting it, and within two years South Australia was on the road to prosperity. In the same year, 1842, the Commissioners were withdrawn, and the new territory became an ordinary Crown colony. Colonisation, it almost seemed, was no longer altogether an unknown art. Wakefield had not persuaded the Commissioners to adopt his sufficient price; but he had done more; he had taught his fellow-countrymen to introduce system into the Empire. And this he had achieved through a group of Radicals and in the zenith of Benthamite *laissez faire*. System in the Individualist eighteen thirties was indeed a portent, but Wakefield's Radicals were Radical imperialists, and the Empire, it seemed, had somehow inspired them with a political philosophy half a century ahead of their times.

§4

Its rich lands, it soon proved, were by no means the only wealth of Australia. In the 'thirties geologists had found signs of gold, but the Governor of New South Wales waved the discovery away— "put it away, Mr. Clarke, or we shall all have our throats cut." All through the 'forties strange finds were reported from time to time; a Port Philip shepherd would come upon gold at the roots of an overturned tree, or a labourer in Gippsland strike his spade upon a nugget. But not till 1851 did the world hear of the rich prospects, first in New South Wales, then, a bare six weeks after it had become a separate province, in Victoria, and later in Queensland and Western Australia. The British Government made no attempt to claim a monopoly either for itself or for British citizens; for the Empire was never exclusive, this was not the age of monopolies, and a monopoly could only have been enforced by bloodshed. And so a horde of miscellaneous adventurers from every country in the world descended upon the goldfields. Between 1850 and 1855 the population of Victoria rose from seventy thousand to three hundred and thirty-three thousand. In the raw townships of Bathurst, Bendigo and Ballarat European revolutionaries, Chinese coolies, Norwegian peasants and the sons of English noblemen jostled each other in the most variegated assemblage of humanity on earth. The most frightful disorders seemed possible. But the worst was a small-scale revolt of Ballarat miners, led by an Irishman and a German, against the licence fee of thirty shillings a month. Was this order and moderation due to the hereditary instincts of the British majority? Lord Robert Cecil, afterwards Lord Salisbury, Queen Victoria's prime minister, suspected something of the sort. He was twenty-two, a long sea voyage had been prescribed for his health, and he landed at Victoria in March, 1852, in "a white top hat and a black suit." Melbourne, he noted in his diary, was "thronged with ephemeral plutocrats who were hurrying to exchange their gold nuggets for velvet gowns for their wives and unlimited whisky for themselves." And in Melbourne there were drunken revels and "crimes of audacious violence." But the diggings proved strangely different. Here he was struck at once by the contrast with the American gold-rush.

> The rush of population was nearly if not quite as great; the temptations to crime were as powerful; the country in which the gold lay was as wild and desolate; but the government was of the Queen, not of the mob; from above, not from below, holding from a supposed right (whether real or not, no matter) and not from "the people, the source of all legitimate power," and therefore instead of murders, rapes and robberies daily, Lynch law and a Committee of Vigilance, there was less crime than in a large English town, and more order and civility than I have myself witnessed in my own native village of Hatfield.

Within sixty-five years of the discovery of the first goldfields Australia would produce nearly six hundred million pounds' worth of gold, and a great wealth of silver and copper, tin, lead and zinc.

This was the country which the Dutch had not thought it worth while to explore, and which the British had stumbled on because a Prime Minister had wished to find a dumping-ground for convicts.

§5

But in Australia as elsewhere British expansion would not be justified until free institutions had taken root. Free institutions, however, were not easily to be combined with transportation, not only because transportation must mean either a very unreliable, or a very restricted, electorate, but because it represented, in an aggravated form, the assumption that a colony is a mere convenience. It was natural accordingly that freedom should only develop as the convict system waned. But convicts were regularly dispatched to New South Wales for fifty years after its foundation; crime there was rampant, and in the middle 'thirties the number of death sentences approached the record of the French Revolutionary Terror. In 1837 a Parliamentary Committee published evidence, "a thousand folio pages reeking with crime and cruelty," on which Charles Reade drew lavishly for *It is Never Too Late to Mend*, and many less conscientious novelists have quarried for sensational material. And in 1840 an Order in Council put an end to the system. The date surely is significant, for in 1840 Durham's report was opening men's eyes to an imperial future, in the light of which transportation could but seem the hateful survival of an outworn past. For some years afterwards "conditionally pardoned" men were sent out to New South Wales, but when in 1849 Earl Grey dispatched two shiploads of convicts on ticket of leave the indignant citizens of Melbourne and Sydney threatened violence if the vessels were unloaded. Western Australia, which was in urgent need of labour, was still accepting convicts in 1868, but with that year transportation finally disappeared from the British Empire, and with it the last ambiguous relics of the purpose for which the British had gone to Australia.

A Governor with a nominated council had sufficed for New South Wales, the sparsely populated convict colony, in the Act of 1823. In 1842, two years after the Order in Council had ended transportation, when Durham's Report was three years old and the first Canadian Assemblies were groping their way towards representative government, Peel's ministry took the next step. The council was enlarged to thirty-six, of whom twenty-four were to be elected; it was to control finance, with the exception of the land fund and the official civil list, and could legislate, subject to the governor's veto. These were liberal terms, and though there was no provision for responsible government, effective responsible government is seldom the direct offspring of a written constitution. It was in 1850, one year after New South Wales had finally rid itself of the last relics of transportation, and two years after, thanks to Elgin, the first genuinely responsible ministry had taken office in Canada, that the Australian Colonies Government Act made responsible government possible in Australia. It was done with that simplicity and growing sureness of touch which now begins to characterise the British handling of political, if not of economic, problems. It is almost as if by teaching it a method in harmony with its instincts, and giving it faith in its own imperial future, Durham had swept away the last inhibitions and released the full political genius of the race. The Act set up councils two-thirds elective, on the New South Wales model, in Western Australia, Tasmania, South Australia and in the new Colony of Victoria, here and now created. It then proceeded to empower all the colonies to constitute their own legislatures, to determine their own franchise and even, subject to the assent of the Crown, to alter their own constitutions. Nothing could be simpler. All the colonies framed for themselves constitutions on the British model, with two chambers, and the Governor representing the Crown; and the few years after 1835 saw them all beginning to practise responsible government on the British model, with cabinets dependent on majorities in the lower chamber. This collective example was followed by Queensland as soon as it achieved separate existence in 1859. Save for Western Australia, which hung back, fatally impeded by its convict system, till near the turn of the century, all Australia was practising the difficult art of responsible Parliamentary government before 1860. The transition had been swift, smooth and, above all, natural. Thanks to Durham, Elgin and her own long schooling Britain was again fulfilling her ancient destiny.

CHAPTER THREE

THE MAKING OF NEW ZEALAND

(1836-1853)

§1

IT WAS in the colonisation of New Zealand that Wakefield and the Radical Imperialists first came into collision, not only with the delays and doubts, the customary lack of system and purpose, in the Colonial Office, but with another policy, as clear-cut as their own, whose advocates were resolute and formidable rivals for the ear of Mr. Mothercountry. It was not long after the foundation of Sydney in 1788 that whalers, traders and lone adventurers began to land upon the northern island—to be reinforced in course of time by runaway felons from New South Wales, and all the heterogeneous riff-raff which will always drift into territory lying just beyond the boundaries of civilisation. And for seventy years after Captain Cook formally annexed it in 1769 New Zealand did lie outside the pale of civilised government. It had, it is true, been included in Phillip's Commission as first Governor of New South Wales, but Phillip might almost as well have been instructed to administer the mountains in the moon. More realistically, an Act of 1817 had recognised its true status by placing its inhabitants, with those of other "savage" countries, under the criminal jurisdiction of the nearest settled colony. By 1836 everything conspired to draw Wakefield's attention to New Zealand. He had just washed his hands of the South Australian project, and here, as he put it to a Select Committee on colonial lands in June, 1836, was "the fittest country in the world for colonisation." Here at last perhaps he might persuade his fellow countrymen to found a colony on a system. Left to themselves, he knew only too well how they would set about it. As he told the Select Committee:

Adventurers go from New South Wales and Van Diemen's Land, and make a treaty with a native chief, a tripartite treaty, the poor chief not understanding a word about it. . . . After a time, in these cases, after some persons have settled, the Government at home begins to receive hints that there is a regular settlement of English people formed in such a place; and then the Government at home generally has been actuated by a wish to appoint a governor, and says, "This spot belongs to England; we will send out a Governor." The act of sending out a Governor, according to our Constitution, or law, or practise constitutes the place to which the governor is sent a British province. We are, I think, going to colonise New Zealand, though we be doing so in a most slovenly and scrambling and disgraceful manner.

"According to our Constitution, or law, or practise"—it is a fair description of empirical methods in the age of Bentham. But this time, surely, colonisation need not be so "slovenly and scrambling." All that was necessary was for Mr. Mothercountry to listen for once to those who had a system. And in 1837 a New Zealand Association was formed; Lord Durham and Sir William Molesworth provided good will, expert knowledge and the indispensable respectability; Wakefield, as usual, the energy behind the scenes. But this time the sluggishness of Mr. Mothercountry was not the only obstacle; there were rivals in the field, rivals who also possessed a system.

Like Wakefield, the Secretary of the Church Missionary Society, had given evidence before the Select Committee of 1836. Mr. Dandeson Coates' views could hardly have been more directly opposed to those of the Radical Imperialists.

I wish to add most distinctly a protest, if I might venture to employ such a term, against the colonisation of New Zealand on the part of the government; because, though I do not conceive colonisation to be necessarily productive of disastrous consequences, yet it has so generally led to that result that there is nothing I should deprecate more than the colonisation of New Zealand by this country.

Here indeed was an impasse. For what interested the Church Missionary Society was not the opportunities in New Zealand for British colonisation but the future of the native population. Samuel Marsden, a clergyman from New South Wales, had founded a mission station in New Zealand in 1814, and the missionaries who had been active among the Maoris ever since were not unnaturally critical of the methods of their fellow countrymen, and particularly of the methods by which they obtained their lands. The fact that the missionaries themselves had found it necessary to buy land on much the same terms did nothing to diminish their disapproval. And it was primarily the influence of the Church Missionary Society which ensured the rejection of the New Zealand Association's Bill in 1838, and induced a Select Committee of the Lords to conclude that the likeliest means of "regulating the settlement of British subjects" in New Zealand was to support the efforts of the missionaries. Both Lord Glenelg, the Colonial Secretary, and Sir James Stephen, the power behind his throne, were very favourably disposed towards the Evangelicals, and their views had just been formidably endorsed by a Report of the Aborigines Committee of 1837, which laid it down that contact with Europeans was inevitably harmful to native races. British public opinion was already disposed, on Benthamite grounds, to be sceptical of all existing colonies, and was in any case prejudiced by the all-pervasive *laissez faire* principles of the day against further systematic colonisation of any sort. And now that this reasoned inertia was reinforced by the exhortations of the Evangelicals the prospects of the New Zealand Association and the Radical Imperialists seemed dark indeed. The Press in general was unfriendly. The *Times* attributed to their project every characteristic, real or imaginary, which seemed likely to discredit it. It was a monopoly, and a monopoly "conceived in the most sordid spirit" at that. Wakefield, always an easy target, was dragged for once from his obscurity and playfully pictured as cherishing grandiose personal ambitions of his own—"that his talents are to be unnapkinned as Governor of the proposed colony—that just before setting sail he is to be knighted . . .—that Sir Gibbon shall have a government-house . . ." And the proposals of the Association were dismissed as "a radical Utopia in the Great Pacific," designed, oddly enough, to promote "the doctrines of Jeremy Bentham and Robert Owen"—two gentlemen who, though, as infidels, they might rouse prejudice in Evangelical circles, would have been more than surprised to hear themselves described as patrons of a colonial enterprise.[1]

Nevertheless two powerful arguments, Wakefield perceived, lay ready to hand, arguments to which, despite their evangelical prejudices, Glenelg and Stephen were bound to pay serious attention. In the first place, however much Mr. Dandeson Coates might deprecate the colonisation of New Zealand, and whatever disastrous consequences he might foresee, New Zealand was indisputably being colonised. Only, since the government had hitherto refused to intervene, it was being colonised haphazard, and in the main by scoundrels. The welfare of the native Maoris, for which the missionary societies were so deeply concerned, could only therefore be ensured by placing settlement under the control of some

[1] *Times*, Feb. 10, 1838.

responsible public body, such as the Company. Moreover plausible evidence had just reached England that an occupation of New Zealand was being actively considered by the French Government. And though the prospect of a French New Zealand might not perturb the missionary societies on imperial grounds, for Evangelical reasons if any government was to intervene they must surely prefer that it should be the British government, on which they could always hope to press their own views as to the treatment of the Maoris. Such were Wakefield's most telling arguments, and it is significant that the substance of his case should have been, not that the national and imperial interest must prevail, but that even the welfare of the Maoris demanded British intervention. It was a nicely balanced problem, only too well calculated to plunge Mr. Mothercountry into a prolonged agony of indecision.

In the summer of 1839, after renewed deadlock with Lord Normanby, the new Colonial Secretary, the Company decided that there was only one way in which to force the Government to act, and without more ado it dispatched a party of settlers on the *Tory*. The ship put in at Plymouth and there were reports that the Colonial Office was about to forbid it to sail. Wakefield resolved that, like Drake when he too was bent on committing a timid government to imperial enterprise, the ship must sail before its orders could be countermanded. He hired a postchaise and drove all night for Plymouth; the *Tory* weighed anchor, and the future of New Zealand within the British Empire was ensured. For even the Colonial Office of 1839 could now delay no longer; "circumstances entirely beyond control," said Lord Normanby solemnly, "have at length compelled us to alter our course." That summer New Zealand was annexed, and the first Lieutenant-Governor was appointed.

§2

Land-ownership had always been one of the chief concerns of the Evangelicals, and the new Lieutenant-Governor of New Zealand found land-ownership already in a pretty tangle. The Maoris possessed a land-system of their own, based upon the collective ownership of the soil by the tribe, but it had been largely effaced by inter-tribal war and conquest, and there were innumerable Maori claimants to the ownership of any land offered for sale. To this complex of illegality and misunderstanding the Company's settlers had already begun to add new complications. And for the Company there was the special difficulty that the Wakefield system was based on the assumption that land in a new country belonged to the Crown, and that white settlement could only succeed if the proceeds of land sales went to assist emigration. How then, unless the British tax-payer was prepared to finance colonisation, could substantial pay-ments be made to a native population? Inevitably the Company held the view, endorsed by a Select Committee of the Commons in 1844, that "the uncivilised inhabitants of any country have but a qualified dominion over it." This however was not the view of the Evangeli-cals or the Colonial Office, and with the assistance of the missionaries the new Lieutenant-Governor at once effected with the Maori chiefs of the North Island the celebrated Treaty of Waitangi, of February 6, 1840. The Treaty, condemned by the Select Committee of 1844 as "injudicious," was certainly not a final solution of a problem of which perhaps no final solution was possible. Under it the Maori chiefs submitted to the authority of the Crown, were guaranteed the undisputed possession of their lands, and in their turn yielded to the Crown "the exclusive right of pre-emption over such lands as the proprietors thereof may be disposed to alienate." The Company thought this a good deal too generous, maintaining that British sovereignty dated from Captain Cook's annexation in 1769 and that no treaty was necessary. The standards of the Colonial Office however were stricter; it had no doubt that since 1769 British sovereignty had been repudiated, and the Treaty was confirmed. New Zealand moreover became a separate colony, with Governor and two nominated councils.

But the settlement was more satisfactory on paper than in practise. To treat the Maoris—rather fewer than a hundred thousand in the North Island and about five thousand in the South Island—as owners in perpetuity of the whole of New Zealand was not much more practical than it would have been to assume that the ownership of all North America was vested for ever in the Red Indian tribes. The Company needed land for incoming settlers, it was European immigration which was creating the new land values and the Company's agents were not disposed to be too scrupulous about their methods. Ugly incidents, in which both sides were usually at fault, began to recur. The third Governor took the line of least resistance and repudiated the Treaty altogether, and war with the Maoris was breaking out, when George Grey, whose firm hand had just rescued South Australia from its early troubles, was sent to perform the same ungrateful task for New Zealand. Once again the man was everything, or almost everything, the moment needed. Together with the sympathy and tact which can conciliate alien peoples, and the imagination and courage for great plans, Grey most notably possessed that rarer quality, the instinct for rule. He was in fact above all else, in the fullest sense of a hackneyed phrase, a born ruler, with the imperious will, the strong passions, the egoism and the ruthlessness of a mediæval autocrat. Shaping the fluid destiny of a new colony, remote from home authority, and constantly flouting such authority as the government attempted to assert, Grey was in his element. In Committee, it is not surprising to learn, he seldom shone. In later years, and in another setting, his qualities became an anachronism and his life ended in shadow. In later life, despite the charm of his face in animation, many observers noted in it an underlying savagery, and even a consciousness of moral defeat. But by then he had rebelled too often and against too great odds. Now and in New Zealand his self-confidence and the field for its exercise were alike virtually limitless. He broke the Maori rebellion with ruthless energy, and promptly conciliated the rebels. He triumphed over the missionaries, in the matter of the lands, of which they had acquired large tracts for their missions or their families. Taking an instantaneous dislike to a highly academic federal constitution received from the Secretary of State in 1847, he calmly refrained from putting it into force. The entire Maori race, he pointed out, although "in natural sense and ability" the equal of most European colonists, would have been disfranchised by the requirement that every elector should be able to read and write the English tongue. Doubtless also he was not unaware that the constitution would have deprived the Governor of the greater part of his powers.

In the meantime he prohibited the sale of Maori lands to private individuals, raised and armed a native police, built hospitals and financed missionary schools, taught the Maoris agriculture and collected and translated their mythology. Together with Bishop Selwyn he would traverse the difficult country between Wellington and Auckland on foot, fording rivers, scaling mountains and lodging in the houses of Maori hosts. They made a curiously contrasted pair, resembling each other in little save their courage. Selwyn devoted twenty years to the conversion and education of the Maoris, and for a while his advocacy of Maori rights earned him bitter opposition from British settlers. But he was a strenuous, simple man, prepared to play any rôle which came his way in those formative years, and his Visitation Journal reveals him now recording an idyllic Sunday among the Maoris—"when the song of the birds was ended, the sound of native voices chanting around our tents carried on the same tribute of praise and thanksgiving; while audible murmurs on every side brought to our ears the passages of the Bible which others were reading to themselves"—and now swimming a river alone, his clothes tied in a bundle on his head, to warn, and protect, a native clergyman before the incursion of British soldiers. On one occasion a fanatical Maori opponent persuaded his fellow villagers not to receive the bishop in their houses but to offer him the use of a pigstye, and Selwyn cheerfully cleaned out the stye, spread clean fern and lay down for the night. With some assistance from Grey he founded the Anglican Church in New Zealand, breathing into it a new and democratic spirit which was to have its influence in Australia and Canada, and eventually on the home Church itself.

Grey's enemies denounced him as the most autocratic Governor in the British Empire, and it was probably no coincidence that 1853, the year of the first constitution, should also have been the year in which he left New Zealand, characteristically enough without permission from the home government. Almost his last act had been to disobey the Colonial Office's latest instructions as to the land sales. But the moment, if not the manner, of his going was doubtless well-chosen, for his task had been to hew out a colony in the rough, and he had completed it. And such enemies as he left behind him were not among the Maoris, who bitterly lamented the departure of a protector and a friend. But it is impossible to imagine a wise and patient Grey presiding, like Elgin, over the birth of representative government. For by 1853 the influence of Durham and Elgin had travelled to the ends of the Empire, and although the constitution had nothing to say of representative government, representative government was bound to come. The constitution provided provincial councils for local affairs and a national assembly of one nominated, and one elected, chamber; the Maoris were to have the franchise, but executive power was to remain with the Governor and his permanent officials. The first assembly, however, knew well enough what had happened in Canada and at once demanded an executive dependent upon its own pleasure. With the British government, too, the Canadian example was bound to be decisive, and it acceded gracefully in 1856. In yet another colony (though New Zealand had yet to shed its provincial councils in 1875) the constitutional problem had been the first to be solved.

§3

Wakefield and the Company meanwhile had organised a good deal of successful colonisation without ceasing to conduct the usual guerilla warfare with the Colonial Office. Warfare with the

Colonial Office indeed was inevitable, almost desirable, for as Wakefield knew only too well, it was the nature of the Colonial Office
at this time only to yield to pressure. And in New Zealand it was
pursuing two policies at the same time. It was attempting to protect the interests of the Maoris, and to promote, or rather perhaps
to appease those who desired to promote, British colonisation. And
although these two objects were not incompatible, the Colonial
Office had certainly not put itself to the trouble of reconciling them.
Nor had Wakefield's theories ever been wholly adopted. There had
been a price for land, but not a sufficient price, emigration but not
systematic emigration, concentration of the settlers but not Wakefield's labour concentration. Under these conditions it is not
surprising that the Company's finances should have been consistently
precarious. In 1850 it surrendered its Charter to the Crown. But the
true and lasting achievement of the New Zealand Company was in
a wider field than New Zealand. It had introduced system into
British colonisation, and had helped to rouse a lethargic public to
interest in imperial issues and optimism as to the imperial future.
"New Zealand altogether, as respects both colonisation and government, is in a miserable mess," wrote Wakefield in a gloomy survey
of the achievements of his school.

> There is no part of the colonial empire of Britain . . . which the
> theorists of 1830 can regard without disappointment and regret.
> The only aspect of the subject that is agreeable to them is the
> present state of opinion both at home and in the colonies. Every-
> where in the British Empire they find ideas about colonisation
> prevailing, and a lively interest in it, which twenty years ago
> were exclusively their own; and when they trace the birth and
> progress of these opinions to their own exertions, they almost
> forget the painful disappointments they have suffered, in the
> hope that the time is now not distant when their conceptions
> may at length be realised.

Yet even in New Zealand the theorists of 1830 had laid surprisingly solid foundations. The very existence of the colony after all was
owed to them. And 1840 had seen the founding of Wellington,
destined to replace Auckland, the first Governor's choice, as capital
in 1865. In 1841 came Nelson, and in the same year New Plymouth,
the work of a subordinate company of Devon gentlemen. Dunedin
was founded by Scottish Presbyterians and the province of Canter-
bury by an Association of Churchmen. The missionary societies,
Wakefield perceived, could hardly oppose a Church colony with

ample provision for religious and educational activities; and with
the strange gift he had developed for picking out and winning over
men with the position and influence which could never be his, he
prompted, persuaded and encouraged till the enterprise was safely
afoot. None of these ventures was everything which Wakefield
could have wished, but all of them were more efficiently organised
than any earlier settlement. For system, even if not always the
Wakefield system complete, had at last been introduced into colonisation. And the source of the system, the perpetual fount of foresight, exhortation and meticulous practical advice had never been a
colonist himself, so that there was a special significance in his own
description of his colleagues and himself—"the theorists of 1830."

But in 1852 the one great omission of his career was repaired; he
emigrated to New Zealand. Here perhaps, in the colony on which
he had spent sixteen years of unremitting labour, and which to him
more than to any man owed its very existence, he might emerge
finally from the long obscurity imposed on him by the streak of
Puritanism in British public life, and wield the public influence
which was his due. Four years earlier in a rare fit of impatience he
had hoped that his *A View of the Art of Colonisation* would break down
the doors of his prison house. "My object has been," he wrote to the
Editor of the *Spectator*,

> (having worked hard for twenty years without ever before
> claiming any right thereby acquired) to now *establish* my claim
> to the real authorship of most of what has been done with respect
> to colonisation during that long period. Many, doubtless, have
> shared my labours, and done much independently of me; but
> more have made profit and reputation out of my slavery, without
> offering me a share. So now I claim my own; and having
> resolved to do it, I have not done it by halves.

It may not have been done by halves, but it was done in vain. There
was no place for him in England save in the twilight, and if there
was no place now, there never would be. In New Zealand perhaps
it would be different. He had sent many to find new careers there,
and it would be strange, it seemed to him, if he could not find a new
career himself. But it was too late. Or perhaps a certain nervous
irritability had grown upon him so far that he must always now
find himself a centre of controversy. In less than six months from
his arrival in New Zealand, it is true, he was elected to the general
assembly, and next summer he was moving a resolution for the
responsible government which he had helped to give to Canada. It

was an intoxicating moment. "I am as happy as any one can be in this world," he wrote to his sister, "having a full realisation of what I have hoped and longed and striven for during so many years." But the moment passed. The acting Governor, searching for a compromise, had formed a government which combined irresponsible officials with responsible ministers, and when the ministers impatiently demanded that the officials should resign, Wakefield, who had become the governor's chief adviser, ruled that he could not dismiss persons appointed by the Crown. This curious reversion to the old rôle of counsellor behind the throne was his undoing. He was bitterly denounced as a traitor to the cause of responsible government, of which he had been an advocate all his life. And soon a score of unmistakable signs—his loss of influence in the assembly, the attacks in the Press, the necessity of resigning his post as unofficial adviser—must have convinced him that there was to be no career for him, even in New Zealand. Before the first responsible ministry was formed in 1856 his health had given way. For eight years he lived the life of an invalid recluse, spending whole days sitting silent and alone. When he died most of the inhabitants of Wellington had forgotten his very existence.

CHAPTER FOUR

BEYOND THE CAPE

(1815-1859)

§1

EVEN in New Zealand the British had as yet only partially solved the ancient riddle, how to do justice to an aboriginal people without doing injustice to their own colonists, for although in the South Island by the end of Grey's governorship all was well, in the North there was trouble still to come. The same riddle in an even more complex form confronted them in South Africa, and not one riddle only, but two, most intricately interlocked. For in South Africa they must come to some accommodation not only with the Hottentot and the Bantu but with the Dutch. Here the problem of immigrant and native had taken shape before the British came, the Dutch had acquired their own methods of handling it, and the conflict between their methods and those which found favour with the British Government would become a main source of friction between the two European peoples. It would not have been easy, but it would have been comparatively easy, to manage the Kaffirs if there had been no Dutch, or to live on friendly terms with the Dutch if there had been no Kaffirs, but to do both seemed sometimes to pass the wit of man. And here the Evangelical influence made one of its most conspicuous, well-intentioned and least successful incursions into politics. For whereas in Canada the Imperialist Radicals had had the field virtually to themselves, and over New Zealand Radicals and missionaries had fought a battle royal, in South Africa it was the missionaries whose influence at first was virtually undisputed.

The British had taken the Cape of Good Hope from the Dutch in 1795, during the Napoleonic wars, handed it back at the Peace of Amiens, and promptly recaptured it in 1806. At the Congress of Vienna it was one of the Dutch possessions which they decided to retain—in return for a handsome indemnity. No one then supposed that in the Cape we were acquiring a colony. For the British statesmen of that day the British Empire meant commerce and the Navy, not colonies, and the men of 1815 would have been profoundly shocked at the notion of acquiring a European settlement in South Africa. The Cape, however, they had every reason to suppose, was not a colony, but a naval station on the road to India. As to its hinterland they knew next to nothing, and cared, if possible, less. But Lord Liverpool's cabinet survived for twelve years after signing the treaty, long enough to realise that in the Cape it had acquired something a good deal more important than a naval station, and very much more troublesome. Even in 1795 there was three hundred years of history behind the stormy Cape which Bartholomew Diaz, or his royal master, had named of Good Hope in 1488. The Portuguese had been there, and Dutch and English interlopers. But not till 1652 had the Dutch founded a European settlement, and when the British decided in 1814 that after its second capture it should not be surrendered there were some twenty-six thousand scattered Europeans in it, and perhaps two million natives. And the native problem was as old as the settlement; indeed, there had been a Hottentot war in 1674. The Dutch had early formed their own views as to the best methods of dealing with the natives, and living in patriarchal isolation from the rest of the world they had seen no reason to change them. Of the Evangelical and humanitarian influences which were steadily acquiring strength in Britain they knew nothing. But the first emissaries of the London Missionary Society had reached the Cape by 1799, and, travelling two by two, had penetrated far into the interior. Several other Societies, including Wilberforce's Church Missionary Society, were not much later in the field. And though the view of the missionaries varied slightly from Society to Society, in general all held that the black races should be treated as brothers. They denounced many undoubted abuses in the treatment of black by white, but they were apt to denounce too much; and to the difficulties and dangers of treating the native population as the equals of the European minority they were often curiously blind. By 1816 the arrest of a Dutchman on a charge of ill-treating a native had led to a miniature local rebellion, and in 1820 serious British colonisation began with the sending by the home government of five thousand emigrants to the new colony of Albany on the eastern frontier. Already the two interlocking problems were fairly posed.

Evangelical influence steadily increased, and in 1835, when Charles Grant, Lord Glenelg, son of the Charles Grant of Wilberforce's Clapham Sect, became Colonial Secretary, the central authority itself passed under Evangelical control. The missionaries had little good to report either of the Dutch or of their own fellow-countrymen, and Dr. John Philip of the London Missionary Society spoke for most of them in his *Researches in South Africa*, published in 1828. Dr. Philip's researches had been far from scientific, and his statements were frequently inaccurate or exaggerated—he was successfully sued for libel in Capetown—but the British authorities found his general thesis irresistible. With the general approval of the Commons the Colonial Secretary instructed the Governor, who was still omnipotent at the Cape, to see that henceforth blacks and whites were equal before the law. This same year, 1828, has been called the *annus mirabilis* of Cape history, and it certainly saw many changes, most of them calculated to antagonise the Dutch. The Dutch had been shocked to hear Hottentots declared their equals; they were irritated when English was adopted as the language of the courts. The abolition of slavery in 1833 was even more provoking, for the compensation allotted them was inadequate and it was only payable, after complicated formalities, in London, where a Dutch farmer had few facilities for collecting it. By now they were convinced that the scales would always be officially weighted against them, in favour of both the natives and their British fellow colonists. They had yet to learn how the British government, under Evangelical guidance, would handle a native rising. They did not have long to wait. In 1834 the Kaffir tribes burst across the eastern frontier, killing and laying waste as far west as Algoa Bay.

§2

At first it was for the men on the spot, as usual, to act as they saw fit, unhampered by instructions from home. The Governor's Chief of Staff, Sir Harry Smith, "a dapper, little man, electric in his every movement," was a veteran of the Peninsular war and of Waterloo. On hearing of the Kaffir outbreak he spent two days embarking troops and stores, and then rode six hundred miles on horseback, from Cape Town to Rondebosch, in six days, gathered what fighting men he could and cleared Albany of the invaders by the beginning of 1835. In the course of these operations he rescued a number of missionaries and their families from the heart of Kaffir land, "the best thing," he said, "I ever did during the war, but one which these holy gentlemen and their Societies never acknowledged as they ought, though always ready to *censure*." The Governor, Sir Benjamin d'Urban, and his Chief of Staff then struck east across the frontier and annexed a new belt of territory, which they named Queen Adelaide. The native chiefs agreed to accept the protection of the British Crown, and Harry Smith was left to act as Governor of the new province. "I told them," he says, "they should soon see the difference in me between a friend and an enemy; that as I had waged vigorous war on them, so would I teach them by every kindness to become men and shake off their barbarism." His account[1] of how he set out to fulfil this ambitious promise is curiously illuminating. For this Waterloo veteran had had no training in colonial administration, and no previous occasion to reflect upon how, if suddenly called upon, he would improvise a system of government among a hundred thousand warlike barbarians. And yet, like many another British officer or official in a similar exacting situation, he succeeded immediately and to admiration. And like many another he seems to have evolved by the light of nature, and on the spur of the moment, the rudiments at least of most of the principles which statesmen and students have since accepted as the basis of colonial administration.

Under the circumstances his own authority, it is true, was necessarily absolute; "I never would admit of any arrangement bordering on a compromise." This last was a principle which would hardly commend itself to the average politician, who, however, was unlikely to be called upon, as Smith had been, to rule a newly conquered tract of barbarous territory with few resources save his own personality. "I was ever inflexible," he said, "and I ever strove most energetically to establish that faith in my word and uncompromising justice which aided me beyond anything to effect what I ultimately did." He realised at once that change must be gradual, and that he must work through the Kaffir chiefs. "Having taught the people to look up to me rather than to their own chiefs, I had next to re-establish the power of the chiefs as derived from myself." He first exposed, and then conciliated, the crestfallen witch-doctors, and established a native police force which was soon held in such wide respect that the neighbours of a delinquent would rally to support it. He reduced oppressive chieftains to obedience and friendship, and began to teach agriculture, the practise of burial and the use of money. Independent chieftains across the frontier were soon petitioning to be allowed to become subjects of the British government, or rather perhaps of Sir Harry Smith. The missionaries had returned, "excellent good men," Smith now called them, and he had begun to confer instantly with them as to the likeliest means of converting the Kaffirs. And then news from home abruptly brought down his house of cards. Glenelg, "an excellent, worthy and able man" (says Smith indulgently),

> but led by a vile party, under the cloak of sanctity and philanthropy, directed the Province of Queen Adelaide to be restored

[1] Autobiography of General Sir Harry Smith, chap. 38.

to barbarism, the allegiance the Kaffirs had sworn to be shaken off, and the full plenitude of their barbarity re-established.

Misled by his natural indignation the worthy soldier seems to have attributed to Glenelg something of his own decisiveness. But that pious statesman was far from incapable "of any arrangement bordering on a compromise," and he certainly had not got so far as ordering the abandonment of the province. But Dr. Philip and the missionaries, though in general they had supported the war, were clamouring at home against d'Urban's policy, and the Commons' Committee on Aborigines was in session to support them. Thus prompted, Glenelg had written excusing the Kaffirs' onslaught as a natural consequence of the wrongs they had suffered in the past, and bidding the Governor, unless he knew of good reasons for acting otherwise, to "prepare the public mind" for the evacuation of the new province. This characteristic missive hardly amounted to instructions to do anything in particular, but d'Urban waited the best part of a year before despatching his apologia, and then in a moment of exasperation, after receiving more communications in which Glenelg appeared to favour withdrawal, suddenly ordered instant evacuation. Smith, however, had no doubts as to who was responsible.

> All rule and just and good government was banished under the influence of the philanthropic party, who, by perversion of facts evidently desire to lead others (this Colony certainly) to the devil for God's sake.

His indignation was natural enough. The ordered community he had been busily creating out of nothing had been swept away, the colonists of Albany had been disappointed of the compensation they were expecting in the new province for the damage done by the Kaffir irruption into the old, and while the Kaffirs of Queen Adelaide province were flocking to entreat Smith never to abandon them he was being held up to execration at home as a monster stained with innocent blood. There had of course been other arguments for withdrawal—the more distant frontier might be harder to defend— but Smith was undoubtedly right; the true source of the policy was philanthropy, the philanthropy of men with strong religious principles and imperfect local information. For though the Aborigines Committee had listened to a number of reasonably expert witnesses, the weakness of the Evangelical case at this time was a recurrent tendency to assume that the black was always right and the white always wrong, and that the sufferings of the natives were the only sufferings to be seriously taken into account. And yet if this was a fault, it was a reaction against a much grosser fault, repeated down the centuries; if it was a fault, it was a fault, surely, on the right side, and one which can all too rarely be laid to the account of an imperial power. And in the clash of opinion between Sir Harry Smith and Lord Glenelg, a clash which in various guises and in other times would so often be repeated, there is something symbolical of one of the fundamental sources of vitality of the British Empire, which has survived because it has produced not only so many men with a natural genius for ruling backward races, but also so many men who did not wish to see backward races being ruled.

§3

The withdrawal from the new province was followed by the Great Trek, which in the course of a few years carried some ten thousand Dutch Boers across the Orange and the Vaal Rivers and into Natal, and at length gave South Africa its familiar political shape, with the two British colonies on the coast and the two Boer republics inland, and beyond them again a ring of native territories, of the Basuto, the Bechuana, the Zulu, the Matabele and the Griqua. The Great Trek was by no means solely due to the distaste of the Boers for British administration. In a sense indeed it was but the sudden concentration of a process which had gone on intermittently time out of mind—the steady drift of a pastoral people across the frontiers in search of new lands. Yet the distaste was certainly there, for the official evacuation of the new province was but the latest reminder of that "ungodly equality" between white and black which so profoundly shocked the Boer, and which the home Government appeared to have made its goal. There were financial grievances, too, and war losses for which there had been no compensation, and complaints of the ubiquity of armed Kaffirs, and of courts which heard the pleas of Hottentots against Boer farmers and their families, and heard them in English. There was the rankling sense that the Missionary Societies were blackening the name of the Boer in Britain, and that he had no means of putting the case for the defence. And there was the hereditary distaste of a wandering pastoral people for government interference of any kind. And so the ungainly tilted waggon creaked into the unknown, carrying wife and children, the family Bible and the household gear, and beside it the patient herds padded on day by day. Over the new regions which they entered ranged wild fighting tribes; some trekkers were massacred, some would flee on to safety, some fought and settled on the lands they won. In the far north of the Transvaal they chased the Matabele over the Limpopo, and on the Blood River in Natal they slew three thousand of Dingaan's Zulu impis. Before long, Pietermaritzburg in Natal, Winburg beyond the Orange and Potchefstroom over the Vaal were the germs of three independent Dutch republics. But as the confused reports filtered down to Cape Town of fighting between Boers and natives all over the hinterland the British took alarm. Their desire to end the Trek and their distaste for the prospect of a Boer republic in Natal coincided with Glenelg's fears that the Boers might be maltreating the natives, and he consented grudgingly to intervene, on the understanding that there was to be no "colonisation." The British government intervened, withdrew and inevitably, as the Boers were drawn into conflict with the natives on their frontier, intervened again. Even then Lord Stanley at the Colonial Office sent orders that Natal must be abandoned with all speed—how could the British government be expected to mother its restless subjects all round the world; was it not enough that they had just compelled it, much against its will, to annex New Zealand? But shots had been exchanged in Natal, the Governor of the Cape refused to budge, the Boer Republic began to break up, and Stanley reluctantly agreed that the British must stand their ground. In 1843 Natal was declared a British Colony.

But could the British stop short at Natal? As report after report came in of confused fighting between trekkers and natives, an ugly picture began to take shape of the inextricable tangle of violence and resentment, claims and counterclaims in the wild hinterland. Were the Boers subject to Griqua law? Why should the Griquas, who had also trekked from the Colony, be treated as independent, if the Boers were not? If the Cape government declined to annex territory beyond the Vaal, by what right did it claim the Boers resident there as British subjects without title to their land? These and a score of cognate questions, unanswered or unanswerable, clamoured for the attention of a reluctant Government, which still, with pathetic obstinacy, continued to regard the Cape as a naval station whose price was an unexpected amount of more or less irrelevant trouble in the interior. By 1847 Pretorius and most of the Natal Boers were trekking out of Natal, north across the Drakensberg into the lands between the Orange and the Vaal. With a Resident at Bloemfontein, the British government had already planted one foot across the Orange, but now, to the men on the spot at least, it began to appear that the other foot would have to follow. And when in December, 1847, Sir Harry Smith, bursting as ever with energy and resolution, reappeared at the Cape as Governor—the Colony was "delirious with joy" at his arrival—it became morally certain that there would be no more compromise. And sure enough, having failed to arrest the trek from Natal, Smith annexed the lands between Orange and Vaal as the Orange River Sovereignty, and defeated the indomitable Pretorius, who fled on northward beyond the Vaal.

But Smith's activity roused no echo of enthusiasm in Downing Street. Earl Grey, at the Colonial Office, had only reconciled himself to the retention of Natal by the reflection that its native population might otherwise have been exterminated, and in general he would scarcely have dissented from the fashionable view that colonies are one of those evils which a resolute and enlightened government should be able to avoid. And so in 1852 the Sand River Convention accorded the emigrants beyond the Vaal complete independence, on condition that they kept no slaves, and Smith sailed for home broken-hearted, knowing that the abandonment of the Orange River Sovereignty was now inevitable. For it was not so much its inhabitants as the British Government which desired separation. For the Government was growing restive. It was tired of the perpetual wars and cattle-lifting, of the land-grabbers, the land speculators and even of the missionaries; for the Evangelical movement had spent its first impetus, and the critics were beginning to whisper that the missionary could now hardly be distinguished from a storekeeper. A Burmese war had just ended and the Crimean war was about to begin; the Government could still see little merit in colonies; it was time to cut its losses in a colony which it had never wanted. And so in 1854 the Convention of Bloemfontein created the Orange Free State, on the same terms as the Transvaal had just obtained. South Africa was beginning to crystallise into recognisable political units. It was Balkanisation, perhaps, but then all the most powerful forces in the country were centrifugal, and at home too many statesmen, despite the Radical Imperialists, could see little on the imperial horizon save that "eventual parting on good terms." The grant of a separate government, with a Lieutenant-Governor of its own, to Natal, and of a Parliamentary constitution to the Cape seemed but to reinforce their views, since they took independence for the pattern of the future, and self-government as but a stage on the road to it. Few outside Wakefield's circle would yet have been prepared to prophesy that self-government within the Empire was in fact the destined goal, and that the independence of the two Boer republics would prove a temporary deviation from which they would before long have to retrace their steps. Despite his impetuosity, Sir Harry Smith had seen further and truer than Earl Grey and the Colonial Office.

§4

Yet at home the tide of opinion was beginning to turn. The younger generation was less content with Bentham and Manchester than were the elderly ministers; and when Sir George Grey returned from his rebellious Governorship of New Zealand to the chill of official disapproval in 1854 he was accorded an honorary degree at Oxford amidst the enthusiastic applause of the undergraduates in the Sheldonian Theatre. And though the Colonial Office so frequently distrusted the judgment of its strongest administrators, it could not so easily dispense with their services, and before the end of 1854 Grey had become Governor of the Cape. Perhaps this too was evidence of the turning of the tide; perhaps the Ministry which had already disavowed both d'Urban and Smith sent out an even more contumacious and a more visionary rebel because, though not yet prepared to follow, it could not resist the temptation to discover where such men would lead. As for Grey, he treated the minister to insubordination from the first, cheerfully exceeding or disregarding his instructions, whenever to exceed or disregard them seemed convenient, in his attempt to reorganise and civilise British Kaffraria, the protected native belt between Natal and the Cape. Nor did he stop at minor irregularities. As soon as news of the Indian Mutiny reached the Cape he began at once, without authority from the War Office, to dispatch imperial troops from Africa to India. He even levied new forces, equally without authority, thus technically laying himself open to a charge of high treason. Whether or not Grey, as he always afterwards claimed, had saved India, the home government was bound to let these irregularities pass. But it could hardly overlook his next display of the same strange combination of courage, insight and recklessness. The government itself had entertained the idea of setting up some unitary authority over the Cape, British Kaffraria and Natal. But Grey had learned in New Zealand to believe in federation, and in South Africa he soon decided that federation must include the Boer republics also; thus, and only thus, South Africa might become "a real power which may hereafter bless and influence large portions of this vast continent." Internal divisions and native troubles in the new Boer states gave some faint hope that they might be willing to listen to proposals of this kind, but there and throughout South Africa there was the ubiquitous obstacle of a divergent native policy. In the Cape the rule had been civil and political equality for all, Natal had gravitated towards racial differentiation, with European magistrates administering native law, while as for the Boers, they traditionally held that the natives were destined by Providence as hewers of wood and drawers of water. The elements of the projected federation were thus certainly far from harmonious, but when the Free State accepted the idea at least of some form of union or alliance Grey leaped at the opportunity, and opened the Cape Parliament in 1859 with a speech recommending the federation of South Africa. This was too much for the Colonial Office. It had put up with a good deal, but it could hardly put up with a Governor who on such an issue publicly recommended a policy of which he must know that it disapproved, and Grey was at once recalled.

In the eyes of the Colonial Office indeed his project had nothing to commend it. For even if the Colonial Office had wished to extend British authority, which it did not, and even if federation had been practical politics, which was more than doubtful, would not a federation of two Dutch republics with two British Colonies, one of them more than half Dutch, soon have declared itself independent of Great Britain, carrying with it not only the hinterland and its vexatious and perpetual troubles, but the Cape itself and its indispensable naval base? So at least argued Authority at home. And yet —might there perhaps be more of essential wisdom in Grey's blundering intuition than in all the Colonial Office's unanswerable logic? Had Grey seized upon principles still beyond the horizon of Authority, principles none the less of greater vitality than any at present actuating Mr. Mothercountry? Might Grey after all be right, at least in his surmise that the destiny of South Africa was union rather than Balkanisation, that thus self-government would come, and that there was room in the Empire for all races and all creeds? Once again, some suspicion of this sort seemed to be stirring in the youth of Britain. For the vessel which carried Grey home was boarded off Southampton by a reporter with the news that Derby was out and Palmerston in, and that Palmerston's government would reinstate him—on condition that no more was heard of federation. And this time it was the undergraduates of Cambridge who cheered lustily as he received another honorary degree—in company with Gladstone.

BOOKS FOR FURTHER READING.

Professor Chester New, *Lord Durham;* J. L. Morison, *The Eighth Earl of Elgin;* Theodore Walrond, *Letters and Journals of Lord Elgin;* Sir John G. Bourinot, *Canada, 1760-1900;* George Bryce, *A Short History of the Canadian People;* Ernest Scott, *A short history of Australia;* J. W. Gregory, *Australasia,* vol. I; Hamilton Hume, *The life of Governor Eyre*; A. J. Harrup, *The amazing career of Edward Gibbon Wakefield;* G. C. Henderson, *Life of Sir George Grey;* Ernest Scott (ed.), *Lord Robert Cecil's Gold Fields diary; New Zealand; Letters from the Bishop together with extracts from his Visitation Journal* (S.P.G., 1847); H. W. Tucker, *Memoir of the Life . . . of George Augustus Selwyn;* Sir Harry Smith, *Autobiography;* E. A. Walker, *History of South Africa;* H. A. Bryden, *A History of South Africa.*

Book VIII

EMPIRE AS CIVILISATION

CHAPTER ONE

THE TRANSFORMATION OF INDIA

(1785-1857)

§1

BEFORE the end of the eighteen fifties, though they did not yet know it, the British had saved that part of their Empire to which fifty years earlier they had supposed themselves to be saying farewell. How self-government and independent nationality could co-exist with Empire—for the British settlements this had been the riddle of the Sphinx; they had begun to solve it, and the gates of the future were open. But meanwhile the vast remainder of the Empire must solve its own Sphinx-riddle or decay—the riddle of the impact of civilisation on subject and backward races, the riddle glimpsed in New Zealand and South Africa but already posed in manifold degrees and guises among the primitive peoples of the Pacific, the Far East and the dark interior of Africa, and now to be encountered in all its majestic magnitude in the rich, arrested semi-civilisation of India. For Burke and Wilberforce, preaching the doctrine of trusteeship and moral responsibility, had not so much solved the problem as found the key to it. It could only be adequately solved upon the distracting plane of action, and how elusive adequate solution could be Wilberforce's disciples had already proved in New Zealand and South Africa. Yet until it too had been adequately solved the Empire as a whole could have no valid claim upon the future. And nowhere, and in India least of all, could a solution come speedily. For most of the Empire was in a state of flux, and India pre-eminently was now one vast and rapid transformation scene, in which no established system, good or bad, was yet to be looked for.

§2

The transformation of India between the resignation of Warren Hastings in 1785 and the outbreak of the Mutiny in 1857 was indeed spectacular. A glance at the map shows British India at the earlier date as a solid block of territory running inland from the delta of the Ganges, below this the long narrow coastal strip of the Northern Circars, Bombay and Madras as ports with no hinterland to speak of, and beyond this no more than a handful of isolated trading stations. But in 1857 it is no longer a question of a few minor lodgments on the huge sub-continent. Save for the central area, where the great tract of Rajputana, and south of it the lesser enclaves of the Nizam's dominions, Mysore and Travancore, stand out as startling exceptions, British India has become virtually coterminous with India itself. In the official correspondence of the period appears an almost equally striking transformation. In the days when Burke was assailing Warren Hastings the British public had grown accustomed to hearing charges of perfidy and corruption hurled against the Governor-General, the Company and its officials: in the nineteenth century the rôles are reversed, and it is the Governors-General whom we find denouncing the treachery, the misrule or the depredations of the native princes. And Parliament and public applaud Lord Wellesley for measures ten times as high-handed as those for which a dozen years earlier Warren Hastings had been impeached. Hitherto, moreover, one of the most familiar Parliamentary charges against the Company had been its propensity for embarking upon unnecessary wars; and the Act of 1784 brought India under Parliamentary control with the avowed intention of restraining the warlike ardour ascribed to the Company's servants, and preventing further extensions of British authority. As the Act of 1793 put it:

> Forasmuch as to pursue schemes of conquest and extension of dominion in India are measures repugnant to the wish, the honour, and the policy of this nation. . . .

And yet scarcely had the Crown superseded the Company as the supreme authority in Indian affairs than a period of constant warfare and unprecedented expansion set in. And now it is the pacific Directors of the Company who look on in impotent horror at the warlike proceedings of Governors-General whose office is a political appointment and whom they are quite unable to control, and Lord Wellesley (who could refer irreverently to the Directors as "a pack of narrow-minded old women") will airily report some expensive campaign or far-reaching annexation many months after it has been successfully concluded.

Was Burke then already forgotten, and all that he had taught of the moral responsibility of Britain for India? Did the influence of Wilberforce—which during these very years could end the Slave Trade and abolish slavery throughout the Empire—stop short at the Indian frontier? No, the vast changes in India during the first half of the nineteenth century did not mean that the doctrines of Burke and Wilberforce had been deliberately abjured. For a great historical process was moving to its inevitable conclusion. India being what it now was, no human ingenuity could have arrested the spread of British authority during these years. The dream of con-servatively minded British citizens, that mere non-intervention would somehow consolidate the fluid anarchy of India into a stable peace, was mere wishful thinking by men who knew nothing of Indian conditions. For the firm acquisition of Bengal had made British rule a permanent focus of stable government in a whirlpool of anarchy far more frightful than that which laid England waste under Stephen and Matilda or the Wars of the Roses. No other formidable power in India was interested in the preservation of order; everywhere the strong preyed upon the weak and lived on violence and injustice. Inevitably the weak gravitated towards the only power which could protect them, and sooner or later the strong had to be coerced. Lord Morley observed that eighteenth century India bore a close resemblance to fifth-century Europe. But in Europe after the fall of Rome many centuries passed before the common man lived in security again, whereas in India the British restored ordered government within fifty years. It was a gigantic task to have accomplished, piecemeal and but half intentionally, in so short a space, and on it all other tasks must wait. For this in itself was Britain's first obligation to the peoples of India, since without ordered government and the security of life and property there can be no welfare.

Moreover from 1793 to 1815, years during which the most far-reaching changes were effected, Britain was almost continuously at war with France, France who had so lately been her deadly rival in India, and whose great autocrat twice—when he descended on Egypt in 1798, and when he allied himself with the Russian Tsar in 1807—deliberately planned the conquest of the East. Nor did the maraud-ing Indian princes live remote, like the Hottentots, the Maoris or even the Boers, from the politics of Europe. Tipu, Sultan of Mysore, sent a secret mission to propose an offensive and defensive alliance to the Revolutionary Directory in Paris, and in 1799 received a letter from Bonaparte, whose headquarters were then in Cairo, promising to liberate him from "the iron yoke of the English." French agents were active in the councils, and French officers in the armies, of most of the powerful native rulers, and in a sense the annexations of Wellesley were but an inevitable minor aspect of the world war, and Britain would occupy an Indian State, much as she has lately occupied Iceland or Syria, as a precautionary measure against a deadly enemy in Europe. And these extensions of the British frontier would be tolerated or applauded by a public opinion in Britain which so recently had been sensitively critical of the least forward movement in India, largely because they represented a satisfactory move in the game against France. Two forces in fact combined to draw the British on. As the only stable authority amid the welter of anarchy in India they would have found it difficult enough, even in peace-time, to avoid intervention; but in the midst of a world war anarchy became much more dangerous and intervention much more attractive.

During this era of expansion and experiment no final answer certainly was to be expected to the many insistent problems which pressed upon the new rulers of India, but rather some evidence, as they grappled with the emergencies which beset them thick and fast, that their ultimate objective would still be the welfare of the native races.

§3

It was of good omen that the new era opened with the Governor-Generalship of Earl Cornwallis, who brought to India in 1786 what India needed even more than ability—character. Cornwallis was exceptionally brave, exceptionally independent and exceptionally honest, and he possessed that fine natural courtesy which is among the most valuable qualities of a ruler, and is nowhere more valuable than in the East. His rank and his character alike placed him above mean personal ambitions. "Here," exclaimed Dundas, who in such a matter was the best of all judges, and, since Pitt's Act of 1784, had begun to send East a long succession of able and ambitious Scotsmen, "here there was no broken fortune to be mended! Here there was no avarice to be gratified! Here there was no beggarly mushroom kindred to be provided for!" Not only did Cornwallis's conduct set an example of the strictest integrity to his successors; his reforms laid the foundations of the incorruptible Civil Service of the future.

Madras, whose internal administration was beyond his reach, continued for some years longer "on the good old principles of Leadenhall-street economy—small salaries and immense perquisites," but in Bengal henceforth the tradition was to be reversed, with generous salaries and no perquisites whatever. Cornwallis, it must be added, was responsible for confining all the higher posts in the administration to Europeans. He feared, not without reason, both the pliant Indian functionary and what Sir G. O. Trevelyan called "the splendid sloth and the languid debauchery" of the Europeans who had taken root in India; and his solution was to bring out a constant supply of well-qualified and high-principled administrators direct from Britain. The defect of his system, later to be redressed, was that, though infinitely preferable to the anarchy which it had replaced (but which later generations would readily forget) it must eventually leave the native population with few worthy objects of ambition.

Cornwallis also presided over the Permanent Settlement of the Bengal land dues, which recognised the Zemindars, hereditary rent-collectors on behalf of the government, as actual owners of the soil, and stabilised their rent as a comparatively small permanent revenue. Land settlements however are seldom popular, and never popular for long, and Cornwallis's was no exception. Indeed the problem was one of those to which no satisfactory solution is possible. Even in England, despite the textbooks, the feudal system was never a system, and in India land tenure was not only mediæval but immensely heterogeneous. What was the exact degree of respect to be paid by the British government to the hotly disputed title of some descendant of one of the Mogul Emperor's rent collectors? Inevitably over delicate problems of this nature opinions differed both in Britain and in India. And in many parts of the country, particularly in the west, the Government eventually ignored the Zemindars and made direct assessments upon the cultivators themselves.

Even Cornwallis, who had come out to India as an apostle of peace and caution, could not avoid war. That picturesque ruffian Tipu, Sultan of Mysore, son of the Company's old enemy Hyder Ali, cherished an implacable hatred of the British, and was known to be planning vengeance. Almost any ruler but Cornwallis would have fought a much earlier preventive war. War, when it did come, he fought reluctantly and with noble humanity, hanging British soldiers for looting, and revolutionising the treatment of wounded sepoys. When Tipu was defeated he lost nearly half his territories, most of them being handed over to his northern neighbour, the Nizam. But although, when Cornwallis left India in 1793, it was still believed at home that he had succeeded in inaugurating an era of stationary frontiers, both the policy of peace and caution, and the balancing of one native power against another which it involved, had ceased to be practicable. Britain stood upon the threshold of a period of constant wars and wide annexations, of which the Governor-General who arrived five years later became the embodiment.

§4

Lord Mornington, better known by his later title of Marquis Wellesley, was elder brother of Arthur Wellesley, Duke of Wellington, then serving as a young colonel in India. Wellesley was well-fitted to inaugurate the new policy. Where Cornwallis had been cautious, patient and considerate, Wellesley was hot-tempered and ambitious. The "low birth, vulgar manners and eastern habits" of his predecessor, the evangelical Sir John Shore, Lord Teignmouth, had "contributed," he thought, "to relax every spring of this government . . . and . . . established a systematical degradation of the person, dignity and authority of the Governor-General." In the new era the Governor-General, he was determined, should live ceremoniously aloof; he was not yet a Viceroy but he must maintain a Viceroy's dignity. "The effect of this state of things on my conduct has been to compel me to entrench myself within forms and ceremonies, to introduce much state into the whole appearance of my establishments and household, and to expel all approaches to familiarity." He even contrived to expel any approaches to familiarity on the part of his brother, Arthur.

His was not a mind readily susceptible to ideas, but what he saw, he saw all the more clearly and tenaciously, and from the first he was convinced that it was his mission to give India the British peace, and that there could be no British peace, and indeed no peace of any kind, without the extension of British control. Cornwallis had left the old enemy, Tipu, independent, and what had been the result? With Bonaparte already in Egypt, and boasting that he would soon drive the British from India, both Tipu and the Nizam of Hyderabad, and by no means they only, were intriguing with France, and preparing French-trained armies for a war of revenge. Wellesley summoned the Nizam to disband his troops, dismiss his Frenchmen and pay for protection by a British force which would enable the Company to guarantee the integrity of his territories. The Nizam yielded without a struggle, and here was the first of Wellesley's celebrated "subsidiary treaties," which in their completest form provided that protection should be paid for by cession of territory instead of money, and that a British Resident, and general super-vision of external policy, should be accepted. Their defect was that they were capable of protecting the most imbecile or corrupt rulers not only against invasion from without but against revolution, which in the East was the customary form of change of government, from within. Tipu preferred to fight, which was what Wellesley intended. Within a month he fell, sword in hand, as the British columns stormed his capital of Seringapatam in 1799. The fall of Tipu marked an epoch. The battle of Plassey had established the Company as a power in India, the capture of Seringapatam made it the power paramount; and Arthur Wellesley standing over Tipu's dead body in the torchlight was inaugurating a new epoch as surely as Arthur Wellesley sixteen years later letting loose the Guards on the field of Waterloo. "It was now that a sense of their Indian destiny took hold of men—not, as formerly of an occasional man only, a Warren Hastings or a Thomas Munro—but of the generality who did the rank-and-file work of fighting and administering."[1]

Like all great revolutions in human affairs, the change now being consummated was compact of both good and evil, and the fall of Tipu, after thirty years of intermittent warfare against the British, was typical of both light and shade in much that was to come. For though Tipu was a villain, he was by no means all villain. He was false, treacherous and abominably cruel, and his dominion over Mysore had no title save the sword. Yet he could be a reformer who stamped out intoxicants, as well as an innovator seeking to introduce Western science, and the peasants of Mysore were more prosperous than those of Madras. India had never known any government but despotism and to many of his own subjects in Mysore the very capriciousness of Tipu's rule might well seem preferable to the monotonous efficiency of an alien administration. And yet for India as a whole, tortured and wasted by generations of internecine anarchy, there could be no welfare without peace and order, and no peace and order save from the British. Peace and order once estab-lished, the test of the British might come to be how much of their power they would bring themselves to resign, but the establishment of peace and order was certainly their first obligation, and to accomplish it they must have power.

Power Wellesley steadily acquired. The outlying territories of Tipu's Mysore became British, the remainder was restored to the original Hindu rulers whom Tipu's father had supplanted. The

---

[1] Edward Thompson, *The making of the Indian Princes*, 144. The author is actually speaking of the year 1806.

Carnatic was annexed, and its bankrupt and oppressive rulers pensioned off. Tanjore was voluntarily surrendered by its Rajah to the Madras Presidency on the same terms, and Surat went to Bombay. In Oudh, whose rôle as buffer state was undermined by endemic anarchy, the Nawab was left with a small central nucleus round his capital, bound by a stringent form of Wellesley's subsidiary alliance. And Wellesley had time, before the protests of the now thoroughly apprehensive Directors led to his departure in 1805, to launch the first of the series of wars with the feudal cluster of Mahratta tribes which had long subsisted on raiding their neighbours and quarrelling among themselves. "They have not left a stick standing at the distance of 150 miles from Poonah," reports Colonel Wellesley to his brother in 1803, "they have eaten the forage and grain, they have pulled down the houses, and have used the materials as firewood. . . . Excepting in one village I have not seen a human creature since I quitted the neighbourhood of Meritch." Such were the results of Mahratta conquests, and India had been exposed to them for generations. War with the Mahrattas had become inevitable, now that the advance of the British frontiers had so drastically circumscribed the areas over which they could plunder or levy toll. In spite of Arthur Wellesley's not particularly scientific victories at Assaye and Argaum ("Somebody said, 'Sir! that is the enemy's line.' The General said, 'Is it? Ha, damme, so it is!'")[1] the Directors were so alarmed by a temporary success of the Mahratta forces under Holkar (which being not yet Europeanised were still formidable) that they decided on a peace of compromise. But Mahratta independence and a tranquil India were not permanently compatible; in 1817 their chiefs were secretly assisting the so-called Pindaris, robber hordes formed by native troops disbanded under the subsidiary alliances; war broke out, the Mahrattas were crushed, and, with the chiefs of Rajputana to the north-west placing themselves under British protection, all central India was pacified. Before this, in 1814, Lord Hastings had launched a three years' war with the Gurkhas on the north-eastern frontier of Nepal, who had been plundering the plain of the Ganges. In the course of their customary initial reverses the British learnt much from these courageous and enterprising opponents, including an abiding respect for the chivalry with which they fought and the strictness with which they kept their promises. Nepal eventually ceded some territory, including Simla, and has since remained both friendly and independent. The British have always found the more warlike peoples of India easiest to like and understand. Even before

[1] From the *Life of Mountstuart Elphinstone*. This and several other quotations on recent pages I owe to Messrs. Garrett and Thompson's *Rise and Fulfilment of British Rule in India*.

the fighting was over, Gurkhas were enlisting in the British army, in which Gurkha regiments have since earned a world-wide renown.

§5

In 1826, at the conclusion of a war on the eastern frontier with the Burmese, who had been raiding Bengal for two decades (and had prepared golden fetters for the Governor-General) there came an interlude of peace, during which it became possible for the British, if they pleased, to do something more for India than establish peace and order by the sword. These were the years during which at home the influence of the Evangelicals was rising to its zenith, and that of the Oxford Tractarians gathering strength, and the leaven was beginning to work among the British community in India. A new type of officer and a new type of official was increasingly to be met with—men who lived strictly, read their Bibles, studied Wilberforce or Hannah More or, after 1833, the *Tracts for the Times* and believed that their first obligation to India was to give it the Christian religion and higher moral standards. Many of them were confident that, if they did their duty, idolatry would disappear within a generation. Such men, at home or in India, were horrified at the loose morals of the old-fashioned Indianised European, and refused to tolerate the Company's tradition of religious neutrality, which would close government offices on Hindu or Muslim religious festivals, but keep them open on Sundays. In the 'thirties a British soldier deliberately absented himself from a ceremonial parade in honour of a Hindu deity, and the commander-in-chief resigned rather than have him punished.

As British officials, among whom this new spirit was stirring, began to move more widely about India, and to know it better, they realised that many customs which had astonished and horrified them were not only widely practised, but endorsed or enjoined by Hindu religion. All over northern India there was *thagi* or thuggery—hereditary criminal gangs, united by strict religious vows, whose speciality was strangling followed by robbery—one *thag* confessed proudly to more than five hundred murders in twenty years. Thuggery was ended in the 'thirties by the resolute action of Colonel Sleeman. The human sacrifices of Orissa were suppressed, with infinite patience, by General Campbell, as was the female infanticide common in all central and western India. The ancient Indian rite of widow-burning, inaccurately Anglicised as "suttee," was a more formidable affair. Hindu *pandits*, consulted on the subject, warned the Government that the practice was "recognised and encouraged by the doctrines of the Hindu religion," the British authorities were nervous as to the effects of interference on the sepoys, and it was not until 1829 that suttee was expressly prohibited. Despite an appeal to the Privy Council by five hundred leading Bengalis, the practice disappeared speedily in British India, but in many parts popular sentiment was hostile to suppression, and to this day instances of "suttee" occur from time to time, and always amidst public enthusiasm.

This long, and in general patient and considerate, campaign against a few monstrous excrescences of the Hindu religion was evidence that the religious revival, and its new moral standards, had reached India. The tradition of moral and religious neutrality had been broken down, and it was appropriate that the change should come just about the time when the renewal of the charter in 1833 finally ended the commercial monopoly and turned the Company into a government pure and simple. There was actually a moment when a mass conversion to the Christian faith seemed likely in India, for enlightened Hindus were profoundly stirred by the British onslaught on the cruelties and superstitions of the Hinduism of that day. But this movement was arrested by the Brahmo Samaj, an organisation which provided the noblest Hindu minds with a Hinduism shorn of gross superstition, and therefore with an alternative both to Christianity and to scepticism. In this indirect manner the impact of the British reforms may be said to have been responsible for the sudden flowering of intellectual and spiritual life in Bengal, which would profoundly affect all India during the rest of the century. Despite the Evangelicals and Tractarians, the British failed to Christianise India, but thanks largely to the Evangelicals and Tractarians they were bent on civilising it. They decided to civilise it through the medium of the English language.

The battle between the advocates of an oriental, and an English, education was fought out in the Committee of Public Instruction, and decided by Macaulay's famous Minute of 1825. His idea was to form a class of educated and Westernised Indians, who would "interpret" the British government to the Indian masses. And since Indians were clamouring for Western science the project seemed reasonable enough. But Macaulay had not realised how effectually the caste system would preclude the spread of ideas from one class to another, or that Locke and Burke against an Indian background might cease to be the Locke and Burke he knew. And, as some of the Evangelicals and Tractarians foresaw, to civilise India within these limits might prove to be a process, largely negative, of sterilisa-tion, conducted by men who remained overblind to the spiritual and intellectual riches of the East itself. The Evangelicals and Tractarians may have known too little of eastern lore, and may have been too ready to write off Hinduism and Islam as mere primitive super-stition, yet at least they had something more than the mere mechanics of civilisation to offer to the East, and were qualified in due course to make more sympathetic and discerning contact with the spiritual and intellectual leaders of India. But at home, as the century wore on, Evangelicals and Tractarians would give way to rationalists, and the crude confidence of the Manchester School that nothing which Manchester did not know was knowledge. To give India peace, order and the science of the West would be a process of civilisation indeed, of the only civilisation now familiar to the West, but of civilisation within strict limits.

For India can never be fully understood by those who approach her with material gifts alone. And the defect, the inevitable defect, of British rule in the nineteenth century would be, not that there were no missionaries in India, for there would be many, nor even that the administrators would be predominantly rationalist, for they would not, but that none the less the administration would be predominantly a rationalist administration, thinking too highly of the civilisation of the West and understanding too little of the civilisation of the East. It was inevitable, for during this century the West itself wore blinkers. It was inevitable too perhaps because the progressive assumption of full responsibility by the British itself transformed the nature of their problem. As a mere community of traders they could live side by side with Indians and tolerate, and even seek to understand, customs which, when they became rulers, it seemed unnecessary to understand and impossible to tolerate. The social and racial gulf between British and Indians was wide enough; to add a spiritual gulf made the cleavage almost insuperable. The reforms of the 'thirties were effected for the most part with great kindliness and discretion, and by religiously-minded men, but they helped to convince British officials that they were dealing with a degenerate race, and so to accentuate the gulf between the two peoples. And the final burst of annexation under Lord Dalhousie, between 1848 and 1856, was largely due to the impossibility of suppressing suttee and infanticide without the expansion of the British frontier.

§6

Inevitably that frontier continued to move forward. Not, however—for the British could never think of themselves as a military power—without the customary reverses, and even one disaster on the grand scale. It was now a question of the north-west frontier, on which lay Sind and the Punjab, and beyond them the wilds of Afghanistan. Alarmed by Russian penetration into Afghanistan, Lord Auckland in 1839 occupied the country and installed an Afghan claimant as Amir. After two years, a massacre, many insults and the murder of two British Residents, Auckland decided to evacuate, and a column of sixteen thousand, three-quarters of them non-combatants, left Kabul in December, 1841, under a safe conduct from the Afghan leader. The retreat at once became a prolonged butchery, and next month a solitary survivor reeled into Jalalalabad, the outpost of British India. As for Sind, it was conquered by Sir Charles Napier in 1843. His famous telegram *Peccavi* (I have sinned) may have been more than a pun, for he may have had some doubts—as the chivalrous Outram certainly had—of the justice of the invasion. But if Napier had doubts, they vanished as he proceeded, with the magnificent directness of a brave and simple ruler wielding absolute power, to the pacification of the conquered country. He was immediately successful. When Brahmins protested that widow-burning, which he had forbidden, was a pious religious custom, Napier replied sardonically that in that case it must certainly continue. But his own nation, he added, also had a custom. "When men burn women alive we hang them." Henceforth, accordingly, beside every pyre there would be a row of gibbets; "let us all act according to national customs." There was no more widow-burning in Sind. Napier had no further doubts, for he knew more now of the dark underside of native despotism, and he could see order and elementary justice taking shape before his eyes. Outram, who saw other and more attractive aspects of native rule, had refused his share of the prize money and went home to plead the cause of Sind. Each, within the limits of his vision, was right, but the tides of history were with Napier.

The warlike Sikhs of the Punjab, the last surviving kingdom of India, had been stirred to contempt by the incompetence and disasters of the British in Afghanistan, and in 1845 they crossed the Sutlej, fully expecting to sweep across India as of old. They were defeated by Sir Hugh Gough at Aliwal and Sobraon, and, when they overthrew the regency installed by the British, were defeated again, after a terrific drawn battle at Chilianwala, at Gujerat. The pacification and reorganisation of the Punjab was handed over to the brothers John and Henry Lawrence, and the famous brotherhood of soldiers and administrators which they gathered round them. They ruled for the time being with absolute power, unbound by the regulations of settled, official India. Such circumstances call out the best in a ruler, or the worst, and these were the best administrators available anywhere in the world, men of action and swift decision, devoutly religious, most of them, in a tradition proceeding from Cromwell and the Ironsides by way of the early nineteenth century revival and the public schools—which now in the late 'forties, thanks to Thomas Arnold, were on the threshold of their golden age. "It is not our system," replied John Lawrence, when asked for a few hints as to his methods in the Punjab, "it is our men." The Lawrences' men could understand and love their new subjects, who, like themselves, were both fighting men and devotees, and they were understood and loved by them.

> What days those were! How Henry Lawrence would send us off to great distances, Edwardes to Bunnoo, Nicholson to Peshawar, Abbott to Hazara, Lumsden somewhere else, etc., giving us a tract of country as big as half of England, and giving us no more helpful directions than these, "Settle the country; make the people happy; and take care there are no rows!"

All these were names famous far beyond the frontier which they pacified and guarded—Edwardes, founder of Abbottabad, who twice, on his own responsibility, routed a rebel prince; Nicholson, whose marches and deeds of valour were almost incredible, so that a brotherhood of fakirs in Hazara founded the worship of the god Nikkul Seyn; Lumsden of Lumsden's frontier guides. And there were many more in the constellation which clustered round the two great men who founded "the Punjab tradition." One of them long afterwards vividly recalled his first meeting with John Lawrence:

> I found him discussing with the Postmaster-General the new times of postal delivery, and settling with the officer command-ing the troops the limits of his cantonments. Harry Lumsden, then a young subaltern, was copying letters. Seated round the small knot of Europeans were scores of Sikh and Mohammedan landholders, arranging with their new lord the terms of their cash assessment. John Lawrence was full of energy—his coat off, his sleeves turned up above his elbows—and was impressing upon

his subjects his principles of a just state demand, and their first elementary ideas of natural equity; for, as each man touched the pen, the unlettered token of agreement to their leases, he made them repeat aloud the new trilogue of the English Government: "Thou shalt not burn thy widow; thou shalt not kill thy daughters; thou shalt not bury alive thy lepers"; and old greybeards, in the families of some of whom there was not a single widow, or a female blood-relative, went away chanting the dogmas of the new Moses, which next year were sternly enforced. Here I learnt my first idea of the energetic order and the rapid execution which make up the sum total of good administration. Here I first knew the man, who was my model, my friend, and my master. . . .

Within three years justice and order were established, a new system of land revenue was functioning smoothly, the Punjab was peaceful and contented. The simplicity of its new rulers and the engrossing character of their work is amusingly illustrated by the celebrated incident of the Koh-i-Noor. This most renowned of jewels, whose fabulous adventures commenced before the dawn of history, had been captured in the Punjab and was destined for the British Queen. It was handed over to the Board of Three, and by them entrusted to John Lawrence, who calmly thrust it into his waistcoat pocket. Six weeks later came orders that it was to be instantly dispatched to the Queen. "Send for it at once," said John. "Why, you've got it," said Henry. John had positively forgotten all about the Koh-i-Noor, but as the appalling probability that by now it had once more vanished flashed into his mind not a muscle of his countenance moved. He calmly finished the business in hand, slipped away and summoned his bearer. "Have you got a small box which was in my waistcoat pocket some time ago?" The bearer had kept the box, little suspecting the nature of its contents, and in due course the Koh-i-Noor reached Queen Victoria.

The two brothers did not work easily together. Henry was courteous, formal and ever sympathetic to the claims of the Sikh landowner, John was brusque and informal—he would receive princes in his shirt sleeves and address them in the familiar singular —and he was more tender of the interests of the masses, and therefore also of the ultimate objects of the British government. Eventually the brothers had to part, and it was Henry, the elder, who was transferred. When he left, "a long cavalcade of aged native chiefs followed him, some for five, some for ten, others for twenty or twenty-five miles out of the city. . . . It was a long, living funeral

procession from Lahore nearly to Amritsar." And it is the biographer of John who says of Henry that "no Englishman who has
been in India has ever influenced other men so much for good;
nobody has ever done so much towards bridging over the gulf that
separates race from race, colour from colour, and creed from creed."

Lord Dalhousie's Governor-Generalship is often said to have
provoked the Mutiny. If so, it was not by his series of peaceful
annexations of small states, culminating with that of the still
unregenerate Oudh, so much as by his manifold reforms. For
Dalhousie laid most of the foundations of modern India. He swept
away bureaucratic formalities, greatly increased the expenditure on
public works of all kinds and on education, introduced the railway
and the telegraph, and relentlessly urged on progress in many a
primitive community. He worked unflinchingly on through
bereavement and crippling ill-health, witty, sympathetic and
vivacious to the last. But the very speed of the advance which he
set going contributed to the coming explosion.

§7

The Indian Mutiny, of 1857, was a tragic episode, which profoundly affected the subsequent history of India, but it was by no
means a large-scale affair. It was certainly nothing remotely
resembling a national rebellion. In 1857 the population of India
was about two hundred million and there were two hundred and
thirty-two thousand Indian soldiers. The British troops, who had
no special advantage in weapons (indeed most of the artillery was in
the hands of the sepoys) amounted to only forty-five thousand,
including the invalids and the non-combatant services. It is obvious
that anything like a national rebellion, or even a general mutiny,
must have overwhelmed them at once. For despite the swift extension of British dominion during the last seventy years, and the
repeated fighting which it had entailed, the British Empire, here as
elsewhere, was fundamentally unmilitary in character. And
although for at least two years there had been plenty of portents
of trouble in the army, no preparation whatever had been made for
holding India down by force. What British troops there were, were
scattered, and not on a war footing. And the magazine at Delhi,
the main ammunition-dump of the north, overlooked by the Mogul's
palace with its five thousand retainers, was still in charge of two
British officers and six sergeants. And it was characteristic of the
terms on which India was ruled that not a single British regiment

was stationed in Oudh, the most recent, the most disorderly and the most resentful of Dalhousie's annexations.

Yet only one of the Company's three provincial armies mutinied, that of Bengal, which was recruited not in Bengal but in the North West Provinces and certain native States, and was thoroughly unpopular wherever it had served. The British were greatly outnumbered—they attacked Delhi with five thousand men when it was defended by forty thousand, and Outram successfully held Lucknow with four thousand against a force estimated at over a hundred thousand—but British commanders remembered that this was the centenary of Plassey, and such odds, though very formidable, were not judged hopeless. And meanwhile the frontier was quiet. Nepal sent troops under Jang Bahadur to join Colin Campbell before Lucknow, the newly annexed Punjab remained loyal, its Sikhs and Muslims enlisted in the government levies, and the inhabitants helped the British to disarm doubtful regiments, and attacked those which mutinied. No powerful prince joined the rebels, and many assisted the government. And although the mutineers proclaimed the restoration of the Mogul Empire, not more than a few thousand Mohammedans out of fifty million rallied to defend it. The comparatively small scale of the disaffection suggests that India as a whole was not anxious to rid itself of British rule. And indeed the course of the Mutiny itself served as only too vivid a reminder of the evils from which British rule had delivered the country. For wherever and whenever British authority temporarily disappeared, there was an immediate revival of ancient feuds, religious fanaticism and the activities of the *thag* and the dacoit. The various rebel leaders could neither combine nor organise, and it soon became obvious that the rising, if successful, could only mean a relapse into the old anarchy of rival war lords.

The Mutiny was primarily a military revolt, due not so much to the reported greasing of cartridges with cow or pig fat as to certain professional grievances of the Bengal army, whose discipline had for some while been notoriously lax. But it was not only a military revolt. And though it revealed India in general as not hostile to British rule it also inevitably focused and ventilated many grievances. There was the all-pervasive suspicion, so flattering to the government, that it was anxious to convert all India to Christianity. And in the light of this ubiquitous misgiving, all the government's innovations were apt to become suspect, particularly among Hindus. For whereas Mohammedanism is fundamentally democratic, approving despotism, but having no objection to the humblest citizen becoming Commander of the Faithful, Hinduism is founded upon a rigid caste system. And since the whole conception of religious caste is alien to Europe, almost any idea or custom imported from the West seemed likely to act as a solvent of orthodox Hinduism, and could therefore be interpreted as a deliberate prelude to some form of mass conversion. It was not only that the reforms of the civil or criminal law had offended the susceptibilities of pious Hindus. Were not the new factories, the new railways and even the reformed gaols forcing the castes into unholy proximity, was not the sacred Ganges being tapped for irrigation, and secular education undermining the ancient faiths? Inevitably the British system presented itself as a threat to the immemorial privileges of all the higher Hindu castes. It was expensive also, and Indians were accustomed to think of taxation as a tribute, not as public revenue to be spent for public purposes.

The grievances were various, but neither deep nor wide enough to turn the Mutiny into a rebellion. And yet the Mutiny was undoubtedly the end of an epoch. Afterwards there might be far-reaching reforms and great administrative achievement, but the ultimate objects of the administration would insensibly change. And something of the old confidence would vanish; it would never be glad, confident morning again. The explanation was partly in the actual fighting. For one thing, the British had been thoroughly alarmed. They never forgot that for a month or two their hold on India had seemed terribly insecure. The mutineers had immediately captured Delhi, where there was not a single British regiment. But three thousand British, with twenty field-guns, clinging desperately to the Ridge outside the city, repeatedly beat back the assaults of overwhelming numbers of mutineers, in command of the arsenal and equipped with far more numerous, and far heavier, guns—until John Lawrence, with the loyalty of his Punjab already assured, could send a column under the legendary Nikkul Seyn to their assistance. There were not wanting voices which counselled withdrawal. But John Lawrence in the Punjab had no doubt. "This," he wrote, "is the crisis of our fate." And the diminutive force embarked on the astonishing enterprise of attacking the vast city, garrisoned by tens of thousands of armed fanatics. They blew in the Kashmir gate, and after six days of street fighting Delhi was in their hands. There was much more heavy fighting and many famous episodes yet to come, including the defence of the Lucknow Residency, but this was the turning-point. The Mutiny was doomed.

But, at least equally with that first shock to British confidence, the savagery of the actual fighting was responsible for the lasting moral consequences of the Mutiny. From the first the mutineers knew that they could expect little mercy, and quarter was seldom given or expected. And the repeated murder by the mutineers, and the criminal elements which soon gathered round them, of British officers, and then of European women and children, turned every British soldier into a pitiless avenger. At Cawnpore the British garrison, which had been promised a safe-conduct down the Ganges, was treacherously shot down, and its women and children first imprisoned and then massacred by Nana Sahib, and this celebrated tragedy is often represented as having been responsible for the ferocity of the rest of the struggle. It certainly burned itself into the memory of the British public; but there had been plenty of murders, and reprisals, before this; the Company's troops, as distinct from the regular "Queen's regiments," were among the toughest in the world, having obvious affinities with the French Foreign Legion; and in morality there was soon not much to choose between the worst excesses on either side, except that, unlike the mutineers, the British forces did not deliberately attack women and children. And as soon as the struggle was over Lord Canning insisted on the "clemency" which earned him his honourable soubriquet.

Such happenings were bound to have lasting consequences. Both races had been profoundly shocked. The British remembered, not that the area of the Mutiny had been so restricted but that its character had been so ferocious. Henceforth they would constantly think of themselves as a small garrison, islanded among a people whom they could not trust. The Indians also nursed their grievances, remembering the prisoners shot out of hand, sewn into pigskins or blown from the cannon's mouth, the plunder after the capture of Delhi. And they could not forget that the Mutiny—which it became the fashion among a later school of nationalist writers to treat as a national rebellion—had been on the whole an ignominious affair. Even those who disapproved the cause which men like Nicholson and the Lawrences served, could scarcely deny that such men as these were born leaders and rulers; but not even the most enthusiastic partisan could say as much of the Nana Sahib, Tantia Topi or Bakht Khan. And the memory of the contrast became particularly bitter to those Indians who eventually persuaded themselves, quite unnecessarily, that the mutineers had represented an "India" which did not in fact exist. And so thinking Indians in general were driven in upon themselves. From the Mutiny can be traced a return, a defiant return, to the old religions. The Brahmo Samaj, though its purpose had been to arrest that mass Christianisation of India which had for a moment seemed likely, was nevertheless a westernising influence, seeking to save the old by means of concession to the new. It would now gradually give way to the aggressive and uncompromising Arya Samaj, and to a deliberate cult of the remote, idealised past.

And if, as a consequence of the Mutiny, many Indians grew to be more self-consciously Indian, the British may be said to have become more self-consciously British, appearing to Indians ever more foreign, more formidable and more remote. It could never have been said before the Mutiny, as it would be said with some plausibility after it, that for the British there were only three genuine points of contact with the life of India—official administration, big business and big game shooting. Before the Mutiny the best minds in Britain had for a while cherished the gigantic ambition of Europeanising India, in order that it might become Christian. After the Mutiny they abandoned the dream, and resigned themselves to the now familiar doctrine that East is East and West is West, and that anything like assimilation is impossible. They would give India peace, law and order, but no longer, they resolved, should the family life and morals of the Indian be their concern. And yet, whether they wished it or not, they could not help bringing Europe, and the ways and thoughts of Europe, to India. Only, Westernisation would now be a process part involuntary, part inevitable, a process shorn of any deep, ulterior motive. Or, if in later years British administrators were asked what long range goal they had in view, they would reply, Self-government. For here too, to a setting which in tradition, heredity, sentiment and circumstance was so alien to democracy, the British would in due course carry the idea of Freedom. Not to have done so would have been to be false to their destiny. But the tragedy of the change which set in with the Mutiny will in time be seen to have been that the most natural and fruitful point of contact between East and West is religion—as the British were only beginning to discover just as industrial civilisation ceased to be able to think or speak naturally in such terms. And so the British came slowly to shape their new course deprived of what might have been a sovereign talisman. They would not only give India justice, order and peace, but acclimatise her to that process of change which they were learning to call progress, and so at length hand her back, thus profoundly altered, to the Hindu and Muslim administrations who should succeed them. Such was their intention, and this self-imposed task, too, was a gigantic conception. Only, it would be undertaken by men who had more than half-closed the door which led most naturally to the future. Only, it had yet to be learned how far Hinduism and Islam, and particularly Hinduism and Islam in their new self-conscious mood, would prove compatible with the economic processes and political philosophy of the West.

One consequence of the revulsion from the optimistic occidentalism of the recent past was that the British frontier was advanced no further. No more petty states were mediatised. The India of 1858 with its seven hundred States, some of them of only a few hundred acres, was crystallised as it stood. British India would exercise a certain overriding control over Indian India, but after 1860 there would be no more annexations. And the final disappearance of the long since shadowy Company, the assumption by the Crown of the Empire of India, was a first step in the new political direction. For not only did it give India the monarchy for which centuries of heredity best fitted her, not only did it bring her for the first time fully within the Empire; it also transformed the relations of British and Indians in India. Henceforth in the last analysis, they were not rulers and ruled; they were fellow-subjects.

CHAPTER TWO

THE FAR EAST: RAFFLES AND RAJAH BROOKE

(1808-1860)

§1

IN INDIA once British rule had, almost involuntarily, obtained a secure foothold, it was bound, whether voluntarily or involuntarily, to extend, since anarchy and a power capable of ending it could not co-exist indefinitely within the peninsula. In the Far East outside India it was not so. To have acquired Mauritius did not make it necessary to enter the Malay Archipelago, and even in the Archipelago a station on one island did not lead inevitably to entry on another. Here therefore in a sense the conduct of the British Government is more revealing, since it could act far more completely at its own untrammelled discretion. And here once again, as in earlier centuries, we find on the part of Authority a constant reluctance to advance. Where nothing would have been easier than to take much, Authority took little, and would have preferred to take nothing. Where it moved, it moved reluctantly and under the impulse of some distant representative whose arguments it was unable to resist, or whose action it could not control. It was, in fact, the old story, of adventurer or pioneer committing a timid government, the story of Drake and Burleigh, or the East India Company and Clive.

But now there is a subtle change in the motives of the pioneers. Stamford Raffles and Rajah Brooke desire neither adventure nor conquest, nor even commerce, for their own sakes. They wish to civilise. Their chief motive is to extend what they believe to be the benefits of British rule to oppressed and backward peoples. And the pioneers are distinguished from their contemporaries not so much by hardihood, energy and courage, although all these qualities they possess, as by a certain gentleness and sympathy, a genuine affection for the native races whom they rule. Protesting in 1815 to the President of the Board of Control against the threatened return of Java to the Dutch, Raffles writes:

of Java and its inhabitants I can speak plainly and decisively; they have felt the advantage of British principles, they acknowledge the benefit, and feel grateful for our interference. I have

348

just returned from a three months' tour throughout the Island, and I can safely say that regret, apprehension, and dismay precede the expected return of the Dutch; that the native population, feeling and profiting by the arrangements of the British Government, are decidedly attached to it; that they will not, for they cannot, understand the wisdom of that policy which . . . would transfer them to their former task-masters, and deliver them up unconditionally to their vengeance.

Nor was Raffles merely selecting the arguments likeliest to appeal to the Colonial Office; his whole record makes it plain that he was putting into official language the motives dominant in his own mind.

§2

Stamford Raffles was a clerk in the office of the East India Company who was sent out in 1805, before he was twenty-four, as assistant secretary to the new Presidency just constituted out of the Island of Penang and a strip on the Malayan mainland. His family's poverty had compelled him to leave school at fourteen, and during the ten years of his clerkship he had devoted every leisure moment to educating himself. And now, soon after his arrival in Penang, he had taught himself to read, write and speak Malay. For he was determined to know and understand the people among whom he lived. And since he possessed a natural courtesy, and an intuitive sympathy and tact, he soon won their hearts. And he in turn took to them at once and became deeply interested in their life and customs. Malays not only from Penang but from all over the Archipelago would visit him and talk of their traditions, their problems and their hopes. In the scanty leisure of an able and conscientious administrator, he wrestled with their various dialects, studied their manuscripts, compiled a code of their laws and even began to compose a history of Malaya. And as he toiled at his self-imposed tasks, or lingered over those charming, interminable Malayan conversations, a new ambition began to form itself in his mind. Why should not British rule one day bring, not to Penang only but to all Malayans, a safety, a happiness and a prosperity which they had never known? It was a dream appropriate enough to the age of Wilberforce, but Raffles, as yet, knew nothing of Wilberforce; his ambition was born of his own knowledge, and love, of the Malayan people.

And then a sudden turn of fortune in the world war seemed to bring Raffles's dream within the scope of practical politics. By 1807 Napoleon, now at the height of his power, had begun to talk openly of invading India—"nothing is so easy," he announced, "as this operation." Nor need the attack be confined to the overland route. Since Holland was one of his vassal states he could threaten British India from many hostile vantage-points, not only the Isles of Mauritius and Reunion, but the Cape of Good Hope, Ceylon and the Malay Archipelago. For once, however, the British government had not been tardy. The Cape and Ceylon and Malacca, commanding the northern gateway of the Malay Archipelago, had been seized, and in 1808 the Moluccas in the heart of the Malay islands. But there was still Java. And visiting Malacca in 1808 Raffles found to his consternation that the Directors were positively proposing to abandon that key point. Its fortifications, it seemed, were to be demolished, its Malay inhabitants evacuated to Penang. Raffles sat down and drafted a memorandum of urgent, and entirely unsolicited, advice to his employers against this disastrous step. An abundance of strategic and commercial arguments lay ready to hand—Malacca, being in the narrows, commanded the Straits, as Penang could not—and these Raffles wisely did not neglect. But characteristically the argument which moved him most, and which he strove to impress most forcibly upon remote Authority, was the effect of an evacuation upon the native population. Malacca, he pointed out, had been their home for centuries, and he did his best to convey to the Directors what home meant to a Malay. In any case the Malays were determined to stay where they were. Could the British, then, desert them? For desertion, he was clear, it would certainly be. "The natives consider the British faith as pledged for their protection." Whether they were moved by this appeal to their honour, or by the commercial and strategic considerations which Raffles did not fail to urge—and after all Malacca was the gateway of all Malay—the Directors actually reversed their policy. For the time being at any rate Malacca was retained. But more was to come.

In India, the Governor-General, Lord Minto, was planning to break the last links in the menacing Franco-Dutch chain. He would capture Mauritius and Reunion, and why not, after them, Java itself? Only, when it came to Java, no one in his entourage knew anything of the Archipelago. And then, a bolt from the blue, the indefatigable Raffles arrived in Calcutta. Lord Minto had read the report on Malacca and knew that Providence had sent him the man he needed. "On the mention of Java," wrote Raffles in later years, "his Lordship cast a look of such scrutiny, anticipation, and kindness upon me that I shall never forget. ' Yes,' said he, ' Java is an interesting island. I shall be happy to receive any information you can give me concerning it.'" Raffles, needless to say, was only too ready to provide all the requisite information, and in 1811 a British expedition, which included the Governor-General, and Raffles as his principal secretary, captured Java. But once again the Directors had no desire for new territory. It was their wish that the fortifications should be destroyed and the island evacuated. Lord Minto, however, like Raffles, was resolved that this could not be—and for the same reasons. Even doubts as to the future of Java after the peace "ought not surely to prevent us from beginning to perform the first duty of governments in improving the condition of a people that has become tributary to our authority." Lord Minto acted, as, before the days of the telegraph, Governors could still act, on his own authority. He appointed Raffles Lieutenant-Governor and departed for Bengal, with the parting exhortation, "while we are in Java let us do all the good we can."

Raffles had only five years in Java, but he was capable of crowding as much work into a given span as any man alive—had he not been consistently overworking ever since he left school? And his present task was his overmastering passion, so that he worked in a constant flow of high spirits, save when one of his paralysing headaches seized him. For overwork and the Malayan climate were steadily undermining his strength, so that at forty he would be an old man. Within his five years in Java he swept away the corrupt and oppressive methods of the Dutch and gave the Javanese a freedom, a dignity and a prosperity which they had never known. Of the subordinates whom he appointed he wrote:

> Placed in situations which, but a few years ago, were considered as a fortune to the individual . . . they have without exception felt the honour and character of the British nation prompt them above every selfish consideration and in six months enabled me to effect a revolution which two centuries of Dutch administration could scarcely dream of.

And even as Governor he continued his familiar intercourse with the native population—a startling breach with official tradition. "The people," admits a Dutch authority, "were satisfied and content." But there were only five years. For the long struggle with Napoleon was drawing to its close. By all the accepted rules of the game the British Government might have retained the Dutch Empire in the Far East at the Peace settlement of Vienna. But

Castlereagh recoiled instinctively from such a prospect. "I am sure," he wrote, "our reputation on the Continent . . . is of more real moment to us than an acquisition thus made." And perhaps Castlereagh was right. For his horizon was wider than Raffles's. Raffles's dream of a benevolent British administration raising the moral and material standards of life throughout Malaya was the nobler conception, but on the long view the cautious moderation of Castlereagh was the wiser. More than once the British Empire has been granted a giant's power; it has survived because it forebore to use it like a giant.

And so, although Ceylon was retained, and French Mauritius for the same reason—that it was necessary to the safety of India—all the Dutch possessions in Malaya were handed back. And Britain retired once more outside the gates of the Archipelago, confining herself to her former stations at Penang, and at Bencoolen on the outer, western, coast of Sumatra.

Raffles became Lieutenant-Governor of Bencoolen, "the most wretched place I ever beheld. . . . The roads are impassable; the highways in the town overrun with rank grass; the Government-house a den of ravenous dogs and polecats." Once again a long vista of reforms stretched ahead of him—slaves to be freed, forced cultivation to be ended, gambling to be suppressed. And why should not all Sumatra become British? For the Dutch, safely re-established in their former possessions, were signally failing to permit the "direct import" which Castlereagh had optimistically expected. Once again they set themselves to exclude British traders from the whole of Malaya. And neither the Directors nor Canning, now President of the Board of Control, were prepared to support Raffles in the stand which he attempted to make against the Dutch monopoly. Before long, however, he found a powerful supporter in the new Governor-General of India. Lord Hastings could not be interested in the acquisition of Sumatra, but he shared Raffles's enthusiasm for some station *inside* the gates of the Archipelago. And with Hastings's authority in his pocket Raffles had soon selected Singapore, at the southern end of the Malay peninsula, and, by agreement with the Sultan of Johore, had planted the British flag there in 1819. There was a storm of protests from the Dutch, a storm before which Directors and ministers in Britain might have bowed, if it had not been for Hastings, and a few friends, such as Charles Grant of the Clapham Sect, at India House. But before long the virtues of Singapore itself were beginning to convert the faint-hearted. For Raffles had selected the perfect site. Singapore commanded the more northerly of the two gates into the Archipelago. Even in Raffles's day the Straits of Malacca were the more important of the two for, though ships which had rounded the Cape from Europe found the Straits of Sunda equally convenient, the northern passage meant a saving of a thousand miles for traffic from India and Ceylon. And fifty years later, when the Suez Canal was opened, all European shipping would take the northern route. The population of Singapore and the tonnage in its harbours rapidly and steadily increased. And Singapore would never have come into existence but for the energy, and, even more perhaps, the knowledge, of Raffles. "But for my Malay studies," he wrote, "I should hardly have known that such a place existed; not only the European but the Indian world was also ignorant of it."

Three years later, after another spell in Bencoolen, he had nine months in which to launch Singapore upon its new career. Only nine months, for he was about to leave the East. Though not yet forty-two, he was physically an old man, and in Bencoolen he had just lost three of the four children to whom he was devoted. But in those nine months he laid both the material and the social foundations of the city. And sometimes, in his absorption in the work, despite bereavement and failing health, his spirits would mount to something like their old liveliness. Slavery and the slave trade were abolished. The cosmopolitan commercial population, already beginning to assemble, was given a sort of Legislative Council of merchant magistrates. Schools for Malay children were founded, and an Institution for higher studies, particularly in Malayan and Chinese. Law courts and the jury system were instituted. And memorably enough, since Malaya was still subject to the East India Company, Singapore was declared "a free port, and the trade thereof open to ships and vessels of every nation, free of duty, equally and alike to all." And it was characteristic of Raffles's orderly and farsighted mind, in so many ways so far ahead of his times, that he should have resolved that the great Singapore which he foresaw should not grow up at random. And so he bought back lands which his deputy had sold, pulled down the buildings on them and made arrangements for controlling and directing the future development of the city. By 1824 the Dutch were ready for an amicable bargain. The British surrendered Bencoolen and their interests in Sumatra, and, receiving Malacca in return, became the mainland wardens of the northern gate. Two hundred years after the massacre of Amboyna the British had established themselves in Malaya.

It was a memorable achievement, this swift growth on a derelict and forgotten site of a huge modern port, free to all the world, in which a vast population of all races, colours and creeds would soon be dwelling together in amity. And it was owed to one man. If he could have foreseen the Malay peninsula a hundred years later Raffles would doubtless have welcomed not so much the prodigious economic development, the rubber plantations and the tin mines, as the placid contentment of the Malayan people. The end of slavery and serfdom, of piracy and internal wars, the hospitals, the schools, the lawcourts—to these he would have turned as the final justification of his lifelong belief that British rule meant civilisation.

§3

Not even the profound distaste of the British government for further responsibilities could long prevent a further extension of British authority in the Archipelago. Often enough in the past adventurous individuals had advanced the imperial frontier, and sooner or later reluctant ministers, muttering impotent expostulations, had been compelled to follow in their wake. This time, for once, Authority would leave the pioneer to his own devices. And this time the performances of the pioneer were so excessively unusual that the government had some justification for displaying an exceptional degree of its customary reluctance. And yet the pioneer himself was not a highly exceptional individual. James Brooke, the son of a prosperous member of the Company's Bengal Civil Service, was a brave soldier and a wise administrator, but hundreds, perhaps thousands, of his contemporaries were capable of being both; and if he was also gentle, courteous and indifferent to personal gain so doubtless were many other young Englishmen of his day. And certainly the most romantic prophet would have hesitated to prophesy over his cradle that he would live to become the ruling Rajah of a Malayan principality. Certainly too he was strangely unlike the traditional carver-out of empires. So far was he from amassing, or desiring, a fortune that when he returned to England seventeen years after becoming a despotic ruler he had spent every penny of his private fortune, was five thousand pounds in debt and could only count on an assured income of seventy pounds a year, the pension for a wound received when he was a young officer in the Indian army. But from the first his ruling motive was that of Stamford Raffles, by whose career he had been profoundly influenced. He believed in what he called "the miseries immediately and prospectively flowing from European rule as generally constituted." "If it please God," he wrote, "to permit me to give a stamp to this country which shall last after I am no more, I shall have lived a life which emperors might envy. If by dedicating myself to the task I am able to introduce better customs and settled laws and to raise the feeling of the people, so that their rights can never in future be wantonly infringed, I shall indeed be content and happy."

Even this, however, was hardly exceptional; many then and since have believed in the civilising power of British rule, and have made that belief the mainspring of their lives. And perhaps his most unusual quality as a ruler was his habit of treating "the natives, as far as possible, as equals; not only equals before the law, but in society." That at least had not as yet been the practice of the Dutch or Spanish who had held sway in the Archipelago, and few of his own fellow-countrymen would have imitated him.

§4

Seriously wounded as a young man in the fighting in Burma in 1825, Brooke had left the army, and, inheriting a modest fortune on his father's death, had sailed in his own yacht on a voyage of discovery in the Archipelago. Chance led him to Sarawak, the north-western strip of the large island of Borneo, which lies north of Java, in the heart of the Archipelago. The Dutch were in the southern parts of the island, but the north and west had been seldom visited by Europeans. Here he led the incompetent troops of the Sultan of Borneo against powerful rebel forces, and so deeply impressed Rajah Muda Hassim, the heir presumptive, that "he begged, he entreated me to stay, and offered me the country, its government and its trade, if I would only stop and not desert him." Brooke would not accept then, but during a third visit, in 1841, when the insurrection had been finally quelled, and the varied peoples of Sarawak had learned to look to him as a friend and protector, he agreed to Muda Hassim's proposals and became Rajah of Sarawak. "It is a grand experiment," he wrote, "which, if it succeeds, will bestow a blessing on these poor people, and their children's children will bless my name." The experiment did not, it is true, reach the scale of which Rajah Brooke, like Raffles, had dreamed, for he had wished the British government to take measures to extend a beneficent influence, though not to seize power, throughout the Archipelago; and in such an enterprise no British Ministry was prepared to interest itself.

Even so, the experiment remains memorable enough. The rule of Sarawak has remained hereditary in the Brooke family. "The old Rajah" established it as "a mild despotism." He possessed absolute powers but, as an official brochure[1] put it in 1879, "this power is however rarely exercised, and for all practical purposes of local and general government he is assisted by a Legislative Council composed of two European and five native Malay chiefs." A British civil service was gradually recruited, but the only troops were native and, until, considerably later, a few Sikhs were introduced, there were no police. But the Sea Dyaks, the ferocious pirates of the coast, were transformed into energetic and law-abiding citizens, and imports and exports slowly expanded. There was no swift modernisation, however, and education, too, spread slowly. Perhaps, however, the steady, slow growth was healthier, and the immigration of natives from other parts of Borneo suggested that Sarawak was providing something which they needed, and that the old Rajah's chief ambition was being fulfilled. Although in 1888 the British Foreign Office assumed control of its external relations, Sarawak did not enter the British Empire. As for the Colonial Office, it desired nothing so little as additional responsibilities, and though there was a time when Brooke wished to hand Sarawak over to the government, his views changed visibly under the Parliamentary attacks of Cobden, Bright and Hume, briefed by a discarded agent of his own. For the Manchester Radicals saw in the British Rajah a specially provocative symbol of the Empire which they disliked, but could never understand. Writing to Bright in 1849, Cobden referred to "the sentimental mania" of the British public, which had given Brooke "all his powers of evil." "It shocks me to think what fiendish atrocities may be committed by British arms without rousing any conscientious resistance at home." No less imaginative was his rendering of the fact that after receiving his principality Brooke (who depended in the early years on three British followers and the intermittent presence of his yacht) had suppressed the coastal pirates with the aid of the Royal Navy—"Sir James Brooke seized on a territory as large as Yorkshire, and then drove out the natives, and subsequently sent for our fleet and men to massacre them."

§5

The Malacca Straits were the gate to China, and as the century wore on, the Chinese trade, which the East India Company had established as long ago as 1684, developed and brought inevitable trouble in its train. Inevitable, for the Chinese, who resented Europeans as intruders, and despised them as barbarians, had

[1] *Sarawak as a Field for Planters* (1879), pp. 43, 4.

adopted neither the sensible course of admitting them to trade on equitable terms nor the equally sensible course of excluding them altogether. The Chinese in fact made the worst of every possible world. They admitted foreigners, but subjected them to oppressive restrictions, constant extortion and occasional violence. And they made no preparations to resist, if themselves attacked. The Company had frequently almost, but never quite, been compelled to abandon the trade altogether. After 1833 it no longer possessed a monopoly, but tea had become a necessity to Britain, and trade, and troubles, were bound to continue. The Chinese now began to treat the old-established opium trade much as they had long been treating the foreigners who were conducting it. Their government forbade the trade, but their mandarins connived at it. And since opium-smoking (which has been described by an expert as "rather worse than cigarette-smoking and less injurious than the habitual consumption of alcohol") was a long-familiar necessity to the ague-ridden worker in the rice-fields its sale continued as briskly as ever. The foreigners, including the British, paid the requisite bribes and continued to import. The patrol boats intercepting the opium drove a roaring trade in its subsequent distribution, and attacked Europeans, whether opium dealers or not, with complete impartiality. The war which followed was creditable to neither side. It resulted in 1842 in the cession of Hong-Kong, and the opening of five "treaty ports" for trade. But the Chinese government continued to resent the presence of foreigners, and from time to time its officials committed acts of open hostility. In 1860 an Anglo-French expedition captured Pekin, a treaty, signed, and then repudiated, by the Chinese two years previously, was ratified, five more treaty ports were opened, and Kowloon, the mainland promontory opposite Hong-Kong, was ceded to the British. This was the occasion on which, in reprisal for the ill-treatment of some British prisoners, Lord Elgin, the Lord Elgin who brought responsible government to Canada, ordered the burning of the Emperor's summer palace, which had already been plundered by the troops.

It is a depressing story. In the middle of the nineteenth century the British, as they had abundantly shown elsewhere, were in no imperialistic mood, they dreaded rather than desired further acquisitions of territory, and it might have been hoped that British influence, which other countries would have been ready enough to follow, would succeed in establishing European trade with China without violence. But though the British did not want territory they did want trade, and they never made sufficient allowances for the paradox of a government which passionately resented, but could not prevent its representatives from exploiting, their intrusion. Both Stamford Raffles and Rajah Brooke had represented the nineteenth century civilisation of the West, which they doubtless overrated, at its best, largely because their first object had been to help and educate the East, and because they had taken endless trouble to understand, and allow for, the prejudices of other peoples. But in China, where all foreigners were regarded as barbarians and inferiors, and where the Europeans were traders with no administrative responsibility, neither sympathy nor the sense of responsibility were easy to awake, and Western civilisation displayed its least attractive traits.

CHAPTER THREE

AFTER SLAVERY: THE WEST INDIES

(1810-1860)

§1

IN MANY WAYS the problem set to a civilising Empire in the West Indian islands, the problem of white settlers among a primitive and subject population, was reminiscent not so much of Malaya as of South Africa. But in the West Indies the problem was at once more acute, in that the West Indian negroes were slaves, and more tractable, in that the white settlers were predominantly British. And yet these British planters were faced with social and economic problems of their own, which to them at least long appeared more urgent than the slavery which loomed so dark on the horizon of Evangelicals at home. For throughout the long history of the West Indian plantations the planters had seldom if ever been content, and the eighty years which followed the loss of the American colonies were for them an unbroken period of economic crisis. For American Independence meant that, for the purpose of the Navigation Acts, America was a foreign country, and that under the enumeration clauses of the Acts most of the planters' products must not be exported to it. Inevitably, but slowly and amidst a constant clamour of discontent, the restrictions on shipping were whittled away piecemeal over the next sixty years, until the Navigation Acts themselves were swept bodily away in 1849. As for the imperial preference in the British market which had been the compensating element in the old mercantilism, it perished in the free-trade decade of 1840 to 1850, and the planters, who seemed fated never to lack a grievance, lamented its passing as lustily as they had once protested against the full mercantilist policy which embodied it. It was thus a community already for quite different reasons believing itself to be constantly on the verge of ruin that the British government, hounded on by the Evangelicals, must deprive of the slaves on whom its economic system rested. Abolition was thus very much an economic as well as a moral problem, and, thanks to an unhealthy climate, much rum, a high mortality and the insidious effects of slave-ownership itself, the planters, even if their own pockets had not been threatened, were hardly the men to put the moral aspects first.

But if the prospect about 1810 was disquieting for the planters, it was heart-breaking for the Evangelicals. The Slave Trade, it was true, had been abolished in 1807, but slaves were still smuggled into the plantations under foreign flags, and reports of cruelty and degradation flowed back to England in an undiminished stream. "I am quite, quite sick of the West Indies as a field of labour in our cause . . ." wrote Stephen to Wilberforce. And the ageing Wilberforce himself sometimes flinched when the planters maltreated some suspect missionary, or slave risings, savagely repressed, seemed to present the opponents of emancipation with arguments ready-made, or some West Indian newspaper published a particularly savage onslaught on himself—"one of his paragraphs was sent me the other day with only these three words, 'Thou vile hypocrite.'" But he refused to be discouraged—"I rely upon the religion of the people of this country." Nothing, he was clear, would be done by the West Indians. If, as a concession to the agitation at home, they passed laws or regulations themselves it would be with the deliberate intention of leaving them unobserved. British public opinion must compel the British government to act, over the heads of the planters. ". . . we shall do nothing effectual to check colonial crimes" thought Stephen, "till we blazon them to the English public and arm ourselves with popular indignation." And there was no lack of crimes to be chronicled. The average sugar estate may have appeared a kindly and tranquil community, whose cheerful negroes, simply incapable of overwork, lived on terms of friendly familiarity with their masters; but there were also the exceptions; and beneath even the most placid surface slumbered terror and cruelty, ever ready to awake. The home government moved cautiously; but its partial and piecemeal reforms were punctuated by intermittent slave-risings in the West Indies, which the planters would ascribe to the "unceasing and unconstitutional interference of His Majesty's Ministers with our local legislature." It became obvious that only abolition of slavery, and the emancipation of the slaves, would suffice. And in 1833 the Abolitionists summoned up all their strength. There were meetings and lectures all over Britain; petitions, with over a million signatures, poured into Parliament; pamphlets flooded from the Press; three hundred delegates, elected by Abolitionist meetings in every populous town in the country, marched to Downing Street. And that August the Act of Emancipation was carried. In was one of the noblest measures ever passed by Parliament, a shining example to the world, and a new stage in the advance of men. But even here the spirit of compromise would not be denied. Twenty million pounds was voted in compensation to the planters; it was rather less than half the value of the slaves.

§2

The social effect on the West Indies was instantaneous. In the smaller islands the negroes mostly continued to work on the estates as free labourers, but in Jamaica and British Guiana, where there was vacant space, they went off to live, by primitive subsistence agriculture, in their own villages. In the main the islands passed gradually into the possession of the negroes. And this under administrations controlled exclusively by whites. For until after the middle of the century the old West Indian colonies retained constitutions of Stuart type—which meant a governor with nominated executive and legislative councils monopolising the administration, and an Assembly, elected by a diminutive constituency of planters, controlling finance. Such at least was the model in the Bahamas, Barbados, Bermuda, Dominica, Grenada, Jamaica, the Leeward Islands, St. Vincent and Tobago. It could hardly prove satisfactory. The government at Westminster, thanks to the influence of the humanitarians, was for ever prodding the island oligarchies towards reform. But the planters were suspicious of the home government and afraid of the negroes, and the political history of the West Indies, and particularly of Jamaica, was for long a succession of controversies and deadlocks. Yet the authority of Westminster remained the best hope for these communities of planters and negro freedmen, in which full democratic self-government was impossible. By no other channel indeed was the tradition of Burke and Wilberforce likely to reach them. It needed a catastrophe, however, to bring about the change.

In 1865 a negro insurrection broke out in Jamaica, and thirty unoffending individuals were brutally murdered. Governor Eyre, the explorer of Australia, repressed it with great promptitude and pitiless severity, executing some four hundred and fifty of the rebels. A society founded on slavery, or even on the aftermath of slavery, is always conscious of living on the edge of catastrophe, and the white community believed that it had peered into the abyss. The dispatches from Jamaica, wrote the Colonial Secretary, who had begun by congratulating Eyre on his "spirit, energy and judgment," "contain abundance of assertion of organised conspiracy to massacre all the white and coloured inhabitants, but nothing in the nature of proof." The planters had no doubt that their Governor had done right. But at home a violent outcry was raised by those who

believed that no crimes and no dangers could justify such widespread
executions—only to be met by a counter-agitation among those who
maintained that Eyre had saved Jamaica from a much greater
tragedy, the very success of his severity inevitably eliminating the
proof of its necessity. After a violent controversy, in the course of
which Carlyle and Tennyson supported Eyre, he was retired on a
pension, not brought to trial, as many wished. But the tragedy had
one significant consequence. The constitution of Jamaica was
suppressed. For the planters were now genuinely alarmed. Only
strong government, they believed, could save them, and strong
government they could not themselves provide. In 1866 the administration of Jamaica was in effect placed in the hands of the Colonial
Office. Democracy, which would have meant the rule of white by
black, was still impracticable; oligarchy, the rule of black by white,
had broken down; the only alternative was administration by the
admirable officials now available in the imperial service. The wheel
indeed had come full circle. Only individual initiative could have
founded and developed these colonies, but, society there being what
it was, in the second half of the nineteenth century only the state
could administer them. Most of the islands followed the example
of Jamaica, accepted nominated governments and shed the elective
element altogether. Only the Bahamas, Barbados and Bermuda
retained the representative institutions of the old Colonial Empire.
The rule of the Colonial Office came about because public opinion
in Britain desired to deal impartially between white and black.
Under it an orderly and harmonious society grew up, a society which
included the Indians who, after 1835, came to do the work of the
plantations, Chinese, French, Spanish, Dutch and Portuguese, but
in which negroes owned the greater part of the islands. Colour-
hatred and race violence came to be almost unknown; Church,
Law, professions and public services all contained outstanding
personalities of every colour and race; "there is no negro problem
. . . . in the sense in which the phrase is used in the southern United
States." In the West Indies the nineteenth century was beginning to
atone for the wrongs done to Africa by Europe during two hundred
years of the slave trade.

BOOKS FOR FURTHER READING.

Edward Thompson and G. T. Garratt, *The rise and fulfilment of British
rule in India;* Edward Thompson, *The making of the Indian Princes;* Sir
Alfred Lyall, *British Dominion in India;* R. Bosworth Smith, *Life of
Lord Lawrence;* Professor R. Coupland, *Raffles;* Sir Spenser St. John,
Rajah Brooke; Hamilton Hume, *Life of Governor Eyre.*

Book IX

IMPERIALISM AND CHAMBERLAIN

CHAPTER ONE

IMPERIALISM

§1

BUT NOW a vast and sombre change comes over the scene. From 1783 to somewhere about 1870 the growth of the British Empire, for the most part unplanned, and even unwelcomed, by the home government, had proceeded virtually without competition from other European powers. British explorers had called a new Continent into existence, and gradually British emigrants had begun to people it. Of the handful of ports of call and naval points of vantage to which Britain had confined her acquisitions after the victory over Napoleon, one had unexpectedly proved the nucleus of a wide new area of white colonisation. British North America had developed into a vigorous new nation, British rule in India had spread swiftly. No hostile European power, even if it had wished to, could have interfered in Australia or Canada, South Africa or India, for British sea power was unchallengeable. But, as it happened, no European power had had any desire to interfere. Russia, it is true, had begun to creep through Turkestan towards the Afghan frontier, and had roused some apprehensions in the breasts of British Viceroys of India; France had conquered Algiers and, more recently, Cochin-China in the Far East. But that was all. The era of greedy and powerful nation-states was not yet. Under such circumstances, the growth of the British Empire had been smooth, natural and, to a degree hitherto unprecedented, bloodless. All this while moreover the greater part of the British public had known little of imperial affairs, and on the whole cared less. For politics had been the concern of a limited constituency dominated by the middle class, and profoundly penetrated by *laissez faire* indifferentism. A limited number of Humanitarians, Evangelicals and Radical Imperialists had had their own reasons for interesting themselves actively in what was happening overseas, but the general public had remained obstinately indifferent.

All this was now to end. Both abroad and at home the scene is transformed. The age of imperialism is about to commence. For it is significant that until about this time the word "imperialism,"[1] when used at all, signified only "Cæsarism," the rule of an emperor. During all the years when the British Empire had been the only Empire the word had not acquired the various derogatory senses which have since then become so familiar; these were the product of the new forces now about to be let loose. For it was in 1870 that Germany defeated France, and for the first time became a united and powerful nation, dominated by a militarist Prussia. Nationality had been one of the main articles in the creed of Victorian Liberals. With democracy, free trade, popular education, a cheap Press and the rising tide of material prosperity, it had gone to constitute the Progress which that highly rational age worshipped with an almost mystic fervour. With the warm approval of their fellow countrymen accordingly, the two great Foreign Secretaries of the century, Canning and Palmerston, had patronised and promoted all over Europe that growth of nationalism of which the climax was the emergence of the German nation under the sinister auspices of Bismarck and his characteristically Prussian doctrine of Blood and Iron. It was disquieting perhaps that Bismarck should so unashamedly have forged the new Germany on the anvil of war, deliberately provoking, and defeating, first Denmark, then Austria and now France. All this, however, was undoubtedly nationalism, and most Victorian Liberals were still prepared to welcome it as Progress. Its consequences were swift, unforeseen and profoundly disturbing.

Germany, and to a lesser degree the new Italy, whose Risorgimento was completed in the same year, was now a powerful, self-conscious and greedy nation state. Cradled in war and self-assertion, the new Germany looked confidently to the same methods to bring her further triumphs in the future. Bismarck, her founder, had declared that the material interests of the state must always take precedence over every other consideration whatsoever, an explicit denial of the gospel of Wilberforce and Burke. Inevitably, since her goal was power, the new Germany (unlike Bismarck himself) desired colonies, not only because industrial development was now the means to power, and colonies would provide the raw materials necessary for it, but because the mere possession of colonies, she believed,

---

[1] "Radical Imperialist," as applied to Gibbon Wakefield and his associates, is a term coined long after their day.

would itself mean additional prestige. Colonies accordingly she would obtain if she could, and to her colonies were likely to mean ruthless competition and jealous monopoly. And Germany would set the pace for Europe. The Conference of 1884 which regularised the Scramble for Africa was held at Berlin, and summoned by Germany—in the very year in which she obtained her first foothold on the African continent. Meanwhile in France memories of the humiliation of 1815 had coloured politics for two generations, *la gloire* had long been the watchword of all Parties, and the humiliation of 1870 did but intensify the readiness of the nation for any enterprise overseas which was likely to restore its self-confidence. And soon there would be the temptation to compensate for the disparity of population which now prevented her from facing a united Germany on equal terms, by organising a great African army overseas. Russia too had long been expanding, and continued to expand; Portugal turned from her memories of the past to plan a new Portuguese Empire which should stretch from coast to coast of Africa; even Italy dreamed of conquests.

§2

Such were the new aspirants, and such the new appetites. A scramble for power and monopoly in Asia, Africa and the Pacific was bound to follow, and some of the motives for it had long been present in the consciousness of Europe. But what had rendered the dormant forces explosive was the rise of the greedy, self-conscious and aggressive nationalism, of which the new Germany was the protagonist. An era was opening in which the very word imperialism would change its meaning and acquire new, and too often sinister, associations. Hitherto, throughout the long era in which Britain had been the one active imperial power there had been no need of such a word. For the essence of imperialism is that, whether for good or ill, it is a deliberate and self-conscious policy. And this is precisely what the expansion of Britain overseas had never been. The British Empire had grown; after 1870 empires would be manufactured. And so the scramble which was about to commence was bound to be altogether alien to the tastes and traditions of this country. For the new imperialists now at the helm in Europe would seek monopoly and exclusion and, as a consequence, absolute sovereignty in their colonial acquisitions, whereas the British tradition had been free trade, with an open door for all comers, and a conspicuous reluctance to assume sovereign control of new territory. Yet when the scramble began Britain could hardly stand aloof. For to stand aloof would have meant commercial and industrial decline, and, before long, the arrest of that benevolent process of collectivist social legislation which was launched in the late 'seventies. Nor was it merely that, like the Empress of Austria at the time of the first Partition of Poland, *elle pleurait mais prenait*—she wept, but took her share. For the British carried into the age of the crude new imperialism the mellowed standards and traditions which they had slowly acquired through the centuries. They might have claimed the lion's share of tropical Africa on the ground that its potentialities had in the main been revealed by British explorers—the greatest of whom had worked solely for humanitarian and religious ends. They might even have used their sea-power to exclude all rivals. But they attempted no such monopoly, and set up no such prior claims. Indeed they were for a long while reluctant and backward participants in the unseemly scramble. When Bismarck inquired point blank whether Britain did or did not claim the south-west coast of Africa Gladstone's government could not bring itself to give a definite answer, and a succession of lengthy and evasive Notes was only terminated by Bismarck's blunt announcement of a German Protectorate. Comparatively, although only perhaps comparatively, Britain played a modest rôle. Save for Portugal she was the only power to open her possessions to the trade of all comers. She showed herself ready to forgo an advantage, co-operate with others and even to recognise a rival claim. And despite the new moral climate she contrived to preserve, and develop, that tradition of trusteeship for backward races which was the legacy of Burke, Wilberforce and the Evangelicals. The outlook for humanity would have been black indeed if so much of the world had now had to be partitioned without the experience of Britain to draw upon, and one or two of her solid achievements on which to build.

§3

But it is not only abroad that the scene is now transformed; at home too profound changes are at hand. In the last two decades of the nineteenth century the masses begin for the first time to interest themselves in Empire. And the new doctrines of Collectivism and State control, which now slowly supersede the once all-pervasive Individualism, begin to suggest wholly novel notions of an organised development of the colonial dependencies. Hitherto the unenfranchised masses had had little contact with politics, and during the first half of the century their horizon was darkened and filled by their own economic distress. But in the second half of the century the golden Victorian prosperity set in, and the working class could think of something besides its daily bread. In 1867 the vote was extended to the artisans of the towns, and in 1885 to the agricultural labourer. A great new democratic electorate was ready to listen to new and wider themes. The tides of political fashion moreover were on the turn. For by 1880 *laissez faire* Individualism was a spent force. By now the substance of the doctrines of Bentham and Mill had been placed upon the statute book. In a final burst of energy Gladstone's great ministry of 1868 to 1874 had reformed the Civil Service, the Universities, the Law Courts and the army, had introduced the Ballot and laid the foundations of free elementary education—and all on the strictest lines of Benthamite orthodoxy. Yet still the problem of poverty remained unsolved; mysteriously, the golden age had not arrived. And now a number of contributory motives inclined men's minds increasingly towards the rival doctrine of Collectivism, to belief, that is, in the paramount claims of the state and a disposition towards state ownership, state interference or state control. Disraeli had already taught a half reluctant Conservative Party first to abandon Protection and then to espouse Reform. He now completed the process of education by committing Conservatism to championship of both the new creeds. It was his government of 1874 to 1880 which began to lay the foundations of Collectivist social legislation. And in a number of speeches from 1872 onwards he proclaimed a wholly novel pride and confidence in the imperial destiny of the country. "I express here my confident conviction," he declared in April, 1872,

> that there never was a moment in our history when the power of England was so great and her resources so vast and inexhaustible. And yet, gentlemen, it is not merely our fleets and armies, our powerful artillery, our accumulated capital, and our unlimited credit on which I so much depend, as upon that unbroken spirit of her people, *which I believe was never prouder of the Imperial country to which they belong.*

This was a remarkable assertion to be heard in the Free Trade Hall, Manchester, the very hearthstone of Cobdenite Radicalism. It was partly perhaps—for Disraeli had the shrewdest sense of the current of opinion—a penetrating estimate of a change which had already set in, but it was certainly also a forecast of the sentiments which he was deliberately setting himself to evoke. For Disraeli not only took long views; he was an opportunist of genius. And he had perceived that the ideals of Benthamite Liberalism were out-worn, and that its long reign was drawing to a close. The new electorate would respond to new motives, motives with which Conservatism, he was resolved, should supply it. In June of the same year, at the Crystal Palace, in a speech from which, it seemed to his official biographers,[1] "the modern conception of the British Empire largely takes its rise," he roundly declared that during the supremacy of Liberalism "there has been no effort so continuous, so subtle, supported by so much energy, and carried on with so much ability and acumen, as the attempts of Liberalism to effect the disintegration of the Empire of England." It had failed, he said, "through the sympathy of the Colonies for the Mother Country." "They have decided that the Empire shall not be destroyed." And he went on:

> In my opinion no Minister in this country will do his duty who neglects any opportunity of reconstructing as much as possible our Colonial Empire, and of responding to those distant sympathies which may become the source of incalculable strength and happiness to this land.

How, in his opinion, the Empire might be reconstructed he suggested in the course of his retrospect of the Liberal failure—a failure, it must be admitted, in which he had fully shared himself—to foresee, or desire, the survival of the imperial connection.

> But self-government, in my opinion, when it was conceded, ought to have been conceded as part of a great policy of Imperial consolidation. It ought to have been accompanied by an Imperial tariff, by securities for the people of England for the enjoyment of the unappropriated lands which belonged to the Sovereign as their trustee, and by a military code which should have precisely defined the means and the responsibilities by which the Colonies should be defended, and by which, if necessary, this country should call for aid from the Colonies themselves. It ought, further, to have been accompanied by the institution of some representative council in the metropolis, which would have brought the Colonies into constant and continuous relations with the Home Government.

These are long views indeed for 1872. And although there is a

[1] Moneypenny and Buckle, *Life of Disraeli*, 535.

vein of partisan exaggeration in his strictures on the Liberal failure in the past—the Tory failure had been no less complete—Disraeli illuminatingly exposed the fundamental weakness of Cobdenism when he derided its constant complaint that we had "lost money by our Colonies," and described it as "viewing everything in a financial aspect, and wholly passing by those moral and political considerations which make nations great." This was in the true Tory tradition, these were the veritable accents of Bolingbroke inveighing against Walpole. Against the temptation to which the school of Cobden, like the school of Walpole, had succumbed, the temptation, which ever besets an age of prosperity, to make the increase of material comfort its supreme aim, he urged, like Bolingbroke, the claims of national greatness:

> The issue is not a mean one. It is whether you will be content to be a comfortable England, modelled and moulded upon Continental principles and meeting in due course an inevitable fate, or whether you will be a great country, an Imperial country, a country where your sons, when they rise, rise to paramount positions, and obtain not merely the esteem of their countrymen, but command the respect of the world.

This is not the noblest of national ideals, for, thus defined, at any rate, it is a summons to power or glory rather than to the service of an Idea. And in some of Disraeli's speeches there is a vein of over-emphasis, of vulgarity even; not thus would Salisbury have spoken of the Empire. None the less this is a nobler ideal than Cobden's, or rather than that into which Cobden's ideal too readily degenerated, for it exalts a more generous ambition than individual self-enrichment, and calls on men to sacrifice their own interests for their country's.

These and similar declarations were received with enthusiasm by the new working-class electorate. On his way south after his Manchester speech Disraeli was cheered through the industrial areas "as far as the Potteries." And the election of 1874 gave him a handsome majority. For the first time since 1846 the Conservatives were not merely in office but in power, and for the next thirty years they are the dominant political Party. For the long process of "educating the Tories" was complete, and Distaeli had armed his followers with the two ascendant creeds. As for the Liberal leader, he disliked and mistrusted Collectivism and was so little concerned with imperial affairs that it is possible to read Lord Morley's monumental *Life of Gladstone* and scarcely be reminded that Britain possessed an Empire. From now on accordingly Gladstonian Liberals found it increasingly difficult to frame a programme of either domestic or foreign policy, and began perforce to concentrate on Irish Home Rule. Nevertheless, although Gladstonian Liberalism was a declining force, for a generation after 1870 there was a steady alternation of Liberal and Conservative administrations, and it was not until 1895 that ten years of unbroken Conservative rule set in, with the reign of Joseph Chamberlain at the Colonial Office and the zenith of the mood of self-conscious imperialism which was the paler British reflection of the new temper in Europe. It would not be difficult to interpret the imperial history of these twenty-five years before 1895 as an alternation of excessive energy and excessive caution, corresponding to the political complexion of the government. None the less a careful examination would disclose a continuity of policy even more striking than the variations in it. For now more than ever before the effective motive force was the instinct of the masses. Often enough in the past, from that moment in the seventeenth century when a mysterious impulse sent thousands of English men and women to found a new civilisation overseas, the people had shown themselves more conscious than their rulers of their country's destiny. And now their influence upon national policy was far more compelling and intimate.

When the scramble for Africa commenced it was popular opinion which compelled the British government to act. "British Africa," writes Lord Lugard, "was acquired not by groups of financiers, nor yet by the efforts of . . . statesmen, but in spite of them. It was the instinct of the British democracy which compelled us to take our share." The great new electorate possessed no expert knowledge and little acquaintance with detail. But on broad moral issues it would usually judge more wisely, perhaps because it judged more instinctively, than the ruler or the expert. In the past the unauthorised initiative of adventurers overseas had repeatedly driven a reluctant minister to action. And governments were a good deal more respectful of the enfranchised masses than they had been of the distant pioneer. In 1893 Mr. Gladstone's cabinet had decided to evacuate Uganda, when his Scottish agent informed him that if he did so he would certainly find that he had to evacuate Downing Street also. Uganda was not evacuated.

§4

It had been the faith of many of the Radical nationalists that popular suffrage and universal free education would together spell the doom of both Empire and monarchy. The immediate consequence of these changes was in fact however precisely the contrary. By the end of the century both monarchy and Empire were more firmly rooted in popular affection than ever before. Republicanism had been a fashionable creed in 1840, and there were moments between 1865 and 1870, during the Queen's long seclusion after the death of the Prince Consort, when it had seemed near to becoming a popular one. But by 1900 Victoria was the mother of her people, universally regarded with an almost superstitious reverence and affection; and any politician who had ventured to repeat the republican sentiments with which Sir Charles Dilke could still win applause in 1870 would have been instantly torn to pieces by any public audience in the country. Many factors had contributed to this far-reaching transformation, and in particular the Queen's own prejudices and personality, at once so unmistakably royal and so essentially middle-class, as well as the complete detachment of the Crown since 1860 from public association with either of the political Parties. But the intimate association of Crown and Empire had undoubtedly done much for the popularity of both. In 1876 Disraeli's Additional Titles Bill had made the Queen Empress of India, and by now the Crown had become the single visible symbol of unity holding together the heterogeneous association of peoples which was the British Empire. To the Indian peasant the Parliament of Westminster was not even a name, to the Canadian merchant, whose ancestors had migrated from the United States because they wished to continue to live under a monarchy, and who had not forgotten how Durham had been betrayed by British politicians, it was too often deeply suspect. But both Indian peasant and Canadian merchant could understand allegiance to the British Crown, as the permanent symbol and the ultimate source of the justice or the freedom which they most valued.

§5

It was during the last decades of the reign of Victoria that the Empire was once more profoundly altered not only by another great increase in extent, but by the first appearance of a conscious popular doctrine of imperialism. For Gibbon Wakefield and the Radical Imperialists had been a small group of experts and enthusiasts, concerned only to press their technical theories of colonisation on ministers and departments, whereas Seeley, Froude and the new imperialists professed a whole philosophy of Empire, and they had a large popular following. British expansion had ceased to be unconscious and instinctive. Now a historical process is seldom at its healthiest when it becomes self-conscious. The trained craftsman works instinctively by second nature, and it is the man who has not yet learned, or is beginning to forget, his craft who is most conscious of his motions, and *thinks* of what he does. And similarly it is often in infancy or decadence that a historical process is most self-conscious. But the new theories of British imperialism, like the new phase of British expansion, represented not so much a normal stage in the evolution of the nation, as a secondary consequence of what had happened on the Continent. Because several European nations, led by Germany, had suddenly embarked upon a scramble for colonies, Britain moved too, although two centuries of experience forbade her even now to think of colonies or Empire as most of the new European fortune-seekers thought of them. And because they perceived that they were now passing into an era of imperial rivalries Seeley and Froude and the rest set out to explain the nature of the British Empire to a people which had hitherto taken its world-wide possessions for granted. They sought to bring home to their fellow-countrymen the potentialities and the power of the Empire, but above all its uniqueness. For whatever else it might be, this outcome of long, unreflecting growth was very different from the Empire about to be manufactured by the greedy and ambitious Hohenzollerns. And it is significant that of all that was said about the British Empire at this time what has been best remembered should be the *mot* that it was acquired in a fit of absence of mind. For that familiar aphorism does at least vividly illuminate a fundamental distinction between the British Empire and those which were now to come into being. The last thing that could be said of the German Empire would be that it was acquired in a fit of absence of mind.

The word imperialism in its familiar modern sense was coined to describe the aggressive self-conscious phase which lasted from 1870 to 1914. The British must take their share of blame for what was to come; for they could hardly compete with the acquisitive without growing acquisitive themselves, and in becoming self-conscious the Empire would sometimes be in danger of becoming vainglorious too. Nor was it to be expected that imperial policy would be magically exempt from the greed and materialism which were the characteristic and ubiquitous vices of the industrial age. Nevertheless the fact remains that the era of imperialism owes its more sinister associations primarily to certain aspects of the policy of the new European empire-builders, that these were wholly alien to the previous record of the British Empire, and that the word imperialism has been too loosely used by many who are quite unaware how recent is its origin and how limited its relevance. And, most significant of all, not only in their administration of backward areas in this phase did the British maintain the standards they had learnt from Burke and Wilberforce, but in Canada, Australia, New Zealand and South Africa they laid the foundations of that enduring Commonwealth which they had failed to establish in America in the eighteenth century.

CHAPTER TWO

LIVINGSTONE

(1840-1874)

§1

LITTLE enough in the history of tropical Africa in the previous century foreshadows the irruption of the new Imperialism in the 'eighties. How wholly alien indeed to the British past was the sudden scramble, and our share in it, stands out clearly from the record of the previous decades. Until well into the nineteenth century virtually nothing had been known of the vast interior. Greeks and Romans had dwelt on the north coast, in Egypt or on the Red Sea littoral. Arabs had their caravan routes across the Sahara in the middle ages, but such knowledge as they acquired did not pass beyond the Moslem world. A little later, the Portuguese knew the coasts, and Jesuit missionaries learned something of Abyssinia and Angola. And there had been the slaving stations on the west coast. But the age of discovery did not dawn until towards the end of the eighteenth century, and here again the British were the pioneers. The first motive was sheer curiosity. For the ancient (and still unsolved) riddle of the sources of the Nile had been replaced by a new one. Where, and indeed what, was the Niger? For in the seventeen-eighties the Niger was no more than a mysterious name. Where it rose, where it ended, in what direction it flowed was totally unknown. The African Association, a dining-club presided over by Sir Joseph Banks, whom we have met before, resolved to find out. Three of its first four emissaries perished, and none of them found the Niger. The fourth, Mungo Park, reached it in 1745 and discovered that it flowed east. But its source and mouth remained unknown, and to discover them a succession of explorers continued to sacrifice their lives. Mungo Park himself went out again in 1805, with more than thirty volunteers. By November only Park and four others survived. On the 19th he wrote a cheerful letter to his wife ("I am afraid that, . . . you may be led to consider my situation as a great deal worse than it really is"), set sail down the Niger and was never heard of again. In 1822 Laing located the sources of the river, and ten years later the brothers Lander sailed down it to its mouth. But by now scientific curiosity was ceasing to be the only, or indeed the chief, motive.

§2

For to the Evangelicals and Abolitionists the opening up of the interior of Africa meant a prospect not of trade or power, but of a short cut to the scotching of the slave trade, which still flourished outside the British Empire. For the diplomatic and naval pressure on which Britain had already embarked would obviously be a lengthy task. How much simpler to cut off the supply of slaves at its source! But most of the Abolitionists realised that they were not likely to put an end to " the trade" unless they could replace it with "legitimate commerce." Foreign merchants must learn to go to Africa not for slaves but for raw materials and undeveloped resources. Let trade relations therefore be developed wherever possible, and where necessary by means of minor annexations—the Government "obtaining from the Chiefs the possession of some convenient districts which may best be adapted to carrying on trade with safety and success." The project was naturally warmly endorsed by merchants suffering from the decline in West Indian sugar production which had followed on the abolition of slavery. Here at once appears the eternal paradox of Empire, the germ of the scramble for Africa which was to come. "Philanthropy and five per cent"—the cynicism which has been, rather doubtfully, attributed to Rhodes, does scant justice to Exeter Hall and the Abolitionists. In their eyes commerce was the only likely means of permanently disposing of the slave trade, and so was even more indispensable for Africa than for Europe. Clearly where there is both philanthropy and five per cent some will concern themselves more with the philanthropy and some with the five per cent, but in general to the British public and the British government at this time the philanthropy mattered a great deal and the five per cent very little. It was in hopes of promoting trade that Lander returned to the Niger in 1832—and perished, with thirty-eight of the forty-seven Europeans he took with him. An even larger expedition in 1841 was no more successful. But in 1849, while the southern Sahara was being traversed by Richardson and two Germans, a new era in the exploration, and indeed in the history, of Africa was opened by Livingstone.

§3

David Livingstone was born at Blantyre, near Glasgow, in 1813, the son of a tea-merchant in a very small way. The father was pious in the old, strict Scots fashion; the son had a deep natural sense of religion, but many other intellectual interests as well, particularly in science and travel, and when working as a boy in the local cotton factory he would poise a book on a portion of his jenny, so that he could glimpse a sentence every now and again as he moved to and fro at his spinning. "To this part of my education," he recorded later, "I owe my present power of completely abstracting my mind from surrounding noises, so as to read and write with perfect comfort amidst the play of children or near the dancing and songs of savages." Science was anathema to the father, and "his last application of the rod," Livingstone records, "was on my refusal to peruse Wilberforce's *Practical Christianity*." But the boy was convinced that "science and religion are not hostile." And science and religion, with a passion for exploration and a profound compassion for human suffering, were to be the motive forces of his strange career.

He qualified as a doctor, and offered his services to the London Missionary Society. The Society did not think much of him at first, for the true Livingstone, a marvellous combination of saintliness, courage and common sense, was less obvious than the fact that he possessed little facility either for preaching or extempore prayer. Eventually, however, he passed his examination, and sailed for Africa in 1840. On the voyage he persuaded the captain, "a well-informed, shrewd Scotsman, but no Christian," to teach him to take astronomical observations, and he landed at Capetown after the three months' voyage a qualified geographical explorer. The use to which Livingstone put the voyage, and his comment on his instructor, were both characteristic, as characteristic as his contriving twelve years later, during a brief stay at Cape Town, to study map-making under the Astronomer Royal. For a synthesis of science and religion was the basis not only of Livingstone's faith but of his practice. "In every conceivable emergency . . ." it has been said, "Livingstone could be relied on to discharge his two daily duties with immaculate efficiency —to say his prayers and take his astronomical bearings."[1]

He would probably by now have found it difficult to say whether exploration or evangelism was his ruling passion. Fortunately, however, it would be easy in Africa to combine the two, for he had no intention of settling into a permanent mission station. Almost at once he was sending a friend his day-dreams of a journey across Africa to Abyssinia, adding almost wistfully, "it might be six or seven years before I should return." He would not, however, be neglecting his duties—"if languages are dialects of the Bechuana,

[1] *Livingstone*, by D. C. Somervell, 27.

I could soon make known a little of the blessed plan of mercy to the different tribes on the way."

Livingstone made his way to Kuruman in Bechuanaland, the missionary headquarters of the celebrated Dr. Moffat, who was to become his father-in-law. Here he began what can best be called a nomadic missionary life, pushing his headquarters steadily north towards the Zambesi. For the call of the unknown heart of Africa grew more irresistible every year. And all the while, remote from white men, he was preaching, healing, learning the native tongues, and studying the fauna, flora and geology of the land. Here already the passion of sympathy and indignation, which would henceforth drive him on, was roused by the cruelties inflicted by the Boers on the native peoples. "It is difficult," he wrote,

> for a person in a civilised country to conceive that any body of men possessing the common attributes of humanity . . . should with one accord set out, after loading their own wives and children with caresses, and proceed to shoot down in cold blood men and women, of a different colour, it is true, but possessed with domestic feelings and affections equal to their own. . . . It was long before I could quite give credit to the tales of bloodshed told by native witnesses, and had I received no other testimony but theirs, I should probably have remained sceptical to this day as to the truth of the accounts; but when I found the Boers themselves, some bewailing and denouncing, others glorying in the bloody scenes in which they had been themselves the actors, I was compelled to admit the validity of the testimony and try to account for the cruel anomaly. They are all traditionally religious, tracing their descent from some of the best men (Huguenots and Dutch) the world ever saw. Hence they claim to themselves the title of "Christians," and all the coloured race are "black property," or "creatures." They being the chosen people of God, the heathen are given to them for an inheritance, and they are the rod of Divine vengeance on the heathen, as were the Jews of old.

The Boers, for their part, protested that Livingstone was making the natives "too saucy," and that he and the other British missionaries must leave the district. And some years later, when Livingstone was away, they raided his Bechuana neighbours and seized the opportunity of plundering his house, destroying his stock of medicine, selling his furniture and clothes at public auction, tearing out the leaves of his books and scattering them far and wide. Livingstone

did not receive any reparation for these robberies; his account with
the Boers was to be settled in another fashion. "The Boers resolved
to shut up the interior," he wrote, "and I determined to open the
country; we shall see who have been the most successful . . . , they
or I."

§4

In 1849 Livingstone, who had been moving his mission station
steadily northward, journeyed across the Kalahari desert and discovered Lake Ngami, beyond it. And now the instincts of the
explorer would no longer be denied. The country to the north of
Lake Ngami was the unknown inmost heart of Africa; moreover
it was well-watered, he now heard, and populous. The attraction
was irresistible. He sent his wife and family home, travelling down
to Capetown with them, and then made his way back to Lake
Ngami, and beyond to Linyanti in the Makololo country. The
Makololo seemed to him specially suited for the introduction of
religion and commerce. But their lines of communication obviously
lay east and west, not north and south. He resolved accordingly to
journey west to the Atlantic, and then, if possible, east to the Indian
Ocean. The Makololo seem to have fully understood and approved
the objects of Livingstone's journey—they too desired trade with the
coast. And when he set out on his formidable journey it was with
twenty-seven Makololo as porters, not hired men but picked
emissaries of the tribe. No other white man accompanied him. He
travelled with very scanty equipment, and astonishingly few provisions, north up the Zambesi and then far west towards Angola
on the Atlantic coast,

> After months of sheer endurance, often so ill that he could not
> move or even think or speak, with nothing to carry him forward
> but his feet or an unsaddled ox, sometimes obstructed by un-
> friendly natives, especially in districts infected by the slave trade,
> but always winning through in the end with no gun fired or
> bloodshed, at last, at the beginning of April, with his company
> of twenty-seven Makololo undiminished, Livingstone reached
> the outlying stations of the Portuguese.[1]

In substance the description would serve for any of Livingstone's
astonishing journeys. In Portuguese territory Livingstone found
great kindness, but no interest in his plans for civilising Africa.

[1] Coupland, *Kirk on the Zambesi*, 67.

He refused all offers of a passage to England, saying that he must take his faithful Makololo safely home. After four months accordingly, though still emaciated by fever, he started back and, after a year's even more arduous travelling, arrived in Linyanti with his party still intact, in September, 1853. Thence, after seven weeks, with a hundred Makololo volunteers he journeyed to Portuguese Mozambique on the east coast, discovering the Victoria Falls on the way.

Livingstone's first two great journeys, solitary among the Africans, had not only displayed an astonishing resourcefulness and ascendancy over the native mind; they had not only discovered much new territory and gathered a vast amount of new knowledge; they had exposed the shocking fact that the huge area he had traversed was devastated by the slave trade. And this was not the slave trade of the west coast, which, thanks to Wilberforce and the British Navy, was now nearing its end. It was the east-coast trade, of which little had hitherto been heard in Europe, though the Arabs had been busy with it since before the days of Mahomet. In the seventeenth century the Portuguese had joined them, and though in 1836 they undertook, by treaty with the British Government, to suppress the trade, the British Navy could not be everywhere at once, and slave trading still flourished, with the Portuguese Governors of Mozambique as its active agents. The island of Zanzibar, where many Indian merchants financed the business, had been a chief centre of the trade for centuries and was now the greatest slave-market in the world, annually exporting some twenty thousand slaves across the Indian Ocean. Livingstone was a profoundly compassionate man and the horrors which he had seen, and was to see, haunted him to the end of his life. From now on he devoted himself to the stamping out of the trade. In England, to which he returned in December, 1856, he repeatedly proclaimed his African policy—a naval squadron on the east coast, and Christianity and commerce in the interior. His influence was immense—Evangelicals, philanthropists, geographers, scientists and even politicians were eager to listen to him. And the great public, fascinated by his rare combination of courage, resourcefulness and scientific gifts and, above all, by his unselfish singleness of purpose and deep spiritual power, had taken him to its heart. Although in 1857 there was no popular Press, he was so well known by sight that, unless he took extravagant precautions, crowds surrounded him whenever he appeared in public. And yet 1857 was a year of tense preoccupation with the Indian Mutiny, the year of Nicholson, Lawrence and Havelock.

The Government sent him out in 1858, in command of an

elaborately equipped expedition, to explore the Zambesi and discover the likeliest means of ending the slave-trade and establishing "legitimate commerce." Officially he went as a Consul, in government pay. But though technically he was no longer a missionary, and in the more conventional sense had perhaps never been a missionary at all, missionary nevertheless undoubtedly remains the most appropriate epithet for his work. The new expedition did not achieve all that Livingstone had hoped; the Zambesi and its tributaries proved disappointingly unnavigable, and he had not discovered a waterway outflanking Portuguese territory. He found it harder too to work with his British colleagues than with the Africans. But it achieved much. It explored the Shire highlands and founded a mission there. It discovered the third of the three great lakes of Central Africa, Nyasa—Burton had reached Lake Tanganyika some eighteen months earlier, and six months after Burton's discovery Speke had found Lake Victoria Nyanza. Livingstone had also seen more than ever before of the terrible work of the slave-traders, with some of whom he had fought a spirited action, and the simple, unemotional account of what he saw, which he subsequently published in his second book, *Narrative of an expedition to the Zambesi*, created a profound impression on the British public. He had now moreover irrevocably dispelled the old belief that Cape Colony and Natal were self-contained territories unconcerned with the rest of Africa. The British had already disabused themselves of their original notion that Cape Town was merely a naval port, and had discovered that it was the gateway to a colony. Livingstone's journeys were the first unmistakable demonstration that it was the gateway not to a colony only, but to a continent.

§5

A final brief interlude in England—during which Livingstone assailed the Portuguese slave trade with pen and tongue—and the last journey began in 1865. By all customary standards it was a prolonged and lonely martyrdom, one of those rare martyrdoms, however, which consecrate a cause. Once more he went without white companions. His porters, from India, the African islands and the coastal mainland, robbed and deserted him early, so that through most of the eight years' toil to come he could rely only upon three or four faithful boys from the interior, who had served him in the Zambesi days. Very soon the journals contain the recurrent entry "Too ill to march." And early in 1867 one of the deserting porters

carried off the medicine chest. "I felt," says Livingstone, "as if I
had received the sentence of death." Indeed he must have known
that he had received sentence of death—unless he were to turn back.
And it is clear that he had made up his mind not to leave Africa
again. Starvation, rheumatic fever, pneumonia, hæmorrhage,
prostration and dysentery follow each other in the pages of his
journal with little intermission. The stores and medicines which he
tried to get sent up country did not reach him, for a barrier of fever
and slave raids cut him off from the coast. No one in Europe knew
where he was. From the moment when he started up the Rovuma
in April, 1866, he had vanished into silence. But even without
medicine the indomitable man struggled on until disease positively
prostrated him—and when it had prostrated him he would contrive
somehow or other to recover. And through it all, limping on
ulcered feet, deserted by all but three followers, or stranded on the
Lualaba without a canoe, whatever his bodily weakness, however
seemingly hopeless the outlook, he continued to fill his journal with
a steady flow of information and lively comment, and to write the
long, cheerful letters which he planned some day to "post." He
discovered two more unknown lakes and (though he did not know
it) the headwaters of the Congo. And he saw the slave-trade at the
closest possible quarters, often perforce travelling in company with
Arab slavers.

But the deepest significance of his journeys was the martyrdom
itself, the slow unflinching sacrifice of a life. Most unexpectedly he
was offered an eleventh hour reprieve. As he was sitting, hopeless
and exhausted, in his house at Ujiji, the upcountry base of the Arab
slave trade, the faithful Susi rushed in to announce the arrival of a
white man. It was Stanley, sent by the *New York Herald* to discover
whether Livingstone were yet alive. For Livingstone was now a
world-celebrity, and his disappearance was headline news in every
continent. As Stanley advanced slowly through the throng of Arabs
and Africans which had assembled at the news of the coming of
another white man, he could hardly contain his excitement. "I
would have run to him," he says,

> only I was a coward in the presence of such a mob—would have
> embraced him, only, he being an Englishman, I did not know
> how he would receive me; so I did what cowardice and false
> pride suggested was the best thing—walked deliberately to him,
> took off my hat, and said: "Dr. Livingstone, I presume?"

The famous meeting is almost the only incident which our present educational traditions have allowed the British public to know of the life of one of its greatest men.

Livingstone could not be persuaded to return with his would-be rescuer. In April, 1873, a year after Stanley had left him, in a village beyond Lake Tanganyika, his two faithful servants, Susi and Chumah, found him dead, kneeling at his bedside as if in prayer. There followed a strange and moving épilogue. For it would be possible from Livingstone's own records to collect an abundance of apparently conclusive evidence that the African is incapable of betterment —even the picked Makololo who had accompanied him to Mozambique had taken there to slave-raiding and murder. But such a conclusion would have been a denial of all that Livingstone had lived for. And now that he was dead, Susi and Chumah, the two servants who had never deserted him, proceeded to display a high degree of the very qualities which it would have been easy to conclude that the African native invariably lacks. It almost seemed as if something of the spirit of the dead man had descended upon them. They made up their minds that it was their duty to carry their master's body to the coast, and hand it over to his formidable and mysterious compatriots. They persuaded some of Stanley's former porters to share the task with them, embalmed the body, collected and inventoried Livingstone's property and journals and set out on their journey of fifteen hundred miles. Some of the party died on the way, they were attacked by wild animals and hostile tribes, but nothing could deter them, not even a British expedition on its way out to relieve Livingstone, whose leader urged them to bury their master on the spot. They struggled on until, after nine months, they reached the coast, and handed over their burden to the British Consul. Two months later, in April, 1874, Susi and Chumah saw Livingstone buried in Westminster Abbey. The leading pallbearers were Stanley and an African negro.

§6

The significance of Livingstone's career was not that he had discovered half a dozen lakes, charted many new mountains and rivers, and added a million square miles to the map of the world. It was not that his death, his servants' journey with his body, and the publication of his *Last Journals* profoundly stirred the British public. Nor even that he had thrown open Central Africa to the world. His supreme achievement was that on the eve of the new imperialism, and the scramble of the Powers for African territory,

he taught his own fellow-countrymen that the true mission of
Europe was to promote the welfare of Africa. For the tradition of
Livingstone lived on. Before his death the House of Commons had
decided that at whatever cost the East African-slave trade must be
ended. John Kirk, Livingstone's right-hand man during the second
journey, and his whole-hearted disciple, was Consul in Zanzibar and
succeeded in negotiating a treaty with the Sultan by which the
slave market was closed without resort to force, and the mainland
trade condemned. Before long the Universities' Mission to Central
Africa, direct outcome of Livingstone's Cambridge Lecture of 1857,
was building its cathedral on the site of the abandoned slave market.
The internal trade which supplied Egypt and the Mahommedan states
of the Mediterranean coast, together with the slave-raiding among
the African tribes themselves, which had gone on from time immemorial, would only be extinguished by the partitioning of Africa
itself. That this process, full of ugly incidents as it was, has undoubtedly on balance brought abundant benefit to the peoples of
Africa is in no small degree due to Livingstone. That in British
territory nothing remotely resembling the cruelties yet to be
perpetrated in the Belgian Congo was now conceivable may be
ascribed to an older tradition than Livingstone's. But it was the
tradition of Livingstone, living on in Kirk and Lugard, which
ensured that even in its least worthy moments the British government never altogether forgot that it first obligation in Africa was
to promote the welfare of Africans. What Livingstone had meant by
Christianity and Commerce was what Lugard would mean by *Dual
Mandate*, and the thread which links the two together, though it
runs through the heyday of the new imperialism, is unbroken.

CHAPTER THREE

THE SCRAMBLE: CENTRAL AFRICA AND THE PACIFIC

§1

SUCH was the British prologue to the new Imperialism in general, and to the scramble for Central Africa in particular. That the Berlin Conference of 1884 should have been summoned—to regulate, and, as it proved, to accelerate, the scramble—within eleven years of Livingstone's death, may appear to be one of the more sombre ironies of history. Yet the life, and death, of Livingstone had ensured that Britian would enter into no arrangements which did not seem likely to benefit the native Africans as well as her own people, and that in what she believed to be their interest she would accept some from which she expected little but inconvenience herself. And indeed even the acquisitiveness of the competing European governments had its advantages for Africans. For Africa, and its natural resources, could by no possibility be permanently isolated from the world, like a vast Red Indian Reserve. The penetration of the continent might indeed have been left to irresponsible private individuals, but what that might have meant in human suffering is sufficiently suggested not only by much past history but by the early story of the Belgian Congo. The alternative to indiscriminate private exploitation was for European governments either to buttress the existing native rulers, not without some degree of control, or else to impose their own direct rule upon all concerned.

Yet it was certainly ironical that Livingstone's missionary journeys should have led indirectly to the most atrocious episode of the partition, the Independent State of the Congo, of which King Leopold of Belgium was personal sovereign. The administrators of the Congo had neither experience nor traditions and it became the scene of appalling misrule and suffering before it was transferred to the Belgian Government in 1908. But the Congo venture proved to be the spark which fired the train. The Portuguese had been stirred to revive their ancient claim to the mouth of the river, and in a treaty of 1884 Great Britain, still herself profoundly unambitious, conceded their right to the coast, provided that navigation on the Congo itself was free to all nations. But it was too late. Such an issue could no longer be settled between Great Britain and Portugal alone. A decade earlier, only four European nations, Spain, Portugal, France and Britain, had owned territory in Africa; and of these Spain held very little, and Portugal was sunk deep in inactivity. But now new appetites were awakening, the eyes of all the great powers of Europe were on Africa, and the Anglo-Portuguese treaty was greeted with a storm of opposition. That same year, 1884, an International Conference met at Berlin, and the scramble for Africa had begun.

In part the new powers of science were responsible; for railways and the manifold advances in sanitation and medicine meant that the white man could now remain and rule where previously he could only pay transient visits and die. But even more than the new science it was the new explosive nationalisms of Europe which set the scramble going. And in particular the new Germany was responsible, a newcomer to Africa but the principal convener of the Conference and the principal gainer by the dispositions which resulted from it. And significantly enough the German gains were chiefly made at the expense of Britain. For though British pioneers had been exploring Africa long before an African, or for that matter the German, Empire had been thought of, and though almost in self-defence, as the partition was hurried on, Britain acquired substantial territories for herself, she had not even now wholly shaken off her reluctance to acquire, she could still think of the administration of a colony as an unwelcome responsibility, and its wealth as available to all the world, and she played her part with little relish. And at point after point she showed herself almost obsequiously ready to yield to German claims. Perhaps the government of Gladstone was to some extent responsible for this backwardness and modesty, for, though public opinion would not have permitted any government to stand wholly aside while Protectionist powers divided the wealth of Africa between them, Gladstone had come into power in 1880 on a wave of reaction against Disraeli's adventurous imperial policy, and had begun his administration by withdrawal in South Africa and on the frontiers of Afghanistan. And his Foreign Minister, Lord Granville, took naturally to abnegation and self-effacement overseas, and in conveying his approval of a project for a large German East Africa, in the area which had been opened up by Livingstone before the German Empire had been heard of, he could write of the proposal for a smaller British East Africa to the north of it:

Her Majesty's Government have the scheme under consideration, but they would not support it unless they were fully satisfied

that every precaution were taken that it would in no way conflict
with the interests of the territory that has been taken under the
German Protectorate.

Certainly the keynote of the British government's policy was
reluctance, and in particular reluctance to add to its existing
responsibilities.   Thus in 1878 the anarchy in Bechuanaland had
made military interference necessary, but the government declined
to set up a Protectorate because "the assumption of such increased
responsibilities would be open to very serious objection in present
circumstances." By 1881 all police forces had been removed and
anarchy set in again, chief attacking chief and Boers fishing in the
troubled waters. The missionary at Kuraman, Livingstone's first
station, hurried home to rouse public opinion, and at crowded public
meetings Nonconformists and Radicals urged a forward policy on
the Gladstone government. The eventual outcome in 1885 was a
Crown Colony south of the Molopo River, and a Protectorate north
of it. But when the native chief proposed to place his whole country,
stretching to the Zambesi, under the protection of the Queen, the
Colonial Secretary was cautiously "not prepared to entertain the
offer." Again, over the long stretch of western coast to the north
of Cape Colony the British government had steadily 'declined to
extend its authority. German missionaries there had asked for
British protection in 1867, but it had been refused. In 1880 Bismarck
himself inquired whether Britain would protect German interests
in that area, and was roundly informed that the British government
recognised no responsibility there. A year or two later awakening
German ambitions pitched upon this region as a likely spot for the
foundation of an African Empire. Again the British government
was asked whether or not it claimed sovereign rights, and Lord
Granville could only fence, hesitate and enter into such lengthy
communications with Cape Colony that before any decision was
come to, Germany had proclaimed her own Protectorate of South
West Africa. In the same year Germany annexed Togoland and the
Cameroons, where there was a British Baptist mission and the chiefs
had long been vainly demanding a British Protectorate. When
Joseph Chamberlain and Dilke, two of Gladstone's junior ministers,
heard of this fresh annexation there was an exasperated exchange of
notes; for Chamberlain and Dilke, unlike their colleagues, knew and
cared for the Empire. "The Cameroons!" wrote Dilke, "I annexed
them at the F.O. three years ago, and I fancy you annexed them in
a Committee of Cabinet about one and a half years ago. Why then
does Bismarck get them after all?" "As you say," replies Chamber-

lain, "we decided to assume the Protectorate eighteen months ago and thought it was all settled. If the Board of Trade and Local Government Board managed their business after the fashion of the Foreign Office and the Colonial Office, you and I would deserve to be hung."

In East Africa it was much the same. Britain had long been the paramount influence in the Sultanate of Zanzibar, where she had put an end to the slave-market on the island and was doing her best to stamp out the slave-trade on the mainland; and at any time after 1875 it would have been easy and natural to declare a British Protectorate. Yet when the German agent Karl Peters began to acquire a great block of territory through treaties with chiefs on the mainland the only anxiety of the British Government seemed to be to expedite his arrangements. Indeed it seems conceivable that but for the tide of public opinion, now setting strongly in favour of imperial expansion, the government might have withdrawn from this area altogether. The eventual outcome, in the comprehensive Anglo-German treaty of 1890 which regulated the boundaries wherever the African possessions of the two countries were contiguous, was a large German East Africa stretching from the Rovuma River, up which Livingstone had set out on his last journey in 1866, to midway up Lake Victoria Nyanza, which Speke had discovered in the previous decade. North of it took shape a smaller British East Africa, administered at first by a British East Africa Company, formed not so much in hope of profit—the modern Chartered Company is allowed no monopoly—as to champion British interests during the fever of partition. Before it was ready for further burdens the Company found itself pushing westward into Uganda to protect British missionaries and keep the country out of French or Arab hands. The financial strain was too great, and in 1894 the Government wearily took over the responsibility, and proclaimed both Uganda and East Africa Protectorates under the Crown.

§2

It was not all a story of reluctance, however, and other new territories came to Britain in other ways. Thus the Shire highlands on the southern shores of Lake Nyasa had been Livingstone's most prized discovery, more prized than the Lake itself, for here he foresaw a centre of civilising Christianity. Hither Scots missionaries had speedily followed him, naming their first centre Blantyre after his birthplace on the Clyde. And after some friction with Portugal, which had claimed a continuous belt across central Africa from Angola to Portuguese East Africa, a treaty of 1891 secured the western and southern shores of Lake Nyasa, as Nyasaland, to Great Britain. On the west coast the delta of the Niger had long been known as a source of palm-oil, and trade to the Oil Rivers, as they were called, was carried on until after 1870 by merchants of various countries without rousing any national ambitions to control a pestilent region, to which shipping companies ominously issued no return tickets. By the end of the 'seventies, however, competition was becoming fiercer, and a British group succeeded in buying out its French rivals. At the Berlin Conference of 1884 the doctrine that "effective occupation" of the coast carried a right to a "sphere of influence" in the hinterland ensured the handing over of the Niger Coast to Great Britain. The coast about Lagos, a port which had been taken over in 1861 in order to expel a nest of slave-traders, was consolidated into a Protectorate, but the main course of the Niger went to the Company, which became the Royal Niger Company and not only traded but administered until the end of the century. On the Gold Coast, west of Togoland, there had been British ports and factories since the seventeenth century. Early in the nineteenth century the government had proposed to abandon them, but in 1828 British interests were handed over to a Committee of London merchants. The governor appointed by them, Captain George Maclean, possessed no legal authority and a mere handful of police, but he set up a court of justice to which natives flocked from far afield so that soon, against all instructions from home, and thanks to the magnetic power of strong personality and good government, he was exercising an unauthorised Protectorate over the coastal area between the forts. In 1843 the Crown finally accepted responsibility. A couple of invasions of the Gold Coast by the powerful inland native kingdom of Ashanti, with which there had been earlier encounters, led to a "little war" in 1895. There were some protests from Exeter Hall, but Chamberlain was now Colonial Secretary and he replied brusquely:

> The attempt to excite English sympathy for the King of Ashanti is a fraud on the British public. He is a barbarous chief, who has broken the Treaty, permitted human sacrifices, attacked friendly chiefs, obstructed trade and failed to pay the fine inflicted on him after the war; and the only proof he has ever given of civilisation is to be found in the fact that he has engaged a London solicitor to advocate his interests.

Kumasi was occupied without the firing of a single shot, and annexation followed in 1901.

Such in Central Africa was the British part in the scramble of the new imperialism. It was not a large share in relation to the part which had been played by British pioneers. But large or small mattered comparatively little, for European administration, by one Power or another, had become inevitable. What would matter, as we shall see, was the nature of the administration. What would matter was that for Britain the prelude to the scramble had been— Livingstone.

§3

The other area in which the new acquisitive imperialism launched a scramble for territory was the Pacific. And here a curiously similar process unfolded. Before the era of the new imperialism Britain could have annexed all the islands in the South Pacific virtually without opposition, but though annexations were repeatedly urged from Australia or New Zealand the British Government stubbornly declined to move. Only when first French, and later German, ambitions had been loosed upon the islands did Britain take a hand in the partition, and with the same curious blend of obsequiousness and reluctance, interspersed with short bursts of acquisitive energy.

From 1796, when missionaries left England for the Society Islands, discovered by Captain Cook, until about 1850, missionaries and merchants were the representatives of Europe in the Pacific; the missionaries bringing with them the Gospel and a number of skilled crafts, the merchants the wares of Europe and its vices. The missionaries swiftly made converts, and in 1825 Queen Pomare was petitioning for British protection, which Canning politely declined. Again, after French intervention on behalf of Catholic missionaries in 1838, Queen Pomare appealed on behalf of "what we have dearest to our hearts—the Protestant faith and our nationality. . . . Take us under your protection. Let your flag cover us and your lion defend us." But again the Foreign Secretary—this time Palmerston —politely but firmly declined, pleading the "great extent of the present dominions of the British Crown in the Southern Ocean." And so there was renewed French intervention followed by annexation in 1843. The island had been discovered by a British navigator and converted and civilised by British missionaries, and at any time a show of force by the British Navy would have scared off the timid ministers of Louis Philippe. But the British government, like

Palmerston, was only too conscious of the "great extent of the present dominions of the British Crown," and discreetly stood aside.

In 1843 also, disappointed of New Zealand, the French landed missionaries in New Caledonia, the island, eastwards of Australia, which Cook had claimed as a British possession by right of discovery. Sir George Grey in New Zealand, and the Governor of New South Wales, warned the home government that a French New Caledonia might prove dangerous, but the Government did not act, and in 1853 France formally occupied it. The Sandwich Islands, which include Hawaii and Honolulu, had been visited by Cook in 1778, and in 1794 a Grand Council of native chiefs had decided to place themselves under British protection, but in 1794 the British government was even more preoccupied than usual, and the cession was never ratified. The offer was repeated in 1822 in a personal letter from King Kamahameha to George IV. But once the Californian coast of America was peopled, the natural destiny of the islands was annexation by the United States.

The uniform reluctance of the British government at this time to add to its great possessions had its grotesque aspects, but it represented that old, wise instinct for moderation which had done so much to ensure the survival of the Empire. Had the British confirmed anything like all the claims of their navigators and explorers, accepted all the proffered cessions of their missionaries' converts or fully exploited a tithe of the opportunities of their paramount sea power, they would have built up an Empire so vast that it would have become a standing challenge to the world.

§4

From 1850 to 1875 the administrative problems of the Pacific multiplied. Trade increased in value, white settlers became more numerous and indentured labour was imported from overseas. Society in fact was rapidly becoming more complex, and the native governments on the European model, which the missionaries did their best to establish, were incapable of administering it. Further annexations were obviously probable, and opinion in Australia and New Zealand became increasingly anxious that Britain should follow the French example. But the British government was still profoundly reluctant to move. To the Fiji Islands in the centre of the south Pacific had come Wesleyan missionaries from Tonga Island, three hundred miles to the east, cotton planters from Australia and indentured labour from the New Hebrides. In 1858, on the advice of the missionaries, King Thakombau offered the sovereignty to Great Britain. The British Consul pointed out the naval value of the harbours of Fiji, on the highroad from Australia to Panama, the Admiralty concurred, and even mid-Victorian Manchester, which took little interest in the Empire but a good deal of interest in cotton, seemed to favour annexation. Under this concerted pressure the Colonial Office consented to send out a representative to investigate, though it was careful to utter a number of preliminary warnings. For one thing, expense must be avoided like the plague, for the British taxpayer, mildly though he was still treated, was beginning to be alarmed by the prospect of widening financial responsibility all over the globe. Moreover, "the hope of the conversion of a people to Christianity, however specious, must not be made a reason for increasing the British dominions." Charged with so many admonitions, the official investigator found little difficulty in reporting against annexation. But the Government had not seen the last of its troubles. By 1870 steady pressure in favour of annexation was being exerted from Australia, and though for the time being the Colonial Secretary held his ground, it could not be for long. Charges of kidnapping and other atrocities were appearing in the British Press; Exeter Hall at home and the Wesleyan missionaries in Fiji were in favour of annexation. The government had resisted all comers long and stoutly, but the sudden revival of the humanitarian motive was too much for it. Ministers, declared the Colonial Office in 1873, were

> not only far from desiring any increase of British territory, but they would regard the extensions of British sovereignty to Fiji as a measure which would in no case be adopted unless it were proved to be the only means of escape from evils for which this Government might be justly held to provide a remedy.

Beneath the obscure departmental jargon it was clear that the official mind had recognised that the long struggle was drawing to a close. And in 1874 Great Britain accepted the sovereignty of Fiji. By that time 120,000 out of a native population of 140,000 had been converted to Christianity, and cannibalism, infanticide and the strangulation of widows had been eradicated, save among a few mountain tribes. And although many motives, economic and strategic among them, had driven the reluctant government to act, the determining factor in its decision, it is clear, had been the desire to protect the native races against exploitation.

§5

Until the coming of Germany and the new imperialism the British government had desired nothing less than to add to British possessions in the Pacific. When partition came it could hardly be expected that a power which had been so long in the Pacific should stand wholly aside; but here, as in Africa, Britain took her share without enthusiasm and with a marked readiness to see the voracious German appetites satisfied. For Britain had sufficient reasons just now for desiring to retain the good-will of Germany, particularly over the delicate question of Egypt, and Bismarck had made it clear that as to Egypt the German attitude was likely to depend upon the degree of consideration shown to her colonial ambitions. In the Pacific German imperialism was not quite so bleakly artificial as in Africa. But the German house of Godefroy, which had been established in the Samoa Islands since 1857, had treated the natives with characteristic arrogance and harshness, and its standing instructions to its agents were said to contain the warning "never assist missionaries either by word or deed. . . . Use your best influence with the natives to obstruct and exclude them." By 1871 New Zealand had begun to petition that Great Britain should annex Samoa, but the government remained adamant. In 1884, with New Zealand still cabling petitions and the King and chiefs of Samoa preparing a spontaneous appeal for annexation to the British Crown, the cabinet assured Germany that it had no intentions whatever of acquiring the island. The exasperated New Zealanders all but took action of their own, and for a while Granville at the Colonial Office was in a fever of anxiety. But soon after this the United States appeared upon the scene, and it was a German and an American squadron, seemingly about to come to blows, which were strewn in fragments on the beach of Apia by the celebrated hurricane of 1889. In 1899 the islands were divided between the United States and Germany; and in return for the withdrawal of Britain, Germany gave up her claims to the Tonga islands to the south, which had petitioned for British protection as early as 1843, and became a Protectorate in 1900.

In Australia the great island of New Guinea off its north-east coast had naturally roused interest and anxiety long before the new imperialism had been heard of in the Pacific. The west of the island clearly belonged to the Dutch, but, although possession had more than once been claimed by British officers, the east equally clearly belonged to no Power. Until the coming of Germany it was the old story. The Queenslanders (for there was as yet no federated Australia) wished the east of the island to be annexed, but not to pay the costs of annexation. In England a New Guinea Colonisation Association proposed to dispatch two hundred men to the island with a view to eventual annexation. But the British government was not interested in annexations, and was determined to incur no expense. And the New Guinea Association horrified Lord Carnavon at the Colonial Office. Why, after all, all this impatience? "The German Government," he confidingly assured Australia, "has . . . very lately intimated that it has no intention of acquiring colonies." Her Majesty's government saw "no reason for hastening a decision on so important a question." The Australian colonies continued to grumble intermittently, and the British Government to see no reason for hastening a decision, until 1883. By that year there had come to be a ring of almost excessive honesty about Germany's protests that she had no designs on New Guinea, and the increasingly suspicious Queenslanders brought themselves at last to offer to pay the expenses of annexation. But even so Gladstone and Derby would not hear of action, and certainly in 1883 there was sufficient trouble brewing in many different quarters of the globe to discourage a government of "Peace, Retrenchment and Reform" from under-taking even a modest adventure in the Antipodes. But the Queens-landers would not be put off, and that April they hoisted the British flag in New Guinea on their own responsibility. Derby at once repudiated the annexation, dispatching a long homily to Australia. Their apprehensions as to Germany, he assured the irritated Queens-landers, were "altogether indefinite and unfounded"; his govern-ment had the strongest reasons for believing that no such step as annexation was contemplated. The outburst of irritation and scepticism in Australia which followed this exhibition of wishful thinking startled Derby into something like conversion, but Gran-ville at the Foreign Office was still concerned to placate Germany rather than Australia, and nothing was done. And in August of the following year, 1884, Germany annexed northern New Guinea and the adjacent islands, henceforth known as the Bismarck Archipelago. The southern coast, all that remained unclaimed, was occupied by Britain in October.

§6

As in Africa, Britain's share of the partition might have been very much greater, but, as in Africa, it was by no means small. And as in Africa the British prologue to the scramble of the new imperialists had been the era of the missionaries. If the Australians had already become a united people there might have been a very different story to tell. For it was much more obviously the interest of Australians than of Britain that the British flag should fly in the Pacific, and if there had been an Australian government to speak and act for a united Australia it would certainly have been more active than the British. But the federation of Australia was yet to come, and in the meanwhile a handful of separate colonies, unused to combined action, could exert little influence over events. Perhaps it was as well, for the colonies were as yet more conscious of the advantages than of the responsibilities of empire.

CHAPTER FOUR

CHAMBERLAIN

§1

By 1895 a conjunction of influences had prepared the way for a new chapter of imperial history. Collectivism was visibly superseding *laissez faire* in domestic policy, and sooner or later the systematic was bound to supersede the haphazard in imperial policy also. Sooner or later, too, the new public consciousness of Empire, stirred by the rivalries loosed in the last decade, and deepened by the speeches of Disraeli, and the writings of Seeley, Dilke and Froude, could not but invade and colour politics. And though, thanks to the manifold lessons learnt during its own long, instinctive expansion overseas, this country would never reproduce the self-conscious and acquisitive artificiality of most of the new Continental imperialisms, it was inevitable that sooner or later it should meet the challenge from Europe with a policy of Empire more self-conscious and deliberate than any it had practised in the past. For the first time, in fact, there would be imperialists in this country, and though the word imperialism has been used in a dozen different senses, and though British imperialism would always be both milder nad mellower than the crude new Continental varieties, the fact remained that it would be imperialism of a kind, and that hostile critics would not find it difficult to associate it with the darker characteristics of its rivals. For good or ill the new forces were ready; only the hand to release them was wanting. And then in 1895 Joseph Chamberlain became Colonial Secretary. Seldom has the man more completely matched the hour.

§2

Chamberlain did not enter the House of Commons till 1876, when he was all but forty, and throughout his political career he remained fundamentally a Birmingham business man. He had first become a successful manufacturer and then, as mayor, he had galvanised and transformed the administration of the city, making Birmingham, it was said, the best governed city in the world, a pattern for municipal progress in Britain and overseas. In factory and mayor's parlour alike he had been the new broom, a reformer with a passion for organisation, and in politics he did not alter—whether as spokesman of Gladstone's Radical left wing, or, after that parting from Gladstone which killed Home Rule, as Liberal-Unionist and Salisbury's most powerful lieutenant. And so as Colonial Secretary in Salisbury's Conservative administration of 1895 he found it natural to see the British Colonies as "undeveloped estates" awaiting "the judicious investment of British money . . . for the benefit of their population and for the benefit of the greater population which is outside." The new Collectivist doctrines demanded system and state authority everywhere, and here surely was the man to systematise imperial policy. It would be easy to see Chamberlain, with the orchid, the eyeglass and the intent, jaunty mien, and with Birmingham and the screw-factory ever in the middle distance, as no more than the hard-headed business man in politics. And perhaps in that somewhat hard, brassy exterior there was something akin to the strain of vulgarity or braggadocio which can be sensed now and again in the new school of British imperialists. But Chamberlain was much more than a highly gifted business-man. To the end he remained a Radical, albeit a John Bull Radical in the tradition not of Cobden but of Cobbett. And behind the alert assurance of his manner was a sensitive nature, liable to self-questioning and black, haunted moods. His courage was as remarkable as his energy; when suffering agonies from gout he would refuse a soft slipper, thrust the affected foot into a hard boot and work through a long day without flinching. He was a Unitarian, and it was the religious issue raised in the Education Bill of 1870 which had first brought him into national politics. He was indeed very much more than a business man, yet he was always a business man, and as Colonial Secretary he set himself at once to organise and develop the "undeveloped estate." His appointment to the Colonial Office, a secondary post as it was then thought, was itself something of a surprise. For until 1854 the Colonial Office had been little more than a subsidiary department of the War Office, and since then as a separate office it had usually been derided, when not forgotten. But Chamberlain had long had his eyes on the Colonial Office and the undeveloped estate. He had studied Seeley, worked with Dilke, and pondered the problems of Egypt and South Africa. He knew that under Salisbury he would have a license which Gladstone would not willingly have allowed a Colonial Secretary. He knew that as Colonial Secretary he would be responsible for ten million square miles and about fifty million human beings. And he knew that, like Birmingham, they badly needed organisation.

"The change at the Colonial Office," said a contemporary observer, "was marvellous; it was a total transformation; the sleeping city awakened by a touch." Symbolically, Chamberlain at once replaced the candles in his Department with electric light. And then he flung himself upon projects for a fast steamship service between Britain and Canada, for a Pacific cable between Canada and Australia, for African railways and improved commercial methods. And in his speeches he began to sound a new note of almost aggressive self-assurance:

We are all prepared to admire the great Englishmen of the past ... but when we come to our own time we doubt, we lose the confidence which I think becomes a great nation such as ours; and yet, if we look even to such comparatively small matters as the expeditions in which Englishmen have recently been engaged, the administrations which Englishmen have recently controlled, I see no reason to doubt that the British spirit still lives. ... A number of young Englishmen, picked up as it were haphazard from the mass of our population, having beforehand no special claims to our confidence and gratitude, have, nevertheless, controlled great affairs, and, with responsibility placed upon their shoulders, have shown a power, a courage, a resolution, and an intelligence which have carried them through extraordinary difficulties. I say that he, indeed, is a craven and poor-spirited creature who despairs of the future of the British race.

It is difficult to say at what moment it was first borne in upon British statesmen that henceforth it would no longer be possible to frame imperial policy without taking public opinion constantly into account; perhaps it was during the storm of popular resentment which beat about Gladstone and his Ministry after the death of Gordon at Khartum in 1885.[1] But it is certain at least that by 1895 the masses, whom as Radical demagogue Chamberlain had once fired with his Unauthorised Campaign, were more than ready to respond to the new note. In 1897 the old Queen's Diamond Jubilee was to be celebrated, and the country moved towards that halcyon summer full of a self-confidence dangerously near to self-satisfaction, and scarcely conscious of the thunder-clouds upon the horizon.

[1] See pp. 404-5.

§3

"I regard many of our colonies as being in the condition of undeveloped estates, . . . estates which never can be developed without imperial assistance." So Chamberlain declared in 1895, when first his instinct for Collectivism, originally directed to municipal and social reform, was diverted to the even wider, and even more neglected, field of Empire. Indeed if he could have had his own way he would have begun on an even more ambitious and systematic scale. For he hit upon the notion of devoting the income from Disraeli's Suez Canal shares,[1] which had now risen to £670,000 a year, as a special fund for loan or investment in the Crown Colonies and dependencies. Why not use the proceeds of that imaginative stroke for so eminently appropriate a purpose, instead of dissipating them among "Miscellaneous Receipts"? Unfortunately the Chancellor of the Exchequer grumbled that this would compel him to raise additional taxation—for Chancellors were still reluctant to raise additional taxation—and this Chancellor, Salisbury thought, was unduly influenced by his civil servants, "the Gladstonian garrison of the Treasury"—and the scheme was timidly abandoned by the cabinet. But though balked of the full system, which would have anticipated the Colonial Development Fund of 1940 by more than forty years, Chamberlain did not fail to launch the development of the neglected estate, a process which henceforth every subsequent Colonial Secretary found himself compelled to continue. In this as in so many other ways his reign at the Colonial Office marks the boundary between two ages. Chamberlain belongs to the era of imperialism, and is commonly labelled an imperialist, but for him, it will be noted, imperialism did not mean acquisition so much as organising, enriching and uniting the vast territories for which we were already responsible.

The West Indies in particular he found in urgent need of assistance. First Emancipation and then, since 1870, the competition of European beet-sugar, which Protectionist Governments supported by export bounties, had all but ruined them. Chamberlain established in the West Indies an Imperial Department of Agriculture which eradicated insect pests, introduced improved canes and developed new crops. He lent cheap money for railway building, and eventually prohibited the import of foreign bounty-supported sugar into Great Britain. By 1911 the West Indies were solvent; system had triumphed. To many another part of the Empire—to

[1] See p. 400.

Malaya, the Sudan and Cyprus—system now brought belated economic development. In West Africa it was obvious that what was most urgently needed was to stay the ravages of disease which had so far made of it the white man's grave. Chamberlain promoted the study of tropical medicine and sanitation, and the foundation, in 1899, of Schools of Tropical Medicine in London and Liverpool. A West African Department of Agriculture began to introduce new methods of agriculture and, even more important, new crops. Harbours were improved and railways were built in Sierra Leone, Lagos and the Gold Coast and, on the other side of Africa, in Uganda. For centuries the tsetse fly had made the use of transport animals impossible; now for the first time the dark interior of Africa was being opened up, and as the railway thrust forward, tribal warfare, slavery and crime began to recede, and chieftains who had started life as admired mass-murderers would end their days as respectable magistrates.

CHAPTER FIVE

EGYPT: GORDON AND BARING

(1875-1885)

§1

Upon Chamberlain, busy planning, as befitted the dawn of a Collectivist age, the orderly development of the vast colonial territories, there soon intruded, as was inevitable, the problems of a world in flux. In North Africa as well as South the past decades had been accumulating trouble. The Turkish Empire had been in dissolution for the best part of a century, and in 1806 its province of Egypt had become independent in all but name, under a military adventurer whose dynasty still rules there. At this time, and for many years afterwards, France was the European power with special interests in Egypt. *Tôt ou tard*, Napoleon had prophesied, *l'Egypte appartiendra à la France*. It was the French who cut the Suez Canal, and opened it in 1869. And it was largely the French investor who financed the misrule of Khedive Said—a corrupt and incompetent oriental tyranny with a European façade. His successor, Khedive Ismail, who enjoyed the special friendship of Napoleon III, raised and squandered even vaster loans. By 1875 Ismail, whose ingenious habit it had long been to pay the interest on his loans out of the principal, found himself compelled to dispose of his last remaining asset, a half-share in the Suez Canal. The French were in two minds, and the British Foreign Secretary, Lord Derby, hesitated, but the Prime Minister, Disraeli, had no doubts. Within a fortnight he had raised the money and acquired the shares.

Britain had thus secured a controlling interest in the waterway which linked her with India and Australia, and through which passed four British ships for every foreign vessel. She had also involved herself, for good or ill, in the fortunes of Egypt. Next year even the versatile Ismail could no longer conceal his bankruptcy, and he was forced to accept two Controllers General of his finances, one British and one French. At the same time a number of European administrators, mainly French and British, were introduced—with the significant distinction that the French officials (like the Italian and Austrian Commissioners of the Debt) were appointed by their own government, whereas Lord Derby, at the Foreign Office, resolutely refused to make any nominations, on the ground that Her Majesty's government declined to interfere in the internal affairs of Egypt. The new functionaries differed from any European with whom Ismail had previously been associated, and notably in one all-important respect—they "were all honest." It was largely no doubt this unfamiliar characteristic which prompted Ismail to intrigue against his new mentors, with the result that in 1879 his nominal overlord, the Sultan of Turkey, was induced to depose him. But soon after the succession of his son Tewfik, a military revolt under Arabi Pasha, followed by riots and murders in the streets of Alexandria, and the flight of the Christian population, made foreign intervention inevitable. Gladstone's government naturally would not hear of an occupation by themselves, and shrank from the notion of a joint Anglo-French intervention, which was proposed by the French. Why not let Turkey, the legitimate suzerain of Egypt, do the occupying? Turkey, it was true, was apparently moribund, but the task, thought Lord Granville, should not be too formidable even for Turkey. And at least Turkish intervention would be preferable to any sort of European interference.

But Turkey was incapable of any sort of effective action, and the dream faded. And when Arabi Pasha persisted, in spite of warnings, in strengthening the fortifications of Alexandria, the British fleet destroyed the defensive works by bombardment from the sea. France had declined to co-operate. French governments were but transitory affairs, and it chanced that M. de Freycinet, the minister of the moment, displayed an exceptional timidity, partly due to reaction against the adventurous policy of his predecessor, Gambetta, and partly to his suspicions as to German designs in Europe. And so Gladstone's of all governments found itself committed, much to its own embarrassment, to single-handed intervention in Egypt. A British army under Lord Wolseley was landed to restore order, and defeated Arabi—or rather Arabi's troops, for their commander judiciously refrained from exercising his command in the field— at Tel-el-Kebir, in September, 1882. Gladstone's declared policy was now to set the hapless Khedive Tewfik on his feet again, and leave the country as expeditiously as possible. When Lord Hartington assured a critical House of Commons that the last British soldier would be quitting Egypt within a few months he was undoubtedly voicing the genuine intentions of the cabinet. But withdrawal was a good deal easier to promise than to effect, for the Egypt of the Khedive was in dissolution, and the interests of several European powers, as well as the safety of the Suez Canal, were at stake. As a first expedient British officials were appointed to reorganise the

Khedive's administration, with Sir Evelyn Baring (afterwards Lord Cromer), the maker of modern Egypt, as British Agent and Consul-General. The corruption and chaos which they found there, and the infinite complexity of the Khedive's financial commitments, made it more obvious than ever that speedy withdrawal was unlikely. But worse was to come. The Arabs in the Egyptian Sudan had risen, under a Mohammedan fanatic, against the corrupt, slave-hunting Pashas who represented the authority of the Khedive. In 1883 the Khedive and his advisers decided to send an Egyptian army under a British officer, Colonel Hicks, to reconquer the Sudan. The Egyptian troops, the mutinous relics of Arabi's disbanded forces, were grotesquely unfit for so formidable a task, and the British government should either have forbidden the undertaking altogether, or assumed responsibility for it. It was an uncongenial dilemma for Gladstone, and with that strange streak of short-sighted casuistry on which he was always apt to fall back in moments of embarrassment, he persuaded himself that he could wash his hands of the whole affair, arguing that the Sudan, though "politically connected with Egypt . . . has not been included within the sphere of our operations, and we are by no means disposed to admit without qualification that it is within the sphere of our responsibilities." The cabinet accordingly refused to commit itself "by giving advice for or against the advance of Hicks" and, as Lord Morley ingenuously puts it, "stood aloof."

To stand aloof however was the one course which was no longer possible for a British government, and when Hicks and his ill-fated expedition had been surrounded and annihilated in the desert the cabinet could no longer avoid coming to some decision. A few ministers wished to withdraw from Egypt, and all its perplexities, altogether and at once. Some were ready to take the field against the Mahdi with British troops. The majority preferred a compromise. They were reluctant to use a British army, and the Egyptian army was manifestly not fit to be used. They would accordingly withdraw the remaining Egyptian garrisons from the Sudan, and instruct Sir Evelyn Baring to see that the foolish old Pashas at the head of the Khedive's government kept Egypt henceforth strictly upon the defensive. But who was to undertake the dangerous and delicate task of extricating the Egyptian garrisons? In a moment of infatuation they selected General Gordon—infatuation, for although Gordon knew the Sudan and there and elsewhere had triumphed almost miraculously over difficulties even more formidable than those which would now confront him, he was liable to violent and unpredictable vagaries, and he thoroughly disapproved of the policy of complete withdrawal.

§2

It was characteristic of the Empire that at this juncture it should have committed the destinies of Egypt to two such strangely dissimilar men; in Cairo Sir Evelyn Baring, cool, clear-sighted, calculating, patiently creating a nation; in the Sudan the unpredictable genius of an erratic soldier-saint. And behind them both Gladstone, by turns as coolly calculating as Baring, and as erratic and other-worldly as Gordon. As for Gordon, he was now fifty-one, a man of profound and unconventional religious convictions and a lifelong student of the Bible, who believed that in Holy Writ he could discover all the necessary guidance as to the smallest particulars of his daily conduct. At the age of thirty he had been entrusted by the Chinese government with the colossal task of crushing the Taiping rebellion, and with a mutinous army of three thousand, recruited from the riff-raff of Shanghai, he had gradually subdued the rebels in a series of brilliant manœuvres over the vast plain of the Yangtse delta. His daring and unconventional generalship was scarcely more remarkable than the extraordinary personal ascendancy which he contrived to establish over the miscellaneous ruffians of his army, and the superstitious awe with which the rebels soon regarded the calm Englishman, who walked smiling into action at the head of his troops with nothing but a light cane in his hand. His great achievements in China were virtually unrecognised by the British authorities, and when he returned home—after characteristically refusing an enormous gift of money offered by the Chinese government—he was set for six years to supervising the erection of forts at the mouth of the Thames. Here he lived with great simplicity, spending most of his income on his poverty-stricken neighbours, among whom he had a wide circle of friends. When short of money for a deserving charity he even gave away, after effacing its inscription, the large gold medal which had been the one reward which he had accepted from the Chinese Government. A few years later Ismail's minister invited him to become Governor of the Equatorial Provinces of the Sudan. "Events will go as God likes," reflected the fatalistic Gordon, and while the Khedive scattered his borrowed millions among the ballet dancers and chorus girls of Paris, the strange Englishman with the brick-red complexion, the childishly innocent blue eyes and the steadily accumulating pile of manuscript annotations on the Bible, was building roads, suppressing insurrections and erecting forts in his remote and pestilential province. Characteristically, he had reduced his own salary from ten thousand to two thousand pounds a year. A few hundred Egyptian soldiers were his only military backing, and on one occasion, when a revolt had flared up in an outlying province, Gordon rode eighty-five miles alone in the blazing desert heat to the enemy's camp, and ordered the rebels to disarm and disband. And, awed by his imperious mien, the whole host actually obeyed.

When the Khedive Ismail was deposed, Gordon felt at liberty to resign. But adventures followed in Abyssinia and China, in Mauritius and South Africa—"I am prepared," wrote the fatalist, "to follow the unfolding of the scroll"—and then came the summons from Gladstone's cabinet. Those irresolute ministers had indeed made a surprising choice. Gordon, it is true, had been Governor-General of the Sudan during his last years in Ismail's service, and he was undoubtedly a man of astonishing gifts, whose simple, elemental character could achieve a strange ascendancy over savage races. But he was now to return to the scene of his former triumphs as the emissary of a defeated power and, though a natural fighter, he was to conduct an embarrassing retreat, whose whole object would be to secure the triumph of the very forces he had spent so long in beating down. Worst of all, he, the most independent and individual of emissaries, who had always acted for himself and by himself, would be required to carry out unquestioningly an ambiguous policy dictated from Downing Street and deeply repugnant to his own deepest instincts. The choice of Gordon is indeed so surprising that it has even been suggested[1] that it was due to a deep laid plot among certain ministers, who were anxious to annex the Sudan and confidently counted on Gordon's going beyond his instructions and involving himself in difficulties from which he would have eventually to be rescued. It is more likely that the decision was but one more compromise between the members of an irresolute and deeply divided cabinet. And certainly if any ministers were counting on the Government's intervening to rescue Gordon they reckoned without the hesitation of their colleagues in general and the obstinacy of Mr. Gladstone in particular.

For the inevitable duly came to pass. Gordon was cut off in Khartum. For weeks, for months he waited there, penning his characteristic journals, full of badinage of Lord Granville, appeals to Isaiah and reflections on the purposes of the Almighty and the future of the Sudan. By the end of March, 1884, the British public had taken alarm. There were mass meetings, leading articles, a relief fund. But the weeks went by, and still the government did not act. Partly it was the usual division of opinion, one leading

---

[1] Cf. e.g. Lytton-Strachey, *Eminent Victorians*, "The End of General Gordon."

minister threatening resignation if there were no expedition in the
autumn, another if there were. At a cabinet meeting on April 7,
six ministers were for an expedition, six, including the Prime
Minister, against it. But the true obstacle was Gladstone himself.
For that extraordinary genius, who already had a plausible case for
procrastination (had not Gordon, whom he himself had never seen,
been originally sent merely to report, had he not grossly exceeded
his instructions, would not an expedition mean war and conquest
on the grand scale?) was busy reinforcing it with all the casuistry
which on such occasions invariably came to his assistance. Gordon
might be hemmed in, but he was not surrounded. He could still
escape if he pleased. He was trying to force the government's hand;
the Mahdi and his Arabs were a people rightly struggling to be free.
In the end it came to something like a personal struggle between
Gladstone and Lord Hartington, and though Hartington was
formidable as the leader of the Whig aristocracy, and though he was
inflexible once his conscience had been roused, he was very slow. It
was not till August 26 that Lord Wolseley was appointed to the
command of the relief expedition. It was not till January 28, 1885,
that it had struggled to within sight of Khartum. It was two days
too late. The Egyptian flag had disappeared, and Gordon had
perished. The indignation in Britain was bitter and lasting, for the
public had taken Gordon, his oddities and his Bible to its heart. The
Queen sent Gladstone an angry telegram, undisguised by the usual
cypher, blaming him personally for the tragedy. Undoubtedly, as so
often before, she was voicing public opinion. For once Gladstone
had misjudged and misunderstood the feelings of the masses. He
was an old man, and it was no longer easy for him to sympathise
with new tendencies. And as he had failed to understand or keep
pace with the Collectivist trend in domestic politics, so he had underrated the growth of imperial sentiment. But as to the Sudan he was
still immovable. He would listen to no pleas for its reconquest.
That year the British expedition withdrew, and the Sudan was left
to the Mahdi. Nevertheless Sir Evelyn Baring was still at work in
Cairo, patiently creating a new Egypt.

CHAPTER SIX

FASHODA

(1885-1899)

§1

SUCH were the origins of the problem which was to confront Chamberlain within a year of becoming Colonial Secretary. Since the withdrawal from the Sudan there had intervened ten years of patiently creative work in Egypt under Baring. A hundred difficulties hampered him. Egypt was not a British possession; at home the British government seemed frequently to be simultaneously pursuing the contradictory policies of reform and evacuation; and in Egypt Baring had not only to govern but to recreate the country "without the appearance of doing so and without any legitimate authority over the agents with whom I had to deal." The Egyptians themselves ranged from Mohammedan sages whose spiritual home was in the seventh century to smart young pseudo-Europeans whose notions of Europe were drawn from the underworld of Paris. And they did not take readily to British methods. "The tendency of every Egyptian official," wrote Baring, "is to shirk responsibility. He thinks less of what should be done than of acting in such a manner that no personal blame can be attached to himself." And consequently he found little comfort in the British preference for a minimum of regulations and the greatest possible scope for personal judgment and initiative. "He flies for refuge to the French system, and there he finds . . . that provision is apparently made for everything, to the most minute detail, in a series of elaborate codes."

The French moreover were alertly jealous and resentful. For though British statesmen repeatedly declared that they intended to withdraw from Egypt, there was little sign of their doing so. To have withdrawn now indeed would have seemed to deprive Britain of every justification for the original intervention. For what had the British come to Egypt if not to transform it from an oriental tyranny, in which corruption and incompetence were universal, into a civilised and efficient modern state? And such a transformation, as they had long since learned, was not to be effected by a paper constitution or the sudden stroke of a pen. It could only be brought

406

about in Baring's way—by a patient grapple with detail, and by the personal influence and example of British administrators. For gradually a new spirit was being instilled, not only into the administration but into the people. Slavery and the corvée disappeared, justice was no longer to be bought, the rule of law was established and Pashas learnt that even peasants have their rights. Hospitals and schools began to appear, taxation was lightened and the tyranny of the usurer ended. The army acquired a new confidence and self-respect. The men who slowly wrought these great changes probably expected, and would certainly receive, little gratitude from the country which they were creating. For a backward people has a short memory, and soon a new generation—knowing little of what their fathers had suffered when the Khedives and their Pashas ruled unchecked—would take the new way of life for granted, and revile those who gave it them as intruders unwarrantably stifling the political genius of the Egyptian people.

In Egypt, as in India, the British found no difficulty in establishing the best of personal relations with the simple and unpolitical masses; but when it came to the vocal and intelligent minority some defect, or quality, in their make-up, perhaps their very inability to conceal their own opinions, was apt to induce a somewhat resentful inferiority complex in those with whom they had to deal. No one who wishes to form some conception either of the magnitude of the British achievement in Egypt, or of the minor flaws in it, can do better than study Lord Cromer's *Modern Egypt.* Let him duly wonder at the prodigious difficulties and the prodigious achievements, at the admirable temper, the courage and the lucid common sense displayed throughout the long adventure. And then let him note how, after disclaiming all intention of criticising the Egyptians, Lord Cromer concludes one of his chapters with

> Rather let us, in Christian charity, make every possible allowance for the moral and intellectual shortcomings of the Egyptians, and do whatever can be done to rectify them.

It is not difficult to understand how some Egyptians might grow restive under the calm, firm, consciously beneficent tuition.

§2

Meanwhile the Sudan, evacuated after Gordon's death, remained remote from British influence. The contrast of its fortunes is a remarkable testimony to the work of Baring and his associates in Egypt. For, though Mr. Gladstone, in a moment of ebullient idealism, had spoken of the Mahdi and his conquering Dervishes as "a people rightly struggling to be free," Dervish rule was, in fact, a cruel and barbaric tyranny. Sir Reginald Wingate estimated that under the Mahdi and his successor, the Khalifa, six and three-quarter millions of the eight and a half million inhabitants of the Sudan perished of war, massacre, famine or disease. In one district, which had contained eight hundred villages in 1882, not a single village remained twenty years later. By 1896 Chamberlain, and the Conservative cabinet, were considering a return to the Sudan. The memory of Gordon was still a living influence with them, and with the public. System, too, beckoned Chamberlain onwards. For the regenerated Egypt was ripe for further development, and the prosperity of Egypt depended upon the waters of the Nile—whose upper reaches were in the Sudan. A French expedition moreover was known to be moving east across Africa towards the upper waters of the Nile. The case for action seemed persuasive. And then early that year an Italian army was overwhelmed by Abyssinians at Adowa, the dervishes besieged an Italian garrison on the southern outskirts of the Sudan, and the government in Rome besought Salisbury's cabinet to see that the Egyptian army created a diversion in the Sudan. Chamberlain was for embarking at once upon a slow, circumspect reconquest by stages, and the cabinet concurred. John Morley and the Liberals prophesied another disaster, but Salisbury and Chamberlain were confident. For Sir Herbert Kitchener should command the expedition, and Kitchener would move no faster than he could build his railway into the desert. And he would take the new machine-guns with him.

Kitchener set forth in 1896. All through the Jubilee year of 1897, while the crowds cheered at home, he was moving silently and relentlessly, with his railway, across the desert. On September 2, 1898, he destroyed the Mahdist army at Omdurman, and two days later the British and Egyptian flags were hoisted over the palace at Khartum in which Gordon had perished. Three days after this, word reached Kitchener that a small force commanded by a white man was at Fashoda, some hundreds of miles further up the Nile. This must be the French expedition under Colonel Marchand. Three days later, the news was published in London and Paris, and France and Britain were on the brink of war. As for Kitchener, with massive common sense he proceeded southward to Fashoda—where his timely arrival saved Marchand and his scanty following from destruction by the dervishes—planted the British and Egyptian flags, with all due courtesy, beside Marchand's tricolour, and waited patiently for the politicians to argue it out.

§3

The Fashoda incident was the culmination of prolonged Anglo-French rivalry. The French design had been to establish a continuous belt of French territory, not only from the Mediterranean south to the Congo, but also from west to east, from the Atlantic to the Red Sea. Already they had been busy seizing the Upper Niger, although the British chartered company was established in its delta. They had not only invaded areas regarded by the British as their own by right of prior treaty with native chiefs, but even territory actually occupied by them. To arrest this constant and ubiquitous infiltration Chamberlain had organised the West African Frontier Force of native troops under Colonel Lugard, and for a while at point after point Union Jack and tricolour had flown provocatively within sight of each other, and it was only by the mercy of Providence, it seemed, that the guns did not go off. At last, after nine months during which the issue of war or peace hung upon a thread, a comprehensive West African settlement was concluded in June, 1898. It was due primarily to the West African Frontier Force and Chamberlain's firmness. And for Chamberlain the task of resisting French incursions had often been scarcely more laborious than that of persuading Salisbury that they ought to be resisted. For it was Chamberlain, the Birmingham business man, who represented the imperialism of the industrial age, while Salisbury was an aristocrat and a scholar who shrank instinctively from driving a hard bargain, and had little more taste for acquisition than had his early Victorian predecessors. The arrangement was satisfactory to both parties. The French ensured the unification of an immense African dominion, stretching for nearly three thousand miles southward from Algiers to the Congo, and for almost as far westward from the Atlantic to the borders of the Anglo-Egyptian Sudan. Britain secured the greater part of the territory disputed during the last two years, and all the main objects for which Chamberlain had contended.

And now three months after the settlement had come Fashoda. After the Niger, the Nile. It was the same policy, of presenting the British Government with a *fait accompli*. The gallant Major Marchand had been dispatched in June, 1896. He had travelled three thousand miles from the Congo to the White Nile, and taken three years over the journey—which hardly bore out the implied French thesis that the Sudan was a hinterland of their own West Africa. With his eight French officers and his hundred and twenty Senegalese he was to stake a claim on the upper waters of the Nile, and so link French West Africa, through a friendly Abyssinia, with the French territory on the Red Sea, and ensure a continuous belt of French possessions from west coast to east. As early as 1894 Lugard had warned Chamberlain of what was likely to come. And in 1895 Sir Edward Grey, on behalf of a Liberal Government, had gone so far as to remind France that the appearance of a French expedition on the upper Nile would be regarded as "an unfriendly act." And now that the unfriendly act had come it reverberated round the world. For Marchand represented a claim not only on the Sudan and the life-sources of Egypt, but for a continuous right of way, along the course of his journey, from the Congo to the Nile.

All through the winter of 1898 the tension remained critical, with French statesmen clinging to the belief that Salisbury would prove more accommodating than Chamberlain, and that he might yet gain the upper hand. But such hopes were illusory. British opinion was unanimous for a refusal to submit to the French incursion, even if a refusal meant war. The Liberal leader, Lord Rosebery, warned the world that Britain was prepared to maintain her rights, and Grey and Campbell-Bannerman were equally out-spoken. As for the Conservative Cabinet, with such support it refused to yield an inch. In mid-February, 1899, M. Delcassé gave way, and the French withdrew. For the first time in its history an era of peace and growing prosperity was in store for the Sudan. The scramble for Africa was over. And still Sir Evelyn Baring was patiently creating a new Egypt.

CHAPTER SEVEN

RHODES

(1871-1902)

§1

SOUTH AFRICA, however, was to occasion a far more searching test of Chamberlain and his system than either Egypt or the Sudan. In July of 1895 he received a short letter written in a large and sprawling hand. It plunged with little ceremony to its purpose:

> I am anxious to take over the Bechuanaland Protectorate at once, and if you give it me I promise to build the Railway from Mafeking to Buluwayo in four years. . . . I hope to hear on Saturday that I can bring in Bill to annex British Bechuanaland to Cape. You will find if you look at correspondence that Protectorate is promised to Charter, it is merely question when you will hand over.

With which the letter ended abruptly, "Yours truly C. J. Rhodes." British Bechuanaland, and the Bechuanaland Protectorate, the two areas which the writer was so bluntly demanding, amounted together to some three hundred and twenty-five thousand square miles, and Chamberlain took some time, a good deal longer than Rhodes liked, to think the matter over. He could hardly help fearing that South Africa was on the verge of an explosion, and may have suspected that Rhodes would fire the train. For it was all but a quarter of a century now since the birth of the new imperialism and, even more pregnant for South Africa, it was all but a quarter of a century since (in 1871) diamonds were discovered at Kimberley.

§2

Between the departure of Sir George Grey and the finding of the diamonds change had remained gradual in a predominantly pastoral country. The Cape had moved slowly and, to a surprising degree, reluctantly, towards responsible government. Natal, now detached from the Cape, with a Lieutenant-Governor of its own, was attracting a considerable influx of settlers from Britain. And in the now independent Transvaal the Boers still showed few signs of achieving any sort of political equilibrium. Their pastoral and nomadic tradition had bred in them few civic instincts, and even without an influx of ambiguous adventurers, lured by early rumours of mineral wealth, their domestic problems were almost too much for them. There were native wars and civil strife, and at one time no less than four disorderly Republics were competing for a precarious existence on the Transvaal territory. And in Britain the Boers' treatment of their native neighbours remained deeply suspect.

It was in 1871 that the flat, parched land between the Vaal and the Modder was found to be rich in diamonds. The diamond lands were promptly claimed both by the Orange Free State and by the Transvaal, which had lately failed to float a loan of three hundred pounds. Also more plausibly by the Griquas, who had made a treaty with the British government as far back as 1834, and now asked for a British Protectorate and offered to cede the disputed territory. The Governor of Natal, called in as arbitrator, disallowed the Transvaal claim. The richest fields were awarded to the Griquas, whose chief surrendered his sovereignty to the British crown— Griqualand West becoming a Crown Colony, and, later, a part of Cape Colony. On paper there was a strong case for the award to the Griquas, and indeed for the subsequent annexation, but when diamonds are at stake, and go to the strongest claimant, the proceedings are bound to wear an ambiguous complexion. Not the least important consequence of these transactions, however, was the setting of a limit to the westward expansion of the Boers, so that space was left for the British to move north.

South Africa might now seem to be standing on the threshold of a new age, but in the 'seventies its diminutive white populations were more apprehensive than hopeful. Within their own frontiers the black races outnumbered them by twenty to one, and beyond them lay great tracts inhabited by warlike and independent savages. With native wars, minor and sporadic, the colonists were familiar enough; but what if there should one day be a general, a concerted, native rising? For in the 'seventies the relative advantages of the white man in warfare were less than they had been for centuries past, or have been since. For it was no longer now a question of spears against muskets. The blacks by now possessed plenty of muzzle-loading firearms, and the whites had by no means all yet taken to the breech-loader. A couple of decades, and the balance would be tilted back again by the machine-gun. But for the moment the outlook seemed ominous, and to many it appeared that one of the most dangerous elements in it was the startling dissimilarity in the treatment of the native races by the four white communities. For in the two Boer states the Kaffirs were a subject people living under primitive tribal organisation, virtually outside the law, while in Natal there were Bantu reserves, within which nevertheless the tribal system was already breaking down. Only in Cape Colony, where the blacks were theoretically at least the equals of the whites, eligible for the vote and subject to European law, had the tribal pattern been obliterated. But if a uniform native policy seemed imperative, how could there be a uniform policy without federation? Considerations such as these, together with the example set by Canada in 1867, persuaded Lord Carnarvon, as Colonial Secretary in 1874, that the time had come to create a Dominion of South Africa. Support for such a project was not lacking in South Africa itself, even in the Boer states, but federation is a task for political giants, and Carnarvon, conscientious rather than clear-headed, always prone to irresolution, and known among his colleagues as "Twitters," was very far from a giant. A Conference in 1876 achieved nothing, partly because Carnarvon had injudiciously transferred its venue to England. But the Transvaal was in a state of crisis, bankrupt and anarchic, yet constantly assaulting its native neighbours, and now threatened by the chief Sekukuni on one frontier and by massed Zulus on the other.

And here Carnarvon thought that he saw his opportunity. At the end of 1876 he drafted a permissive Bill, authorising in advance a federation of South Africa, and dispatched a Commissioner to investigate the troubles of the Transvaal, and annex it, if annexation appeared, as he confidently believed that it would, to be what the burghers desired. The Commissioner, Sir Theophilus Shepstone, found it difficult to discover what was in the minds of the burghers, but he knew very well what was in Carnarvon's, and after long and indecisive discussions he proclaimed annexation. No force was used —Shepstone indeed had no troops—and there was no resistance; indeed if annexation had been speedily followed by responsible government and generous economic treatment, all might have been well. Denied these consolations however, the Dutch in the Transvaal and elsewhere were alienated, and though Carnarvon remained obstinately optimistic, and sent Sir Bartle Frere as High Commissioner to carry through federation, it became obvious to almost every one else that the prospects of federation had receded into the remote distance. Disraeli by now had quite lost confidence in his Colonial Secretary; "every day," he wrote irritably to Lady Bradford, "brings forward a new blunder of Twitters. The man he swore by was Sir T. Shepstone. . . . We sent him out entirely for Twitters's sake, and he has managed to quarrel with Eng., Dutch, and Zulus; and now he is obliged to be recalled, but not before he has brought on, I fear, a new war." The new war was with the Zulus. Conscious that trouble was brewing in India, the cabinet repeatedly urged caution, "a spirit of forbearance and a strictly defensive policy," but to Frere it seemed that all white South Africa was threatened by Cetewayo and his Zulus, lusting to "wash their spears," preferably in the blood of their hereditary foes, the Boers, but, if even the Boers were now to be protected by the British peace, then at least by an onslaught at some point on the ring of white men which seemed to be closing in on them.

War, to the secret consternation of the cabinet, began in January, 1879, and like all British wars, it began disastrously—with the slaughter of a column surrounded in its camp at Isandhlwana. And though the campaign was successfully finished off by July, and Zululand thereafter turned into a Protectorate, public opinion at home had been profoundly disturbed, and the general impression that Disraeli had been dangerously adventurous was largely responsible for his defeat at the election next year. During the election campaign Gladstone made several caustic references to the annexation of the Transvaal, "by means dishonourable to the character of the country." If he had not been carried away at the moment by the fervours of his Midlothian tour he might perhaps have recollected that on the strength of such words President Kruger might reasonably expect him, when Prime Minister himself, to reverse the policy which he had condemned. On succeeding Disraeli, however, he refused, despite a confident appeal from the Transvaal, to do anything of the kind—largely, no doubt, because Exeter Hall was convinced that, left to themselves, the Boers would always treat the natives with injustice and cruelty. And not only did Gladstone's government refuse to restore independence to the Transvaal Dutch; it promised them "the fullest liberty" to manage their own affairs, and then, despite repeated pressure from Bartle Frere, failed completely to honour the pledge. Finally, it recalled Frere himself—unpopular as the symbol of a forward policy, yet the one man who might have held the four South African communities together. Gladstone and his colleagues had thus done almost everything possible to provoke the Boer rising which duly followed in December, 1880.

As usual, the British were completely unprepared for war, and as usual war opened with disasters. So far all was proceeding according to the customary pattern; but this time there was a startling variation. The familiar defeats had been sustained, but the equally familiar muddling through to victory did not follow. After the disaster of Majuba Hill, and while the reinforcements necessary for a serious war were on their way to the Cape, the Liberal government decided to make peace. It was a difficult and, on the whole, a courageous decision. Negotiations had opened before Majuba. Were we, Gladstone demanded, to say to the Boers, "Although we might have treated with you before these military miscarriages, we cannot do so now, until we offer up a certain number of victims in expiation of the blood that has been shed"? It would have been even more pertinent to ask how Gladstone's government, within a few months of an election won largely on the plea that Disraelian Conservatism was dangerously aggressive, could launch major operations to conquer the Transvaal, and hold it down by force. The truth was that Gladstone had made his crucial mistakes before the fighting began; there was no escaping the dilemma now; no answer to the taunt of his opponents that he had conceded to three defeats what he had refused to a score of peaceful petitions. But at least the government's proceedings, whether evidence, as Lord Morley believed, of exceptional moral courage, or, as its critics maintained, of unusual political cowardice, were certainly not characteristic of the new aggressive imperialism. The Pretoria Convention of 1881 gave the Transvaal what Lord Morley calls "quasi-independence, subject to the suzerainty of the Queen." Three years later, however, it was accorded the style of "South African Republic."

It was with a new confidence that the Boers now invaded the territories of their native neighbours. In the east their claims rose eventually to some three-quarters of all Zululand, so that Britain first intervened to reduce them, and then, to forestall further aggressions, annexed what was left of Zulu territory in 1887. On the west there were Boer incursions into Bechuanaland, and an appeal to Britain from the natives. The intruders were turned back and a British Protectorate was proclaimed over all Bechuanaland, while a smaller southern portion of it was declared a Crown Colony in 1885. British Bechuanaland was thus the Crown Colony which, in 1895, Rhodes proposed, in his abrupt letter to Chamberlain, to annex to the Cape; through it the railway ran already as far as Mafeking. And Bechuanaland was the Protectorate which he was "anxious to take over at once"; through it the railway must pass on its way from Mafeking to Rhodesia. Rhodes had spoken in 1895 in a twofold capacity. It was as head of the Chartered Company that he proposed to take over the Protectorate, and as Prime Minister of the Cape that he was about to annex the Colony.

§3

Cecil Rhodes, son of the Vicar of Bishop's Stortford in Hertford-shire, left England for South Africa at the age of seventeen, in 1870, because his health had broken down, or, as he sometimes preferred to put it, because he " could no longer stand the eternal cold mutton." And soon the tall, fair, blue-eyed boy with the aquiline, somewhat predatory, profile was to be seen industriously sorting diamonds at Kimberley. At nineteen he was a man of means, and surprisingly enough he betook himself to Oxford and proceeded intermittently over a period of eight years to combine the rôles of undergraduate and diamond magnate—the exquisite, sheltered life among the old grey palaces of Oxford and the raw jostle of the jetsam of thirty nations amid the dust and the corrugated iron of Kimberley. For he was already possessed by his overmastering idea. It had probably been born in him during a solitary eight months' ox-waggon journey through Bechuanaland and the Transvaal, a journey during which the high veld, and the veld nights, had entered into his blood. And at Oxford there had been not only lectures on Aristotle but lectures by Ruskin; and Ruskin, who had long been the dominant authority on Art and Socialism, had recently had his attention drawn to the Empire, so that at Oxford he spoke of:

a destiny now possible to us, the highest ever set before a nation to be accepted or refused. Will you youths of England make your Country again a royal throne of Kings, a sceptred isle, for all the world a source of light, a centre of peace . . .? This is what England must do or perish. She must found colonies as fast as and as far as she is able, formed of the most energetic and worthiest of men; seizing any piece of fruitful waste ground she can set her foot on, and there teaching her colonists that their chief virtue is to be fidelity to their country, and that their first aim is to be to advance the power of England by land and sea.

However unlooked for from the author of *Modern Painters* and *Unto this Last*, such exhortations as these, together with Rhodes's reading, his Oxford conversations (for unlike the strong man of tradition he was far from silent) and his solitary self-questionings, all served to illumine and endorse, and also to deepen and extend, the purpose which had already taken possession of him. Rhodes's purpose, like Rhodes himself, and like all compelling ideas, was profoundly simple—to extend the influence of the English-speaking race as widely as possible. It had all begun with that long, solitary trek across the veld. He had then resolved that it was his task, working with the Dutch settlers, and with the assent of the Cape Dutch, to federate South Africa under British rule.

Africa, not Oxford, had given him his life's inspiration; but at Oxford he had worked out, with something like the directness and the naïveté of a child, a simple philosophic foundation for his gigantic aims. Winwood Reade's *Martyrdom of Man* and Darwin's theories of evolution were the principal elements in this strange private creed. Assuming the existence of a God, God, he argued, must wish man to serve His purpose. And this purpose, it appeared, was to perfect humanity through natural selection, for ever eliminating the unfit, and giving new power to the fit. And who were fittest to survive? The answer of history, it seemed to Rhodes, was unmistakable. The English-speaking peoples, the peoples of Great Britain, her colonies and of the United States, had come nearest to achieving justice, liberty and peace. The highest duty of man therefore must be to promote the unity, and extend the influence, of the Anglo-Saxon race. Such was the simple creed evolved between Oxford and Kimberley, so characteristic not only of its author, but of its age. And yet not only perhaps of its age; for beneath the echoes of Darwinism and imperialism it is not difficult to detect an older and less strident influence, that of the Hertfordshire parsonage. From Kimberley during the long vacation of 1877 Rhodes could write:

I contend that we are the first race in the world, and that the more of the world we inhabit, the better it is for the human race. I contend that every acre added to our territory provides for the birth of more of the English race who otherwise would not be brought into existence. Added to which the absorption of the greater portion of the world under our rule simply means the end of all wars.

He will work accordingly " for the furtherance of the British Empire, for the bringing of the whole civilised world under British rule, for the recovery of the United States, for the making of the Anglo-Saxon race into one Empire." And that same year he drew up the first and most extraordinary of the six wills which he was to frame at intervals throughout the rest of his life. In this document the young man of twenty-four leaves the fortune which he has not yet acquired to establish a secret society whose aim shall be no less than to make Britain omnipotent by colonising the greater part of the globe. The later wills, up to that last version, of 1899, which creates the famous scholarships, would grow steadily more practical, but through them all runs the same relentless purpose. For Rhodes himself had become an embodied idea; indeed it was in the strength of that idea that the dreamy young man with the weak heart and the tendency to tuberculosis became almost at once the dominant personal force in South Africa. For where others desired wealth or power for themselves, Rhodes set himself to become rich and powerful solely "for the furtherance of the British Empire." "You have to give in to him," said Barney Barnato, the Whitechapel Jew whom Rhodes ousted from control of the diamond fields.

His ascent was very swift. When he graduated at Oxford in 1881 he had already floated the de Beers Mining Company and been elected to the Cape Parliament. By the time that he was thirty-five he had amalgamated all the Kimberley diamond mines, ninety per cent of the world's output, under his own control. He might have established the same sort of predominance on the Rand goldfields, discovered in the Transvaal in 1886, but, as he told his agent, "I cannot calculate the power in these claims"—and it was characteristic of Rhodes to say "power," and not "wealth." Moreover, for once he allowed his affections to obstruct his affairs. When the crucial option awaited his signature at Johannesburg, word reached him that an intimate friend was dying at Kimberley, and Rhodes hastened away. To his frantic agent's telegrams he returned no answers, the option lapsed, and a few months later the young clerk to whom he had hurried back died in his arms. Nevertheless in Johannesburg too Rhodes had acquired important interests, and soon from diamonds and gold his annual income was at least a million pounds a year. He had armed himself with the personal power necessary for the pursuit of his vast impersonal ends.

§4

His first and most urgent task was to keep open the path, Livingstone's path, to the North—"my North" Rhodes would soon call it. "I look upon this Bechuanaland territory," he told the Cape Parliament, "as the Suez Canal of the trade of this country, the key of its road to the interior." Now as then the Boers were the obstacle. The Boers, and, in a sense, the Parliament at Westminster. "We want to get rid of the Imperial factor in this question," said Rhodes, "and to deal with it ourselves, jointly with the Transvaal." The observation at first sight is surprising, and it puzzled and irritated Chamberlain, but Rhodes (who subscribed to the funds of the Irish Party) always believed that "the key of the Federal System" was "perfect Home Rule in every part of the Empire"; and he was only too familiar with the reluctance of the Colonial Office, not yet galvanised into new life by Chamberlain, to venture on even the most cautious advance. "We want to get rid of the imperial factor"—it was Rhodes's prescient version of the Dominion status which was to be. And soon he would be dreaming of linking the Cape not with the interior only, but with Egypt.

As the Cape leads north to Bechuanaland, so Bechuanaland leads north to the country of the Matabele and the Mashona. And as soon as Bechuanaland, thanks largely to his energies, was secure, and Boer claims had been withdrawn, Rhodes looked beyond it to the country which had fired his imagination from the first, the country of close on half a million square miles, healthy, fertile, rich, he believed, in minerals, and magnificently suitable for European settlement, which was ruled over by Lobengula, *he that drives like the wind*, son of Moselikatze, *the pathway of blood*. In Lobengula was to be re-enacted the tragedy of Tipu Sahib, and many another chieftain of backward races who stood in the path of oncoming civilisation. Lobengula was a Zulu; his father had been chief of the armies of the terrible Chaka, and, becoming too powerful and too popular, had been forced to flee. With his followers he had crossed the Drakensberg and been defeated in Basutoland, where they earned their new name of Matabele, *the people with the long shields*. They had turned north, killing as they went, so that in ten years not a Hottentot or a Bushman was left in the country they traversed, killing Griquas, killing, and being killed by, Boers. They encountered and fought other Zulus, and moved north again into the country of the Bechuana and conquered them. They were attacked by the Boers and made north once more, and at last settled down between the Limpopo and the Zambesi, "eating up" its feebler occupants the Mashona, whose survivors they had not ceased to harry and destroy. Their principal settlement they had named, appropriately enough, Gebuluwayo, *the place of killing*. Such were the Matabele, with their captured slaves, their military organisation, their witch doctors and witchcraft executions, and their story will serve for that of a score of other African tribes; noble savages in their way, but savages; a pattern of society with small prospect of survival in a swiftly changing world, and little title to its lands save that of conquest. What rights of ownership has an uncivilised people against oncoming civilisation—a civilisation of machine-guns and gold-prospectors, it is true, but also, if we are to be fair, of the Bible, the school, the hospital and the railway?

He would be a bold man who gave a confident answer. It is less difficult to pass judgment on the methods of the intruders. Rhodes was an urgent man, always conscious of a race against time; for the powers were scrambling for Africa; Portuguese, Germans and even Boers were all, in one way or another, active in the neighbourhood. And Rhodes was always conscious that he had not long to live. His emissaries obtained from Lobengula a concession, a concession which Lobengula certainly did not fully understand, and soon regretted, and Rhodes thereupon formed the British South Africa Company to exploit it. It was a revival of a time-honoured method—the association of merchant adventurers ready to go where the government would not venture. Then Rhodes moved swiftly. In June of next year, 1890, a hundred and seventy-nine pioneers and some hundreds of police set off from Bechuanaland with Selous, the hunter, as guide, and natives to cut their road before them as they travelled. Meanwhile Dr. Jameson, old friend of Rhodes, a chivalrous, nonchalant, courageous and highly capable Scot, with a cool head and a taste for gambling, sat in Lobengula's kraal, engaged in the delicate task of pacifying the bewildered and irritated savage. There was no fighting. The pioneers let the Matabele be, made for the country of the Mashona, and founded Salisbury, and next spring, without drugs, food or doctors, were deluged by the heaviest rains within memory. Rhodes meanwhile had become Prime Minister of the Cape, for he believed that the future of South Africa lay with that Colony—"I have undertaken that northern development as a Cape Colonist." He made Jameson administrator of Mashonaland, and Jameson reduced the Company's expenditure there from twenty thousand pounds a month to three thousand, and the police from seven hundred to forty. The new Colony was saved—"Zambesia," Rhodes called it, Jameson preferred "Charterland"; but before long it became officially "Rhodesia." Thus far the Company had occupied only Mashonaland. In 1893 came the inevitable war with the Matabele, swiftly over. Old Lobengula fled and died. Almost with his last words he had bidden his indunas seek Rhodes and his protection—"he will be your chief and friend." The end of Lobengula and his Matabele kingdom is a minor tragedy, and not less a tragedy because it was inevitable, and of great advantage to Africa. In a few years Rhodesia was an orderly territory, and the railways were moving steadily north and east. And in due course Rhodes did not fail to become the "chief and friend" of the Matabele.

§5

Such was the man who wrote to Chamberlain in July, 1895, and such were his achievements. Chamberlain was slower than Rhodes expected in allowing him "to take over the Bechuanaland Protectorate." But in November he handed over the Protectorate to the Chartered Company, first with a meticulous blue pencil marking off on the map ample tribal reserves to be solely subject to the Crown. Grateful Bechuana chiefs, who had conferred with him in London on the settlement, named the Colonial Secretary Moatlhodi, *the man who rights things.* But Chamberlain's blue pencil had linked Bechuanaland with a crisis which was about to overshadow Africa, the Empire and the world. For the Company now possessed not only the strip of land required for its northward railway along the western frontier of the Transvaal, but a base, if a base should be needed, from which that frontier could be crossed. Chamberlain had no reason to suspect, as he plied his methodical pencil, that the chiefs of the Company were already maturing plans for crossing it. He was very soon to be enlightened.

For inevitably the discovery of gold on the Rand had bred formidable problems in the Transvaal. President Kruger and the Boers held aloof from the goldfields, despising the ungodly rabble there as the Chosen People despised the Philistines. The Uitlanders, as the Boers called them, outnumbered the Dutch burghers by more than two to one, and contributed nineteen-twentieths of the taxes, but were allowed no vote, civic rights or educational opportunities, yet were liable to conscription, and subject to numerous humiliating and capricious exactions. When they petitioned for the franchise they were told that if they wanted the vote they could fight for it. All over the rest of South Africa under the British flag the Dutch enjoyed complete equality; and the Transvaal's treatment of the Uitlanders, who were predominantly, though by no means exclusively, of British stock, seemed to stamp them as an inferior race. The Boers' case might have been overwhelming: for they protested that they had a prior right to the Republic for which they had trekked and fought, and were resolved to preserve their pastoral way of life uncontaminated by the corruptions of the modern world from which they had so often fled. Unfortunately there was a flaw in this biblical theme; for Kruger too was now dependent upon the money extracted from the oppressed Philistines. He wanted in fact the gold without the gold-diggers. And increasingly he was looking for support to Germany. He had "asked Her Majesty's Government for bigger clothes," he told the German Club in January of this same 1895, and he had been refused. "I feel certain when the time comes for the Republic to wear still larger clothes you Germans will have done much to bring it about." It was very largely this speech that set Rhodes secretly preparing to aid and abet the Uitlander rising which all South Africa was now awaiting. For Rhodes was still in a hurry, conscious that he might not have long to live, and determined to see a federated South Africa before he died. Before the end of 1895 there was a revolutionary conspiracy brewing among the Uitlanders, and Rhodes was a party to it. The Uitlanders were to rise in Johannesburg, and an irregular force under Jameson would ride over the border to assist them. It was a sad political blunder. Only, Rhodes dared not wait. Often enough ere now he had been compelled to become a law to himself, and he had always triumphed; he felt confident that he would triumph now. At the last moment there was a dispute. At Johannesburg the Uitlanders preferred to use the Transvaal flag, Rhodes and Jameson were determined on the British. The Uitlanders hung back, but even so Jameson would not wait. His little column crossed the frontier on December 29: on January 2, 1896, it was rounded up and captured by a Boer commando. Word came to Chamberlain at Highbury that Jameson had ridden into the Transvaal; it was the night of the annual servants' ball. He was seen to clench his hands. "If this succeeds," he said, "it will ruin me. I am going up to London to crush it."

But it was too late; Jameson was overtaken by a messenger from the High Commissioner, ordering him back in the Queen's name, but by then he was half-way to Johannesburg, and he went on. A last-moment wire from Rhodes, "On no account whatever must you move," had never reached him. The story of the raid, and its ignominious failure, roused the execration and derision of the world. Germany threatened armed intervention, and the Kaiser telegraphed congratulations to Kruger. His arrogant message was Rhodes's salvation. For Germany had suddenly bared her teeth, and the storm of resentment which swept Britain sprang from the profound instinct which warned her people that danger lay ahead. It was resentment against the Kaiser, not Rhodes. Rhodes indeed fell; the Dutch Afrikander Bond, formerly his political mainstay, drove him from office; but he was not broken. Jameson served a brief term of imprisonment in Britain, but the Raid, it has been said, did not lose him a friend. He lived to be Prime Minister of the Cape, and, later, leader of the Opposition in the Parliament of the Union. Rhodes lost his Dutch political allies, and was driven into the arms of the aggressive Loyalists. And he had dangerously exposed himself to those who were already his enemies in Britain, who henceforth would always speak of him as a mere filibustering adventurer and stockjobber, grasping at the basest personal gain. But the Select Committee of Enquiry, though it condemned Rhodes and his principal associates for political misconduct and duplicity, nevertheless found that Rhodes had not directed or approved the final act, and acquitted them all of any sort of mercenary motive. And in the subsequent debate, with the extreme Radicals clamouring that Rhodes must be broken, Chamberlain paid him a ringing tribute, despite his "one gigantic mistake." In much the same mood an earlier House had censured Clive, yet resolved "that Lord Clive has at the same time rendered great and meritorious services to his country."

As for Rhodes, after the first phase of dazed grief—for five nights after Jameson's catastrophe he walked up and down his bedroom sleepless behind locked doors—he soon recovered his energy and resolution. Two months after the Raid on the Transvaal the Matabele and Mashona rose in Rhodesia. They had been hardly treated after the occupation, and now they spread over the countryside, butchering and mutilating lonely settlers. For Rhodes, as it proved, the rising was providential. He was determined to save his settlers, or perish. He joined a relief column, and displayed a cool and even reckless courage in the fighting. And then he did better. For the guerilla warfare might have dragged on for months, and ruined both the Company and Rhodesia. He went unarmed, and with three companions only, among the desperate Matabele warriors, and talked with them. He listened to their grievances, and promised redress, and they threw down their arms. And after this for many weeks he camped among them and discussed, interminably, patiently discussed, their troubles; until the last chief had vowed that Rhodes was his father and sworn perpetual peace. Rhodes kept his promises to the Matabele. Their grievances were redressed. But one thing he could not do. He could not give them back the lordly savage life, as they had lived it before the white man came.

§6

After the Raid the Boers began to import arms steadily from Germany, so that by April, 1897, Chamberlain was warning Salisbury that the Transvaal "has a stock of artillery, rifles and ammunition of all sorts, enough to furnish a European army." The British, as always, were hopelessly unprepared. "Meanwhile we have only one battery at the Cape; and the War Office agreed that in the event of war . . . they could not defend the Cape Colony." There were three years of fruitless negotiation, circling round British "suzerainty," and Boer infringements of the existing Convention, but always returning to the claims of the Uitlanders, whom Kruger rigidly refused to admit to anything like equal citizenship. War was inevitable; Dutch and British could live together in South Africa, but not two incompatible political systems. For it had long been clear that the destiny of South Africa was union, and every project of union hitherto had foundered on the pseudo-biblical oligarchy of the Boers. Sir Alfred Milner wrote, as High Commissioner, in a dispatch from the Cape which stirred British opinion acutely in 1899,

> South Africa can prosper under two, three or six governments, though the fewer the better, but not under two absolutely conflicting social and political systems, perfect equality for Dutch and British in the British Colonies, side by side with permanent subjection of British to Dutch in one of the Republics.

War came in October, 1899, and to much of Europe, and to a small but vocal minority in Britain, it seemed that a powerful and greedy Empire was coercing a small Republic of unworldly farmers, at the prompting of a ring of sinister financiers. "It is our country you want," Kruger had cried passionately, and there is a certain majesty about the old man's stubborn struggle. But he struggled to keep too much. Kruger was both too narrow and too greedy. Chamberlain did not want the Transvaal, nor did the British government. And by fighting to preserve not only the independence of his burghers but the subservience of the Uitlanders Kruger had ensured the ruin of all his aims. It was the old problem over again. What are the rights of a backward enclave against the oncoming tides of history? Chamberlain, like so many others before him, wanted union and he wanted union under British suzerainty. But for a long while he believed that in due time union would come without war. He was, after all, the same Chamberlain who, as a Radical in Gladstone's government, had been ready to make peace after the humiliation of Majuba in 1881; throughout the long and irritating negotiations the general theme of his instructions to Milner had been the desirability of peace; as he summed up an exhaustive memorandum in March, 1898, "our greatest interest in South Africa is peace and . . . all our policy must be directed to this object." But by now Kruger was not the only obstacle; there were jingoes on both sides, not only in the Cape or Britain, but in both the Boer Republics. The brother of the State Secretary of the Orange Free State spoke for many burghers when he said, "The only thing we are afraid of now is that Chamberlain . . . will cheat us out of the war, and consequently the opportunity of annexing the Cape Colony and Natal and forming the Republican United States of South Africa."

The war began with even more than the usual tale of disasters. For the Boers were numerous, well equipped and past masters in the tactics of the veld, and the British War Office, as usual, had not been allowed to make adequate preparations, and what preparations it had made had been, as usual, preparations for the wrong kind of war. During the first four months the Boers invaded Natal and Cape Colony, and crossed their western frontier into Bechuanaland and Griqualand West. They inflicted a series of crushing reverses on the plodding British generals, and enveloped and besieged British armies in Ladysmith, Mafeking and Kimberley. Under the shock of these humiliations not only Britain but the whole Empire braced itself for effort. Australia, New Zealand and Canada sent more than thirty thousand men to the front, and the British in South Africa thirty thousand more. The professional soldiers, incredibly enough, did not want them; Aldershot regarded colonial troops, the Secretary of State for War reported, as "necessary evils," and hoped that there would as few as possible. But Chamberlain saw to it that they came, and that they were not merged, as the War Office would have liked, in other units. This rally from overseas was a portent, political even more than military. For the first time the whole Empire was at war, and it kindled to a new sense of organic unity. After the opening catastrophes Lord Roberts, of Afghan fame, was sent out to take command, with Lord Kitchener, of Khartum, as his second in command. In four months Roberts entered Pretoria, and Orange Free State and Transvaal were annexed. Two years of tedious guerilla warfare followed against the far-ranging Boer commandos, and peace was not concluded until May, 1902. The terms were clement in the extreme. British sovereignty over both Republics was acknowledged. But they were to have representative institutions, and, in due course, responsible government. And the British government undertook to pay three million pounds to resettle the Boers on their farms, and to see that the Dutch language was safeguarded. All this foreshadowed the equality of the two white races. Had Kruger triumphed, there would have been a Dutch ascendancy.

Before the war was over Rhodes was dead. He had arrived in Kimberley, somewhat to the embarrassment of its garrison, by the last train before the siege closed in. Until the Raid estranged them, Rhodes had always worked closely with the Dutch, and before he died he spoke some prophetic words to his new supporters, the Loyalists of Cape Town:

> You think you have beaten the Dutch. It is not so. The Dutch are not beaten. What is beaten is Krugerism, a corrupt and evil government, no more Dutch in essence than English. No! The Dutch are as vigorous and unconquered to-day as they have ever been; the country is still as much theirs as yours, and you will have to live and work with them hereafter as in the past.

In the long history of the British Empire Rhodes is perhaps the only great figure who can be called a conscious imperialist: yet his last warning was against all thought of racial ascendancy. He had died young, as he expected to die. But long after his death his "immense and brooding spirit," in Kipling's words, still "quickened and controlled."

BOOKS FOR FURTHER READING.

Sir C. P. Lucas, *The Partition of Africa;* A. L. P. Martin, *Missionaries and annexation in the Pacific;* G. H. Scholefield, *The Pacific: its past and future;* D. C. Somervell, *Livingstone;* Professor Coupland, *Kirk on the Zambesi;* M. Perham and J. Simmons, *African discovery;* J. L. Garvin, *Life of Joseph Chamberlain;* The Earl of Cromer, *Modern Egypt;* Lord Morley, *Life of Gladstone;* Moneypenny and Buckle, *Life of Disraeli;* Essay on *Gordon* in Lytton Strachey, *Eminent Victorians;* H. A. Bryden, *A History of South Africa;* G. A. Walker, *A History of South Africa; Lives* of Cecil Rhodes by Basil Williams, Sarah Gertrude Millin and William Plomer; Sir J. G. McDonald, *Rhodes, a heritage.*

Book X

THE CLAIM TO SURVIVAL

CHAPTER ONE

FROM COLONY TO DOMINION

(1850-1914)

§1

1897 was the year of Victoria's Diamond Jubilee, the sixtieth of her astonishing reign, and the flawless summer months were thronged with changing pageantry. It was essentially an imperial ceremony and in the military parades and processions, led by Life Guards or Dragoons, Maori, Dyak, Haussa and Sikh would march with Canadian, Afrikander and Australian. Affection, and almost superstitious reverence, for the mother of so many peoples, thankfulness for their own great prosperity, pride in the wide Empire over which the Queen ruled, so much of which seemed to have grown all but unbidden during her reign and which so far outdistanced all comparison that if it had not come into being no mind would have conceived its possibility—all these emotions mingled in the mood of the moment. And if a certain strain of bombast could be detected in the high pageantry of those halcyon months that too perhaps was not altogether inappropriate to a moment of unwonted selfconsciousness, and though it may have derived partly from the phase of international rivalry bred by the new imperialism it is possible to see in it also a transient revival of the youthful Elizabethan mood, in which courage and vainglory were often wedded. Yet in the minds of many, it is clear, even while the crowds shouted and the processions passed, an undercurrent of foreboding was not absent. Chamberlain himself had little doubt that sterner days lay ahead, and that the Empire must soon be subjected to a more searching ordeal than ever before. Viewing, with the Colonial Premiers, the line of warships stretching far out of sight at the Jubilee Naval Review, he was conscious, with them, that only the Navy stood between the Empire and a world of foes. And Kipling, the poet of the new Empire, struck a solemn, an almost penitential, note in his Jubilee *Recessional*.

The tumult and the shouting dies—
The captains and the kings depart—
Still stands Thine ancient sacrifice,
An humble and a contrite heart.
Lord God of Hosts, be with us yet,
Lest we forget, lest we forget.

It was the climax of a golden age, the poised moment before the breaking of the wave, an occasion such as the oldest had never seen before and the youngest would never see again. But it was also for an imperialist a great opportunity, and Chamberlain was determined to use it. He had invited the Prime Ministers of the self-governing colonies, all of which had reached self-government during Victoria's reign, to come to England as state guests, and to bring with them contingents of their troops. They were sumptuously feted, and were at the centre of every great ceremony. Chamberlain had doubtless calculated on the spontaneous warmth of the British crowds' reception of these visitors, and in their letters and reminiscences[1] it is still easy to trace the readiness with which they kindled to their reception. More perhaps was done for Empire unity in the streets than at the Conference table, but with the coming of the Colonial Premiers another Colonial Conference—there had been one in 1887— was inevitable. For during the last four decades the colonies had grown swiftly towards maturity.

§2

Canada, as we now call it, had headed the march towards self-government. It had developed rapidly since the days of Elgin. So rapidly in fact that before long it became obvious that the Union of the two Canadas in 1840 had not solved their political problems. They were free; indeed in 1859 substantial duties were levied on certain imports from Britian, so that it was apparent that the wheel was coming full circle, and that the colonies would soon be taxing the mother country, without representation. But though the Canadas were free they were in difficulties. Immigration from Britain rose sometimes to a flood—a hundred thousand Irish arrived in a single year after the famine of 1845—and it set strongly towards Ontario. Within fifteen years the population of the western province, which had been less than that of Quebec by 170,000, exceeded it by a quarter of a million, and new controversies embittered the

---

[1] e.g. especially *My Reminiscences* by Sir George Reid.

jealousies and deadlocks already inevitable in the joint administration of two such dissimilar constituents. The idea of federation—union for national purposes, separation for local affairs—was born of this dilemma. It was a purely Canadian project, a practical solution of a particular problem. No inspired jurist, no academic fathers of the constitution, planned it. George Brown (from Edinburgh) and John Macdonald (from Sutherland), the Liberal and Conservative leaders, combined for this purpose only—and thereafter never spoke to each other again. Fourteen days' conference at Quebec in 1864 proved sufficient to hammer out a workmanlike project. The executive would be the Governor-General acting for the British Crown. The legislature would consist of a nominated Senate and an elected House of Commons. The relations of legislature and government would naturally be modelled on those of Parliament and Crown in Britain. One significant contrast distinguished the Canadian project from the Union of the United States. The thirteen American colonies had come together as sovereign states and remained the chief repositories of power, automatically retaining all functions not expressly transferred to the nation. Despite their mutual differences the Canadian provinces wisely preferred a strong central government.

Indeed they had very lately been sharply reminded of some of the disadvantages of the American alternative. And not only by the breakdown of central authority in the United States which led to the civil war of 1861 to 1865. For at the close of the civil war some discharged Irish soldiers had organised a Fenian Brotherhood, which planned an invasion of Canada, and drilled openly in several cities in the United States. In 1866 bodies of Fenians crossed the frontier at several places and there was fighting—repeated in 1870 and 1871. The unconvincing excuse pleaded by the authorities at Washington —that they had no power to interfere in the individual states—did little to commend the American version of confederation to Canadian federalists. And so unlike the founders of the United States they proposed that all powers should be vested in the central government, unless expressly handed over to the provinces. The two Canadas, New Brunswick and Nova Scotia agreed to enter the projected Confederation, and the British Parliament gave it statutory authority in the British North America Act of 1867—first taking the precaution of altering " Kingdom of Canada," the title for the united country preferred by Canadians, to " Dominion of Canada," in deference to the supposed susceptibilities of the United States. Bright and the Radicals sneered at the Confederation, and suggested that the Canadian provinces ought either to set up on their own or join the United States, but theirs was the only dissentient note. It was of good omen for the Empire that Canada should thus early have set the example of consolidation, on the eve of an age in which, as Seeley would soon be insisting, the future would be with the great states. And it was in full harmony with the developing British tradition that the political structure thus empirically evolved should have been one which organised diversity in unity, and made it possible for Frenchmen to remain Canadians without ceasing to be French. Thirty years later the Catholic French Canadian premier of Canada,[1] speaking to Frenchmen in Paris, could say of his own country:

> We have liberty, absolute, complete, more complete—pardon my national pride for the affirmation I am making—more complete than in any country whatsoever in the world: liberty for our religion, with its worship, its ceremonies, its prayers, its costumes: liberty for our language, which is the official language as English is: liberty for all the institutions that our ancestors brought from France, and which we regard as a sacred heritage. Equality is ours. What other proof of it could I give you than this? In this country, where the majority is of English descent and of the Protestant religion, the last general elections have brought to power a man of French descent and Catholic religion, who has always strongly affirmed his race and his religion. . . .

There were more provinces to join the Confederation, for Canada was growing fast. Of the older territories Prince Edward Island was admitted in 1873. As for the great North West, its development had been hastened, from 1766 onwards, by the challenge of rivals from Montreal to the long-standing monopoly of the Hudson's Bay Adventurers. Competition for a while was in both senses of the word, cut-throat. Most of the newcomers were Scots, "their names . . . sound like a roll-call of the clans at Culloden"; they covered vast distances in their birch-bark canoes; they founded trading-posts all over the wild interior; and they built up a commercial empire across half a continent. One of them, Alexander Mackenzie (from Stornoway), travelled in 1789 to the Great Slave Lake, and thence down the river which now bears his name, until, first of white men, he stood on the northern shores of Canada, and looked out across the Polar Sea. Four years later he crossed the Rocky Mountains and on a rock on the Pacific Coast painted in vermilion letters "Alexander Mackenzie, from Canada by land, July 22nd, 1793." After him many

[1] Sir Wilfred Laurier (Skelton, *Life and Letters of Sir Wilfred Laurier*, ii, 80).

others, men for the most part with Scottish names, explored the country west of the Rockies. Mackenzie's plea for a British North America stretching from sea to sea did not interest the British government, but by 1820, exhausted by rivalry, the North West Company based on Montreal and its older rival, Charles II's Company of Adventurers of England trading into Hudson's Bay, combined in the Hudson's Bay Company, and for a generation the vast territories between Ontario and the Pacific coast lay under its nominal control. For almost forty years after the amalgamation the fortunes of the Company were autocratically directed by George Simpson, "the little Emperor," who travelled tirelessly over its vast territories in canoes paddled by scarlet-shirted Iroquois, and ruled his trade-Empire with a rod of iron. But the fur trade was the Company's concern, not administration; it even discouraged agriculture. And as the waste places began to fill, its authority was bound to be curtailed. West of the Rockies, after a dispute with the United States, the territory above latitude 49° north, including Vancouver Island, was assigned to Britain by the Oregon Treaty of 1846. Ten years later gold was discovered on the Fraser River, and with the rush of immigrants which followed it became obvious that the population was outgrowing a trading Company's jurisdiction. In 1858 all this western territory became the Crown Colony of British Columbia, which united with Vancouver Island in 1866 and joined the Dominion of Canada in 1871. Much the same was bound to happen as the wide lands between Ontario and the Rockies began to fill. The Fenian raids moreover were fresh in the memory of the new Dominion Government; clearly a strong central administration was desirable, and in 1869 the Company (it retained its trading rights) was bought out, if buying be the word for the purchase of many hundreds of thousands of square miles of some of the richest land in the world for £300,000. At this time settlement had scarcely pushed further west than what is now Manitoba, where a sparse population of French and British half-breeds represented the survivors of the Red River Settlement founded by the Earl of Selkirk in 1812. Manitoba became a province of the confederated Dominion in 1870.

But federation did more than extend the authority of the central government; it bred population. For federation meant railways, and railways meant new settlers. An "intercolonial" line between Ontario and the eastern provinces was a condition of the original Confederation. British Columbia made a similar stipulation. But a railway from ocean to ocean, a railway to cover three thousand five hundred miles, and cross the Rockies, this was a much more formidable proposition. Of the thousand miles of it which would run north of Lake Superior nothing whatever was known; of its illimitable bog and crag the glimpses caught from an occasional canoe, gliding on some fur-trader's waterway, were all that human eye had lighted on since time began. Successive governments recoiled from the project; it hung fire tantalisingly, and became a controversial issue in politics. At last in 1880 the Macdonald Government handed over the whole undertaking to a private syndicate— Scotsmen again, with Donald Smith, later Lord Strathcona, as the dominating influence. They asked for ten years, and completed the line in five. It became a political as well as an economic link. And soon it was carrying immigrants to the empty lands of Manitoba and beyond. Further and further west farmers turned the virgin soil, Indians were shepherded into their reserves, and Canada began to assume the shape we know. Alberta and Saskatchewan, the new western provinces, entered the Dominion in 1905.

Confederation and the gradual peopling of the west gave the new Canada both the bulk and the national self-consciousness to resist absorption by the United States. And naturally enough the new sense of nationhood bred the "national policy"—including tariffs to protect the infant industries needed for a self-sufficient community—with which John Macdonald won a sweeping electoral victory in 1878. On the rock of this new sense of Canadian nationality foundered all subsequent movements for economic, which must have meant political, union with the States. When gold was discovered (in 1894) in Klondyke, in the far north-west, and the Alaska boundary became a subject of controversy with the United States, the Canadians were a good deal more excited than the British. For it was their own territory which was at stake.

§3

Canada had achieved unity a generation and more before the other self-governing colonies. Unfederated Australia still needed six Prime Ministers to represent her at Chamberlain's Diamond Jubilee Conference, Canada only one. And for Chamberlain Canada was the key to all plans for the future. But in Canada the Liberals under the eloquent Laurier had lately routed the Conservatives, and were known to be toying with the notion of commercial union with the United States. For a while Chamberlain, and therefore Salisbury, doubted whether even in the Queen's year the times were propitious for a Colonial Conference. But Chamberlain was not given to excessive caution and he had soon decided on his imaginative invitation to the Colonial premiers; their unanimous acceptance made a Conference inevitable. In the previous year he had declared:

> The recent isolation of the United Kingdom, the dangers which seemed to threaten us, have evoked from all our colonies . . . an outburst of loyalty and affection which has reverberated throughout the world. . . . I ask you now, gentlemen, is this demonstration, this almost universal expression of loyalty from all our Colonies, to pass away without a serious effect upon the part of both colonial and Imperial statesmen to transform these sentiments into practical results ?

And he went on to outline the practical results which, for a moment, seemed to him attainable—no less than an Imperial Zollverein, free trade, that is, within the Empire, and duties on all foreign goods. Closer imperial union was his ultimate object, and "to organise an Empire . . . greater and more potent for peace and the civilisation of the world than any that history has ever known." It was characteristic of Chamberlain to approach such a goal through a commercial proposition, characteristic too perhaps that the commercial arrangement proposed should have been one which, in the manner of the Continental exponents of the new imperialism, would have made of the Empire something like a closed fist, menacing the rest of the world. The project ran counter to British tradition; hitherto other nations had looked with a tolerant eye upon the prolonged expansion of Britain overseas largely because the doors of its commerce were open to all the world. The project ran counter to British tradition, nor was it practicable; colonial tariffs were already too deep-rooted. The project ran counter to British tradition, but in variant forms we shall meet it again.

The desire for some sort of closer imperial union had been for some while in the air. An Imperial Federation League had been founded in 1884, but though it succeeded in diffusing a vague sense of the desirability of a more intimate political connection it did not succeed in recommending an agreed plan for federation. And in the deliberations of the first Colonial Conference, which had met in 1887, the year of the first Jubilee, federation was expressly ruled out as not ripe for discussion. At Chamberlain's Conference of 1897 the delegates continued to grope their way towards closer union in one form or another, political, commercial or military. For the first time all the Colonial members were Prime Ministers, and they met in the intervals of the Jubilee whirl of ceremony, spectacle and

I.C. 2 E

entertainment, distracted perhaps by their crowded engagement-books and the tumultuous streets—"I am not sure whether the British Empire needs a new constitution," wrote Laurier to a Canadian friend, "but I am certain that every Jubilee guest will need one"—yet undoubtedly full of a special and heightened friendliness. Laurier had said, "it would be the proudest moment of my life if I could see a Canadian of French descent affirming the principles of freedom in the Parliament of Great Britain," and more than once during his visit he recurred to the same theme. The Conference however set up no machinery for closer union, political, military or commercial. Imperial federation and an imperial Zollverein it did not regard as practical politics, and the burden of imperial defence was left, where it had always been, with the mother country. Only towards commercial union was a step taken, with the decision that, in order to implement the recent Canadian offer of preference for British goods, and make it possible for other colonies to imitate it, the British government should denounce the old treaties with Germany and Belgium, whose "most favoured nation" clauses prevented any colony from giving preferential treatment to imports from the mother country. But the Conference had done something which was both more important and more characteristic than the setting up of machinery. It had resolved to reassemble at regular intervals. Chamberlain may have been over-optimistic when he exclaimed, "that is the beginning of it—the beginning of a Federal Conference"; the fact remained, the imperial constitution was growing a new limb. And progress, according to the British custom, had been instinctive and experimental; no formal instrument would regulate or restrict the future activities of the Conference; it had come into being because it was needed and in due course would doubtless do whatever proved to be needful. The next Conference was to meet in 1902. By then the Australian colonies too would be federated.

§4

Australia moved towards federal unity slowly and reluctantly. Its component colonies were widely scattered, and so unused to co-operation that they did not even build their railways to the same gauge. Confederation in Canada had been hastened by racial rivalries within and danger from without; in Australia there was no racial cleavage, and throughout the nineteenth century the colonies were shielded from any danger of foreign aggression by

British sea power. Australian democracy indeed grew up under exceptionally, and in a sense, unnaturally, favourable conditions. For Britain had ceased to control the policy of the Australians without ceasing to protect them. The British Navy and the British taxpayer between them relieved the colonists of both the political problems, and the financial burdens, of security. Their political adolescence accordingly was exceptionally sheltered, and they could devote an unusual degree of attention to domestic legislation. At first their interests were political; many of the immigrants during the gold rush were men who had taken part in, or been influenced by, the Chartist agitation in England, and though the origins of Chartism were social its programme was purely political. All the Chartists' Six Points, save the ridiculous proposal for annual Parliaments, were accepted in Australia long before they became law in Britain. It was largely thanks to Chartist influence also that the demand for a system of public education, when it came, was for education not only "free and compulsory," but "secular." But in due course, as an industrial population developed in the towns, Australians would turn to social legislation, and feel themselves free to concentrate on the pursuit of high economic standards, even to the point of restricting immigration, as no people trained to self-defence could have ventured to do.

It is impossible to watch the growth of colonies such as these to political maturity without admiration, not only for the youthful Parliaments taking their first uncertain steps along the difficult path of self-government, but for the ancient mother and instructress, to whom, despite a natural taste for asserting their own personalities, they turn from time to time for guidance or admonition. For the British Parliamentary system is complex and subtle, and demands notable virtues, and in particular the virtue of moderation, from those who practise it. So much in it depends upon unwritten usage, upon tact and instinct and toleration, upon moral and social environment, that it is not the least of the achievements of the Empire to have planted flourishing Parliaments in four of the five continents. Nor, in most instances, was the achievement due solely to hereditary aptitude modelling itself upon the British archetype. Often enough there would be practical guidance from Whitehall. Thus in 1878 when the second of two bitter and protracted disputes between the Council and the Assembly in Victoria seemed to be reaching deadlock it was resolved to send a deputation to England to invite the imperial Parliament somehow or other to solve their problems for them. It was clear that Victoria had much to learn; in the twenty years from 1856 there had been no less than eighteen administrations and in

South Australia twenty-nine. The Secretary of State, however, did not consider that the imperial Parliament should intervene; intervention, he pointed out, would imply that Victoria was incapable of governing itself "from a general want of the moderation and sagacity essential to the success of constitutional government." And he proceeded to suggest that the two Houses in Victoria should be "guided in this matter, as in others, by the practice of the Imperial Parliament." After a brief excursus on the mutual relations of Lords and Commons at Westminster he concluded with the pregnant reflection that "the clearest definition of the relative position of the two Houses . . . would not suffice to prevent collisions, unless interpreted with the discretion and mutual forbearance which have been so often exemplified in the history of the Imperial Parliament." The sage advice bore fruit. The British model could not be exactly imitated in a colonial setting, nor can a colonial governor precisely reproduce the functions of the Crown; but the analogies are very close, and "discretion and mutual forbearance" is at least as essential overseas. The dispute in Victoria duly ended in compromise, and a reform of the Council, in 1881.

The comparatively simple pattern of early Australian politics was dictated by the texture of Australian colonisation itself. In each colony the population was distributed into three clearly-marked zones—first town and seaport, then the farming belt which fed them, and finally the deep hinterland of the great grazing estates of the squatters. On this clear-cut pattern the goldfields appeared an almost adventitious excrescence, whose population however on the whole shared the economic interests of the towns. More wool and more gold meant more capital, and more manufactures; and as the towns grew, the farming zone which supplied them had to grow also. It could only grow at the expense of the squatters in the interior. Political conflict between farmers and squatters was therefore inevitable. The various governments were interested parties to the dispute, for whereas originally they had encouraged the squatters by making it easy to acquire vast grazing lands, with a growing population their aim was now to settle a yeoman population on the soil. Despite differential taxation and a variety of ingenious spoliatory devices, and although the squatters were not so much owners as Crown tenants, it did not prove easy to break up the great estates. However the expansion of the agricultural belt contrived to keep pace with the needs of the expanding towns, and in due course the growth of manufactures, and of an industrial population, decreased the pressure on the land.

In Australia as in other colonies self-government necessarily brought protection in its train—for without protection against British imports the colony could not hope to establish a balanced economy, and must remain a mere producer of raw materials. It took the Australians some while indeed to see where their interests lay, and when David Syme, a lanky Scot, "reared on oatmeal and philosophy," who had made some money in the goldfields, bought the Melbourne *Age* for two thousand pounds in 1856, and resolved to convert Australia to protection, "there was not," he afterwards wrote, "so far as I knew, a man in the whole country but was a free trader." But the pull of economic interest was even more irresistible than Syme's dour polemics, and, though New South Wales lagged behind until the turn of the century, the other colonies soon followed the example of Victoria and set up tariff barriers, against the outer world, against Britain and indeed against each other. In yet another colony the wheel had come all but full circle. Henceforth with the British taxpayer shouldering Australian defence, and the British exporter contributing through tariffs to Australian industrial reorganisation, there would be something not unlike taxation without representation. But this time it was the mother country which was paying the taxes.

Behind the new tariff wall urban industries began to multiply, and with them an industrial population, trade unions, industrial conflicts and, in due course, at about the same time as in England, the conception of a political Labour Party. Before long the new Party would impose on all Australia the ideal of a high standard of living, never more dangerous than in a country not normally conscious of the full political responsibilities of its own defence. At the end of the last century it was confidently expected that within fifty years the population of Australia would have risen to thirty millions; at the outbreak of the second world war it stood at a mere seven millions. To few nations has that most ubiquitous of democracy's temptations, the illusion that it can enjoy comfort without sacrifice, been presented more insidiously than to the Australians. But they were a young and vigorous people and though they would harbour the illusion they would survive it. Nevertheless the colonies passed stringent measures to exclude Chinese immigrants, and when Lord Salisbury's government showed signs of disapproval, announced that they were not school children and "neither for Her Majesty's ships of war, nor for Her Majesty's representatives, nor for the Secretary of State, do we intend to turn aside from our purpose, which is to terminate the landing of the Chinese on these shores for ever." Common feeling and common action on this issue, at an inter-colonial conference in 1888, marked an unconscious step along the road to federation. So did the steady improvement of world communications. During Australia's first half century the sea voyage to Britain usually lasted four months; in the eighteen-fifties it was halved by the sailing clippers and the scientific study of winds and currents. Almost at once came steam, and in 1869 the opening of the Suez Canal took five thousand miles off the length of the journey and halved the time again. In 1871 the submarine cable brought London within an hour or two of Australia, Perhaps it was well for the growth of self-government that during the early years of the colonial Parliaments British Secretaries of State were still a couple of months distant.

By the early 'eighties French and German activity in the Pacific, and the manifest British reluctance to acquire new possessions, and responsibilities, there, had set unwonted speculations as to the advantages of a united Australia stirring in the minds of a few colonial statesmen. By the end of the decade the quickening tempo of world imperialism made a divided Australia seem yet more of an anachronism. In 1889 Sir Henry Parkes, the veteran premier of New South Wales, reopened the question of federation. It was an unexpected lead, for New South Wales still believed in free trade while the rest of Australia was becoming increasingly protectionist. But about Parkes, the son of a Warwickshire labourer, there was a touch of the visionary, not confined, as in some of his contemporaries, to the hirsute profile of a major prophet; and the Convention which he succeeded in promoting in 1891 drafted a constitution which became the basis of the eventual federation. Thereafter the movement languished until 1897, when a new Convention, with wider popular backing, framed a constitution which was accepted, on its second submission to the people by referendum, in 1899. Only still remote West Australia stood aside for some while longer. In one respect Australians preferred the model of the United States to that of Canada. They permitted the Federal government only those powers deliberately surrendered by the federating states and, to safeguard the rights of the constituent colonies, set up a High Court as sole interpreter of the constitution. But, like all the other self-governing members of the Empire, they retained the British Parliamentary system, with a Senate, in which all states, large and small, were to be equally represented, taking the place of the House of Lords.

It was a memorable political achievement, this first and only constitution framed for a whole continent, this federation which had not, like other federations, needed the threat of conflict within, or serious danger from without, to spur it on. It is not too much to say that without the hereditary British instinct for political organisation it would have been impossible. By now there were many Australian citizens of foreign extraction, but every one of the names of the fifty members of the Convention which framed the federation is of British origin.

§5

The colonies whose Premiers, united Australia's among them, met in London for the Imperial Conference of 1902 were by now not so much colonies as young, self-conscious nations, and the significance of the Conference lay mainly in its failures to agree. The optimistic imperialists who had expected far-reaching agreements or closer union were shocked and disappointed; yet the pessimists who, like most foreign observers, forthwith rashly concluded that the Empire was doomed to slow disintegration failed even more signally to see beneath the surface. The mother country, it is true, failed to persuade the colonies to shoulder anything like a proportionate share of the burdens of imperial defence. One-quarter of the sea-borne trade of the Empire, the Admiralty pointed out, belonged to the colonies, yet even after they had all made their new offers of assistance, Britain's share of the naval expenses was not merely, as was natural, much larger, but wholly disproportionate even for her much larger population—15s. 2d. per head, as against Australia's 1s. 0¼d., New Zealand's 1s. 0¾d., and Canada's refusal to make any contribution whatever.

Chamberlain felt more keenly than ever that new political machinery was needed to hold the Empire together, and he once more proposed a grand federal Council. But the young nations would have none of it. They had no wish to surrender any part of their new-found autonomy to a federation. The way to closer union, they suggested, lay through reciprocity in trade. There could be no Empire free trade, for there were already tariffs, but there might be even higher tariffs against foreigners. And Canada at least had already granted preference to British trade as against other imports, although even against Britain the tariff was high enough to be almost insurmountable. The Conference pointedly suggested that Britain might follow suit by granting the colonies exemption from "duties now or hereafter imposed." The words stirred Chamberlain's imagination. At present there were no duties from which to grant exemption. But what of duties "hereafter imposed"? The colonies had shied away from political union and from military union; he was a business man; why not commercial union?

And yet perhaps all of them, the imperialists with their high hopes of spectacular agreements, Chamberlain and his federal Council, the colonial premiers and their commercial union, were in varying degrees mistaking the form for the spirit. For the true significance of the Conference was not the search for machinery, whether political or commercial. At this Coronation-tide gathering the young, self-conscious nations from overseas were feeling their way towards equality of status. Britain and her colonies were on the last stages of that path towards freedom within the Empire from which they had strayed in the eighteenth century. With that goal reached, commercial or political innovations might, or might not, prove desirable for added strength or efficiency, but for union it would suffice that all were conscious of the Empire as custodian of a unique way of life, precious not only for Britain but for the future of mankind.

In the following winter Chamberlain was in South Africa, arranging a customs union between the four colonies, and delivering a series of powerful speeches. Imperial unity was still his goal; he had tried an imperial council, he had tried imperial defence, and now that phrase "duties now or hereafter imposed" was stirring in his mind. At home there was a small "registration" duty on corn; might it be remitted on Empire-grown corn? That at least would be a first step, a gesture of good will. Yet how reluctantly, even now, he fell back upon commercial union was shown by the frequency with which, in South Africa, he warned his audiences against any attempt to turn the Empire into a business concern; "the conception of Empire is not to be gained if you treat it in a huckstering spirit." He returned to England in March, 1903, a greater public figure than ever, to find that in his absence the Chancellor of the Exchequer had persuaded the cabinet to repeal the corn-duty. There was accordingly no prospect now of any cautious first step towards imperial preference, and after weeks of altercation in the cabinet Chamberlain crossed his Rubicon. On May 15, at Birmingham, he proclaimed his belief in imperial preference, and, what would soon be inextricably confused with it, retaliation against foreign tariffs. Balfour did his subtle best to maintain the unity of his cabinet and his Party with a compromise, but by October the cabinet had broken up and been remodelled; and Chamberlain, freed from office, loosed his campaign upon the country. But it ceased almost from the first to be a campaign for imperial preference. Chamberlain himself, it is true, never forgot that his ultimate objective was imperial unity. Thus that October he was saying at Newcastle:

I have ventured to speak on behalf of my countrymen here, and to say to our kinsmen beyond the seas, "We want your aid. We call you to our Councils; come and take part in them," and they have decided they will not advance along that line and federate in that way. . . . I tried next in connexion with imperial defence. Again I was beaten by the difficulties of the situation; but I did not on that account give it up, and I come back, therefore, to this idea of commercial union, which will bring us together, which will necessitate the Council, which Council in time may do much more than it does in the beginning, and may leave us, though it will not find us, a great, loyal and federated Empire.

Nothing could be clearer or franker. But unfortunately the colonies could not support his campaign, and his backing came mainly from such British industrialists as happened to desire a tariff. Imperial preference for the sake of the Empire, tariffs, that is, against all the world in order that we might lower them in favour of our own colonies, slid insensibly into protection for its own sake—tariffs to save "dying" British industries. The two, wholly different, propositions were soon inextricably confused upon the public platform, and have remained inextricably confused in the public mind ever since. Only, the domestic aspect, tariffs to protect British industry, inevitably loomed largest for an electorate trained to interest itself primarily in domestic affairs.

The split among the Conservatives was a godsend to the Liberal Party, itself constantly crippled by internal feuds, the latest of which, over the South African war, was hardly yet healed. But in defence of free trade all Liberals could unite, and Asquith followed Chamberlain round the country, answering him speech by speech with persuasive and telling lucidity. At the general election of 1906 the Liberals were triumphant, and imperial preference and protection went down, together with many other policies with which they had no necessary connection but with which they had become inextricably entangled. Unfortunately in the course of the confused controversy the victors had devoted themselves to denouncing not only Chamberlain and tariffs, but the Empire and the imperial connection. The imperialism of the last quarter of a century offered a tempting target, particularly when politicians imputed to their fellow countrymen all the characteristic failings of the harsh new German-inspired imperialism of the Continent. Neither the eager controversialists nor their audiences knew much of the history of the Empire, and in the heat of the electoral struggle many went further, and were soon assuming that for three hundred years

Britain had been displaying that coldblooded acquisitive imperialism, whose very name had only been coined within the last few decades and to describe the forces let loose by the new Germany. The tariff controversy, and, it must be added, the universal ignorance of imperial history, were together mainly responsible for a strange, one-sided misconception of the Empire, which would work power-fully upon the nation's consciousness for a generation.

In this crude new version the British Empire was the British Empire of 1880 to 1900, and even the Empire was not understood. It was Rhodes and the Boer War, not Burke and Wilberforce, Durham or Livingstone. It was Rhodes and the Boer War without any notion that Rhodes had been the embodiment of a selfless idea, and the Boer War the inevitable and fruitful solution of an intolerable dilemma. Many who now learned to think of the typical repre-sentative of Empire as some grasping industrialist prompting aggression for his own sordid ends, would have ridiculed the notion that, to the eye of history, the truly characteristic figure was rather the settler, the adventurer, the missionary or the explorer, or perhaps some harassed Victorian Secretary of State desperately seeking a plausible excuse for not adding to British responsibilities overseas. There was virtue no doubt in this revision of values; it represented, for one thing, a healthy reaction against the braggadocio and false sentiment of some recent popular imperialism, and, at a profounder level, a stirring of the national conscience, an uneasy suspicion that there were ideals worth cherishing which had been vulgarised or half-forgotten in recent years. Nevertheless it was sheer misfortune that what can only be called a distorted version of so brief a phase should have been so deeply imprinted on the public imagination as an accepted picture of all imperial history.

At the Colonial Conference of 1907 all the members, save one, again affirmed their desire for imperial preference, but since the one dissentient was Great Britain it was evident that the road was blocked. A good deal of useful business, however, was transacted and it was resolved to set up an Imperial General Staff. And henceforth the Conference was to be styled the Imperial Conference. It would meet every fourth year, and would consist of the Prime Ministers of the United Kingdom and of " the self-governing Dominions beyond the seas." From this moment, with the creation of a new Dominions Division in the Colonial Office, may be reckoned the first formal recognition of a new " Dominion" status. It was well timed. For as the Conference ended, the shadow of Germany's coming power began to creep out across the world, and a first faint chill fell upon the air.

§6

In this same 1907 New Zealand had become a Dominion. The change of title represented here no change of political organisation. For all but fifty years there had been self-government in New Zealand, and its structure had always been unitary. The new style represented rather the belated recognition that an adult nation, yet another, was already active within the Commonwealth.

Sir George Grey's first governorship had left New Zealand with some of the problems of adolescence still unsolved. Guerilla warfare with the Maoris, provoked by the land quarrel, blazed or smouldered in the North Island from 1860 to 1866. The New Zealanders sniped and skirmished in the still largely unexplored interior; their women-folk, grotesquely hampered by stiff mid-Victorian dresses, huddled in redoubts in moments of danger, or cooked and cleaned in their wooden houses. The Maoris fought with skill, courage and remark-able chivalry. They would send food and ammunition to beleaguered settlers, and there is a story of Maori warriors, who had conceived an admiration for the British 65th Regiment, calling "Keep your heads down, Sikkitifif. We're going to fire." Grey, who had been summoned to wrestle with so many an imperial crisis, had been called back from South Africa in 1861, but he failed to stave off the war, and it blazed up again after he had been curtly recalled in 1868. Not until 1870 did the Maori wars finally end. The Maoris had shown themselves fine fighters, a quarrel with an aboriginal people is seldom wholehearted, and it was with relief that most New Zealanders saw Sir Donald McLean, as Native minister, skilfully establish a lasting peace. Certain parts of the island he left discreetly alone, but else-where, with road, railway and a rising tide of settlement, the Queen's writ ran secure. By the end of the century the numbers of the Maoris, who returned four Members to the New Zealand Parliament, had fallen to somewhere about forty thousand, from an estimated seventy thousand at the time of the treaty of Waitangi, but before long they began slowly to increase again. Maori doctors, lawyers and engineers became numerous. The Maoris had come to terms with civilisation.

Gold discovered in 1861 brought a flood of immigrants. Even the sober Presbyterians of Dunedin flocked to dig at Tuapeka, so that many a country kirk was emptied of its congregation. With such ingredients it is not surprising that the goldfields of New Zealand were more law-abiding, even than those of Australia. After 1870 power passed steadily to the central authority, and New Zealand crystallised from a number of separate settlements into a nation

Like Australia, New Zealand was able to spare all the more time and money for social legislation because it had been relieved of the problems of diplomacy and the burdens of defence. Radical influence was potent in its early politics as in those of Australia, and New Zealand was not long in adopting both women's suffrage and secular education. But in character it was the most British of the colonies. Similarity of environment was partly responsible, for the climate of New Zealand is temperate and every New Zealander lives within reach of the sea. But racially too the people were homogeneous and the direct influence of Britain lasted long. By 1898 no native of the country had yet become its Prime Minister, and all its leading Members of Parliament, professors, clergy and professional men without exception were British born. More obviously than in Canada, Africa or even Australia the British way of life had taken root overseas.

§7

At the Imperial Conference of 1911 yet fewer premiers were needed to represent the Empire overseas, but they represented wider territories and an expanded population. For already South Africa was united. For what was accomplished in the eight years between the Peace of Vereeniging and the Act of Union it is not easy to find a parallel. Seldom indeed has victory in war been used with so noble and fortunate a wisdom. The credit of one of the most remarkable political achievements in history must go first to the sage instincts, the humanity and the good nature of the British people. The war itself had been singularly humane; it is not difficult to imagine by what ruthless measures against the families of the commandos a totalitarian power would have shortened the long guerilla struggle which followed the collapse of the main Boer armies. A totalitarian power moreover would assuredly have used victory to found, and necessarily on force, the sort of racial ascendancy which, as fostered by President Kruger, had provoked the war. But the British were not interested in racial ascendancy, and had never been able to cherish enmities for long. Their forebears indeed had long since contrived to reckon Joan of Arc, George Washington and almost, once he had capitulated, Napoleon himself as something very like national heroes of their own; and when, soon after the peace, the Boer generals Botha, de la Rey and de Wet went to London to seek for a modification of the terms the good-humoured public took them to its heart. They returned home determined to make the best of the Treaty. How much there was to be made of it even now they hardly yet realised.

That one of the main complaints of the Boer generals had been that the British government had not made permanent provision for the widows and children of Boer burghers killed in battle is striking evidence of the humanity of the post-war settlement. But it was by no means only the British tradition of tolerance and humanity which transformed the outlook. At this critical juncture South Africa was peculiarly fortunate in its leaders, both British and Boer. At first the conquered republics were constituted as Crown Colonies; and there could have been no more fruitful prologue than the administrative genius of Lord Milner, who now became Governor of both, and the energy and vision of the band of gifted young men who under his direction toiled, against time, to repatriate the Boers, settle newcomers, replace the vanished administrative machine, repair the devastated countryside, build railways and introduce scientific agriculture. "Milner's Kindergarten" contained a remarkable galaxy of talent. Some of its members fell prematurely in the first German world war, but of the rest were Philip Kerr, later Marquis of Lothian, an illustrious ambassador to Washington, Patrick Duncan, Governor-General of South Africa, John Buchan, afterwards Lord Tweedsmuir, Governor-General of Canada, Lionel Hichens, one of the most enlightened of great industrialists, Geoffrey Dawson, long editor of the *Times*, and Lionel Curtis, whose philosophy of Empire was a power behind the scenes for two generations. Long after the Kindergarten itself was disbanded, its members were held together by loyalty to Milner and his creed, and through their quarterly *Round Table*, and countless other channels, diffused an enlightened and liberal imperial doctrine which shared almost nothing with the imperialism of the scramble for Africa save its now tarnished name.

Milner and his Kindergarten, like the band of brilliant young men who reorganised Sind and the Punjab under the Lawrence brothers, were not working within the ruts of a departmental system, and under such conditions the British genius for administration always flowers most freely. At almost any other period of British history it would no doubt have been equally possible to collect, as Milner did, a body of promising young men from outside the government service, and turn them loose to recreate a country within two years. But even so they owed their success to the great man who chose and led them. One of the finest scholars of his time, Milner had been inspired by Arnold Toynbee to dedicate his life to the state, and later experience had enlarged his instinct for radical social reform to embrace the Empire as a whole. To a singular degree his mind united breadth of vision with mastery of detail. He was perhaps too perfect an administrator to be a perfect diplomatist, and his critics maintained that if in his fervour for a modern democracy in South Africa he had made more sympathetic allowances for Kruger's ideal of an Old Testament patriarchy, the Bloemfontein Conference might have averted the Boer War. But as an administrator he was unequalled. In a double sense he was responsible for the rebirth of a nation, for he reconstructed South Africa from the foundations, and everywhere—whether in joint institutions for Transvaal and Orange Free State or in inter-Colonial Conferences and Commissions—his rebuilding was designed for Union. Indeed Milner believed himself to be working for an even more distant goal; confessedly "an imperialist more than an Englishman," he never ceased to dream of federation of the Empire.

In South Africa federation, his ultimate objective, must wait upon reconstruction; but economic federation, of the sort for which Rhodes had worked, was an obvious and necessary preliminary to it, and was already within reach; and in 1903 Milner called a second Conference at Bloemfontein, which established a customs system for the whole of South Africa, including Southern Rhodesia and the Native Protectorates. It was this Conference which decided to import indentured Chinese labour to the goldfields—a mistake with far-reaching repercussions, for the conditions under which the segregated Chinese immigrants were forced to live shocked opinion at home and made a powerful contributory factor in the defeat of the Conservative Government in the election of 1906.

Responsible self-government was introduced into both Transvaal and Orange Free State in 1907, and Boer administrations resulted from the first elections in each Colony. The traditional preliminary of representative government without executive powers had been omitted. Thus within five years of the signing of peace Boer Prime Ministers were ruling their own country with virtually untrammelled powers. But during those five years their country had become a modern democracy, in place of a patriarchal tyranny founded upon racial ascendancy. And now the Boers made to the great transformation a contribution no less remarkable than that of the British. In the Transvaal Botha took office, "built on lines of primitive simplicity, and wise with an elemental wisdom." His presence at the Imperial Conference of 1907, and his declaration that he was prepared to fight for Britain as whole-heartedly as he had once fought against her, had profoundly impressed Sir Wilfred Laurier, of Canada. "Such a consummation," he said, "would be possible nowhere except within the bounds of the British Empire." Botha's Colonial Secretary was J. C. Smuts. Smuts was now thirty-seven; at thirty-one he had been in supreme command of the Boer forces in Cape Colony. But for the war he might have lived and died a Johannesburg lawyer. The war, and the defeat of his people, which he would do more than any other man to turn to victory, transformed him into a statesman who would shape the new South Africa and profoundly influence the destinies of the Empire and the world. He had read Law at Cambridge, where he headed both parts of the Law Tripos; he liked and understood the British, and he combined an acute practical intelligence with that philosophic bent which sees every problem in the light of eternal principles. Three years after the Boer War he had been sent to England to ask the new Liberal cabinet for responsible government. "I saw," he said,

> Churchill, Morley, Elgin, Lloyd George, Campbell Bannerman. The only one I had met before was Churchill. I came across him when he was taken prisoner at Ladysmith. He asked me if I had ever known of a conquered people being allowed to govern themselves. I said no. But we did not want to govern ourselves. We could not govern ourselves without England's assistance. . . .

His talk with Campbell Bannerman "settled the future of South Africa." Responsible government was ensured.

The passing of three of the four colonies under Afrikander control—for early in 1908 the Afrikander Bond, renamed South African Party, defeated Jameson and resumed power in the Cape—brought Union nearer, for no Afrikander need now fear that Union would mean British domination. "We do not know what lies ahead of us," said Smuts.

> To-day we are standing under the majesty and the power of the British flag, but we do not know what will be the case a hundred years hence, and there is only one thing the people of South Africa can do—become a united people.

And it was becoming increasingly obvious that the main political problems of South Africa could only be satisfactorily solved by a unitary government. There was the threat of a native rising in Natal, a rising which Natal would not be strong enough to master and which might imperil all South Africa. There were sharp differences of opinion over customs and railways. And there were the Indians. Imported into Natal as coolies since 1860, they had since played a not inconsiderable economic rôle both there and in the Transvaal. Both Colonies now wished to restrict the entrance and activities of Asiatics, and one of the first measures of the new Transvaal Parliament was an immigration law providing for an education test and thumb-print registration. Against this passive resistance was already being organised by a prosperous Indian barrister in Johannesburg named Gandhi, who was soon to figure on a wider stage. All these more or less intractable problems clearly needed the hand of a central authority. Lord Selborne, who had succeeded Milner as High Commissioner in 1905, was able and approachable and knew his Bible as well as any Boer farmer. And he shared the enthusiasm for Union of Lionel Curtis and those members of the Kindergarten who had been studying Oliver's *Life* of the great American Federalist, Alexander Hamilton.

In 1907 they drafted the historic Selborne Memorandum, whose lucid and tactful survey of the case for Union served to crystallise public opinion at a crucial moment. Discreetly "dropped in the path of South African statesmen," it set politicians and Closer Union Societies everywhere discussing Union. A National Convention met in the summer of 1908. The delegates of Het Volk, the Dutch Party of the Transvaal, and the Cape Colony Progressives, came fully briefed and armed with a constitution drafted by Smuts and the Kindergarten, and the discussions centred naturally round their proposals. Gradually the more explosive problems were solved, or else, like education and native policy, discreetly shelved—only reluctantly, and under stringent safeguards, was the Cape permitted to retain its non-European franchise. But before the end of 1909 the Act for the Union of South Africa had passed the imperial Parliament.

The Union, which came into being in 1910, is not a federation. The Union Parliament, and not the written constitution, is the supreme authority, and the four colonies, now Provinces, each with a Provincial Council, exercise their limited powers at the pleasure of the central authority. In general the now familiar imperial model was followed, with a Governor-General to represent the Crown, a Senate of ten members for each of the four provinces, and an Assembly whose numbers are proportioned to population. Botha took office as the first Prime Minister of the Union. There were many lions in the path of the new South Africa, most of them, like racial jealousies and the old divisions over native policy, legacies of the past. The fact remained that as a direct consequence of their defeat in war, and within a decade of it, the Boer leaders were ruling not only the Transvaal but all South Africa. There had been wisdom, generosity and courage in the policy of Britain, and the presence of Botha and Smuts was a sufficient guarantee that there would be wisdom, generosity and courage in the response to it. Moreover when the Union Bill had reached Westminster all Parties had been agreed that it was not for them to introduce amendments of substance. Another stage in imperial evolution had been reached. The imperial Parliament claimed now no more than to give legal form to the agreements already arrived at by the self-governing colonies. Not only had the tradition of free nationality within the Empire been greatly fortified and enlarged, but the elastic imperial structure had once more accommodated itself to changing circumstance, on the eve of an ordeal which only a political organism manifestly serving the present needs of mankind could hope to survive.

§8

When the Imperial Conference (for so it was now styled) met in 1911 the threat of the coming world war with Germany was already taking shape. The Committee of Imperial Defence conducted its military and naval discussions in secret, but in open session Sir Joseph Ward, of New Zealand, put forward a proposal which went to the roots of the problem of defence and indeed of the whole imperial structure. Why not an imperial parliament, of two Houses, and an executive council, with jurisdiction over defence and diplomacy, and power to apportion the costs among the constituent nations? The proposal was only perfunctorily discussed. In Britain the present generation had heard, and thought, little of imperial federation. And the young self-governing nations overseas prized their new autonomy too highly to be prepared to sacrifice a substantial part of it to a central authority. Nor was it yet apparent that the British taxpayer could not indefinitely maintain the defence of the Empire virtually unaided. But the dangers of aggression from without would grow steadily more formidable, and the military and economic scale of the leading world powers would steadily expand. The British Navy had kept the peace of the world since 1815; could it continue to prevent a world war—with the acquisitive passions of a century of materialism soon to be unleashed —unless the full military and economic resources of all its members could somehow be integrated? Could the Empire, as at present organised, even rely upon winning a world war, if a world war should come? In an age of great and increasing concentrations of force could it even rely upon maintaining itself much longer among the two or three leading world powers, so long as its defensive system rested ultimately upon the resources of the British Isles? Such questions as these would become increasingly insistent, but in 1911 they were not insistent yet. The fact that the colonies had outgrown political tutelage was already felt to carry with it certain implications as to foreign policy, and the Conference resolved that whenever possible they should be informed as to transactions with foreign powers before these were irrevocably concluded—the modest rudiments of a principle not yet fully recognised, but destined to develop far and swiftly. But political maturity, though it implied further rights was not held to involve further obligations, and Britain continued to hold over the Dominions the shield of the Royal Navy, as in the days of their infancy, almost unaided. There were some who, in default of Chamberlain's imperial preference, saw in British sea-power and the Dominions' naval weakness the one all-potent bond of material interest between the scattered units of the Empire. But the true bond of Empire in the years of trial to come would be the sense of community which springs from a common history, a common loyalty and a common way of life.

CHAPTER TWO

BACKWARD PEOPLES

(1870-1914)

§1

IN THE DARK and prolonged ordeal which Britain and the British Empire were now so soon to face the chief title to survival of the self-governing communities overseas would be that they had spread the idea of freedom across the world. In this way most palpably they were serving the interests of mankind. Could any comparable claim be made on behalf of all those elements of the Empire which were not self-governing? Were these too in some analogous fashion serving the interests of mankind? On no other terms could they too hope to survive the decades to come.

§2

In many ways, and in particular as most backward, the African Crown Colonies and Protectorates may be said to afford the most searching test. Nowhere did ancient and deeply rooted-savagery present a more novel and exacting problem, nowhere had authority on the spot freer scope for evolving its own solution. In Africa there was no question, as in the Dominions or in India, of the slow increment of generations of growth; here swift improvisation was inevitable. The opportunity for initiative was perhaps unparalleled, even in the annals of the Empire. It was for these pioneer administrators, with scanty funds and an underpaid and inadequate staff,[1] to control vast areas without roads or communications, to put down the internal slave trade, of whose very existence the British public was hardly aware, to stamp out the domestic warfare which had been endemic since time immemorial, to create an administration and a system of justice out of chaos. Nowhere was the problem more formidable, or its solution more fruitful, than in Nigeria. The colony and Protectorate of Nigeria had grown out of the territories of the Royal Niger Company (whose political jurisdiction passed to the Crown in 1899-1900) the old Niger Coast Protectorate and the colony and Protectorate of Lagos. When British administrators

---

[1] In 1903 there were 44 administrative officers in Northern Nigeria, 1 to every 400,000 of the population.

began their work, Northern Nigeria had long been subject to the Fulani, Mahommedans more capable of rule than the indigenous peoples.

> The subject races near the capital were then serfs, and the victims of constant extortion. Those dwelling at a distance were raided for slaves, and could not count their women, their cattle, or their crops their own. Punishments . . . included impalement, mutilation and burying alive.[1]

The picture only needs darkening to serve for almost any of these African territories. When Uganda, for example, passed under British control in 1891 a triangular civil war was raging, Christians were burnt at the stake and the population of wide areas was decimated by slave-raids.

To grapple with these deep-rooted and complex problems the British government was wise enough to trust in the main to the men on the spot. And indeed it was the sort of situation in which the British administrator is apt to be at his best. A distinguished Frenchman, M. Cambon, has observed that "in colonisation the English have method but not system," and in Africa, as elsewhere, that fortunate characteristic was their salvation; for instead of enforcing a rigid, theoretic system, they would gradually and empirically mould their administration to the peculiar needs of the African peoples. It was a task for which there was virtually no precedent, one of the milestones in the history of man, this introduction, so sudden and on so vast a scale, of the African negro to the civilisation of Europe. Fortunately, as so often before in imperial history, the man to match a great occasion was forthcoming. Sir Frederick (afterwards Lord) Lugard had commanded an expedition against the slave traders of Lake Nyasa when he was thirty; he had led the expedition which brought distracted Uganda under British control in 1890, and had laid the foundations of its administration during the next two years; he had raised and commanded the West African Frontier Force; he had conquered and pacified the warlike Mohammedan states of North Nigeria; and for two fruitful periods of six years, after 1900 and again after 1913, he ruled over the whole colony and Protectorate of Nigeria. His profound knowledge of Africa had long since convinced him that the purpose of British rule must not be to turn the African into an inferior imitation of the European. Somehow Western civilisation must enrich and refashion, but not overwhelm, the ancient traditions of the negro. As early as 1893 he had written of Uganda, "the object to be aimed at in the

---

[1] Lord Lugard *The Dual Mandate in British Tropical Africa*, 198-9.

administration of this country is to rule through its own executive government." That sentence embodied the whole principle of indirect rule, whereby the shock of the impact of Europe would be partially absorbed, and its lessons rendered both more palatable and more intelligible for the African, by the intervention of his own hereditary institutions. And so in Nigeria each Emir, or paramount chief, each district and village Headman, became an active and responsible ruler. The British Resident supervised, assisted and advised the leading prince, as did District Officers the district and village Headmen; but the whole, British and Africans together—and it was this which gave the system its unique character—formed a single, indivisible administration. Indirect rule through dependent princes is a very ancient imperial device, but never before had imperial officials and native rulers been welded into one organic whole. Within the British Empire there had been premonitions of indirect rule as it developed under Lugard in Nigeria—in Natal, for example, under Shepstone in the 'fifties, under the first Governor of Fiji in the 'seventies and under the first administrator of British New Guinea, and more recently, in Africa, in Buganda and Barotseland. But it was in the Moslem states of Northern Nigeria that indirect rule first attained its full stature. For soon Emirs and headmen who had so lately raided their neighbours for slaves, and impaled their prisoners or buried them alive, were poring industriously over plans for schools and dispensaries, or supervising the construction of court houses and roads. In the courts, under British supervision, native judges administered native law. Native rulers were not permitted to raise armed forces, legislate or impose (though they could assess) taxation. But in general they had become the trusted delegates of the Governor, integral elements in a single government, with a status as clearly defined as that of the British officials themselves.

By such means and without any abrupt convulsion the moral and material texture of life in Nigeria was swiftly and steadily transformed. Native Emirs vied with each other in the progress of the schools, some of them residential, which the government, following here in the wake of the missionaries, was actively developing. The gulf for education to bridge was prodigious. The childish memories of the young Africans of the coming generation who would one day take advanced degrees at a British or American University would be of smoky huts shared by goats, of medicine men and rain-makers and tabus. The material framework of society changed even more conspicuously. The new and undreamed-of security of life and property caused an exodus from the towns. The railway, which had penetrated a mere hundred and twenty-five miles inland from Lagos by 1901, was pushed through the interior. The huge, primitive Protectorate was entering on the first stage of organised economic life, the stage of commerce rather than industry, of exported raw materials rather than domestic manufactures. Both Africa and Europe were gainers. The oil-nuts which had grown wild and rotted, ungarnered, in the forests, were cultivated and exported overseas. Africa had begun to send out the food supplies and raw materials increasingly demanded by the rising economic standards of Europe; in return it was not only the native African merchants and middlemen who profited; nor only the influx of manufactured goods by which the native population benefited. All Nigeria, all British tropical Africa indeed, was being transformed from a race of slaves and serfs, helplessly subject to the caprice of irresponsible tyrants, into an ordered society of communal proprietors and wage-earners, in which saving and social advancement were possible.

§3

Lugard's indirect rule became the basis of British administration throughout tropical Africa. Its effects on the moral and material texture of native life were swift and salutary. On the plane of the spirit it moved, in the tradition of its age, with less conviction. In most of tropical Africa trade preceded the flag, and missionaries had preceded both. Missionaries had set up their schools many decades before the government's, they had trained the greater part of the government's subordinate native staff, and in many unspectacular ways, despite unedifying sectarian rivalry, they had done the civilising work of the government for it. Yet, in general, as the great Lugard himself put it, "the attitude which British governments have endeavoured to assume is that of strict neutrality, impartiality and tolerance in all religious matters—but ' every man should be free to worship God as he chooses.'" In the context[1] Lugard was thinking primarily of Islam, and there were special difficulties, it is true, about the presence of Christian missions in Moslem states, for they were inevitably assumed by the native to be instruments of the British government, and it has been alleged that "a genuine conversion of a genuine Mussulman has never taken place." But even in pagan regions the government was apt to produce the impression that it stood deliberately aloof, admitting missionaries on sufferance, and subject always to the paramount interests of the secular administration. Matters spiritual it was content to leave, as it had once left trade, industry and colonisation

[1] *The Dual Mandate in British Tropical Africa*, 594.

itself, to individual initiative. The conversion of the heathen had always been a dominant motive among the early colonists, it was never a dominant motive with the state. For it was in an age of materialism that the state assumed paramount authority in the Empire. The missionary, and the spread of Christianity, had initiated profound changes in the moral texture of African life, and particularly a transformation in many regions of the status of women, but with the now paramount state standing deliberately aloof from religion much of the responsibility for the moral education of the native came to rest upon the British official. Recruited for the most part from the English public schools, themselves traditionally training grounds of character, he possessed the now familiar qualities which since about 1850 had rendered incalculable service to the Empire, as well as their less numerous defects. Unrivalled as a leader of primitive and martial peoples, fertile in initiative, incorruptible, courageous and humane, towards superiors and inferiors alike he displayed an instinctive loyalty which would often sacrifice health, and life itself, to his service. A certain lack of imagination was his chief defect. The Westernised native and his ambitions he found it hard to understand or indulge, he was sometimes too ready to confuse legitimate criticism with sedition, and he seldom made effective contact with the religious and artistic life of a foreign people. And with him religion was seldom, as it had so often been with the early British administrators of India, a dominant inspiration. No one in short could have been better qualified to train the character of a primitive people—except a Livingstone.

The system did not always commend itself to the educated native, since it gave authority to chiefs who in the early years lacked all class-room education and were often unable even to speak the English language, and rendered them largely independent of the native lawyer and expert with his Western training. It is true also that by supporting native rule the British government accepted some degree of responsibility for the failures inevitable at first in a system with a long tradition of tyranny behind it, supervised by so meagre a staff of British officials. But that indirect rule produced loyal chiefs and a contented and increasingly prosperous people there can be no doubt, and the evidence is written large across the records. In Nigeria by 1914 both population and revenue were steadily increasing, the bandits of the North Nigerian hilltops were coming down to live peacefully in well-planned villages in the plains, and violence and disorder were fading memories of the past. When during the coming war Northern Nigeria was thought to be threatened by a powerful Moslem army, when the people of the neighbouring

French territories to the north had risen in revolt, and most of the British forces in Nigeria had already been withdrawn for service elsewhere, there was never any doubt of the country's loyalty. Twenty-nine years after Lugard left Uganda he was still regularly receiving letters from the chiefs whose friendship and devotion he had won there.

After the first German war indirect rule would spread yet further in British Africa—to Tanganyika, the southern Sudan, Northern Rhodesia and Kenya. Already on the eve of the ordeal, all through the varied pattern of life in British tropical Africa can be traced the steady growth of the doctrine of trusteeship, of the principle that the paramount interest is that of the native population, the heir-apparent of its own recreated country. The doctrine could hardly extend to the regions in which the white man himself had taken root and whose future he naturally considered primarily his own concern. Indeed one of the most intractable of African problems would soon be the contrast between the practice of trusteeship in the British colonies and Protectorates and the repressive native policy of self-governing South Africa.

But in the meantime if there were many shortcomings in the administration of British tropical Africa as the hour of another struggle for survival drew near, and although a considerable proportion of them could be ascribed, in the last analysis, to the ignorance and apathy of the British public itself, there was none the less no lack either of the seeds of growth. The British were in process of discovering in the Dependencies, as they had discovered in the Dominions, a new political secret.

§4

In the further East the organisation of Malaya had in a sense been the prototype of indirect rule in tropical Africa. At the time of the treaty with the Dutch in 1824, the British Settlements in the Straits—Singapore, Malacca and Penang—had been of insignificant area, dotted about the broad southern extremity of the peninsula, the greater part of which was occupied by a number of native sultanates, whose tin was already being mined by industrious Chinese immigrants. Their rulers were arbitrary tyrants perpetually at war with each other, plundering and crushing their peoples with excessive taxation and forced labour. Under these conditions, their subjects seldom abandoned their natural indolence save to embark upon piracy or brigandage. Even the Chinese fought savagely with each other and against their Malay overlords. The potential wealth of the country was well known; its anarchy was perpetual and flagrant; it was defenceless—the situation, in short, might have been purposely designed to invite the intervention of a predatory imperialism. But this was an epoch in which the word imperialism, in its modern sense, had yet to be coined, the pre-German era. And if the condition of Malaya marked it out as a potential prey for the appetites of imperialism at its worst, it equally invited the assistance of imperialism at its best.

In 1867 the Straits Settlements passed from the Indian government to the control of the Colonial Office. For many years the independent Malay States of Perak, Selangor and Negri Sembilan (the Nine States) had been devastated by perpetual anarchy. They had repeatedly implored the East India Company, and then Great Britain, to intervene and rule, but their requests had always been curtly refused. At last in 1874 disorder had become so formidable, and the coast so unsafe for shipping, that the British government reluctantly yielded, so far as to attempt a compromise. Even now it would not itself rule, but it would dispatch a Resident adviser to Perak and Selangor and to Sungei Ujong, one of the Nine small states. This was to expect a great deal from the Resident. "It is one thing," wrote Sir Frank Swettenham,

> to send two or three white men into a country where none of their kind has ever been seen before: to tell them to advise those whose minds and traditions are crooked to follow the straight path and never deviate; to endow them with the sole authority to collect and expend all revenues and to regulate the general administration of the country with no force behind them but their courage, tact, ability and the spectre of British power miles away in the dim and shadowy background. It is quite another thing to evolve peace and order and prosperity. . . .

Yet this is in effect what was achieved. The Resident at Perak was murdered in 1875, but thereafter there was no serious disturbance; unobtrusively the Pax Britannica took root, with prosperity in its wake. Thanks largely to the influence of Sir Hugh Low, Resident at Perak from 1877 to 1889, the Malays were governed through their own chiefs and headmen, and here too indirect rule prospered. British officials encouraged immigration from India, China and other parts of Malaya, made the personal acquaintance of the immigrants, nursed them through their early difficulties, encouraged them to build and plant, and taught them "a pride in their surroundings which amounted to the gift of a new sense." Modern institutions were gradually built up, without laying an axe to the roots of the traditional social system. Malayan tin and rubber were steadily developed, to the benefit no doubt of merchants and investors in Britain and elsewhere, but to the no less certain, and even greater, benefit of Malaya itself, transformed within a few decades from an impoverished and fever-stricken jungle of pirates and brigands to a free, prosperous and contented community attracting immigrants from all over the Far East. In this new Malaya the life and property of the humblest Malayan were for the first time secure. For the first time he owned a permanent title to his land. Free education, free hospitals and free medicine were his, banks for his savings, and rail and roads for his travel. The government helped him to build his mosque and to drain and irrigate his fields. Arbitrary taxation and forced labour, slavery and piracy were no more. Cholera and smallpox had virtually disappeared. The courts of law dispensed equal justice to men of every colour and creed. And thanks to the natural wealth of Malaya, all that was asked of the Malayan in return was a small quit-rent, if he owned land. Perhaps indeed too little was asked, for the Malay is careless and indolent by nature and the Dutch in Java had found that only taxation would spur the population to industry. Yet the contrast between the old Malaya and the new was the contrast between pre-Norman England and the England of the twentieth century.

And there had been no conquest ; indeed, save for a minor punitive expedition after the murder in Perak in 1875, there had been no fighting. Order had been evolved without the use of force, by the personal influence of the British Residents and officials. The hereditary rulers of Malaya had not been displaced, nor the texture of Malayan life abruptly unravelled. If these were not the highest gifts which one nation can conceivably bestow upon another they were the highest which any nation in that age was capable of bestowing, and almost inevitably the British system spread. Between 1883 and 1895 supervision was extended to the rest of the Negri Sembilan, and in 1887-8 to Pahang. In 1896 the four Protected states were federated in one administration. In 1914 a British administration was given to Johore, at the southern tip of the peninsula; and in 1909 four states to the northward, previously under Siamese jurisdiction, similarly became Protectorates. Here too indirect rule transformed the native potentates from primitive tyrants to enlightened servants of their peoples. Of what was being done in their name in Malaya, as elsewhere in the Empire, the British at home remained almost completely ignorant. Yet here too on the eve of their ordeal, they held a key to the future in their hands.

CHAPTER THREE

INDIA AFTER THE MUTINY

(1857-1914)

§1

IN THE Dominions their new status and in the Colonial Empire the growing conception of trusteeship and the practise of indirect rule represented patterns of growth which were full of life because in them a practical genius for government was working in harmony with deep-seated natural tendencies. In India between the Mutiny and the opening of the great ordeal with the first German war we are not conscious of this sense of steady development, natural yet deliberately planned, towards some significant and ever more clearly defined goal—unless indeed modern methods of administration can be accounted such. India, it is true, was unique, a continent rather than a country, a vast kaleidoscope of nations without racial or religious unity, which as yet only Europeans, and not its own natives, even thought of as India. Yet it is difficult to resist the impression that, whereas in Canada or Nigeria the British, grappling, as was their habit, with the problem as it arose, had nevertheless all the while half-unconsciously been steering, by the compass of their own political instincts, for distant goals, goals implicit almost from the first in their most empirical solution of the immediate problem, in India on the other hand during the greater part of this period they are merely governing. Their rule, if often aloof and unimaginative, is superbly incorruptible and highly efficient and it achieves many prodigious results, yet it does not seem to contain within it, in the same sense as elsewhere, the impulse of organic growth. This may be but another way of saying that in India the British were working in a more recalcitrant medium. Or more probably that it was impossible for any ultimate political goal to define itself until, as a direct consequence of British rule, India had covered some of the vast distance which separated her from self-conscious nationhood.

In British India no analogy was forthcoming to the indirect rule of the Colonial Empire—save in the restricted sense that, in the native states, the British government had constituted itself adviser and protector of the Indian princes, and would on occasion intervene, or even, as in Baroda in 1875, remove an oppressive ruler, in the interests of his subjects. "Clemency" Canning, the Viceroy of the Mutiny, had, it is true, conceived the idea of turning the landed classes in British India into magistrates and administrators on the English model, of "increasing the consequence of and placing trust in the native chiefs and gentry generally." It was a remarkable project for the Viceroy of the Mutiny to have entertained at a time when the prevailing impression in Britain was that no Indian official could be trusted, and if it had proved possible to make of the zemindar a counterpart of the British Justice of the Peace, not only Indian administration, but, later, Indian nationalism might perhaps have developed to an altogether different and more indigenous pattern.

§2

Inevitably, as we have seen,[1] the Mutiny left its mark, but neither the Mutiny nor the transfer of the government to the Crown had occasioned any profound heart-searchings at home or anything resembling a revolution in the administration of India. Perhaps if the men who had had the actual suppressing of the Mutiny had been a trifle more alarmed by it, its moral and intellectual effects would have gone deeper. But the British had preserved their proverbial calm, and the *Times* even observed how, with Lucknow still in the hands of the rebels, officers travelling up country would complain of the absence of tablecloths and the incivility of the native servants in the *dak* bungalows. But though the Mutiny provoked no administrative revolution it was not without lasting effects. The years which followed were the heyday of paternalism, but it was a paternalism which held notably aloof, taking little interest in the tastes and opinions of educated Indians; for the Mutiny had put an end to the notion that India was to be transformed by the infiltration of western ideas through the educated classes. The Indian Councils Act of 1861 added to the Viceroy's executive council of five from six to twelve members for legislative purposes only, and there were a number of analogous provincial Councils; all of them, both central and provincial, included some Indians, but there was no election until 1892. And Indians were permitted no key positions in the great new administrative machine which resulted from the methodical unification of the vast diversity of India during the two decades which followed the Mutiny. Virtually no Indians

[1] See pp. 342-347 above.

had reached the highest ranks of the Civil Service by 1885, and even by 1915 only five per cent of it was Indian. The object of the British government was not so much to repress Indian aspirations as to maintain efficiency. It was as if after the shock of the Mutiny the British had set themselves resolutely to *govern* India—effectively, conscientiously and benevolently, but across a gulf. As always, British officials and British officers could make loyal followers or friends of the simple folk among whom their duties took them, but the system as a whole was impersonal. With a native population which by 1872 had reached two hundred and fifty millions, a vast majority of whom had never set eyes upon a European, a certain effect of aloofness was doubtless inevitable; indeed it was one of the merits of British rule, and clear evidence that it was not resented by the masses, that three thousand British officials, spread over all the various public services, supported by a British army of no more than sixty thousand men, should be sufficient to govern India and keep the peace.[1]

Nevertheless other and less healthy symptoms helped to set a gulf between government and people. During the 'sixties and 'seventies the foundations of the industry and commerce of modern India were being laid apace; the cotton industry was developing in Bombay, and the jute industry in Bengal, tea-planting in Assam and coffee-planting in the Nilgiris, and foreign trade was expanding. Industry and commerce alike were bringing a steady influx of business men to India; and most of these new arrivals had been permanently, if not always consciously, prejudiced by the Mutiny. They came out to India ready to suspect, and sometimes to despise, all things Indian, and with a new sense of racial cleavage and racial superiority. The business community was soon numerous enough to live a separate social life of its own, to develop a communal sense and sometimes to exercise organised pressure on the government. If the chief defect of most British officials and officers in India was a certain lack of sensitiveness and imagination, these qualities were much more conspicuously lacking in British business men; and, what in India mattered even more, their manners were much less courteous. They never wielded powerful or permanent influence over the government, but they were capable on occasion of violent agitation, and it is said that their campaign against the Ilbert Bill of 1883 (which proposed to abolish the privilege that for a criminal offence a European could only be tried by Europeans) taught nascent Indian nationalism a lesson which it never forgot—that even the

[1] In 1881 the total "British-born" population, including the army and the business men, was 99,738.

powerful British government could be induced to compromise by newspaper abuse and public insult. In the same way the long tradition, dating from the early days of the Company, that the Press was free to attack, and to misrepresent, the government was a precedent on which the earliest Indian vernacular newspapers fastened with avidity.

§3

By 1885 the new administrative machine had been assembled and was running smoothly. It may have been somewhat unimaginative and aloof, it may have been insufficiently conscious of moving towards any defined goal, save its own goal of just and effective administration, but undisputably it governed. For the first time a resolute and well-equipped administration was grappling with the age-old afflictions of India. In some ways its most formidable problem was the recurrent famine, to which many parts of the peninsula had been subject since time immemorial. For centuries famine had been thought of as an inevitable natural calamity, virtually impossible to avert or relieve; even the East India Company had so regarded the fourteen major famines of the ninety years between 1660 and 1750. But the cause was clearly the periodical drought, to which many areas were liable, and the complete failure of crops which would ensue. Since relief had always depended upon animal transport, which was immobilised by a drought, and since in the era of disorder no government had possessed the necessary authority, relief had hitherto been virtually unknown. Now with the new security of life and property population increased steadily and tended, more than ever, to spread out into the areas of precarious rainfall. But now irrigation could reduce the risks, and railways transport foodstuffs into the devastated areas. When famine fell upon the North West Provinces in 1860, the New Jumna Canals saved a million acres in the heart of the afflicted area, and the new railway brought in grain from Calcutta. In the Orissa famine of 1867 on the other hand the government was virtually helpless, for Orissa had not yet been opened up, and no adequate roads, railways or harbours linked it with the lands of plenty. Between one and two millions of the population perished. There was still much to learn. Threatened with a crop failure in densely populated Bihar and Bengal in 1873 the government took exaggerated precautions, spent six and a half millions on importing and distributing grain, and was left with a hundred thousand tons of rice rotting on its hands. Sir

Richard Temple came to the conclusion that "the task of saving life irrespective of cost" was beyond any government's power; the consequent debt and taxation, he thought, must eventually prove more fatal than the famine itself. The government accordingly went about the next famine, in 1876, more cautiously. Unfortunately it proved to be the greatest of all famines, affecting 200,000 square miles and a population of thirty-six millions in southern and central India. The government eventually spent eleven million pounds, but the monsoon rains failed in two successive years and the resulting catastrophe dwarfed the relief measures, and indeed all the available resources, into insignificance. The government had learnt its lesson. A prolonged and systematic study of famine and famine relief was now undertaken, and the new Famine Code was the outcome, with its methodical preparations for combining prevention with cure. The consequences were spectacular. In the famine of 1896 three-quarters of a million persons died, but relief measures saved four millions. In 1899 a million died but six millions were saved. And henceforth famines, as India had once known them, were no more. The population, no longer diminished as of old by violence and civil war. steadily increased—it rose by eighteen million between 1901 and 1911—and pressed continuously upon the margin of subsistence. But a new network of irrigation-canals steadied and extended the output of wheat; and although the race between irrigation and the careless fecundity of the Indian peasant was never-ending, so that sooner or later irrigation must be outstripped, for the time being it greatly decreased the incidence of famine. The death-rate in some of the later famines scarcely exceeded the normal, and the contrast with the heavy mortality in a number of the Native States, where mediæval methods lingered, was sufficient evidence of what British rule had achieved. Before the age-old problem could be mastered India had needed internal peace, modern science and an administration capable of planning for the whole sub-continent. The British had given her all three.

§4

But if India was to be modernised, and this goal at least the British had set themselves long since, it was not sufficient to forestall or mitigate natural disasters; she must be equipped with the mechanism—her rulers scarcely aimed at providing her with the soul—of a modern state. How could education be diffused among that vast diversity of race and creed, which ranged from the noblest spiritual culture to the most primitive savagery? A Department of Education was one of the first creations of the Crown government, and India possessed an organised system of state education earlier than England itself, and half a century before the Dutch East Indies. But it was of a strictly limited character. The obstacles indeed were very formidable. For the Indian peasant saw little advantage in sending his sons to school, and none in sending his daughters. And even if his children did acquire literacy, soon after their return to the fields, with nothing to read and virtually nothing to write, they were usually soon illiterate again. Tradition moreover forbade either Hindu or Mohammedan women to become teachers, and many Mohammedans had strong objections to secular teaching of any kind. By the end of the century little more had been achieved than to systematise under public control and inspection, and with the aid of public funds, the various private institutions through which the small minority of castes and classes which already desired education had always achieved a certain standard of literacy. India in general was as illiterate as ever, and showed no desire whatever for a change. In 1904 the Government set itself resolutely to extend primary education. The new campaign had behind it ample funds, a formidable administrative machine and the confident energies of Lord Curzon. It had been launched at an Education Conference which passed, without a dissentient voice, a hundred and fifty resolutions drafted by the Viceroy's own indefatigable pen. But to extend education from the castes and classes which had always desired it to those, so vastly more numerous, to which it had always been a matter of complete indifference, this, it soon appeared, was a task before which the most powerful bureaucracy might well quail. "Harassed subordinates prepared maps and schemes and went round begging villages to accept schools"; and schools seemed to grow up, and too often to disappear, almost overnight. In 1921 only seventeen, out of the two hundred and forty-seven, millions in British India could read and write. Curzon seems to have divined that for Indian tastes there was a certain bleakness, almost a lack of soul, about a state-controlled Western education. "Ever since the cold breath of Macaulay's rhetoric passed over the field of the Indian languages and Indian textbooks," he wrote, "the elementary education of the people in their own tongues has shrivelled and pined." But even so he was unable to provide a curriculum capable of charming the vast illiterate majority of Indians out of their age-long indifference to education. Perhaps learning centred more directly upon religion, the age-long preoccupation of the old India, or upon politics, the increasing cult of the new, might have fired more imaginations;

but it would not have been education as education is known in the West. Perhaps no unitary administration, modelled upon that of a homogeneous Western state, could have provided intellectual fare flexible enough for the infinite diversities of India. Perhaps much more than a century was needed to persuade the Indian peasant and his priests that secular education could bring him any good.

The Universities it seemed easier to reform. For to Curzon, of Balliol and All Souls, the institutions originally set up by Lord Canning in Calcutta, Bombay and Madras, scarcely appeared to be Universities at all. The Indian University was "not even a collection of buildings; it was scarcely even a site"; it was a mere examining body, empowered to grant degrees. The result had been to stimulate not, as Canning had hoped, the teaching in the schools, but a vast industry of cramming and a portentous flood of candidates for matriculation, only one in seventeen of whom eventually acquired the degree, so coveted as a passport to clerical employment that even the unsuccessful were apt to describe themselves proudly as "failed B.A." Curzon's reforms were designed to substitute a wider education for a smaller number of students, with some sort of corporate University life, in place of what had become a mercenary scramble, by way of the examination room, for government posts and openings at the Bar. His proposals were hotly resisted by all, and there were many, whose vested interests in the old system were threatened, and though they were duly enacted, a new Commission, thirteen years later, found Calcutta University still predominantly an examining body.

§5

But of all the tasks which faced the Government of India at once the most symbolic and the most insoluble was that of breaking down the age-long oriental indifference of its peoples to the most elementary principles of sanitation, hygiene and health. For the worst of the traditional practices were those consecrated by religion or enjoined by tabu. It was religion which preserved the sacred cow —starving, tortured, diseased or browsing on garbage, but alive— which made of childbirth a nightmare medley of filth, cruelty and witchcraft, and the death-rate of both mothers and infants the highest in the world; which taught men to drink from the river putrid with sewage and human corpses; which substituted black magic for medicine, charms for disinfectants, and astrology for diagnosis; which forbade the Hindu meat, taught him that unbridled sexual indulgence was a religious virtue and enjoined child-marriage, so that with every generation he became physically more feeble; which made of every widow an outcast, approved infanticide and consecrated mendicancy and prostitution; which condemned sixty million Untouchables to fantastic deprivations—so that some, forbidden to pollute the earth by lying on it, roosted like bats in the trees. A government which after the Mutiny held itself pledged not to interfere with the religious customs of the people could make little headway against customs so deeply rooted. *Suttee* and thuggery had been abolished, before the Mutiny, by force and the edict of the sovereign power; it seemed unlikely that persuasion would suffice to end child-marriage or infanticide. And if some well-intentioned Westernising measure were placed upon the statute book, such as that which in 1891 raised the legal age for the consummation of marriage to twelve, the prospects of its being obeyed were dubious in the extreme. Public sanitation was slowly forced upon the towns, so that the death-rate in the army, British and Indian, fell from some twenty per thousand in the 'seventies to under five per thousand in the last years before the first world war. But the inroads of science upon the vast medley of superstition and suffering were painfully slow, so slow that sometimes there seemed to be no movement at all. When the bubonic plague came to India in 1896 the Government's insistence on inspection, quarantine and disinfection was passionately denounced by educated Indian nationalists in the name of religion and of caste. The old customs might have been swept away by an administration which had succeeded in converting India to Christianity, or in reforming the old religions, or which was prepared to deal with child-marriage as it had once dealt with *suttee*, and as, on a grander scale, oriental societies have since been dealt with by ruthlessly modernising governments in Turkey, Russia and Japan. But so long as the reign of the most ancient oriental superstition endured unbroken, western science could do comparatively little to give the teeming Hindu masses physical stamina or a normal span of life.

§6

The administrative machine continued however to govern—and to reform. The elective principle in municipal government was extended, "not primarily," as Lord Ripon pointed out in 1883, "with a view to improvement in administration" but rather "as a measure of political and popular education." Election was introduced into the central and provincial Councils by an Act of 1892. Tenants were protected and rents fixed. And no longer was there constant bloodshed between Hindu and Moslem. But in India, even more than in Egypt, it was inevitable that growing discontent should be the measure of the government's success. By the last decade of the century internal peace and the rule of law, which for centuries had been scarcely dreamed of even as remote ideals, were taken for granted, and some of the ruling castes at least were now conscious of few consequences of British rule save that it had robbed them of their influence. In particular the Mahratta Brahmins looked impatiently for further power. For the Mahrattas had not forgotten that when their predatory aggressions were ended by the British sword, power over all India had seemed to be within their grasp. And the members of the privileged Brahmin caste were hereditarily not only spiritual, but intellectual and political, leaders of all Hindus; it was their offices which had passed to the agents of British rule. Moreover revolution in every age and country has been originated by the middle class, and it was one of the earliest signs of the Westernisation of India that there too British rule had begun to create what may be called a professional middle class, recruited largely from the Brahmins but also from the sons of the smaller *zemindars*, from merchants and moneylenders, and from the unemployed B.A.s, and failed B.A.s, of the University examinations. It was the caste tradition that all educated persons were entitled to a salaried, sedentary and privileged occupation. But middle-class unemployment appeared early in India, the government machine and the clerical labour market very soon failed to absorb the flood of University graduates, comparatively few of whom were prepared to interest themselves in commerce or industry, in medicine, agriculture, science or engineering. Already in this unemployed and discontented middle-class any student of revolutions will readily recognise the potential elements of a revolutionary agitation. Moreover the culture of this new class was largely based upon ill-digested theories of democracy derived from Western philosophers, who wrote against a social and political background of whose nature the Eastern student could have little conception. And the victory of Abyssinia over Italy in 1896, and of Japan over Russia eight years later, and even Britain's unexpectedly protracted struggle with the Boer farmers, inspired the intoxicating reflection that Europe was not invincible after all. Nor had the British war of 1878 to 1880 with Afghanistan been forgotten, in the course of which there had been signs that once again the British columns, though they could conquer the country, were not strong enough to hold it down.

The first leader to organise and focus the revolutionary sentiment of the diminutive but vocal minority was a Mahratta Brahmin, Bal Gangadhar Tilak. A plump man, heavy-lidded and thick-lipped, he had the air of a sedentary dreamer, but he set himself to organise active revolt. Numbers he could not command, but he could at least make his followers formidable. The dagger and the bomb should be their weapons, and the strictest Hindu orthodoxy the basis of their creed. For orthodoxy and violence were far from incompatible. " The divine Krishna," Tilak pointed out, " tells us that we may kill even our teachers and our kinsmen, and no blame attaches if we are not actuated by selfish desires." And since the youthful members of his secret societies, raising their funds by violence and dacoity, were naturally not actuated by selfish desires, all was clearly well. And religious, as well as political, leaders soon joined in the hero-worship of convicted assassins. The too familiar doctrine that the end justifies the means quickly spread beyond assassination. In 1897 Tilak denounced a Moderate leader, G. K. Gokhale, as a traitor to his country because he had apologised for an accusation against the army, which he had subsequently found to be inaccurate. The truth or falsity of the charge, Tilak explained, was irrelevant, since in war any weapon is permissible. The tempting doctrine that their own propaganda, being wartime propaganda, was entitled, wherever convenient, to ignore the truth, spread from Tilak to his fellow extremists, and, much later, from them to the Hindu National Congress, which had been founded in 1885.

But the Congress at its outset, and until the first world war, was controlled by Moderates. An English Liberal, A. O. Hume, who had been offered a Lieutenant-Governorship but had preferred to further the political training of India in a less official manner, had a prominent hand in its foundation, which was encouraged by the Viceroy, Lord Dufferin. "If you . . . cannot . . . make a resolute struggle to secure greater freedom for yourselves and your country," wrote Hume to the Indian students, ". . . then we, your friends, are wrong, and our adversaries right." He toured England to stir public interest in Indian reform, and succeeded in enlisting the enthusiasm of the veteran Radical John Bright, who, however, was so imperfectly acquainted with the Indian scene that he could speak, in the jargon of the British political platform, of the "unanimous demands" of the Indian masses. The President at the second meeting of Congress, a Parsee, made a candid and remarkable avowal:

I ask whether in the most glorious days of Hindu rule you could imagine the possibility of a meeting of this kind, whether even Hindus of all different provinces of the kingdom could have collected and spoken as one nation. . . . It is under the civilising rule of the Queen and people of England that we meet here together, hindered by none and allowed to speak our minds without the least fear and the least hesitation. Such a thing is possible under British rule and British rule only. . . . We are thoroughly sensible of the numberless blessings conferred upon us, of which the very existence of this Congress is a proof in a nutshell. Were it not for those blessings of British rule I could not have come here to-day . . . without the least fear that my children might be robbed and killed in my absence; nor could you have come from every corner of the land.

The extremists, though they made repeated attempts, did not succeed in capturing Congress until after 1914. But in the meantime they were themselves undergoing a significant transformation. They were becoming not only, perhaps not so much, extremists as Nationalists. The earliest followers of Tilak were Mahrattas and Hindus rather than Indians; the very conception of an Indian nation was wholly novel and unfamiliar, for there had been no India until British rule created it. Indeed it was the custom of Tilak to refer to Mohammedans as "foreigners," and to encourage his followers to provoke the religious riots which seldom needed much provoking, in the hopes of embarrassing the British authorities. But in Bengal, among whose clerkly castes Tilak found his readiest pupils, it was easy to revive vague traditions of a Golden Age, and a Motherland once prosperous but now despoiled by foreigners. And steadily the insurgents became less religious and more political, less provincial and more conscious of an Indian nationhood. Curzon's partition of Bengal into two Provinces, carried through against fierce opposition in 1905, was denounced as an insult not only to the Bengali "nation" but to the newly imagined Indian motherland, and the old invocation to the goddess Kali, *Bande Mataram*, "Hail to the mother," became the accepted war-cry of Indian nationalism. Swiftly but imperfectly the Indian malcontent, like the administration of India, was being Westernised. Britain had brought to India much of the science and the current political fashions of the West, but little enough of its religion, which indeed the West itself had so largely forgotten, and in India of all countries the ill-proportioned gift was bound to breed trouble.

The reforms of Lord Morley in 1909 were not due to sympathy with the Indian nationalists, still less to any desire to transform India into a Parliamentary democracy. Indeed, despite his long career as a Gladstonian Radical, Morley proved "the most autocratic . . .

Secretary of State ever seen in Whitehall." His Indian Councils Act admitted an Indian member to that innermost shrine, the Viceroy's executive council, and to the executive councils of the provinces; and it extended the powers and size of all the legislative councils, multiplying the number of elected members by four. In effect these changes set up a permanent Opposition, representative but not responsible, a body of critics which could never exchange criticism for authority. "If it could be said that this chapter of reforms," declared Morley, "led directly or necessarily up to the establishment of a Parliamentary system in India, I, for one, would have had nothing at all to do with it." But this chapter of reforms was avowedly not the final chapter, and towards what other goal, if not to a Parliamentary system, it could be leading he did not explain. Like most rulers of India since the Mutiny he was content to see that India was governed as beneficently as might be, and to yield gradually to Indians those powers which the history of the West had taught them to demand. Sufficient for present needs was his own chapter of reforms; what chapters might lie beyond, what manner of Finis might one day close the volume, he did not closely consider.

India on the eve of the great ordeal was thus moving towards goals which those who directed her journey had not clearly imagined. Yet the distance already traversed, the distance which separated British India from the multifarious mediæval anarchy of the dissolving Mogul Empire, was prodigious. And the journey was among the most ambitious ever undertaken in the course of human history. The goal might still be veiled, yet that during the past hundred years India had travelled far no impartial observer could deny. Here too the Empire had surely earned survival.

BOOKS FOR FURTHER READING.

J. L. Garvin, *Life of Joseph Chamberlain;* Sir George Reid, *My reminiscences;* O. D. Skelton, *Life and Letters of Sir Wilfred Laurier;* John Macnaughton, *Lord Strathcona;* Sarah Gertrude Millin, *General Smuts;* Richard Jebb, *The Imperial Conference;* John Buchan, *Memory hold the Door;* Lord Lugard, *The dual mandate in British Tropical Africa;* The Earl of Ronaldshay, *Life of Lord Curzon;* Edward Thompson and G. T. Garratt, *The rise and fulfilment of British rule in India;* Sir Alfred Lyall, *British Dominion in India.*

Book XI

THE GRAND ORDEAL

CHAPTER ONE

THE FIRST GERMAN WAR

(1914-1918)

§1

THROUGHOUT history war has served as the supreme recurrent test of a nation's fitness to bear rule. Cruel, wasteful as well as infinitely irrelevant though such an ordeal may appear—for the qualities of the wise ruler may be very different from those of the successful soldier—war yet remains the one ordeal which the powerful or wealthy among the nations must from time to time survive, or perish. And just as no feeble constitution can survive severe disease, so the decadent or disorganised succumb to the searching strains of war. Especially is this true of a modern conflict upon the grand scale, which demands so comprehensive an effort from the entire social organism that only a nation possessing high qualities can expect to conduct it successfully. Moreover since in world-wide conflicts, such as those which Germany was about to unleash, no nation could count upon survival through its own unaided strength, the world's judgment of the British record would soon be of sovereign importance. The Empire could hardly have survived the thirty years of varied conflict which commenced in 1914 if it had offended the conscience of mankind. For it would be only too easy to underestimate the cumulative strain to which the British system was now about to be subjected. The Empire-Commonwealth had grown to the pattern of peace. Time after time it had neglected to arm itself for war. The most insignificant conflicts had almost invariably found it unprepared. And now the most formidable military power in the world was bent upon destroying it; and the onslaught would be prolonged over more than the span of a generation.

For fundamentally the war of 1914, like the war of 1939, and the uneasy interlude which separated them, was a German effort to overthrow the British Empire. This time, it is true, the Germans marched first on France, and would gladly have bribed or bluffed the British government to stand aside. But the avowed purpose of the Day, so long prepared, so often toasted and so impatiently awaited, was to win world-domination with the German sword; and for Germany there could be no world-domination until the British Empire had been destroyed. It was for this purpose that the nation which already possessed the mightiest army in the world had deliberately set itself, at whatever financial sacrifice, to create the mightiest fleet.

It was not chance that once again the challenge had come from a military autocracy, and that William of Hohenzollern filled the rôle once played by the King of Spain, by the French Bourbons and by Napoleon. For despotism is the primitive, the natural, social pattern, above which a nation rises with difficulty, and to which it readily reverts. It is peculiarly suited to a people bred to warfare or bent on conquest. And those who submit to it are specially prone to misunderstand the nature of a free community, so that they exaggerate the significance of its more obvious defects and greatly underestimate its invisible reserves of strength.

Never had two such dissimilar antagonists fought for so great a stake. Moulded and ruled by Prussia, the new Germany was a continental power, concentrated and homogeneous. The world-wide British community was sea-based, widely scattered and infinitely diverse. The German Empire was new and profoundly artificial, the recent product of the appetite of its rulers for power and prestige. The British Empire was old, and its growth had been spontaneous and unplanned. Germany was elaborately organised for war, the British Empire had instinctively shaped itself for peace. Apart from its Navy it was relatively unarmed. Even the tension of the last few years had scarcely stirred it to serious preparations. "Popular governments," wrote Mahan, "are not generally favourable to military expenditure," and democracy in Britain, as elsewhere, had shown an impatience of discipline or sacrifice in time of peace, a readiness to embrace the tempting doctrine that to prepare for war makes war more likely and a scepticism as to expert warnings of danger ahead which had gone far to persuade the German warlords that their hour was indeed at hand. And to German eyes the steady growth of independence in the British Dominions overseas was but further evidence of decadence in the mother-country. In brief, imperial Germany was an empire of the most ancient and primitive type, armed with weapons of terrible modernity, the

British Empire a world society of a wholly unprecedented and still evolving pattern, relatively unprepared for war.

The German plan was simple and ferocious. Three wars in swift succession had made Germany one, under Prussia, Prussia of which it had been said long since that its only industry was war. From their own recent history Germans had learnt to identify war with a swift, victorious campaign yielding immense rewards. The new campaign was to be no less swift and would yield them, they believed, the greatest prize of all, the world-domination to which all Germany believed herself to be entitled. This was the doctrine not only of the army and the militarist ruling class, but of professors and historians, merchants and industrialists, Socialists and school-boys, in effect of the entire German nation. World power was to be won by a single perfectly timed and coldly calculated stroke, without the long apprenticeship, the trial and error, the centuries of rivalry with other nations which had gone to the making of the Empire which was to be destroyed.

§2

The Empire had not been strong enough to fulfil that first obligation, which during the past century, thanks to the Royal Navy, it had so often conspicuously discharged. It had not prevented war. And so once again the existence of the world-wide community was staked upon a more searching trial than any before endured of the quality and endurance of its citizens. In Britain at least a century of peace and growing prosperity, and the too ready assumption that growing prosperity is progress, might well have sapped the moral fibre of the people, but although they had failed, as always, to prepare for war it soon appeared that their ancient valour had not, as their enemies supposed, deserted them. For the first time indeed it was a citizens' army that went to war, not a professional army, like Wellington's, of ruffians and fire-eaters officered by aristocrats, and some of the most splendid records were those of homespun county regiments of sober taxpayers, grimly resolved to go through with a distasteful duty to the bitter end. And for the first time too the whole Empire was at war.

The Dominions indeed entered the conflict instantly and without hesitation. The recent loosening of formal ties had not, as German observers supposed, relaxed the subtler bonds of kinship, sympathy and a common way of life. On August 1, three days before the outbreak of war, Sir Robert Borden, as Prime Minister, cabled that

Canada would make every sacrifice in the coming conflict. And in the Canadian House of Commons Sir Wilfrid Laurier, the French-Canadian leader of the Opposition, said "it is our duty . . . at once . . . to let Great Britain know, and to let the friends and foes of Great Britain know, that there is in Canada but one mind and one heart, and that all Canadians stand behind the mother country." On July 31 the Parliament of New Zealand unanimously agreed to organise an expeditionary force, for service overseas. Australia had already offered twenty thousand men before war was declared. And from South Africa Botha had cabled that the Union would at least be responsible for its own defence. A few days later he agreed, before he could consult his own Parliament, to attack German South West Africa. A white population in the four Dominions of fifteen millions, men, women and children, had produced a million and a quarter armed men before the war was over, and each Dominion, save South Africa, would equip, train and pay for its own forces.

The non-British races of the Empire were no less ready. For even the least contented were well aware of the world of difference between the British system, with its tolerance and cult of freedom, and German rule, based on German belief in force and racial superiority. And looking into the gulf which seemed to be opening at their feet, even the most astringent critics of British administration realised suddenly how much they had to be thankful for. German observers, from the Crown Prince downwards, had toured India freely before the war and were well aware that Indian nationalists aimed at complete independence; they had little doubt that war with Germany would be the signal for immediate revolt. In the event it occasioned a swift and spontaneous expression of loyalty which astonished the British themselves. Every Indian community offered its resources and service. "Let not the world mistake us," said an Indian member of the Viceroy's Council, "should any outside danger threaten us, we stand shoulder to shoulder round our mighty mother, England, and her enemies will find us arrayed in solid phalanx by her side, ready to meet any danger for the sake of the great and glorious Empire of which we are proud to call ourselves citizens." And it was a politician of the Opposition, Surenden Nath Banerjee, at one time not a little influenced by Tilak, who said, "We are loyal because we are patriotic; because we believe that with the stability and permanence of British rule are bound up the best prospects of Indian advancement."

A German victory would have strangled not only the established democracies of the Dominions, but freedom wherever it was growing throughout the Empire. In the hour of trial it was the salvation of the British system that it enshrined an ideal which mankind would not willingly allow to perish. At the end of the war the contrast between what was and what had been threatened was pointedly summed up by a spokesman of the Maoris, who had long since fully shared the privileges and responsibilities of New Zealand citizenship:

> We know of the Samoans, our kin; we know of the Eastern and Western natives of German Africa; and we know of the extermination of the Hereros, and that is enough for us. For seventy-eight years we have been, not under the rule of the British, but taking a part in the ruling of ourselves, and we know by experience that the foundations of British sovereignty are based upon the eternal principles of liberty, equity and justice.

§3

Almost everywhere throughout the dependencies and Protectorates, among the negroes of Africa and the West Indies, in Malaya and the Pacific Islands, the story was the same. The impact of war stirred not revolt or disaffection, but protestations of loyalty and eagerness to help. Inevitably in a community so diverse and so vast there were exceptions, as indeed there must always be even within a homogeneous nation embarking on so terrible a war. But the exceptions were relatively so few and so insignificant, as to seem rather to illumine the general unanimity. Only in South Africa was there for a brief while something like real danger. Here a minority of irreconcilables among the Boers was for a war on the Empire which should re-establish the Boer republics, while others, with General Herzog, were for standing aside to await the outcome in Europe. Commandant Maritz of the Union defence force put himself in touch with the Governor of German South West Africa, and marched for the frontier with his immediate command. But Botha and Smuts, the leaders of the majority, were abler men, and they had no doubts as to their duty. When Beyers, the Commandant-General, resigned his post in a letter comparing the German treatment of Belgium to barbarous acts by the British during the Boer War, Smuts wrote that his attack on Great Britain was baseless. "You forget to mention," he added,

> that since the South African War the British people gave South Africa her entire freedom under a constitution which makes it

possible for us to realise our national ideals along our own lines, and which, incidentally, allows you to write with impunity a letter for which you would, without doubt, be liable in the German Empire to the supreme penalty.

Botha crushed the rebellion before the end of the year, using only his own Dominion forces, over two-thirds of the thirty thousand of them loyalist Dutch. As Smuts said, when the government asked for troops, "regiment after regiment rose as at a wizard's wand. . . . The Dutch people of South Africa feel that their honour is touched and they are determined to wipe out this disgrace." But South Africa remained too deeply divided for effort on a large scale. Herzog and his Nationalists steadily opposed effective participation in the war, and a small body of Labour extremists busily fostered social unrest. After the conquest of South West Africa a considerable number of South Africans fought under Smuts and Van Deventer in German East Africa, and a South African brigade was maintained in France, but that was all; and the greater part of the expenses of these forces had to be met by the British taxpayer.

The chief contribution of the Union to the imperial cause was Smuts himself. Despite the ferocious abuse of Boer Nationalists, and several attempts on his life during the election of 1915, he had not flinched from his resolve; "Briton and Boer must combine to make one great nation." During 1916 he commanded the imperial forces in German East Africa in a campaign, thanks to the climate and the nature of the country, "probably," as he said, "without parallel in the history of war." He was the inspiration and the idol of his polyglot army, and his daring strategy had driven the Germans from the most fertile parts of the colony when he was summoned to London to the Imperial Conference of 1917. It was the darkest hour of the war; Russia was giving up the struggle, and the United States had not yet entered it, and to the British public the arrival of this former enemy, confident, sagacious and undefeated, came as a tonic reassurance. Introduced by Mr. Lloyd George into the Imperial War Cabinet he immediately displayed his profound genius for affairs. On all sides was heard the demand that he should be retained in the inner councils of the Empire. Not only a new stage in his own career but a new milestone in Empire history had been reached. He was the first Dominion statesman to exercise throughout the Empire an influence different in kind but scarcely less in degree than that which he had achieved in his own country.

§4

South Africa's was the most formidable episode of disaffection. In Egypt, which was declared a Protectorate when Turkey, its nominal suzerain, went to war with Britain, nationalism among the educated and half-educated grew more embittered under the prolonged stresses of war-time. Egypt had prospered under the British occupation. Since 1904, when France recognised the British occupation as part of that comprehensive settlement of differences which constituted the *entente cordiale*, reform had moved swiftly. Lord Cromer himself, after retiring from his long, benevolent despotism in 1907, summed up the transformation wrought by British rule:

A new spirit has been instilled into the population of Egypt. Even the peasant has learnt to scan his rights. Even the Pasha has learnt that others besides himself have rights which must be respected. The *courbash* may hang on the walls of the Moudirieh, but the Moudir no longer dares to employ it on the back of the *fallahin*. For all practical purposes, it may be said that the hateful *corvée* system has disappeared. Slavery has virtually ceased to exist. The halcyon days of the adventurer and the usurer are past. Fiscal burdens have been greatly relieved. Everywhere law reigns supreme. Justice is no longer bought and sold. The soldier has acquired some pride in the uniform which he wears. He has fought as he never fought before. The sick man can be nursed in a well-managed hospital. The lunatic is no longer treated like a wild beast. The punishment awarded to the worst criminal is no longer barbarous. Lastly the school-master is abroad with results which are as yet uncertain, but which cannot fail to be important.

It is an impressive, but a studiously accurate, catalogue. And to it must be added the revivifying miracle of the harnessing of the waters of the Nile. For many years before the British came both irrigation and drainage had been steadily decaying, but British engineers first rendered the barrage below Cairo effective, and then improved the canals and built the great dam at Assouan in Upper Egypt and the barrages at Assint and Zifta. And so not two, but ten blades of grass grew where one grew before. This alone, if the British had achieved nothing else, would have justified their presence in Egypt.

In spite of which, needless to say, the men who had conferred these great benefits were soon bitterly vilified by those who had received them. Needless to say—for it was not merely that, as Lord Cromer bluntly put it, "We are not liked anywhere. . . . There is no getting out of the fact that we are not Mohammedans, that we neither eat, drink nor intermarry with them." More than this, as always, another generation had forgotten the bondage from which their fathers had been delivered, and remembered only that their country was now administered by Christians and aliens. Moreover, as in India, the educated classes had learnt from the British example to assume that any adult and civilised people must needs practise Parliamentary government, and as in India they had little conception of the long centuries of experiment and experience, or of the homogeneous texture of society, out of which the Parliamentary system had slowly developed in the country of its birth. That the Egyptian masses were still deep in primitive ignorance, still bowed by the memories of centuries of serfdom, seemed to the new Egyptian nationalists no barrier to their desire. Shortly before the outbreak of world war, under Lord Kitchener, government became more representative. And as was natural the partial change inflamed the impatience, and added to the resentment, of those who desired more. And so war found Egypt with an eastern heart still beating to ancient rhythms beneath the administrative framework of a modern state —and a restive minority clamouring to be allowed to crown all with their own version of the politics of the West.

In Southern Ireland, too, though it furnished some of the Empire's most gallant soldiers, nationalism became envenomed as the slow years of war dragged by. And the French Canadians in general, despite their veteran leader, Sir Wilfrid Laurier, professed the view that the war was no concern of theirs, and, though continually emphasising their French origin and culture, remained equally indifferent to the desperate plight of France. Of the 365,000 who had gone from Canada to serve overseas by March, 1918, only 16,000 were French Canadians.

Many obstacles peculiar to their country prevented the peoples of India from at once translating their first spontaneous enthusiasm into a war-effort worthy of it. Caste is an insuperable barrier to swift collective action; and the sense of unity which war demands can hardly be expected in a land in which a high-caste soldier would rather die than accept a cup of water from a person of low caste. Again the army in India, like all British land forces, had been organised for defensive purposes only, and there were special difficulties about now converting it into a reserve for imperial uses overseas. Yet before the war was over, India, whose native army in 1914 did not exceed 160,000, had put about a million men into the field. From a population of three hundred and twenty millions a million may seem no high proportion, but it has to be remembered that many of the peoples of India are profoundly unmilitary in character—349,688 fighting men volunteered in the Punjab out of a population of twenty millions, and only 7117 from the teeming millions of Bengal. Comradeship in arms on this unprecedented scale should have done much to help British and Indians to understand each other, for if the great and inevitable defect of British rule in India had been to bring not only peace, justice and the rule of law, but many of the materialist limitations with which Western civilisation has paid for its material advances, to lands in which the spiritual ideals of poverty, resignation and contemplation still reigned as potent as in mediæval Europe, nevertheless courage, discipline and self-sacrifice, the military virtues, are themselves spiritual ideals. Yet the immediate effect of the war, particularly among the unmilitary population of Bengal, was to breed unrest.

In relation to the Empire as a whole such discords were proportionately of no more account than the opposition to the war of a small minority within Britain itself. And in comparison with what Germany had so confidently expected they were as nothing. This strange world society of something like a third of the human race had already achieved one political miracle; it had established lasting peace within its own wide frontiers. And now another miracle was being enacted. After a generation, during which, by common consent of foreign observers, it had shown every sign of steady disintegration, it had been presented with the supreme opportunity of disintegration, and to the astonishment of the world its infinitely diverse membership was seen to be more closely and resolutely united than ever before.

§5

But the rising of the Empire to meet the new challenge to its ancient purpose was more than a revelation to the world; it was a revelation to the British, contributing incalculably to their determination and their confidence. For even the least instructed citizen was now dimly aware that the stake in the conflict was something greater than Britain or Britain's possessions; and that Britain and her daughter nations were defending a way of life, first nurtured in these islands, which now commanded the allegiance, or enshrined the hopes, of men of every race all over the world. Had the British been fighting only for their own power, their own wealth or even for their own freedom, it is possible that their hearts might have failed them, or their vigour flagged, before the end. But they knew now that they were fighting for the principle of freedom everywhere, and that of this principle their own world-community was the metropolis and citadel, and in this knowledge they found assurance that they must survive. And all too ignorant though they still remained of their own imperial history, and prone enough, as we have seen, to a sense of guilt even for crimes which they had not committed, yet in the spontaneous unanimity of constituent nations so diverse the most critical and the most uninstructed could see both a tribute to the past and a promise for the future. For a while at least the horizon of the nation widened. And to the Empire itself its own uprising was a veritable rebirth, pregnant with growth, so that it emerged from four years of war already transformed, and conscious that it stood upon the threshold of further change.

§6

Some of the outlying campaigns were easily recognised as imperial enterprises, but the main military effort of both Germany and the allies was spent upon the four years of close-locked trench fighting in France, in which the life-blood of a generation ebbed away. Here, if anywhere on land, the fate of the Empire was decided, and here, inevitably, Britain, with Canada, bore the brunt of the Empire's sacrifice. And once again the Navy, in whose youthful strength the Empire was cradled, played an all-but decisive rôle in its defence. Like Bonaparte and Bourbons before them Hohenzollern Germany was throttled by the slow stranglehold of the blockade, and the ships it never saw. And, though an Australian squadron did lively service, clearing the German flag from the Pacific in the first weeks of war, the Navy was still in substance the product of the mother country.

But wars are not won by armed forces alone. Ordeal by battle is the most searching of all tests of the whole structure and organisation which gives the armed forces birth, and of the spirit which inspires them. In the last analysis we may perhaps say that the Empire survived in 1918 because it deserved to survive; because it embodied, and indeed personified, an Idea which many peoples now held precious. Nevertheless it could not have survived unless its structure, social and economic, had been adequate to resist the penetrating stresses of war. And it was inevitable that under those stresses that structure, both imperial and domestic, should be profoundly modified. For war serves always as a forcing house, swiftly maturing tendencies which would otherwise have long remained rudimentary, to meet its continuous but ever-changing emergencies.

CHAPTER TWO

THE STRUCTURE OF EMPIRE

(1914-1939)

§1

THERE WAS a moment in 1917 when it almost seemed as if the supreme direction of the Empire's war had been placed in commission between three distinct bodies, all then in session in England. There was the War Cabinet, an inner council of the normal larger executive. There was the Imperial Conference, which had been summoned by Mr. Lloyd George, soon after he displaced Asquith at the end of 1916, to concert measures for winning the war; it was attended by various British ministers, although not by members of the War Cabinet, and by spokesmen of all the Dominions save Australia, whose political leaders were preoccupied just then with domestic politics. And for the first time representatives of India had been included. And there was the Imperial War Cabinet, an amalgam of War Cabinet and Imperial Conference sitting together. There was a sense in which all three bodies revolved round Smuts. He was the only member who sat in all of them, for alone of the Dominion statesmen he had become a member of the British War Cabinet itself, a notable anomaly, since he sat in neither British Houses of Parliament, but, like many others, readily accepted under the shadow of crisis.

For it was not merely that Smuts was both a soldier and a statesmen, nor merely that Mr. Lloyd George had speedily recognised his singular wisdom. In a dark hour many saw in this former enemy who had become so loyal a servant of the Empire a heartening reassurance as to their own past. "Nothing has impressed the world more," said one newspaper, "and nothing has strengthened the Allies' cause more than the fact that in this struggle the enemies of yesterday are beside us in defending the principles we share in common." "He has done more," said another, "than any man to recall this country to its great tradition." And indeed to the British public Smuts almost seemed in his own person to moralise the Empire's cause. The narrow traditions of their education had allowed them to know almost nothing of its history: in moments of disquiet vague memories would revive of charges of oppression or exploitation, bandied about by politicians almost as ignorant as themselves. And yet here was this leader of the little Republic to which critics of the Empire had so often pointed as the outraged victim of imperialist aggression, in speech after speech bidding Britian take heart, and remember that her Empire was the hope of the world. "We are not an Empire," Smuts told them. "Germany is an Empire, and so was Rome, and so is India; but we are a system of nations, a community of states and of nations far greater than any Empire that has ever existed." As Rome had guided European civilisation for close on two thousand years, so might the ideas struggling to maturity within the British system guide civilisation for centuries to come. "All the nations that we have known in the past and that exist to-day are founded on the idea of assimilation, of trying to force human material through one mould so as to form one nation. Your whole idea and basis is entirely different. You want to develop them into greater nationhood." To this moment we may ascribe the popular acceptance of a new conception of Empire as "this community of nations which I prefer to call" (Smuts said) "the British Commonwealth of Nations." The idea of a British world society which was also a nursery of free nationhood, diverse yet united, had been implicit for more than a century in the evolution of the Empire, and had long been familiar to the few enthusiasts who had studied its history or reflected on its future. But it was the war and the menace of the primitive German ambitions which first stirred the general public to a sense of the full British destiny, and then the voice of Smuts, reminding them in a dark hour that on the Empire, which had conquered his fatherland, rested the hopes of mankind. During the first years of war even British statesmen still thought, and spoke, of the Dominions as if they had chivalrously come to the assistance of the mother country. By the end of it even the general public had come to realise that the Dominions were fighting for the British Empire.

The Prime Minister had declared in Parliament that the members of the Imperial War Cabinet hoped "that the holding of an annual Imperial Cabinet to discuss foreign affairs and other aspects of imperial policy will become an accepted convention of the British Constitution," and the hopes of the advocates of federation ran high. Might this not prove a step towards the permanent imperial Parliament of which they dreamed? But despite Mr. Lloyd George's announcement, the Imperial Cabinet was not destined to meet annually after the war, nor, in all the pride of their swiftly matured nationhood, had the Dominions any desire for federation. At the same time war had taught them how necessary was concerted action.

All that they could do before the Conference dispersed in 1917 was
to pass a constitutional resolution which embodied their two
apparently contradictory aspirations, for unity and independence.
They made no attempt to resolve the contradiction; after all they
were not drafting a constitution, they were grappling with an
emergency. Somehow or other in practice, they trusted, like many
other constitutional dilemmas in British history, it would resolve
itself. And so they spoke of "a full recognition of the Dominions as
autonomous nations of an Imperial Commonwealth, and of India
as "an important portion of the same," and also of "the right of the
Dominions and India to an adequate voice in foreign policy" without
further defining what they meant by "adequate," or elaborating
the difficulty that, since decisions on foreign policy must be arrived
at by somebody, in the absence of an imperial Parliament the only
body competent to pronounce them remained the Parliament of
Great Britain.

§2

By November the world scene was transformed; Germany's
allies were prostrate, German civilians were rising in revolution and
the German Emperor was in flight. Ten million fighting men had
perished, and the first German bid for world domination was at an
end. Soon the peacemakers were descending on Paris. And here
while politicians took their first dubious soundings in the conflicting
currents of allied policy the Empire recorded a clearcut constitutional
advance. For India and each of the four Dominions was separately
represented at the Peace Conference, with two delegates for Canada,
Australia, South Africa and India, and one for New Zealand. Since,
save for the declaration of war, there is no more important transaction in diplomacy than the negotiation of peace this arrangement
represented more than "an adequate voice in foreign policy," and
proclaimed to the world that the Dominions at least had achieved
the status of full nationhood. Something more than the "adequate
voice in foreign policy" resolved on by the Imperial Conference of
1917 had been fully achieved in practise—if not so fully yet in theory,
as future anomalies would show. The Dominions were content.
"The Dominions have been well launched on their great career,"
said Smuts; "their status of complete nationhood has now received
international recognition." And he went on, "the successful launching of her former Colonies among the nations of the world, while
they remain members of an inner Britannic circle, will ever rank

as one of the most outstanding achievements of British political genius."

§3

Many British citizens would have liked to see a generous peace with Germany. The mere presence of Smuts on the British delegation was a reminder that generous peacemaking had been a habit with the British, and that it had rewarded them. And the old, humane tradition of war as a sort of daemonic cricket match, after which victor and vanquished shook hands and settled down to be good neighbours, still survived from the last century. Smuts himself was all for clemency, for he remembered the Peace of Vereeniging. "Do nor forget," said Botha in Paris, "that Smuts and I are the only people here who have ever been in the position in which the Germans are to-day." It is probable that no one in Britain, even among those who were for severity, had yet realised that for the true rulers of Germany the war which they had just lost was only the first round in a conflict which they were determined to renew as often as necessary, until they, or their descendants, had won it; still less that Germans were already calculating that if they played their cards wisely Germany, despite her defeat, would prove to have finished her first world war relatively stronger than she began it. The most extreme generosity would scarcely have turned Germany from her purpose, but extreme generosity was out of the question. For the French were much more concerned than the British to prevent another German invasion, though even the French foresaw rather a war of revenge than the fanatical renewal of a struggle for world power temporarily broken off, but never finally abandoned. And in Britain mass opinion, which was now the ultimate arbiter of foreign policy, was much less disposed to make "a gentleman's" peace than Castlereagh and the handful of aristocrats who had been left with so free a hand at the Congress of Vienna. Generosity at the Conference-table on the full-blooded Vereeniging pattern was out of the question, but both in the terms of the peace, and increasingly in the handling of Germany after it, the traditional British reluctance to press a fallen foe too hard was strong enough to prevent any measures which might have lastingly disabled the German war machine. Another treaty like that of Brest-Litovsk, in which the Germans had carved up Eastern Europe when Russia collapsed in 1917, was no more possible than another Peace of Vereeniging. And in the upshot the Germans found it possible both to begin almost at once preparing their next war, and to remain convinced that they had been treated with inhuman severity.

§4

The treaties of Versailles considerably increased the extent of the British Empire by allotting German and Turkish possessions, as mandates from the new League of Nations, usually to those who had conquered them. On these terms Australia acquired New Guinea with the neighbouring islands, New Zealand received Samoa, and South Africa took German South West Africa. Britain received mandates for Palestine and Mesopotamia, and in Africa for German East Africa, renamed the Tanganyika Territory, and for part of Togoland. The mandatory principle had itself been borrowed from the British Empire. Its essence was the idea of trusteeship, and it involved a public pledge to administer the mandated territory in the interests of its native population and to admit the commerce of other nations—to pursue, in short, the traditional policy of the British Empire. The subtlest theorist found it hard to say where under the mandatory system sovereignty resided, whether in the League, which had allotted the mandate, and listened every year to the mandatory power's report, in the mandatory power itself, or in some indeterminate region midway between the two. In practise, however, the problem was less insoluble; there was no doubt as to who in fact governed the mandated territories, and when in due course the League itself vanished into limbo, the same Powers continued to exercise the same authority.

§5

That the League of Nations, which so many enthusiasts hailed as the political salvation of mankind, should have perished almost unnoticed after a precarious existence of twenty years, while the three-centuries-old Empire which it seemed about to supersede lived on to save the world from yet another tyranny—this would indeed have seemed a strange and disheartening paradox to the idealists of 1919. Yet the fate of the League was assured from the moment of its birth. For although it set out to do for the whole of mankind what the British Empire was already doing for a quarter of it, its founders ignored every lesson which they might have learned from British experience. The Empire had grown, the League was manufactured.

The pliable constitution of the Empire was for ever changing, the rigid constitution of the League made change all but impossible. The Empire had survived largely because it was a League without a Covenant. "Yours is the only system that has ever worked in history," said Smuts of the British Empire, "where a large number of nations have been living together in unity. Talk about the League of Nations—you are the only league of nations that has ever existed." Above all, like so many earlier dreams of world peace assured by a stroke of the pen, the League sought not to provide a substitute for war but to repress warmakers. And it had no means of repressing them. Yet despite its manifest and fatal deficiencies the highest hopes of the most generous idealists of many countries were concentrated on it for the best part of two decades. And among the British the most sterile controversy at Geneva would for a while attract more respectful attention than the most urgent problems of their own world community. For the British knew next to nothing of their imperial history, and what they had lately learnt of the Empire in the hard school of war they soon allowed themselves to forget. This indeed was one of the few indisputable achievements of the League, that in Britain for the generation between the two German onslaughts it overshadowed and outmoded the Empire, and engrossed much of the energy and idealism which, had it been devoted to imperial opportunities, might have gone far to ensure the peace of the world.

Yet during its brief heyday the League did something too to hasten the evolution of the Empire. Indeed the mere existence, even on paper, of an organisation setting out to embrace all mankind was bound to affect the constitution of a community in which a quarter of mankind had long been included. India and the Dominions had signed the peace treaties as separate nations, yet on the Council of the League it was the Empire that was represented, not its constituent peoples, for otherwise they would have become not only separate but independent. The spectacle of the Dominions represented by a British spokesman, not amenable to the will of Dominion electorates, was greeted by some enthusiasts as a temporary anomaly obviously heralding an Imperial Parliament and an imperial federation. Again, the Covenant of the League committed member nations, or those of them at least who might one day have to fight the League's wars, to responsibilities far more formidable than their electorates, or most of their politicians, had realised. Indeed from the first there were not wanting British observers who roundly declared that if the British public should ever grasp the full extent of its obligations under the Covenant it would instantly repudiate them. Meanwhile, however, not only Britain but the Dominions stood pledged, under Article X of the Covenant, to go to war to resist aggression in any quarter of the globe. Almost unawares they had undertaken responsibilities to foreign states greater than any they had yet been willing to shoulder on behalf of Britain or the British Empire. In a sense they were merely being over-optimistic, for in the hopeful infancy of the League it seemed plausible to suppose that the mere pledge of so many nations to fight if need be had made it infinitely unlikely that fighting would ever have to be done. Few had yet realised that it was in the last degree improbable that any of the small nations would be prepared to give any assistance in fighting the battles of the League. But for the moment the prospect of serious aggression appeared remote, it was assumed that the League would endure, and to many it seemed that, so far from encouraging, as the federalists had surmised, the development of a federal Parliament, it had relieved the Empire of the necessity even of perfecting its existing mechanism. What need, after all, to organise closer imperial co-operation in foreign policy or defence, when responsibility for foreign policy and defence was so clearly passing to the League?

The League moreover did not only seem to dispense the Empire from the necessity of defending itself or of pursuing a foreign policy of its own; it also masked the delicate problems which, on the approach of war, might spring from the Balfour Declaration and the Statute of Westminster. What matter if, from 1925 onwards, despite the promise of the war-time Conferences, imperial foreign policy had dwindled to British foreign policy once again—so long as the system of Collective Security endured? For the League was the counterpart and, in the eyes of many, the heir-presumptive, of the Empire, and if the Empire had no foreign policy, the League had. Again the prospect that "autonomous communities within the British Empire, equal in status, in no way subordinate one to another" would clearly be entitled, if confronted with the prospect of war, to prefer neutrality or even secession, seemed to matter little so long as it could be assumed that henceforth all wars would be League Wars, as to their duty in which the Covenant left its signatories no option. There could be no conflict of loyalties for the autonomous members of the Commonwealth so long as all remained loyal members of the League. And in 1935 even Eire supported the British policy of economic sanctions against Italy, not because it was the policy of Britain but because it was the policy of the League.

But from 1936 onwards, as the League swiftly disintegrated, the imperial problems which it had once shrouded in a golden haze re-emerged with uncomfortable clarity. A League which could not halt Mussolini in 1936, still less Hitler in 1938, could clearly no longer serve the Empire as an alternative bond of union. The British Empire stood forth once again as the only system of collective security in existence, and since it lacked the comprehensive written constitution which had simplified, and destroyed, the League, its members found themselves taking anxious stock of their mutual relations. At first sight the prospect was gloomy, with numerous apparently centrifugal forces standing out bleakly against a background of general disillusionment. It seemed clear that in the event of war powerful elements in Canada, South Africa and perhaps Australia would be for neutrality. Yet the forces of cohesion, though less conspicuous, were still immensely powerful. Interest and sentiment both made for unity, and Herzog, the South African nationalist, could express them both. In 1935 he had hailed the British Navy as the guardian of the liberties of South Africa. And on the eve of war he reminded his followers that Britain had been "the greatest benefactor to South Africa in the last three hundred years."

§6

In the years of increasingly uneasy peace after 1919 to many foreign observers the Empire, which had so recently astonished the world, and itself, by its unity, appeared once again to be slowly disintegrating. For few foreign observers had sounded the full implications of the idea of freedom, or accustomed themselves to the conception that an Empire could subsist on consent in place of authority. Yet on the political plane all that was now happening was that the self-governing Dominions, that inner core of the Empire which Smuts had called the Commonwealth, were covering the last stages of the journey on which they had been travelling for many decades, or being accorded formal recognition of principles already for some while established in practice. And it was not its political structure which held the Empire together.

Only in its organisation for defence was the Empire, now as always, backward and inert. Once again, as immediate danger vanished, the British democracies assumed that danger would never revive, and proceeded to concentrate their attention on their own domestic affairs. Lord Jellicoe was sent to visit the Dominions in 1919, in the hopes that in the rough school of war they would have learnt the wisdom of a more equal sharing of the burden of naval defence. But the German Navy had sunk itself at Scapa Flow, Japan was still an ally, no immediate danger could be discerned; and he met with a chilly response. And so while constitutionally the Dominions were reaching equality and autonomy, full and final, as far as defence was concerned the traditions of their infancy lingered on, and they remained immature and dependent still.

The Imperial Conference of 1921 declined to investigate the constitution of the Empire, as had been prescribed by the Conference of 1917. The constitution had developed too far since 1917, they held, for that to be necessary. And at the last moment they instinctively recoiled from the prospect of definitions. "You are defining life itself," said Mr. Lloyd George, "when you are defining the British Empire. You cannot do it. . . ." The members contented themselves accordingly with pronouncing for frequent and direct, but not continuous, consultation. The federalists realised that the moment of opportunity had passed. "The present system" the *Round Table* pointed out,

> leaves on Great Britain the responsibility of conducting the foreign policy of a Commonwealth which contains a quarter of the people of the globe, and of maintaining, at its own cost, the diplomatic service and the Army and Navy needed for the purpose, and that without knowing whether its policy is approved and its acts will be supported by the peoples for whom it is supposed to speak.

Nevertheless federation seemed more than ever remote. Indeed, later that year at a Conference at Washington, although the main topic for discussion was the Navies of the world, to which they contributed little, the Dominions would have nothing less than the status they had achieved at Paris, and insisted on receiving separate invitations.

During the next five years the natural forces of growth, themselves easily mistaken for slow disruption, and punctuated by misunderstandings and mischances which emphasised the centrifugal process, prepared the way for the "decisive formula" of 1926. The Dominions had taken no hand in negotiating the Treaty of Lausanne with Turkey in 1923, and in the same year Canada composed its own Halibut Fisheries Treaty with the United States without a British signature to the document. In 1924 the Irish Free State, now heading at full speed for virtual secession from the Empire, set the example of separate diplomatic representation in a foreign capital—followed by Canada and South Africa, though not by New Zealand and Australia.

And in 1925 the Dominions shared neither in the Conference at Locarno nor in the subsequent Pact which pledged Britain to serious military responsibilities, for which her disarmament was steadily disqualifying her, on the continent. In due course, since Germany would soon be strong enough to ignore treaties with impunity once more, the Treaty of Locarno would go the way of other Scraps of Paper, but in the meantime it seemed to Smuts, as to many others, to lend impetus to the forces of disruption. The stage was set for the decisive formula.

§7

For so it was described. It is needless to say perhaps that since it was a formula it was not likely, in the British Empire, to be decisive. But a formula it certainly was. A committee of the Imperial Conference of 1926, after repeating that any attempt to provide the British Empire with a constitution would be superfluous, proceeded to define the "position and mutual relation" of Great Britain and the Dominions:

They are autonomous Communities within the British Empire, equal in status, in no way subordinate one to another in any aspect of their domestic or external affairs though united by a common allegiance to the Crown and freely associated as members of the British Commonwealth of Nations.

There is an Athanasian flavour about this celebrated formula, composed by the metaphysical Balfour, which reaches a veritably theological subtlety in a later sentence: "but the principles of equality and similarity, appropriate to status, do not universally extend to function." Here it is possible that the Committee was thinking of the British Navy, for in this respect it was certainly true that the members of the Commonwealth, although avowedly now equal in status, did not, and could not, perform equal functions. But the Committee, while insisting that "every Dominion is now and must always remain the sole judge of the nature and extent of its co-operation," stoutly and sensibly declared that "no common cause will, in our opinion, be thereby imperilled." And the formula was in truth only summarising a constitutional situation already reached in practise. Naturally no theory could exactly fit an empirical process, and "in no way subordinate one to another in any aspect of their . . . external affairs" hardly represents the inevitable primacy of the mother country; as the Conference itself put it, for foreign affairs " the major share of responsibility rests now and must for some time continue to rest with His Majesty's Government in Great Britain." After a subsequent meeting of experts, the work of the Conference was embodied in the Statute of Westminster of 1931, which gives equality of status legal form. The Parliament of Great Britain cannot now legislate for a Dominion save "at the request and with the consent of that Dominion."

Did any vestige of imperial unity, foreign observers asked themselves, now survive? And all those who could only think of Empire as domination decided that the British Empire had committed suicide. "A passive renunciation of world-dominion," a proof that Britain had lost "the flair for rule" and was "now only a pseudo-Power"—such was the verdict in that new Germany which was in truth but the old Germany in modern battledress. "The very day war broke out it would become manifest that Great Britain had already lost her world dominion." The future belonged to the "dynamic" powers who had not lost the "will to rule." The German view was perfectly reasonable, granted the persistent German assumption that force rules, and ought to rule, the world. Yet the declaration of 1926 and the statute of 1931, the process which by German standards so inevitably seemed to spell surrender, had in fact made no essential change. It had finally and formally recognised the maturity of the Dominions, that is all. For a century and more the unity of Britain and the Dominions had depended in the last resort solely upon their will to remain united. Upon their will to remain united it depended still.

§8

The final disappearance of political tutelage had thus been formally recorded, and the dangerous problems of imperial defence conveniently shelved. But this was not all. The bewildered years between the two German onslaughts saw the Empire attempt, with chequered results, a closer integration of its economic structure.

First came an attempt by the state to promote the peopling of the empty spaces overseas. During the last three years before the war of 1914 emigration from the United Kingdom to the Empire had been proceeding, with little state assistance, at the rate of 304,000 a year. The intervention of the state, which certainly was not likely to inspire the individual, with the spirit of adventure, did not even succeed in overcoming the social and economic factors which now told against emigration. In the Empire Settlement Act of 1922 the government undertook to shoulder half the cost of any emigration scheme concerted with Dominion authorities; but between 1919 and 1922 the average migration was only 180,000 a year, and the Act achieved next to nothing. For at home, despite the economic slump, unemployment insurance and steadily expanding social services made life in familiar surroundings preferable, in the eyes of countless potential emigrants, to adventure overseas. And the Dominions, with social and economic troubles of their own, were fastidious about their acceptance of immigrants, and apt to regard all newcomers as unwelcome competitors. In the ten years which followed the Act of 1922 only a million persons left Britain for some other part of the Empire, while 610,000 came from Empire territories into the United Kingdom. And with the great depression of the nineteenthirties the homeward flow rapidly increased.

But the economic integration of the Empire was sought chiefly through tariff and preference. Towards some sort of imperial preference there had been, at the instance of the Dominions, a tentative and, on the whole, on the part of the mother country at least, a reluctant, approach since the beginning of the century—culminating in the Imperial Economic Conference of 1923 and the subsequent legislation of Mr. Baldwin's government. Thus encouraged, the advocates of protection dwelt insistently on the advantages of that economic imperialism which other Empires pursued as a matter of course. Foreign tariffs, and the repeated default of foreign debtors, reinforced their arguments. Might not the pursuit of mutual economic advantage go far to supplement those political ties which, in the light of the Declaration of 1926, seemed now so tenuous? The world-wide economic catastrophe of 1931, with the downward plunge in the prices of primary products, and the dumping on Britain and the Empire of the surplus products of nations with depreciating currencies, set the Dominions clamouring for help. The new National government responded with a number of tariffs, and, at the Ottawa Conference of 1932, with a wide extension of imperial preference, in which the colonies were not forgotten. There were not inconsiderable benefits, particularly at first, for all concerned. During the next five years British exports to the Empire rose by 52 per cent, and exports to foreign countries by 35 per cent, while the trade between nations of the Empire other than the United Kingdom actually increased by 124 per cent. None the less both Britain and the Dominions needed world trade as well as Empire trade, and world trade was steadily drying up. Moreover tariff and preference seemed to breed jealousy and divergent interest almost as conspicuously as they fostered good will. And more than one colonial people had protested against duties which virtually amounted to taxation without their consent. And the apparent closing of the traditionally open door into her colonies seemed to deprive Britain of the right to claim that she was developing her "imperial estate" in the interests of all the world. Apparent closing rather than real, for many of the colonial dependencies had remained outside the Ottawa system, and, all told, scarcely three per cent of Britain's exports to her colonial Empire received tariff or quota advantages. None the less the mere gesture towards Empire trade had been sufficient to enrage Liberals and internationalists, and to provide the self-styled Have-not Powers with serviceable arguments for aggression. And by 1937 the Empire was turning its back on the Ottawa policy, and at the Imperial Conference of that year it was the Dominions, once the enthusiastic sponsors of imperial preference, who insisted that everything possible should be done to stimulate international trade. Once more the Empire had learnt that its true interests were the interests of the world. But there appeared to be another lesson too to be learned, not at first sight altogether compatible. In this disordered world, it seemed, little could be hoped of promiscuous and unregulated trade and investment; they must be regulated if they were to prosper, and it was very much easier to regulate trade and investment within the Empire than for the world at large. And might not the organisation of the Empire be of itself a service to the world? Might not the Empire indeed, and the slowly emerging pattern of its political and economic life, be in some sense the prologue and archetype, conceivably even one day the nucleus, of a wider world community yet to be?

CHAPTER THREE

§1

IT MIGHT have been expected that the war, and their own narrow escape from destruction, would have roused in the British a new and lasting zeal for the Empire, a fuller sense of its obligations and opportunities and a determination that henceforth it should be strong enough to make another world war unlikely. Unfortunately the war had no such consequences. Indeed it is probable that during the twenty years which were to pass before Germany was once more ready to spring at the throat of Europe the British public knew and cared less about the Empire than at any time since 1880. A century hence a scholar might study the controversial literature issued during the six general elections of these years, and for all that four-fifths of it concerned itself with imperial affairs might remain under the impression that it was addressed to the electorate of a country without interests or responsibilities overseas. Indeed he would be forced to conclude that powerful currents of political opinion regarded the Empire as positively discreditable.

There were many reasons for this surprising aftermath of a war in which the Empire had once again saved freedom, and astonished the world with its solidarity. In a sense it was but one aspect of the swift moral reaction which set in almost as soon as the last shot had been fired. For the first time in history war had demanded a supreme effort, moral and physical, from the whole people, and it left them exhausted, and, before long, disillusioned. For it soon became apparent that the expected fruits of victory, prosperity at home and security abroad—or, in the political jargon of the day, "homes fit for heroes" and "a world safe for democracy"—were to be denied them. And soon it became the literary fashion to complain that the war had "settled" nothing. "The only victory that had resulted was in fact the victory of death over life, of stupidity over intelligence, of hatred over humanity," such was a novelist's characteristic verdict. That the war had at least saved Britain and the world from the Prussian jackboot, and that neither prosperity nor security could be expected without further effort, effort of almost the same intensity, and involving, in one way or another, the entire Empire, this few then perceived and still fewer still proclaimed.

And besides all this there were special reasons for the general indifference with which the Empire was now regarded. For a surprising proportion of the most influential writers during these years were men who had deliberately stood aside from the national effort and were now in more or less conscious revolt not only against the war itself but against the moral standards and political ideals which had commended themselves to a nation at war. And so, for a small but highly influential enclave of opinion the Empire followed the military virtues into the shades of popular disfavour, and while Britain once more eagerly discarded her material weapons, she seemed for a while to be in some danger of dispensing with her moral and political defences also. Once again the most critical imperial problems would rouse little interest in the general public, increasingly preoccupied with its own domestic appetites; and for good or ill both controversy and solution would be confined to a narrow circle of experts and enthusiasts. And in school, college and University the rising generation continued to be brought up in almost total ignorance of its own imperial history, and therefore of its vast obligations and opportunities, and indeed of the nature of the modern world.

The war was over, but not the grand ordeal which the Empire must survive or perish. And although, as the uneasy years between the two wars drew on, the danger changed its shape, it did not grow less deadly. For it is not merely the fact that both wars were but stages in the unfolding of a continuous German design which gives the years between the wars their likeness to an uneasy armistice, or even to a new phase of war. It is difficult not to see the press of problems and emergencies, moral, political and economic, which beset the Empire between 1918 and 1939 as embodying, together with the wars from which so many of them sprang, or into which they led, one supreme coherent test of the Empire's fitness to endure, one grand ordeal so formidable and searching that merely to survive it would furnish an answer to every critic. And that despite all, the Empire would survive, would be owed not to its political and intellectual leaders, but first and foremost to the stout hearts and steady nerves of its common folk. For in these dark years while politicians grew ever more timid and shortsighted, and intellectuals followed darkness like a dream, the courage, the shrewd instinctive common sense and the simple decency of the rank and file did not abate. And so it would come about that as, long since, the private citizen had created the Empire in his own government's despite, so in due course, despite his leaders, he would save it.

§2

The grand ordeal continued. Even while throughout the Dominions the imperial structure was once more adapting itself swiftly to changing needs—so swiftly that by many change was mistaken for decay—in the dependent Empire manifold problems of adaptation to an era of rapid change loomed even more formidable.

Even before the war had ended, India was entering upon the most troubled era of political controversy in all her long history. In the dispute soon to reach its climax neither British nor Indians would be seen at their best. For India, the land of the Vedas and the Upanishads, of Buddha and Asoka, is not politically minded; prophets, saints and soldiers she has bred in abundance, but of statesmen very few. And as for the British they seemed to be paying now the penalty of not having earlier and more clearly chosen their objective and marked out the road to it. For increasingly during these distressful decades the observer is conscious of a sense of frustration, as if the protagonists on both sides were beginning to suspect that the obvious, the only, path, the path on which they were so painfully toiling, might after all not be leading them towards the desired goal.

In 1917 Edwin Montagu, as Secretary of State, announced that the British prescription for India was responsible self-government. In 1918, with Lord Chelmsford, he published a Report foreshadowing gradual advance towards that goal. As recently as 1912 Lord Crewe, as Liberal Secretary of State, had been saying of the demand for Dominion status that "he saw no future for India on these lines. The experiment of a measure of self-government was one which could not be tried." But at last the British government had crossed its Rubicon. It was a momentous decision, from which there could be no turning back, one of those decisions which to contemporaries suddenly seem inevitable, and, whatever controversy may have gone before, are reached almost without argument, like the decision in Britain, at about the same time, to extend the franchise to women. "We have ourselves made sacrifices," wrote a commentator in England a few years later, "to an idea in our hour of victory such as few Empires, even in defeat, have offered to the triumphant victor." The idea for which the sacrifices had been accepted was the Idea—of freedom through Parliamentary self-government—which had so long been the dominant political inspiration of the British Empire, and through it had taken root in every continent save Asia. But now for the first time it was to try its fortunes in Asia also, among an oriental people, and amid conditions fantastically remote from any which it had hitherto encountered. And the idea of Parliamentary self-government, for which Montagu, Chelmsford and then, in the Act of 1919, Parliament itself, made their sacrifices, embodies other ideas not a few, to which also accordingly, even if unconsciously, the sacrifices were devoted. Unity, for one. For from the first it would be a dogma of the extreme Indian nationalism which had captured Congress in 1916, that the self-governing India of the future must be one, and its government unitary. And if unity, homogeneity.

Yet how was the India of the future to be either united or homogeneous, seeing that in the India of the present virtually the only unifying force was British authority? What homogeneity or unity was to be looked for in a land which, before the British began to rule there, had been a vast kaleidoscope of petty, warring princedoms, and in which even to-day there were still two hundred and twenty-two languages spoken by more than a million people each, but no common tongue; a land in which there were two thousand strictly segregated castes, and fifty million persons so far beyond the pale of all caste that their very shadow polluted the food of orthodox Hindus; in which even now, despite the heavy hand of British authority, no year passed without widespread bloodshed between Hindu and Moslem; in which tens of millions knew less of each others' tastes, prejudices and habits than a Yorkshire shepherd knows of life in a Buddhist monastery; in which millions of Hindus so revered idols that they would worship the very tables off which they ate, while millions of Moslems detested idolatry so fiercely that they would not tolerate a picture on a wall? And if the Parliamentary system, at least as hitherto practised, had always required in the nation a homogeneity and a mutual tolerance unattainable, and indeed unimaginable, among India's warring creeds and segregated castes, democracy had always hitherto implied a social structure in which, although there might be class distinctions, men could yet pass easily from one social plane to another. In a land where intermarriage, and even social intercourse, between caste and caste was unthinkable, and untouchables were expected to leave the road on the approach of a Brahmin, how, it might be wondered, could democracy take root?

Self-government, yes; to the goal of self-government for India the British Empire stood pledged by its entire past. But self-government through Parliament and democracy on the British model? Had it perhaps been too hastily assumed that India could be fitted into moulds slowly fashioned in that West against so much of whose philosophy India's nationalists themselves were in revolt? Might it not prove impossible to build Parliament and democracy where the only known foundations for Parliament and democracy did not, perhaps could never, exist? Would the British, had they marked out their goal, and reflected on it sufficiently and betimes, have taken now some other path, towards self-government indeed but self-government of another kind? "I would turn the whole of British India into Indian states," a British civil servant, much loved in India, had written in 1914; and such a stroke would at least have meant at first a more developed form of the indirect rule which had done so much for other parts of the Empire. Again, the Indian masses have always preferred a person to a system, and had there been a Disraeli at hand to advise, George the Fifth might conceivably have become a second Asoka to the Hindus of India, another Sulei-man the Magnificent to the Moslems. Among the martial castes and races of India there was already a profound contempt and suspicion for the middle-class intelligentsia of their own country, to whom power under a Parliamentary system would inevitably pass. "We ask that you do not school us in a highly centralised form of Parliamentary rule," said a brilliant Bengali, Chitra Ranjan Das. It must break down, he prophesied, because it would concentrate power in the middle class, and because it would run counter to "the economic, social and religious nature of India."

But the British preferred the natural and the obvious path, for it is natural that a Parliamentary democracy should choose Parliamentary and democratic forms, and Parliamentary and democratic forms were what the leaders of Indian nationalism, so many of them educated in the West, were now clamorously demanding. And so the Act of 1919 left the central executive much as it had been, but entrusted legislation to a new Council of State and Legislative Assembly, each containing an official *bloc* but an elected majority. And the Provinces were to have Legislative Councils, elected on a wider franchise. "Central Subjects," including defence, customs and foreign relations, were reserved for the Governor in Council, with some of the "Provincial Subjects"; but a number of the "Provincial Subjects" were "transferred" to elected ministers, responsible to the legislature. Such was "dyarchy," by which the Act proposed to achieve its declared purpose of promoting "the increasing association of Indians in every branch of Indian administration, and . . . the gradual development of self-governing institutions."

§3

The experiment opened ominously. The Rowlatt Acts, passed to enable the executive to deal with revolutionary terrorism, had authorised arrest without trial, and other restrictive measures, in areas where political murders had been committed. The Acts were never in fact enforced, but they became the occasion of an agitation which, in accordance with Tilak's doctrine that nationalist propaganda need not be truthful, translated their strictly limited intentions into proposals for universal state inspection before marriage, and for the prohibition of all assemblies of more than three persons. And they introduced Mr. Gandhi to the centre of the Indian stage. A combination, it has been said, of St. Francis and Lord Beaverbrook, Mr. Gandhi had spent twenty years defending the rights of Indians in Natal, and though a Tolstoyan pacifist had nevertheless been ready to recruit for the British cause during the recent war. Now, however, he put himself at the head of a campaign of what he described as non-violent non-co-operation, a characteristic combination which resulted in a good deal of non-co-operation but extremely little non-violence. Mr. Gandhi was genuinely and profoundly disturbed by the bloodshed to which his doctrines invariably gave rise, but nothing would deter him from preaching them. And henceforth he was the embodiment of Indian nationalism, perhaps because he came so near to being the embodiment of India—at once a Mahatma, a great spirit, and (despite his immense intelligence and his *bania* caste) most typical of the Hindu peasant, shrewd, simple and persistent.

1919, the year of the new Act, saw also widespread unrest in the Punjab, due partly to the prospective partition of Mohammedan Turkey and a brief conflict with Mohammedan Afghanistan, where a Holy War against Britain had been proclaimed. It saw also the tragedy of Amritsar. In April there was rioting in that city and a mob murdered all the Europeans on whom it could lay hands. British banks were looted and the Anglican Church, the Mission Hall, the railway station, the telegraph office and the town hall were set on fire. Two British women were attacked, one of them, a missionary, being savagely beaten and left for dead in the streets. In the Mutiny also assaults on British women had always provoked the more savage reprisals. There were riots, burnings and lootings throughout the Punjab, and railway and telegraph lines were cut. The stage seemed set for widespread revolt. It was under these conditions that General Dyer marched through Amritsar city with a small body of troops on April 13th, and read aloud at various points an order forbidding public meetings. In the afternoon, however, a huge crowd assembled in the Jallianwala Bagh, to hear inflammatory orations from Congress leaders. General Dyer at once marched to the scene with sixty-five Gurkha riflemen, twenty-five Baluchis and two armoured cars, which last a narrow entrance prevented him from using. There was a brief, tense pause and then he ordered his men to open rapid fire on the crowd. Some four hundred persons were killed and sixteen hundred wounded. General Dyer marched his men back to barracks, leaving the dead and wounded where they lay.

Some say that to condone his action it is only necessary to have had some experience of the April sun in the Punjab, and of commanding a handful of soldiers among a vast mob seething with revolt. Others that what he did was fully justified, since only instant and ruthless action could have saved the Punjab, and perhaps India, from revolt, and bloodshed on a much more terrible scale. Others that even so no British general should have fired so long upon an unarmed crowd, or failed to attempt at least to assist the wounded. And yet others that the whole affair was an unforgivable medley of brutality and misjudgment. It was said also that neither the shooting in the Jallianwala Bagh, nor the subsequent order that men passing through the street in which the woman missionary had been assaulted should go upon hands and knees, would have been conceivable in one of the British Dominions—which was true enough; but then the whole scene, and the murder and arson which preceded it, would also have been unthinkable in a British Dominion. But in India perhaps the deepest resentment was caused by the apparent assumption throughout a good deal of the subsequent controversy that Indians were an inferior race. In the event General Dyer was censured, and his career was broken. But he was warmly supported by many members of both Houses at Westminster, and by a powerful section of the Press. It was the story of Governor Eyre over again; the same sudden tragedy, the same arguments and the same inconclusive ending. But it made an ominous prologue for dyarchy.

§4

Throughout the next few years Mr. Gandhi, who had proclaimed in 1919 that his trust in the soul-force of his followers had been a "Himalayan blunder," nevertheless returned repeatedly to the non-co-operation which, despite its name, was never non-violent. By 1922 he was in prison, and his leadership had passed to the more extreme leaders of the Hindu Congress, who now decided, instead of boycotting the legislatures, to enter them, and wreck them from within. In 1924 began a lengthy phase of Commissions and consultations, moving ponderously across a background heavy with the sense of impending change. For, as de Tocqueville pointed out long since, no era is so prone to revolutionary sentiment as that in which a conservative government begins to reform. Yet in 1926 there dawned a transient prospect that the path taken in 1919 might soon lead to the promised land, and, as was natural in India, hope centred upon a person, not a project. For soon after the arrival of Lord Irwin as Viceroy an electrifying rumour ran round the bazaars. There was "a holy man," it was whispered, in Government House. For Britain had for once sent to India as Viceroy not a mere statesman or administrator, although Irwin was both, but a Christian who obviously and deeply believed in Christianity. In India, where saints are more highly esteemed than in Birmingham or Glasgow, and where the medley of creeds makes for a marked tolerance as to the particular tenets of the saint, this unaccustomed phenomenon had an instant effect. Gandhi, who had recovered his old influence, held Lord Irwin to be the one Englishman who had understood the mind and spirit of India. And stories of how, when the Viceroy was travelling, his train would be stopped at small wayside stations to enable him to attend service in church were soon repeated all over India. "I want to see Irwin the man," said Gandhi, with a flash of his penetrating insight, and the celebrated personal interview between the two, after Lord Irwin had released him unconditionally from gaol, might even have found the path through the maze—if only Gandhi had been able to speak for all India. "The nauseating and humiliating spectacle," another great man called it, "of this one-time Inner Temple lawyer, now seditious fakir, striding half-naked up the steps of the Viceroy's palace, there to negotiate and parley on equal terms with the representative of the King Emperor." Mr. Churchill may be pardoned his outburst, for he had long foreseen the inevitable frustrations of the journey commenced in 1919, but there was assuredly no humiliation in that unwontedly intimate conference of two men who could understand each other so much better than could the vast aggregates of humanity which they represented.

But the agreement which they reached in 1931 was still-born. Hindu-Moslem tension in India was now too strong, and the Congress leaders too weak; and ministerial changes at home had altered the emphasis of British policy. And in the meantime the

Simon Commission had toured India, had been boycotted and had produced the brilliant Report, which—since it elaborately explained that the profound communal and religious differences which divided India were still an insuperable obstacle to normal Parliamentary democracy—was disliked by most politicians at Westminster and ignored by most officials at Delhi. There had followed the series of three autumn Round Table Conferences in London, which began in 1930, and were still in progress when Lord Irwin left India in 1931. The Conferences, it had been announced, would "end for ever the old tutelage of India," but before they had concluded, the political world was beginning belatedly to recognise that the true conflict was not between Britain and India, but between Hindu and Moslem, between high caste and low caste, between Congress and the Princes. On the complex issues raised at the Conference Mr. Gandhi, the sole Congress representative, could neither expound a clear-cut view, on which that body had palpably failed to agree, nor even reconcile the opinions of the other Indian delegates. Where then was the India on which Britain was to confer self-government?

§5

Faced not with one India, but many, the Conference turned towards federation. In 1933, after Congress had been proscribed and Gandhi had again been committed to gaol, a White Paper foreshadowed the coming reforms. The Government of India Act of 1935 was an honest attempt to solve the insoluble, and to placate the extremists without antagonising their opponents, but it had the air of being addressed primarily to British sceptics, and roused little interest in India. A federation of all India was to be approached in two stages. First there were to be autonomous governments in eleven provinces, and then their federation with the Indian states. The project was beset with "safeguards," allowing Provincial governors to override their Ministers and the Viceroy the Central Legislature. But despite lengthy negotiation the Indian States persisted in regarding federation on such terms as "fundamentally unsound." The Moslem League would have no constitution based on the "economic and political unity of India," which was the basis of the Hindu Congress creed; it put forward its own "Pakistan plan," for two Indias, with the areas in which Moslems were a majority as independent states. And the Hindu fighting races, and the Hindu Depressed Classes, betrayed increasing scepticism as to their prospects under a democratic All-India government, which would inevitably be controlled by the Congress Working Committee. And so while, mesmerised by a new and more terrible German menace, the world moved helplessly into the preliminaries of another world war, the road of the reformers of 1919 reached its destined goal, deadlock within politically conscious India, deadlock therefore among the unconscious masses, deadlock, let us say, between the hundred and eighty millions for whom Congress spoke, eighty million who would welcome "Pakistan," eighty million subjects of the native states, fifty million members of the Depressed Classes.

§6

Yet reform had not slackened. "The increasing association of Indians in every branch of Indian administration" did not cease. And when war came again there would be only six hundred and thirty British among five thousand five hundred higher officials, only six thousand out of a hundred and eighty-seven thousand in the police forces, less than two hundred British doctors among the six thousand in the civil medical departments, only two hundred and thirty out of two thousand five hundred judges. An Indian tariff protected India from the competition of British goods. The jute industry had largely passed into the hands of Indian shareholders. The non-productive debt of the Indian government was less than that of any other nation in the world. The machine still governed, efficiently and beneficently governed, so that the population, which in 1891 had reached two hundred and fourteen millions, mounted dizzily during the next fifty years by a hundred and seventy-four millions more. British administrators had treated India as one, and it had prospered, but when British statesmen sought to do likewise, they found it impossible. Too much had been left out of their calculations.

§7

The blocked path in India provoked all the more impatience when Indians observed how swiftly after the war self-government could grow up elsewhere. Mesopotamia, a desolation long blighted by the unvarying misrule of the Turkish Empire, was transferred, under Mandate, to the British Government in 1920. For twelve years a British High Commissioner and British officials laboured to efface a tradition of misgovernment little younger than the ruined arch

of the dead Greek city amidst whose dust the battle of Ctesiphon had
been so lately fought. And once again, as at so many other times
and in so many other places, young Englishmen toiled good-
humouredly in desert outposts, or were killed in frontier affrays,
intent upon their hereditary art of improvising order out of chaos.
An Arab king was elected, and an Arab administration, and then a
Parliamentary system, was set up. A civil service and a police force
were organised, schools and hospitals sprang up, roads and railways
were built. And in 1932 the Mandate was determined, and Iraq, as
the new kingdom was named, entered the League of Nations as an
independent state, at the instance of the British government.

§8

In Egypt too the advance to self-government, by Indian standards,
was swift. Only since 1914, when Turkey joined Germany, had
Egypt, as a British Protectorate, been formally a part of the British
Empire. In Egypt, as elsewhere, the war bred both irritation and
impatience. It brought unexpected riches, and not only to un-
scrupulous Mudirs and Omdehs; even the fellaheen grew prosperous
for the first time in their long history; and strange stories circulated
of peasants purchasing motor cars in villages from which only two
miles of road were accessible, or, with their families, squatting on
the floor of luxurious hired flats in Cairo, with the rococo chairs
ranged, unused, along the walls. For all this the fellaheen were not
ungrateful; but they were also conscripted for labour battalions,
in which they not only acquired a grievance but caught a disturbing
glimpse of the larger world. The politically conscious minority was
even more discontented and even more impatient. They had been
caught up, they felt, in a quarrel not their own. They lacked the
dignity of combatants, yet Egypt became a base for British operations and a source of British supplies. And some Egyptian
politicians had lived throughout the war in Constantinople or
Vienna, or served in the Turkish army. All were roused by the
current talk of self-determination, and later by the national revival
in Turkey under Mustapha Kemal. Nor was it unimportant that
Egyptians were accustomed to the habits of a hot climate, and had
little liking for the traditions of industry, punctuality and discipline
which had accompanied the British. Nationalist pamphlets circulated widely, one quoting more than sixty separate British promises
to leave Egypt. An insurrection in 1919 was easily suppressed, but
soon afterwards Lord Milner succeeded in opening negotiations with

the leader of the nationalists, and in 1922 the Protectorate was abolished, and Egypt was declared "an independent sovereign state." Reservations, however, qualified both the independence and the sovereignty. Imperial communications, defence, the protection of foreign interests and minorities and the status of the Sudan were "reserved absolutely" for Britain.

Years of negotiation and agitation followed, with politics a triangular argument on the reservations of 1922, conducted between the King, the popular Parties and the British government. The presence of British troops made it easy both for the Egyptian government to decline responsibility for keeping agitators in order, and for agitators to claim that but for the British they would be making short work of the abuses in their own Egyptian government. In 1936 complete Egyptian sovereignty was acknowledged, and military occupation became "permanent military defensive alliance." The treaty entrusted the defence of the Suez Canal to the British, and maintained the Anglo-Egyptian *condominium* in the Sudan, which is still administered by a civil service mainly British. And in Egypt too, though the Protectorate was no more, there remained a certain number of British civil servants. Egyptians in general were not sorry to have it so, for they were aware that they were still in need of some assistance, and that if the British were not there some other, and less welcome, foreign power would take their place. And with the irritation of the occupation and the Protectorate removed, they were conscious of a not inconsiderable respect for British administration. Had it not given Egypt since 1882 an irrigation system ten times more efficient than the dams built with foreign aid before 1882, and ten times less expensive? Had it not indeed bequeathed a more intangible but a more fundamental legacy, to measure which it was perhaps only necessary to compare Egypt with Syria, ruled by the French since 1920. For in 1914 Syria had been economically, culturally and politically far in advance of Egypt, its literature the most vigorous in the Near East, its Press the most effective, its intelligentsia dominant throughout the Arab world. Yet since 1920 in all these respects Egypt had left it far behind. Such had been the quickening power of the idea of freedom. "The fact is," wrote one of the British Empire's more astringent critics,[1] "that countries like Iraq, Turkey, Iran and various Baltic states have discovered after experimenting with officials and experts from all over the world that the British give far more devoted and disinterested and useful service."

[1] The American Albert Viton, *Great Britain*, p. 326.

CHAPTER FOUR

TRUSTEESHIP IN THE INTERLUDE

(1918-1939)

§1

IN WHAT were once the colonies of settlement, grown now to political equality, the once unimaginable goal had been triumphantly attained. And in the East the Empire had crossed its Rubicon and set itself one of the most ambitious tasks yet attempted in the political history of man. And it is tempting to think of the remaining nations of the Empire as a vast and various convoy moving towards the same goal. The metaphor, it is true, is hardly exact, for if this was a convoy the vessels in it were travelling at very different speeds, and were already strung out at irregular, and lengthy, intervals. Yet if, as official utterances often suggested, all were moving towards the same eventual harbour, there is a certain attraction in the conception of a convoy, anxiously shepherded by the ministers and officials of the mother of democracies. Were all, however, in fact making for the same port? Perhaps a more accurate official description of the process was that of the Colonial Secretary who said in June, 1939, "The main objective of our government in all the Colonies is to train the people to stand always a little more securely on their own feet." A little more securely on their own feet; that at least is true of all the diverse process. A movement, regular or intermittent, fast or slow, towards greater self-government; not inevitably towards complete self-government, nor necessarily towards the British Parliamentary system; that perhaps is as far as generalisation can safely go.

For the diversity within the imperial unity is so startling as to defy classification. At the head of the procession, if we choose to think of a procession, would come Southern Rhodesia, with its white settlers and stable Parliamentary system, and, since 1923, its all-but-Dominion status. Very near it might rank Burma, separated from India in 1937, with its two-chamber legislature and, subject to the overriding powers of the Governor, its responsible executive. But what of Ceylon? Here, in 1931, the advance deliberately ignores the familiar pattern of Parliament and Party, and a constitution is modelled on the procedure of the London County Council. The experiment was not destined for a long life, but it was at least evidence that the Empire was learning from experience in the East that the Parliamentary system is not necessarily or always the ideal shape of self-government.

In the more backward dependencies the normal constitutional pattern during this period came to be a Council, in which, in varying proportions, official members were balanced against unofficial, elected or nominated, subject to the casting vote, or overriding powers, of the Governor. In some, as Jamaica, Mauritius and all the islands of the Windward and Leeward groups, the scales were tilted in favour of the unofficial members; in some (Grenada, the Straits Settlements, Lagos and Southern Nigeria are examples) the balance became equal; in a few, such as Sierra Leone and the Gold Coast, officials were in the majority. It may be (who can say?) that none of these dependencies was heading for a Parliament, yet all were making towards increasing self-government, standing "always a little more securely on their own feet."

At two points at least on the long line of advance there was retreat. In Cyprus (occupied in 1878 and annexed when its nominal suzerain, the Sultan of Turkey, went to war with Britain in 1914) control by the Governor was restored, after serious rioting, in 1931. And in Malta, where a two-chamber legislature and a responsible executive had been introduced in 1921, trouble, stirred up by a small pro-Fascist bourgeoisie, led to the abrogation of the constitution in 1933.

After all, there is little resemblance to a convoy. Nor is it easy to classify the constitutions or to generalise as to the nature of the advance. The movement is slow, irregular and occasionally reluctant. Yet it is impossible to examine the constitutions of the Empire in all their diversity without a sense that these are growing organisms, seeking, like life itself—and like life itself not without failure and recoil—to adapt themselves to the changing circumstance of a world in flux. And the principle of life within them is unmistakable. The movement is slow, but the coming war will soon transform its *tempo*. The movement is slow, but the principle is there. It is the principle which has animated the Empire from the first, the Idea of self-government, closely akin to the doctrine of trusteeship, and now, by one of the most notable advances in man's history, extended from the white colonies of settlement to the whole world-wide association of communities of every colour and creed.

§2

Yet the twentieth century had almost ceased to be able to see political advance in isolation from its economic background. Even in Britain the emphasis on material welfare was steadily increasing, had already indeed, in the light of the international situation, reached the point of danger. And certainly many of the backward peoples of the Empire needed prosperity more than self-government. Here was a clear summons to the doctrine of trusteeship. Yet in the trough of the uneasy years of armistice, when the whole world, and every nation, great or small, after its own fashion and degree, was racked and distempered, it began to seem as if even with the practise of trusteeship all was not well. In part no doubt this was but a reflection of the world malaise, in which every people had its inevitable share. After 1931, for example, with the downward plunge in the prices of the primary products on which their prosperity depended, there was widespread distress in the Colonies and dependencies.

Yet the sudden and abnormal depression was but intensifying, and exposing, symptoms already latent or half-revealed. Lord Hailey's exhaustive *African Survey* of 1938, and the Report of the West India Royal Commission in 1939, were the most conspicuous and searching of a number of inquiries which went to show that for some while the colonial peoples had not been reaping the social and economic benefits which the Empire's avowed policy was intended to confer on them. And from 1934 onwards strikes in the copperbelt of North Rhodesia, and among the cocoa-growers of the Gold Coast, complaints of low wages on the plantations of Malaya and a continuous rumble of dissatisfaction from the West Indies left no doubt that there were grave deficiencies somewhere. In some respects, it seemed, these troubles might be more deep-seated than the world depression itself, and they certainly did not square with the doctrine of trusteeship. Moreover the growing prospect of a second German challenge to the very existence of the Empire now began grimly to emphasise the urgency of the need for reform.

In the nineteen-thirties the Colonial Office set a new precedent. During these years the long-suffering British taxpayer was called upon for twelve million pounds to meet colonial deficits, as well as for the advance of large sums to bankrupt Newfoundland, which in 1934 had been compelled by the world depression and its own long maladministration to leave the ranks of the self-governing Dominions, and accept the rule of a joint British and Newfoundland

Commission. Meanwhile an intense colonial activity sprang up. Education, health, child-welfare, agriculture, nutrition and land-settlement—against their varying regional backgrounds these problems were studied and attacked anew. Organised campaigns against soil-erosion in Tanganyika and Ceylon, and sleeping-sickness in Nigeria, pasture-improvements in Mauritius and the Falklands, small-holdings in Jamaica and new Education Departments in Aden and Somaliland—such were some of the first-fruits of the government's reviving energy. The development of secondary industries was encouraged. A growing body of trade union and industrial welfare legislation began to appear upon the statute-book at Westminster, and in the dependencies. And who was to finance reform? In Africa, at least, said Lord Hailey, the mining companies ought to be made to contribute more substantially to colonial revenue. But in general the colonies could not provide the necessary funds. And the main burden, it was clear, must be shouldered once more by the British taxpayer. For the revolution was at last complete. The old mercantilist Empire (with all its contemporaries) had unhesitatingly assumed that colonies were an asset, to be administered in her own interest by the mother-country. There had followed an era in which it was judged sufficient to provide dependent peoples with decent and orderly government. But now it had been publicly acknowledged that colonies might be sheer liability, and none the less an imperial power must put their interests before its own. That much ridiculed phrase "the white man's burden" took on a new significance. And on the eve of the last and darkest phase of its greatest ordeal the Empire was feeling its way towards a new practise which would at last clothe the doctrine of trusteeship with full reality.

§3

Yet trusteeship demanded even more than political tutelage and social development. How was the ideal to survive where black and white lived side by side in the same community? The British government at least had no hesitation. No British government, said a minister, could tolerate a colour-bar in a British colony. Yet the domestic policy of the Union of South Africa, which was steadily extending its influence northwards, was founded upon the most rigid of colour-bars. The Union held firmly to the traditional Boer view that "the supremacy of the white man's rule in South Africa is essential if he is to retain either his birthright or his civilisation." And in 1925, General Hertzog, at the head of a Nationalist-Labour

coalition, had set out to establish thorough-going native segregation, so that by 1937 the natives of the Union, who formed two-
thirds of its population, could be shut out, save as visitors or
employees, from all towns, were debarred altogether from many
occupations, and could acquire land only in scattered areas, representing some twelve and a half per cent of the Union's territory.
The natives in the Cape Province had held the Parliamentary franchise
since 1853, though even there they were not admitted to Parliament;
but in Natal and the former Boer Republics no black man was
entitled to the normal vote; and all were represented by three
Europeans in the House of Assembly, and eight in the Senate. The
white minorities in the Rhodesias, in Kenya, Uganda and Tanganyika had pursued a very similar policy. And so when the Union
Government pressed for the transfer to itself of the reluctant
Protectorates, Swaziland, Basutoland and Bechuanaland, or when
Europeans in North Rhodesia and Nyasaland talked of federation,
largely in the hopes of shaking off the more clement native policy
of the British government, ministers at Westminster found themselves compelled politely but firmly to decline. The doctrine of
trusteeship had not yet spread overseas.

BOOKS FOR FURTHER READING.

Sir Charles Lucas (ed.), *The Empire at war;* Sarah Gertrude Millin,
General Smuts; Henry Borden (ed.), *Robert Laird Borden: his Memoirs;*
The Earl of Cromer, *Modern Egypt; The Round Table;* Sir A.
Zimmern, *The Third British Empire;* A. B. Keith, *The Dominions as
Sovereign States . . .;* "L.S.A.," *Imperial preference and expansionist policy*
(pamphlet); Edward Thompson and G. T. Garratt, *The rise and fulfilment
of British rule in India;* J. T. Gwynn, *Indian politics;* Lord Hailey (ed.),
An African Survey.

EPILOGUE

§1

"He that wrestles with us strengthens our will, and sharpens our wits. Our antagonist is our helper." So wrote Burke. In each one of her previous great ordeals the Empire had learnt wisdom from suffering and failure; and now the supreme ordeal was upon her. For Germany was ready again; ready for the new war, for which her rulers had begun to prepare as soon as the last shot of the old war was fired. And in relation to France and Britain Germany were now far stronger than in 1914. To German eyes indeed the prospect was enticing. The public life of France had been rotten for a century, and, as Germans had good cause to know, it was honeycombed with treachery and corruption now. And as for Britain, this time, surely, her disintegrating Empire would dissolve at the first blow. "The very day war broke out it would become manifest that Great Britain had already lost her world dominion," so had run the German prophecy; and so, the rulers of Germany had no doubt, it would fall out.

And so it must have fallen out, if the life of the Empire had not been quick and vigorous beneath the superficial malaise of the distempered years, if it had not still nourished traditions big with promise for the future of mankind, and still been able to learn from suffering and defeat. Arms alone would not save Britain. Indeed she had done almost everything possible to ensure that arms should not save her. After all her wars she had been quick to fling away her weapons, and after the last war the mere existence of the League of Nations had rendered the temptations which always beset a democratic state well-nigh irresistible. With the readiest optimism politicians and public alike had assumed that the League would relieve them of their obligations, some being all the readier to disarm because they believed in the League, others all the more anxious to believe in the League because they were eager to disarm. The process had been all the more thorough because the Dominions had so soon reverted to the tempting old tradition that the defence of the Empire was the responsibility of the British taxpayer, while the British taxpayer, footing the bill of his own expanding social services, had been only too eager to economise on self-defence.

The complete and terrible significance of the new German war was only gradually revealed. As if reluctant to unloose the full horrors of such a conflict upon humanity, or to commit themselves finally to a gamble for such tremendous stakes, the protagonists began with what seemed a half-hearted sparring for position. The Germans at once attacked British sea communications, but there was no fighting on land and no bombing of inland targets. And after he had overrun Poland, and as torture and massacre in their most brutal form returned to that often martyred land, Hitler even declared that he saw no good reason why the war should continue. That much however the British people could see. They were still in considerable bewilderment as to what they were fighting for, but by now they had no doubts whatever as to what they were fighting against. Only, they could hardly yet be said to be fighting at all, and the eerie unreality of a war which seemed not so much war as an intenser phase of the long pre-war distemper left public opinion a prey to its too familiar confusion and disunity. The United States, too, found the spectacle of distressful Europe, from which America had strictly isolated herself, as incomprehensible as ever. Even the British government remained comprehensively blind to the nature and dimensions of the dangers confronting it, and early in 1940 Mr. Chamberlain went so far as to announce that "Hitler has missed the bus." Many buses in the course of his strange career Hitler might indeed be said to have missed, but not assuredly the bus which he now designed to catch; and within a few weeks the Germans had occupied Denmark, and were overrunning Norway. Then came the onslaught in the west. The German army, proclaimed Hitler, was about to decide the destiny of Europe for a thousand years; in this war the defeated would disappear from the pages of history. At last the full scope and pattern of the ancient German design stood out more unmistakably than ever, for all the world to see. After this war, if Germany won it, there were to be no return matches. Germany was to achieve world dominion, more complete and decisive than any dreamed of by previous conquerors. The British way of life, the ideal of freedom and what was left of Christian civilisation would be extinguished for ever. In their place, the primitive Prussian conception of regimented force would hold the world in thrall. It was a breath-taking design; so breath-taking indeed that, though so much was hardly yet apparent, it may be said to have ensured its own frustration. For since it left the conquered no hope, it made it certain that free men everywhere would prefer death to defeat.

And for a while Germany seemed irresistible. Crushing the

would-be neutrals, Belgium and Holland, like egg-shells, the mechanised hordes swept on into France. That unhappy land now paid the penalty, long-deferred and terrible, for the vices which had poisoned her public life since the Revolution. Ill-armed, bewildered, half-hearted and betrayed, her armies reeled back in confusion. Convinced that the war was all but over, and roaring once more from his balcony that the day of the effete democracies was ended, and that the future was for the virile young powers, with the new Italy in their van, Mussolini allied himself with Germany, to ensure the Italian share of the vast expected spoils. And soon the aged Petain was seeking an armistice for France, in the vain hope of some sort of accommodation with Hitler's Germany, and some sort of place in Hitler's Europe. Meanwhile the British army had scrambled back from Dunkirk, and the spirit of Britain had been transformed overnight. Gone were the days of half-hearted warfare; here at last was the challenge, naked and mortal.

§2

The nation settled down to fight for its life under Mr. Churchill's new National administration, to which Parliament, in a three-hour sitting, gave dictatorial powers of the antique Roman pattern for the saving of the state. The equipment of the army, such as it was, had been lost in France, and seven years after Hitler became ruler of Germany the British Empire began the new war virtually unarmed. But at least in this dark hour, Britain did not stand alone. Even less than the mother country was the Empire organised for war, yet the Empire was a quarter of the world, a far wider citadel of freedom than the little island now in such urgent peril, and from the Empire, should the mother country fall, the struggle to save freedom might conceivably be carried on. But for the moment the fate of the world for centuries to come hung upon the fate of Britain, and the world held its breath to watch Britain fall. But Britain was now not only determined to fight to the end; mysteriously, against every apparent probability, she was convinced that once again she would triumph in the end. Partly it was the sheer wickedness of National Socialist Germany which inspired this seemingly irrational confidence; partly some potent current of national heredity; partly the series of incomparable orations with which the Prime Minister enshrined the new spirit of the nation in language as splendid as Chatham's or Pitt's, but to an audience far vaster than Chatham or Pitt could command. To no small degree it was a new consciousness of the

Empire, the sense that, with every other ally struck down or fallen away, Britain was yet sustained by a world-wide community. But above all it was the belief of that community in itself. If the instinct of its citizens, the whole world over, had not told them that they were guardians of long-descended traditions on which the destiny of civilisation now depended, first Britain, and then the Empire, would surely have perished.

The world held its breath to watch Britain fall, but Britain did not fall. Doggedly she settled down to save herself, once more, by her own exertions, in the hope that so one day she might, once again, save this time not Europe only but the world by her example. For the present, at whatever cost, time must be bought for the great democracy beyond the Atlantic to perceive that the survival of her way of life also was at stake. And so during the late summer of 1940, in the glare of her burning cities, friends and enemies alike saw Britain more clearly than ever before. Lessons to which they had been blind for a century stood out suddenly unmistakable. Even those who had supposed themselves hostile could now perceive that the Empire was infinitely preferable to the regimented tyranny which it was defying, and were even ready to admit that it had done the world some service in saving it from the would-be tyrants of the past. Citizens of the United States and in the republics of South America realised abruptly that for generations past they had been taking the unobtrusive screen of the Royal Navy for granted, and that they might soon be deprived of it for ever. For two centuries intermittent victims of continental tyranny had been finding in Britain an asylum of safety, but the great tide of refugees which made for Britain now, and the exiled continental governments established in London and pooling their territories and resources with those of the Empire, made it clear to many who had scarcely suspected it before that this ancient league of freedom-loving nations might well be the prototype of the international organisation of the future. All over the world millions of simple folk saw that the British Empire was for the time being their only hope, and learnt something as to its essential nature which centuries of history had failed to teach them.

All through the summer and early autumn, as in the days when the Armada was awaited in the Channel, or when Napoleon assembled his invasion barges at Boulogne, hastily mustered volunteer defences waited all but unarmed at their posts. But by the end of October the fighter pilots of the Royal Air Force, heavily outnumbered, had shot the *Luftwaffe* out of the daylight British sky, uncomplainingly paying with their lives for the unreadiness of their fellow-countrymen.

§3

Nor was it only foreign peoples who learnt something of the true nature of the British Empire for the first time in that summer of 1940. Once again the Empire itself was learning the lessons of suffering and defeat. If indeed it had been unable to learn, it could not have survived. But the mortal threat of 1940, and even more perhaps the capitulation of Singapore to the Japanese, in February, 1942, launched through the Empire an impulse of self-questioning and self-reform which future students will mark as the dawn of a new phase in history. For though there were excuses for the loss of the great Far Eastern base—Britain could scarcely have reckoned upon having to fight Germany and Japan together, without the assistance of France in the West or the United States in the East, nor yet upon the treacherous readiness with which the new French government opened for the enemy the road to a landward assault—yet the disaster, the largest, said Mr. Churchill, in British military history, was a profound and salutary shock.

In the new and unsparing light of crisis all the intractable problems, the failures and the partial successes of recent decades took on a new urgency. The government addressed itself to such drastic reforms that it could almost be said to be building a new imperial structure. With Dominion status the colonies of white settlement had reached their goal, but what of the goals which had not been reached? The movement of the dependent Empire towards self-government, it now seemed in retrospect, had been marked by slowness, reluctance and indecision. Abruptly the tempo accelerated. Franchises were extended and constitutions liberalised, and native administrators were given extended responsibilities. The constitution offered to Jamaica early in 1943 was characteristic of the new process. There was to be universal adult suffrage and a wholly elective lower House; and further progress was promised in five years' time if, in the meanwhile, the Jamaicans had proved adequate to their new responsibilities. Similar advances were planned for Cyprus, Ceylon, Burma and Malta, fresh-laurelled from her heroic air-siege. As for the backward African dependencies Mr. Herbert Morrison rightly observed that to grant such colonies self-rule would be "like giving a child of ten a latch-key, a bank-account and a shot-gun." They had yet to be hustled across the prodigious interval of time, the equivalent of four or five centuries, which separated them from the van of the Empire's advance. But in September, 1942, the Colonial Secretary instructed the colonial governments to increase the employment of natives in their administrations; "there should be no discrimination on the ground of colour." Of some 250,000 officials in the colonial Empire less than six thousand came from Great Britain and the Dominions.

§4

In India the war had not masked the constitutional quarrel for long, or bridged for a moment the communal schism which underlay it. Before long Congress had resolved to renew civil disobedience, and the Moslem League had retorted that civil disobedience would mean civil war. Islam and Hinduism, said Mr. Jinnah, were not only profoundly contrasted cultures but separate nations, incapable of uniting under a single political government. Politically there was still no India, only a confused clamour of communal dissension.

In the first flush of its heightened resolve, Mr. Churchill's administration offered more Indian seats in the Central Executive Council, a new, broad-based War Council and an all-Party convention to devise a new constitution after the war. It was a promising overture, in that long-tried tradition of experimental advance, through which so many nations of the Empire, like the United Kingdom itself, had won their liberties. Congress however had little taste for the practical accommodations by which, in the political life of the countries in which political life has flourished, the great constitutional advances have been achieved. It continued to prefer all or nothing, and to require concessions immediate, complete and precisely defined. Before the end of the year Gandhi had launched a pacifist campaign against the war effort, three thousand of his followers had been arrested, and Moslems and Hindus were at each others throats in Bombay. Yet nothing, neither communal schism nor doctrinaire politicians, could prevent India from steadily acquiring the status of a world power in her own right. In June, 1941, the British government tried again, giving eight of the twelve executive offices in an enlarged Central Executive Council to Indians, and creating a National Defence Council, of whose thirty-one members thirty were Indians. It was of no avail. Congress remained profoundly suspicious, and the Moslem members of the Defence Council abandoned it for a session in formal protest against British subservience to Hindu pressure. Even the Japanese irruption into

Malaya did not startle the dissidents into harmony. Sir Stafford Cripps arrived in Delhi to offer wide powers forthwith, and after the war complete self-government, even independence, if it pleased, to all India willing to accept a constitution framed by Indians; but his mission failed. For the fundamental dilemma remained unresolved: Britain might offer self-government to India, but there was still no India to accept it. Administrative and economic unity Britain had given India, but without the mass conversion to Christianity of which there had once seemed to be a transient possibility, social and political unity must one day be forged by India for herself. Until then only two alternatives remained—some form of tutelage indefinitely prolonged, or anarchy, with its inevitable sequel of subjection to some foreign invader.

§5

Already, before the war, the British government had recognised that henceforth, at a time of heavy burdens, it must shoulder an additional burden, the financing of social development in the colonies. And in 1940 the Colonial Development and Welfare Act authorised spending up to five million pounds a year, and cancelled ten million pounds of loans already advanced to the poorer colonies. Within a century and a half of the decease of the mercantilist Empire the British were taxing themselves in war time for the benefit of the native peoples of the colonies. And not only taxing themselves. As a British newspaper pointed out, when it came to a conflict between the need of the home market for more raw materials and the need of colonial peoples to grow more food for themselves, "the need of the colonial peoples must come first." And if native peoples were to acquire the habit of responsibility in economics as well as in politics there would have to be freer spending "of money which cannot be found by the colonies themselves and from which the British taxpayer cannot hope for any immediate return." That this was imperialism is certain, but it is equally certain that it bore no resemblance to the imperialism of familiar and contemptuous parlance, or to the policy of any Empire of the past, and that of such imperialism the world stood in sore and increasing need.

Two of the great outstanding problems of Empire, of all Empire everywhere, were thus being slowly mastered. There remained at once the most intractable and the least far-reaching, the problem of the colour bar. Most intractable because its solution was only partly within the competence of the British Government, least far-reaching because it was a strictly local phenomenon, restricted to some, though not all, of the areas in which white minorities inter-mingled with, and were outnumbered by, a numerous black population. And yet in a sense, like all moral issues, the problem of the colour bar must be called far-reaching, touching the life of the Empire at many points beyond the areas of its own immediate origin, so that (for example) it became less easy to grant complete self-government to certain colonies because complete self-govern-ment, and the unrestricted rule of white minorities, might conceiv-ably mean the collapse of the existing safeguards of the interests of the black population. Such a problem cannot be solved at a distance, and perhaps its eventual solution must come from the one self-governing Dominion confronted with it. There are signs that here too the war may have brought new perspectives. In 1942, impressed certainly by the mutual respect of South African and native troops in North Africa, and possibly by the social results of the neglect of native health and housing in the Union, Smuts declared that segregation had been tried and had failed, and that European and Bantu must learn to "live together in helpful harmony."

§6

In the United States the unveiling of the full German menace in the summer of 1940 affected the attitude of the public to the war almost as profoundly, though less swiftly, than in the British Empire. The sense there of blessed isolation was natural, ancient and deep-rooted. Was it not to escape the wrath to come that the Pilgrim Fathers had left Stuart England? And since then generation after generation of immigrants had crossed the Atlantic, minded to turn their backs for ever on Europe and its ancient ills. And for more than a century now the Monroe doctrine, warning Europe off the American Continent, had been the central pillar of American policy. To many Americans it now became startlingly apparent for the first time that it was the British Navy which had made the Monroe doctrine possible. Indeed it was the American Secretary for War, Colonel Stimson, who reminded both Americas, North and South, that they owed their freedom and the survival of their way of life to the friendly control of the Royal Navy over the north Atlantic. And though the will to isolation was deep-seated in the social structure, and the very constitution, of the United States, the tradition of liberty ran deeper still. And the tradition of liberty in the United States was the tradition of Britain—derived thence and still closely akin, so that the threat to the freedom of Britain and the British Commonwealth was not difficult to recognise as a threat to freedom in the United States. Nor was it freedom only that was threatened. Beneath many superficial contrasts, the way of life of the United States was still fundamentally akin to that of the islands which had given them birth. From Chaucer, through Shakespeare, King James' Bible, Milton and Bunyan to Gray's Elegy, the well-springs of their literature were the same; their law was founded upon the English common law; state, federal and local, their political institutions were substantially those of the British everywhere; they cherished the same ideas of right and wrong. Despite their ancient cult of isolation, Americans, as they gazed across the Atlantic, were beginning uneasily to suspect that for them too the issue of the conflict might be a matter of life and death.

Slowly the two great English-speaking communities drew together. Sometimes the American President gave the lead, sometimes, with patient wisdom, he waited to be thrust on. But always the movement was in the same direction. And when the President had been accorded a third term, the pace quickened. Short of war, there would be all practicable aid to the fighting democracies.

In June, 1941, in a final and fatal miscalculation, Hitler flung the German armies upon his Russian associate; Britain within the day, and the Dominions on the morrow, promised the Soviet Republics all possible assistance, and for the first time far ahead, beyond how much further human suffering who could yet tell, the shape of an eventual allied victory became dimly discernible. Less than six months later the Japanese fell upon the American Pacific fleet at Hawaii without declaration of war. The British war in Western Europe and Africa, the Russian war in Eastern Europe and the Chinese war in Asia were all now fused in one gigantic conflict. And all the nations of the English-speaking world were fighting it together.

"If we had kept together after the last war," said Mr. Churchill at Washington, at Christmas, 1941, "if we had taken common measures for our safety, then this renewal of the curse need never have fallen upon us." And one day far hence it may be that in the long perspective of history the renewed association of the British Empire and the United States may be judged to have been the most significant aspect of the most terrible war by which the world has so far been desolated. That renewed association would not have been possible if Britain had not now so manifestly crossed the moral Rubicon from which she had recoiled in the eighteenth century. It was because the Dominions had been freely accorded the full self-government for which American citizens had had to fight against the British in 1776 that American citizens found it natural to fight beside the British in 1943. Once more the Empire could survive because it had learnt the lessons of failure and defeat.

§7

But that is not all. If Britain and the British Empire survive the present conflict it will be because they have doubly earned survival. It will be because tested by the most fiery and searching of all ordeals, the people of the Empire, and in particular the people of Britain, the heart of the Empire, were found to retain their ancient virtues. But it will also be because the Empire still gives to the world something of which the world stands in need, and which it cannot obtain elsewhere; and because its existence is still agreeable to the conscience of mankind.

"The time came," said Mr. Churchill at the Mansion House in 1943,

when this loosely and variously knit world-spread association, where so much was left unwritten and undefined, was confronted with the most searching test of all. The Mother Country, the home of the Kingship, this famous island, seemed to enter the very jaws of death and destruction. . . . Then, surely, was the moment for the Empire to break up, for each of its widely dispersed communities to seek safety on the winning side, for those who thought themselves oppressed to throw off their yoke and make better terms betimes with the conquering Nazi and Fascist power. Then was the time. But what happened? It was proved that the bonds which unite us, though supple and elastic, are stronger than the tensest steel. It was proved that they were the bonds of the spirit and not of the flesh and thus could rise superior alike to the most tempting allurements of surrender and the harshest threats of doom. In that dark, terrific, and also glorious hour we received from all parts of His Majesty's Dominions, from the greatest to the smallest, from the strongest and from the weakest, from the most modern and the most simple, the assurance that we would all go down or come through together. You will forgive me if on this occasion, to me so memorable, here in the heart of mighty London, I rejoice in the soundness of our institutions and proclaim my faith in our destiny.

The Empire in the past has played many rôles, and as we look back from this watershed of history their sovereign importance stands out more clearly than ever before. To have spread organised political freedom across the world; three times to have saved Europe, and twice the world as well, from a tyrant; to have ended slavery, and taught other nations to end it too; to have been so reluctant to acquire territory, and so often to have acquired it in the interests of others; to have learnt wisdom from adversity and to have held a giant's power without using it like a giant; to have grown unplanned, and in so many different fashions that growth seemed to be a response to the demands of nature herself; to have learnt to put the interests of primitive peoples before those of their rulers; to have nursed four Dominions to maturity, and essayed an experiment in the East so vast and pregnant that of it, despite all its shortcomings, the great de Tocqueville could write, "for every man who believes in the legitimate progress of the human race what a consoling and marvellous spectacle is that of the English dominion in India!"—all this has richly earned the Empire survival hitherto, and has given it abundant titles to the gratitude of mankind. But even this may not of itself suffice to ensure survival in a new age, in which new opportunities and new obligations will swiftly unfold. Much, it is true, of what the Empire has achieved still stands on the highroad of the world's needs. The lessons which Burke and Wilberforce and Livingstone taught Britain, and which have issued in the accepted and expanding practise of trusteeship on behalf of backward peoples, the prodigious Indian experiment, founded upon the triumphs and the tragedies of Clive and Warren Hastings—these will surely be woven into the texture of the future, whatever pattern the future may assume. But more than this will be needed. And is not the British Empire a living example of what in the new age the world will need most—the peaceful and enduring association of free nations within a world community? A distinguished Spaniard[1] wrote of Britain:

Not in vain does she control the lion's share of the world. . . . Not in vain has she been allowed centuries of insular concentration, so that the collective virtues she has cultivated in her island of peace should be spread by her over the whole world when the time for universality is ripe. Not in vain is it assumed everywhere, even where it is not said, even where it is not liked, that the main responsibility is hers. In the beginning is the Word. The world must have a solemn, clear, simple word from Great

[1] Professor S. de Madariaga.

Britain. The Nations of the King's peace, the Fatherland of self-government must say to the world: "I believe in the World Commonwealth."

Such abstract *credos* however are hardly in the British tradition. And the gift of the British Empire to the future is likely rather to be of the Empire-Commonwealth itself as the pattern, and, it may even be, the nucleus, of some wider organisation yet to be. Britain "is the single country in the world," wrote a German scholar, "that, looking after its own interest with meticulous care has at the same time something to give to others; the single country where patriotism does not represent a threat or challenge to the rest of the world; the single country that invariably summons the most progressive, idealistic and efficient forces in other nations to co-operate with it." And it may well be that the island from which the world learnt the art of freedom will yet teach it the art of unity. It may well be that her present sufferings have finally fitted Britain for that rôle. But history cannot read the future. All that history can say is that such an outcome would match the pattern of the past. One who pored, towards the end of the fifteenth century, among the scrolls and Tritons of some fantastic map of the world as men then believed the world to be, found little enough to warn him that three hundred years later other maps would show the insignificant island off the north-west angle of Europe as metropolis of a world-wide society. And one who scans an atlas of the world in 1944 can see the great oceanic Empire-Commonwealth sprawled across the five continents plain enough, but, no more than that other, can he guess what wider destiny waits to be unrolled.

THE END

Proclamation line 1763 — · — · —

THE GREAT LAKES

F R A N C E

R. St. Lawrence

THE

MAINE

MASSACHUSETTS

Falmouth
NEW. HAMP!
Saratoga
Naumkeag Salem!
NEW YORK
Boston
C. Ann
C. Cod
ymouth
RHODE I.
CONNECTICUT
Newhaven
New York

Delaware R.
Hudson R.

PENNSYLVANIA

Philadelphia
NEW JERSEY

Washington
MARYLAND
DELAWARE

VIRGINIA

James R.
Jamestown
Yorktown

Ohio R.
Allegheny R.

Alleghenies

N E W

NORTH CAROLINA

Roanoke I.

SOUTH
CAROLINA

NORTH

GEORGIA
Charleston

ATLANTIC

FLORIDA

OCEAN

Miles

0   100   200   300   400   500

THE THIRTEEN ORIGINAL AMERICAN COLONIES

INDIA

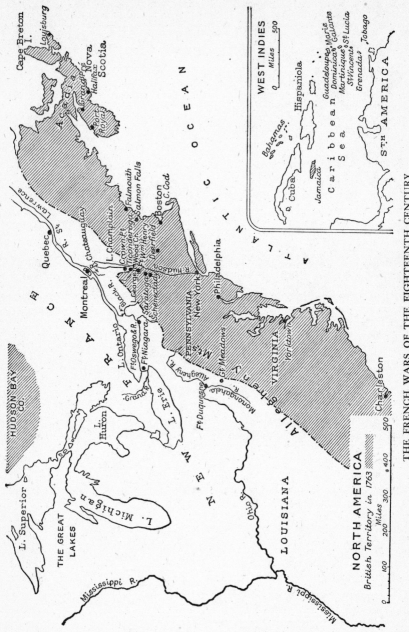

THE FRENCH WARS OF THE EIGHTEENTH CENTURY

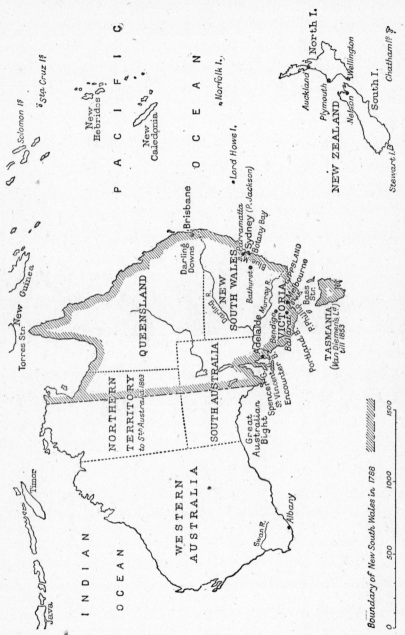

THE SETTLEMENT OF AUSTRALIA AND NEW ZEALAND

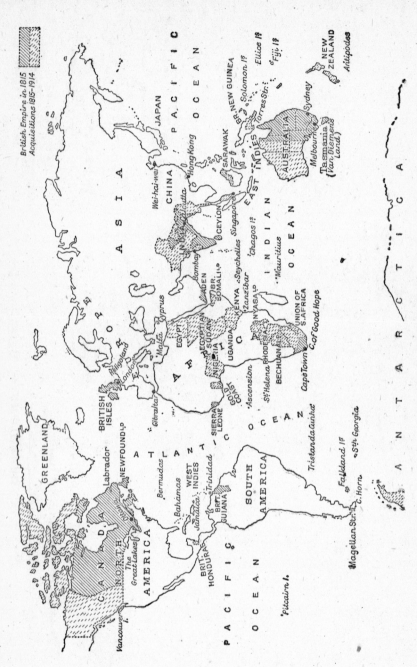

THE BRITISH EMPIRE, 1815-1914

British Empire in 1815
Acquisitions 1815-1914

GREENLAND

NORTH AMERICA
CANADA
Vancouver I.
Labrador
NEWFOUND'L'D
The Great Lakes

Bermudas
Bahamas
WEST INDIES
Jamaica
Trinidad
BRIT. HONDURAS
BRIT. GUIANA

SOUTH AMERICA

ATLANTIC OCEAN

PACIFIC OCEAN

Pitcairn I.

Magellan Str.
C. Horn
Falkland Is.
St. Georgia
Tristan da Cunha

BRITISH ISLES
London
Gibraltar
Heligoland

EUROPE

ASIA

Malta
Cyprus
EGYPT
EGYPTIAN SUDAN
NIGERIA
SIERRA LEONE
GOLD COAST
Ascension
St. Helena
AFRICA
UGANDA
KENYA
BR. SOMALI'D
ADEN
Aden
Zanzibar
NYASA L'D
RHODESIA
BECHUANAL'D
UNION OF S. AFRICA
Cape Town
C. of Good Hope
Seychelles
Mauritius
Chagos Is.

Bombay
Madras
Calcutta
CEYLON
Singapore
EAST INDIES
INDIAN OCEAN

CHINA
Wei-hai-wei
JAPAN
Hong Kong
SARAWAK
BR. NEW GUINEA
Solomon Is.
Torres Str.

PACIFIC OCEAN

AUSTRALIA
Melbourne
Sydney
Tasmania
(Van Diemen's Land)

Ellice Is.
Fiji Is.
NEW ZEALAND
Antipodes

ANTARCTICA

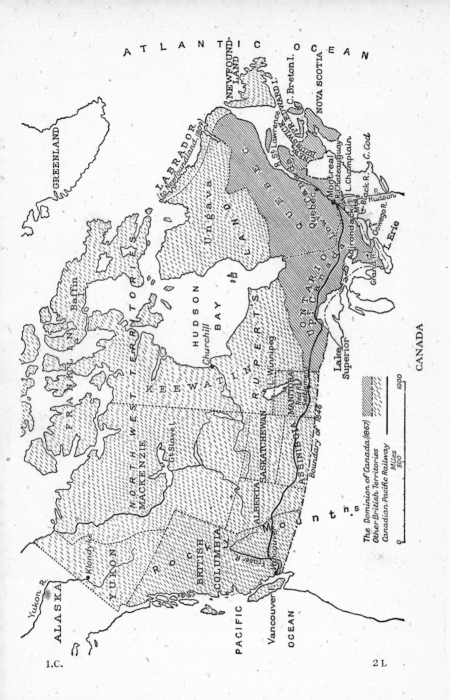

ATLANTIC OCEAN

GREENLAND

NEWFOUNDLAND

NOVA SCOTIA

C. Breton I.

PRINCE EDWARD I.

NEW BRUNSWICK

R. St. Lawrence

Saguenay R.

Montreal

L. Champlain

C. Cod

Black R.

Hudson R.

Oswego R.

L. Erie

Grand R.

Adirondacks Mts.

Quebec

QUEBEC

LABRADOR

(to Newfoundland 1809)

Ungava

UPPER CANADA

ONTARIO

LAND

HUDSON

BAY

Churchill R.

Lake Superior

Baffin I.

F R A N K L I N

N O R T H   W E S T   T E R R I T O R I E S

K E E W A T I N

M A C K E N Z I E

Gt. Slave L.

R U P E R T S   L A N D

Winnipeg

MANITOBA

Red R.

Settlement

L. Winnipeg

SASKATCHEWAN

ASSINIBOIA

Boundary of 1846

ALBERTA

R O C K Y

M o u n t a i n s

BRITISH COLUMBIA

Fraser R.

Vancouver

YUKON

Klondyke

ALASKA

Yukon R.

PACIFIC OCEAN

CANADA

The Dominion of Canada (1867)
Other British Territories
Canadian Pacific Railway

Miles

0   500   1000

I.C.

2 L

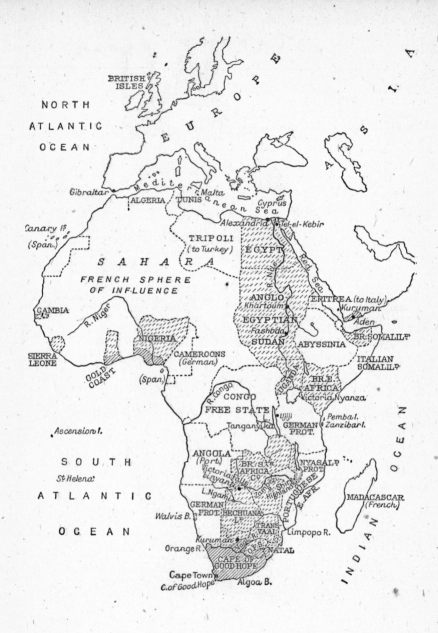

NORTH
ATLANTIC
OCEAN

BRITISH
ISLES

EUROPE

ASIA

Gibraltar

Mediterranean Sea

ALGERIA   TUNIS   Malta   Cyprus

Alexandria   Tel-el-Kebir

Canary Is.
(Span.)

TRIPOLI
(to Turkey)

EGYPT

Red Sea

SAHARA

FRENCH SPHERE
OF INFLUENCE

ANGLO

Khartoum

ERITREA (to Italy)
Kuruman

GAMBIA

R. Niger

EGYPTIAN

Fashoda

Aden

BR. SOMALIL?

NIGERIA

SUDAN

ABYSSINIA

SIERRA
LEONE

CAMEROONS
(German)

ITALIAN
SOMALIL?

GOLD
COAST

(Span.)

UGANDA

BR. E.
AFRICA

Victoria Nyanza

R. Congo

CONGO

FREE STATE

Ascension I.

Tanganyika

Ujiji

GERMAN
PROT.

Pemba I.
Zanzibar I.

SOUTH

St Helena

ANGOLA
(Port.)

Victoria Falls
Zambezi

BR. S.A.
AFRICA
Co.

NYASAL?
PROT.

ATLANTIC

L. Ngami

Zambezi
High lands
Shire

PORTUGUESE

E. AFR.

MADAGASCAR
(French)

GERMAN
PROT.

OCEAN

Walvis B.

BECHUANA-
LP

TRANS-
VAAL

Limpopo R.

INDIAN

Kuruman

O.F.S.

NATAL

OCEAN

Orange R.

CAPE OF
GOOD HOPE

Cape Town
C. of Good Hope

Algoa B.

British Possessions, Protectorates etc. before 1884

  ,,   ,,   ,,   since   ,,

Miles
0   500   1000   1500

AFRICA

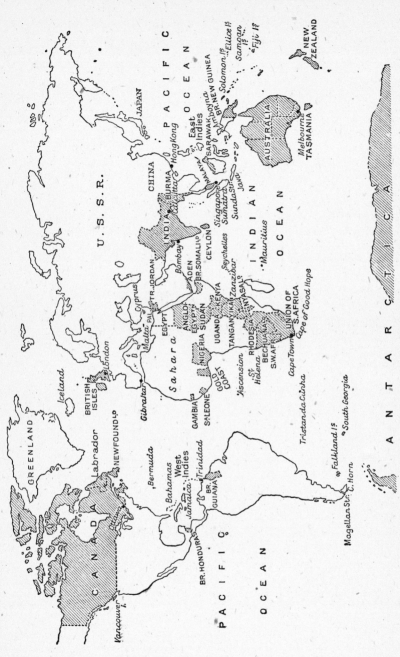

THE BRITISH EMPIRE, 1939 (INCLUDING MANDATED TERRITORIES)

INDEX

533

015 R